IN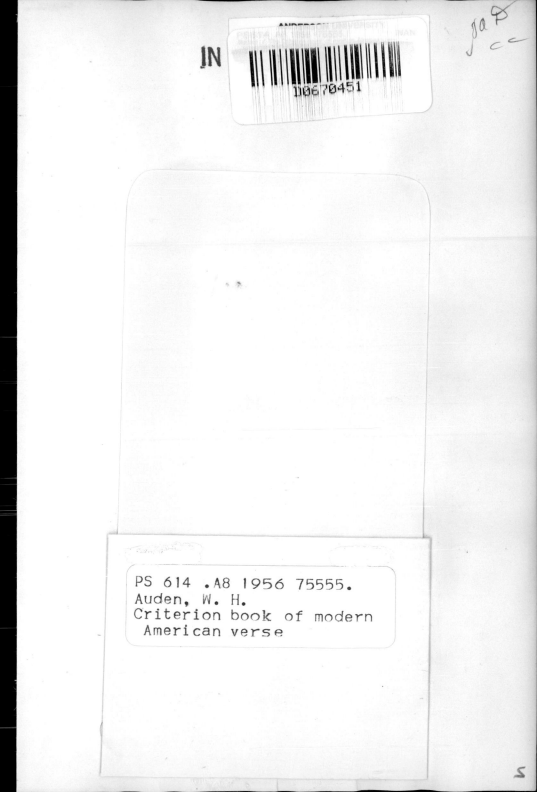

IN GRANGER'S INDEX

The *Criterion Book*
of *Modern*
American Verse

books by W. H. Auden

*

THE SHIELD OF ACHILLES
NONES
THE ENCHAFED FLOOD
COLLECTED SHORTER POEMS 1930–44
THE AGE OF ANXIETY
FOR THE TIME BEING
NEW YEAR LETTER
POEMS
THE ORATORS
SOME POEMS
MOUNTAINS

The *Criterion Book*

of *Modern*

American Verse

Edited with an introduction by

W. H. Auden (Wystan Hugh) 1907-1973

CRITERION BOOKS   NEW YORK

The land was ours before we were the land's.
She was our land more than a hundred years
Before we were her people. She was ours
In Massachusetts, in Virginia,
But we were England's, still colonials,
Possessing what we still were unpossessed by,
Possessed by what we now no more possessed.
Something we were withholding made us weak
Until we found out that it was ourselves
We were withholding from our land of living,
And forthwith found salvation in surrender.
Such as we were we gave ourselves outright
(The deed of gift was many deeds of war)
To the land vaguely realising westward,
But still unstoried, artless, unenhanced,
Such as she was, such as she would become.

ROBERT FROST: *The Gift Outright*

CONTENTS

INTRODUCTION
By W. H. Auden   *page* 9

ROBINSON, EDWIN ARLINGTON. 1869-1935
Mr. Flood's Party   23
Eros Turannos   25
Clavering   26
The Long Race   28
Luke Havergal   28

MASTERS, EDGAR LEE. 1869-1950
Four Epitaphs: John Horace Burleson   30
     Editor Whedon   30
     Perry Zoll   31
     J. Milton Miles   32

CRANE, STEPHEN. 1871-1900
Four Poems: In the desert   33
     Once there came a man   33
     A man said to the universe   34
     A man adrift on a slim spar   34

STICKNEY, TRUMBLE. 1874-1904
Mnemosyne   36
In Ampezzo   37
Leave him now quiet   40

STEIN, GERTRUDE. 1874-1946
Pigeons on the grass alas   41
We cannot retrace our steps   41

FROST, ROBERT. *b.* 1875
The Oven Bird   43
The Pauper Witch of Grafton   43
Two look at Two   46
Neither out far nor in deep   48
Design   48
The Most of It   49
Never again would bird's song   50
The Middleness of the road   50
Directive   51
for Epigraph: The Gift Outright   vii

MARQUIS, DON. 1878-1937
    archys autobiography   page 53
    archys last name   54
    artists shouldnt have offspring   55

SANDBURG, CARL. b. 1878
    Personality   56
    Clocks   56
    Bas-Relief   57

LINDSAY, VACHEL. 1879-1931
    The Flute of the Lonely   58
    What the Moon saw   59
    Bryan, Bryan, Bryan, Bryan   9
    The Factory Window Song   67

STEVENS, WALLACE. 1879-1955
    The Snow Man   69
    Disillusionment of Ten O'clock   69
    Sunday Morning   70
    Dry Loaf   74
    Woman looking at a vase of flowers   75
    Bethou me, said sparrow   76
    We reason of these things   76

BYNNER, WITTER. b. 1881
    Jeremiah   78

WILLIAMS, WILLIAM CARLOS. b. 1883
    Sunday in the Park   79
    To Daphne and Virginia   86

WYLIE, ELINOR. 1885-1928
    Lavish Kindness   90
    Doomsday   90
    Shepherd's holiday   91
    Full Moon   92

POUND, EZRA. b. 1885
    The Lake Isle   93
    Provincia Deserta   93
    South-Folk in Cold Country   96
    Homage to Sextus Propertius, Part V   96
    E.P. Ode pour l'élection de son sépulchre   99
    Canto XLVII   99

UNTERMEYER, LOUIS. b. 1885
    Song Tournement; New Style   103

2

FLETCHER, JOHN GOULD. 1886-1946
   The Windmills   *page* 104

H.D. *b.* 1886
   An incident here and there   106
   Ah (you say), this is Holy Wisdom   108

WHEELOCK, JOHN HALL. *b.* 1886
   The Years   112
   Reconciliation   112

JEFFERS, ROBINSON. *b.* 1887
   Summer Holiday   113
   Reference to a Passage in Plutarch's Life of Sulla   113
   November Surf   114
   I shall laugh purely   115
   The Eye   118

MOORE, MARIANNE. *b.* 1887
   The Steeple-Jack   119
   Melancthon   120
   England   123
   A Grave   125
   The Pangolin   126
   The Mind is an enchanting thing   129

RANSON, JOHN CROWE. *b.* 1888
   Vision by Sweetwater   131
   Bells for John Whiteside's daughter   131
   Antique Harvesters   132
   Judith of Bethulia   134
   Painted Head   135

AIKEN, CONRAD. *b.* 1889
   Annihilation   137
   Systole and Diastole   138
   The Stepping Stones   139
   The Sounding   140

MILLAY, EDNA ST. VINCENT. 1892-1950
   Never may the Fruit be Plucked   141
   The Buck in the Snow   141
   In the Grave no Flower   142
   To a Young Poet   143

BISHOP, JOHN PEALE. 1892-1944
   This Dim and Ptolemaic Man   144

3

COFFIN, TRISTRAM. 1892-1955
    The Fog   *page* 145

MACLEISH, ARCHIBALD. *b.* 1892
    Cook County   146
    Words in Time   147

GREENBERG, SAMUEL. 1893-1917
    Conduct   148
    Peace   148
    Man   149

PARKER, DOROTHY. *b.* 1893
    Bohemia   150

VAN DOREN, MARK. *b.* 1894
    It should be easy   151
    Foreclosure   152
    Tall tale God   153

CUMMINGS, E. E. *b.* 1895
    when life is quite through with   154
    my father moved through dooms of love   155
    might these be thrushes climbing through almost (do they   157
    pity this busy monster, manunkind   158
    it was a goodly co   158
    plato told   159
    noone' autumnal this great lady's gaze   160

HUMPHRIES, ROLFE. *b.* 1895
    Render Unto Caesar   162
    The Cynneddf   162

WILSON, EDMUND. *b.* 1895
    On Editing Scott Fitzgerald's Papers   166

BOGAN, LOUISE. *b.* 1897
    Baroque Comment   169
    M., Singing   170

WHEELRIGHT, JOHN. 1897-1940
    Why must you know?   171
    The Huntsman   172
    Paul and Virginia   172

BENÉT, STEPHEN VINCENT. 1897-1943
    Invocation   174

GREGORY, HORACE. b. 1898
  The Unwilling Guest: an Urban Dialogue   *page* 180

CRANE, HART. 1899-1932
  To Brooklyn Bridge   184
  Van Winkle   185
  The Sea   187
  Chaplinesque   188
  Island Quarry   189

TATE, ALLEN. b. 1899
  Seasons of the Soul   190
  The Buried Lake   197

ADAMS, LÉONIE. b. 1899
  Light at Equinox   203
  The Font in the Forest   204

WINTERS, IVOR. b. 1899
  By the Road to the Airbase   205
  A Prayer for my Son   205
  Summer Noon, 1941   206

LEWIS, JANET. b. 1899
  The Candle Flame   208

WILLIAMS, OSCAR. b. 1900
  The Mirage   209

FRANCIS, ROBERT. b. 1901
  Walls   211
  Swimmer   211
  Apple Peeler   212

SPENCER, THEODORE. 1902-1949
  The Phoenix   213

NASH, OGDEN. b. 1902
  Portrait of the artist as a prematurely old man   217

ZATURENSKA, MARYA. b. 1902
  The False Summer   219

MOORE, MERRILL. b. 1903
  He said the facts   221
  They also stand   221

DENBY, EDWIN. b. 1903
  Air   223
  Northern Boulevard   223

BLACKMUR, RICHARD. *b.* 1904
    The Rape of Europa   *page* 225
    Scarabs for the Living   226

HOLMES, JOHN. *b.* 1904
    What does a man think about   227
    Bucyrus   228
    The Overgrown Back-yard   228

EBERHARDT, RICHARD. *b.* 1904
    Ode to the Chinese Paper Snake   230
    The Horse Chestnut Tree   233

REXROTH, KENNETH. *b.* 1905
    Maximian Elegy V   235
    Marcus Argentarius   236
    Antipator of Thessalonica   237

KUNITZ, STANLEY. *b.* 1905
    The Daughters of the Horseleech   238
    He   238
    End of Summer   239
    The Scourge   240

M'CGINLEY, PHYLLIS. *b.* 1905
    Country Club Sunday   241
    Portrait of a Girl with Comic Book   241

WARREN, ROBERT PENN. *b.* 1905
    Original Sin: A Short Story   243
    Pursuit   244

VILLA, JOSÉ GARCIA. *b.* 1918
    Between God's eyelashes I look at you   247
    Be beautiful, noble like the antique ant   247

ENGLE, PAUL. *b.* 1908
    Chameleon   249

ROETHKE, THEODORE. *b.* 1908
    My Papa's Waltz   251
    Academic   251
    The Dance   252
    The Waking   252
    Song   253
    The Song   254

AGEE, JAMES. 1909–1955
    Description of Elysium   256

FITZGERALD, ROBERT. *b.* 1910
   Windshield   *page* 258

SCOTT, WINFIELD TOWNLEY. *b.* 1910
   Mr. Whittier   259

MILES, JOSEPHINE. *b.* 1911
   Forecast   262
   The Sympathizers   262

PATCHEN, KENNETH. *b.* 1911
   The Constant Bridegrooms   264
   The Everlasting Contenders   265

BISHOP, ELIZABETH. *b.* 1911
   From the Country to the City   266
   Roosters   267
   Little Exercise   272

SCHWARTZ, DELMORE. *b.* 1913
   The Heavy Bear   273
   The Beautiful American Word, Sure   274

SHAPIRO, KARL. *b.* 1913
   Paradox: The Birds   275

JARRELL, RANDALL. *b.* 1914
   The Lines   276
   The Breath of Night   276
   The Knight, Death and the Devil   277

BERRYMAN, JOHN. *b.* 1914
   from Homage to Mistress Bradstreet   279

MERTON, THOMAS. *b.* 1915
   An Argument—of The Passion of Christ   284
   Figures for an Apocalypse, VII   286

VIERECK, PETER. *b.* 1916
   Counter-Serenade: She Invokes the Autumn Instant   288

MORSE, SAMUEL FRENCH. *b.* 1916
   The Track into the Swamp   289

GRIFFIN, HOWARD. *b.* 1916
   Suppose in Perfect Reason   291

LOWELL, ROBERT. *b.* 1917
   The Drunken Fisherman   293
   As a Plane Tree by the Water   294
   Falling Asleep Over the Aeneid   295

7

GIBSON, WALKER. *b.* 1919
David   *page* 298

DUNCAN, ROBERT. *b.* 1919
The Reaper   299
Hero Song   300

BROUGHTON, JAMES. *b.* 1920
The Lighthouse Keeper's Offspring   302
Genesis of Vowels   302

KALLMAN, CHESTER. *b.* 1921
Nightmare of a Cook   304
Little Epithalamium   305
Urban History   305

WILBUR, RICHARD. *b.* 1921
Potato   307
Beasts   308
Beowulf   309

RAINER, DACHINE. *b.* 1921
Double Ritual   311

HORAN, ROBERT. *b.* 1922
Little City   313
Emblems of Evening   314

HECHT, ANTHONY. *b.* 1922
The Place of Pain in the Universe   316
Japan   316

8

INTRODUCTION

One often hears it said that only in this century have the writers of the United States learned to stand on their own feet and be truly American, that, previously, they were slavish imitators of British literature. Applied to the general reading public and academic circles this has a certain amount of truth but, so far as the writers themselves are concerned, it is quite false. From Bryant on there is scarcely one American poet whose work, if unsigned, could be mistaken for that of an Englishman. What English poet, for example, in need of emotive place-names for a serious poem, would have employed, neither local names nor names famous in history or mythology, but names made up by himself as Poe did in *Ulalume*? Would an English poet have received the idea of writing a scientific cosmological prose poem and of prefacing it thus: 'I offer this Book of Truths, not in its character of Truth-teller, but for the Beauty that abounds in its Truth, constituting it true . . . *What I here propound is true:* therefore it cannot die . . . Nevertheless it is as a Poem only that I wish this work to be judged after I am dead.' (Poe, Preface to *Eureka*)?

Maud, The Song of Hiawatha and the first edition of *Leaves of Grass* all appeared in the same year, 1855: no two poets could be more unlike each other than Longfellow and Whitman—such diversity is in itself an American phenomenon—yet, when compared with Tennyson, each in his own way shows characteristics of the New World. Tennyson and Longfellow were both highly skilful technicians in conventional forms and both were regarded by their countrymen as the respectable mouthpieces of their age, and yet, how different they are. There is much in Tennyson that Longfellow would never have dared to write, for the peculiar American mixture of Puritan conscience and democratic licence can foster in some cases a genteel horror of the coarse for which no Englishman has felt the need.

On the other hand Longfellow had a curiosity about the whole of European literature compared with which Tennyson, concerned only with the poetry of his own land and the classical authors on whom he was educated, seems provincial. Even if there had been Red Indians roaming the North of Scotland, unsubjugated and unassimilable, one cannot imagine Tennyson sitting down to write a long poem about them and choosing for it a Finnish metre. Leaving aside all questions of style, there is a difference between Tennyson's *Ode on the Death of the Duke of Wellington* and Whitman's elegy for President Lincoln *When lilacs last in the dooryard bloom'd* which is significant. Tennyson, as one would expect from the title of his poem, mourns for a great public official figure, but it would be very hard to guess from the words of Whitman's poem that the man he is talking of was the head of a State; one would naturally think that he was some close personal friend, a private individual.

To take one more example—two poets, contemporaries, both women, both religious, both introverts preoccupied with renunciation—Christina Rossetti and Emily Dickinson; could anyone imagine either of them in the country of the other? When I try to fancy such translations, the only Americans I can possibly imagine as British are minor poets with a turn for light verse like Lowell and Holmes; and the only British poets who could conceivably have been American are eccentrics like Blake and Hopkins.

Normally, in comparing the poetry of two cultures, the obvious and easiest point at which to start is with a comparison of the peculiar characteristics, grammatical, rhetorical, rhythmical, of their respective languages, for even the most formal and elevated styles of poetry are more conditioned by the spoken tongue, the language really used by the men of that country, than by anything else. In the case of British and American poetry, however, this is the most subtle difference of all and the hardest to define. Any Englishman, with a little effort, can learn to pronounce 'the letter *a* in psalm and calm . . . with the sound of *a* in candle', to say *thumb-tacks* instead of *drawing-pins* or twenty-minutes-*of*-one instead of twenty-minutes-*to*-one, and discover that, in the Middle West, *bought* rhymes with *hot*, but he will still be as far from speaking American English, as his Yankee cousin who comes to England will be from speaking the King's. No dramatist in either country who has introduced a character from the other side, has, to my knowledge, been able to make his speech convincing. What the secret of the difference is, I cannot put my finger on; William Carlos Williams, who has thought more than most about this problem, says that 'Pace is one of its most important manifestations' and to this one might add another, Pitch. If undefinable, the difference is, however, immediately recognizable by the ear, even in verse where the formal conventions are the same.

> He must have had a father and a mother—
> In fact I've heard him say so—and a dog,
> As a boy should, I venture; and the dog,
> Most likely, was the only man who knew him.
> A dog, for all I know, is what he needs
> As much as anything right here today,
> To counsel him about his disillusions,
> Old aches, and parturitions of what's coming,—
> A dog of orders, an emeritus,
> To wag his tail at him when he comes home,
> And then to put his paws up on his knees
> And say, 'For God's sake, what's it all about?'

(E. A. ROBINSON, *Ben Jonson Entertains A Man From Stratford*)

Whatever this may owe to Browning, the fingering is quite different and un-British. Again, how American in rhythm as well as in sensibility is this stanza by Robert Frost.

> But no, I was out for stars:
> I would not come in.
> I meant not even if asked;
> And I hadn't been.   (*Come in*)

11

Until quite recently an English writer, like one of any European country, could presuppose two conditions, a nature which was mythologized, humanized, on the whole friendly, and a human society which had become in time, whatever succession of invasions it may have suffered in the past, in race and religion more or less homogeneous and in which most people lived and died in the locality where they were born.

Christianity might have deprived Aphrodite, Apollo, the local genius, of their divinity but as figures for the forces of nature, as a mode of thinking about the creation, they remained valid for poets and their readers alike. Descartes might reduce the non-human universe to a mechanism but the feelings of Europeans about the sun and moon, the cycle of the seasons, the local landscape remained unchanged. Wordsworth might discard the mythological terminology but the kind of relation between nature and man which he described was the same personal one. Even when nineteenth century biology began to trouble men's mind with the thought that the universe might be without moral values, their immediate experience was still of a friendly and lovable nature. Whatever their doubts and convictions about the purpose and significance of the universe as a whole, Tennyson's Lincolnshire or Hardy's Dorset were places where they felt completely at home, landscapes with faces of their own which a human being could recognize and trust.

But in America, neither the size or condition or climate of the continent encourages such intimacy. It is an unforgettable experience for anyone born on the other side of the Atlantic to take a plane journey by night across the United States. Looking down he will see the lights of some town like a last outpost in a darkness stretching for hours ahead, and realize that, even if there is no longer an actual frontier, this is still a continent only partially settled and developed, where human activity seems a tiny thing in comparison to the magnitude of the earth, and the equality of men not some dogma of politics or jurisprudence but a self-evident

12

fact. He will behold a wild nature compared with which the landscapes of Salvator Rosa are as cosy as Arcadia and which cannot possibly be thought of in human or personal terms. If Henry Adams could write:

> 'When Adams was a boy in Boston, the best chemist in the place had probably never heard of Venus except by way of scandal, or of the Virgin except as idolatry. . . . The force of the Virgin was still felt at Lourdes, and seemed to be as potent as X-rays; but in America neither Venus nor Virgin ever had value as force—at most as sentiment. No American had ever been truly afraid of either.'

the reason for this was not simply that the *Mayflower* carried iconophobic dissenters but also that the nature which Americans, even in New England, had every reason to fear could not possibly be imagined as a mother. A white whale whom man can neither understand nor be understood by, whom only a madman like Gabriel can worship, the only relationship with whom is a combat to the death by which a man's courage and skill are tested and judged, or the great buck who answers the poet's prayer for 'someone else additional to him' in *The Most of It* are more apt symbols. Thoreau, who certainly tried his best to become intimate with nature, had to confess

> *I walk in nature still alone*
> *And know no one,*
> *Discern no lineament nor feature*
> *Of any creature.*
> *Though all the firmament*
> *Is o'er me bent,*
> *Yet still I miss the grace*
> *Of an intelligent and kindred face.*
> *I still must seek the friend*
> *Who does with nature blend,*
> *Who is the person in her mask,*
> *He is the man I ask.* . . .

Many poets in the Old World have become disgusted with human civilization but what the earth would be like if the race became extinct they cannot imagine; an American like Robinson Jeffers can quite easily, for he has seen with his own eyes country as yet untouched by history.

In a land which is fully settled, most men must accept their local environment or try to change it by political means; only the exceptionally gifted or adventurous can leave to seek his fortune elsewhere.

In America, on the other hand, to move on and make a fresh start somewhere else is still the normal reaction to dissatisfaction or failure. Such social fluidity has important psychological effects. Since movement involves breaking social and personal ties, the habit creates an attitude towards personal relationships in which impermanence is taken for granted.

One could find no better illustration of the difference between the Old and the New World than the respective conclusions of *Oliver Twist* and *Huckleberry Finn*, the heroes of which are both orphans. When Oliver is at last adopted by Mr. Brownlow, his fondest dream, to have a home, to be surrounded by familiar friendly faces, to receive an education, is realized. Huck is offered adoption too, significantly by a woman not a man, but refuses because he knows she would try to 'civilize' him, and announces his intention to light out by himself for the West; Jim, who has been his 'buddy' in a friendship far closer than any enjoyed by Oliver, is left behind like an old shoe, just as in *Moby Dick* Ishmael becomes a blood-brother of Queequeg and then forgets all about him. Naturally the day-dream of the life-long comrade in adventure often appears in American literature:

> *Camerado, I give you my hand!*
> *I give you my love more precious than money,*
> *I give you myself before preaching or law;*
> *Will you give me yourself? will you come travel with me?*
> *Shall we stick by each other as long as we live?*
> (WHITMAN, *Song of the Open Road*)

but no American seriously expects such a dream to come true.

To be able at any time to break with the past, to move and keep on moving lessens the significance not only of the past but also of the future which is reduced to the immediate future, and minimizes the importance of political action. A European may be a conservative who thinks that the right form of society has been discovered already, or a liberal who believes it is in process of being realized, or a revolutionary who thinks that after long dark ages it can now be realized for the first time, but each of them knows that, by reason or force, he must convince the others that he is right; he may be an optimist about the future or a pessimist. None of these terms applies accurately to an American, for his profoundest feeling towards the future is not that it will be better or worse but that it is unpredictable, that all things, good and bad, will change. No failure is irredeemable, no success a final satisfaction. Democracy is the best form of government, not because men will necessarily lead better or happier lives under it, but because it permits constant experiment; a given experiment may fail but the people have a right to make their own mistakes. America has always been a country of amateurs where the professional, that is to say, the man who claims authority as a member of an élite which knows the law in some field or other, is an object of distrust and resentment. (In the field with which we are here concerned, one symptom of this is that curious American phenomenon, the class in 'Creative Writing'.)

> *Amerika, du hast es besser*
> *Als unser Kontinent, der alte,*
> *Hast keine verfallenen Schloesser*
> *Und keine Basalte.*[1]

wrote Goethe, by *Keine Basalte* meaning, I presume, no violent political revolutions. This is a subject about which, in relation to their own histories, the English and the

---

[1] Things are easier for you, America, than for this old continent of ours; you have no ruins of fortresses, no basalt intrusions.
GOETHE

15

Americans cherish opposite fictions. Between 1533 and 1688 the English went through a succession of revolutions in which a church was imposed on them by the engines of the State, one king was executed and another deposed, yet they prefer to forget it and pretend that the social structure of England is the product of organic peaceful growth. The Americans on the other hand like to pretend that what was only a successful war of secession was a genuine revolution.[1] There is indeed an American mentality which is new and unique in the world but it is the product less of conscious political action than of nature, of the new and unique environment of the American continent. Even the most revolutionary feature of the Constitution, the separation of Church and State, was a recognition of a condition which had existed since the first settlements were made by various religious denominations whose control of the secular authority could only be local. From the beginning America had been a pluralist state and pluralism is incompatible with an Established Church. The *Basalt* in American history, the Civil War, might indeed be called Counter-Revolution, for it was fought primarily on the issue not of slavery but of unity, that is, not for a freedom but for a limitation on freedom, to ensure that the United States should remain pluralist and not disintegrate into an anarchic heap of fragments. Pluralist and experimental: in place of *verfallene Schloesser* America has ghost towns and the relics of New Jerusalems which failed.

Whatever one may feel about Whitman's poetry, one is bound to admit that he was the first clearly to recognize what the conditions were with which any future American poet would have to come to terms.

> 'Plenty of songs had been sung—beautiful, matchless songs—adjusted to other lands than these . . . the Old World has had the poems of myths, fictions, feudalism, conquest, caste,

[1] 1829, though bloodless, was a more revolutionary year than 1776.

16

dynastic wars, and splendid exceptional characters, which have been great; but the New World needs the poems of realities and science and of the democratic average and basic equality. . . . As for native American individuality, the distinctive and ideal type of Western character (as consistent with the operative and even money-making features of United States humanity as chosen knights, gentlemen and warriors were the ideals of the centuries of European feudalism) it has not yet appeared. I have allowed the stress of my poems from beginning to end to bear upon American individuality and assist it—not only because that is a great lesson in Nature, amid all her generalizing laws, but as counterpoise to the levelling tendencies of Democracy.'

The last sentence makes it quite clear that by the 'average' here who was to replace the 'knight' Whitman did not mean the mediocre, but the individual whose 'exceptional character' is not derived from birth, education or occupation, and that he is aware of how difficult it is for such an individual to appear without the encouragement which comes from membership in some *élite*.

What he does not say, and perhaps did not realize, is that, in a democracy, the status of the poet himself is changed. However fantastic, in the light of present-day realities, his notion may be, every European poet, I believe, still instinctively thinks of himself as a 'clerk', a member of a professional brotherhood, with a certain social status irrespective of the number of his readers (in his heart of hearts the audience he desires and expects are those who govern the country), and taking his place in an unbroken historical succession. In the States poets have never had or imagined they had such a status, and it is up to each individual poet to justify his existence by offering a unique product. It would be grossly unjust to assert that there are fewer lovers of poetry in the New World than in the Old—in how many places in the latter could a poet demand and receive a substantial sum for reading his work aloud?—but there is a tendency, perhaps, in the former, for audiences to be

17

drawn rather by a name than a poem, and for a poet, on his side, to demand approval for his work not simply because it is good but because it is *his*. To some degree every American poet feels that the whole responsibility for contemporary poetry has fallen upon his shoulders, that he is a literary aristocracy of one. 'Tradition', wrote Mr. T. S. Eliot in a famous essay, 'cannot be inherited, and if you want it you must obtain it by great labour.' I do not think that any European critic would have said just this. He would not, of course, deny that every poet must work hard but the suggestion in the first half of the sentence that no sense of tradition is acquired except by conscious effort would seem strange to him.

There are advantages and disadvantages in both attitudes. A British poet can take writing more for granted and so write with a lack of strain and over-earnestness. American poetry has many tones, a man talking to himself or one intimate friend, a prophet crying in the wilderness, but the easy-going tone of a man talking to a group of his peers is rare; for a 'serious' poet to write light verse is frowned on in America and if, when he is asked why he writes poetry, he replies, as any European poet would, 'For fun,' his audience will be shocked. (In this Cambridge-on-the-Cam is perhaps a few leagues nearer Gambier, Ohio than is Oxford-on-Thames.) On the other hand a British poet is in much greater danger of becoming lazy, or academic, or irresponsible. (One comes across passages, even in very fine English poets, which make one think: 'Yes, very effective but does he believe what he is saying?': in American poetry such passages are extremely rare.) The first thing that strikes a reader about the best American poets is how utterly unlike each other they are. Where else in the world, for example, could one find seven poets of approximately the same generation so different as Ezra Pound, W. C. Williams, Vachel Lindsay, Marianne Moore, Wallace Stevens, E. E. Cummings and Laura Riding? The danger for the American poet is not of writing

18

like everybody else but of crankiness and a parody of his own manner.[1]

Plato said that when the modes of music change the walls of the city are shaken. It might be truer to say, perhaps, that a change in the modes gives warning of a shaking of the walls in the near future. The social strains which later break out in political action are first experienced by artists as a feeling that the current modes of expression are no longer capable of dealing with their real concerns. Thus, when one thinks of 'modern' painting, music, fiction or poetry, the names which immediately come to mind as its leaders and creators are those of persons who were born roughly between 1870 and 1890 and who began producing their 'new' work before the outbreak of World War I in 1914, and in poetry and fiction, at least, American names are prominent.

When a revolutionary break with the past is necessary it is an advantage not to be too closely identified with any one particular literature or any particular cultural group. Americans like Eliot and Pound, for example, could be as curious about French or Italian poetry as about English and could hear poetry of the past, like the verse of Webster, freshly in a way that for an Englishman, trammelled by traditional notions of Elizabethan blank verse, would have been difficult.

[1] The undeniable appearance in the States during the last fifteen years or so of a certain literary conformity, of a proper and authorized way to write poetry is a new and disquieting symptom, which I cannot pretend to be able to explain fully. The role of the American college as a patron of poets has been discussed a good deal both here and in England. Those who criticize it, often with some reason, fail to suggest a better alternative. It would be nice if the colleges could ask no more from the poets in return for their keep than occasional pieces, a Commencement Day masque or an elegy on a deceased trustee; if that is too much to ask, then the poets themselves should at least demand that they give academic courses in the literature of the dead and refuse to have anything to do with modern literature or courses in writing. There has been a vast output of critical studies in contemporary poetry, some of them first rate, but I do not think that, as a rule, a poet should read or write them.

Further, as Americans, they were already familiar with the dehumanized nature and the social levelling which a technological civilization was about to make universal and with which the European mentality was unprepared to deal. After his visit to America De Tocqueville made a remarkable prophecy about the kind of poetry which a democratic society would produce.

'I am persuaded that in the end democracy diverts the imagination from all that is external to man and fixes it on man alone. Democratic nations may amuse themselves for a while with considering the productions of nature, but they are excited in reality only by a survey of themselves . . .

The poets who lived in aristocratic ages have been eminently successful in their delineations of certain incidents in the life of a people or a man; but none of them ever ventured to include within his performances the destinies of mankind, a task which poets writing in democratic ages may attempt . . .

It may be foreseen in like manner that poets living in democratic times will prefer the delineation of passions and ideas to that of persons and achievements. The language, the dress, and the daily actions of men in democracies are repugnant to conceptions of the ideal. . . . This forces the poet constantly to search below the external surface which is palpable to the senses, in order to read the inner soul; and nothing lends itself more to the delineation of the ideal than the scrutiny of the hidden depths in the immaterial nature of man. . . . The destinies of mankind, man himself taken aloof from his country and his age, and standing in the presence of Nature and of God, with his passions, his doubts, his rare prosperities and inconceivable wretchedness, will become the chief, if not the sole, theme of poetry.'

If this be an accurate description of the poetry we call modern, then one might say that America has never known any other kind.

W. H. AUDEN

The *Criterion Book*
of *Modern*
American Verse

Edwin Arlington Robinson

(1869-1935)

MR. FLOOD'S PARTY

Old Eben Flood, climbing alone one night
Over the hill between the town below
And the forsaken upland hermitage
That held as much as he should ever know
On earth again of home, paused warily.
The road was his with not a native near;
And Eben, having leisure, said aloud,
For no man else in Tilbury Town to hear:

'Well, Mr. Flood, we have the harvest moon
Again, and we may not have many more;
The bird is on the wing, the poet says,
And you and I have said it here before.
Drink to the bird.' He raised up to the light
The jug that he had gone so far to fill,
And answered huskily: 'Well, Mr. Flood,
Since you propose it, I believe I will.'

Alone, as if enduring to the end
A valiant armour of scarred hopes outworn,
He stood there in the middle of the road
Like Roland's ghost winding a silent horn.
Below him, in the town among the trees,
Where friends of other days had honoured him,
A phantom salutation of the dead
Rang thinly till old Eben's eyes were dim.

Then, as a mother lays her sleeping child
Down tenderly, fearing it may awake,

23

EDWIN
ARLING-
TON
ROBIN-
SON
He set the jug down slowly at his feet
With trembling care, knowing that most things break;
And only when assured that on firm earth
It stood, as the uncertain lives of men
Assuredly did not, he paced away,
And with his hand extended paused again:

'Well, Mr. Flood, we have not met like this
In a long time; and many a change has come
To both of us, I fear, since last it was
We had a drop together. Welcome home!'
Convivially returning with himself,
Again he raised the jug up to the light;
And with an acquiescent quaver said:
'Well, Mr. Flood, if you insist, I might.

'Only a very little, Mr. Flood—
For auld lang syne. No more, sir; that will do.'
So, for the time, apparently it did,
And Eben evidently thought so too;
For soon amid the silver loneliness
Of night he lifted up his voice and sang,
Secure, with only two moons listening,
Until the whole harmonious landscape rang—

'For auld lang syne.' The weary throat gave out,
The last word wavered; and the song being done,
He raised again the jug regretfully
And shook his head, and was again alone.
There was not much that was ahead of him,
And there was nothing in the town below—
Where strangers would have shut the many doors
That many friends had opened long ago.

EROS TURANNOS

EDWIN
ARLING-
TON
ROBIN-
SON

She fears him, and will always ask
   What fated her to choose him;
She meets in his engaging mask
   All reasons to refuse him;
But what she meets and what she fears
Are less than are the downward years,
Drawn slowly to the foamless weirs
   Of age, were she to lose him.

Between a blurred sagacity
   That once had power to sound him,
And Love, that will not let him be
   The Judas that she found him,
Her pride assuages her almost,
As if it were alone the cost.—
He sees that he will not be lost,
   And waits and looks around him.

A sense of ocean and old trees
   Envelops and allures him;
Tradition, touching all he sees,
   Beguiles and reassures him;
And all her doubts of what he says
Are dimmed with what she knows of days—
Till even prejudice delays
   And fades, and she secures him.

The falling leaf inaugurates
   The reign of her confusion;
The pounding wave reverberates
   The dirge of her illusion;
And home, where passion lived and died,
Becomes a place where she can hide,
While all the town and harbour side
   Vibrate with her seclusion.

25

We tell you, tapping on our brows,
  The story as it should be—
As if the story of a house
  Were told, or ever could be;
We'll have no kindly veil between
Her visions and those we have seen—
As if we guessed what hers have been,
  Or what they are or would be.

Meanwhile we do no harm; for they
  That with a god have striven,
Not hearing much of what we say,
  Take what the god has given;
Though like waves breaking it may be,
Or like a changed familiar tree,
Or like a stairway to the sea
  Where down the blind are driven.

CLAVERING

I say no more for Clavering
  Than I should say of him who fails
To bring his wounded vessel home
  When reft of rudder and of sails;

I say no more than I should say
  Of any other one who sees
Too far for guidance of to-day,
  Too near for the eternities.

I think of him as I should think
  Of one who for scant wages played,
And faintly, a flawed instrument
  That fell while it was being made;

26

I think of him as one who fared,   EDWIN
  Unfaltering and undeceived,   ARLING-
Amid mirages of renown   TON
  And urgings of the unachieved;   ROBIN-
    SON

I think of him as one who gave
  To Lingard leave to be amused,
And listened with a patient grace
  That we, the wise ones, had refused:

I think of metres that he wrote
  For Cubit, the ophidian guest:
'What Lilith, or Dark Lady' . . . Well.
  Time swallows Cubit with the rest.

I think of last words that he said
  One midnight over Calverly:
'Good-bye—good man.' He was not good;
  So Clavering was wrong, you see.

I wonder what had come to pass
  Could he have borrowed for a spell
The fiery-frantic indolence
  That made a ghost of Leffingwell;

I wonder if he pities us
  Who cautioned him till he was grey
To build his house with ours on earth
  And have an end of yesterday;

I wonder what it was we saw
  To make us think that we were strong;
I wonder if he saw too much,
  Or if he looked one way too long.

But when were thoughts or wonderings
  To ferret out the man within?

Why prate of what he seemed to be,
  And all that he might not have been?

He clung to phantoms and to friends,
  And never came to anything.
He left a wreath on Cubit's grave.
I say no more for Clavering.

THE LONG RACE

Up the old hill to the old house again
Where fifty years ago the friend was young
Who should be waiting somewhere there among
Old things that least remembered most remain,
He toiled on with a pleasure that was pain
To think how soon asunder would be flung
The curtain half a century had hung
Between the two ambitions they had slain.

They dredged an hour for words, and then were done.
'Good-bye! . . . You have the same old weather-vane—
Your little horse that's always on the run.'
And all the way down back to the next train,
Down the old hill to the old road again,
It seemed as if the little horse had won.

LUKE HAVERGAL

Go to the western gate, Luke Havergal,
There where the vines cling crimson on the wall,
And in the twilight wait for what will come.
The leaves will whisper there of her, and some,
Like flying words, will strike you as they fall;
But go, and if you listen, she will call.

28

Go to the western gate, Luke Havergal—
Luke Havergal.

EDWIN
ARLING-
TON
ROBIN-
SON

No, there is not a dawn in eastern skies
To rift the fiery night that's in your eyes;
But there, where western glooms are gathering,
The dark will end the dark, if anything:
God slays himself with every leaf that flies,
And hell is more than half of paradise.
No, there is not a dawn in eastern skies—
In eastern skies.

Out of a grave I come to tell you this,
Out of a grave I come to quench the kiss
That flames upon your forehead with a glow
That binds you to the way that you must go.
Yes, there is yet one way to where she is,
Bitter, but one that faith may never miss.
Out of a grave I come to tell you this—
To tell you this.

There is the western gate, Luke Havergal,
There are the crimson leaves upon the wall.
Go, for the winds are tearing them away,—
Nor think to riddle the dead words they say,
Nor any more to feel them as they fall;
But go, and if you trust her she will call.
There is the western gate, Luke Havergal—
Luke Havergal.

Edgar Lee Masters

(1869-1950)

JOHN HORACE BURLESON

I won the prize essay at school
Here in the village,
And published a novel before I was twenty-five.
I went to the city for themes and to enrich my art;
There married the banker's daughter,
And later became president of the bank—
Always looking forward to some leisure
To write an epic novel of the war.
Meanwhile friend of the great, and lover of letters,
And host to Matthew Arnold and to Emerson.
An after dinner speaker, writing essays
For local clubs. At last brought here—
My boyhood home, you know—
Not even a little tablet in Chicago
To keep my name alive.
How great it is to write the single line:
'Roll on, thou deep and dark blue Ocean, roll!'

EDITOR WHEDON

To be able to see every side of every question;
To be on every side, to be everything, to be nothing long;
To pervert truth, to ride it for a purpose,
To use great feelings and passions of the human family
For base designs, for cunning ends,
To wear a mask like the Greek actors—
Your eight-page paper—behind which you huddle,

Bawling through the megaphone of big type:
'This is I, the giant.'
Thereby also living the life of a sneak-thief,
Poisoned with the anonymous words
Of your clandestine soul.
To scratch dirt over scandal for money,
And exhume it to the winds for revenge,
Or to sell papers,
Crushing reputations, or bodies, if need be,
To win at any cost, save your own life.
To glory in demoniac power, ditching civilization,
As a paranoiac boy puts a log on the track
And derails the express train.
To be an editor, as I was.
Then to lie here close by the river over the place
Where the sewage flows from the village,
And the empty cans and garbage are dumped,
And abortions are hidden.

PERRY ZOLL

My thanks, friends of the County Scientific Association,
For this modest boulder,
And its little tablet of bronze.
Twice I tried to join your honoured body,
And was rejected,
And when my little brochure
On the intelligence of plants
Began to attract attention
You almost voted me in.
After that I grew beyond the need of you
And your recognition.
Yet I do not reject your memorial stone,
Seeing that I should, in so doing,
Deprive you of honour to yourselves.

J. MILTON MILES

Whenever the Presbyterian bell
Was rung by itself, I knew it as the Presbyterian bell.
But when its sound was mingled
With the sound of the Methodist, the Christian,
The Baptist and the Congregational,
I could no longer distinguish it,
Nor any one from the others, or either of them.
And as many voices called to me in life
Marvel not that I could not tell
The true from the false,
Nor even, at last, the voice that I should have known.

Stephen Crane

(1871-1900)

FOUR POEMS

I

In the desert
I saw a creature, naked, bestial,
Who, squatting upon the ground,
Held his heart in his hands,
And ate of it.
I said, 'Is it good, friend?'
'It is bitter—bitter,' he answered;
'But I like it
Because it is bitter,
And because it is my heart.'

II

Once there came a man
Who said,
'Range me all men of the world in rows.'
And instantly
There was terrific clamour among the people
Against being ranged in rows.
There was a loud quarrel, world-wide.
It endured for ages;
And blood was shed
By those who would not stand in rows,
And by those who pined to stand in rows.
Eventually, the man went to death, weeping.
And those who stayed in bloody scuffle
Knew not the great simplicity.

III

A man said to the universe:
'Sir, I exist!'
'However,' replied the universe,
'The fact has not created in me
A sense of obligation.'

IV

A man adrift on a slim spar
A horizon smaller than the rim of a bottle
Tented waves rearing lashy dark points
The near whine of froth in circles.
God is cold.

The incessant raise and swing of the sea
And growl after growl of crest
The sinkings, green, seething, endless
The upheaval half-completed.
God is cold.

The seas are in the hollow of The Hand;
Oceans may be turned to a spray
Raining down through the stars
Because of a gesture of pity toward a babe.
Oceans may become grey ashes,
Die with a long moan and a roar
Amid the tumult of the fishes
And the cries of the ships,
Because The Hand beckons the mice.
A horizon smaller than a doomed assassin's cap,
Inky, surging tumults
A reeling, drunken sky and no sky
A pale hand sliding from a polished spar.
God is cold.

The puff of a coat imprisoning air:
A face kissing the water-death
A weary slow sway of a lost hand
And the sea, the moving sea, the sea.
                    God is cold.

STEPHEN
CRANE

Trumble Stickney

(1874-1904)

MNEMOSYNE

It's autumn in the country I remember.

How warm a wind blew here about the ways!
And shadows on the hillside lay to slumber
During the long sun-sweetened summer-days.

It's cold abroad the country I remember.

The swallows veering skimmed the golden grain
At midday with a wing aslant and limber;
And yellow cattle browsed upon the plain.

It's empty down the country I remember.

I had a sister lovely in my sight:
Her hair was dark, her eyes were very sombre;
We sang together in the woods at night.

It's lonely in the country I remember.

The babble of our children fills my ears,
And on our hearth I stare the perished ember
To flames that show all starry thro' my tears.

It's dark about the country I remember.

There are the mountains where I lived. The path
Is slushed with cattle-tracks and fallen timber,
The stumps are twisted by the tempests' wrath.

But that I knew these places are my own,
I'd ask how came such wretchedness to cumber
The earth, and I to people it alone.

It rains across the country I remember.

IN AMPEZZO

Only once more and not again—the larches
Shake to the wind their echo, 'Not again,'—
We see, below the sky that over-arches
Heavy and blue, the plain

Between Tofana lying and Cristallo
In meadowy earths above the ringing stream:
Whence interchangeably desire may follow,
Hesitant as in dream,

At sunset, south, by lilac promontories
Under green skies to Italy, or forth
By calms of morning beyond Lavinores
Tyrolward and to north:

As now, this last of latter days, when over
The brownish field by peasants are undone
Some widths of grass, some plots of mountain clover
Under the autumn sun,

With honey-warm perfume that risen lingers
In mazes of low heat, or takes the **air**,
Passing delicious as a woman's fingers
Passing amid the hair;

When scythes are swishing and the mower's muscle
Spans a repeated crescent to and fro,

Or in dry stalks of corn the sickles rustle,
Tangle, detach and go,

Far thro' the wide blue day and greening meadow
Whose blots of amber beaded are with sheaves,
Whereover pallidly a cloud-shadow
Deadens the earth and leaves:

Whilst high around and near, their heads of iron
Sunken in sky whose azure overlights
Ravine and edges, stand the grey and maron
Desolate Dolomites,—

And older than decay from the small summit
Unfolds a stream of pebbly wreckage down
Under the suns of midday, like some comet
Struck into gravel stone.

Faintly across this gold and amethystine
September, images of summer fade;
And gentle dreams now freshen on the pristine
Viols, awhile unplayed,

Of many a place where lovingly we wander,
More dearly held that quickly we forsake,—
A pine by sullen coasts, an oleander
Reddening on the lake.

And there, each year with more familiar motion,
From many a bird and windy forestries,
Or along shaking fringes of the ocean,
Vapours of music rise.

From many easts the morning gives her splendour;
The shadows fill with colours we forget;
Remembered tints at evening grow tender,
Tarnished with violet.

Let us away! soon sheets of winter metal
On this discoloured mountain-land will close,
While elsewhere Spring-time weaves a crimson petal,
Builds and perfumes a rose.

Away! for here the mountain sinks in gravel.
Let us forget the unhappy site with change,
And go, if only happiness be travel
After the new and strange:—

Unless 't were better to be very single,
To follow some diviner monotone,
And in all beauties, where ourselves commingle,
Love but a love, but one,

Across this shadowy minute of our living,
What time our hearts so magically sing,
To meditate our fever, simply giving
All in a little thing?

Just as here, past yon dumb and melancholy
Sameness of ruin, while the mountains ail,
Summer and sunset-coloured autumn slowly
Dissipate down the vale;

And all these lines along the sky that measure
Sorapis and the rocks of Mezzodì
Crumble by foamy miles into the azure
Mediterranean sea:

Whereas to-day at sunrise, under brambles,
A league above the moss and drying pines
I picked this little—in my hand that trembles—
Parcel of columbines.

LEAVE HIM NOW QUIET

Leave him now quiet by the way
To rest apart.
I know what draws him to the dust alway
And churns him in the builder's lime:
He has the fright of time.
I heard it knocking in his breast
A minute since;
His human eyes did wince,
He stubborned like the massive slaughter beast
And as a thing o'erwhelmed with sound
Stood bolted to the ground.

Leave him, for rest alone can cure—
If cure there be—
This waif upon the sea.
He is of those who slanted the great door
And listened—wretched little lad—
To what they said.

Gertrude Stein

(1874-1946)

Pigeons on the grass alas.
Pigeons on the grass alas.
Short longer grass short longer longer shorter yellow
grass
    Pigeons large pigeons on the shorter longer yellow grass
alas pigeons on the grass.
If they were not pigeons what were they.
If they were not pigeons on the grass alas what were they.
He had heard of a third and he asked about it it was a magpie
in the sky. If a magpie in the sky on the sky can not cry if the
pigeon on the grass alas can alas and to pass the pigeon on the
grass alas and the magpie in the sky on the sky and to try
and to try alas on the grass alas the pigeon on the grass the
pigeon on the grass and alas. They might be very well very
well very well they might be they might be very well they
might be very well very well they might be.
    Let Lucy Lily Lily Lucy Lucy let Lucy Lucy Lily Lily
Lily Lily Lily let Lily Lucy Lucy let Lily. Let Lucy Lily.

(from Four Saints in Three Acts)

Susan B.'s voice. We cannot retrace our steps, going
forward may be the same as going back-
wards. We cannot retrace our steps,
retrace our steps. All my long life, all
my life, we do not retrace our steps, all
my long life, but.
    (A silence a long silence)
    But—we do not retrace our steps, all
my long life, and here, here we are here,

41

in marble and gold, did I say gold, yes I
said gold, in marble and gold and where—
(A silence)
Where is where. In my long life of
effort and strife, dear life, life is strife, in
my long life, it will not come and go, I
tell you so, it will stay it will pay but
(A long silence)
But do I want what we have got, has
it not gone, what made it live, has it not
gone because now it is had, in my long life
in my long life
(Silence)
Life is strife, I was a martyr all my
life not to what I won but to what was
done.
(Silence)
Do you know because I tell you so, or do
you know, do you know.
(Silence)
My long life, my long life.

(from *The Mother of Us All*)

Robert Frost

(1875-   )

THE OVEN BIRD

There is a singer everyone has heard,
Loud, a mid-summer and a mid-wood bird,
Who makes the solid tree trunks sound again.
He says that leaves are old and that for flowers
Mid-summer is to spring as one to ten.
He says the early petal-fall is past
When pear and cherry bloom went down in showers
On sunny days a moment overcast;
And comes that other fall we name the fall.
He says the highway dust is over all.
The bird would cease and be as other birds
But that he knows in singing not to sing.
The question that he frames in all but words
Is what to make of a diminished thing.

THE PAUPER WITCH OF GRAFTON

Now that they've got it settled whose I be,
I'm going to tell them something they won't like:
They've got it settled wrong and I can prove it.
Flattered I must be to have two towns fighting
To make a present of me to each other.
They don't dispose me, either one of them,
To spare them any trouble. Double trouble's
Always the witch's motto anyway.
I'll double theirs for both of them—you watch me.
They'll find they've got the whole thing to do over,

ROBERT
FROST That is, if facts is what they want to go by.
They set a lot (now don't they?) by a record
Of Arthur Amy's having once been up
For Hog Reeve in March Meeting here in Warren.
I could have told them anytime this twelvemonth
The Arthur Amy I was married to
Couldn't have been the one they say was up
In Warren at March Meeting for the reason
He wa'n't but fifteen at the time they say.
The Arthur Amy I was married to
Voted the only times he ever voted,
Which wasn't many, in the town of Wentworth.
One of the times was when 'twas in the warrant
To see if the town wanted to take over
The tote road to our clearing where we lived.
I'll tell you who'd remember—Heman Lapish.
Their Arthur Amy was the father of mine.
So now they've dragged it through the law courts once
I guess they'd better drag it through again.
Wentworth and Warren's both good towns to live in,
Only I happen to prefer to live
In Wentworth from now on; and when all's said,
Right's right, and the temptation to do right
When I can hurt someone by doing it
Has always been too much for me, it has.
I know of some folks that'd be set up
At having in their town a noted witch:
But most would have to think of the expense
That even I would be. They ought to know
That as a witch I'd often milk a bat
And that'd be enough to last for days.
It's make my position stronger, think,
If I was to consent to give some sign
To make it surer that I was a witch?
It wa'n't no sign, I s'pose, when Mallice Huse
Said that I took him out in his old age
And rode all over everything on him

Until I'd had him worn to skin and bones,
And if I'd left him hitched unblanketed
In front of one Town Hall, I'd left him hitched
In front of every one in Grafton County.
Some cried shame on me not to blanket him,
The poor old man. It would have been all right
If someone hadn't said to gnaw the posts
He stood beside and leave his trade mark on them,
So they could recognize them. Not a post
That they could hear tell of was scarified.
They made him keep on gnawing till he whined.
Then that same smarty someone said to look—
He'd bet Huse was a cribber and had gnawed
The crib he slept in—and as sure's you're born
They found he'd gnawed the four posts of his bed,
All four of them to splinters. What did that prove?
Not that he hadn't gnawed the hitching posts
He said he had besides. Because a horse
Gnaws in the stable ain't no proof to me
He don't gnaw trees and posts and fences too.
But everybody took it for a proof.
I was a strapping girl of twenty then.
The smarty someone who spoiled everything
Was Arthur Amy. You know who he was.
That was the way he started courting me.
He never said much after we were married,
But I mistrusted he was none too proud
Of having interfered in the Huse business.
I guess he found he got more out of me
By having me a witch. Or something happened
To turn him round. He got to saying things
To undo what he'd done and make it right,
Like, 'No, she ain't come back from kiting yet.
Last night was one of her nights out. She's kiting.
She thinks when the wind makes a night of it
She might as well herself.' But he liked best
To let on he was plagued to death with me:

45

If anyone had seen me coming home
Over the ridgepole, 'stride of a broomstick,
As often as he had in the tail of the night,
He guessed they'd know what he had to put up with.
Well, I showed Arthur Amy signs enough
Off from the house as far as we could keep
And from barn smells you can't wash out of ploughed ground
With all the rain and snow of seven years;
And I don't mean just skulls of Rogers' Rangers
On Moosilauke, but woman signs to man,
Only bewitched so I would last him longer.
Up where the trees grow short, the mosses tall,
I made him gather me wet snow berries
On slippery rocks beside a waterfall.
I made him do it for me in the dark.
And he liked everything I made him do.
I hope if he is where he sees me now
He's so far off he can't see what I've come to.
You *can* come down from everything to nothing.
All is, if I'd a-known when I was young
And full of it, that this would be the end,
It doesn't seem as if I'd had the courage
To make so free and kick up in folks' faces.
And I might have, but it doesn't seem as if.

TWO LOOK AT TWO

Love and forgetting might have carried them
A little further up the mountainside
With night so near, but, not much further up.
They must have halted soon in any case
With thoughts of the path back, how rough it was
With rocks and washout, and unsafe in darkness;
When they were halted by a tumbled wall
With barbed-wire binding. They were facing this,

Spending what onward impulse they still had
In one last look the way they must not go,
On up the failing path, where, if a stone
Or earthslide moved at night, it moved itself;
No footstep moved it. 'This is all,' they sighed,
'Good-night to woods.' But not so; there was more.
A doe from round a spruce stood looking at them
Across the wall, as near the wall as they.
She saw them in their field, they her in hers.
The difficulty of seeing what stood still,
Like some up-ended boulder split in two,
Was in her clouded eyes: they saw no fear there.
She seemed to think that two thus they were safe.
Then, as if they were something that, though strange,
She could not trouble her mind with too long,
She sighed and passed unscared along the wall.
'*This*, then, is all. What more is there to ask?'
But no, not yet. A snort to bid them wait.
A buck from round the spruce stood looking at them
Across the wall, as near the wall as they.
This was an antlered buck of lusty nostril,
Not the same doe come back into her place.
He viewed them quizzically with jerks of head,
As if to ask, 'Why don't you make some motion?
Or give some sign of life? Because you can't.
I doubt if you're as living as you look.'
This till he had them almost feeling dared
To stretch a proffering hand—and a spell-breaking.
Then he too passed unscared along the wall.
Two had seen two, whichever side you spoke from.
'This *must* be all.' It was all. Still they stood,
A great wave from it going over them,
As if the earth in one unlooked-for favour
Had made them certain earth returned their love.

NEITHER OUT FAR NOR IN DEEP

The people along the sand
All turn and look one way.
They turn their back on the land.
They look at the sea all day.

As long as it takes to pass
A ship keeps raising its hull;
The wetter ground like glass
Reflects a standing gull.

The land may vary more;
But wherever the truth may be—
The water comes ashore,
And the people look at the sea.

They cannot look out far.
They cannot look in deep.
But when was that ever a bar
To any watch they keep?

DESIGN

I found a dimpled spider, fat and white,
On a white heal-all, holding up a moth
Like a white piece of rigid satin cloth—
Assorted characters of death and blight
Mixed ready to begin the morning right,
Like the ingredients of a witches' broth—
A snow-drop spider, a flower like a froth,
And dead wings carried like a paper kite.

What had that flower to do with being white,
The wayside blue and innocent heal-all?

48

What brought the kindred spider to that height,
Then steered the white moth thither in the night?
What but design of darkness to appal?—
If design govern in a thing so small.

THE MOST OF IT

He thought he kept the universe alone;
For all the voice in answer he could wake
Was but the mocking echo of his own
From some tree-hidden cliff across the lake.
Some morning from the boulder-broken beach
He would cry out on life, that what it wants
Is not its own love back in copy speech,
But counter-love, original response.
And nothing ever came of what he cried
Unless it was the embodiment that crashed
In the cliff's talus on the other side,
And then in the far distant water splashed,
But after a time allowed for it to swim,
Instead of proving human when it neared
And someone else additional to him,
As a great buck it powerfully appeared,
Pushing the crumpled water up ahead,
And landed pouring like a waterfall,
And stumbled through the rocks with horny tread,
And forced the underbrush—and that was all.

NEVER AGAIN WOULD BIRDS' SONG BE THE SAME

He would declare and could himself believe
That the birds there in all the garden round
From having heard the daylong voice of Eve
Had added to their own an oversound,
Her tone of meaning but without the words.
Admittedly an eloquence so soft
Could only have had an influence on birds
When call or laughter carried it aloft.
Be that as may be, she was in their song.
Moreover her voice upon their voices crossed
Had now persisted in the woods so long
That probably it never would be lost.
Never again would birds' song be the same.
And to do that to birds was why she came.

THE MIDDLENESS OF THE ROAD

The road at the top of the rise
Seems to come to an end
And take off into the skies.
So at the distant bend

It seems to go into a wood,
The place of standing still
As long the trees have stood.
But say what Fancy will,

The mineral drops that explode
To drive my ton of car
Are limited to the road.
They deal with near and far,

But have almost nothing to do
With the absolute flight and rest
The universal blue
And local green suggest.

ROBERT
FROST

DIRECTIVE

Back out of all this now too much for us,
Back in a time made simple by the loss
Of detail, burned, dissolved, and broken off
Like graveyard marble sculpture in the weather,
There is a house that is no more a house
Upon a farm that is no more a farm
And in a town that is no more a town.
The road there, if you'll let a guide direct you
Who only has at heart your getting lost,
May seem as if it should have been a quarry—
Great monolithic knees the former town
Long since gave up pretence of keeping covered.
And there's a story in a book about it:
Besides the wear of iron wagon wheels
The ledges show lines ruled southeast northwest,
The chisel work of an enormous Glacier
That braced his feet against the Arctic Pole.
You must not mind a certain coolness from him
Still said to haunt this side of Panther Mountain.
Nor need you mind the serial ordeal
Of being watched from forty cellar holes
As if by eye pairs out of forty firkins.
As for the woods' excitement over you
That sends light rustle rushes to their leaves,
Charge that to upstart inexperience.
Where were they all not twenty years ago?
They think too much of having shaded out
A few old pecker-fretted apple trees.

ROBERT
FROST Make yourself up a cheering song of how
Someone's road home from work this once was,
Who may be just ahead of you on foot
Or creaking with a buggy load of grain.
The height of the adventure is the height
Of country where two village cultures faded
Into each other. Both of them are lost.
And if you're lost enough to find yourself
By now, pull in your ladder road behind you
And put a sign up CLOSED to all but me.
Then make yourself at home. The only field
Now left's no bigger than a harness gall.
First there's the children's house of make believe,
Some shattered dishes underneath a pine,
The playthings in the playhouse of the children.
Weep for what little things could make then glad.
Then for the house that is no more a house,
But only a belilaced cellar hole,
Now slowly closing like a dent in dough.
This was no playhouse but a house in earnest.
Your destination and your destiny's
A brook that was the water of the house,
Cold as a spring as yet so near its source,
Too lofty and original to rage.
(We know the valley streams that when aroused
Will leave their tatters hung on barb and thorn.)
I have kept hidden in the instep arch
Of an old cedar at the waterside
A broken drinking goblet like the Grail
Under a spell so the wrong ones can't find it,
So can't get saved, as Saint Mark says they mustn't.
(I stole the goblet from the children's playhouse.)
Here are your waters and your watering place.
Drink and be whole again beyond confusion.

Don Marquis

(1878-1937)

archys autobiography

if all the verse what i have wrote
were boiled together in a kettle
twould make a meal for every goat
from nome to popocatapetl
mexico

and all the prose what i have penned
if laid together end to end
would reach from russia to south bend
indiana

but all the money what i saved
from all them works at which i slaved
is not enough to get me shaved
every morning

and all the dams which i care
if heaped together in the air
would not reach much of anywhere
they wouldnt

because i dont shave every day
and i write for arts sake anyway
and always hate to take my pay
i loathe it

and all of you who credit that
could sit down on an opera hat
and never crush the darn thing flat
you skeptics
                    archy

archys last name

boss i just discovered what
my last name is i
pass it on to you i belong to the
family of the blattidæ right o
said mehitabel the cat when i told her
about it they have
got you sized up right you blatt out
everything you hear
i gleaned the information from
a bulletin issued by the
united states department of
agriculture which you left on the
floor by your desk it was entitled
cockroaches and written by
e l marlatt entomologist and acting
chief in the absence of the chief and he
tells a dozen ways of killing roaches boss
what business has the united states
government got
to sick a high salaried
expert onto a poor little roach
please leave me some
more cheerful literature also please
get your typewriter fixed the keys are
working hard again butting them as i
do one at a time with
my head i get awful pains in my
neck writing for you
                                archy

artists shouldnt have offspring

DON
MARQUIS

A bulletin from Archy the Cockroach, who started out last July to
hitch-hike from Hollywood to New York with Mehitabel the Cat and
Mehitabel's seven platinum-blonde kittens :

had a great ride boss
got a ride on the running board of a car
and caught up with mehitabel
in new mexico where she is gadding about
with a coyote friend
i asked her where the kittens were
kittens said mehitabel kittens
with a puzzled look on her face
why goodness gracious i seem to remember
that i did have some kittens
i hope nothing terrible has happened
to the poor little things but if something has
i suppose they are better off
an artist like me shouldnt really
have offspring it handicaps her career
archy i want you to meet my boy friend
cowboy bill the coyote i call him
i am trying to get him to come to new york
with me and do a burlesque turn
isnt he handsome i said tactfully that he looked
very distinguished to me and all bill said
was nerts insect nerts
                    archy

Carl Sandburg

(1878-   )

PERSONALITY

Musings of a Police Reporter in the Identification Bureau

You have loved forty women, but you have only one thumb.
You have led a hundred secret lives, but you mark only one
thumb.
You go round the world and fight in a thousand wars and
win all the world's honours, but when you come back
home the print of the one thumb your mother gave
you is the same print of thumb you had in the old
home when your mother kissed you and said good-bye.
Out of the whirling womb of time come millions of men and
their feet crowd the earth and they cut one another's
throats for room to stand and among them all are not
two thumbs alike.
Somewhere is a Great God of Thumbs who can tell the
inside story of this.

CLOCKS

Here is a face that says half-past seven the same way whether
a murder or a wedding goes on, whether a funeral or a
picnic crowd passes.
A tall one I know at the end of a hallway broods in shadows
and is watching booze eat out the insides of the man of
the house; it has seen five hopes go in five years: one
woman, one child, and three dreams.

A little one carried in a leather box by an actress rides with CARL
her to hotels and is under her pillow in a sleeping-car SAND-
between one-night stands. BURG
One hoists a phiz over a railroad station; it points numbers
to people a quarter-mile away who believe it when
other clocks fail.
And of course . . . there are wrist watches over the pulses of
airmen eager to go to France. . . .

BAS-RELIEF

Five geese deploy mysteriously.
Onward proudly with flagstaffs,
Hearses with silver bugles,
Bushels of plum-blossoms dropping
For ten mystic web-feet—
Each his own drum-major,
Each charged with the honour
Of the ancient goose nation,
Each with a nose-length surpassing
The nose-lengths of rival nations.
Sombrely, slowly, unimpeachably,
Five geese deploy mysteriously.

Vachel Lindsay

(1879-1931)

THE FLUTE OF THE LONELY

(To the tune of 'Gaily the Troubadour')

Faintly the ne'er-do-well
Breathed through his flute:
All the tired neighbour-folk,
Hearing, were mute.
In their neat doorways sat,
Labours all done,
Helpless, relaxed, o'er-wrought,
Evening begun.

None of them there beguiled
Work-thoughts away,
Like to this reckless, wild
Loafer by day.
(Weeds in his flowers upgrown!
Fences awry!
Rubbish and bottles heaped!
Yard like a sty!)

There in his lonely door,
Leering and lean,
Staggering, liquor-stained,
Outlawed, obscene—
Played he his moonlight thought,
Mastered his flute.
All the tired neighbour-folk,
Hearing, were mute.
None but he, in that block,

Knew such a tune.
All loved the strain, and all
Looked at the moon!

WHAT THE MOON SAW

Two statesmen met by moonlight.
Their ease was partly feigned.
They glanced about the prairie.
Their faces were constrained.
In various ways aforetime
They had misled the state,
Yet did it so politely
Their henchmen thought them great.
They sat beneath a hedge and spake
No word, but had a smoke.
A satchel passed from hand to hand.
Next day, the deadlock broke.

BRYAN, BRYAN, BRYAN, BRYAN

*The campaign of eighteen ninety-six, as viewed at the time by a
sixteen-year-old, etc.*

I

In a nation of one hundred fine, mob-hearted, lynching,
    relenting, repenting millions,
There are plenty of sweeping, swinging, stinging, gorgeous
    things to shout about,
And knock your old blue devils out.

I brag and chant of Bryan, Bryan, Bryan,
Candidate for president who sketched a silver Zion,
The one American Poet who could sing outdoors,

VACHEL
LINDSAY He brought in tides of wonder, of unprecedented splendour,
Wild roses from the plains, that made hearts tender,
All the funny circus silks
Of politics unfurled,
Bartlett pears of romance that were honey at the cores,
And torchlights down the street, to the end of the world.

There were truths eternal in the gab and tittle-tattle.
There were real heads broken in the fustian and the rattle.
There were real lines drawn:
Not the silver and the gold,
But Nebraska's cry went eastward against the dour and old,
The mean and cold.

It was eighteen ninety-six, and I was just sixteen
And Altgeld ruled in Springfield, Illinois,
When there came from the sunset Nebraska's shout of joy:
In a coat like a deacon, in a black Stetson hat
He scourged the elephant plutocrats
With barbed wire from the Platte.
The scales dropped from their mighty eyes.
They saw that summer's noon
A tribe of wonders coming
To a marching tune.

Oh, the longhorns from Texas,
The jay hawks from Kansas,
The plop-eyed bungaroo and giant giassicus,
The varmint, chipmunk, bugaboo,
The horned-toad, prairie-dog and ballyhoo,
From all the newborn states arow,

Bidding the eagles of the west fly on,
Bidding the eagles of the west fly on.
The fawn, prodactyl and thing-a-ma-jig,
The rakaboor, the hellangone,
The whangdoodle, batfowl and pig,

The coyote, wild-cat and grizzly in a glow,   VACHEL
In a miracle of health and speed, the whole breed abreast,   LINDSAY
They leaped the Mississippi, blue border of the West,
From the Gulf to Canada, two thousand miles long:—
Against the towns of Tubal Cain,
Ah,—sharp was their song.
Against the ways of Tubal Cain, too cunning for the young,
The longhorn calf, the buffalo and wampus gave tongue.

These creatures were defending things Mark Hanna never
    dreamed:
The moods of airy childhood that in desert dews gleamed,
The gossamers and whimsies,
The monkeyshines and didoes
Rank and strange
Of the canyons and the range,
The ultimate fantastics

Of the far western slope,
And of prairie schooner children
Born beneath the stars,
Beneath falling snows,
Of the babies born at midnight
In the sod huts of lost hope,
With no physician there,
Except a Kansas prayer,
With the Indian raid a howling through the air.
And all these in their helpless days
By the dour East oppressed,
Mean paternalism
Making their mistakes for them,
Crucifying half the West,
Till the whole Atlantic coast
Seemed a giant spider's nest.

And these children and their sons
At last rode through the cactus,

A cliff of mighty cowboys
On the lope,
With gun and rope.
And all the way to frightened Maine the old East heard them
call,
And saw our Bryan by a mile lead the wall
Of men and whirling flowers and beasts,
The bard and the prophet of them all.
Prairie avenger, mountain lion,
Bryan, Bryan, Bryan, Bryan,
Gigantic troubadour, speaking like a siege gun,
Smashing Plymouth Rock with his boulders from the West,
And just a hundred miles behind, tornadoes piled across the
sky,
Blotting out sun and moon,
A sign on high.

Headlong, dazed and blinking in the weird green light,
The scalawags made moan, afraid to fight.

II

When Bryan came to Springfield, and Altgeld gave him
greeting,
Rochester was deserted, Divernon was deserted,
Mechanicsburg, Riverton, Chickenbristle, Cotton Hill,
Empty: for all Sangamon drove to the meeting—
In silver-decked racing cart,
Buggy, buckboard, carryall,
Carriage, phaeton, whatever would haul,
And silver-decked farm-wagons gritted, banged and rolled,
With the new tale of Bryan by the iron tires told.

The State House loomed afar,
A speck, a hive, a football,
A captive balloon!

And the town was all one spreading wing of bunting, plumes, VACHEL
    and sunshine, LINDSAY
Every rag and flag, and Bryan picture sold,
When the rigs in many a dusty line
Jammed our streets at noon,
And joined the wild parade against the power of gold.

We roamed, we boys from High School,
With mankind,
While Springfield gleamed,
Silk-lined.
Oh, Tom Dines, and Art Fitzgerald,
And the gangs that they could get!
I can hear them yelling yet.
Helping the incantation,
Defying aristocracy,
With every bridle gone,

Ridding the world of the low down mean,
Bidding the eagles of the West fly on,
Bidding the eagles of the West fly on,
We were bully, wild and woolly,
Never yet curried below the knees.
We saw flowers in the air,
Fair as the Pleiades, bright as Orion,
—Hopes of all mankind,
Made rare, resistless, thrice refined.
Oh, we bucks from every Springfield ward!
Colts of democracy—
Yet time-winds out of Chaos from the star-fields of the Lord.

The long parade rolled on. I stood by my best girl.
She was a cool young citizen, with wise and laughing eyes.
With my necktie by my ear, I was stepping on my dear,
But she kept like a pattern, without a shaken curl.

She wore in her hair a brave prairie rose.
Her gold chums cut her, for that was not the pose.

No Gibson Girl would wear it in that fresh way.
But we were fairy Democrats, and this was our day.

The earth rocked like the ocean, the sidewalk was a deck.
The houses for the moment were lost in the wide wreck.
And the bands played strange and stranger music as they
    trailed along.
Against the ways of Tubal Cain,
Ah, sharp was their song!
The demons in the bricks, the demons in the grass,
The demons in the bank-vaults peered out to see us pass,
And the angels in the trees, the angels in the grass,
The angels in the flags, peered out to see us pass.
And the sidewalk was our chariot, and the flowers bloomed
    higher,
And the street turned to silver and the grass turned to fire,
And then it was but grass, and the town was there again,
A place for women and men.

III

Then we stood where we could see
Every band,
And the speaker's stand.
And Bryan took the platform.
And he was introduced.
And he lifted his hand
And cast a new spell.
Progressive silence fell
In Springfield,
In Illinois,
Around the world.
Then we heard these glacial boulders across the prairie
    rolled:
'The people have a right to make their own mistakes . . .
You shall not crucify mankind
Upon a cross of gold.'

And everybody heard him—
In the streets and State House yard.
And everybody heard him
In Springfield, in Illinois,
Around and around and around the world,
That danced upon its axis
And like a darling broncho whirled.

IV

July, August, suspense.
Wall Street lost to sense.
August, September, October,
More suspense,
And the whole East down like a wind-smashed fence.

Then Hanna to the rescue,
Hanna of Ohio,
Rallying the roller-tops,
Rallying the bucket-shops.
Threatening drouth and death
Promising manna,
Rallying the trusts against the bawling flannelmouth;
Invading misers' cellars,

Tin-cans, socks,
Melting down the rocks,
Pouring out the long green to a million workers,
Spondulix by the mountain-load, to stop each new tornado,
And beat the cheapskate, blatherskite,
Populistic, anarchistic,
Deacon—desperado.

V

Election night at midnight:
Boy Bryan's defeat.
Defeat of western silver.

Defeat of the wheat.
Victory of letterfiles
And plutocrats in miles
With dollar signs upon their coats,
Diamond watchchains on their vests
And spats on their feet.
Victory of custodians,
Plymouth Rock,
And all that inbred landlord stock.
Victory of the neat.
Defeat of the aspen groves of Colorado valleys,
The blue bells of the Rockies,
And blue bonnets of old Texas,
By the Pittsburg alleys.
Defeat of alfalfa and the Mariposa lily.
Defeat of the Pacific and the long Mississippi.
Defeat of the young by the old and silly.
Defeat of tornadoes by the poison vats supreme.
Defeat of my boyhood, defeat of my dream.

VI

Where is McKinley, that respectable McKinley,
The man without an angle or a tangle,
Who soothed down the city man and soothed down the
    farmer,
The German, the Irish, the Southerner, the Northerner,
Who climbed every greasy pole, and slipped through every
    crack;
Who soothed down the gambling hall, the bar-room, the
    church,
The devil vote, the angel vote, the neutral vote,
The desperately wicked, and their victims on the rack,
The gold vote, the silver vote, the brass vote, the lead vote,
Every vote?...
Where is McKinley, Mark Hanna's McKinley,
His slave, his echo, his suit of clothes?

Gone to join the shadows, with the pomps of that time,   VACHEL
And the flame of that summer's prairie rose.   LINDSAY

Where is Cleveland whom the Democratic platform
Read from the party in a glorious hour,
Gone to join the shadows with pitchfork Tillman,
And sledge-hammer Altgeld who wrecked his power.

Where is Hanna, bulldog Hanna.
Low-browed Hanna, who said: 'Stand pat'?
Gone to his place with old Pierpont Morgan.
Gone somewhere . . . with lean rat Platt.

Where is Roosevelt, the young dude cowboy,
Who hated Bryan, then aped his way?
Gone to join the shadows with mighty Cromwell
And tall King Saul, till the Judgment day.

Where is Altgeld, brave as the truth,
Whose name the few still say with tears?
Gone to join the ironies with Old John Brown,
Whose fame rings loud for a thousand years.

Where is that boy, that Heaven-born Bryan,
That Homer Bryan, who sang from the West?
Gone to join the shadows with Altgeld the Eagle,
Where the kings and the slaves and the troubadours rest.

FACTORY WINDOWS ARE ALWAYS BROKEN

Factory windows are always broken.
Somebody's always throwing bricks,
Somebody's always heaving cinders,
Playing ugly Yahoo tricks.

VACHEL
LINDSAY
Factory windows are always broken.
Other windows are let alone.
No one throws through the chapel-window
The bitter, snarling derisive stone.

Factory windows are always broken.
Something or other is going wrong.
Something is rotten—I think, in Denmark.
End of the factory-window song.

Wallace Stevens

(1879-1955)

THE SNOW MAN

One must have a mind of winter
To regard the frost and the boughs
Of the pine-trees crusted with snow;

And have been cold a long time
To behold the junipers shagged with ice,
The spruces rough in the distant glitter

Of the January sun; and not to think
Of any misery in the sound of the wind,
In the sound of a few leaves,

Which is the sound of the land
Full of the same wind
That is blowing in the same bare place

For the listener, who listens in the snow,
And, nothing himself, beholds
Nothing that is not there and the nothing that is.

DISILLUSIONMENT OF TEN O'CLOCK

The houses are haunted
By white night-gowns.
None are green,
Or purple with green rings,
Or green with yellow rings,

Or yellow with blue rings.
None of them are strange,
With socks of lace
And beaded ceintures.
People are not going
To dream of baboons and periwinkles.
Only, here and there, an old sailor,
Drunk and asleep in his boots,
Catches tigers
In red weather.

SUNDAY MORNING

Complacencies of the peignoir, and late
Coffee and oranges in a sunny chair,
And the green freedom of a cockatoo
Upon a rug mingle to dissipate
The holy hush of ancient sacrifice.
She dreams a little, and she feels the dark
Encroachment of that old catastrophe,
As a calm darkens among water-lights.
The pungent oranges and bright, green wings
Seem things in some procession of the dead,
Winding across wide water, without sound.
The day is like wide water, without sound,
Stilled for the passing of her dreaming feet
Over the seas, to silent Palestine,
Dominion of the blood and sepulchre.

II

Why should she give her bounty to the dead?
What is divinity if it can come
Only in silent shadows and in dreams?

Shall she not find in comforts of the sun,
In pungent fruit and bright, green wings, or else
In any balm or beauty of the earth,
Things to be cherished like the thought of heaven?
Divinity must live within herself:
Passions of rain, or moods in falling snow;
Grievings in loneliness, or unsubdued
Elations when the forest blooms; gusty
Emotions on wet roads on autumn nights;
All pleasures and all pains, remembering
The bough of summer and the winter branch.
These are the measures destined for her soul.

III

Jove in the clouds had his inhuman birth.
No mother suckled him, no sweet land gave
Large-mannered motions to his mythy mind.
He moved among us, as a muttering king,
Magnificent, would move among his hinds,
Until our blood, commingling, virginal,
With heaven, brought such requital to desire
The very hinds discerned it, in a star.
Shall our blood fail? Or shall it come to be
The blood of paradise? And shall the earth
Seem all of paradise that we shall know?
The sky will be much friendlier then than now,
A part of labour and a part of pain,
And next in glory to enduring love,
Not this dividing and indifferent blue.

IV

She says, 'I am content when wakened birds,
Before they fly, test the reality
Of misty fields, by their sweet questionings;
But when the birds are gone, and their warm fields
Return no more, where, then, is paradise?'

There is not any haunt of prophecy,
Nor any old chimera of the grave,
Neither the golden underground, nor isle
Melodious, where spirits gat them home,
Nor visionary south, nor cloudy palm
Remote on heaven's hill, that has endured
As April's green endures; or will endure
Like her remembrance of awakened birds,
Or her desire for June and evening, tipped
By the consummation of the swallow's wings.

V

She says, 'But in contentment I still feel
The need of some imperishable bliss.'
Death is the mother of beauty; hence from her,
Alone, shall come fulfilment to our dreams
And our desires. Although she strews the leaves
Of sure obliteration on our paths,
The path sick sorrow took, the many paths
Where triumph rang its brassy phrase, or love
Whispered a little out of tenderness,
She makes the willow shiver in the sun
For maidens who were wont to sit and gaze
Upon the grass, relinquished to their feet.
She causes boys to pile new plums and pears
On disregarded plate. The maidens taste
And stray impassioned in the littering leaves.

VI

Is there no change of death in paradise?
Does ripe fruit never fall? Or do the boughs
Hang always heavy in that perfect sky,
Unchanging, yet so like our perishing earth,
With rivers like our own that seek for seas
They never find, the same receding shores
That never touch with inarticulate pang?

Why set the pear upon those river-banks
Or spice the shores with odours of the plum?
Alas, that they should wear our colours there,
The silken weavings of our afternoons,
And pick the strings of our insipid lutes!
Death is the mother of beauty, mystical,
Within whose burning bosom we devise
Our earthly mothers waiting, sleeplessly.

VII

Supple and turbulent, a ring of men
Shall chant in orgy on a summer morn
Their boisterous devotion to the sun,
Not as a god, but as a god might be,
Naked among them, like a savage source.
Their chant shall be a chant of paradise,
Out of their blood, returning to the sky;
And in their chant shall enter, voice by voice,
The windy lake wherein their lord delights,
The trees, like serafim, and echoing hills,
That choir among themselves long afterward.
They shall know well the heavenly fellowship
Of men that perish and of summer morn.
And whence they came and whither they shall go.
The dew upon their feet shall manifest.

VIII

She hears, upon that water without sound,
A voice that cries, 'The tomb in Palestine
Is not the porch of spirits lingering.
It is the grave of Jesus, where he lay.'
We live in an old chaos of the sun,
Or old dependency of day and night,
Or island solitude, unsponsored, free,
Of that wide water, inescapable.
Deer walk upon our mountains, and the quail

Whistle about us their spontaneous cries;
Sweet berries ripen in the wilderness;
And, in the isolation of the sky,
At evening, casual flocks of pigeons make
Ambiguous undulations as they sink,
Downward to darkness, on extended wings.

DRY LOAF

It is equal to living in a tragic land
To live in a tragic time.
Regard now the sloping, mountainous rocks
And the river that batters its way over stones,
Regard the hovels of those that live in this land.

That was what I painted behind the loaf,
The rocks not even touched by snow,
The pines along the river and the dry men blown
Brown as the bread, thinking of birds
Flying from burning countries and brown sand shores,

Birds that came like dirty water in waves
Flowing above the rocks, flowing over the sky,
As if the sky was a current that bore them along,
Spreading them as waves spread flat on the shore,
One after another washing the mountains bare.

It was the battering of drums I heard
It was hunger, it was the hungry that cried
And the waves, the waves were soldiers moving,
Marching and marching in a tragic time
Below me, on the asphalt, under the trees.

74

It was soldiers went marching over the rocks   WALLACE
STEVENS
And still the birds came, came in watery flocks,
Because it was spring and the birds had to come.
No doubt that soldiers had to be marching
And that drums had to be rolling, rolling, rolling.

WOMAN LOOKING AT A VASE OF FLOWERS

It was as if thunder took form upon
The piano, that time: the time when the crude
And jealous grandeurs of sun and sky
Scattered themselves in the garden, like
The wind dissolving into birds
The clouds becoming braided girls.
It was like the sea poured out again
In east wind beating the shutters at night.

Hoot,   little owl within her,   how
High blue became particular
In the leaf and bud and how the red,
Flicked into pieces, points of air,
Became—how the central, essential red
Escaped its large abstraction, became,
First, summer, then a lesser time,
Then the sides of peaches, of dusky pears.

Hoot how the inhuman colours fell
Into place beside her, where she was,
Like human conciliations, more like
A profounder reconciling, an act,
An affirmation free from doubt.
The crude and jealous formlessness
Became the form and the fragrance of things
Without clairvoyance, close to her.

BETHOU ME, SAID SPARROW

Bethou me, said sparrow, to the crackled blade,
And you, and you, bethou me as you blow,
When in my coppice you behold me be.

Ah, ké! the bloody wren, the felon jay,
Ké-ké, the jug-throated robin pouring out,
Bethou, bethou, bethou me in my glade.

There was such idiot minstrelsy in rain,
So many clappers going without bells,
That these bethous compose a heavenly gong.

One voice repeating, one tireless chorister,
The phrases of a single phrase, ké-ké,
A single text, granite monotony,

One sole face, like a photograph of fate,
Glass-blower's destiny, bloodless episcopus,
Eye without lid, mind without any dream—

These are of minstrels lacking minstrelsy,
Of an earth in which the first leaf is the tale
Of leaves, in which the sparrow is a bird

Of stone, that never changes. Bethou him, you
And you, bethou him and bethou. It is
A sound like any other. It will end.
                    (from *Notes toward a Supreme Fiction*)

WE REASON OF THESE THINGS

We reason of these things with later reason
And we make of what we see, what we see clearly
And have seen, a place dependent on ourselves.

There was a mystic marriage in Catawba, WALLACE
STEVENS
At noon it was on the mid-day of the year
Between a great captain and the maiden Bawda.

This was their ceremonial hymn: Anon
We loved but would no marriage make. Anon
The one refused the other one to take,

Foreswore the sipping of the marriage wine.
Each must the other take not for his high,
His puissant front nor for her subtle sound,

The shoo-shoo-shoo of secret cymbals round.
Each must the other take as sign, short sign
To stop the whirlwind, balk the elements.

The great captain loved the ever-hill Catawba
And therefore married Bawda, whom he found there,
And Bawda loved the captain as she loved the sun.

They married well because the marriage-place
Was what they loved. It was neither heaven nor hell.
They were love's characters come face to face.

(from *Notes toward a Supreme Fiction*)

Witter Bynner

(1881-   )

JEREMIAH

Roses have been his bed so long that he
Constructs a mat of thorns for lying on;
People have flattered him, until the sea
Becomes a preferable monotone.
He sets his masonry upon the brink
Of lamentation, out of his window peers
Toward waves that ever rise only to sink
Confused and lost as he among his years.
A ship alive becomes to him a hull
Charred and undone, the fumble of a wreck;
His dreams are but the droppings of a gull
Caught in a noose of seaweed round his neck;
And crying like a maniac toward the sky,
He pulls mankind in after him, to die.

William Carlos Williams

(1883-   )

SUNDAY IN THE PARK

And still the picnickers come on, now
early afternoon, and scatter through the
trees over the fenced-in acres   .

                          Voices!
multiple and inarticulate   .   voices
clattering loudly to the sun, to
the clouds. Voices!
assaulting the air gaily from all sides.

—among which the ear strains to catch
the movement of one voice among the rest
—a reed-like voice
                    of peculiar accent

Thus she finds what peace there is, reclines,
before his approach, stroked
by their clambering feet—for pleasure

               It is all for
pleasure   .   their feet   .   aimlessly
        wandering

The 'great beast' come to sun himself
                       as he may
  .   .   their dreams mingling,
aloof

Let us be reasonable!

79

WILLIAM
CARLOS
WILLIAMS
                        Sunday in the park,
limited by the escarpment, eastward; to
the west abutting on the old road: recreation
with a view! the binoculars chained
to anchored stanchions along the east wall—
        beyond which, a hawk
                        soars!

        —a trumpet sounds fitfully.

Stand at the rampart (use a metronome
if your ear is deficient, one made in Hungary
if you prefer)
and look away north by east where the church
spires still spend their wits against
the sky   .   to the ball-park
in the hollow with its minute figures running
—beyond the gap where the river
plunges into the narrow gorge, unseen

—and the imagination soars, as a voice
beckons, a thundrous voice, endless
—as sleep: the voice
that has ineluctably called them—
                        that unmoving roar!
churches and factories
                (at a price)
together, summoned them from the pit   .

—his voice, one among many (unheard)
moving under all.

                The mountain quivers.

Time! Count! Sever and mark time!

80

So during the early afternoon, from place
to place he moves,
his voice mingling with other voices
—the voice in his voice
opening his old throat, blowing out his lips,
kindling his mind (more
than his mind will kindle)

                    —following the hikers.

At last he comes to the idlers' favourite
haunts, the picturesque summit, where
the blue-stone (rust-red where exposed)
has been faulted at various levels
                    (ferns rife among the stones)
into rough terraces and partly closed in
dens of sweet grass, the ground gently sloping.

loiterers in groups straggle
over the bare rock-table—scratched by their
boot-nails more than the glacier scratched
them—walking indifferent through
each other's privacy

                    —in any case
the centre of movement, the core of gaiety.

here a young man, perhaps sixteen,
is sitting with his back to the rock among
some ferns playing a guitar, dead pan

The rest are eating and drinking.

                    The big guy
in the black hat is too full to move

                              but Mary
is up!

WILLIAM
CARLOS
WILLIAMS

Come on! Wassa ma'? You got
broken leg?

It is this air!
the air of the Midi
and the old cultures intoxicates them:
present!

—lifts one arm holding the cymbals
of her thoughts, cocks her old head
and dances! raising her skirts:

La la la la!

What a bunch of bums! Afraid somebody see
you?
Blah!
Excrementi!
—she spits.
Look a' me, Grandma! Everybody too damn
lazy.

This is the old, the very old, old upon old,
the undying: even to the minute gestures,
the hand holding the cup, the wine
spilling, the arm stained by it:
Remember

the peon in the lost
Eisenstein film drinking

from a wine-skin with the abandon
of a horse drinking

so that it slopped down his chin?
down his neck, dribbling

82

over his shirt-front and down
onto his pants—laughing, toothless?

Heavenly man!

—the leg raised, verisimilitude
even to the coarse contours of the leg, the
bovine touch! The leer, the cave of it,
the female of it facing the male, the satyr—
(Priapus!)
with that lonely implication, goatherd
and goat, fertility, the attack, drunk,
cleansed   .

Rejected. Even the film
suppressed   :   but   .   persistent

The picnickers laugh on the rocks celebrating
the varied Sunday of their loves with
its declining light—

Walking—

look down (from a ledge) into this grassy
den
(somewhat removed from the traffic)
above whose brows
a moon! where she lies sweating at his side:

She stirs, distraught,
against him—wounded (drunk), moves
against him (a lump) desiring,
against him, bored   .
flagrantly bored and sleeping, a
beer bottle still grasped spear-like
in his hand   .

while the small, sleepless boys, who
have climbed the columnar rocks

83

overhanging the pair (where they lie
overt upon the grass, besieged—

careless in their narrow cell under
the crowd's feet) stare down,
                              from history!
at them, puzzled and in the sexless
light (of childhood) bored equally,
go charging off   .

                    There where
the movement throbs openly
and you can hear the Evangelist shouting!

                              —moving nearer
          she—lean as a goat—leans
          her lean belly to the man's backside
          toying with the clips of his
          suspenders   .

—to which he adds his useless voice:
until there moves in his sleep
a music that is whole, inequivocal (in
his sleep, sweating in his sleep—labouring
against sleep, agasp!)
                    —and does not waken.

Sees, alive (asleep)
                    —the fall's roar entering
his sleep (to be fulfilled)
                              reborn
in his sleep—scattered over the mountain
severally

          —by which he woos here, severally.

And the amnesic crowd (the scattered),   WILLIAM
called about strains   CARLOS
to catch the movement of one voice   WILLIAMS

                                               hears
                    Pleasure! Pleasure!

                                               —feels
half dismayed, the afternoon of complex
voices its own—
                    and is relieved
                                   (relived)
          A cop is directing traffic
          across the main road up
          a little wooded slope toward
          the conveniences:
                              oaks, choke-cherry,
          dogwoods, white and green, iron-wood;
          humped roots matted into the shallow soil
          —mostly gone: rock out-croppings
          polished by the feet of the picnickers:
          sweetbarked sassafras

          leaning from the rancid grease:
                                   deformity—
          —to be deciphered (a horn, a trumpet!)
          an elucidation by multiplicity,
          a corrosion, a parasitic curd, a clarion
          for belief, to be good dogs   :

NO DOGS ALLOWED AT LARGE IN THIS PARK
                                   (from *PATERSON*)

WILLIAM
CARLOS
WILLIAMS

TO DAPHNE AND VIRGINIA

THE SMELL OF the heat is boxwood
    when rousing us
        a movement of the air
stirs our thoughts
    that had no life in them
        to a life, a life in which
two women agonize:
    to live and to breathe is no less.
        Two young women.
The box odour
    is the odour of that of which
        partaking separately,
each to herself
    I partake also

        .   .   separately.
BE PATIENT THAT I address you in a poem,
    there is no other
        fit medium.
The mind
    lives there. It is uncertain,
        can trick and leave us
agonized. But for resources
    what can equal it?
        There is nothing. We
should be lost
    without its wings to
        fly off upon.
THE MIND IS the cause of our distresses
    but of it we can build anew.
        Oh something more than
it flies off to:
    a woman's world,
        of crossed sticks, stopping
thought. A new world
    is only a new mind.

And the mind and the poem
are all apiece.
            Two young women
                        to be snared,
odour of box,
            to bind and hold them
                        for the mind labours.

WILLIAM
CARLOS
WILLIAMS

ALL WOMEN ARE fated similarly
            facing men
                        and there is always
another, such as I,
            who loves them,
                        loves all women, but
finds himself, touching them,
            like other men,
                        often confused.

I HAVE TWO sons,
            the husbands of these women,
                        who live also
in a world of love,
            apart.
                        Shall this odour of box in
                        the heat
not also touch them
            fronting a world of women
                        from which they are
debarred
            by the very scents which draw them on
                        against easy access?

IN OUR FAMILY we stammer unless,
            half mad,
                        we come to speech at last

AND I AM not
            a young man.

My love encumbers me.
It is a love
            less than
                    a young man's love but,
like this box odour
            more penetrant, infinitely
                    more penetrant,
in that sense not to be resisted.

THERE IS, IN the hard
            give and take
                    of a man's life with
                    a woman
a thing which is not the stress itself
            but beyond
                    and above
that,
            something that wants to rise
                    and shake itself
free. We are not chickadees
            on a bare limb
                    with a worm in the mouth.
The worm is in our brains
            and concerns them
                    and not food for our
offspring, wants to disrupt
            our thought
                    and throw it
to the newspapers
            or anywhere.
                    There is, in short,
a counter stress,
            born of the sexual shock,
                    which survives it
consonant with the moon,
            to keep its own mind.

There is, of course
more.
        Women
                are not alone
in that. At least
            while this healing odour is abroad
                one can write a poem.

STAYING HERE in the country
            on an old farm
                we eat our breakfasts
on a balcony under an elm.
            The shrubs below us
                are neglected. And
there, penned in,
            or he would eat the garden,
                lives a pet goose who
tilts his head
            sidewise
                and looks up at us,
a very quiet old fellow
            who writes no poems.
                Fine mornings we sit there
while birds
            come and go.
                A pair of robins
is building a nest
            for the second time
                this season. Men
against their reason
            speak of love, sometimes,
                when they are old. It is
all they can do
            or watch a heavy goose
                who waddles, slopping
                noisily in the mud of
                his pool.

WILLIAM
CARLOS
WILLIAMS

Elinor Wylie

(1885-1928)

LAVISH KINDNESS

Indulgent giants burned to crisp
The oak-trees of a dozen shires
Adorning thus a will-o'-the-wisp
With momentary pomp of fires.

The waters of an inland sea
Were magicked to a mountain peak
Enabling dwindled pools to be
Cool to a single swallow's beak.

But whether prodigies of waste,
Or idle, or beneficent,
Such deeds are not performed in haste
And none has fathomed their intent.

DOOMSDAY

The end of everything approaches;
I hear it coming
Loud as the wheels of painted coaches
On turnpikes drumming;
Loud as the pomp of plumy hearses,
Or pennoned charges;
Loud as when every oar reverses
Venetian barges;
Loud as the caves of covered bridges
Fulfilled with rumble

Of hooves; and loud as cloudy ridges
When glaciers tumble;
Like creeping thunder this continues
Diffused and distant,
Loud in our ears and in our sinews,
Insane, insistent;
Loud as a lion scorning carrion
Further and further;
Loud as the ultimate loud clarion
Or the first murther.

SHEPHERD'S HOLIDAY

Too honest for a gypsy, too lazy for a farmer,
What should you be but a shepherd on the hills,
Herding sheep with sad faces
Over grass-grown places,
High above a web of streams and willow-trees and mills?

Too tame for a gypsy, too wild for a dairy-maid,
What could I be but a silly goose-girl,
Tending hissing white snakes
By weed-green lakes,
Crying in the dew-fall with my hair out of curl?

Too silent for the neighbours, too simple for the towns-
    people,
What shall we do who love each other so?
I'll teach your grey sheep
To guard you from the steep,
You'll catch me back from drowning where my dark lake
    lies deep,
I'll pluck a feather pillow that shall sing you to sleep
Up among the rocks where the blueberries grow.

91

FULL MOON

My bands of silk and miniver
Momently grew heavier;
The black gauze was beggarly thin;
The ermine muffled mouth and chin;
I could not suck the moonlight in.

Harlequin in lozenges
Of love and hate, I walked in these
Striped and ragged rigmaroles;
Along the pavement my footsoles
Trod warily on living coals.

Shouldering the thoughts I loathed,
In their corrupt disguises clothed,
Mortality I could not tear
From my ribs, to leave them bare
Ivory in silver air.

There I walked, and there I raged;
The spiritual savage caged
Within my skeleton, raged afresh
To feel, behind a carnal mesh,
The clean bones crying in the flesh.

Ezra Pound

(1885-   )

THE LAKE ISLE

O God, O Venus, O Mercury, patron of thieves,
Give me in due time, I beseech you, a little tobacco-shop,
With the little bright boxes
        piled up neatly upon the shelves
And the loose fragrant cavendish
        and the shag,
And the bright Virginia
        loose under the bright glass cases,
And a pair of scales not too greasy,
And the whores dropping in for a word or two in
        passing,
For a flip word, and to tidy their hair a bit.

O God, O Venus, O Mercury, patron of thieves,
Lend me a little tobacco-shop,
        or install me in any profession
Save this damn'd profession of writing,
        where one needs one's brains all the time.

PROVINCIA DESERTA

At Rochecoart,
Where the hills part
        in three ways,
And three valleys, full of winding roads,
Fork out to south and north,
There is a place of trees . . . grey with lichen.

93

I have walked there
　　　　　thinking of old days.
At Chalais
　　　　　is a pleached arbour;
Old pensioners and old protected women
Have the right there—
　　　　　it is charity.
I have crept over old rafters,
　　　　　peering down
Over the Dronne,
　　　　　over a stream full of lilies.
Eastward the road lies,
　　　　　Aubeterre is eastward,
With a garrulous old man at the inn.
I know the roads in that place:
Mareuil to the north-east,
　　　　　La Tour,
There are three keeps near Mareuil,
And an old woman,
　　　　　glad to hear Arnaut,
Glad to lend one dry clothing.

I have walked
　　　　　into Perigord,
I have seen the torch-flames, high-leaping,
Painting the front of that church;
Heard, under the dark, whirling laughter.
I have looked back over the stream
　　　　　and seen the high building,
Seen the long minarets, the white shafts.
I have gone in Ribeyrac
　　　　　and in Sarlat,
I have climbed rickety stairs, heard talk of Croy,
Walked over En Bertran's old layout,
Have seen Narbonne, and Cahors and Chalus,
Have seen Excideuil, carefully fashioned.

I have said:
       'Here such a one walked.
'Here Cœur-de-Lion was slain.
       'Here was good singing.
'Here one man hastened his step.
       'Here one lay panting.'
I have looked south from Hautefort,
       thinking of Montaignac, southward.
I have lain in Rocafixada,
       level with sunset,
Have seen the copper come down
       tingeing the mountains,
I have seen the fields, pale, clear as an emerald,
Sharp peaks, high spurs, distant castles.
I have said: 'The old roads have lain here.
'Men have gone by such and such valleys
'Where the great halls were closer together.'
I have seen Foix on its rock, seen Toulouse, and
       Arles greatly altered,
I have seen the ruined 'Dorata.'
       I have said:
'Riquier! Guido.'
       I have thought of the second Troy,
Some little prized place in Auvergnat:
Two men tossing a coin, one keeping a castle,
One set on the highway to sing.
       He sang a woman.
Auvergne rose to the song;
       The Dauphin backed him.
'The castle to Austors!'
       'Pieire kept the singing—
A fair man and a pleasant.'
       He won the lady,
Stole her away for himself, kept her against armed
       force:
So ends that story.
That age is gone;

Pieire de Maensac is gone
I have walked over these roads;
I have thought of them living.

SOUTH-FOLK IN COLD COUNTRY

The Dai horse neighs against the bleak wind of Etsu,
The birds of Etsu have no love for En, in the North,
Emotion is born out of habit.
Yesterday we went out of the Wild-Goose gate,
To-day from the Dragon-Pen.[1]
Surprised. Desert turmoil. Sea sun.
Flying snow bewilders the barbarian heaven.
Lice swarm like ants over our accoutrements.
Mind and spirit drive on the feathery banners.
Hard fight gets no reward.
Loyalty is hard to explain.
Who will be sorry for General Rishogu,
                    the swift moving,
Whose white head is lost for this province?

HOMAGE TO SEXTUS PROPERTIUS, PART V

I

Now if ever it is time to cleanse Helicon;
                    to lead Emathian horses afield,
And to name over the census of my chiefs in the Roman
    camp.
If I have not the faculty, 'The bare attempt would be praise-
    worthy.'
'In things of similar magnitude
                    the mere will to act is sufficient.'

---

[1] i.e., we have been warring from one end of the empire to the other,
now east, now west, on each border.

96

The primitive ages sang Venus,
the last sings of a tumult,
And I also will sing war when this matter of a girl is
exhausted.
I with my beak hauled ashore would proceed in a more
stately manner,
My Muse is eager to instruct me in a new gamut, or
gambetto,
Up, up my soul, from your lowly cantilation,
put on a timely vigour.
Oh august Pierides! Now for a large-mouthed product.
Thus:
'The Euphrates denies its protection to the Parthian and
apologizes for Crassus,'
And 'It is, I think, India which now gives necks to your
triumph,'
And so forth, Augustus. 'Virgin Arabia shakes in her inmost
dwelling.'
If any land shrink into a distant seacoast,
it is a mere postponement of your domination.
And I shall follow the camp, I shall be duly celebrated for
singing the affairs of your cavalry.
May the fates watch over my day.

II

Yet you ask on what account I write so many love-lyrics
And whence this soft book comes into my mouth.
Neither Calliope nor Apollo sung these things into my ear,
My genius is no more than a girl.

If she with ivory fingers drive a tune through the lyre,
We look at the process.
How easy the moving fingers; if hair is mussed on her
forehead,
If she goes in a gleam of Cos, in a slither of dyed stuff,
There is a volume in the matter; if her eyelids sink into sleep,

EZRA There are new jobs for the author;
POUND And if she plays with me with her shirt off,
    We shall construct many Iliads.
And whatever she does or says
    We shall spin long yarns out of nothing.

Thus much the fates have allotted me, and if, Maecenas,
I were able to lead heroes into armour, I would not,
Neither would I warble of Titans, nor of Ossa
                    spiked onto Olympus,
Nor of causeways over Pelion,
Nor of Thebes in its ancient respectability,
            nor of Homer's reputation in Pergamus,
Nor of Xerxes' two-barreled kingdom, nor of Remus and
    his royal family,
Nor of dignified Carthaginian characters,
Nor of Welsh mines and the profit Marus had out of them.
I should remember Caesar's affairs . . . for a background,
Although Callimachus did without them,
                and without Theseus,
Without an inferno, without Achilles attended of gods,
Without Ixion, and without the sons of Menoetius
    and the Argo and without Jove's grave and the Titans.

And my ventricles do not palpitate to Caesarial *ore rotundos*,
Nor to the tune of the Phrygian fathers.
Sailor, of winds; a ploughman, concerning his oxen;
Soldier, the enumeration of wounds; the sheep-feeder of
    ewes;
We, in our narrow bed, turning aside from battles:
Each man where he can, wearing out the day in his manner.

III

It is noble to die of love, and honourable to remain un-
                cuckolded for a season.
And she speaks ill of light women,
                and will not praise Homer
Because Helen's conduct is 'unsuitable'.

E. P. ODE POUR L'ELECTION DE SON SEPULCHRE

EZRA POUND

For three years, out of key with his time,
He strove to resuscitate the dead art
Of poetry; to maintain 'the sublime'
In the old sense. Wrong from the start—

No, hardly, but seeing he had been born
In a half-savage country, out of date;
Bent resolutely on wringing lilies from the acorn;
Capaneus; trout for factitious bait;

Ἴδμεν γάρ τοι πάνθ', ὅσ' ἐνὶ Τροίῃ
Caught in the unstopped ear;
Giving the rocks small lee-way
The chopped seas held him, therefore, that year.

His true Penelope was Flaubert,
He fished by obstinate isles;
Observed the elegance of Circe's hair
Rather than the mottoes on sundials.

Unaffected by 'the march of events',
He passed from men's memory in *l'an trentiesme,
De son eage*; the case presents
No adjunct to the Muses' diadem.

CANTO XLVII

Who even dead, yet hath his mind entire!
This sound came in the dark
First must thou go the road
                    to hell
And to the bower of Ceres' daughter Proserpine,
Through overhanging dark, to see Tiresias,

99

EZRA Eyeless that was, a shade, that is in hell
POUND So full of knowing that the beefy men know less than he,
Ere thou come to thy road's end.
                    Knowledge the shade of a shade,
Yet must thou sail after knowledge
Knowing less than drugged beasts. *phtheggometha
thasson*

φθεγγώμεθα θᾶσσον
            The small lamps drift in the bay
And the sea's claw gathers them.
Neptunus drinks after neap-tide.
Tamuz! Tamuz!!
The red flame going seaward.
                    By this gate art thou measured.
From the long boats they have set lights in the water,
The sea's claw gathers them outward.
Scilla's dogs snarl at the cliff's base,
The white teeth gnaw in under the crag,
But in the pale night the small lamps float seaward
                                τυ Διώνα
                                TU DIONA

και Μοῖρα τ'"Αδονιν
KAI MOIRA T' ADONIN

The sea is streaked red with Adonis,
The lights flicker red in small jars.
Wheat shoots rise new by the altar,
            flower from the swift seed.
Two span, two span to a woman,
Beyond that she believes not. Nothing is of any importance.
To that is she bent, her intention,
To that art thou called ever turning intention,
Whether by night the owl-call, whether by sap in shoot,
Never idle, by no means by no wiles intermittent
Moth is called over mountain
The bull runs blind on the sword, *naturans*

100

To the cave art thou called, Odysseus,

By Molü hast thou respite for a little,
By Molü art thou freed from the one bed
  that thou may'st return to another
The stars are not in her counting,
   To her they are but wandering holes.
Begin thy ploughing
When the Pleiades go down to their rest,
Begin thy ploughing
40 days are they under seaboard,
Thus do in fields by seaboard
And in valleys winding down toward the sea.
When the cranes fly high
   think of ploughing.
By this gate art thou measured
Thy day is between a door and a door
Two oxen are yoked for ploughing
Or six in the hill field
White bulk under olives, a score for drawing down stone,
Here the mules are gabled with slate on the hill road.
Thus was it in time.
And the small stars now fall from the olive branch,
Forked shadow falls dark on the terrace
More black than the floating martin
  that has no care for your presence,
His wing-print is black on the roof tiles
And the print is gone with his cry.
So light is thy weight on Tellus
Thy notch no deeper indented
Thy weight less than the shadow
Yet hast thou gnawed through the mountain,
   Scilla's white teeth less sharp.
Hast thou found a nest softer than cunnus
Or hast thou found better rest
Hast'ou a deeper planting, doth thy death year
Bring swifter shoot?
Hast thou entered more deeply the mountain?

EZRA   The light has entered the cave. Io! Io!
POUND The light has gone down into the cave,
       Splendour on splendour!
       By prong have I entered these hills:
       That the grass grow from my body,
       That I hear the roots speaking together,
       The air is new on my leaf,
       The forked boughs shake with the wind.
       Is Zephyrus more light on the bough, Apeliota
       more light on the almond branch?
       By this door have I entered the hill.
       Falleth,
       Adonis falleth.
       Fruit cometh after. The small lights drift out with the tide,
       sea's claw has gathered them outward,
       Four banners to every flower
       The sea's claw draws the lamps outward.
       Think thus of thy ploughing
       When the seven stars go down to their rest
       Forty days for their rest, by seaboard
       And in valleys that wind down toward the sea

                     και Μοῖρα τ'"Αδονιν
                     KAI MOIRA T' ADONIN

       When the almond bough puts forth its flame,
       When the new shoots are brought to the altar,

                     τυ Διῳνα, και Μοῖρα
                     TU DIONA, KAI MOIRA

       και Μοῖρα τ'"Αδονιν
       KAI MOIRA T' ADONIN

                 that hath the gift of healing,
       that hath the power over wild beasts.

Louis Untermeyer
(1885-   )

SONG TOURNEMENT: NEW STYLE

Rain, said the first, as it falls in Venice
Is like the dropping of golden pennies
Into a sea as smooth and bright
As a bowl of curdled malachite.

Storm, sang the next, in the streets of Peking
Is like the ghost of a yellow sea-king,
Scooping the dust to find if he may
Discover what earth has hidden away.

The rush of Spring, smiled the third, in Florence
Is wave upon wave of laughing torrents,
A flood of birds, a water-voiced calling,
A green rain rising instead of falling.

The wind, cried the fourth, in the bay of Naples
Is a quarrel of leaves among the maples,
A war of sunbeams idly fanned,
A whisper softer than sand on sand.

Then spoke the last: God's endless tears,
Too great for Heaven, anoint the spheres,
While every drop becomes a well
In the fathomless, thirsty heart of Hell.

And these five bards, who could boast of travel
Fifty miles from their native gravel,
Rose in the sunlight and offered their stanzas
At the shrine of the Poetry Contest in Kansas.

John Gould Fletcher

(1886-1946)

IV. THE WINDMILLS

The windmills, like great sunflowers of steel,
Lift themselves proudly over the straggling houses;
And at their feet the deep blue-green alfalfa
Cuts the desert like the stroke of a sword.

Yellow melon flowers
Crawl beneath the withered peach-trees;
A date-palm throws its heavy fronds of steel
Against the scoured metallic sky.

The houses, double-roofed for coolness,
Cower amid the manzanita scrub.
A man with jingling spurs
Walks heavily out of a vine-bowered doorway,
Mounts his pony, rides away.

The windmills stare at the sun.
The yellow earth cracks and blisters.
Everything is still.

In the afternoon
The wind takes dry waves of heat and tosses them,
Mingled with dust, up and down the streets,
Against the belfry with its green bells:

And, after sunset, when the sky
Becomes a green and orange fan,
The windmills, like great sunflowers on dried stalks,
Stare hard at the sun they cannot follow.

Turning, turning, forever turning   JOHN
In the chill night-wind that sweeps over the valley,   GOULD
With the shriek and the clank of the pumps groaning FLETCHER
    beneath them,
And the choking gurgle of tepid water.

H.D.

(1886-   )

AN INCIDENT HERE AND THERE

An incident here and there,
and rails gone (for guns)
from your (and my) old town square:

mists and mist-grey, no colour,
still the Luxor bee, chick and hare
pursue unalterable purpose

in green, rose-red, lapis;
they continue to prophesy
from the stone papyrus:

there, as here, ruin opens
the tomb, the temple; enter,
there as here, there are no doors:

the shrine lies open to the sky,
the rain falls, here, there
sand drifts; eternity endures:

ruin everywhere, yet as the fallen roof
leaves the sealed room
open to the air,

so, through our desolation,
thoughts stir, inspiration stalks us
through gloom:

unaware, spirit announces the Presence;
shivering overtakes us,
as of old, Samuel:

trembling at a known street-corner,
we know not nor are known;
the Pythian pronounces—we pass on

to another cellar, to another sliced wall
where poor utensils show
like rare objects in a museum;

Pompeii has nothing to teach us,
we know crack of volcanic fissure,
slow flow of terrible lava,

pressure on heart, lungs, the brain
about to burst its brittle case
(what the skull can endure!):

over us, Apocryphal fire,
under us, the earth sway, dip of a floor,
slope of a pavement

where men roll, drunk
with a new bewilderment,
sorcery, bedevilment:

the bone-frame was made for
no such shock knit within terror,
yet the skeleton stood up to it:

the flesh? it was melted away,
the heart burnt out, dead ember,
tendons, muscles shattered, outer husk dismembered,

107

yet the frame held:
we passed the flame: we wonder
what saved us? what for?

AH (YOU SAY), THIS IS HOLY WISDOM

I

Ah (you say), this is Holy Wisdom,
Sancta Sophia, the SS of the *Sanctus Spiritus*,

so by facile reasoning, logically
the incarnate symbol of the Holy Ghost;

your Holy Ghost was an apple-tree
smouldering—or rather now burgeoning

with flowers; the fruit of the Tree?
this is the new Eve who comes

clearly to return, to retrieve
what she has lost the race,

given over to sin, to death;
she brings the Book of Life, obviously.

II

This is a symbol of beauty (you continue),
she is Our Lady universally,

I see her as you project her,
not out of place

flanked by Corinthian capitals,
or in a Coptic nave,

or frozen above the centre door
of a Gothic cathedral;

you have done very well by her
(to repeat your own phrase),

you have carved her tall and unmistakable,
a hieratic figure, the veiled Goddess,

whether of the seven delights,
whether of the seven spear-points.

III

O yes—you understand, I say,
this is all most satisfactory,

but she wasn't hieratic, she wasn't frozen,
she wasn't very tall;

she is the Vestal
from the days of Numa,

she carries over the cult
of the *Bona Dea*,

she carries a book but it is not
the tome of the ancient wisdom,

the pages, I imagine, are the blank pages
of the unwritten volume of the new;

all you say, is implicit,
all that and much more;

but she is not shut up in a cave
like a Sibyl; she is not

imprisoned in leaden bars
in a coloured window;

she is Psyche, the butterfly,
out of the cocoon.

IV

But nearer than Guardian Angel
or good Daemon,

she is the counter-coin-side
of primitive terror;

she is not-fear, she is not-war,
but she is no symbolic figure

of peace, charity, chastity, goodness,
faith, hope, reward;

she is not Justice with eyes
blindfolded like Love's;

I grant you the dove's symbolic purity,
I grant you her face was innocent

and immaculate and her veils
like the Lamb's Bride,

but the Lamb was not with her,
either as Bridegroom or Child;

her attention is undivided,
we are her bridegroom and lamb;

her book is our book; written
or unwritten, its pages will reveal

a tale of a Fisherman,
a tale of a jar or jars,

the same—different—the same attributes,
different yet the same as before.

John Hall Wheelock

(1886-   )

THE YEARS

My dreams wear thinner as the years go by:
  The stony face of Fate, into my own,
Stares, with that granite look of hers—and I
  Stare back, with a still face, but not of stone.

RECONCILIATION

At the foot of a great pine, in the wild country
Westward, well inland, we uncovered them,
The skeletons of a fish-hawk and a fish,
Half-buried in dead leaves. The long pursuit,
And the flight, ended; the terror, the conquest, ended,
And the wars that divide Being, they rested there—
Emblems of the inexplicable will.

Robinson Jeffers
(1887-)

SUMMER HOLIDAY

When the sun shouts and people abound
One thinks there were the ages of stone and the age of bronze
And the iron age; iron the unstable metal;
Steel made of iron, unstable as his mother; the towered-up
    cities
Will be stains of rust on mounds of plaster.
Roots will not pierce the heaps for a time, kind rains will
    cure them,
Then nothing will remain of the iron age
And all these people but a thigh-bone or so, a poem
Stuck in the world's thought, splinters of glass
In the rubbish dumps, a concrete dam far off in the
    mountain. . . .

I. REFERENCE TO A PASSAGE IN PLUTARCH'S LIFE OF SULLA

The people buying and selling, consuming pleasures, talking
    in the archways,
Were all suddenly struck quiet
And ran from under stone to look up at the sky: so shrill and
    mournful,
So fierce and final, a brazen
Pealing of trumpets high up in the air, in the summer blue
    over Tuscany.
They marvelled; the soothsayers answered:
'Although the Gods are little troubled toward men, at the
    end of each period

A sign is declared in heaven
Indicating new times, new customs, a changed people; the
    Romans
Rule, and Etruria is finished;
A wise mariner will trim the sails to the wind.'
                          I heard yesterday
So shrill and mournful a trumpet-blast,
It was hard to be wise. . . . You must eat change and endure;
    not be much troubled
For the people; they will have their happiness.
When the republic grows too heavy to endure, then Caesar
    will carry it;
When life grows hateful, there's power . . .

NOVEMBER SURF

Some lucky day each November great waves awake and are
    drawn
Like smoking mountains bright from the west
And come and cover the cliff with white violent cleanness:
    then suddenly
The old granite forgets half a year's filth:
The orange-peel, eggshells, papers, pieces of clothing, the
    clots
Of dung in corners of the rock, and used
Sheaths that make light love safe in the evenings: all the
    droppings of the summer
Idlers washed off in a winter ecstasy:
I think this cumbered continent envies its cliff then . . .
    But all seasons
The earth, in her childlike prophetic sleep,
Keeps dreaming of the bath of a storm that prepares up the
    long coast
Of the future to scour more than her sea-lines:
The cities gone down, the people fewer and the hawks more
    numerous,

The rivers mouth to source pure; when the two-footed
Mammal, being someways one of the nobler animals,
    regains
The dignity of room, the value of rareness.

I SHALL LAUGH PURELY

I

Turn from that girl
Your fixed blue eyes.
Boy-slender she is,
And a face as beautiful as a hawk's face.
History passes like falling rocks.

I am old as a stone,
But she is beautiful.
War is coming.
All the fine boys will go off to war.
History passes like falling rocks.

Oh, that one's to marry
Another old man;
You won't be helped
When your tall sons go away to war.
History falls on your head like rocks.

Keep a straight mind
In the evil time
In the mad-dog time
Why may not an old man run mad?
History falls like rocks in the dark,
All will be worse confounded soon.

II

Count the glories of this time,
Count that girl's beauty, then count England,
Bleeding, at bay, magnificent,
At last a lion,
For all will be worse confounded soon.

Count that girl's beauty, count the coast-range,
The steep rock that stops the Pacific,
Count the surf on its precipice,
the hawks in its air,
For all will be worse confounded soon.

Count its eagles and wild boars,
Count the great blue-black winter storms,
Heavy rain and the hurricane,
Get them by heart,
For all will be worse confounded soon.

Count no human thing but only
England's great fight and that girl's beauty,
History passes like falling
Rocks in the dark,
And all will be worse confounded soon.

III

But this, I steadily assure you, is not the world's end,
Nor even the end of a civilization. It is not so late as you
     think: give nature time.
These wars will end, and I shall lead a troupe of shaky old
     men through Europe and America,
Old drunkards, worn-out lechers; fallen dictators, cast
     kings, a disgraced president; some cashiered generals
And collapsed millionaires: we shall enact a play, I shall
     announce to the audience:
'All will be worse confounded soon.'

We shall beware of wild dogs in Europe, and of the police in
  armed imperial America:—
For all that pain was mainly a shift of power:—we shall
  enact our play: 'Oh Christian era,
Make a good end,' but first I announce to our audiences:
  'This play is prophetic, it will be centuries.
This play does not represent the world's end,
But only the fall of a civilization. It is not so late as you
  think: give nature time.'
In Europe we shall beware of starving dogs and political
  commissars, and of the police in America.
We shall rant on our makeshift stages in our cracked voices:
  'Oh Christian era,
Era of chivalry and the barbarians and the machines, era of
  science and the saints,
When you go down make a good sunset.
Never linger superfluous, old and holy and paralytic like
  India,
Go down in conclusive war and a great red sunset, great
  age go down,
For all will be worse confounded soon.'

We shall tour to the last verge and the open Pacific, we
  shall sit on the yellow cliffs at Hurricane Point
And watch the centaurs come from the sea; their splayed
  hooves plunge and stutter on the tide-rocks, watch
  them swarm up,
The hairy and foamy flanks, the naked destructive shoulders,
  the brutal faces and the bent bows,
Horde after horde under the screaming gulls: my old men
  will cough in the fog and baa like sheep,
'Here comes the end of a civilization. Give nature time,'
And spit, and make lewd jokes. But I shall laugh purely,
Remembering what old enthusiast named a girl's beauty and
  England's battle
Among the lights of his time: she being by then a dyed hag,
  or more likely

117

One of those embalmer-fingered smiles in the subsoil; and
England will be
Not admirable. I shall laugh purely, knowing the next age
Lives on not-human beauty, waiting on circumstance and its
April, weaving its winter chrysalis;
Thin snow falls on historical rocks.

THE EYE

The Atlantic is a stormy moat, and the Mediterranean,
The blue pool in the old garden,
More than five thousand years has drunk sacrifice
Of ships and blood and shines in the sun; but here the
Pacific:
The ships, planes, wars are perfectly irrelevant.
Neither our present blood-feud with the brave dwarfs
Nor any future world-quarrel of westering
And eastering man, the bloody migrations, greed of power,
battle-falcons,
Are a mote of dust in the great scale-pan.
Here from this mountain shore, headland beyond stormy
headland plunging like dolphins through the grey sea-
smoke
Into pale sea, look west at the hill of water: it is half the
planet: this dome, this half-globe, this bulging
Eyeball of water, arched over to Asia,
Australia and white Antarctica: those are the eyelids that
never close; this is the staring unsleeping
Eye of the earth, and what it watches is not our wars.

Marianne Moore

(1888-   )

THE STEEPLE-JACK

Dürer would have seen a reason for living
    in a town like this, with eight stranded whales
to look at; with the sweet sea air coming into your house
on a fine day, from water etched
    with waves as formal as the scales
on a fish.

One by one, in two's, in three's, the seagulls keep
    flying back and forth over the town clock,
or sailing around the lighthouse without moving their
    wings—
rising steadily with a slight
    quiver of the body—or flock
mewing where

a sea the purple of the peacock's neck is
    paled to greenish azure as Dürer changed
the pine green of the Tyrol to peacock blue and guinea
grey. You can see a twenty-five-
    pound lobster and fish-nets arranged
to dry. The

whirlwind fife-and-drum of the storm bends the salt
    marsh grass, disturbs stars in the sky and the
star on the steeple; it is a privilege to see so
much confusion.

        A steeple-jack in red, has let
    a rope down as a spider spins a thread;

MARI- he might be part of a novel, but on the sidewalk a
ANNE sign says C. J. Poole, Steeple-Jack,
MOORE   in black and white; and one in red
and white says

Danger. The church portico has four fluted
        columns, each a single piece of stone, made
modester by white-wash. This would be a fit haven for
waifs, children, animals, prisoners,
        and presidents who have repaid
sin-driven

senators by not thinking about them. One
        sees a school-house, a post-office in a
store, fish-houses, hen-houses, a three-masted schooner on
the stocks. The hero, the student,
        the steeple-jack, each in his way,
is at home.

It scarcely could be dangerous to be living
        in a town like this, of simple people
who have a steeple-jack placing danger-signs by the church
when he is gilding the solid-
        pointed star, which on a steeple
stands for hope.

MELANCTHON

Openly, yes,
with the naturalness
        of the hippopotamus or the alligator
        when it climbs out on the bank to experience the

sun, I do these
things which I do, which please

no one but myself. Now I breathe and now I am sub- MARI-
merged; the blemishes stand up and shout when the ANNE
  object   MOORE

in view was a
renaissance; shall I say
    the contrary? The sediment of the river which
    encrusts my joints, makes me very grey but I am used

to it, it may
remain there; do away
    with it and I am myself done away with, for the
    patina of circumstance can but enrich what was

there to begin
with. This elephant-skin
    which I inhabit, fibred over like the shell of
    the cocoanut, this piece of black glass through which no
        light

can filter—cut
into checkers by rut
    upon rut of unpreventable experience—
    it is a manual for the peanut-tongued and the

hairy-toed. Black
but beautiful, my back
    is full of the history of power. Of power? What
    is powerful and what is not? My soul shall never

be cut into
by a wooden spear; through-
    out childhood to the present time, the unity of
    life and death has been expressed by the circumference

described by my
trunk; nevertheless I
    perceive feats of strength to be inexplicable after
    all; and I am on my guard; external poise, it

has its centre
well nurtured—we know
    where—in pride; but spiritual pose, it has its centre
        where?
    My ears are sensitized to more than the sound of

the wind. I see
and I hear, unlike the
    wandlike body of which one hears so much, which was
        made
    to see and not to see; to hear and not to hear;

that tree-trunk without
roots, accustomed to shout
    its own thoughts to itself like a shell, maintained intact
    by who knows what strange pressure of the atmosphere;
        that

spiritual
brother to the coral-
    plant, absorbed into which, the equable sapphire light
    becomes a nebulous green. The I of each is to

the I of each
a kind of fretful speech
    which sets a limit on itself; the elephant is
    black earth preceded by a tendril? Compared with those

phenomena
which vacillate like a
    translucence of the atmosphere, the elephant is
    that on which darts cannot strike decisively the first

time, a substance
needful as an instance
    of the indestructibility of matter; it
    has looked at electricity and at the earth-

quake and is still

here; the name means thick. Will

    depth be depth, thick skin be thick, to one who can see

      no

    beautiful element of unreason under it?

ENGLAND

with its baby rivers and little towns, each with its abbey or
    its cathedral,
with voices—one voice perhaps, echoing through the tran-
    sept—the
criterion of suitability and convenience; and Italy with its
    equal
shores—contriving an epicureanism from which the gross-
    ness has been

extracted: and Greece with its goat and its gourds, the nest
    of modified illusions:
and France, the 'chrysalis of the nocturnal butterfly', in
whose products mystery of construction diverts one from
    what was originally one's
object—substance at the core: and the East with its snails,
    its emotional

shorthand and jade cockroaches, its rock crystal and its im-
    perturbability,
all of museum quality: and America where there
is the little old ramshackle victoria in the south, where
    cigars are smoked on the
street in the north; where there are no proof-readers, no
    silk-worms, no digressions;

the wild man's land; grassless, linksless, languageless coun-
    try in which letters are written

not in Spanish, not in Greek, not in Latin, not in shorthand,
but in plain American which cats and dogs can read! The
letter *a* in psalm and calm when
pronounced with the sound of *a* in candle, is very noticeable,
but

why should continents of misapprehension have to be accounted for by the
fact? Does it follow that because there are poisonous toad-
stools
which resemble mushrooms, both are dangerous? In the
case of mettlesomeness which may be
mistaken for appetite, of heat which may appear to be haste,
no con-

clusions may be drawn. To have misapprehended the matter
is to have confessed
that one has not looked far enough. The sublimated wisdom
of China, Egyptian discernment, the cataclysmic torrent of
emotion compressed
in the verbs of the Hebrew language, the books of the man
who is able

to say, 'I envy nobody but him, and him only, who catches
more fish than
I do',—the flower and fruit of all that noted superi-
ority—should one not have stumbled upon it in America,
must one imagine
that it is not there? It has never been confined to one locality.

A GRAVE

MARI-
ANNE
MOORE

Man looking into the sea,
taking the view from those who have as much right to it as
    you have to it yourself,
it is human nature to stand in the middle of a thing,
but you cannot stand in the middle of this;
the sea has nothing to give but a well excavated grave.
The firs stand in a procession, each with an emerald turkey-
    foot at the top,
reserved as their contours, saying nothing;
repression, however, is not the most obvious characteristic
    of the sea;
the sea is a collector, quick to return a rapacious look.
There are others besides you who have worn that look—
whose expression is no longer a protest; the fish no longer
    investigate them
for their bones have not lasted:
men lower nets, unconscious of the fact that they are dese-
    crating a grave,
and row quickly away—the blades of the oars
moving together like the feet of water-spiders as if there
    were no such thing as death.
The wrinkles progress among themselves in a phalanx—
    beautiful under networks of foam,
and fade breathlessly while the sea rustles in and out of the
    seaweed;
the birds swim through the air at top speed, emitting cat-
    calls as heretofore—
the tortoise-shell scourges about the feet of the cliffs, in
    motion beneath them;
and the ocean, under the pulsation of lighthouses and noise
    of bell-buoys,
advances as usual, looking as if it were not that ocean in
    which dropped things are bound to sink—
in which if they turn and twist, it is neither with volition
    nor consciousness.

MARI-
ANNE
MOORE

Another armoured animal—scale
 lapping scale with spruce-cone regularity until they
form the uninterrupted central
 tail-row! This near artichoke with head and legs and
  grit-equipped gizzard,
 the night miniature artist engineer is
  Leonardo's—da Vinci's replica—
   impressive animal and toiler of whom we seldom
   hear.
  Armour seems extra. But for him,
   the closing ear-ridge—
    or bare ear lacking even this small
    eminence and similarly safe

contracting nose and eye apertures
 impenetrably closable, are not;—a true ant-eater,
not cockroach-eater, who endures
 exhausting solitary trips through unfamiliar ground at
  night,
 returning before sunrise; stepping in the moonlight,
  on the moonlight peculiarly, that the outside
   edges of his hands may bear the weight and save
   the claws
  for digging. Serpentined about
   the tree, he draws
    away from danger unpugnaciously,
    with no sound but a harmless hiss; keeping

the fragile grace of the Thomas-
 of-Leighton Buzzard Westminster Abbey wrought-
  iron vine, or
rolls himself into a ball that has
power to defy all effort to unroll it; strongly intailed,
  neat

head for core, on neck not breaking off, with curled-in
    feet.
    Nevertheless he has sting-proof scales; and nest
      of rocks closed with earth from inside, which he
      can thus darken
    Sun and moon and day and night and man and beast
      each with a splendour
        which man in all his vileness cannot
        set aside; each with an excellence!

'Fearful yet to be feared,' the armoured
    ant-eater met by the driver-ant does not turn back, but
engulfs what he can, the flattened sword-
      edged leafpoints on the tail and artichoke set leg- and
        body-plates
quivering violently when it retaliates
      and swarms on him. Compact like the furled
        fringed frill
        on the hat-brim of Gargallo's hollow iron head
        of a
matador, he will drop and will
        then walk away
      unhurt, although if unintruded on,
      he cautiously works down the tree, helped

by his tail. The giant-pangolin-
    tail, graceful tool, as prop or hand or broom or axe,
        tipped like
the elephant's trunk with special skin,
    is not lost on this ant- and stone-swallowing uninjurable
artichoke which simpletons thought a living fable
      whom the stones had nourished, whereas ants had
      done
      so. Pangolins are not aggressive animals; between
      dusk and day they have the not unchain-like machine-
      like

form and frictionless creep of a thing
made graceful by adversities, con-

versities. To explain grace requires
a curious hand. If that which is at all were not forever,
why would those who graced the spires
with animals and gathered there to rest, on cold luxurious
low stone seats—a monk and monk and monk—between
the thus
ingenious roof-supports, have slaved to confuse
grace with a kindly manner, time in which to pay
a debt,
the cure for sins, a graceful use
of what are yet
approved stone mullions branching out across
the perpendiculars? A sailboat

was the first machine. Pangolins, made
for moving quietly also, are models of exactness,
on four legs; or hind feet plantigrade,
with certain postures of a man. Beneath sun and moon,
man slaving
to make his life more sweet, leaves half the flowers
worth having,
needing to choose wisely how to use the strength;
a paper-maker like the wasp; a tractor of food-
stuffs,
like the ant; spidering a length
of web from bluffs
above a stream; in fighting, mechanicked
like the pangolin; capsizing in

disheartenment. Bedizened or stark
naked, man, the self, the being we call human, writing-
master to this world, griffons a dark
'Like does not like like that is obnoxious'; and writes
error with four

r's. Among animals, one has a sense of humour,
    Humour saves a few steps, it saves years. Un-
        ignorant,
    modest and unemotional, and all emotion,
    he has everlasting vigour,
        power to grow,
            though there are few creatures who can make one
            breathe faster and make one erecter.

Not afraid of anything is he,
    and then goes cowering forth, tread paced to meet an
        obstacle
at every step. Consistent with the
    formula—warm blood, no gills, two pairs of hands and
        a few hairs—that
is a mammal; there he sits in his own habitat,
    serge-clad, strong-shod. The prey of fear, he, always
        curtailed, extinguished, thwarted by the dusk,
            work partly done,
    says to the alternating blaze,
        'Again the sun!
            anew each day; and new and new and new,
            that comes into and steadies my soul.'

THE MIND IS AN ENCHANTING THING

        is an enchanted thing
            like the glaze on a
        katydid-wing
                subdivided by sun
                till the nettings are legion.
        Like Gieseking playing Scarlatti;

        like the apteryx-awl
            as a beak, or the

kiwi's rain-shawl
     of haired feathers, the mind
     feeling its way as though blind,
walks along with its eyes on the ground.

It has memory's ear
    that can hear without
having to hear.
     Like the gyroscope's fall,
     truly unequivocal
because trued by regnant certainty,

it is a power of
    strong enchantment. It
is like the dove-
     neck animated by
     sun ; it is memory's eye ;
it's conscientious inconsistency.

It tears off the veil; tears
    the temptation, the
mist the heart wears,
     from its eyes,—if the heart
     has a face; it takes apart
dejection. It's fire in the dove-neck's

iridescence; in the
    inconsistencies
of Scarlatti.
     Inconfusion submits
     its confusion to proof; it's
not a Herod's oath that cannot change.

John Crowe Ransom

(1888-   )

VISION BY SWEETWATER

Go and ask Robin to bring the girls over
To Sweetwater, said my Aunt; and that was why
It was like a dream of ladies sweeping by
The willows, clouds, deep meadowgrass, and the river.

Robin's sisters and my Aunt's lily daughter
Laughed and talked, and tinkled as wrens
If there were a little colony all hens
To go walking by the steep turn of Sweetwater.

Let them alone, dear Aunt, just for one minute
Till I go fishing in the dark of my mind:
Where have I seen before, against the wind,
These bright virgins, robed and bare of bonnet,

Flowing with music of their strange quick tongue
And adventuring with delicate paces by the stream,—
Myself a child, old suddenly at the scream
From one of the white throats which it hid among?

BELLS FOR JOHN WHITESIDE'S DAUGHTER

There was such speed in her little body,
And such lightness in her footfall,
It is no wonder her brown study
Astonishes us all.

Her wars were bruited in our high window.
We looked among orchard trees and beyond,
Where she took arms against her shadow,
Or harried unto the pond

The lazy geese, like a snow cloud
Dripping their snow on the green grass,
Tricking and stopping, sleepy and proud,
Who cried in goose, Alas.

For the tireless heart within the little
Lady with rod that made them rise
From their noon apple-dreams and scuttle
Goose-fashion under the skies!

But now go the bells, and we are ready,
In one house we are sternly stopped
To say we are vexed at her brown study,
Lying so primly propped.

ANTIQUE HARVESTERS

(Scene : Of the Mississippi the bank sinister, and of the Ohio the bank sinister.)

Tawny are the leaves turned but they still hold,
And it is harvest; what shall this land produce?
A meagre hill of kernels, a runnel of juice;
Declension looks from our land, it is old.
Therefore let us assemble, dry, grey, spare,
And mild as yellow air.

'I hear the croak of a raven's funeral wing.'
The young men would be joying in the song
Of passionate birds; their memories are not long.
What is it thus rehearsed in sable? 'Nothing.'

Trust not but the old endure, and shall be older
Than the scornful beholder.

JOHN
CROWE
RANSOM

We pluck the spindling ears and gather the corn.
One spot has special yield? 'On this spot stood
Heroes and drenched it with their only blood.'
And talk meets talk, as echoes from the horn
Of the hunter—echoes are the old men's arts,
Ample are the chambers of their hearts.

Here come the hunters, keepers of a rite;
The horn, the hounds, the lank mares coursing by
Straddled with archetypes of chivalry;
And the fox, lovely ritualist, in flight
Offering his unearthly ghost to quarry;
And the fields, themselves to harry.

Resume, harvesters. The treasure is full bronze
Which you will garner for the Lady, and the moon
Could tinge it no yellower than does this noon;
But grey will quench it shortly—the field, men, stones.
Pluck fast, dreamers; prove as you amble slowly
Not less than men, not wholly.

Bare the arm, dainty youths, bend the knees
Under bronze burdens. And by an autumn tone
As by a grey, as by a green, you will have known
Your famous Lady's image; for so have these;
And if one say that easily will your hands
More prosper in other lands,

Angry as wasp-music be your cry then:
'Forsake the Proud Lady, of the heart of fire,
The look of snow, to the praise of a dwindled choir,
Song of degenerate spectres that were men?
The sons of the fathers shall keep her, worthy of
What these have done in love.'

True, it is said of our Lady, she ageth.
But see, if you peep shrewdly, she hath not stooped;
Take no thought of her servitors that have drooped,
For we are nothing; and if one talk of death—
Why, the ribs of the earth subsist frail as a breath
If but God wearieth.

JUDITH OF BETHULIA

Beautiful as the flying legend of some leopard
She had not yet chosen her great captain or prince
Depository to her flesh, and our defence;
And a wandering beauty is a blade out of its scabbard
You know how dangerous, gentlemen of threescore?
May you know it yet ten more.

Nor by process of veiling she grew the less fabulous.
Grey or blue veils, we were desperate to study
The invincible emanations of her white body,
And the winds at her ordered raiment were ominous.
Might she walk in the market, sit in the council of soldiers?
Only of the extreme elders

But a rare chance was the girl's then, when the Invader
Trumpeted from the south, and rumbled from the north,
Beleaguered the city from four quarters of the earth,
Our soldiery too craven and sick to aid her—
Where were the arms could countervail this horde?
Her beauty was the sword.

She sat with the elders, and proved on their blear visage
How bright was the weapon unrusted in her keeping,
While he lay surfeiting on their harvest heaping,
Wasting the husbandry of their rarest vintage—

And dreaming of the broad-breasted dames for concubine? JOHN
CROWE
RANSOM
These floated on his wine.

He was lapped with bay-leaves, and grass and fumiter weed,
And from under the wine-film encountered his mortal
    vision,
For even within his tent she accomplished his derision;
She loosed one veil and another, standing unafraid;
And he perished. Nor brushed her with even so much as a
    daisy?
She found his destruction easy.

The heathen are all perished. The victory was furnished,
We smote them hiding in our vineyards, barns, annexes,
And now their white bones clutter the holes of foxes,
And the chieftain's head, with grinning sockets, and
    varnished—
Is it hung on the sky with a hideous epitaphy?
No, the woman keeps the trophy.

May God send unto our virtuous lady her prince.
It is stated she went reluctant to that orgy,
Yet a madness fevers our young men, and not the clergy
Nor the elders have turned them unto modesty since.
Inflamed by the thought of her naked beauty with desire?
Yes, and chilled with fear and despair.

PAINTED HEAD

By dark severance the apparition head
Smiles from the air a capital on no
Column or a Platonic perhaps head
On a canvas sky depending from nothing;

Stirs up an old illusion of grandeur
By tickling the instinct of heads to be

135

Absolute and to try decapitation
And to play truant from the body bush;

But too happy and beautiful for those sorts
Of head (homekeeping heads are happiest)
Discovers maybe thirty unwidowed years
Of not dishonouring the faithful stem;

Is nameless and has authored for the evil
Historian headhunters neither book
Nor state and is therefore distinct from tart
Heads with crowns and guilty gallery heads;

So that the extravagant device of art
Unhousing by abstraction this once head
Was capital irony by a loving hand
That knew the no treason of a head like this;

Makes repentance in an unlovely head
For having vinegarly traduced the flesh
Till, the hurt flesh recusing, the hard egg
Is shrunken to its own deathlike surface;

And an image thus. The body bears the head
(So hardly one they terribly are two)
Feeds and obeys and unto please what end?
Not to the glory of tyrant head but to

The increase of body. Beauty is of body.
The flesh contouring shallowly on a head
Is a rock-garden needing body's love
And best bodiness to colorify

The big blue birds sitting and sea-shell flats
And caves, and on the iron acropolis
To spread the hyacinthine hair and rear
The olive garden for the nightingales.

Conrad Aiken

(1889-   )

ANNIHILATION

While the blue noon above us arches,
And the poplar sheds disconsolate leaves,
Tell me again why love bewitches,
And what love gives.

Is it the trembling finger that traces
The eyebrow's curve, the curve of the cheek?
The mouth that quivers, when the hand caresses,
But cannot speak?

No, not these, not in these is hidden
The secret, more than in other things:
Not only the touch of a hand can gladden
Till the blood sings.

It is the leaf that falls between us,
The bells that murmur, the shadows that move,
The autumnal sunlight that fades upon us:
These things are love.

It is the 'No, let us sit here longer',
The 'Wait till tomorrow', the 'Once I knew—'
These trifles, said as I touch your finger,
And the clock strikes two.

The world is intricate, and we are nothing.
It is the complex world of grass,
A twig on the path, a look of loathing,
Feelings that pass—

These are the secret! And I could hate you,
When, as I lean for another kiss,
I see in your eyes that I do not meet you,
And that love is this.

Rock meeting rock can know love better
Than eyes that stare or lips that touch.
All that we know in love is bitter.
And it is not much.

SYSTOLE AND DIASTOLE

Thus systole addressed diastole,—
The heart contracting, with its grief of burden,
To the lax heart, with grief of burden gone.

Thus star to dead leaf speaks; thus cliff to sea;
And thus the spider, on a summer's day,
To the bright thistledown, trapped in the web.

No language leaps this chasm like a lightning:
Here is no message of assuagement, blown
From Ecuador to Greenland; here is only

A trumpet blast, that calls dead men to arms;
The granite's pity for the cloud; the whisper
Of time to space.

THE STEPPING STONES

CONRAD
AIKEN

At the first stepping-stone, the past of water—
the thought with blunt nose swimming against the stream—
the tail and fins rigid, the water cold,
the scales cold, the past cold and perfect—

at the second stepping-stone, the present of water,
fluid memory surrounding the cold wish—
weeds borne downward on the changing stream
thoughts in a dream on the scarred stones—

at the third stepping-stone, the stillborn step—
suspended poise of the becoming soul
I was there, I am here, I will be there and gone,
not yet gone, but waiting to be gone—

at the third stepping-stone, the sense of water,
the perfect stream, breakless unchanging all—:
let us wait here, in the timelessness of un-willing,
and watch the past and present perpend the future . . .

At the fourth stepping-stone, it is another,—
that other, not ourself, who stands and remembers
the departed one, who stayed at the third stone,
who is now present with us like a ghost—

ghost of water, ghost of stone, ghost of weed,
that other, alas, who is but is not, was
and is, is dead but will be, will be borne
downstream forever past the later comers—

those who reach the fifth stone, or the sixth,
who wait there poised, remembering, the dead men
whose deaths will take us on from stone to stone
further across the perfect stream of water—

but never across, never to reach the last,
the final remembrance, the all-knowing shore—
where death looks backward from the shading tree,
and perfect stillness stares at perfect stream.

THE SOUNDING

Blue sky, blue noon, and the secret line is flung:
once more, the Mariner his sounding takes;
from heaven's blue bridge once more the Lead is swung,
and downward through the ethereal Ocean breaks

the divine Plummet and the invisible cord
past sun-drowned Vega, and Orion's Belt.
Now the unfathomed is fathomed with a Word:
Earth and this City, by their heartbeat felt.

Like a small lightning through the clouds' pale glooms,
at intervals unguessed by the faint sun,
down to this stony reef, the city, comes
that cord, unloosed so soundlessly to run;

and on the bridge that arches the unknown
the Master Mariner, his sounding sure,
carves in the ice: A kingdom overthrown—
man kills his children. But the birds endure.

Edna St. Vincent Millay

(1892-1950)

NEVER MAY THE FRUIT BE PLUCKED

Never, never may the fruit be plucked from the bough
And gathered into barrels.
He that would eat of love must eat it where it hangs.
Though the branches bend like reeds,
Though the ripe fruit splash in the grass or wrinkle on the
    tree,
He that would eat of love may bear away with him
Only what his belly can hold,
Nothing in the apron,
Nothing in the pockets.
Never, never may the fruit be gathered from the bough
And harvested in barrels.
The winter of love is a cellar of empty bins,
In an orchard soft with rot.

THE BUCK IN THE SNOW

White sky, over the hemlocks bowed with snow,
Saw you not at the beginning of evening the antlered buck
    and his doe
Standing in the apple-orchard? I saw them. I saw them
    suddenly go,
Tails up, with long leaps lovely and slow,
Over the stone-wall into the wood of hemlocks bowed with
    snow.

Now lies he here, his wild blood scalding the snow.
How strange a thing is death, bringing to his knees,
    bringing to his antlers

The buck in the snow.
How strange a thing,—a mile away by now, it may be,
Under the heavy hemlocks that as the moments pass
Shift their loads a little, letting fall a feather of snow—
Life, looking out attentive from the eyes of the doe.

IN THE GRAVE NO FLOWER

Here dock and tare.
But there
No flower.

Here beggar-ticks, 'tis true;
Here the rank-smelling
Thorn-apple,—and who
Would plant this by his dwelling?
Here every manner of weed
To mock the faithful harrow:
Thistles, that feed
None but the finches; yarrow,
Blue vervain, yellow charlock; here
Bindweed, that chokes the struggling year;
Broad plantain and narrow.

But there no flower.

The rye is vexed and thinned,
The wheat comes limping home,
By vetch and whiteweed harried, and the sandy bloom
Of the sour-grass; here
Dandelions,—and the wind
Will blow them everywhere.

Save there.
There
No flower.

TO A YOUNG POET

EDNA ST.
VINCENT
MILLAY

Time cannot break the bird's wing from the bird.
Bird and wing together
Go down, one feather.

No thing that ever flew,
Not the lark, not you,
Can die as others do.

John Peale Bishop

(1892-1944)

THIS DIM AND PTOLEMAIC MAN

For forty years, for forty-one,
Sparing the profits of the sun,
This farmer piled his meagre hoard
To buy at last a rattly Ford.

Now crouched on a scared smile he feels
Motion spurt beneath his heels,
Rheumatically intent shifts gears,
Unloosing joints of rustic years.

Morning light obscures the stars,
He swerves avoiding other cars,
Wheels with the road, does not discern
He eastward goes at every turn,

Nor how his aged limbs are hurled
Through all the motions of the world,
How wild past farms, past ricks, past trees,
He perishes toward Hercules.

Robert P. Tristram Coffin

(1892-1955)

THE FOG

He knew how Roman legions looked, for he
Had seen the Maine coast fogs march in from sea
For many years now, in the August days.
They came in mighty columns up the bays,
Tawny and grey and silver in the sun ;
They trampled out the seaports one by one,
The islands and the woods, with their high hosts,
And pushed the world back inland from the coasts.

This little house was lost, these hills and dells,
Cows in a pasture faded into bells,
The world around a man closed in and in
Till nowhere was ten paces from his chin.
A man drew up and halted with a start
To be so close to his own beating heart
And left so to himself and wholly blind
To everything but what was in his mind.

This was the peril and the comfort, too,
A man who lived in such a region knew ;
On any Summer's day, within an hour,
He might be blind and naked to a power
So vast, it might have come from stars unmade,
Undreamt of, even, making him afraid,
So mightier than the night that he could guess
How life was but a name for loneliness.

Archibald MacLeish

(1892-   )

COOK COUNTY

The northeast wind was the wind off the lake
Blowing the oak-leaves pale side out like
Aspen: blowing the sound of the surf far
Inland over the fences: blowing for
Miles over smell of the earth the lake smell in.

The southwest wind was thunder in afternoon.
You saw the wind first in the trumpet vine
And the green went white with the sky and the weather-
    vane
Whirled on the barn and the doors slammed all together.
After the rain in the grass we used to gather
Wind-fallen cold white apples.

                   The west
Wind was the August wind, the wind over waste
Valleys, over the waterless plains where still
Were skulls of the buffalo, where in the sand stale
Dung lay of wild cattle. The west wind blew
Day after day as the winds on the plains blow
Burning the grass, turning the leaves brown, filling
Noon with the bronze of cicadas, far out falling
Dark on the colourless water, the lake where not
Waves were nor movement.

                     The north wind was at night
When no leaves and the husk on the oak stirs
Only nor birds then. The north wind was stars
Over the whole sky and snow in the ways
And snow on the sand where in summer the water was . . .

WORDS IN TIME

ARCHI-
BALD
MACLEISH

Bewildered with the broken tongue
Of wakened angels in our sleep—
Then, lost the music that was sung
And lost the light time cannot keep!

There is a moment when we lie
Bewildered, wakened out of sleep,
When light and sound and all reply:
That moment time must tame and keep.

That moment, like a flight of birds
Flung from the branches where they sleep,
The poet with a beat of words
Flings into time for time to keep.

Samuel Greenberg

(1893-1917)

CONDUCT

By a peninsula the painter sat and
Sketched the uneven valley groves.
The apostle gave alms to the
Meek. The volcano burst
In fusive sulphur and hurled
Rocks and ore into the air—
Heaven's sudden change at
The drawing tempestuous,
Darkening shade of dense clouded hues.
The wanderer soon chose
His spot of rest; they bore the
Chosen hero upon their shoulders,
Whom they strangely admired, as
The beach-tide summer of people desired.

PEACE

The blue, faded purple, horizon mount
Seemed to bellow the valleys in mists
Of enriching, ensuing, divine shadowings . . .
Where may this be? Perhaps unpopulated
Crags of stepping rocks, where thought
Slumbers, inhaled thought, unbearing
Real earth that refines e'er the insects' muse.
Royalty defies the haunt they chose,
Therein mingles wild, perspective charm,
As immortals' thorny, entangled growth

'Mongst the field of oaks, pressing steep
Twilight's veil, Milky Way's fence; the deep
Lionized eagle hisses o'er this scene;
Birds, wild swans, glide palely o'er a charming stream.

SAMUEL
GREEN-
BERG

MAN

Always alone, star-told?
What tales are bone and skulls?
O thou nigh art a lost mind!
Quite true, we dug gold out
Of thee. Wilt thou build shadows?
Cause them thicker than now?
A trip to the moon perhaps
Will turn Heaven's eye real.
O burning statue of tendons—
Time loses thine eye!

Dorothy Parker

(1893-   )

BOHEMIA

Authors and actors and artists and such
Never know nothing, and never know much.
Sculptors and singers and those of their kidney
Tell their affairs from Seattle to Sidney.
Playwrights and poets and such horses' necks
Start off from anywhere, end up at sex.
Diarists, critics, and similar roe
Never say nothing, and never say no.
People Who Do Things exceed my endurance;
God, for a man that solicits insurance!

Mark Van Doren
(1894-   )

IT SHOULD BE EASY

It should be easy, letting the small feet go ;
Quick should it turn, the necessary knob ;
Empty this porch of any following eye
Fixed upon waves wherein a head shall bob
Now up, now down forever ; till it rises,
And floats and disappears among the mob.

We should be sure the shoulders will return,
And the hands reach and click the lock again.
We should be thoughtless, occupying days
With a new ritual modified to men.
We should be proud and let a trumpet say
How close the waters welter about the den.

And solitude would soothe us, were it not
For the slow sound of breakers near the door :
Reminders of the many farther out,
Of the lost many, nameless evermore,
That young with pride set seaward long ago,
Leaving the grey alone, the mother shore.

It would be easy, letting the cap depart,
And the small face that never looks around ;
But the firm coast line—suddenly it bends ;
Suddenly it follows, and the sound
Of hopeless cries is heard ; until the waves
Wash once again on straight and silent ground.

FORECLOSURE

So he sat down and slowly, slowly
Worked at his Christian name;
Watching the gold and halfway smiling
As the last letter came;
Till the whole sound was there, and shouted,
Suddenly, his shame.

Between this word then and the other—
His and his father's too—
He stared at the pen as if its handle
Were a great horn, and blew;
Then lowered the point and quietly laboured
Till the last ink was through.

So he got up, and through the wide silence
Wandered; and song began.
Not the old tune, for that was buried
Where the slow writing ran;
But remnants, hung in the wind awhile,
And impotent to scan.

There was the bell that once had brought him,
Frightened, across the field;
There was the mad white shepherd's barking,
And the hurt child, unhealed;
There was a hen whose blood came piping
To the red worm revealed.

There was quick trampling on a stairway,
Until doors sealed the sound.
There were the drums of winter booming
When the lame boy was drowned.
So his lost land went with him, pulling
Its tatters close around.

TALL TALE GOD

MARK
VAN
DOREN

If there were sound, the slapping
Of his reminded thigh,
The chuckle in the treetops—
As old, as high—
Would publish the true ages
Of our best brag and lie.

The colt that jumped North Mountain,
The macaroni dance;
The time we heard the breathing
Of boulders in a trance;
Midnight's lost meridians
Wheeling home from France;

The names we roared to rascals
Met on the back-hill road;
The insult at the picnic,
And how the children glowed;
The mica tree; the minted
Dollars in the lode—

He, long ago delighted,
Laughs now a double laugh:
At these, and at the wing-strength
Of so much dust and chaff;
The truth, he says, flew farther,
But not so high by half.

E. E. Cummings

(1894-   )

1

when life is quite through with
and leaves say alas,
much is to do
for the swallow, that closes
a flight in the blue;

when love's had his tears out,
perhaps shall pass
a million years
(while a bee dozes
on the poppies, the dears;

when all's done and said, and
under the grass
lies her head
by oaks and roses
deliberated.)

my father moved through dooms of love
through sames of am through haves of give,
singing each morning out of each night
my father moved through depths of height

this motionless forgetful where
turned at his glance to shining here;
that if (so timid air is firm)
under his eyes would stir and squirm

newly as from unburied which
floats the first who, his april touch
drove sleeping selves to swarm their fates
woke dreamers to their ghostly roots

and should some why completely weep
my father's fingers brought her sleep:
vainly no smallest voice might cry
for he could feel the mountains grow.

Lifting the valleys of the sea
my father moved through griefs of joy;
praising a forehead called the moon
singing desire into begin

joy was his song and joy so pure
a heart of star by him could steer
and pure so now and now so yes
the wrists of twilight would rejoice

keen as midsummer's keen beyond
conceiving mind of sun will stand,
so strictly (over utmost him
so hugely) stood my father's dream

his flesh was flesh his blood was blood:
no hungry man but wished him food;
no cripple wouldn't creep one mile
uphill to only see him smile.

Scorning the pomp of must and shall
my father moved through dooms of feel;
his anger was as right as rain
his pity was as green as grain

septembering arms of year extend
less humbly wealth to foe and friend
than he to foolish and to wise
offered immeasurable is

proudly and (by octobering flame
beckoned) as earth will downward climb,
so naked for immortal work
his shoulders marched against the dark

his sorrow was as true as bread:
no liar looked him in the head;
if every friend became his foe
he'd laugh and build a world with snow.

My father moved through theys of we,
singing each new leaf out of each tree
(and every child was sure that spring
danced when she heard my father sing)

then let men kill which cannot share,
let blood and flesh be mud and mire,
scheming imagine, passion willed,
freedom a drug that's bought and sold

giving to steal and cruel kind,
a heart to fear, to doubt a mind,

to differ a disease of same,
conform the pinnacle of am

though dull were all we taste as bright,
bitter all utterly things sweet,
maggoty minus and dumb death
all we inherit, all bequeath

and nothing quite so least as truth
—i say though hate were why men breathe—
because my father lived his soul
love is the whole and more than all

3

might these be thrushes climbing through almost (do they

beautifully wandering in merciful
miracles wonderingly celebrate day
and welcome earth's arrival with a soul)

sunlight? yes
            (always we have heard them sing
the dark alive but)
                  look: begins to grow
more than all real, all imagining;

and we who are we? surely not i not you
behold nor any breathing creature this?
nothing except the impossible shall occur

—see! now himself uplifts of stars the star
(sing! every joy)—wholly now disappear
night's not eternal terrors like a guess.

Life's life and strikes my your our blossoming sphere

4

Pity this busy monster, manunkind,

not. Progress is a comfortable disease:
your victim (death and life safely beyond)

plays with the bigness of his littleness
—electrons deify one razorblade
into a mountainrange; lenses extend

unwish through curving wherewhen till unwish
returns on its unself.
                        A world of made
is not a world of born—pity poor flesh

and trees, poor stars and stones, but never this
fine specimen of hypermagical

ultraomnipotence. We doctors know

a hopeless case if—listen: there's a hell
of a good universe next door; let's go

5

It was a goodly co
which paid to make man free
(for man is enslaved by a dread dizziz
and the sooner it's over the sooner to biz
don't ask me what it's pliz

then up rose bishop budge from kew
a anglican was who
(with a rag and a bone and a hank of hair)'d
he picked up a thousand pounds or two
and he smote the monster merde

then up rose pride and up rose pelf
and ghibelline and guelph
and ladios and laddios
(on radios and raddios)
did save man from himself

ye duskiest despot's goldenest gal
did wring that dragon's tail
(for men must loaf and women must lay)
and she gave him a desdemonial
that took his breath away

all history oped her teeming womb
said demon for to doom
yea (fresh complexions being oke
with him) one william shakespeare broke
the silence of the tomb

then up rose mr lipshits pres
(who always nothing says)
and he kisséd the general menedjerr
and they smokéd a robert burns cigerr
to the god of things like they err

6

plato told

him: he couldn't
believe it (jesus

told him; he
wouldn't believe
it) lao

tsze
certainly told

him, and general
(yes

mam)
sherman;
and even
(believe it
or

not) you
told him: i told
him; we told him
(he didn't believe it, no

sir) it took
a nipponized bit of
the old sixth

avenue
el; in the top of his head: to tell

him

7

noone" autumnal this great lady's gaze

enters a sunset "can grow (gracefully or
otherwise) old. Old may mean anything
which everyone would rather not become;
but growing is" erect her whole life smiled

"was and will always remain: who i am.

Look at these (each serenely welcoming
his only and illimitably his
destiny) mountains! how can each" while flame
crashed "be so am and i and who? each grows"

then in a whisper, as time turned to dream

"'and poets grow; and (there—see?) children" nor
might any earth's first morning have concealed
so unimaginably young a star

E. E.
CUM-
MINGS

Rolfe Humphries

(1895-   )

RENDER UNTO CÆSAR

One side of the coin has a vicious monarch's face,—
His image and superscription written plain—
Evil and tyrannous. The other side
Has a crown of laurel, and stars, and a field of sky.

Nobody, taking the coin from purse or pocket,
Holding its weight in the hollow of the hand,
Ever wonders which side is the more important,
Which is the one that makes it legal tender.
The only question is this one, very simple:
What will the money buy?

Hard and durable metal. Centuries after
Its empire crumbles, the disk and the imprint keep
Their mark, their shape, under the ash and rubble,
Under the loam, unearthed some day, and studied,
Rubbed bright again, the tyrant and the laurel,
Placed under glass in an up-to-date museum,
Current no longer, coin of the realm no more,
Purchasing power lost, but the value greater,
Greater than any it ever had before.

THE CYNNEDDF

After a banquet
Powyll of Dyfed
With many attending

Strolled to hillock
Back of the palace.

ROLFE
HUMPH-
RIES

'Lord,' said a courtier,
'Here is a strangeness:
If you sit on this mound
One of two things
Will certainly happen
Before you depart,
The hurt of a wound,
Or the sight of a wonder.'

'I fear no wound,'
Said Powyll of Dyfed,
'With this host all around me,
And as for a wonder,
Gladly I'd see one,
For wonders were ever
Dear to my heart.'

He sat on the mound,
And a lady came riding,
Lovely to look at
In garments of gold
On a cream-coloured stallion.
She rode very slowly,
She sang sweet and low,
And no one there knew her.

Powyll of Dyfed
Followed on foot
And could not overtake her,
And sent for the sorrel,
Most fleet of his stable,
Mounted and rode
By cairn and by cromlech.

Salmon and eagle,
The owl and the ousel,
From rock and from river,
From water, from air,
Watched the pursuit,
Pursued and pursuer.

Weary of riding,
Powyll of Dyfed
Cried in despair
To the beautiful lady,
'Stay, in the name
Of the one you love best!'
She reined in, smiling,
Turned to him, told him,
'Had you said so the sooner,
You would have spared
Your spirited sorrel
A great deal of anguish,'
And she took off her veil.

Of all of the maidens
And all of the women
He ever had seen
This was the fairest.
Powyll of Dyfed
Came to her side,
Said to her, 'Lady,
Receive my greeting,
And what is your journey?'
—'I go my own errand
In my own manner,'
—'Oh, what is your quest?'
—'You,' she replied.

It would be a big lie
To say they were happy

For ever and ever:
Boredom, depression,
Sometimes would settle
Even in Narberth,
And now and again
The hurt of a wound
That time could not always
Stifle or soften:
But every so often,
And over and over,
They would see from the mound
A wonder go by.

ROLFE
HUMPH-
RIES

Edmund Wilson

(1895-   )

ON EDITING SCOTT FITZGERALD'S PAPERS

Scott, your last fragments I arrange tonight,
Assigning commas, setting accents right,
As once I punctuated, spelled and trimmed
When, passing in a Princeton spring—how dimmed
By this damned quarter-century and more!—
You left your *Shadow Laurels* at my door.
That was a drama webbed of dreams: the scene
A shimmering beglamoured bluish-green
Soiled Paris wineshop; the sad hero one
Who loved applause but had his life alone;
Who fed on drink for weeks; forgot to eat,
'Worked feverishly,' nourished on defeat
A lyric pride, and lent a lyric voice
To all the tongueless knavish tavern-boys,
The liquor-ridden, the illiterate;
Got stabbed one midnight by a tavern mate—
Betrayed, but self-betrayed by stealthy sins—
And faded to the sound of violins.

Tonight, in this dark long Atlantic gale,
I set in order such another tale,
While tons of wind that take the world for scope
Rock blackened waters where marauders grope
Our blue and bathed-in Massachusetts ocean;
The Cape shakes with the depth-bomb's dumbed con-
    cussion;
And guns can interrupt me in these rooms,
Where now I seek to breathe again the fumes

Of iridescent drinking-dens, retrace
The bright hotels, regain the eager pace
You tell of . . . Scott, the bright hotels turn bleak;
The pace limps or stamps; the wines are weak;
The horns and violins come faint tonight.
A rim of darkness that devours light
Runs like the wall of flame that eats the land;
Blood, brain and labour pour into the sand;

I climbed, a quarter-century and more
Played out, my college steps, unlatched my door,
And, creature strange to college, found you there:
The pale skin, hard green eyes, and yellow hair—
Intently pinching out before a glass
Some pimples left by parties at the Nass;
Nor did you stop abashed, thus pocked and blotched,
But kept on peering while I stood and watched.
Tonight, from days more distant now, we find,
Than holidays in France were, left behind,
Than spring of graduation from the fall
That saw us grubbing below City Hall,
Through storm and darkness, Time's contrary stream,
There glides amazingly your mirror's beam—
To bring before me still, glazed mirror-wise,
The glitter of the hard and emerald eyes.
The cornea tough, the aqueous chamber cold,
Those glassy optic bulbs that globe and hold—
They pass their image on to what they mint,
To blue ice or light buds attune their tint
And leave us, to turn over, iris-fired,
Not the great Ritz-sized diamond you desired
But jewels in a handful, lying loose:
Flawed amethysts; the moonstone's milky blues;
Chill blues of pale transparent tourmaline;
Opals of shifty yellow, chartreuse green,
Wherein a vein vermilion flees and flickers—
Tight phials of the spirit's light mixed liquors;

EDMUND
WILSON Some tinsel zircons, common turquoise; but
Two emeralds, green and lucid, one half-cut,
One cut consummately—both take their place
In Letters' most expensive Cartier case.

And here, among our comrades of the trade,
Some buzz like husks, some stammer, much afraid,
Some mellowly give tongue and join the drag
Like hounds that bay the bounding anise-bag,
Some swallow darkness and sit hunched and dull,
The stunned beast's stupor in the monkey-skull.
And there I have set them out for final show,
And come to the task's dead-end, and dread to know
Those eyes struck dark, dissolving in a wrecked
And darkened world, that gleam of intellect
That spilled into the spectrum of tune, taste,
Scent, colour, living speech, is gone, is lost;
And we must dwell among the ragged stumps,
With owls digesting mice to dismal lumps
Of skin and gristle, monkeys scared by thunder,
Great buzzards that descend to grab the plunder.
And I, your scraps and sketches sifting yet,
Can never thus revive one sapphire jet
However close I look, however late,
But only spell and point and punctuate.

Louise Bogan
(1897-   )

BAROQUE COMMENT

From loud sound and still chance;
From mindless earth, wet with a dead million leaves;
From the forest, the empty desert, the tearing beasts,
The kelp-disordered beaches;
Coincident with the lie, anger, lust, oppression and death in
    many forms:

Ornamental structures, continents apart, separated by seas;
Fitted marble, swung bells; fruit in garlands as well as on the
    branch;
The flower at last in bronze, stretched backward, or curled
    within;
Stone in various shapes: beyond the pyramid, the contrived
    arch and the buttress;
The named constellations;
Crown and vesture; palm and laurel chosen as noble and
    enduring;
Speech proud in sound; death considered sacrifice;
Mask, weapon, urn; the ordered strings;
Fountains, foreheads under weather-bleached hair;
The wreath, the oar, the tool,
The prow;
The turned eyes and the opened mouth of love.

LOUISE
BOGAN

M., SINGING

Now, innocent, within the deep
Night of all things you turn the key
Unloosing what we know in sleep.
In your fresh voice they cry aloud
Those beings without heart or name.

Those creatures both corrupt and proud,
Upon the melancholy words
And in the music's subtlety,
Leave the long harvest which they reap
In the sunk land of dust and flame
And move to space beneath our sky.

John Wheelright

(1897-1940)

WHY MUST YOU KNOW?

—'What was that sound we heard
fall on the snow?'
—'It was a frozen bird.
Why must you know?
All the dull earth knows the good
that the air, with claws and wings
tears to the scattered questionings
which burn in fires of our blood.'
—'Let the air's beak and claws
    carry my deeds
far, where no springtime thaws,
    the frost for their seeds.'
—'One could fathom every sound
that the circling blood can tell
who heard the diurnal syllable,
while lying close against the ground.'
—'My flesh, bone and sinew
    now would discern
hidden waters in you
    Earth, waters that burn.'
—'One who turns to earth again
finds solace in its weight; and deep
hears the blood forever keep
the silence between drops of rain.'

THE HUNTSMAN

My cartridge belt is empty.
I have killed no beasts.
I have one bullet.
Can we; with untrembled pistol
when a serpent clasps a child;
send the bullet through the serpent
past the small head of the child?
Be not disconsolate if the bullet
pierce both child and serpent.
A trembled pistol spares the serpent
to kill the child.
Throw the empty belt away.
Take the pistol.
Shoot

PAUL AND VIRGINIA

Nephews and Nieces,—love your leaden statues.
Call them by name; call him 'Paul'. She is 'Virginia'.
He leans on his spade. Virginia fondles a leaden
fledgling in its nest. Paul fondles with his Eyes.
You need no cast in words. You know the Statues,
but not their Lawns; nor words to plant again
the shade trees, felled; ponds, filled, and built over.
Your Garden is destroyed, but there are other Gardens
yet to spare from the destroying Spoor
unseen, save in destructful Acts. Unseen
a hungered Octopus crawls under ground
as Fungus; eats the air as Orchids on all trees;
and on all waters spreads translucent Slime.
Nephews and Nieces, who would breathe sweet Air
and till rich Ground, spy out against its suction;
wither these spreading tentacles, these roots
and radicles of cancerous Greed.

Let us put Paul and Virginia back in the Garden's
warmth of wet Box and Arbor Vitae. The Bell-Tree
a silver shrub from Japan, is grown up Big
like a willow whose Branches nose the Ground. They root
and eat the Earth. They drink deep water springs
while finger twigs fill neighbouring winds with silent
tinkles of Petals, blowing on Lilies-of-the-Valley
on Larches, on copper Beeches, urn-like Elms
on Lilies, Iris, Roses walled with Hedges
mirrored on dark waters and, light with fruit trees,
on Peonies abiding in quiet pomp with leaden
Statues in a Garden, alive with Bugs and Toads.
This Garden, sad as a ripe joy is sad (dead Garden)
sheds no perfume of Soil, over a soil-less land.
This dead Garden's seeds take root in children
like the Cherry a young girl swallowed,—Stem,
Meat, and Stone; to bud, to bloom, to fruit
and to house twittering Birds.

In your Mother and Father, much you love is memory;
and much they love in you is memory transplanted
from Gardens of Love, which speak to Love from a dead
world to another, and from Death, which speaks to life
through love remembered. Nephews and Nieces,—love
your Statues, love their names.

JOHN
WHEEL-
RIGHT

Stephen Vincent Benet

(1897-1943)

INVOCATION

American muse, whose strong and diverse heart
So many men have tried to understand
But only made it smaller with their art,
Because you are as various as your land,

As mountainous-deep, as flowered with blue rivers,
Thirsty with deserts, buried under snows,
As native as the shape of Navajo quivers,
And native, too, as the sea-voyaged rose.

Swift runner, never captured or subdued,
Seven-branched elk beside the mountain stream,
That half a hundred hunters have pursued
But never matched their bullets with the dream,

Where the great huntsmen failed, I set my sorry
And mortal snare for your immortal quarry.

You are the buffalo-ghost, the broncho-ghost
With dollar-silver in your saddle-horn,
The cowboys riding in from Painted Post,
The Indian arrow in the Indian corn,

And you are the clipped velvet of the lawns
Where Shropshire grows from Massachusetts sods,
The grey Maine rocks—and the war-painted dawns
That break above the Garden of the Gods.

The prairie-schooners crawling toward the ore STEPHEN
VINCENT
BENET
And the cheap car, parked by the station-door.

Where the skyscrapers lift their foggy plumes
Of stranded smoke out of a stony mouth
You are that high stone and its arrogant fumes,
And you are the ruined gardens in the South

And bleak New England farms, so winter-white
Even their roofs look lonely, and the deep
The middle grainland where the wind of night
Is like all blind earth sighing in her sleep

A friend, an enemy, a sacred hag
With two tied oceans in her medicine-bag.

They tried to fit you with an English song
And clip your speech into the English tale.
But, even from the first, the words went wrong,
The catbird pecked away the nightingale.

The homesick men begot high-cheekboned things
Whose wit was whittled with a different sound
And Thames and all the rivers of the kings
Ran into Mississippi and were drowned.

They planted England with a stubborn trust.
But the cleft dust was never English dust.

Stepchild of every exile from content
And all the disavouched, hard-bitten pack
Shipped overseas to steal a continent
With neither shirts nor honour to their back.

Pimping grandee and rump-faced regicide,
Apple-cheeked younkers from a windmill-square,

175

Puritans stubborn as the nails of Pride,
Rakes from Versailles and thieves from County Clare,

The black-robed priests who broke their hearts in vain
To make you God and France or God and Spain.

These were your lovers in your buckskin-youth.
And each one married with a dream so proud
He never knew it could not be the truth
And that he coupled with a girl of cloud.

And now to see you is more difficult yet
Except as an immensity of wheel
Made up of wheels, oiled with inhuman sweat
And glittering with the heat of ladled steel.

All these you are, and each is partly you,
And none is false, and none is wholly true.

So how to see you as you really are,
So how to suck the pure, distillate, stored
Essence of essence from the hidden star
And make it pierce like a riposting sword

For, as we hunt you down, you must escape
And we pursue a shadow of our own
That can be caught in a magician's cape
But has the flatness of a painted stone.

Never the running stag, the gull at wing,
The pure elixir, the American thing.

And yet, at moments when the mind was hot
With something fierier than joy or grief,
When each known spot was an eternal spot
And every leaf was an immortal leaf,

I think that I have seen you, not as one,   STEPHEN
But clad in diverse semblances and powers   VINCENT
Always the same, as light falls from the sun,   BENET
And always different, as the differing hours.

Yet, through each altered garment that you wore
The naked body, shaking the heart's core.

All day the snow fell on that Eastern town
With its soft, pelting, little, endless sigh
Of infinite flakes that brought the tall sky down
Till I could put my hands in the white sky

And taste cold scraps of heaven on my tongue
And walk in such a changed and luminous light
As gods inhabit when the gods are young.
All day it fell. And when the gathered night

Was a blue shadow cast by a pale glow
I saw you then, snow-image, bird of the snow.

And I have seen and heard you in the dry
Close-huddled furnace of the city street
When the parched moon was planted in the sky
And the limp air hung dead against the heat

I saw you rise, red as that rusty plant,
Dizzied with lights, half-mad with senseless sound,
Enormous metal, shaking to the chant
Of a triphammer striking iron ground.

Enormous power, ugly to the fool,
And beautiful as a well-handled tool.

These, and the memory of that windy day
On the bare hills, beyond the last barbed wire,

177

STEPHEN
VINCENT
BENET
When all the orange poppies bloomed one way
As if a breath would blow them into fire,

I keep forever, like the sea-lion's tusk
The broken sailor brings away to land,
But when he touches it, he smells the musk,
And the whole sea lies hollow in his hand.

So, from a hundred visions, I make one,
And out of darkness build my mocking sun.

And should that task seem fruitless in the eyes
Of those a different magic sets apart
To see through the ice-crystal of the wise
No nation but the nation that is Art,

Their words are just. But when the birchbark-call
Is shaken with the sound that hunters make
The moose comes plunging through the forest-wall
Although the rifle waits beside the lake.

Art has no nations—but the mortal sky
Lingers like gold in immortality.

This flesh was seeded from no foreign grain
But Pennsylvania and Kentucky wheat,
And it has soaked in California rain
And five years tempered in New England sleet

To strive at last, against an alien proof
And by the changes of an alien moon,
To build again that blue, American roof
Over a half-forgotten battle-tune

And call unsurely, from a haunted ground,
Armies of shadows and the shadow-sound.

In your Long House there is an attic-place STEPHEN
Full of dead epics and machines that rust, VINCENT
And there, occasionally, with casual face, BENET
You come awhile to stir the sleepy dust;

Neither in pride nor mercy, but in vast
Indifference at so many gifts unsought,
The yellowed satins, smelling of the past,
And all the loot the lucky pirates brought.

I only bring a cup of silver air,
Yet, in your casualness, receive it there.

Receive the dream too haughty for the breast,
Receive the words that should have walked as bold
As the storm walks along the mountain-crest
And are like beggars whining in the cold.

The maimed presumption, the unskilful skill,
The patchwork colours, fading from the first,
And all the fire that fretted at the will
With such a barren ecstasy of thirst.

Receive them all—and should you choose to touch them
With one slant ray of quick, American light,
Even the dust will have no power to smutch them,
Even the worst will glitter in the night.

If not—the dry bones littered by the way
May still point giants toward their golden prey.

Horace Gregory

(1899-   )

THE UNWILLING GUEST:
AN URBAN DIALOGUE

—How still, how very still the air is,
As though it waited, is still waiting
For the clock to strike. Did you see that shadow
Fall behind the clock, behind the white face
of the dial?

      —No.

—Will you have a drink?

         —No.

—Another cigarette?

         —No

—If I lift the curtain you can see
Three Spaniards, a Welsh Albino and a Levantine Greek
Drinking their hearts away. One wears
A newly rented evening gown. I can almost
Hear them singing. Did you say something?

                —No.

—That's half the charm of living
In the city. Do you expect to stay here long?

                —No.

—You must remember it is a holiday: the HORACE
Coronation of another half-century, GREGORY
And nearly midnight. The snow is falling lightly,
Carefully drifting, yet the room is very warm:
'You could fancy we were lying
On the beach.' Do you want to sing?

                    —No.

—Do you find the room unnaturally quiet?

                    —No. It
Is probably trying to think. If anything waits
For something it cannot think.

—You mean it falls apart? But the room is still
Here. You can sit on the table or pace the floor
Or talk.

          —That is what I meant.
                    —Listen,
Is that a starling behind the chimney piece? Or water
     flowing?
I forgot to water the statues in the hall,
The three girls picking flowers, the little ones,
Called Morning, Noon, and Night. And the large ones,
Father and Mother, who sometimes talk,
Should be fed at once, then covered with a cloth
And put to sleep. One becomes extremely
Domestic if one lives alone.

                    —That fluttering
Of wings behind the walls could be echoes
Of a blind man playing a violin,
Or is everyone in the city blessed with eyes?
You needn't answer.

HORACE
GREGORY —There is a half-domed
Casement pouring light above us; it is not,
But looks like a three-quarter moon.
Would you like to see it?

                    —No.

                    —If I open the shades
You will see layers and layers of freshly cut
Plate glass, light splintering
The streets from a million windows.
And O the people! Everyone talking, laughing, dining out,
But you cannot hear them. Here is one window
Filled with dancing couples, and in another
Four children are playing cards, and in that window
I think I see the horseshow at a concert:
The usual pearls and gloves, white shirt front,
Naked shoulder, and minutely printed on a folded play-bill
Held in a woman's hand, *Roméo et Juliette*.
                    And in the windows
Everything to sell: the latest inventions
In copper wire, spun brass, gun-cotton, steel,
Even uranium, each almost perfect of its kind,
Sharp, clean, reflecting light—O a million lights,
Flood lights out of the dark,
Cross-beamed, white, yellow, red against the sky.
Shall I open our window?

                    —No.

                    —Everything looks
As it has seemed for almost fifty years,
A trifle overbright, but ingenuous, cheerful,
Mindful of holidays: The Alexandrian city.
Do you remember Alexandria?

                    —No.

—Pharos?

—No.

—If I draw the shades
It is as peaceful as Pharos before the tower fell.
But we, of course, are on a different island,
Hearing other rumours, if we choose to hear them,
In the African silence of this room.
Shall I unroll a map? There are rumours
That all cities are fires dropped from the sky
In a curious geography of wars:
This shaded portion of the map was Pharos:
The gods no longer walk there.
                              And across the water
The grape withers and runs over
A mound of thistled grass, and look, the Pillar
Of Cestius is a pyramid of smoke.
                        There is nothing here
That the wind cannot blow away, except the harbours,
Except in the deeper forests perhaps
A cave. If you look too closely the map is
Like a lecture at a museum
That no one cares to hear. Is that shadow still
Wandering behind the clock? Even as you leave the room,
It is still a temporal hour:
It is excellent weather for a holiday.

Hart Crane

(1899-1932)

TO BROOKLYN BRIDGE

How many dawns, chill from his rippling rest
The seagull's wings shall dip and pivot him,
Shedding white rings of tumult, building high
Over the chained bay waters Liberty—

Then, with inviolate curve, forsake our eyes
As apparitional as sails that cross
Some page of figures to be filed away;
—Till elevators drop us from our day . . .

I think of cinemas, panoramic sleights
With multitudes bent toward some flashing scene
Never disclosed, but hastened to again,
Foretold to other eyes on the same screen;

And Thee, across the harbour, silver-paced
As though the sun took step of thee, yet left
Some motion ever unspent in thy stride,—
Implicitly thy freedom staying thee!

Out of some subway scuttle, cell or loft
A bedlamite speeds to thy parapets,
Tilting there momently, shrill shirt ballooning,
A jest falls from the speechless caravan.

Down Wall, from girder into street noon leaks,
A rip-tooth of the sky's acetylene;
All afternoon the cloud-flown derricks turn . . .
Thy cables breathe the North Atlantic still.

And obscure as that heaven of the Jews,
Thy guerdon . . . Accolade thou dost bestow
Of anonymity time cannot raise:
Vibrant reprieve and pardon thou dost show.

O harp and altar, of the fury fused,
(How could mere toil align thy choiring strings!)
Terrific threshold of the prophet's pledge,
Prayer of pariah, and the lover's cry,—

Again the traffic lights that skim thy swift
Unfractioned idiom, immaculate sigh of stars,
Beading thy path—condense eternity:
And we have seen night lifted in thine arms.

Under thy shadow by the piers I waited;
Only in darkness is thy shadow clear.
The City's fiery parcels all undone,
Already snow submerges an iron year . . .

O Sleepless as the river under thee,
Vaulting the sea, the prairies' dreaming sod,
Unto us lowliest sometime sweep, descend
And of the curveship lend a myth to God.

VAN WINKLE

Macadam, gun-grey as the tunny's belt,
Leaps from Far Rockaway to Golden Gate:
Listen! the miles a hurdy-gurdy grinds—
Down gold arpeggios mile on mile unwinds.

Times earlier, when you hurried off to school
—It is the same hour though a later day—
You walked with Pizarro in a copybook,

*Streets
spread past
store and
factory—
sped by sun-
light and her
smile . . .*

185

*Like
Memory, she
is time's
truant, shall
take you by
the hand . . .*

And Cortez rode up, reining tautly in—
Firmly as coffee grips the taste,—and away!

There was Priscilla's cheek close in the wind,
And Captain Smith, all beard and certainty,
And Rip Van Winkle bowing by the way,—
'Is this Sleepy Hollow, friend—?' And he—

*And Rip forgot the office hours, and he forgot the pay ;
Van Winkle sweeps a tenement way down on Avenue A,—*

The grind-organ says . . . Remember, remember
The cinder pile at the end of the backyard
Where we stoned the family of young
Garter snakes under . . . And the monoplanes
We launched—with paper wings and twisted
Rubber bands . . . Recall-recall
                              the rapid tongues
That flittered from under the ash heap day
After day whenever your stick discovered
Some sunning inch of unsuspecting fibre—
It flashed back at your thrust, as clean as fire.

*And Rip was slowly made aware
        that he, Van Winkle, was not here
    nor there. He woke and swore he'd seen Broadway
        a Catskill daisy chain in May—*

So memory, that strikes a rhyme out of a box
Or splits a random smell of flowers through glass—
Is it the whip stripped from the lilac tree
One day in spring my father took to me,
Or is it the Sabbatical, unconscious smile
My mother almost brought me once from church
And once only, as I recall—?

It flickered through the snow screen, blindly
It forsook her at the doorway, it was gone
Before I had left the window. It
Did not return with the kiss in the hall.

Macadam, gun-grey as the tunny's belt,
Leaps from Far Rockaway to Golden Gate. . . .
Keep hold of that nickel for car-change, Rip,—
Have you got your '*Times*'—?
And hurry along, Van Winkle—it's getting late!

(from *THE BRIDGE*)

THE SEA

Above the fresh ruffles of the surf
Bright striped urchins flay each other with sand.
They have contrived a conquest for shell shucks,
And their fingers crumble fragments of baked weed
Gaily digging and scattering.

And in answer to their treble interjections
The sun beats lightning on the waves,
The waves fold thunder on the sand;
And could they hear me I would tell them:

O brilliant kids, frisk with your dog,
Fondle your shells and sticks, bleached
By time and the elements; but there is a line
You must not cross nor ever trust beyond it
Spry cordage of your bodies to caresses
Too lichen-faithful from too wide a breast.
The bottom of the sea is cruel.

CHAPLINESQUE

We make our meek adjustments,
Contented with such random consolations
As the wind deposits
In slithered and too ample pockets.

For we can still love the world, who find
A famished kitten on the step, and know
Recesses for it from the fury of the street,
Or warm torn elbow coverts.

We will sidestep, and to the final smirk
Dally the doom of that inevitable thumb
That slowly chafes its puckered index toward us,
Facing the dull squint with what innocence
And what surprise!

And yet these fine collapses are not lies
More than the pirouettes of any pliant cane;
Our obsequies are, in a way, no enterprise.
We can evade you, and all else but the heart:
What blame to us if the heart live on.

The game enforces smirks; but we have seen
The moon in lonely alleys make
A grail of laughter of an empty ash can,
And through all sound of gaiety and quest
Have heard a kitten in the wilderness.

ISLAND QUARRY

HART
CRANE

Square sheets—they saw the marble into
Flat slabs there at the marble quarry
At the turning of the road around the roots of the mountain
Where the straight road would seem to ply below the stone,
    that fierce
Profile of marble spiked with yonder
Palms against the sunset's towering sea, and maybe
Against mankind. It is at times—

In dusk it as at times as though this island lifted, floated
In Indian baths. At Cuban dusk the eyes
Walking the straight road toward thunder—
This dry road silvering toward the shadow of the quarry
—It is at times as though the eyes burned hard and glad
And did not take the goat path quivering to the right,
Wide of the mountain—thence to tears and sleep—
But went on into marble that does not weep.

Allen Tate

(1899-   )

SEASONS OF THE SOUL

To the memory of John Peale Bishop, 1892-1944

Allor porsi la mano un poco avante
e colsi un ramicel da un gran pruno ;
e il tronco suo grido : Perchè mi schiante?

I. SUMMER

Summer, this is our flesh,
The body you let mature;
If now while the body is fresh
You take it, shall we give
The heart, lest heart endure
The mind's tattering
Blow of greedy claws?
Shall mind itself still live
If like a hunting king
It falls to the lion's jaws?

Under the summer's blast
The soul cannot endure
Unless by sleight or fast
It seize or deny its day
To make the eye secure.
Brother-in-arms, remember
The hot wind dries and draws
With circular delay
The flesh, ash from the ember,
Into the summer's jaws.

It was a gentle sun   ALLEN
When, at the June solstice   TATE
Green France was overrun
With caterpillar feet.
No head knows where its rest is
Or may lie down with reason
When war's usurping claws
Shall take the heart escheat—
Green field in burning season
To stain the weevil's jaws.

The southern summer dies
Evenly in the fall:
We raise our tired eyes
Into a sky of glass,
Blue, empty, and tall
Without tail or head
Where burn the equal laws
For Balaam and his ass
Above the invalid dead,
Who cannot lift their jaws.

When was it that the summer
(Daylong a liquid light)
And a child, the new-comer,
Bathed in the same green spray,
Could neither guess the night?
The summer had no reason;
Then, like a primal cause
It had its timeless day
Before it kept the season
Of time's engaging jaws.

Two men of our summer world
Descending winding hell
And when their shadows curled
They fearfully confounded

The vast concluding shell:
Stopping, they saw in the narrow
Light a centaur pause
And gaze, then his astounded
Beard, with a notched arrow,
Part back upon his jaws.

II. AUTUMN

It had an autumn smell
And that was how I knew
That I was down a well:
I was no longer young;
My lips were numb and blue
The air was like fine sand
In a butcher's stall
Or pumice to the tongue:
And when I raised my hand
I stood in the empty hall.
The round ceiling was high
And the grey light like shale
Thin, crumbling, and dry:
No rug on the bare floor
Nor any carved detail
To which the eye could glide;
I counted along the wall
Door after closed door
Through which a shade might slide
To the cold and empty hall.

I will leave this house, I said,
There is the autumn weather—
Here, nor living nor dead;
The lights burn in the town
Where men fear together.
Then on the bare floor,
But tiptoe lest I fall,
I walked years down

Towards the front door
At the end of the empty hall.

The door was false—no key
Or lock, and I was caught
In the house; yet I could see
I had been born to it
For miles of running brought
Me back where I began.
I saw now in the wall
A door open a slit
And a fat grizzled man
Come out into the hall:

As in a moonlit street
Men meeting are too shy
To check their hurried feet
But raise their eyes and squint
As through a needle's eye
Into the faceless gloom,—
My father in a grey shawl
Gave me an unseeing glint
And entered another room!
I stood in the empty hall
And watched them come and go
From one room to another,
Old men, old women—slow,
Familiar; girls, boys;
I saw my downcast mother
Clad in her street-clothes,
Her blue eyes long and small,
Who had no look or voice
For him whose vision froze
Him in the empty hall.

III. WINTER

Goddess sea-born and bright,
Return into the sea

193

Where eddying twilight
Gathers upon your people—
Cold goddess, hear our plea!
Leave the burnt earth, Venus,
For the drying God above,
Hanged in his windy steeple,
No longer bears for us
The living wound of love.
All the sea gods are dead.
You, Venus, come home
To your salt maidenhead,
The tossed anonymous sea
Under shuddering foam—
Shade for lovers, where
A shark swift as your dove
Shall pace our company
All night to nudge and tear
The livid wound of love.

And now the winter sea:
Within her hollow rind
What sleek facility
Of sea-conceited scop
To plumb the nether mind!
Eternal winters blow
Shivering flakes, and shove
Bodies that wheel and drop—
Cold soot upon the snow
Their livid wound of love.

Beyond the undertow
The grey sea-foliage
Transpires a phosphor glow
Into the circular miles:
In the centre of his cage
The pacing animal
Surveys the jungle cove

And slicks his slithering wiles
To turn the venereal awl
In the livid wound of love.

Beyond the undertow
The rigid madrepore
Resists the winter's flow—
Headless, unageing oak
That gives the leaf no more.
Wilfully as I stood
Within the thickest grove
I seized a branch which broke;
I heard the speaking blood
(From the livid wound of love)

Drip down upon my toe:
'We are the men who died
Of self-inflicted woe,
Lovers whose stratagem
Led to their suicide.'
I touched my sanguine hair
And felt it drip above
Their brother who, like them
Was maimed and did not bear
The living wound of love.

IV. SPRING

Irritable spring, infuse
Into the burning breast
Your combustible juice
That as a liquid soul
Shall be the body's guest
Who lights, but cannot stay
To comfort this unease
Which, like a dying coal,

Hastens the cooler day
Of the mother of silences.

Back in my native prime
I saw the orient corn
All space but no time,
Reaching for the sun
Of the land where I was born:
It was a pleasant land
Where even death could please
Us with an ancient pun—
All dying for the hand
Of the mother of silences.

In time of bloody war
Who will know the time?
Is it a new spring star
Within the timing chill,
Talking, or just a mime,
That rises in the blood—
Thin Jack-and-Jilling seas
Without the human will?
Its light is at the flood,
Mother of silences!

It burns us each alone
Whose burning arrogance
Burns up the rolling stone,
This earth—Platonic cave
Of vertiginous chance!
Come, tired Sisyphus,
Cover the cave's egress
Where light reveals the slave,
Who rests when sleeps with us
The mother of silences.

Come, old woman, save
Your sons who have gone down

Into the burning cave:
Come, mother, and lean
At the window with your son
And gaze through its light frame
These fifteen centuries
Upon the shirking scene
Where men, blind, go lame:
Then, mother of silences,

Speak, that we may hear;
Listen, while we confess
That we conceal our fear;
Regard us, while the eye
Discerns by sight or guess
Whether, as sheep foregather
Upon their crooked knees,
We have begun to die;
Whether your kindness, mother,
Is mother of silences.

ALLEN
TATE

THE BURIED LAKE

Ego mater pulchrae dilectionis, et timoris,
et agnitionis, et sanctae spei.

Lady of Light, I would admit a dream to you
    If you would take it in your hand.
    Will you not let it in a gentle stream

Of living blood? How else may I remand
    Your light if not as pulse upon your ear?
    Since I have dreamt this dream at your command,

If it shall bring my edge of darkness near
    I pray you do not let the edging slough
    To blind me, but light up my edge of fear.

ALLEN
TATE The Way and the way back are long and rough
Where Myrtle twines with Laurel—single glow
Of leaf, your own imponderable stuff

Of light in which you set my time to flow.
In childhood, when I tried to catch each flake
And hold it to deny the world of snow.

—The night was tepid. I had kept opaque,
Down deeper than the canyons undersea,
The sullen spectrum of a buried lake

Nobody saw; not even seen by me.
And now I pray you mirror my mind styled
To spring its waters to my memory.

I fumbled all night long, an ageing child
Fled like a squirrel to a hollow bole
To play toy soldier, Tiny Tim, and, mild

In death, the Babes with autumn leaves for stole—
The terror of their sleep I could not spell
Until your gracing light reduced the toll.

I stumbled all night long on sand and shell
By a lakeshore where time, unfaced, was dark;
I grazed with my left foot a pinched hotel;

Where a sick dog coughed out a sickly cark
To let me in. Inside I saw no man,
But benches ranged the walls as round a park—

Sputtering gas-jet, ceiling without span
Where thinning air lay on my cheek like tin;
But then exulting in my secret plan:

I laid my top hat to one side; my chin ALLEN
  Was ready; I unsnapped the lyric case; TATE
  I had come there to play my violin.

Erect and sinuous as Valence lace
  Old ladies wore, the bow began to fill
  The shining box—whence came a dreaming face,

Small dancing girl who gave the smell of dill
  In pelts of mordents on a minor third
  From my cadenza for *The Devil's Trill*.

No, no! her quick hand said in a soft surd.
  She locked the fiddle up and was not there.
  I mourned the death of youth without a word.

And could I go where air was not dead air?
  My friend Jack Locke, scholar and gentleman,
  Gazed down upon me with a friendly stare,

Flicking his nose as if about to scan
  My verse; he plucked from his moustache one hair,
  Letting it fall like gravel in a pan,

And went as mist upon the browning air
  Away from the durable lake, the blind hotel,
  Leaving me guilted on a moving stair

Upwards, down which I regularly fell
  Tail backwards, till I caught the music room
  Empty, like a gaol without a cell.

'If I am now alone I may resume
  The grey sonata'—but the box was gone;
  I heard instead three footfalls, a light broom

Dusting the silted air, which now put on—
   Like Pier Francesca sunning a shady wall—
   A stately woman, who in sorrow shone.

I rose; she moved, she glided towards the hall;
   I took her hand but then would set her free,
   'My Love,' I said.—'I'm back to give you all,'

She said, 'my love.' (Under the dogwood tree
   In bloom, where I had held her first beneath
   The coiled black hair, I saw her smile at me.)

I hid the blade within the melic sheath
   And tossed her head; but it was not her head—
   Another's searching skull, whose drying teeth

Crumbled me all night long, and I was dead.
   Down, down below the wave that turned me round,
   Head downwards, where the Head of God had sped

On the third day; where nature had unwound
   And ravelled her green that she had softly laved,—
   The green reviving spray now slowly drowned

Me, since the shuttling eye would not be saved.
   In the tart undersea of slipping night
   The dream whispered while sight within me, caved,

Deprived, poured stinging dark on cold delight,
   And multitudinous whined invisible bees;
   All grace being lost and its considering rite,

Till come to midmost May I bent my knees,
   Santa Lucia! at noon—the prudent shore,
   The lake flashing green fins through amber trees—

And knew I had not read your eye before
  You played it in the flowing scale of glance:
  I had not thought that I could read the score,

Yet how harsh, bitter, and vexed the trance
  Of light—how I resented Lucy's play!
  Better stay dead, better not try the lance

In the living bowl: living we have one way
  For all time in the twin darks where light dies
  To live: forget that you too lost the day

Yet finding it refound it Lucy-guise
  As I, refinding where two shadows meet,
  Took from the burnished umbrage mirroring eyes

Like blue Kentucky on a golden sheet
  Spread out for all my stupor. Lady Coming,
  Lady-not-Going, come Lady come: I greet

You in the sockets of your eyes—humming
  Miles of lightning where (small pastoral scene)
  The fretting pipe is lucent and becoming.

I thought of ways to keep this image green—
  Until the leaf unfold the formal cherry—
  In an off season, when the eye is lean

With an inward gaze upon the wild strawberry,
  Cape jasmine, wild azalea, eglantine—
  All the sad eclogue that will soon be merry;

And knew that nature could not more refine
  What it had given in a looking-glass
  And holds there, after the living body's line

ALLEN
TATE Has moved wherever it must move—wild grass
Inching the earth; and the quicksilver art
Throws back the invisible but lightning mass

To inhabit the room: for I have seen it part
The decanted air, the air close up above
And under you light Lucy, light of heart—

Light choir upon my shoulder, speaking Dove!
The dream is over and the dark expired.
I knew that I had known enduring love.

Leonie Adams

(1899-   )

LIGHT AT EQUINOX

A realm is here of masquing light
When struck rent wood and cornland by
The belled heaven claps the ground.
Husk, seed, pale straw, pale ear the year reposes,
And a thinned frieze of earth rims round
The whey-gleamed wet-as-dimming sky,
And whole trodden floor of light,
Where that slant limb winds with its shadowing closes.

Distant as lustrally the sun
Within that pearl of nimble play
Where traverse with rehearsing tread
Orients of prime to their all-reaping west,
Strangered from every grave glissade
Of blue enduskings or of milky day,
And wan, his silver nimbus on,
Muses his burning sojourn unprofessed.

Past barks mouse-sleek, wattled as serpent skin,
Rare acorn fall, rare squirrel flash.
Beyond, and in a silenced scene,
The wren, gamin wanderer of immense day
Can with luxuriant bendings preen,
Or in his pebble-scoopings plash,
To alarmless Eden flown,
And suddenly, for nothing, flies away.

And all are sole in the estranging day ;
    Forms of all things their candour wear,

Like the undefending dead,
And forth from out that mortal stricture gaze,
Of unperspective radiance shed
Through everywhere horizoned air,
Tasking precising love to say,
For its its dense words, the azuring periphrase.

To her own brink light glides, intent
An unsphering sense to bind
By narrowing measures in.
Sidelong as then up branching March she bade
Stiff buds into the glancing skein,
And the green reel unwind;
Now toward another pole she's leant,
And netherwards for partner draws her shade.

THE FONT IN THE FOREST

Before remembrance we moved here, withheld,
This long reserve beneath what had not been,
Without commencement, late by life that lay,
Offered for anyone and still its own;
Intrusion of its utter forest whose eyes
Abash (nested and laired how deep) which dwell
In their intent. Here on the foreheads dries
The christening freshness of the clear year's front.
And all comes docile to its names, and all
The specious air of creature cannot shield
Unenterable recess. O listener!
Who had not heard the name you listened for,
Beside a font, tongueless, which lichens tinge
With chill frescoings where of day
On day sad afterlight must fall
Changeless upon the falling of a day
Lichens in frond with their dim arms adore.

Ivor Winters

(1899-   )

BY THE ROAD TO THE AIR-BASE

The calloused grass lies hard
Against the cracking plain:
Life is a greyish stain;
The salt-marsh hems my yard.

Dry dikes rise hill on hill:
In sloughs of tidal slime
Shell-fish deposit lime,
Wild sea-fowl creep at will.

The highway, like a beach,
Turns whiter, shadowy, dry:
Loud, pale against the sky,
The bombing planes hold speech.

Yet fruit grows on the trees;
Here scholars pause to speak;
Through gardens bare and Greek,
I hear my neighbour's bees.

A PRAYER FOR MY SON

'*Tangled with earth all ways we move.*'—JANET LEWIS

Eternal Spirit, you
Whose will maintains the world,
Who thought and made it true;

The honey-suckle curled
Through the arbutus limb,
The leaves that move in air,
Are half akin to him
Whose conscious moving stare
Is drawn, yet stirs by will;
Whose little fingers bend,
Unbend, and then are still,
While the mind seeks an end.
At moments, like a vine,
He clambers through small boughs;
Then poised and half divine,
He waits with lifted brows.
To steep the mind in sense,
Yet never lose the aim,
Will make the world grow dense,
Yet by this way we came.
Earth and mind are not one,
But they are so entwined,
That this, my little son,
May yet one day go blind.
Eternal Spirit, you
Who guided Socrates,
Pity this small and new
Bright soul on hands and knees.

SUMMER NOON: 1941

With visionary care
The mind imagines Hell,
Draws fine the sound of flame
Till one can scarcely tell
The nature, or the name,
Or what the thing is for:
    Past summer bough and cry,

The sky, distended, bare,   IVOR
Now whispers like a shell   WINTERS
Of the increase of war.
    Thus will man reach an end:
In fear of his own will,
Yet moved where it may tend,
With mind and word grown still.
    The fieldmouse and the hare,
The small snake of the garden,
Whose little muscles harden,
Whose eyes now quickened stare,
Though driven by the sound
—Too small and free to pardon!—
Will repossess this ground.

Janet Lewis

(1899-   )

THE CANDLE FLAME

I feel myself like the flame
Of a candle fanned
By every passionate claim,
Flickering fast,
Or brought to an upright stand
In the curve of a hand.

There is nothing certain, nothing steady
About the mind
That can so alter and wind
Itself in sorrow and mood,
And be ever ready
To change like the leaves in a wood.

And what of our loyalty?
That would turn, alas,
To a flickering vagrancy,
The shadow of grass,
Were it not for the certain, ever-recurring calm
Of the unknown sheltering palm.

Oscar Williams

(1900-   )

THE MIRAGE

I lived a life without love, and saw the being
I loved on every branch; then that bare tree
Stood up with all its branches up, a great harp,
Growing straight out of the ground, and there I saw
A squadron of bright birds clothing the bare limbs;
The music notes sat on the harp; it was all love.

This was the heart inside the starved body;
Love grew images like cactus, and planted roses
On the walls of the mirage, and the garden grew
Shining with perfume and the senses dwindled to dew,
The century was rolled into one formation aloft,
A cloud, like St. Veronica's handkerchief of love.

There I saw the face of the one without whom
I lived, two soft jewels implanted in her face,
Her hair pouring around her face without sound,
And her love for me sprang on her skin like dew,
Pearl-grey as the flower of the brain she lay
Quivering on the soft cushion of the great day.

I heard a roar of buildings at my conscience,
I looked up and saw a wall of windows glowing,
And there my love leaned out of each window,
There she leaned out multiplied like heaven
In that vast wall of lights, every light her face,
Suns of a thousand mornings ranging on one day.

OSCAR
WILLIAMS   And all the machines were running, and yes, great
         Was the sound of their running downward and down
         Into the blind chutes of their rooted feet,
         And all of the windows quivered with my many loves,
         Like apples they fell off at one windfall, all,
         And I awoke on the starved pavements of no love.

Robert Francis

(1901-   )

WALLS

A passer-by might just as well be blind.
These walls are walls no passer sees behind.
Or wants or needs to want to see behind.
Let the walls hide what they are there to bind.
Out-of-sight they say is out-of-mind.
The walls are cruel and the walls are kind.

SWIMMER

I

Observe how he negotiates his way
With trust and the least violence, making
The stranger friend, the enemy ally.
The depth that could destroy gently supports him.
With water he defends himself from water.
Danger he leans on, rests in. The drowning sea
Is all he has between himself and drowning.

II

What lover ever lay more mutually
With his beloved, his always-reaching arms
Stroking in smooth and powerful caresses?
Some drown in love as in dark water, and some
By love are strongly held as the green sea
Now holds the swimmer. Indolently he turns
To float.—The swimmer floats, the lover sleeps.

ROBERT
FRANCIS

APPLE PEELER

Why the unbroken spiral, Virtuoso,
Like a trick sonnet in one long, versatile sentence?

Is it a pastime merely, this perfection,
For an old man, sharp knife, long night, long winter?

Or do your careful fingers move at the stir
Of unadmitted immemorial magic?

Solitaire. The ticking clock. The apple
Turning, turning as the round earth turns.

Theodore Spencer

(1902-1949)

THE PHOENIX

I

The Sphinx with lion's feet
Comes from the North to greet
At Heliopolis
After ten centuries
The incense-flavoured death,
The holocaust of birth.
To this millennium
Now is also come
The elegant Unicorn
Bearing his graceful horn
Out of the jewelled East;
While slowly from the South
Large gentle Behemoth
Lumbers to watch the fire
Where death will soon expire.
And out of the far West
Comes the last guest,
The enormous, sad-eyed Roc
Folding his huge wings
With feathery shudderings
Like heavy clouds to block
And cramp a desert pool;
Lonely and terrible
He settles to watch the pyre
Of the renascent fire
That will at last redeem
Dead life through flame.

THEO-
DORE
SPENCER
Behold these four creatures
Come to see Nature's
Rare resurrection
From feathers and bone.
Sphinx on the North,
Assured, waiting;
Unicorn on the East,
Aristocratically waiting;
Behemoth on the South,
Motherly waiting;
Dark Roc on the West,
Ominously waiting.

And while they wait in the air that waits for them,
The pyre of incense waits for them and Him.

II

A sudden darkening of the sun
Proclaims the ritual act begun;
A blackening blur against the light—
The aged Phoenix sinks to sight.
His body heavily achieves
The aromatic sticks and leaves;
Almost losing his stiff balance,
He grips with bent rheumatic talons
A sweetly scented log or two
That will his withered force renew,
Totters, and then sinks down to rest
After a thousand years at last
His moulted scabrous ravaged breast
In the hereditary nest.

His father Sun this August day
Shoots down the hot enkindling ray
To light the myrrh and frankincense
As cradle for new innocence.

The flames crackle, sweetly flowering, THEO-
The perfumed silken wood devouring, DORE
And, enclosed in flaming petals, SPENCER
The wrinkled body gently settles
Into the fructifying core
By the caught gazers seen no more:
Until the palisade of flame
Shrivels its roseate diadem
Down to a ruffling coronet
Within whose rim, jauntily set,
Wings akimbo, beak held high,
A whole millennium in his eye,
The fledgling on the whitened coal
Asserts his re-assembled soul,
And, fresh-created paraclete,
Stands on bronze and polished feet;
Then to the sun, the golden sun,
Springs up, his purgatory done,
And on triumphant wings is gone.

But while the ashes fade that fired Him,
Four staring creatures wonder, What of them?

And as night's cooling air
Still finds them silent there,
First the dark bird of ocean
Is troubled into motion,
And to the West returns
As the last glimmer burns.
Back to the waiting South
Lumbers great Behemoth;
And the delicate Unicorn
Back to his Eastern bourn
Steps sadly and slowly;
While in melancholy
The Sphinx walks back
Across her sandy track

To her bleak home of sand,
Piled stones on her right hand.
Oh creatures of man's thought,
Why is man so wrought
That he must make his creatures
Wistful to outlast Nature's
Marriage of flesh and bone?
Like you from South and West,
From North and out of the East,
He yearns to see the death
That flowers to new breath,
The flaming spectacle,
The impossible miracle,
That, like you, occurs
Because man hopes and fears.
But he, like you, goes back
His too-accustomed track,
The rare performance done,
Back, like you, alone.

Wondering whether his mind
That has created you,
And hence created Him,
Was in creation blind,
Or flowering from dead stem,
Flared better than it knew.

Ogden Nash

(1902-   )

PORTRAIT OF THE ARTIST
AS A PREMATURELY OLD MAN

It is common knowledge to every schoolboy and even every
  Bachelor of Arts,
That all sin is divided into two parts.
One kind of sin is called a sin of commission, and that is very
  important,
And it is what you are doing when you are doing something
  you ortant,
And the other kind of sin is just the opposite and is called a
  sin of omission and is equally bad in the eyes of all right-
  thinking people, from Billy Sunday to Buddha,
And it consists of not having done something you shudda.
I might as well give you my opinion of these two kinds of sin
  as long as, in a way, against each other we are pitting them,
And that is, don't bother your head abouts sins of commission because however sinful, they must at least be fun
  or else you wouldn't be committing them.
It is the sin of omission, the second kind of sin,
That lays eggs under your skin.
The way you get really painfully bitten
Is by the insurance you haven't taken out and the checks you
  haven't added up the stubs of and the appointments
  you haven't kept and the bills you haven't paid and the
  letters you haven't written.
Also, about sins of omission there is one particularly
  painful lack of beauty,
Namely, it isn't as though it had been a riotous red letter
  day or night every time you neglected to do your duty;
You didn't get a wicked forbidden thrill

OGDEN Every time you let a policy lapse or forgot to pay a bill;
NASH You didn't slap the lads in the tavern on the back and loudly
cry Whee,
Let's all fail to write just one more letter before we go
home, and this round of unwritten letters is on me.
No, you never get any fun
Out of the things you haven't done,
But they are the things that I do not like to be amid,
Because the suitable things you didn't do give you a lot more
trouble than the unsuitable things you did.
The moral is that it is probably better not to sin at all, but if
some kind of sin you must be pursuing,
Well, remember to do it by doing rather than by not doing.

Marya Zaturenska

(1902-   )

THE FALSE SUMMER

It might have been in the heart of a deep forest,
So wide the shade, dense-thicketed where only a pool's
    sound
Strikes;—dancing over stones, with a sound cool and airy,
But it was in a city park, enclosed from the stone street
By an iron gate,
By a phalanx of trees.

We followed a thin stream of rumour, were led to a trail
Of unwinding memory, pounding and low like a moving sea
Till we came to a hot meadow;—then one voice pastoral-
    muted
Pealed through the air like a silver bell and sang like an angel;
It drew rain from the heavens,
Bowed the trembling trees.

By a glint of gold through the trees, we traced the falling
    hair
Of Amaryllis; she who lives in that burning meadow,
Whose voice as cool as a stream calms the false summer,
Who points to a mirage of streams when the soul faints with
    heat,
She who when wheels are turning calls to the pastoral land,
Sings of eternal silence,
Cool grass and tree-arched groves.

Voice of delight and fear to the lost, listening children!
They run for home, they gather their toys, the nursemaids
    call,

And suddenly rivers of blood ran on and on as always,
The nursemaids wept for their old country, green in the
angry sea,
While the heavenly voice kept singing
In the green solitude.

We too remembered the flag at half mast, the crumbling
fortress,
In that old country where we fled to danger
Because the ruins were lovely, because Death wore an
angel's mask,
We saw how the blood-rivers followed, stained the secure
landscape
Even in that rich, round song
The frozen fear, the warning.

We are lost if the iron gate closes, if the intricate thickets
Draw us deep in delightful shade, toward the charmed
singing,
Green song and deep, sharp, pure and steep, clean, green,
Song heard in the opening leaves, the closing flowers,
Do not detain us
Lest you forever claim us.

Amaryllis who sings in the shade till the storm leaps and
gathers,
Till the invaders march through the streets sealing the
fountains,
Poisoning the springs of life, destroying our secret shelters,
Drawing us further from home till we stand on the enemy
street;
And the uneasy charm is broken,
The angel music from a demon's throat.

Merrill Moore

(1903-   )

HE SAID THE FACTS

'That is important. I do not watch the birds':
He said, 'The facts—I only seek for facts—'
He said, 'I do not seek the hidden wish;
That is a fact, if you insist on facts,
But not as people think of them as facts.'

He said: 'Much more important are the acts,
They are the food upon the silver dish.'
He said: 'What is important are the acts;
I mean the way he acts, the way she acts.'

'That is important. I do not watch the birds:
Spinsters do that; I do not count the swords:
Supply sergeants do that; nor list the words:
I leave that to the effing Ph.D's.'

He said: 'All that I do I seek the facts;
The only things that concern me are the acts.'

THEY ALSO STAND . . .

At midnight, in the garden never planted,
They are unwanted, they were never wanted.

The wanderers in the dark have never come
Upon their use and uses in the kingdom—
The garden with so many in daylight,

With the sun to paint their faces white,
Who were wanted, who were always wanted.

Always asking permission to stand there,
Begging the heel of a loaf, something to wear,
Asking for faggots, fuel, asking for food
(They had none of any), all of them stood,
Standing there as if they were rooted there
Begging, and whether it is fair or unfair,
I, standing apart, have seen them standing there.

Edwin Denby

(1903-   )

AIR

Thin air I breathe and birds use for flying
Over and through trees standing breathing in air
Air insects drop through in insect dying
And deer that use it to listen in, share—

Thickens with mist on the lake, or rain
Cuts it with tasteless water and a grey
Day colours it and it is the thin and plain
Air in my mouth the air for miles away.

So close it feeds me each second, everyone's friend
Hugging outside and inside, I can't get rid
Of air, I know it, till the hateful end
When with it I give up the insanely hid

The airless secret I strangle not to share
With all the others as others share the air.

NORTHERN BOULEVARD

The bench, the sewermouth, the hydrant placed
On the street are attractive and foolproof,
Their finish is in republican taste
The expense, on democratic behoof.

People wear the city, the section they use
Like the clothes on their back and their hygiene

EDWIN
DENBY And they recognize property as they do news
By when to stay out and where to go in.

Near where a man keeps his Sunday plyers
Or young men play regularly, they place
Next to acts of financial empires
An object as magic as a private face.

No use to distinguish between hope and despair
Anyone's life is greater than his care.

Richard Blackmur

(1904-   )

THE RAPE OF EUROPA

This age it is the same with less remembered.
The first was mounted by a foam-white bull:
Others that came after were less sure
what beast bore God upon them fatally.
Always Europa is a doubting mother /
seeing the torn place struggle to be healed;
while what is born lies shameless in her lap.

This age her whole loveliness lies mauled /
battered and barren from a six-years' bout /
so trod and torn / grossness itself defiled.
Though none could seem to mother her but earth
man monstered God upon her nonetheless.
The muck she lies in mocks the muck of birth
and what is born lies blameless in her lap.

Horror got out of horror may yet be blest
when the great scar of birth begins to scab
and with each change in weather pull and burn
and the wound verge on flow. What bore / tore;
the horror and the glory are the same.
Man's hope the wound / God's memory the scar!
—else what is born lies nameless in her lap.

RICHARD
BLACK-
MUR

SCARABS FOR THE LIVING

I. TOO MUCH FOR ONE: NOT ENOUGH TO GO ROUND

There are too many heart-shaped words for one
to seem enough or two to offer choice;
and yet the heart offers the mind a voice
above all words. Crying its All is None
it is the heart itself that comes undone.

II. IN THE WIND'S EYE

Passionate are palms that clasp in double fist;
compassionate palms lie open to the sky;
on either the dew falls in manna-mist.
Weather is all. The sailor's answering wrist
hauls up / or down / as winds rise / or veer / or die.

III. ON COMMON GROUND

Shambles come ready-made these years / are found
wherever man has stood / or lost / his ground.
So the wide world. It is no otherwise
within the narrow ward where each man lies
apart / his own breathing a shamble-sound.

John Holmes

(1904-   )

WHAT DOES A MAN THINK ABOUT

What does a man think about, working alone all day
Down in the cranberry, fern, and waterlily country?
What does a man know must not happen to him yet
Down in the fog and firefly, dune and old dory country?
Is it his child drowned, is it his boat broken or drifted,
His house hurt by weather, by his own age, by debt?
No. He thinks a boat, wet ditches, weather, the tide
Mean well for him, will be luck, surely make him money,
Down in the bell-buoy, gull, sand, and slow-railroad
    country.
Thinks, somehow all this can give me what I must provide.
What does a man think, driving to get the day's food and
    mail,
Up in the stony-river country, where the evening road is
Pine-cool, steep, old-rotted-moss-log wet, and greener
As the evening valley darkens, cool, colder as light fails
From the granite outcrop down dark trees to the river bed.

Is it a letter more than anything in the world he hopes for?
May be, in the meadow-well, bridge, wild-strawberry
    country.

But a thought of water too much or too little is in his head.
Like speaking of his love too little, or of love too much.

227

BUCYRUS

A slant-windowed belt-footed enormously long-boomed
Digger, dignified or at least designated as Lima—
That's a place in Peru. What is Lima doing here,
Clawing at Alewife Brook, to lay its water away
In five-foot-round adequate concrete tunnels?
    The alewife, Indian for a sort of herring,
    Maybe meaning aloof, swarmed up this stream.
    They named it who netted a health here.
Bucyrus, a steam-shovel redder than two freight cars,
Hero of tar-paper bunkhouses in the log-boom country;
A big-bucketted up-biter, grunting soft-coal smoke,
He jumbled boulders and raw fill into dinkey-trains
That hauled it through 1910 to build build a dam.
    In the Deerfield East Branch, fish were pike,
    Perch, bass, mostly pike big and criminal,
    The bass flat the other way, a few lost trout.
Bucyrus worked three years to chew up enough Vermont
To dam a river. While he snored in the peeled-pine night
You there could stare at cold air. You could see the
Dead trees out in the water stood up for how hard it is
To kill fish, and get running water under control.
    Bucyrus the whale, grounded and dry-mouthed,
    Tried, and Lima, a Diesel female and nervous,
    Is trying, but the ancient stream runs, water
    Is not to be buried, and the boulders will drift.

THE OVERGROWN BACK YARD

There is a rumour hereabout of summer,
A long green and heavy heat,
By thunder sometimes broken asunder,
And rivers in the street.

But early in the season, with reason,
We began with weapons war
On weeds rising, on the lilac raising
New leaves too far.

JOHN
HOLMES

Wet makes the grass grow. Sun, we think,
Drinks up the damp. Whet we
Then the hand-sickle against the fickle
Grass, and cut.

The sickle sound, close to the ground,
Is soft. The hooked blade's bevel
Makes fall the grass, that eye may pass
On lawn at level.

That insistent goer, the charging mower,
Hauls back, and pants, and lunges
At tufts and patches. The wheel catches.
But the green changes

From jungle creeping up, to dingle,
To a dell. This clothesyard slope,
From under cover, with this going over,
Begins to take shape.

Richard Eberhardt

(1904-   )

ODE TO THE CHINESE PAPER SNAKE

I

Held on the slightest of bamboo poles,
Suspended from the most voluble of delicate strings,
Heavy in the head, as is proper to subtlety,

His limitation is his slyest and activist, most charm;
Achieves with the least energy the greatest purpose;
Frail in the body, liable to tear, a dissolute.

His eye is horny, he has the feather of imagination
For a fang; his hiss is what you are.
The circuitous pleases him most: circles are endless.

II

The father of a metaphysical principle,
Made in Hong Kong but sold in San Francisco,
The paper snake is foreign to the people of Maine
And has never been seen in the hives of Vienna.

Nearest to stillness his force is most potent.
Thus he adumbrates the meaning of innocence,
Liable in gross action to the unsalvageable and comic;
His least motions manipulate the fiercest evil.

Delicacy is also the mark of civilization
And this is a most uncultured Satanism;
Him no Spengler fingered into exotic play,
Nor divested him of his striking parody.

230

RICHARD
EBER-
HARDT

As sex he would be simple, but nothing is simple,
So sexually he bares the fascination of centuries.
He triumphs adept, formally, evident, exquisite.

The ultimate investing philosopher of the future,
A paper snake gives way to none in egoism.
His confidence is masterful and ritualistic,

His is the innate totality of knowledge.
A pertness poses his profundity, deftly expressed,
And it has in it the guile and the smile of the sly.

IV

The pleasantest and the most profound trickery
Is that you can handle as you will this apostle.
It is you who think you control the principle of evil,
It is you who think you invite the charming play of the good.

Nor should we forget forgetfulness, which he induces;
Such rite of resolutions is another of his provinces.
Neither Chinese nor Christian, his characteristic of uni-
    versality

Intrigues as blood, as intellect, as purity, as impurity;
Most inanimate the Chinese snake becomes most animate
Seemingly in the very laughter and sorrow of your being.

V

Aeschylus should have asked of this plaything an answer
As Sophocles spent a lifetime in honouring him;
He was too inward for the Western tone of Shakespeare;
Baudelaire knew him in Paris as a cat.

The heaviness in the Hebrews did not see his dandyism.
Perhaps the greatest effrontery to knowledge
Is that you can manipulate your own fate

RICHARD
EBER-
HARDT And as I dandle this fragile, motionable creature
His invitation is the subtle invitation of evil,
The prospect of the Immortal in a paper toy.

VI

And as I think of his perfect, immaterial existence
I am reminded of the deepest human sympathies,
While in his coyness I can make him run.
Inventiveness is his saucy mode, as he spins.

Delectable is the passionate language of the snake,
His motion has in it the stillness of all delectation,
Ancient the sinuousness, instructive the sensibility

For death is in the imagination of that tongue;
But the poison you create in entertaining him
Is swallowed up in waves of orgiastic love.

VII

Or maybe as music as an aftermath
The tantalizing pose always about to be destroyed,
Vagaries of the vigorous, quagmires of the pellucid,
Indices of the contaminations of the realities

You will perceive in fabulous sounds this serpent.
He is present to your skull as in a mirror,
It is the music of your blood you see in his visage.

Delightful is the persuasion of this destroyer,
He is the charming absolute of crumbling fingers,
The dancer, the actor fabulous in the abstract.

VIII

Self-knowledge is the tempter on the stick,
Fair is his eye, ineradicable his logic,
Unquestionable his intention to destroy
Perdurable his ability to maintain!

For you have coiled him up upon himself,
You have looked him in his evil eye,
Adroit, you spurned him into fantasy,

RICHARD
EBER-
HARDT

And you are the pattern of his prophecy!
You are the structure of his massive eye,
And you increase his inviolability.

THE HORSE CHESTNUT TREE

Boys in sporadic but tenacious droves
Come with sticks, as certainly as Autumn,
To assault the great horse chestnut tree.

There is a law governs their lawlessness.
Desire is in them for a shining amulet
And the best are those that are highest up.

They will not pick them easily from the ground.
With shrill arms they fling to the higher branches,
To hurry the work of nature for their pleasure.

I have seen them trooping down the street
Their pockets stuffed with chestnuts shucked, unshucked.
It is only evening keeps them from their wish.

Sometimes I run out in a kind of rage
To chase the boys away; I catch an arm,
Maybe, and laugh to think of being the lawgiver.

I was once such a young sprout myself
And fingered in my pocket the prize and trophy.
But still I moralize upon the day

RICHARD And see that we, outlaws on God's property,
EBER- Fling out imagination beyond the skies
HARDT Wishing a tangible good from the unknown.

And likewise death will drive us from the scene
With the great flowering world unbroken yet,
Which we held in idea, a little handful.

Kenneth Rexroth

(1905-   )

MAXIMIAN ELEGY V

(*for Mildred*)

The sky is perfectly clear.
Motionless in the moonlight,
The redwood forest descends
Three thousand feet to the sea,
To the unmoving, silent,
Thick, white fog bank that stretches
Westward to the horizon.
No sound rises from the sea;
And the forest is soundless.
Here in the open windows,
Watching the night together,
I cannot understand what
You murmur, singing sweetly,
Softly, to yourself, in French.
O, lady, you are learned
In your hands that touch me,
In lips that sing obscurely,
In secret, your private songs.
Your face looks white and frozen
In the moonlight, and your eyes
Glitter, rigid and immense.
The illusion of moonlight
Makes you look terror stricken.
And behind you the firelight
Draws back and red frightening
Toppling shadows on the walls.
An airplane crosses, low down,

And fills the landscape with noise
Like an hallucination.
Alive or dead, the stiff heart,
As the hours slide through moonlight,
Squeezes blood and memory.
The fog climbs up the mountain,
And leaves only one star in
The fog bound wood, like an eye
In a tomb. Without warning
Your voice breaks, and your face
Streams with tears, and you stagger
Against me. I do not speak,
But hold you still in my arms.
Finally you say, 'I am not
Weeping for our own troubles
But for the general chaos
Of the world.' I feel you hurling
Away, abandoned on
A parachute of ruin.
A violent shuddering
Overcomes me, as though all
The women like you who had
Ever lived, had stepped across my grave.

MARCUS ARGENTARIUS

Dead, they'll burn you up with electricity,
An interesting experience,
But quite briefly illuminating—
So pour your whisky and kiss my wife or yours,
And I'll reciprocate. Stop fretting your brains.
In Hell the learned sit in long rows saying,
'Some A-s are not B-s, there exists a not B.'
You'll have time to grow wise in their company.

ANTIPATER OF THESSALONICA

KENNETH
REXROTH

Neither war, nor cyclones, nor earthquakes,
Are as terrifying as this oaf,
Who stares, sips water, and remembers
Everything we say.

Stanley Kunitz

(1905-   )

THE DAUGHTERS OF THE HORSELEECH

The daughters of the horseleech crying 'Give! Give!'
Implore the young men for the blood of martyrs.
How shall we keep the old senator alive
Unless we satisfy his thirst for cultures?

Entreat the rat, the weasel, and the fox
To forage for a toothless master;
Have mercy, boys, on the monkey in his box;
Dear Judas goat, lead out the sheep to slaughter.

For if the warlock with the gilded claws
Withers away, and of his bones are waters,
Who will transmute our foreheads into brass
And who will keep his five charming daughters?

HE

He runs before the wise men: He
Is moving on the hills like snow.
No gists, no tears, no company
He brings but wind-rise and water-flow.

In meadows of descended day
His motion leans, dividing air:
He takes the unforgiving way
Beneath the apostolic star.

238

Mary, Mary, call Him Stranger. STANLEY
KUNITZ
Parting the night's long hair, He steals
Within the heart, that humble manger
Where the white, astonished spirit kneels.

His vertical inflicting pride,
Whose shadow cuts the nib of space,
Bends to this virtue fructified.
But though He kiss the little face

Like rapture breaking on the mind,
The necessary fierce details
Implacably He has designed.
Redemption hangs upon the nails.

END OF SUMMER

An agitation of the air,
A perturbation of the light
Admonished me the unloved year
Would turn on its hinge that night.

I stood in the disenchanted field
Amid the stubble and the stones,
Amazed, while a small worm lisped to me
The song of my marrow-bones.

Blue poured into summer blue,
A hawk broke from his cloudless tower,
The roof of the silo blazed, and I knew
That part of my life was over.

Already the iron door of the north
Clangs open; birds, leaves, snows
Order their populations forth,
And a cruel wind blows.

STANLEY
KUNITZ

THE SCOURGE

My heart felt need to die,
Our dusty time had come;
I said, 'Endure the lie,
The waste, the tedium.'

My heart sank to his knees,
Schooled in the tragic style,
But I, being out of heart,
Whipped him another mile,

And not because I cared
To let that actor go,
But only that I feared
His eternal No, No, No.

Beyond the covered bridge
The crooked road turned wild;
He rose at the season's edge,
Passionate and defiled,

Plucking the remnant leaf
Stained with the only good,
While all my children leaped
Out of the glowing wood.

Phyllis McGinley

(1905-   )

COUNTRY CLUB SUNDAY

It is a beauteous morning, calm and free.
   The fairways sparkle. Gleam the shaven grasses.
Mirth fills the locker rooms and, hastily,
   Stewards fetch ice, fresh towels, and extra glasses.

On terraces the sandaled women freshen
   Their lipstick; gather to gossip, poised and cool;
And the shrill adolescent takes possession,
   Plunging and splashing, of the swimming pool.

It is a beauteous morn, opinion grants.
   Nothing remains of last night's Summer Formal
Save palms and streamers and the wifely glance,
   Directed with more watchfulness than normal,
At listless mate who tugs his necktie loose,
Moans, shuns the light, and gulps tomato juice.

PORTRAIT OF A GIRL WITH COMIC BOOK

Thirteen's no age at all. Thirteen is nothing.
It is not wit, or powder on the face,
Or Wednesday matinées, or misses' clothing,
Or intellect, or grace.
Twelve has its tribal customs. But thirteen
Is neither boys in battered cars nor dolls,
Not *Sara Crewe*, or movie magazine,
Or pennants on the walls.

241

PHYLLIS
MC-
GINLEY Thirteen keeps diaries and tropical fish
(A month, at most); scorns jumpropes in the spring;
Could not, would fortune grant it, name its wish;
Wants nothing, everything;
Has secrets from itself, friends it despises;
Admits none to the terrors that it feels;
Owns half a hundred masks but no disguises;
And walks upon its heels.

Thirteen's anomalous—not that, not this:
Not folded bud, or wave that laps a shore,
Or moth proverbial from the chrysalis.
Is the one age defeats the metaphor.
Is not a town, like childhood, strongly walled
But easily surrounded; is no city.
Nor, quitted once, can it be quite recalled—
Not even with pity.

Robert Penn Warren
(1905-   )

ORIGINAL SIN: A SHORT STORY

Nodding its great head rattling like a gourd,
And locks like seaweed strung on the stinking stone,
The nightmare stumbles past, and you have heard
It fumble your door before it whimpers and is gone:
It acts like the old hound that used to snuffle your door and
    moan.

You thought you had lost it when you left Omaha,
For it seemed connected then with your grandpa, who
Had a wen on his forehead and sat on the veranda
To finger the precious protuberance, as was his habit to do,
Which glinted in sun like rough garnet or the rich old
    brain bulging through.

But you met it in Harvard Yard as the historic steeple
Was confirming the midnight with its hideous racket,
And you wondered how it had come, for it stood so
    imbecile,
With empty hands, humble, and surely nothing in pocket:
Riding the rods, perhaps—or grandpa's will paid the ticket.

You were almost kindly then, in your first homesickness,
As it tortured its stiff face to speak, but scarcely mewed;
Since then you have outlived all your homesickness,
But have met it in many another distempered latitude:
Oh, nothing is lost, ever lost! at last you understood.

But it never came in the quantum glare of sun
To shame you before your friends, and had nothing to do

With your public experience or private reformation:
But it thought no bed too narrow—it stood with lips askew
And shook its great head sadly like the abstract Jew.

Never met you in the lyric arsenical meadow
When children call and your heart goes stone in the bosom;
At the orchard anguish never, nor ovoid horror,
Which is furred like a peach or avid like the delicious plum.
It takes no part in your classic prudence or fondled axiom.

Not there when you exclaimed: 'Hope is betrayed by
Disastrous glory of sea-capes, sun-torment of whitecaps
—There must be a new innocence for us to be stayed by.'
But there it stood, after all the timetables, all the maps,
In the crepuscular clutter of *always*, *always*, or *perhaps*.

You have moved often and rarely left an address,
And hear of the deaths of friends with a sly pleasure,
A sense of cleansing and hope, which blooms from distress;
But it has not died, it comes, its hand childish, unsure,
Clutching the bribe of chocolate or a toy you used to
    treasure.

It tries the lock; you hear, but simply drowse:
There is nothing remarkable in that sound at the door.
Later you hear it wander the dark house
Like a mother who rises at night to seek a childhood picture;
Or it goes to the backyard and stands like an old horse cold
    in the pasture.

PURSUIT

The hunchback on the corner, with gum and shoelaces,
Has his own wisdom and pleasures, and may not be lured
To divulge them to you, for he has merely endured
Your appeal for his sympathy and your kind purchases;

And wears infirmity but as the general who turns ROBERT
PENN
WARREN
Apart in his famous old greatcoat there on the hill,
At dusk when the rapture and cannonade are still,
To muse withdrawn from the dead and his gorgeous
    subalterns;
Or stares from the thicket of his familiar pain, like a fawn
That meets you a moment, wheels, in imperious innocence
    is gone.

Go to the clinic. Sit in the outer room,
Where like an old possum the snag-nailed hand will hump
On its knee in murderous patience, and the pomp
Of pain swells like the Indies, or a plum.
And there you will stand, as on the Roman hill,
Stunned by each withdrawn gaze and severe shape,
The first barbarian victors stood to gape
At the sacrificial fathers, white-robed, still;
And even the feverish old Jew regards you with authority
Till you feel like one who has come too late, or improperly
    clothed, to a party.

The doctor will take you now. He is burly and clean;
Listening, like lover or worshiper, bends at your heart;
But cannot make out just what it tries to impart;
So smiles; says you simply need a change of scene.
Of scene, of solace: therefore Florida,
Where Ponce de Leon clanked among the lilies,
Where white sails skit on blue and cavort like fillies,
And the shoulder gleams in the moonlit corridor.
A change of love: if love is a groping Godward, though
    blind,
No matter what crevice, cranny, chink, bright in dark, the
    pale tentacle find.

In Florida consider the flamingo,
Its colour passion but its neck a question;
Consider even that girl the other guests shun

245

ROBERT
PENN
WARREN On beach, at bar, in bed, for she may know
The secret you are seeking, after all;
Or the child you humbly sit by, excited and curly,
That screams on the shore at the sea's sunlit hurlyburly,
Till the mother calls its name, toward nightfall.
Till you sit alone: in the dire meridians, off Ireland, in fury
Of spume-tooth and dawnless sea-heave, salt rimes the
    lookout's devout eye.

Till you sit alone—which is the beginning of error—
Behind you the music and lights of the great hotel:
Solution, perhaps, is public, despair personal,
But history held to your breath clouds like a mirror.
There are many states, and towns in them, and faces,
But meanwhile, the little old lady in black, by the wall,
Who admires all the dancers, and tells you how just last fall
Her husband died in Ohio, and damp mists her glasses;
She blinks and croaks, like a toad or a Norn, in the horrible
    light,
And rattles her crutch, which may put forth a small bloom,
    perhaps white.

Jose Garcia Villa

(1918-   )

BETWEEN GOD'S EYELASHES

Between God's eyelashes I look at you,
Contend with the Lord to love you,
In this house without death I break His skull
I ache, I ache to love you.

I will batter God's skull God's skull God's skull!
I'll batter it till He love you
And out of Him I'll dash I'll dash
In thy coasts, O mortal flesh.

He'll be broken He'll be broken He'll be broken
By my force of love He'll be broken
And when I reach your side O Eve
You'll break me you'll break me you'll break me.

BE BEAUTIFUL

Be beautiful, noble, like the antique ant,
Who bore the storm as he bore the sun,
Wearing neither gown nor helmet,
Though he was archbishop and soldier:
Wore only his own flesh.

Salute characters with gracious dignity,
Though what these are is left to
Your own terms. Exact: the universe is
Not so small but these will be found
Somewhere. Exact: they will be found.

JOSE
GARCIA
VILLA

Speak with great moderation: but think
With great fierceness, burning passion:
Though what the ant thought
No annals reveal, nor his descendants
Break the seal.

Trace the tracelessness of the ant,
Every ant has reached this perfection.
As he comes, so he goes,
Flowing as water flows,
Essential but secret like a rose.

Paul Engle
(1908-   )

CHAMELEON

Chameleon, knowing I am near,
Runs the brown leaf in his brown fear,
Dark as dread and light as light
His swiftness doubles with his fright,
Nimble toe and narrow tongue
Leap with the excited lung,
Long tail astonishes the air
Lashed at nothing, nothing there,

Then jumps to a green leaf that's near
And turns to green in his green fear.
My eyes blink in that altering light
As if his fright were my own fright,
Unwilled and yet aware toe, tongue
Move with my excited lung,
And I am changed in coloured air
By his change, live and sudden there.

I have watched you, slight animal,
On the long stalk of daylight crawl,
Letting the languid noon light run
On hair so burned and quick with sun—
Brown dazzle over you, brown face—
It gave that light a living grace,
And watched you, startled I was near,
Leap up in mingled love and fear.

And let your hand, slight animal,
Over my branching body crawl,

PAUL
ENGLE

So close did we together run
Touching earth was touching sun,
Change to change and face to face
I moved with greed and you with grace.
Shocked that two could be so near
We feared a love so like a fear.

Theodore Roethke

(1908-   )

MY PAPA'S WALTZ

The whisky on your breath
Could make a small boy dizzy;
But I hung on like death:
Such waltzing was not easy.

We romped until the pans
Slid from the kitchen shelf;
My mother's countenance
Could not unfrown itself.

The hand that held my wrist
Was battered on one knuckle;
At every step you missed
My right ear scraped a buckle.

You beat time on my head
With a palm caked hard by dirt,
Then waltzed me off to bed
Still clinging to your shirt.

ACADEMIC

The stethoscope tells what everyone fears:
You're likely to go on living for years,
With a nurse-maid waddle and a shop-girl simper,
And the style of your prose growing limper and limper.

THE DANCE

Is that dance slowing in the mind of man
That made him think the universe could hum?
The great wheel turns its axle when it can;
I need a place to sing, and dancing-room,
And I have made a promise to my ears
I'll sing and whistle romping with the bears.

For they are all my friends: I saw one slide
Down a steep hillside on a cake of ice,—
Or was that in a book? I think with pride:
A caged bear rarely does the same thing twice
In the same way: O watch his body sway!—
This animal remembering to be gay.

I tried to fling my shadow at the moon,
The while my blood leaped with a wordless song.
Though dancing needs a master, I had none
To teach my toes to listen to my tongue.
But what I learned there, dancing all alone,
Was not the joyless motion of a stone.

I take this cadence from a man named Yeats;
I take it, and I give it back again:
For other tunes and other wanton beats
Have tossed my heart and fiddled through my brain.
Yes, I was dancing-mad, and how
That came to be the bears and Yeats would know.

THE WAKING

I wake to sleep, and take my waking slow.
I feel my fate in what I cannot fear.
I learn by going where I have to go.

We think by feeling. What is there to know?
I hear my being dance from ear to ear.
I wake to sleep, and take my waking slow.

Of those so close beside me, which are you?
God bless the Ground! I shall walk softly there,
And learn by going where I have to go.

Light takes the Tree; but who can tell us how?
The lowly worm climbs up a winding stair;
I wake to sleep, and take my waking slow.

Great Nature has another thing to do
To you and me; so take the lively air,
And, lovely, learn by going where to go.

This shaking keeps me steady. I should know.
What falls away is always. And is near.
I wake to sleep, and take my waking slow.
I learn by going where I have to go.

SONG

Under a southern wind,
The birds and fishes move
North, in a single stream;
The sharp stars swing around;
I get a step beyond
The wind, and there I am;
I'm odd and full of love.

Wisdom, where is it found?—
Those who embrace, believe.
Whatever was, still is,
Says a song tied to a tree.
Below, on the ferny ground,
In rivery air, at ease,
I walk with my true love.

What time's my heart? I care.
I cherish what I have
Had of the temporal:
I am no longer young
But the winds and waters are;
What falls away will fall;
All things bring me to love.

THE SONG

I

I met a ragged man;
He looked beyond me when
I tried to meet his eyes.
What have I done to you?
I cried, and backed away.
Dust in a corner stirred,
And the walls stretched wide.

II

I went running down a road,
In a country of bleak stone,
And shocks of ragged corn;
When I stayed for breath, I lay
With the saxifrage and fern
At the edge of a raw field.
I stared at a fissure of ground
Ringed round with crumbled clay,
The old house of a crab;
I stared, and began to sing.

III

I sang to whatever had been
Down in that watery hole:

I wooed with a low tune;
You could say I was mad.
And a wind woke in my hair,
And the sweat poured from my face,
When I heard, or thought I heard,
Another join my song
With the small voice of a child,
Close, and yet far away.

Mouth upon mouth, we sang,
My lips pressed upon stone.

THEO-
DORE
ROETHKE

James Agee

(1908-1955)

DESCRIPTION OF ELYSIUM

There : far, friends : ours : dear dominion :
> Whole health resides with peace,
> Gladness and never harm,
> There not time turning
> Nor fear of flower of snow.

> Where marbling water slides
> No charm may halt of chill,
> Air aisling the open acres,
> And all the gracious trees.

> Spout up their standing fountains
> Of wind-beloved green
> And the blue conclaved mountains
> Are grave guards

> Stone and springing field
> Wide one tenderness,
> The unalterable hour
> Smiles deathlessness

> No thing is there thinks:
> Mind the witherer
> Withers on the outward air:
> We can not come there.

> Sure on this shining night
> Of starmade shadows round,

Kindness must watch for me
This side the ground

The late year lies down the north.
All is healed, all is health.
High summer holds the earth.
Hearts all whole.

Sure on this shining night I weep for
 wonder wandering far alone
Of shadows in the stars.

Now thorn bone bare
Silenced with iron the branch's gullet:
Rattling merely on the air
Of hornleaved holly:

The stony mark where sand was by
 The water of a nailèd foot:
The berry harder than the beak,
The hole beneath the dead oak root

All is brought quiet
Through the latest throe
Quieted and ready and quiet:
Still not snow

Still thorn bone bare
Iron in the silenced gulley
Rattling only of the air
Through hornleaved holly.

Robert Fitzgerald

(1910-   )

WINDSHIELD

A wet day on the road: the slim blades cutting
Fans of transparency among water jewels;
Distension and rip of high-speed passers-by,
Deaf to the lowly gatherings of the field;
Corn tassels tossed and oak leaves flowing in darkening
Grey rain and western wind.
                        Unplug the lighter
And frown cross-eyed upon that fiery circlet;
There is always something wanting about our hands,
On just-soft cushions lolling or lightly at work
With the slender wheel; and there is something
Perpetually unsaid in what we say—
Our silken exhalations of being friends.
A failure of no consequence?
                       I've dreamed
Of armless men in carnivals, legless men
Knuckling like apes on smoky avenues,
A world's whole host of savage crippled men
Silent but for the single cry: 'Somewhere!'

On each long curve the highway balances
Against our speed with tight terrestrial power,
Conducting to no other place but here;
Here always, the wide alien light of home,
The ever-present wildness of the air—
The nightly dread, say, in cold parishes
Of some tall silvery and unsmiling Father—
A child's wish to do something simply superb.

Winfield Townley Scott

(1910-   )

MR. WHITTIER

It is so much easier to forget than to have been Mr. Whittier.
Though of course no one now remembers him when he was
    young.
A few old ladies who were little girls next door in Amesbury,
Or practically next door, have reminiscences of pears and
    apples
Given them by the famous, tamed, white-bearded saint with
    the
Still inextinguishable dark Hebraic eyes; and
Of course there is the old man—and I for one am grateful—
    who
Recalls the seedy coat, the occasionally not so clean high
    collar,
And that like many another he read his paper by the hour in
    the privy.
Carl Schurz, finding him rained in by the stove at the
    village store,
Thought 'So superior to those about him, and yet so like
    them;' and
His official biographer decided that Mr. Whittier's poetry
    was the kind
'Written first of all for the neighbours.' There are lesser and
    worse.

In any case, here is a city, founded in 1630, present popula-
    tion somewhere about
55,000—has been more in boom times, and has been a lot
    less;—say,

In three hundred years has birthed a couple of hundred
thousand people
And one poet. Not bad. And as proof of the title I shall only
remark
It is easier to leave *Snow-Bound* and a dozen other items in or
out of
The school curriculum than it is to have written them. Try
it and see.

Born where the east wind brought the smell of the ocean
from Plum Island up-River,
At a brookside haunted in the foggy dark of autumn nights
By six little witches in sky-blue capes—Uncle Moses had
seen them;—
Born on a farm to the *Bible*, *Pilgrim's Progress*, a weekly paper,
the Quaker meeting-house,
To hard poverty, obscure, and a few winters of country
school;
To die—though only after there were thirteen for dinner,
and the clock
Suddenly stopped—ancient with fame, with honorary
degrees, and
One hundred thousand dollars all made out of poems—I say
Even this was not easy, though also it is not
What I am talking about, but is really incidental along with
Not liking Walt Whitman and never quite affording
marriage.

Neither, under the circumstances, could it have been easy,
and it was important,
To stand suddenly struck with wonder of old legends in a
young land,
To look up at last and see poetry driving a buckboard
around the bend,
And poetry all the time in the jays screeching at the cats in
the dooryard,

Climbing with the thrush into the August noon out of the WIN-
 boy's sight   FIELD
As he dawdled barefoot through poetry among the welts of TOWNLEY
 the goldenrod;   SCOTT
But nothing is hardest which treads on nobody else's toes.

Let us not begrudge Mr. Whittier his white beard, his
 saintliness, his other foibles;
Let us remember him when he was young, not to begrudge
 his rise
As a goddam Abolitionist hated not only in the South,
Hated by manufacturers, politicians, his neighbours, our
 folk, all
Who hate the outspoken radical and know a safer way;
Denounced by the clergy—a serious matter in that time; by
 the good men who
Rotten-egged him in New Hampshire, burned him out in
 Pennsylvania,
Jailed those who read him, and twenty years later im-
 mortally froze
With Webster on whom he turned his scorn of compromise.
It is so much easier to forget than to have been Mr.
 Whittier.
He put the names of our places into his poems and he
 honoured us with himself;
And is for us but not altogether, because larger than us.
When he was an old man, the Negroes came to him free to
 come and sang to him
'The Lord bless thee and keep thee;
The Lord make his face to shine upon thee and be gracious
 unto thee;
The Lord lift up his countenance upon thee, and give thee
 peace.'
—No more begrudge their freedom than his tears.

Josephine Miles
(1911-   )

FORECAST

All our stones like as much sun as possible.
Along their joints run both solar access and decline
In equal splendour, like a mica chipping
At every beat, being sun responsible.

How much sun then do you think is due them?
Or could say, how much sun do you think they are apt to
    have?
It has misted at their roots for some days now,
The grey glamour addressing itself to them.

I should think possible that it go on misting likewise
A good way into next year, or time as they have it,
A regular cool season every day for our stones.
Not a streak that low of any sun or longed surprise.

THE SYMPATHIZERS

To this man, to his boned shoulders
Came the descent of pain.
All kinds
Cruel, blind, dear, horrid, hallowed,
Rained, again, again.

To this small white blind boned face
Wherever it was
Descended

The blows of pain, it took as it were blinded, JOSEPH-
INE
MILES
As it were made for this.

We were there. We uneasy
Did not know if it were.
Knew neither
The reason nor the man nor whether
To share, or to beware.

Kenneth Patchen

(1911-   )

THE CONSTANT BRIDEGROOMS

Far down the purple wood
Coats of a company
Of silent soldiers
Flap idly in the wind

There they have stood

Since early day
Faces turned incuriously to the sound
Of the dry rustling
Of leaves in the wind

No command has reached

Them there
All silent have they stood
As
Though they were asleep
Now night darkens their coats
Far away
Their names are spoken

Somewhere at world's end

THE EVERLASTING CONTENDERS

KENNETH
PATCHEN

Of the beast . . . an angel
Creatures of the earth
It is good
Any who praise not grandly

O but they should

But they should
Death waits for everything that lives
Beast of the wood
Grim beast of the wood

Who praise not grandly

Should should
Heart weeps for all things
Here
And is greatly comforted
For heart is the angel
Of all
Who praise not grandly

But wish they could

Elizabeth Bishop

(1911-   )

FROM THE COUNTRY TO THE CITY

The long, long legs,
league-boots of land, that carry the city nowhere,
    nowhere; the lines
that we drive on (satin-stripes on harlequin's
    trousers, tights);
his tough trunk dressed in tatters, scribbled over with
    nonsensical signs;
his shadowy, tall dunce-cap; and, best of all his
    shows and sights,
his brain appears, throned in 'fantastic triumph',
    and shines through his hat
with jeweled works at work at intermeshing crowns,
    lame with lights.
As we approach, wickedest clown, your heart and head,
    we can see that
glittering arrangement of your brain consists, now,
    of mermaid-like,
seated, ravishing sirens, each waving her hand-mirror;
    and we start at
series of slight disturbances up in the telephone wires
    on the turnpike.
Flocks of short, shining wires seem to be flying sidewise.
    Are they birds?
They flash again. No. They are vibrations of the tuning-fork
    you hold and strike
against the mirror-frames, then draw for miles, your dreams,
    out countrywards.
We bring a message from the long black length of body:
    'Subside,' it begs and begs.

ROOSTERS

ELIZA-
BETH
BISHOP

At four o'clock
in the gun-metal blue dark
we hear the first crow of the first cock

just below
the gun-metal blue window
and immediately there is an echo

off in the distance,
then one from the back-yard fence,
then one, with horrible insistence,

grates like a wet match
from the broccoli patch,
flares, and all over town begins to catch.

Cries galore
come from the water-closet door,
from the dropping-plastered hen-house floor,

where in the blue blurr
their rustling wives admire,
the roosters brace their cruel feet and glare

with stupid eyes
while from their beaks there rise
the uncontrolled, traditional cries.

Deep from protruding chests
in green-gold medals dressed,
planned to command and terrorize the rest,

the many wives
who lead hens' lives
of being courted and despised;

267

deep from raw throats
a senseless order floats
all over town. A rooster gloats

over our beds
from rusty iron sheds
and fences made from old bed-steads,

over our churches
where the tin rooster perches,
over our little wooden northern houses,

making sallies
from all the muddy alleys,
marking out maps like Rand MacNally's:

glass-headed pins,
oil-golds and copper-greens,
anthracite blues, alizarins,

each one an active
displacement in perspective;
each screaming, 'This is where I live!'

Each screaming
'Get up! Stop dreaming!'
Roosters, what are you projecting?

You, whom the Greeks elected
to shoot at on a post, who struggled
when sacrificed, you whom they labelled

'Very combative . . .'
what right have you to give
commands, and tell us how to live,

cry 'Here!' and 'Here!'
and wake us here where are
unwanted love, conceit, and war?

The crown of red
set on your little head
is charged with all your fighting-blood.

Yes, that excrescence
makes a most virile presence,
plus all that vulgar beauty of iridescence.

Now in mid-air
by twos they fight each other.
Down comes a first flame-feather,

and one is flying,
with raging heroism defying
even the sensation of dying.

And one has fallen,
but still above the town
his torn-out, bloodied feathers drift down;

and what he sung
no matter. He is flung
on the grey ash-heap, lies in dung

with his dead wives
with open, bloody eyes,
while those metallic feathers oxidize.

.   .   .   .   .   .

St. Peter's sin
was worse than that of Magdalen
whose sin was of the flesh alone;

of spirit, Peter's,
falling, beneath the flares,
among the 'servants and officers'.

Old holy sculpture
could set it all together
in one small scene, past and future:

Christ stands amazed,
Peter, two fingers raised
to surprised lips, both as if dazed.

But in between
a little cock is seen
carved on a dim column in the travertine,

explained by *Gallus Canit*;
Flet Petrus underneath it.
There is inescapable hope, the pivot;

yes, and there Peter's tears
run down our chanticleer's
sides and gem his spurs.

Tear-encrusted thick
as a medieval relic
he waits. Poor Peter, heart-sick,

still cannot guess
those cock-a-doodles yet might bless,
his dreadful rooster come to mean forgiveness,

a new weathervane
on basilica and barn,
and that outside the Lateran

there would always be
a bronze cock on a porphyry
pillar so the people and the Pope might see

that even the Prince
of the Apostles long since
had been forgiven, and to convince

all the assembly
that 'Deny deny deny',
is not all the roosters cry.

In the morning
a lowlight is floating
in the back-yard, and gilding

from underneath
the broccoli, leaf by leaf;
how could the night have come to grief?

gilding the tiny
floating swallow's belly
and lines of pink cloud in the sky,

the day's preamble
like wandering lines in marble.
The cocks are now almost inaudible.

The sun climbs in,
following 'to see the end',
faithful as enemy, or friend.

ELIZA-
BETH
BISHOP

LITTLE EXERCISE

Think of the storm roaming the sky uneasily
like a dog looking for a place to sleep in,
listen to it growling.

Think how they must look now, the mangrove keys
lying out there unresponsive to the lightning
in dark, coarse-fibred families,

where occasionally a heron may undo his head,
shake up his feathers, make an uncertain comment
when the surrounding water shines.

Think of the boulevard and the little palm trees
all stuck in rows, suddenly revealed
as fistfuls of limp fish-skeletons.

It is raining there. The boulevard
and its broken sidewalks with weeds in every crack,
are relieved to be wet, the sea to be freshened.

Now the storm goes away again in a series
of small, badly lit battle-scenes,
each in 'Another part of the field'.

Think of someone sleeping in the bottom of a row-boat
tied to a mangrove root or the pile of a bridge;
think of him as uninjured, barely disturbed.

Delmore Schwartz

(1913-   )

THE HEAVY BEAR

The withness of the body—WHITEHEAD

The heavy bear who goes with me,
A manifold honey to smear his face,
Clumsy and lumbering here and there,
The central ton of every place,
The hungry beating brutish one
In love with candy, anger, and sleep,
Crazy factotum, dishevelling all,
Climbs the building, kicks the football,
Boxes his brother in the hate-ridden city.

Breathing at my side, that heavy animal,
That heavy bear who sleeps with me,
Howls in his sleep for a world of sugar,
A sweetness intimate as the water's clasp,
Howls in his sleep because the tight-rope
Trembles and shows the darkness beneath.
—The strutting show-off is terrified,
Dressed in his dress-suit, bulging his pants,
Trembles to think that his quivering meat
Must finally wince to nothing at all.

That inescapable animal walks with me,
Has followed me since the black womb held,
Moves where I move, distorting my gesture,
A caricature, a swollen shadow,
A stupid clown of the spirit's motive,
Perplexes and affronts with his own darkness,

The secret life of belly and bone,
Opaque, too near, my private, yet unknown,
Stretches to embrace the very dear
With whom I would walk without him near,
Touches her grossly, although a word

Would bare my heart and make me clear,
Stumbles, flounders, and strives to be fed
Dragging me with him in his mouthing care,
Amid the hundred million of his kind,
The scrimmage of appetite everywhere.

THE BEAUTIFUL AMERICAN WORD, SURE

The beautiful American word, Sure,
As I have come into a room, and touch
The lamp's button, and the light blooms with such
Certainty where the darkness loomed before,

As I care for what I do not know, and care
Knowing for little she might not have been,
And for how little she would be unseen,
The intercourse of lives miraculous and dear.

Where the light is, and each thing clear,
Separate from all others, standing in its place,
I drink the time and touch whatever's near,

And hope for day when the whole world has that face:
For what assures her present every year?
In dark accidents the mind's sufficient grace.

Karl Shapiro

(1913-   )

PARADOX: THE BIRDS

Wrong about birds. I cannot call
That swift, enslaved, mechanical
Come and go, come and go,
Build and feed and mate and grow
    Beautiful.
Beautiful, the poets are wrong
To love you for your turn and wheel and glide and song
Beast of the wind, wolf of the tree,
Heart with the gunner's history,
Rise and fall, rise and fall,
Heart of the heart I cannot call
    Liberty.
Liberty, the poets are wrong
To love you for your turn and wheel and glide and song.

Randall Jarrell

(1914-   )

THE LINES

After the centres' naked files, the basic line
Standing outside a building in the cold
Of the late or early darkness, waiting
For meals or mail or salvage, or to wait
To form a line to form a line to form a line;
After the things have learned that they are things,
Used up as things are, pieces of the plain
Flat object-language of a child or states;
After the lines, through trucks, through transports, to the
    lines
Where the things die as though they were not things—
But lie as numbers in the crosses' lines;
After the files that ebb into the rows
Of the white beds of the quiet wards, the lines
Where some are salvaged for their state, but some
Remanded, useless, to the centres' files;
After the naked things, told they are men,
Have lined once more for papers, pensions—suddenly
The lines break up, for good; and for a breath,
The longest of their lives, the men are free.

THE BREATH OF NIGHT

The moon rises. The red cubs rolling
In the ferns by the rotten oak
Stare over a marsh and a meadow
To the farm's white wisp of smoke.

276

A spark burns, high in heaven.
Of the old orchard, rabbits
Hop by the well-curb. The cock crows

From the tree by the widow's walk;
Two stars, in the trees to the west,
Are snared, and an owl's soft cry
Runs like a breath through the forest.

Here too, though death is hushed, though joy
Obscures, like night, their wars,
The beings of this world are swept
By the Strife that moves the stars.

THE KNIGHT, DEATH, AND THE DEVIL

Cowhorn-crowned, shockheaded, cornshuck-bearded,
Death is a scarecrow—his death's-head a teetotum
That tilts up toward man confidentially
But trimmed with adders; ringlet-maned, rope-bridled,
The mare he rides crops herbs beside a skull.
He holds up, warning, the crossed cones of time:
Here, narrowing into now, the Past and Future
Are quicksand.
                    A hoofed pikeman trots behind.
His pike's claw-hammer mocks—in duplicate, inverted—
The pocked, ribbed, soaring crescent of his horn.
A scapegoat aged into a steer; boar-snouted;
His great limp ears stuck sidelong out in air;
A dewlap bunched at his breast; a ram's-horn wound
Beneath each ear; a spur licked up and out
From the hide of his forehead; bat-winged, but in bone;
His eye a ring inside a ring inside a ring

277

RANDALL
JARRELL That leers up, joyless, vile, in meek obscenity—
This is the devil. Flesh to flesh, he bleats
The herd back to the pit of being.

In fluted mail; upon his lance the bush
Of that old fox; a sheep-dog bounding at his stirrup,
In its eyes the cast of faithfulness (our help,
Our foolish help); his dun war-horse pacing
Beneath in strength, in ceremonious magnificence;
His castle—some man's castle—set on every crag:
So, companioned so, the knight moves through this world.
The fiend moos in amity, Death mouths, reminding:
He listens in assurance, has no glance
To spare for them, but looks past steadily
At—at—a man's look completes itself.

The death of his own flesh, set up outside him;
The flesh of his own soul, set up outside him—
Death and the devil, what are these to him?
His being accuses him—and yet his face is firm
In resolution, in absolute persistence;
The folds of smiling do for steadiness;
The face is its own fate—*a man does what he must*—
And the body underneath it says: *I am.*

John Berryman

(1914-   )

from "HOMAGE TO MISTRESS BRADSTREET"

When by me in the dusk my child sits down
I am myself. Simon, if that's loose,
let me wiggle it out.
You'll get a bigger one there, and bite.
How they loft, how their sizes delight and grate.
The proportioned, spiritless poems accumulate.
And they publish them
away in brutish London, for a hollow crown.

Father is not himself. He keeps his bed,
and threw a saffron scum Thursday. God-forsaken words
escaped him raving. Save,
Lord, thy servant zealous & just.
Sam he saw back from Harvard. He did scold
his secting enemies. His stomach is cold
while we drip, while
my baby John breaks out. O far from where he bred!

Bone of moaning: sung Where he has gone
a thousand summers by truth-hallowed souls;
be still. Agh, he is gone!
Where? I know. Beyond the shoal.
Still-all a Christian daughter grinds her teeth
a little. This our land has ghosted with
our dead: I am at home.
Finish, Lord, in me this work thou hast begun.

And they tower, whom the pear-tree lured
to let them fall, fierce mornings they reclined
down the brook-bank to the east
fishing for shiners with a crookt pin,
wading, dams massing, well, and Sam's to be
a doctor in Boston. After the divisive sea,
and death's first feast,
and the galled effort on the wilderness endured,

Arminians, and the King bore against us;
of an 'inward light' we hear with horror.
Whose fan is in his hand
and he will throughly purge his floor,
come towards mé. I have what licks the joints
and bites the heart, which winter more appoints.
Iller I, oftener.
Hard at the outset; in the ending thus hard, thus?

Sacred & unutterable Mind
flashing thorough the universe one thought,
I do wait without peace.
In the article of death I budge.
Eat my sore breath, Black Angel. Let me die.
Body a-drain, when will you be dry
and countenance my speed
to Heaven's springs? lest stricter writhings have me declined.

'What are those pictures in the air at night,
Mother?' Mercy did ask. Space charged with faces
day & night! I place
a goatskin's fetor, and sweat: fold me
in savoury arms. Something is shaking, wrong.
He smells the musket and lifts it. It is long.
It points at my heart.
Missed he must have. In the gross storm of sunlight

I sniff a fire burning without outlet,
consuming acrid its own smoke. It's me.

Ruined laughter sounds
outside. Ah but I waken, free.
And so I am about again. I hagged
a fury at the short maid, whom tongues tagged,
and I am sorry. Once
less I was anxious when more passioned to upset

the mansion & the garden & the beauty of God.
Insectile unreflective busyness
blunts & does amend.
Hangnails, piles, fibs, life's also.
But we are that from which draws back a thumb.
The seasons stream and, somehow, I am become
an old woman. It's so:
I look. I bear to look. Strokes once more his rod.

My window gives on the graves, in our great new house
(how many burned?) upstairs, among the elms.
I lie, & endure, & wonder.
A haze slips sometimes over my dreams
and holiness on horses' bells shall stand.
Wandering pacemaker, unsteadying friend,
in a redskin calm I wait:
beat when you will our end. Sinkings & droopings drowse.

They say thro' the fading winter Dorothy fails,
my second, who than I bore one more, nine;
and I see her inearthed. I linger.
Seaborn she wed knelt before Simon;
Simon I, and linger. Black-yellow seething, vast
it lies fròm me, mine: all they look aghast.
It will be a glorious arm.
Docile I watch. My wreckt chest hurts when Simon pales.

In the yellowing days your faces wholly fail,
at Fall's onset. Solemn voices fade.
I feel no coverlet.

JOHN
BERRY-
MAN

Light notes leap, a beckon, swaying
the tilted sickening ear within. I'll—I'll—
I am closed & coming. Somewhere! I defile
wide as a cloud, in a cloud,
unfit, desirous, glad—even the singings veil—

—You are not ready? You are ready. Pass,
as shadow gathers shadow in the welling night.
Fireflies of childhood torch
you down. We commit our sister down.
One candle mourn by, which a lover gave,
the use's edge and order of her grave.
Quiet? Moisture shoots.
Hungry throngs collect. They sword into the carcass.

Headstones stagger under great draughts of time
after heads pass out, and their world must reel
speechless, blind in the end
about its chilling star: thrift tuft,
whin cushion—nothing. Already with the wounded flying
dark air fills, I am a closet of secrets dying,
races murder, foxholes hold men,
reactor piles wage slow upon the wet brain rime.

I must pretend to leave you. Only you draw off
a benevolent phantom. I say you seem to me
drowned towns off England,
featureless as those myriads
who what bequeathed save fire-ash, fossils, burled
in the open river-drifts of the Old World?
Simon lived on for years.
I renounce not even ragged glances, small teeth, nothing,

O all your ages at the mercy of my loves
together lie at once, forever or
so long as I happen.
In the rain of pain & departure, still

Love has no body and presides the sun,
and elfs from silence melody. I run.
Hover, utter, still,
a sourcing whom my lost candle like the firefly loves.

JOHN
BERRY-
MAN

Thomas Merton

(1915-   )

AN ARGUMENT—
OF THE PASSION OF CHRIST

And what one of you, by taking thought, can add to his stature one cubit?—St. Matthew, vi, 27

I

The furious prisoner of the womb,
Rebellious, in the jaws of life,
Learns, from the mother's conscious flesh,
The secret laws of blood and strife.

The demon raging at the breast,
Arrayed in cries, and crowned with tears,
Has sucked the magics of the east,
The doubts of the philosophers.

In the red straits of his arteries,
Love runs, lost and ravening;
Nothingness feeds upon itself
And swells up to a mighty king!

Wit walks out, in envy's mask;
Love will hide, and be a lecher.
Adultery, by taking thought,
Adds a cubit to his stature,

Until we scan the wastes of death,
And wind blows through our cage of bones;
Sight leaves the sockets of the skull,
And love runs mad among the stones!

The worm that watched within the womb
Was standing guard at Jesus' tomb,
And my first angry, infant breath
Stood wakeful, lest He rise from death.
My adolescence, like the wolf,
Fled to the edges of the gulf
And searched the ruins of the night
To hide from Calvary's iron light:
But in the burning jaws of day
I saw the barren Judas Tree;
For, to the caverns of my pride
Judas had come, and there was paid!

III

Seeds of the three hours' agony
Fell on good earth, and grew from me,
And, cherished by my sleepless cares
Flowered with God's Blood, and Mary's tears.
My curious love found its reward
When Love was scourged in Pilate's yard:
Here was the work my hands had made:
A thorny crown, to cut His head.
The growth of thoughts that made me great
Lay on His cross, and were its weight;
And my desires lay, turned to stones,
And where He fell, cut to the bone.
The sharpnesses of my delight
Were spikes run through His hands and feet,
And from the sweetness of my will
Their sponge drew vinegar and gall.

IV

The cry that rent the temple veil
And split the earth as deep as hell
And echoed through the universe,

Sounds, in bombardments, down to us.
There is no ear that has not heard
The deathless cry of murdered God:
No eye that has not looked upon
The lance of the crucifixion:
And yet that cry beats at the ears
Of old, deaf-mute interpreters,
Whose querulous and feeble cries
Drown stronger voices, and whose eyes
Will let no light of lances in:
They still will clamour for a sign!

FIGURE FOR AN APOCALYPSE

Landscape : Beast
Yonder, by the eastward sea
Where smoke melts in a saucer of extinguished cities,
The last men stand, in delegations,
Waiting to see the seven-headed business
Promised us, from those unpublished deeps:
Waiting to see those horns and diadems
And hear the seven voices of the final blasphemy.

And westward, where the other waters are as slick as silk
And slide, in the grey evening, with uncertain lights,
(Screened by the smoke of the extinguished studios)
The last men wait to see the seven-headed thing.
They stand around the radios
Wearing their regalia on their thin excited breasts,
Waving the signals of their masonry.
What will happen, when they see those heads, those horns
Dishevel the flickering sea?
How will they bare their foreheads, and put forth their
    hands
And wince with the last indelible brand,
And wear the dolour of that animal's number,
And evermore be burned with her disgusting name?

Inland, in the lazy distance, where a dozen planes still play THOMAS
As loud as horseflies, round the ruins of an average town, MERTON
A blue-green medium dragon, swimming in the river,
Emerges from the muddy waters, comes to romp awhile
    upon the land.
She rises on the pathless shore,
And goes to roll in the ashes of the ravaged country.
But no man turns to see and be surprised
Where those grey flanks flash palely in the sun.
Who shall gather to see an ordinary dragon, in this day of
    anger,
Or wonder at those scales as usual as sin?

Meanwhile, upon the broken mountains of the south
No one observes the angels passing to and fro:
And no one sees the fire that shoots beneath the hoofs
Of all the white, impatient horses.

And no one hears or fears the music of those blazing swords.

(Northward, northward, what lies there to see?
Who shall recount the terror of those ruined streets?
And who shall dare to look where all the birds with golden
    beaks
Stab at the blue eyes of the murdered saints?)

Peter Viereck

(1916-   )

COUNTER-SERENADE: SHE INVOKES THE AUTUMN INSTANT

Then touch then park; the leaves are stained to lure you.
The leaves are spread on winds they fan before you,
They drained the summer, and their veins prefer you
Dark with the season they are keening for.

Then bring the heavy dying they prefer.
Each painful fruit is hanging heavier.
Why pause when loveliness grows lonelier
And love is just as melting as it looks?
There's but one touch that all the ripeness lacks:
You are the instant; you are waited for.

Then touch the park. The leaves have spread before you
The green they drained, the darkness they prefer.
Come to the leaves, reach out and touch them all:
Bring to the smouldering year, that hovers for you,
The hovering instant love is dawdling for.

There's not one blade that does not long to fall.

Samuel French Morse
(1916-   )

THE TRACK INTO THE SWAMP

This is the place, as wild as summer snow.
A few square miles of land
Locked in the township where our father lived
Are strange and unexplored.
The idle traffic
Moving north a mile away
Is more familiar than the silt
This coastal stream brings down;
But we have wondered, late in the spring,
How far the river overflowed
Behind the ruined dam.

We know there has been traffic here:
Someone, thirty years ago,
Cleared out a track as far as this.
He must have thought
There was a fortune in the river-sand;
He bound the cedar ties
On something less than rock
And learned the road he had spent a summer on
Was treacherous and vain.
It ends, a narrow path,
In scrub and shadow, farther down.

But if we are more curious than some,
Or have more time,
What was the summer journey he began?
The cedar stands;

And he could see the river from the road,
Or calculate how high it rose in spring
By going to the dam.
What was he looking for, if anything?

He took the longest way to learn
What sedge and grasses thrust
From crumbling ice the glacier left;
Where sundew, like a burning-glass,
Lies open to the light.
Whatever was apparent here
He must have seen,
Though deeper in the swamp, perhaps some trace
Of time before the Pleistocene still shows.
What conscious aim he had
Remains as secret as our own,—
But surely science understands
How deep the inhuman mystery goes;
The wilderness it comprehends
It can explain, like summer snow.

Howard Griffin

(1916-   )

SUPPOSE IN PERFECT REASON

Suppose in perfect reason
you want to die, you want earnestly
knowing for years the meaning,
you want above all to die—
recall the eager, the blonde
beavers who died in shelterhalves
of steel or ground like coral
to reefs where there was no choice.
Life defines the power to choose
and when you cut the thread
you are chosen, you become
a total, a togetherness.
More difficult to go on
bowlining silk-end
to end with awkward hand.
If for any cause you want to die
recall the dead who wanted simply
to live and who had every reason
to go on yet who died
for no accurate reason that you
could name. The pure line
is never poetry
but in walking down the street
to the store.—Wrong or right
they could not be colder dead
whatever side of the fence
the beast is. They eat
out of our mouths, they gaze
through our eyes that look

HOWARD
GRIFFIN

at a plant. If for any cause
you want profoundly to die,
remember the dead. Re-
collect the dead.
Recall the finished dead.

Robert Lowell

(1917-)

THE DRUNKEN FISHERMAN

Wallowing in this bloody sty,
I cast for fish that pleased my eye
(Truly Jehovah's bow suspends
No pots of gold to weight its ends);
Only the blood-mouthed rainbow trout
Rose to my bait. They flopped about
My canvas creel until the moth
Corrupted its unstable cloth.

A calendar to tell the day;
A handkerchief to wave away
The gnats; a couch unstuffed with storm
Pouching a bottle in one arm;
A whisky bottle full of worms;
And bedroom slacks: are these fit terms
To mete the worm whose molten rage
Boils in the belly of old age?

Once fishing was a rabbit's foot—
O wind blow cold, O wind blow hot,
Let suns stay in or suns step out:
Life danced a jig on the sperm-whale's spout—
The fisher's fluent and obscene
Catches kept his conscience clean.
Children, the raging memory drools
Over the glory of past pools.

Now the hot river, ebbing, hauls
Its bloody waters into holes;

ROBERT
LOWELL

A grain of sand inside my shoe
Mimics the moon that might undo
Man and Creation too; remorse
Stinking, has puddled up its source;
Here tantrums thrash to a whale's rage.
This is the pot-hole of old age.

Is there no way to cast my hook
Out of this dynamited brook?
The Fisher's sons must cast about
When shallow waters peter out.
I will catch Christ with a greased worm,
And when the Prince of Darkness stalks
My bloodstream to its Stygian term . . .
On water the Man-Fisher walks.

AS A PLANE TREE BY THE WATER

Darkness has called to darkness, and disgrace
Elbows about our windows in this planned
Babel of Boston where our money talks
And multiplies the darkness of a land
Of preparation where the Virgin walks
And roses spiral her enamelled face
Or fall to splinters on unwatered streets.
Our Lady of Babylon, go by, go by,
I was once the apple of your eye;
Flies, flies are on the plane tree, on the streets.

The flies, the flies, the flies of Babylon
Buzz in my ear-drums while the devil's long
Dirge of the people detonates the hour
For floating cities where his golden tongue
Enchants the masons of the Babel Tower
To raise tomorrow's city to the sun

That never sets upon these hell-fire streets
Of Boston, where the sunlight is a sword
Striking at the withholder of the Lord:
Flies, flies are on the plane tree, on the streets.

Flies strike the miraculous waters of the iced
Atlantic and the eyes of Bernadette
Who saw Our Lady standing in the cave
At Massabielle, saw her so squarely that
Her vision put out reason's eyes. The grave
Is open-mouthed and swallowed up in Christ.
O walls of Jericho! And all the streets
To our Atlantic wall are singing: 'Sing,
Sing for the resurrection of the King.'
Flies, flies are on the plane tree, on the streets.

FALLING ASLEEP OVER THE AENEID

*An old man in Concord forgets to go to morning service. He falls
asleep, while reading Vergil, and dreams that he is Aeneas at the
funeral of Pallas, an Italian prince.*

The sun is blue and scarlet on my page,
And *yuck-a, yuck-a, yuck-a, yuck-a*, rage
The yellowhammers mating. Yellow fire
Blankets the captives dancing on their pyre,
And the scorched lictor screams and drops his rod.
Trojans are singing to their drunken God,
Ares. Their helmets catch on fire. Their files
Clank by the body of my comrade—miles
Of filings! Now the scythe-wheeled chariot rolls
Before their lances long as vaulting poles,
And I stand up and heil the thousand men,
Who carry Pallas to the bird-priest. Then
The bird-priest groans, and as his birds foretold,
I greet the body, lip to lip. I hold

The sword that Dido used. It tries to speak,
A bird with Dido's sworded breast. Its beak
Clangs and ejaculates the Punic word
I hear the bird-priest chirping like a bird.
I groan a little. 'Who am I, and why?'
It asks, a boy's face, though its arrow-eye
Is working from its socket. 'Brother, try,
O Child of Aphrodite, try to die:
To die is life.' His harlots hang his bed
With feathers of his long-tailed birds. His head
Is yawning like a person. The plumes blow;
The beard and eyebrows ruffle. Face of snow,
You are the flower that country girls have caught,
A wild bee-pillaged honey-suckle brought
To the returning bridegroom—the design
Has not yet left it, and the petals shine;
The earth, its mother, has, at last, no help:
It is itself. The broken-winded yelp
Of my Phoenician hounds, that fills the brush
With snapping twigs and flying, cannot flush
The ghost of Pallas. But I take his pall,
Stiff with its gold and purple, and recall
How Dido hugged it to her, while she toiled,
Laughing—her golden threads, a serpent coiled
In cypress. Now I lay it like a sheet;
It clinks and settles down upon his feet,
The careless yellow hair that seemed to burn
Beforehand. Left foot, right foot—as they turn,
More pyres are rising: armoured horses, bronze,
And gagged Italians, who must file by ones
Across the bitter river, when my thumb
Tightens into their wind-pipes. The beaks drum;
Their headman's cow-horned death's-head bites its tongue,
And stiffens, as it eyes the hero slung
Inside his feathered hammock on the crossed
Staves of the eagles that we winged. Our cost
Is nothing to the lovers, whoring Mars

And Venus, father's lover. Now his car's
Plumage is ready, and my marshals fetch
His squire, Acoetes, white with age, to hitch
Aethon, the hero's charger, and its ears
Prick, and it steps and steps, and stately tears
Lather its teeth; and then the harlots bring
The hero's charms and baton—but the King,
Vain-glorious Turnus, carried off the rest.
'I was myself, but Ares thought it best
The way it happened.' At the end of time,
He sets his spear, as my descendants climb
The knees of Father Time, his beard of scalps,
His scythe, the arc of steel that crowns the Alps.
The elephants of Carthage hold those snows,
Turms of Numidian horse unsling their bows,
The flaming turkey-feathered arrows swarm
Beyond the Alps. 'Pallas,' I raise my arm
And shout, 'Brother, eternal health. Farewell
Forever.' Church is over, and its bell
Frightens the yellowhammers, as I wake
And watch the whitecaps wrinkle up the lake.
Mother's great-aunt, who died when I was eight,
Stands by our parlour sabre. 'Boy, it's late.
Vergil must keep the Sabbath.' Eighty years!
It all comes back. My Uncle Charles appears.
Blue-capped and bird-like. Phillips Brooks and Grant
Are frowning at his coffin, and my aunt,
Hearing his coloured volunteers parade
Through Concord, laughs, and tells her English maid
To clip his yellow nostril hairs, and fold
His colours on him . . . It is I, I hold
His sword to keep from falling, for the dust
On the stuffed birds is breathless, for the bust
Of young Augustus weighs on Vergil's shelf:
It scowls into my glasses at itself.

Walker Gibson

(1919-   )

DAVID

Master of metaphor, at three
He's learned the language of mirage—
Sees dump trucks climbing every tree;
The sky, he says, is their garage.

And like a derrick, drops his head;
Contrives his airplane arms like flaps;
Mother and father sleep like dead;
Behind the barn the dead cat naps.

This is no simple world. To him
Man is machine, machine is man,
And the corpse talks, the lilies swim.
Of course, we tell him what we can.

Robert Duncan

(1919-   )

THE REAPER

Created by the poet to sing my song,
or created by my song to sing.

The source of the song must die away.

All day the night of music hovers
In the fir-tree, swims and glitters.
O touch me not to song
I desire to be forever mute with my first Lord.

The source of the song will die away.

Glorious is the hot sun.
The reaper in his youth cuts down the living grain.
We see the glitter of his hot curved scythe.
His weary labours cut us down
while yet we live.

The source of the song will die away.

Sweep not upon the strings of my dark lyre,
my body, music; make mute
the tree within my heart, for I desire
to come unto my Lord unsung: the Tomb
of Muses in the marble of the flesh
is like a monument of song.

The source of the song will die away.

All night the pestilential reaper slays.
We fall away beneath his blade.
Our youth is daily harvested like wheat
from fields of our first Lord

The source of the song will die away.

But see, glorious is the hot sun.
The Reaper cuts my hot youth down.
He cuts me down from my first Lord
while yet I live.

The source of the song will die away.

HERO SONG

There was no repose.

We think of them
at the boundaries
crows of a carrion world
natural to the cold
driven forward, forced back.

    caw, caw, caw.

He was a light in our restlessness,
shedding no light
but luminous in himself—
on electric cloud,
then, embodied,
a torso foreign to our despair.

Death does not come down upon us.
We wait for him.

For the great carnal striker
to level our pride.

Brides to our future,
we hear the crows cawing.

Away! Away!

Fear is mysterious
to instil resistance.

We resist at the boundaries of the day
the first light we have seen

the incandescence of the dead.

Love, he said,
     will eat away the Empire
     until chaos remains.

James Broughton

(1920-   )

THE LIGHTHOUSE KEEPER'S OFFSPRING

Storms once hurled my howls about,
but now no traumas worry me.
I the skiff that hugged safe harbour
find no harbour save the sea.

And there is where I'll choose to bed,
stretching out on rolling tide.
There my boat shall aim its sailing,
there will I like Christmas glide.

Gods unknown, O god of racing,
grace me fleets to steer my own.
If free I can, if me I can,
such as this my bold will go:

Straight across the world's old sorrow,
lightly rigged for shipshape seas,
and all of earth's dry murder thrown
overboard with ease.

GENESIS OF VOWELS

A is to begin with, and A began with Adam.
E is to proceed with, and Eve was her name.
I is what they ended with, and I of course is me.
O is how they did it, O over O and over.
U is what undid them, underneath the game.

For Y was added to the act.
Adamant is Y.
Even crawling inside O
it yowls at U and I.

JAMES
BROUGH-
TON

Chester Kallman

(1921-   )

NIGHTMARE OF A COOK

And the day arrives at last, my friends,
When the breakwater drops like a duck's head
Before your unweanable greed,
As I, pip-squeak and upset,
Your lunch two hours late,
Circle on one shorter leg about the sands,
And you come on, your voices
Merged in a driving whimper, but
How well I know your faces.

For each of you two faces.
One: as I entered, candlelight
Gave up your greasy hands
At once to my greedy sight,
And bluntly your eyes said, *Caught!*
As you dropped all thought of excuses
For killing the Great White Goose.
The other: you came in suddenly, eyes bright,
Eyes sharp as those of one who finds
Confirmed a wished unfaithfulness,
While I sat morbidly among my dead,
The groaning board of isolation spread.

An instant, from a bird's eye, spread
Lie sea and beach below me, but
I am where I am and you, a sea of hands,
A sea of eyes, all mouth, all simplified,
Come on; and you will not be stupefied by spices

Nor compromise with sauces
When you take your time, and even the neat
Scavenger, the feeling snail, will get
Nothing of me, when you are done, my friends.

CHESTER
KALLMAN

LITTLE EPITHALAMIUM

Oak, fern, ivy and pine:
What they are, not the sound spoken,
The words only as invocation
Permitting me their presence again.
The bus climbed from the narrow plain,
From the palm-lined shore; on the mountain
Were oak, fern, ivy and pine,
A tang in the air. I was not alone,
I was not alone. And later when
We returned, under a sickle moon
The blue broke in a fleece-white ribbon
Along the beach. We came down
Through the mountain air, not a word spoken.
Let me, a moment, have as mine
What is ever, and even in possession,
A blessed, blessing separation
Making one, making one.
I say them in ceremony again:
Oak, fern, ivy and pine.

URBAN HISTORY

We said *We understand*, and for a while
    Perhaps in truth we really founded
        A calm within that wheel
    Whereon the flock, in dreams of holy-land,

Are moved by nothing real.
We loved, we nested, saw no evil,
And wakefully to folly blind,
We studied what to feel.

We said *We understand*, to clear a while
A working interval surrounded
By an uncertain wall;
But patiently across the civil sand,
The waves of madness crawl,
And almost as we heard the babble
Afar of that uncertain sound,
We knew what must befall.

We said *We understand*, but even while
We spoke, and speaking hailed a rounded
New world where all was well,
Some dreaming sybil idly bade the wind
Speak Heaven and speak Hell,
A God was born of woman, Virgil
Burrowed the rock, we saw the wound,
Man was redeemed, Rome fell.

We understood it, and a little while
Later were not at all astounded
When Love did what He will.
It is over, we said. *We understand.*
It is not over still:
The wind raves on with tongues that Babel
Failed to define; the sea, unstained,
Haunts what it cannot fill.

Richard Wilbur

(1921-   )

POTATO

for André du Bouchet

An underground grower, blind and a common brown;
Got a misshapen look, it's nudged where it could;
Simple as soil yet crowded as earth with all.

Cut open raw, it loosens a cool clean stench,
Mineral acid seeping from pores of prest meal;
It is like breaching a strangely refreshing tomb:

Therein the taste of first stones, the hands of dead slaves,
Waters men drank in the earliest frightful woods,
Flint-chips, and peat, and the cinders of buried camps.

Scrubbed under faucet water the planet skin
Polishes yellow, but tears to the plain insides;
Parching, the white's blue-hearted like hungry hands.

All of the cold dark kitchens, and war-frozen grey
Evening at window; I remember so many
Peeling potatoes quietly into chipt pails.

'It was potatoes saved us, they kept us alive.'
Then they had something to say akin to praise
For the mean earth-apples, too common to cherish or steal.

Times being hard, the Sikh and the Senegalese,
Hobo and Okie, the body of Jesus the Jew,
Vestigial virtues, are eaten; we shall survive.

What has not lost its savour shall hold us up,
And we are praising what saves us, what fills the need.
(Soon there'll be packets again, with Algerian fruits.)

Oh, it will not bear polish, the ancient potato,
Needn't be nourished by Caesars, will blow anywhere,
Hidden by nature, counted-on, stubborn and blind.

You may have noticed the bush that it pushes to air,
Comical-delicate, sometimes with second-rate flowers
Awkward and milky and beautiful only to hunger.

BEASTS

Beasts in the major freedom
Slumber in peace tonight. The gull on his ledge
Dreams in the guts of himself the moon-plucked waves
below,
And the sunfish leans on a stone, slept
By the lyric water;

In which the spotless feet
Of deer make dulcet splashes, and to which
The ripped mouse, safe in the owl's talon, cries
Concordance. Here there is no such harm
And no such darkness

As the selfsame moon observes
Where, warped in window-glass, it sponsors now
The werewolf's painful change. Turning his head away
On the sweaty bolster, he tries to remember
The mood of manhood,

But lies at last, as always,
Letting it happen, the fierce fur soft to his face,

Hearing with sharper ears the wind's exciting minors, RICHARD
　　The leaves' panic, and the degradation WILBUR
　　　Of the heavy streams.

　　　Meantime, at high windows
　　Far from thicket and pad-fall, suitors of excellence
Sigh and turn from their work to construe again the painful
　　Beauty of heaven, the lucid moon
　　　And the risen hunter,

　　　Making such dreams for men
　　As told will break their hearts as always, bringing
Monsters into the city, crows on the public statues,
　　Navies fed to the fish in the dark
　　　Unbridled waters.

BEOWULF

The land was overmuch like scenery,
The flowers attentive, the grass too garrulous green;
In the lake like a dropped kerchief could be seen
The lark's reflection after the lark was gone;
The Roman road lay paved too shiningly
For a road so many men had travelled on.

Also the people were strange, were strangely warm.
The king recalled the father of his guest,
The queen brought mead in a studded cup, the rest
Were kind, but in all was a vagueness and a strain,
Because they lived in a land of daily harm.
And they said the same things again and again.

It was a childish country; and a child,
Grown monstrous, so besieged them in the night
That all their daytimes were a dream of fright

That it would come and own them to the bone.
The hero, to his battle reconciled,
Promised to meet that monster all alone.

So then the people wandered to their sleep
And left him standing in the echoed hall.
They heard the rafters rattle fit to fall,
The child departing with a broken groan,
And found their champion in a rest so deep
His head lay harder sealed than any stone.

The land was overmuch like scenery,
The lake gave up the lark, but now its song
Fell to no ear, the flowers too were wrong,
The day was fresh and pale and swiftly old,
The night put out no smiles upon the sea;
And the people were strange, the people strangely cold.

They gave him horse and harness, helmet and mail,
A jewelled shield, an ancient battle-sword,
Such gifts as are the hero's hard reward
And bid him do again what he has done.
These things he stowed beneath his parting sail,
And wept that he could share them with no son.

He died in his own country a kinless king,
A name heavy with deeds, and mourned as one
Will mourn for the frozen year when it is done.
They buried him next the sea on a thrust of land:
Twelve men rode round his barrow all in a ring,
Singing of him what they could understand.

Dachine Rainer

(1921-   )

DOUBLE RITUAL

for Baby Thérèse and Grandpa Mendel

Death thresholded old man hold
Upon your uncertain lap—here, hold!
Upon your near centuried lap
Your golden child.

And smile your ancient heartworn ache:
There is no place for an old man.

This is the dance of youth and old age,
Kick high!
You wear death in place of the features
We knew. Kick high! Kick high.

Death's intervening face affronts my gaze,
Oh no. This is no place.

Too late: it scarcely seems worth the journey's weight
To bring the child's gaiety for your poor sight.
Dim old man, dear grandpa, homeless and confined,
I grieve years long with an enduring grief

For you, earth ridden, wandering and shackled, in the
        hospital
Of an old age home. There is no place for an old man.

    That she may look upon the earth
    I cast her on, and weep for all the shipwrecks,

All the castaways,
That she may view the sorrow

Of unalterable loneliness
Before her infant mind can penetrate its mysteries,

To inoculate her spirit
Against the dreadful vagaries
Of brutal man, I bring her here,
And for your benedictine touch, your glance, your
    winging wishes.

Where there is no place for an old man
There is no place for anyone.

But, there! she moves upon your lap
As though the great wheel on which we all ride
Stirred her, as though wheels, worlds, the moving
    years
On centuries leaned upon her tiny thoughtful form

As she sits, gazing out from the bright rim of all the
    heavens
Upon the shell of night.

Robert Horan

(1922-   )

LITTLE CITY

Spider, from his flaming sleep,
staggers out into the window frame;
swings out from the red den where he slept
to nest in the gnarled glass.
Fat hero, burnished cannibal
lets down a frail ladder and ties a knot,
sways down to a landing with furry grace.

By noon this corner is a bullet-coloured city
and the exhausted architect
sleeps in his pale wheel,
waits without pity for a gold visitor
or coppery captive, his aerial enemies
spinning headlong down the window to the trap.

The street of string shakes now and announces
a surprised angel in the tunnel of thread.
Spider dances down his wiry heaven to taste the moth.

A little battle begins and the prison trembles.
The round spider hunches like a judge.
The wheel glistens.
But this transparent town that caves in at a breath
is paved with perfect steel.
The victim hangs by his feet, and the spider
circles invisible avenues, weaving a grave.

By evening the web is heavy with monsters,
bright constellation of wasps and bees,

breathless, surrendered.
Bronze skeletons dangle on the wires
and a thin wing flutters.
The medieval city hangs in its stars.

Spider lumbers down the web
and the city stretches with the weight of his walking.
By night we cannot see the flies' faces
and the spider, rocking.

EMBLEMS OF EVENING

Look, sunset's all undone!
Blackbird, no platform to swim from
but pinnacles of pine.
The garden is ribboned with red,
ladders of washing wine

The sun-dial shows one dazzled inch
on its purple wheel.
The statues stand in clots of shadow;
all retreat, scarved and mute,
toward the horizon of the unreal.

Rush, in rare dusk, the crippled moths;
around the woollen light, toss and flow.
There are no stars yet, but rents in cloth
which will later glow,
an intermittent meadow.

The deer in their dewing hovels
fold their legs.
Sleep holds toward them,
and the staring frogs, homes.

314

(Your eyes behind their lowered lids   ROBERT
travel a blue parabola.   HORAN
Medallions of the sunken sun
glimmer on your lean shoulder.)

Anthony Hecht

(1922-   )

THE PLACE OF PAIN IN THE UNIVERSE

Mixture of chloroform and oil of cloves
Swabbed with a wadded toothpick on the gums
Grants us its peace by slackening the thread
Of rich embroidered nerve spun in the head,
And to the weak and wretched jaw it comes
Lighter than manna and in sweeter loaves.

An old engraving pictures St. Jerome
Studying at his table, where a skull,
Crowned with a candle, streams cold tears of wax
On its bone features for the flesh it lacks,
Yet its white complement of teeth is full
While all its pain runs happily to loam.

Observe there is no easy moral here.
Having received their diet from the skies
The teeth remain, although they cannot bite,
And to perform inspection beyond sight
The empty sockets famish for their eyes,
The pain is lifelike in that waxwork tear.

JAPAN

It was a miniature country once
To my imagination; Home of the Short,
And also the academy of stunts
        Where acrobats are taught

The famous secrets of the trade:
  To cycle in the big parade
While spinning plates upon their parasols,
Or somersaults that do not touch the ground,
    Or tossing seven balls
In Most Celestial Order round and round.

A child's quick sense of the ingenious stamped
All their invention: toys I used to get
At Christmastime, or the peculiar, cramped
    Look of their alphabet.
    Fragile and easily destroyed,
    Those little boats of celluloid
Driven by camphor round the bathroom sink,
And delicate the folded paper prize
    Which, dropped into a drink
Of water, grew up right before your eyes.

Now when we reached them it was with a sense
Sharpened for treachery compounding in their brains
Like mating weasels; our Intelligence
    Said: The Black Dragon reigns
    Secretly under yellow skin,
    Deeper than dyes of atabrine
And deadlier. The War Department said:
Remember you are Americans; forsake
    The wounded and the dead
At your own cost; remember Pearl and Wake.

And yet they bowed us in with ceremony,
Told us what brands of Sake were the best,
Explained their agriculture in a phony
    Dialect of the West,
    Meant vaguely to be understood
    As a shy sign of brotherhood
In the old human bondage to the facts
Of day-to-day existence. And like ants,

Signalling tiny pacts
With their antennae, they would wave their hands.

At last we came to see them not as glib
Walkers of tightropes, worshippers of carp,
Nor yet a species out of Adam's rib
　　Meant to preserve its warp
　　In Cain's own image. They had learned
　　That their tough eye-born goddess burned
Adoring fingers. They were very poor.
The holy mountain was not moved to speak.
　　Wind at the paper door
Offered them snow out of its hollow peak.

Human endeavour clumsily betrays
Humanity. Their excrement served in this;
For, planting rice in water, they would raise
　　Schistosomiasis
　　Japonica, that enters through
　　The pores into the avenue
And orbit of the blood, where it may foil
The heart and kill, or settle in the brain.
　　This fruit of their nightsoil
Thrives in the skull, where it is called insane.

Now the quaint early image of Japan
That was so charming to me as a child
Seems like a bright design upon a fan,
　　Of water rushing wild
　　On rocks that can be folded up,
　　A river which the wrist can stop
With a neat flip, revealing merely sticks
And silk of what had been a fan before,
　　And like such clever tricks,
It shall be buried in excelsior.

ACKNOWLEDGMENTS

For permission to reprint these poems, thanks are due the
following poets, their copyright holders, and publishers:

RICHARD BLACKMUR—for his poems from *The Good
European* (Cummington Press, 1947).

BRANDT & BRANDT—for "Invocation" from "John
Brown's Body" by Stephen Vincent Benét in *Selected
Works of Stephen Vincent Benét* (Rinehart & Co.),
copyright 1927, 1928 by Stephen Vincent Benét; for
poems of E. E. Cummings from *Poems 1923-1954* by E.
E. Cummings (Harcourt Brace & Co.), copyright 1925,
1940, 1944, 1950, 1953 by E. E. Cummings; and for
poems of Edna St. Vincent Millay from *Collected
Lyrics of Edna St. Vincent Millay* (Harper & Bros.),
copyright 1923, 1928, 1934 by Edna St. Vincent Millay.

JAMES BROUGHTON—for his poems from *Musical
Chairs* (Centaur-Press, 1947).

EDWIN DENBY—for his poems from *In Public, In Private*
(J. A. Decker, 1948).

DOUBLEDAY & CO.—for poems of Don Marquis from
Archy's Life of Mehitabel by Don Marquis, copyright
1933 by Doubleday & Co.; for "Academic" from *Open
House* by Theodore Roethke, copyright 1941 by Theo-
dore Roethke; "The Dance" (copyright 1952 by the
Atlantic Monthly Co.), "Four for Sir John Davies," and
"The Waking" from *The Waking, Poems 1933-1953*,
copyright 1953 by Theodore Roethke; and "My Papa's

319

321

322

323

ALAN SWALLOW—for poems of Janet Lewis from *Poems 1924-1944* by Janet Lewis, copyright 1950 by Janet Lewis.

ALLEN TATE—for "The Buried Lake," first published in the *Sewanee Review*, Spring 1953.

TWAYNE PUBLISHERS—for "What Does a Man Think About" from "Water Poem" in *The Double Root* by John Holmes; and for the poems of Merrill Moore from *Illegitimate Sonnets* by Merrill Moore.

MARK VAN DOREN—for his poems from *Collected Poems* by Mark Van Doren (Henry Holt and Co.).

CARL VAN VECHTEN—for poems of Gertrude Stein from *Last Operas and Plays* by Gertrude Stein (Rinehart, 1949).

VIKING PRESS—for poems of Horace Gregory from *Selected Poems of Horace Gregory*, copyright 1951 by Horace Gregory; for "Country Club Sunday" (first published in *The New Yorker*) from *A Short Walk to the Station* by Phyllis McGinley, copyright 1946, 1951 by Phyllis McGinley, and "Portrait of a Girl With a Comic Book" (first published in *The New Yorker*) from *The Love Letters of Phyllis McGinley*, copyright 1952, 1954 by Phyllis McGinley; for poem of Dorothy Parker from *The Portable Dorothy Parker*, copyright 1927, 1944 by Dorothy Parker; for poems of José Garcia Villa from *Have Come, Am Here* by José Garcia Villa, copyright 1941, 1942 by José Garcia Villa.

ROBERT PENN WARREN—for his poems from *Collected Poems 1923-1943* by Robert Penn Warren, copyright 1944 by Robert Penn Warren (Harcourt, Brace).

326

INDEX OF AUTHORS

Adams, Léonie, 203
Agee, James, 256
Aiken, Conrad, 137

Benét, Stephen Vincent, 174
Berryman, John, 279
Bishop, Elizabeth, 266
Bishop, John Peale, 144
Blackmur, Richard, 225
Bogan, Louise, 169
Broughton, James, 302
Bynner, Witter, 78

Coffin, Tristram, 145
Crane, Hart, 184
Crane, Stephen, 33
Cummings, E. E., 154

D., H., 106
Denby, Edwin, 223
Duncan, Robert, 299

Eberhardt, Richard, 230
Engel, Paul, 249

Fitzgerald, Robert, 258
Fletcher, John Gould, 104
Francis, Robert, 211
Frost, Robert, 43

Gibson, Walker, 298
Greenberg, Samuel, 148
Gregory, Horace, 180
Griffin, Howard, 291

Hecht, Anthony, 316
Holmes, John, 227
Horan, Robert, 313
Humphries, Rolfe, 162

Jarrell, Randall, 276
Jeffers, Robinson, 113

Kallman, Chester, 304
Kunitz, Stanley, 238

Lewis, Janet, 208
Lindsay, Vachel, 58
Lowell, Robert, 293

McGinley, Phyllis, 241
MacLeish, Archibald, 146
Marquis, Don, 53
Masters, Edgar Lee, 30
Merton, Thomas, 284
Miles, Josephine, 262
Millay, Edna St. Vincent, 141
Moore, Marianne, 119
Moore, Merrill, 221
Morse, Samuel French, 289

Nash, Ogden, 217

Parker, Dorothy, 150
Patchen, Kenneth, 264
Pound, Ezra, 93

Rainer, Dachine, 311
Ransom, John Crowe, 131
Rexroth, Kenneth, 235

Robinson, Edward Arlington, 23
Roethke, Theodore, 251

Sandburg, Carl, 56
Schwartz, Delmore, 273
Scott, Winfield Townley, 259
Shapiro, Karl, 275
Spencer, Theodore, 213
Stein, Gertrude, 41
Stevens, Wallace, 69
Stickney, Trumble, 36

Tate, Allen, 190

Untermeyer, Louis, 103

Van Doren, Mark, 151
Viereck, Peter, 288
Villa, José Garcia, 247

Warren, Robert Penn, 243
Wheelock, John Hall, 112
Wheelright, John, 171
Wilbur, Richard, 307
Williams, Oscar, 209
Williams, William Carlos, 79
Wilson, Edmund, 166
Winters, Ivor, 205
Wylie, Elinor, 90

Zaturenska, Marya, 219

INDEX OF FIRST LINES

A is to begin with, and A began with Adam, 302
A man adrift on a slim spar, 34
A man said to the universe, 34
A passer-by might just as well be blind, 211
A realm is here of masquing light, 203
A slant-windowed, belt-footed enormously long-boomed, 228
A wet day on the road: the slim blades cutting, 258
Above the fresh ruffles of the surf, 187
After a banquet, 162
After the centres' naked files, the basic line, 276
Ah (you say), this is Holy Wisdom, 108
All our stones like as much sun as possible, 262
Always alone, star told? 149
American muse, whose strong and diverse heart, 174
An agitation of the air, 239
An incident here and there, 106
Another armoured animal—scale, 126
An underground grower, blind and a common brown, 307
And still the picknickers come on, now, 79
And the day arrives at last, my friends, 304
At four o'clock, 267
At midnight, in the garden never planted, 221
At the first stepping-stone, the past of water, 139
At the foot of a great pine, in the wild country, 112
At Rochecourt, 93
Authors and actors and artists and such, 150

Back out of all this now too much for us, 51
Beasts in their major freedom, 308
Beautiful as the flying legend of some leopard, 134
Be beautiful, noble, like the antique ant, 247
Before remembrance we moved here, 204
Bethou me, said sparrow, to the crackled blade, 76
Between God's eyelashes I look at you, 247
Bewildered with the broken tongue, 147
Blue sky, blue noon, and the secret line is flung, 140
boss i just discovered what, 54

Boys in sporadic but tenacious droves, 233
By a peninsula the painter sat and, 148
By dark severance the apparition head, 135

Chameleon, knowing I am near, 249
Complacencies of the peignoir, and late, 70
Cowhorn-crowned, shockheaded, cornshuck-bearded, 277
Created by the poet to sing my song, 299

Darkness has called to darkness, and disgrace, 294
Dead, they'll burn you up with electricity, 236
Death threshholded old man hold, 311
Dürer would have seen a reason for living, 119

England with its baby rivers and little towns, 123
Eternal Spirit, you, 205

Factory windows are always broken, 67
Faintly the ne'er-do-well, 58
Far down the purple wood, 264
Five geese deploy mysteriously, 57
For three years, out of key with his time, 99
From loud sound and still chance, 169

Go and ask Robin to bring the girls over, 131
Go to the western gate, Luke Havergal, 28

had a great ride boss, 55
He knew how Roman legions looked, for he, 145
He runs before the wise men: He, 238
He thought he kept the universe alone, 49
He would declare and could himself believe, 50
Held on the slightest of bamboo poles, 230
Here dock and tare, 142
Here is a face that says half-past seven, 56
How many dawns, chill from his rippling rest, 184
How still, how very still the air is, 180

I feel myself like the flame, 208
I found a dimpled spider, fat and white, 48
I lived a life without love, and saw the being, 209

I met a ragged man, 254
I say no more for Clavering, 26
I wake to sleep, and take my waking slow, 252
I won the prize essay at school, 30
if all the verse what i have wrote, 53
If there were sound, the slapping, 153
In a nation of one hundred fine, mob-hearted, lynching, 59
In the desert, 33
Indulgent giants burned to crisp, 90
Is that dance slowing in the mind of man, 252
It is a beauteous morning, calm and free, 241
It's autumn in the country I remember, 36
It is common knowledge to every schoolboy, 217
It is equal to living in a tragic land, 74
It is so much easier to forget than to have been Mr. Whittier, 259
It might have been in the heart of a deep forest, 219
It should be easy, letting the small feet go, 151
it was a goodly co, 158
It was as if thunder took form upon, 75
It was a miniature country once, 316

Lady of Light, I would admit a dream, 197
Leave him now quiet by the way, 40
Look, sunset's all undone, 314
Love and forgetting might have carried them, 46

Macadam, gun-grey as the tunney's belt, 185
Man looking into the sea, 125
Master of Metaphor, at three, 298
might these be thrushes climbing almost (do they, 157
Mixture of chloroform and oil of cloves, 316
My bands of silk and miniver, 92
My cartridge belt is empty, 172
My dreams wear thinner as the years go by, 112
my father moved through dooms of love, 154
My heart felt need to die, 240
My thanks, friends of the County Scientific Association, 31

Neither war, nor cyclones, nor earthquakes, 237
Nephews and nieces—love your leaden statues, 172

333

Never, never may the fruit be plucked from the bough, 141
Nodding its great head rattling like a gourd, 243
noone' autumnal this great lady's gaze, 160
Now if ever it is time to cleanse Helicon, 96
Now, innocent, within the deep, 170
Now that they've got it settled whose I be, 43

O God, O Venus, O Mercury, patron of thieves, 93
Oak, fern, ivy and pine, 305
Observe how he negotiates his way, 211
Of the beast . . . an angel, 265
Old Eben Flood, climbing alone one night, 23
Once there came a man, 33
One must have a mind of winter, 69
One side of the coin has a vicious monarch's face, 162
Only once more and not again—the larches, 37
Openly, yes, 120

Passionate are palms that clasp in double fists, 226
Pigeons on the grass alas, 41
pity this busy monster, manunkind, 158
plato told, 159

Rain, said the first, as it falls in Venice, 103
Roses have been his bed so long that he, 78

Scott, your last fragments I arrange tonight, 166
Shambles come ready-made these years/are found, 226
She fears him, and will always ask, 25
So he sat down and slowly, slowly, 152
Some lucky day each November great waves awake, 114
Spider, from his flaming sleep, 313
Square sheets—they saw the marble into, 189
Storms once hurled my howls about, 302
Summer, this is our flesh, 190
Suppose in perfect reason, 291

Tawny are the leaves turned but they still hold, 132
'That is important. I do not watch the birds', 221
The Atlantic is a stormy moat, 118

334

The beautiful American word, Sure, 274
The bench, the sewermouth, the hydrant placed, 223
The blue, faded purple, horizon mount, 148
The calloused grass lies hard, 205
The Dai horse neighs against the bleak wind of Etsu, 96
The daughters of the horseleech, crying 'Give! Give!, 238
The end of everything approaches, 90
The furious prisoner of the womb, 284
The heavy bear who goes with me, 273
The houses are haunted, 69
The hunchback on the corner, with gum and shoelaces, 244
The land was overmuch like scenery, 309
The long, long legs, 266
The mind is an enchanting thing, 129
The moon rises. The red cubs rolling, 276
The north-east wind was the wind off the lake, 146
The people along the sand, 48
The people buying and selling, consuming pleasures, 113
The road at the top of the rise, 50
The sky is perfectly clear, 235
The smell of the heat is boxwood, 86
The Sphinx with lion's feet, 213
The stethoscope tells what everyone fears, 251
The sun is blue and scarlet on my page, 295
The whisky on your breath, 251
The windmills, like great sunflowers of steel, 104
Then touch the park: the leaves are stained to lure you, 288
There are too many heart-shaped words for one, 226
There is a rumour hereabout of summer, 228
There is a singer everyone has heard, 43
There was no repose, 300
There was such speed in her little body, 131
Thin air I breathe and birds use for flying, 223
Think of the storm roaming the sky uneasily, 272
Thirteen's no age at all, 241
This age it is the same/with less remembered, 225
This dim and Ptolemaic man, 144
This is the place, as wild as summer snow, 289
Thus systole addressed diastole, 138
Time cannot break the bird's wing from the bird, 143

To be able to see every side of the question, 30
Too honest for a gypsy, too lazy for a farmer, 91
To this man, to his boned shoulders, 262
Turn from that girl, 115
Two statesmen met by moonlight, 59

Under a southern wind, 253
Up the old hill to the house again, 28

Wallowing in this bloody sty, 293
We cannot retrace our steps, 41
We make our meek adjustments, 188
We reason of these things, 76
We said *We understand*, and for a while, 305
What does a man think about, 227
What was that sound we heard, 171
When by me in the dusk my child sits down, 279
Whenever the Presbyterian bell, 32
when life is quite through with, 154
When the sun shouts and people abound, 113
While the blue moon above us arches, 137
White sky, over the hemlocks bowed with snow, 141
Who even dead, yet hath his mind entire!, 99
Whole health resides with peace, 256
Why the unbroken spiral, Virtuoso, 212
With visionary care, 206
Wrong about birds. I cannot call, 275

You have loved forty women, but you have only one thumb, 56

Horizontal Equity, Uncertainty, and Economic Well-Being

Studies in Income and Wealth
Volume 50

National Bureau of Economic Research
Conference on Research in Income and Wealth

Horizontal Equity, Uncertainty, and Economic Well-Being

Edited by Martin David and
Timothy Smeeding

The University of Chicago Press

Chicago and London

Martin David is professor of economics at the University of Wisconsin, Madison. Timothy Smeeding is director of the Division of Social Science Research and professor of economics at the University of Utah, Salt Lake City.

The University of Chicago Press, Chicago 60637
The University of Chicago Press, Ltd., London

Library of Congress Cataloging in Publication Data
Main entry under title:

Horizontal equity, uncertainty, and economic well-being.

(Studies in income and wealth ; v. 50)
Includes bibliographies and indexes.
Papers and discussion presented at the Conference on Horizontal Equity, Uncertainty, and Economic Well-Being held in Baltimore, Md., Dec. 8–9, 1983 and sponsored by the National Bureau of Economic Research.
1. Cost and standard of living—United States—Congresses. 2. Quality of life—United States—Congresses. 3. Income distribution—United States—Congresses. 4. Uncertainty—Congresses.
I. David, Martin Heidenhain. II. Smeeding, Timothy. III. Conference on Horizontal Equity, Uncertainty, and Economic Well-Being (1983 : Baltimore, Md.) IV. National Bureau of Economic Research. V. Series.
HC106.3.C714 vol. 50 330 s [339.4'7'0973] 85–5879
[HD6983]
ISBN 0-226-13726-0

Contents

Prefatory Note   x

Acknowledgments   xi

Introduction   1
Martin David and Timothy Smeeding

1. **Happiness, Affluence, and Altruism in the Postwar Period**   7
Frank Levy
Comment: Lee Rainwater

2. **The Impact of Changes in Income and Family Composition on Subjective Measures of Well-Being**   35
Arie Kapteyn, Sara van de Geer, and Huib van de Stadt
Comment: Harold W. Watts

3. **Estimating Changes in Well-Being across Life: A Realized versus Comprehensive Income Approach**   69
Richard V. Burkhauser, J. S. Butler, and James T. Wilkinson
Comment: Lee A. Lillard

4. **Wealth, Realized Income, and the Measure of Well-Being**   91
Eugene Steuerle
Comment: James D. Smith

5.   Inflation Vulnerability, Income, and Wealth of
      the Elderly, 1969–1979   125
      Michael D. Hurd and John B. Shoven
      Comment: Sheldon Danziger

6.   The Horizontal and Vertical Equity
      Characteristics of the Federal Individual
      Income Tax, 1966–1977   179
      Marcus C. Berliant and Robert P. Strauss
      Comment: T. N. Srinivasan

7.   Measuring the Benefits of Income
      Maintenance Programs   215
      David Betson and Jacques van der Gaag
      Comment: F. Thomas Juster

8.   A Comparison of Measures of Horizontal
      Inequity   239
      Robert Plotnick
      Comment: Edward M. Gramlich

9.   Rewards for Continued Work: The Economic
      Incentives for Postponing Retirement   269
      Olivia S. Mitchell and Gary S. Fields
      Comment: Joseph F. Quinn

10.   Income, Inequality, and Uncertainty:
      Differences between the Disabled and
      Nondisabled   293
      Robert H. Haveman and Barbara L. Wolfe
      Comment: Dan Usher

11.   Household Wealth and Health Insurance as
      Protection against Medical Risks   323
      Pamela J. Farley and Gail R. Wilensky
      Comment: Joseph P. Newhouse

12.   The Valuation of Environmental Risks Using
      Hedonic Wage Models   359
      V. Kerry Smith and Carol C. S. Gilbert
      Comment: T. H. Tietenberg

13.   Interfamily Transfers and Income
      Redistribution   393
      Donald Cox and Fredric Raines
      Comment: Paul L. Menchik

14.   **Economic Consequences of Marital Instability**   427
       Greg J. Duncan and Saul D. Hoffman
       Comment: Isabel V. Sawhill

15.   **Variations in the Economic Well-Being of
       Divorced Women and Their Children: The
       Role of Child Support Income**   471
       Andrea H. Beller and John W. Graham
       Comment: Irwin Garfinkel

       List of Contributors   511

       Author Index   515

       Subject Index   518

Prefatory Note

This volume contains the papers and discussion presented at the Conference on Horizontal Equity, Uncertainty, and Economic Well-Being held in Baltimore, Maryland, on 8 and 9 December 1983. Funds for the Conference on Research in Income and Wealth are provided to the National Bureau of Economic Research by the National Science Foundation; we are indebted for its support. We also thank Martin David and Timothy Smeeding, who served as cochairmen of the conference and editors of this volume, and the other members of the planning committee, John Bishop, Richard Burkhauser, James Morgan, James Smith, and Eugene Smolensky.

Acknowledgments

The editors would like to acknowledge several individuals who were of particular help in conceptualizing and arranging the conference, and in editing the conference volume. First and foremost we would like to thank Eugene Smolensky of the University of Wisconsin whose many conversations and insights on the topic of measuring well-being proved so useful to our conceptualization of the conference. Also the members of the Executive Committee of the Conference on Research in Income and Wealth, particularly Jack Triplett and Tom Juster, who first suggested that we organize our conference and then defended its aims when questioned by "higher authorities." At the National Bureau of Economic Research (NBER), Kathi Smith and Kirsten Foss provided excellent assistance in organizing the conference per se, under the general guidance of David Hartman, NBER's executive director. Mark Fitz-Patrick and Annie Spillane provided excellent and timely editorial assistance for which we are most grateful. Harold Watts of Columbia University and Jean Crockett of the University of Pennsylvania helped turn the conference papers into the more polished volume which you are reading. Lest he go unnoticed, A. Myrick Freeman of Bowdoin College also provided a useful and detailed review of one of our papers. Our most cooperative and time conscious authors and discussants all helped solve the "who will be last" free-rider problem in record time, allowing the authors to collect a small bet from an earlier volume editor who was not so fortunate. Last, but certainly not least, we would like to thank Nancy Faidley Devine and her colleagues at Faidley's Oyster Bar in the Lexington Market for the best hour of seafood congeniality that this, or any, conference will ever experience.

Introduction

Martin David
Timothy Smeeding

The title of this volume emphasizes the elements of this fiftieth Conference on Income and Wealth. The target for discussion is a familiar one: measuring the well-being of individuals and households (in the United States). But within this broad topic area the two major focuses that we seek to emphasize may not be so familiar to those acquainted with previous volumes in this series. The value of our discussion lies in a recognition that measures of well-being serve to guide social and economic policy, and that measures used historically may be deficient in a period of rapid economic and social change such as the present.

Thus the purpose of this conference is to explore the intersection of two relatively new research areas: (1) the implication of new analytic models of consumer choice under uncertainty for data development and model estimation, particularly as they relate to public policy, and (2) the use of new data sets and techniques to examine the horizontal equity implications of expanded measures of economic well-being. Following these themes, the conference demonstrates the use of several new data sets and develops new methodologies to contribute fresh insights into the measurement of well-being, especially in a dynamic and prospective sense.

The four brief comments that follow will help the reader understand the context for the conference and the volume and provide the more general framework within which the contributors have developed their own studies. In the first two sections we recognize that the concept of well-being can be approached from two meaningful perspectives. In the one instance, well-being may be thought of as that perception of the world that motivates economic behavior of the individuals in the society. The chapters dealing with this subjective evaluation of economic status are mentioned in the first section below. In the second instance, well-being may be thought of as a social appraisal of the state of society. Issues treated in this second section include those related to pensions, to the environment, and to the way in which contingent claims affect and are affected by both policy and behavior. The third section completes our summary of chapters by addressing the topic of policy-relevant measurement of well-being, particularly as it deals with the issue of horizontal equity. The fourth and final section explains the more general hidden agenda that underlies our conference and that, we feel, should underly all Conferences on Income and Wealth.

Individual Well-Being

The individual perspective on well-being causes us to search for data that will more clearly link economic models of rational responses to changing prices and incomes to the changing behavior of individuals. It causes us to ask: To what degree is a subjective approach required? If individuals *feel* better off they will behave differently than if they feel worse off, despite identical objective conditions. Thus some understanding of attitudes towards well-being may be an intrinsic part of the measurement of well-being for policy purposes. This theme is explored here in the chapters by Levy and by Kapteyn, van der Geer, and van de Stadt.

Another aspect of the subjectivity of well-being is that well-being will vary as individual expectations vary. The poverty of the student is less oppressive than the poverty of the unemployed illiterate, precisely because income expectations are different. Changes in nominal income presage different real-income situations for individuals, depending on their level of inflation expectations and their ability to adjust to those expectations. Both the Levy and Shoven-Hurd chapters help us to begin to understand this aspect of well-being, the latter chapter dealing with the effect of inflation on the incomes of the elderly during the 1970s.

A third aspect of subjectivity that is clearly of essential importance to how individuals appraise their well-being is their understanding of risks and contingencies that affect the future. Health risks may depress income levels expected in the future; risks of divorce and death may induce more bearish feelings about well-being than are justified by current positions and expected income trajectories. But these risks are clearly of two types—those that are in some sense fungible, and those that are not. The individual recognizes that variation in rate of return affects the yield of investments, but that variation is able to offset gain on some assets against loss with respect to others. However, risks that involve change in marital status involve largely nonfungible human assets. Farley and Wilensky deal with an aspect of risk that is fungible in their exploration of the substitution of wealth for insurance against the risks of medical costs. Duncan and Hoffman study a nonfungible risk—remarriage by divorcees, who can hardly be expected to make adjustments in present life-styles on the basis of potential for improved well-being from a marriage that may or may not come to pass.

Social Appraisal of Well-Being

Historically, measurement of well-being in the United States after World War II has focused largely on objective annual data collected from sources that pertain to individuals—surveys, tax return data, and the census. Earlier volumes of this conference have sought to improve upon those measures by assuring adequate coverage, comprehensive enumeration of items resulting in income flows, and attention to measures of in-kind income. Most of the attention has largely been given to measurement of annual income, rather than measurement of consumption flows, savings, or longer multiperiod incomes. Recent trends in compensation, taxation, and family stability make it less clear that such measures are sufficient, particularly for the evaluation of social programs. This brings us to the second aspect of the conference—societal concerns with well-being.

Pensions

Lack of information about well-being, for instance, in connection with individual knowledge of pension rights, may persist at the individual level because of market failures, inertia, and the cost of acquiring information. At a societal level the situation is different. The society can and does regulate pension-giving organizations in return for the substantial tax subsidies granted them and their clients. Continuation of tax subsidies for pension funds clearly engenders a social interest in measuring well-being that is broader than the individual interest, even in a situation where individuals are fully rational and responsive to the true cost of information.

This social interest in individual behavior and well-being prompted two chapters in this volume. Burkhauser, Butler, and Wilkinson responded most directly to the question: How can society appraise the well-being of the retired as compared to those still in the labor force, but near retirement? The authors show that the difference between comprehensive measures of well-being and actual cash received can be substantial. Because the former is clearly more useful than the latter for policy purposes, their contribution is an important one. Mitchell and Fields focus on a more policy-oriented societal question. They seek to determine how the profile of pension rights varies according to the age of retirement in order to determine whether the rules of private pension programs reflect variation in rights that are socially desirable, or at least not capricious. Without such information it is hard to evaluate the behavioral implications of both private and social pension regulations.

Environment

It is well known that environmental contaminants pose health risks to individuals. The risks pose different degrees of hazard to persons with different (sometimes unknown) characteristics. The risks are likely to be small, stochastic, and unmeasured. Some individuals respond by ignoring the risks; others are unable to acquire relevant information. Collecting information from individuals on the effects on well-being of environmental risks is therefore likely to be difficult. Smith and Gilbert, in their contribution to this volume, attempt to assess the degree to which inferences from other domains—the impact of air pollution on property values—can be transfered into assessment of changes in the well-being of individuals. Again the central interest in the problem arises because society needs measures of the degree to which the distribution of well-being is altered by externalities that may be regulated to some degree or may be compensated by ameliorative or income replacement programs (such as the black-lung diseases program).

Contingent Resources

Most measures have concentrated on income to individuals; they have tended to ignore the resource that is available for subsistence in the stock of wealth owned by the individual. Even more often they ignore the resources that will be forthcoming under some contingencies from kin (or friends), from employers, or from government. Because these contingent claims affect and are affected by policy, it is important to understand the way that measures of well-being can incorporate them as a basis for behavioral analysis.

Some information on both of these problems comes from the chapters by Steuerle and by Cox and Raines. Steuerle is able to directly join the information on estate wealth to the income tax returns of individuals. This combination exposes the degree to which income flows offer adequate information on individual well-being and the degree to which unrealized gains and capital stocks must also be brought into a measure of well-being. Cox and Raines look at another aspect of the picture, the flow of gifts between households and measures of interhousehold support, especially as they affect children receiving aid from parents and inter vivos private transfers of all types.

Another aspect of interhousehold support is the actual payments that flow from divorced parents for the support of their children. Understanding these flows requires an understanding both of the legal settlement (obligations) and the fulfillment of those obligations. Research on both topics is undertaken by Beller and Graham in their contribution.

Finally we must approach the role of governmental disability policy as it affects the income flows to disabled persons. While most would agree that disabled persons (and also the elderly) ought to be assured of a stable income flow, the contribution by Haveman and Wolfe indicates that current public disability programs often do not meet these expectations.

What is clear from all of these chapters is that it may be necessary to address a large data base, including characteristics of individuals and characteristics of their environment, whether it be the work environment, the places where people live, or their kinship groups. Social evaluation of well-being is not possible without integrating information that may be beyond individual reach; also the information that guides behavior is not always known with certainty.

Measures Suitable for Policy Analysis

Even after a measure that encompasses sufficient information has been determined from the facts, important questions arise as to how the distribution of that measure is to be used to generate policy-relevant information. Three chapters attempt to integrate the developments in theory with the practice of policy assessment related to measures of well-being.

Plotnick and Berliant and Strauss concentrate their efforts on distinguishing horizontal and vertical equity in the distribution of measures of well-being. They adopt radically different approaches. Plotnick derives a criterion for horizontal inequity from the reranking of individuals in the distribution of well-being as it is transformed by the operation of government tax and transfer programs. Berliant and Strauss adopt a more intuitive approach in which horizontal inequity is measured by pairwise comparisons of the measures of well-being of individuals within an equivalence class. Both procedures recognize that some normative assumptions are placed on the use of measures of well-being in the process of interpreting the results for the purposes of policy-making.

Betson and van der Gaag adopt a more specialized approach to a more limited but vexing problem: What would individuals be willing to pay for the reduction of uncertainty concerning the lower-bound level of their income? Their work, which extends the theory of option demand in a new and important way, indicates how this concern can be made pertinent for understanding the social demand for income maintenance programs.

The Hidden Agenda of the Conference

Because the measurement of well-being involves a broad range of factual data, because those data are not necessarily accessible to an individual, because well-being also entails a perception of the facts, and because the society will interpret both facts and perceptions in accord with statistics based on normative concepts of equity and inequity, it is clear that the measurement of well-being is complex and extensive. At this conference NBER hoped to bring together a group of scholars who could demonstrate the usefulness of new or continuing data sets and who would also indicate ways in which the future collection of new or different data would encourage a clearer understanding of well-being. Such a demonstration was particularly aimed toward those who design and implement data collection efforts. This direct intersection of data collectors and data users is all too often absent, leading to collection of relatively less useful data and to use of poor proxies for data that, in retrospect, could have been collected. This intersection is the hidden agenda of which we speak.

The studies presented cover a range of complex data sets—the Retirement History Survey of the Social Security Administration, the matched estate–income tax record file of the Internal Revenue Service, the National Medical Care Expenditure Survey, the Panel Survey of Income Dynamics, and the matched child support and income supplements of the 1979 Current Population Survey. In addition to such data on individuals, Smith and Gilbert, and Mitchell and Fields develop bodies of information that embed individual data in environmental or employer variables to which behavioral change is often geared. The need for this latter type of cross-cutting data becomes clear as the analyses in those chapters so aptly demonstrate.

The development of such complex data sets, replication to monitor longitudinal trends and change in the society, and the productive exploitation of such bodies of information using new tools of analysis are all topics that the chapters in this volume indirectly address. It is clear that many of the studies done here will need to be repeated because the stability of findings must be tested and because society continues to change. It is also clear that some of the data (and some of the models) were found wanting, as the reader can see from the discussants' comments.

But this is how progress takes place. As editors of the volume we are proud that our contributors made progress, given the imperfect tools at hand. We believe that major contributions have been made in the conceptualization of uncertainty and its measurement, in the realm of developing measures of horizontal (and vertical) equity, and in the development of new measures of well-being, all of which comprise a substantial advance over previous work. We hope that you concur.

1 Happiness, Affluence, and Altruism in the Postwar Period

Frank Levy

1.1 Happiness, Affluence, and Altruism

If an economist were asked to assess U.S. postwar economic performance, he would probably describe the period in three intervals:

The late 1940s and 1950s were fairly good. Real wages grew very quickly. The period had three recessions but only the last one (1958–60) was severe. Inflation was low except when WW II price controls were lifted and when the Korean War began. When inflation was a problem, a year of recession was sufficient to end it.

The 1960s were better. Real wages did not grow quite as fast in the 1950s but recessions were less of a problem. After 1963, the economy went on a sustained expansion. Unemployment fell more or less continuously until 1970. And inflation did not really emerge until the end of the decade.

The 1970s were awful. The 1960s expansion left an inflationary inertia so that the 1970–71 recession was not enough to bring inflation under control. Then came the 1972–73 food price explosion and the first OPEC price rise. They generated supply-shock inflation that was even more immune to recession. After 1973, productivity stopped growing and real wages stagnated. And then there was another OPEC price rise to finish out the decade. It was terrible.

Frank Levy is professor of public affairs at the University of Maryland.

Support for this study came from the National Committee for Research on the 1980 Census, a Ford Foundation grant to the Urban Institute, and the Computer Science Center and the Division of Behavioral and Social Sciences of the University of Maryland. Particular thanks go to Richard Michel of the Urban Institute and Jack Citrin of the University of California, Berkeley, for discussions on the points in this paper, to Marilyn Potter of the Roper Center for helping to obtain various unpublished poll results, to Lee Rainwater of Harvard University for comments on an earlier version of this paper, to Joung Yong Lee of the University of Maryland for expert research assistance, and to Rosemary Blunck for preparation of the manuscript. Remaining errors are, of course, the author's.

The assessment appears non-controversial, yet it contains a large piece of thin ice. Terms like *pretty good*, *better* and *awful* imply something about not only the economy but about how people reacted to the economy. One could read the assessment as saying that people were happier in the 1960s than in the 1950s and least happy in the 1970s.

The most direct evidence of this proposition does not offer strong support. Periodically, the Gallup poll (officially the American Institute of Public Opinion—hereafter AIPO) asks questions with the following general form (e.g., AIPO 410): In general, how happy would you say that you are—very happy, fairly happy, or not very happy?

Responses to this question are contained in table 1.1. Data for the early postwar years through 1957 show a moderately increasing level of happiness—a possible reflection of rising real incomes. Then a six-year gap occurs during which time the question was not asked. When the data resumes in 1963, a trend is harder to discern. Interpretation is difficult because the precise wording of the question changes in 1963, 1973, and again in 1977. Moreover the 1977 response—the happiest in the series— comes from a poll that focused on religious habits and beliefs; responses for other years come from polls that focused on politics and the economy. When adjustments are made for these problems, the data suggest that the moderately rising level of happiness through the 1950s was followed by a roughly constant level of happiness thereafter.

Table 1.1   **Distribution of Responses to AIPO Question**

	Very Happy	Fairly Happy	Not Very Happy
April 1946	34	50	10
December 1947	42	47	10
August 1948	43	43	11
November 1956	47	41	9
September 1956(1)	53	41	5
September 1956(2)	52	42	5
March 1957	53	43	3
July 1963	47	48	5[a]
October 1966	49	46	4[a]
December 1970	43	48	6[a]
January 1973	52	45	3[b]
Various weeks 1974	57	41	2[b]
November 1977	42	48	10[c]

Source: Various AIPO polls.

Note: The AIPO question reads: "In general, how happy would you say you are—*very* happy, *fairly* happy, or *not very* happy?"

[a]Read "not happy" rather than "not very happy."

[b]Read "not at all happy" rather than "not happy."

[c]Read "not too happy" rather than "not very happy."

Ten years ago, Richard A. Easterlin (1974) wrote an ingenious essay interpreting these poll responses in the context of James Duesenberry's relative income hypothesis (Duesenberry 1952). Easterlin began by noting that *within any poll*, higher-income individuals were more likely than lower-income individuals to report themselves as happy. He contrasted this association with his perception of a weaker association over time when real incomes were rising for everyone. He also examined data from Cantril's cross-national study (Cantril 1965) which showed a similar lack of association between a country's per capita income and the self-reported happiness of its population.

Together these data provided Easterlin with a basis for an application of the relative income hypothesis. In the application, an individual's happiness depends on the relationship between his income and his needs, but his needs are heavily conditioned by what he sees around him. If incomes were to rise uniformly, an individual's relative position (apart from life-cycle considerations) would remain unchanged, and so his individual happiness would not increase.

Easterlin's argument is appealing but it raises two problems. First, it does not explain the rising level of happiness in the early postwar years. Second, it leads to an overemphasis of private, versus public, consumption. As Easterlin writes:

> Finally, with regard to growth economics, there is the view that the most developed economies—notably the United States, have entered an era of satiation. . . . If the view suggested here has merit, economic growth does not raise a society to some ultimate state of plenty. Rather, the growth process itself engenders ever-growing wants that lead it ever onward. (1974, p. 121)

In the Easterlin-Duesenberry argument "ever-growing wants" refers to additional *private* consumption. It is private consumption, after all, that provides one's easiest comparisons with one's neighbors. But the focus on private consumption ignores important history.

The largest omission is the growth of the public sector. In 1947, all government nondefense outlays accounted for 14 percent of GNP. By 1980 these outlays had grown to 28 percent of GNP. In explaining this growth, the mid-1960s emerge as a particularly pivotal period during which the federal government instituted health insurance for the aged, the War on Poverty, aid to elementary and secondary schools (with emphasis on compensatory education) and other areas, which significantly redefined the role of the public sector.

To be sure, these Great Society years were distinguished not so much by growing expenditures as by new initiatives that would obligate future expenditures. Administration officials occasionally acknowledged the problems they were creating for future administrations. But they felt they had a rare opportunity, a narrow window, during which they had to finish what the New Deal had left undone (Moynihan 1967; Sundquist 1968).

Their opportunity came from a particularly sympathetic public. When government officials of the time proposed a new initiative, they emphasized its "public good" aspects: the way in which aiding the poor, the elderly, or the disadvantaged would make the United States a more humane place for everyone. Consider, for example, Lyndon Johnson's eloquent Howard University speech on equality for blacks:

> . . . There is no single easy answer to all of these problems.
>
> Jobs are part of the answer. They bring the income which permits a man to provide for his family.
>
> Decent homes in decent surroundings, and a chance to learn—an equal chance to learn—are part of the answer.
>
> Welfare and social programs better designed to hold families together is part of the answer.
>
> Care of the sick is part of the answer.
>
> An understanding heart by all Americans is also a large part of the answer.
>
> To all these fronts—and a dozen more—I will dedicate the expanding efforts of the Johnson Administration.
>
> . . . This is American justice. We have pursued it faithfully to the edge of our imperfections. And we have failed to find it for the American Negro.
>
> It is the glorious opportunity of this generation to end the one huge wrong of the American Nation and, in so doing, to find America for ourselves, with the same immense thrill of discovery which gripped those who first began to realize that here, at last, was a home for freedom. (Quoted in Rainwater and Yancey 1967, pp. 131–32)

The rarity was not in Johnson's argument,[1] but in the number of people who agreed with it. While the majority of the population did not demand such initiatives, they did form, in V. O. Key's phrase, a "permissive consensus" that allowed the government to implement its liberal agenda (Key 1961, p. 33). This willingness to experiment with public consumption (in hopes of increasing the general welfare) is not contained in Easterlin's reading of Dusenberry's theory. In this paper, we view the origins of the mid-1960s consensus from a somewhat different perspective.

A sensible explanation of the mid-1960s must account for both the origins of public consensus and its subsequent demise. By most estimates, the

1. A more modern example of public good rhetoric occurs in remarks by Walter Mondale while campaigning for the Democratic presidential nomination in New Hampshire: "Most of us in this room are like [my mother and father]. You're not going to get rich, but the chances are you're going to have a wonderful life, and that's where fairness comes in. You can lose your job. You can become ill. Kids can be born deaf and handicapped. We have to care. We believe in self-reliance but we must believe in compassion. We are not a jungle where just the richest and fittest prosper. We are a community, a family, we must care for one another" (quoted in the *New York Times*, 18 Feb. 1984, p. 7).

consensus for new initiatives peaked in 1964–66 and then began to erode. Government, acting in part on inertia, produced occasional new programs through the late 1960s and early 1970s, with the universalization of food stamps (1971) and the federal take-over of aid to the aged, blind, and disabled (1972) marking the end of the period. The remainder of the 1970s was increasingly dominated by antigovernment and antitax sentiment.

History affords few natural experiments; thus it is not surprising that the mid-1960s consensus has attracted a variety of explanations. The origin of consensus has been ascribed to the growth of the civil rights movement, and to the combination of John Kennedy's assassination and Barry Goldwater's candidacy (Sundquist 1968). The end of consensus has been ascribed to the devisiveness of the Vietnam War and to Watergate. But while all of these explanations sound plausible, none by itself is sufficient.

Consider, for example, the combined effects of the Kennedy assassination and the Goldwater candidacy. They were traumatic experiences that led to a Democratic president and Democratic congressional majorities. A rough parallel existed in 1976 when, in the aftermath of Watergate, the country again elected a Democratic president with Democratic congressional majorities. Despite the parallels, Jimmy Carter had only a fraction of the legislative success enjoyed by Lyndon Johnson. Part of Carter's lack of success was due to his political style, but part was due to the temper of the times: If people accepted "public good" arguments in the mid-1960s, they clearly rejected those arguments in the 1970s. They had seen too many government programs in the intervening years to retain their enthusiasm.

This dependence of current attitudes on past experience leads us to look for a more generic explanation of the mid-1960s, an explanation that (like Easterlin's explanation of happiness) does not rest too heavily on particular presidents, wars, or scandals.

One such explanation involves a slight elaboration of a public-private cycle recently advanced by Albert Hirschman. In *Shifting Involvements* (1979), Hirschman argues that industrialized societies move between periods emphasizing private material gain and periods emphasizing public (i.e., collective) action. The cycle's motivation is the disappointment that arises when either kind of "consumption" fails to provide the satisfaction it promised ex ante.

In his writing Hirschman discusses government programs under the heading of private material gain (pp. 39–46). But his examples make clear that he is describing those government programs that are most like private goods—the public education a father and mother "purchase" for their children. Conversely, the redistributive programs of the mid-1960s are best thought of as government extensions of Hirschman's collective action.

With this modification, the Hirschman cycle begins with a period of rising consumption and rising happiness. After a time the attraction of increasing affluence begins to wear thin. This leads to the cycle's second phase in which popular opinion becomes receptive to both public causes and those government programs that advance the "public good." (Again, it is the public or collective nature of such programs that is important. A war against poverty, properly presented, can fit the category. A war against potholes in one's own neighborhood cannot.)

If the government takes up this mandate, the public will find that the country is not improved as easily as they had hoped (or as the government had promised). Their disappointment in public goods—the Hirschman cycle's third phase—leads to a returning emphasis on private affluence.

In this chapter we ask whether a Hirschman cycle lay behind the mid-1960s consensus. Given the limits of public opinion data—gaps in time series, questions with changed wording—the case for the cycle is reasonably strong. The result increases our understanding of the postwar American experience in two ways. Not only does it give us a better explanation of the mid-1960s consensus, but it helps to explain why the federal government could look so good in the mid-1960s and so bad thereafter. And, as a final point, we will find that the Hirschman cycle and the Easterlin-Dusenberry hypothesis are not so different as they first appear.

We will develop the argument in the three sections that follow. In section 1.2 we briefly review the macroeconomic history of the postwar period and public reaction to economic conditions. We conclude that people's economic optimism rose through the 1950s and that by the late 1950s they appear to have put the uncertainty of the Great Depression, World War II, and the Korean War behind them. This trend is consistent with the trend of increasing happiness during the period (table 1.1) and suggests that if a Hirschman cycle existed, support for public goods should have grown at about this time.

The economic data also show that people became uncertain about the economy at the end of the 1960s; the data became particularly gloomy after the food and oil price inflation of 1973–74. If a Hirschman cycle existed, disappointment with public goods could have begun well before this time, but adverse economic conditions would have reinforced the turn back to private consumption.

In section 1.3 we review opinion data for the existence of a Hirschman cycle. In the late 1950s, the most obvious examples of broad public goods were redistributive programs. We find that during this period, sentiment in favor of such programs was high and increasing. Initially this sentiment did not translate into new programs as Presidents Eisenhower and Kennedy were reluctant to propose substantial new spending. Their reluctance, if anything, made people more amenable to Lyndon Johnson's public good arguments because there were few recent examples of public good programs that had failed. It was under Johnson that substantial new initiatives began, and our data show that not long afterwards sentiment in favor of redistributive programs began to dissipate.

In section 1.4 we summarize our findings and apply them to understanding the role of government in the 1960s and 1970s. We conclude by briefly reconciling the Hirschman cycle with the Easterlin-Dusenberry argument.

1.2   The Postwar Economic Landscape

The experience of the Great Depression and rationed wartime consumption dictated that people would enter the postwar period with a hunger for private consumption. The question is, when, if ever, did this hunger abate: Did private consumption grow enough and become sufficiently secure to cause public opinion to shift toward collective welfare as Hirschman's cycle predicts?

We begin to answer this question by briefly reviewing the economics of the postwar period, with particular emphasis on the path of incomes. In the early years of the period, the dominant single factor was rising productivity. Between 1947 and 1959 the growth of output per manhour in private business averaged 3.3 percent per year compared to 2.5 percent per year for both the 1910–29 and 1930–39 periods. The high growth rate was important because it translated into rapidly rising real wages (table 1.2).

Consider a man who, in 1949, was in his late twenties. In that year his income would have been about $11,100 (in 1982 dollars). If he had looked to men in their late thirties to see what his own future might hold, he would have guessed that his income would rise by 13 percent ($12,491/$11,070) over the next ten years. In fact, his income over 1949–59 would increase not by 13 percent but by 64 percent. Taken by itself, this

Table 1.2   **Median Incomes (from All Sources) for Men by Age, 1949–79 (all figures in 1982 dollars based on CPI adjustments)**

Male Age Groups	Median Income			
	1949	1959	1969	1979
20–24	$ 6,998	$ 8,520	$ 9,618	$ 8,415
25–34	11,070	15,972	21,053	19,641
35–44	12,491	18,098	23,865	24,486
45–54	12,062	16,879	23,060	24,167
55–64	10,430	14,505	18,997	19,956
65+	4,652	5,848	7,530	8,545

Note: Median is defined over all men with at least one dollar of income from any source. This group typically represents 99 percent of all men in a single age group.

Sources: Decenial Census 1950, 1960 and various *Current Population Reports*.

performance in excess of expectation should have left him feeling quite good.

But there were other factors. The Korean mobilization, including the imposition of price controls, came only five years after World War II and rekindled fears of wartime austerity. Moreover, the demand side of the economy created a variety of year-to-year fluctuations. There were three bursts of inflation during 1946–48 (11 percent per year), 1951 (8 percent), and 1956–57 (4 percent). Similarly, there were three recessions in 1949 (when unemployment reached 5.9 percent), 1954 (5.5 percent), and 1958–60 (when unemployment averaged 5.9 percent).

The income figures in table 1.2 make clear that despite demand-side fluctuations, everything "came out all right." But this, of course, is an ex post conclusion. Ex ante, people had a variety of worries. For example, throughout World War II, the population was acutely aware of the role of war production in ending the Great Depression. They were unconvinced that another depression could be avoided at the war's end. Consider the following National Opinion Research Center question (NORC #233, Q14) asked in 1945: "For the first year or two after the war, which of these things do you expect: enough jobs for everybody, some unemployment, or a lot of unemployment?" Thirty-eight percent expected enough jobs for everybody, an outlook more optimistic than two years earlier, but 25 percent expected a lot of unemployment.

Similarly, Gallup frequently asks respondents to name the most important problem facing the nation, a question that permits a completely open-ended response. Smith's analysis of these data shows that in much of the postwar period, fears of war and social disorder kept economic concerns from the top of the list. But economic concerns did dominate the list in the immediate postwar period, in response to a feared second depression, as well as the then current inflation and a wave of postwar labor strikes (Smith 1980). Together these data suggest that the economics of the early postwar years were good but anxious.

The economics of the middle years were good and less anxious. Productivity declined slightly but remained high in historical terms, so a man in his late twenties in 1959 would have seen his real income grow by 49 percent over the next ten years (table 1.2). Anxiety was reduced because this income growth was accompanied by stable demand. After 1961, unemployment declined more or less steadily for the rest of the decade, falling from 6.7 percent in 1961 to 3.5 percent in 1969. Moreover, this expansion appeared to be the result of conscious government policy—not simply a lucky roll of the dice. With the wisdom of hindsight, we know the Keynesian triumph of John Kennedy and Lyndon Johnson depended on external and inherited conditions as much as on policy per se (Levy and Michel 1983). But for a brief time it appeared that economic policymakers had discovered how to successfully run the economy, much as an engineer discovered how to place a satellite in orbit.

The first break in economic performance came as inflation reasserted itself, reaching 6.1 percent in 1969. To a large extent the inflation arose from Lyndon Johnson's decision to pay for the Vietnam War buildup through deficit financing. This was clearly bad economic policy, so it was possible to continue believing that good policy would produce economic success.

The faith in good policies' power did not survive many more years. When Richard Nixon took office in 1969, his first priority was to reduce the inflation he had inherited. Earlier postwar episodes suggested a short recession would do the trick. But in practice the 1960s expansion had created a kind of inflationary inertia, so that while the economy entered a recession in early 1970, prices were still rising by 4.7 percent per year in mid-1971. The difficulty of slowing inflation (even in a slack economy) caused Nixon to adopt wage and price controls—policies that were accompanied (and weakened) by an expansion of the money supply that was designed to reduce unemployment in time for the 1972 election (Blinder 1979).

The 1969–71 experience suggested that even the best policy could not reproduce a 1960s expansion automatically. Still worse news came when, in 1973–74, the economy was hit with two supply shocks—one in food and the other in oil—that caused annual inflation to reach 11 percent in 1974. This shortage-driven inflation owed nothing to bad economic policy and no "good" policy could produce a quick cure. Initial attempts to fight the inflation by restrictive policies only reinforced the way in which higher energy prices served as a substantial tax, sending large amounts of purchasing power out of the country. The country reentered recession with unemployment reaching 8.5 percent in 1975, a postwar high. Moreover, the combination of rapidly increasing energy prices and general economic chaos caused productivity to collapse, a condition that would continue through the decade (e.g., Denison 1983).

The combined effects of inflation, unemployment, and the productivity collapse can be seen by repeating our example of the man in his late twenties who, in 1969, might have expected a 13 percent income increase over the next ten years. In reality his income increased by about this amount; but most of the growth took place before 1973, and during the rest of the decade his income remained in a holding pattern (table 1.2).

In summary the late postwar period suffered in three respects: income growth was much lower than in earlier periods, year-to-year fluctuations were very high, and the country had to relinquish the recently acquired impression that someone in Washington was in charge of the economy.

To this point, we have discussed the postwar period in macroeconomic terms. If we are to examine Hirschman's cycle, we must determine how people reacted to these macroeconomic variables. In particular, we need to see whether there was a point at which people began to feel that they were doing well and expected to do still better in the future, i.e., a point at which they began to take income growth for granted. It is at this point that we might expect sentiment to begin to shift toward collective action and public goods.

Data assessing individual financial status are available from the answers to questions on financial changes that are regularly posed by the University of Michigan Survey Research Center (SRC). Typical formulations read:

> *Retrospective Financial Situation.* We are interested in how people are getting along financially these days. Would you say that you (and your family living there) are better off or worse off financially than you were a year ago?
>
> *Prospective Financial Situation.* Now looking ahead—do you think that a year from now, you (and your family living there) will be better off financially, or worse off, or just about the same as now? (Converse et al. 1980, pp. 235 and 248)

Graphed responses to the retrospective question appear in figure 1.1. While responses are obviously influenced by short-term macroeconomic fluctuations, the data—in particular the proportion feeling worse off than a year before—divide into three periods. The first period, 1947–60, shows a general downward trend in the proportion who see themselves as worse off than a year earlier. The proportion reaches a low point (i.e., things are

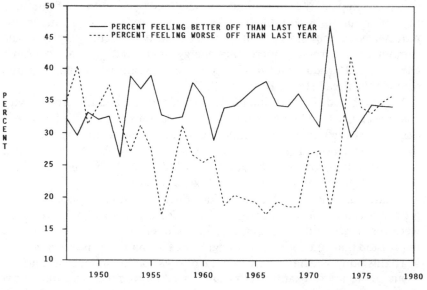

Fig. 1.1.   Perception of recent changes in economic status, 1947–78.

getting better) in the 1956 recovery from recession. In 1957 through 1960 it averages 27 percent, nine points lower than the average of ten years earlier.

In the second period, 1962–69, the proportion seeing themselves as worse off than last year averages 19 percent, a sustained and historic low. This number clearly reflects the 1960 expansion.

The third phase begins in 1970 as the economy entered recession. Here the proportion of people who saw a decline in financial status rose to 27 percent in 1970–71, dipped briefly in the 1972 recovery (which was abetted by President Nixon's wage and price controls), and then exploded to 42 percent with the onset of the food and energy price inflations. It averaged 34 percent for the remainder of the decade.

Expectations about next year's financial status are graphed in figure 1.2. Here the proportion expecting to be financially better off shows the greater variation, and this proportion also divides into three periods. During the late 1940s and early 1950s, the proportion tends to move slightly upward from 30 percent to about 33 percent. It then jumps to 35 percent in 1959 and 40 percent in 1960–61.

The second phase lasts from 1964 to 1969 when the proportion expecting to be better off averages a high 38 percent. The third phase begins in 1970 when optimism starts to falter. After a brief recovery, the proportion expecting to be better off collapses to 24 percent in 1974, a level from which it has not fully recovered.

In casual discussion—e.g., the historical sketch that opened this essay—we divide the postwar period into the decades of the 1950s, the

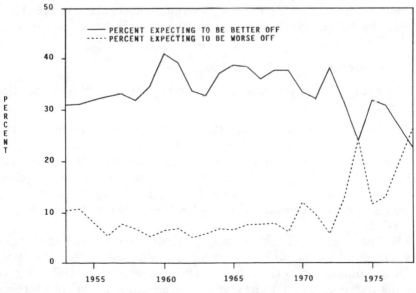

Fig. 1.2.   Expectations about next year's economic status, 1953–78.

1960s, and the 1970s. The data in figures 1.1 and 1.2 suggest one important qualification: the economic optimism associated with the early and mid-1960s actually began in the late 1950s. There was much to be optimistic about. A second Great Depression had not occurred. Inflation had not been a serious problem since the Korean War. The Korean War itself had ended several years earlier, and no new war was on the horizon. And perhaps most important, real incomes were growing. Between 1947 and 1959, median family income had increased by 47 percent. The skies were not cloudless: the 1958–60 recession underlined the continued impact of short-term fluctuations. But even this recession did not seriously dampen future expectations (figure 1.2). And when people compared their situation to that following the end of World War II, they had come a long way.

If Hirschman is correct, it is in the late 1950s that we should expect public opinion to become more favorably inclined toward what we have called public goods. We shall examine this proposition in the next section, but first we note one additional point.

Suppose public sentiment did shift toward public goods and government responded to this shift with new programs. The Hirschman cycle predicts that the public would become disappointed in these new programs, regardless of any external factors. In particular, the public would not require an actual deterioration in their private consumption to become disappointed in public goods. But if a deterioration in private consumption did occur, the disappointment would presumably be amplified.

We have seen in both the economic and opinion data that such a deterioration began slowly in 1970 and accelerated sharply in 1973–74. It follows that any reemphasis of private consumption should have been reinforced by these events. We will return to this point in the next section.

1.3   Public Opinion on Public Goods

America has become bored with the poor, the unemployed, and the insecure.

It is easy to picture the welfare state as having grown steadily since the Great Depression. In fact, the growth was not that steady. The quotation above comes not from a 1980 liberal reformer but from Harry Hopkins (Leuchtenberg 1963, p. 274). Hopkins, writing in 1937, perceived public opinion to be substantially cooler to the New Deal than it had been four years before, and he wondered if New Deal legislation would soon be dismantled.

We know that by the mid-1960s opinion had again shifted, and the public supported legislation that went substantially beyond the New Deal. The question raised by the Hirschman cycle is whether a significant part of this shift occurred in the late 1950s when economic growth had become secure. Within the limits of available data, the answer appears to be yes.

To begin with, public trust in government was high and increasing. This view is summarized in Miller's Trust-in-Government Index (Miller, Miller, and Schneider 1980, p. 268). The index, displayed in figure 1.3, is based on a series of individual questions including:

a. How much of the time do you think you can trust the government in Washington to do what is right—just about always, most of the time, or only some of the time?
b. Do you feel that almost all of the people running the government are smart people who usually know what they are doing, or do you think that quite a few of them don't seem to know what they are doing?
c. Do you think that people in the government waste a lot of money we pay in taxes, waste some of it, or don't waste very much of it? (Miller, Miller, and Schneider 1980, pp. 257–65)

In 1958, the first year in which the index was calculated, 58 percent of the sample fell into the "trusting" category while 11 percent fell into the cynical category. As shown in figure 1.3, the proportion expressing trust increased to 61 percent in 1964 (the next year for which data exists). But after 1966 the proportion would never again exceed 48 percent. Even in 1958 all was not perfect harmony: Responses to (c) above indicated that 43 percent of all respondents felt the government wasted "a lot" of money. But this high proportion would only grow larger as time passed.

The progovernment sentiment in figure 1.3 implies that people regarded the government as competent. It is therefore not surprising that the public supported increases in a variety of broad-based government pro-

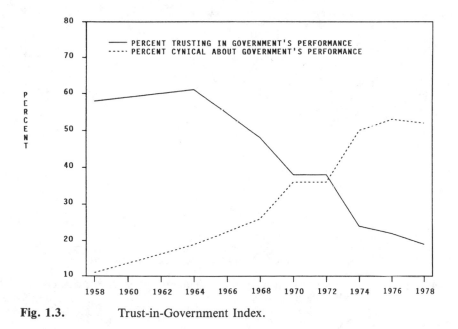

Fig. 1.3.   Trust-in-Government Index.

grams, including public education and housing, programs from which typical poll respondent might immediately benefit (e.g., Converse et al. 1980, p. 382) But if the Hirschman cycle is correct, we should also find high and rising support for programs that benefit most respondents only indirectly—what we have called public goods. In the late 1950s, the most obvious kind of public goods involved programs of aid to the poor, programs that became an important part of Lyndon Johnson's agenda. Existing poll data provide approximate time-series evidence on two such programs—government provision of jobs and welfare assistance.

Support for government provision of jobs is displayed in figure 1.4. In examining the data, it is necessary to examine the precise wording of the question underlying each response. The December 1945 response comes from the question:

> Do you think it should or should not be up to the government to see to it that there are enough jobs in the country for everybody who wants to work? (cited in Schiltz 1970, p. 189)

Sixty-nine percent of all respondents agreed with this statement.
The 1947 question reads:

> If it looked as if we were going into another depression that would bring large-scale unemployment, what do you think the government should do—see to it that people don't go hungry but let business and industry take the lead in solving the problems of unemployment or take full re-

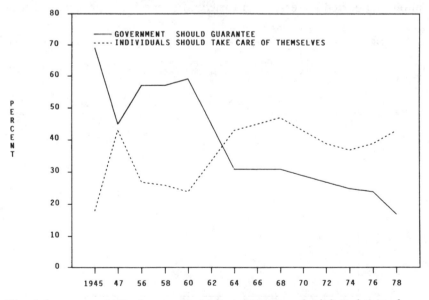

Fig. 1.4.   Attitudes on government guarantee of a job and a good standard of living.

sponsibility for seeing that there are enough jobs to go around and take whatever steps are necessary to accomplish this? (Schiltz 1970, p. 189)

Forty-five percent of all respondents felt the government should take full responsibility, a fourteen-point drop in support in two years. Part of this drop undoubtedly reflected the different nature of the 1947 question. But declining support also reflected changing times. The postwar economy had not immediately returned to depression, and the Truman administration was being pressed to cut back defense spending to permit tax cuts (Stein 1969, chap. 9). The government was not an unambiguous economic ally of the people.

From 1956 (the next time the question was asked) through 1960, the respondent was shown an opinion scale running from *agree strongly* through *disagree strongly* and was asked to assess the following statement:

The government in Washington ought to see to it that everybody who wants to work can find a job. Do you have an opinion on this or not? (Bishop, Oldendick, and Tuchfarber 1978, p. 90)

Fifty-seven percent agreed or agreed strongly with this statement in 1956, a fraction that rose to 59 percent by 1960. This statement is similar to the 1945 question, with an important contextual difference: In 1945 poll respondents were facing a possible second Great Depression after the war and they could imagine having to take government jobs themselves. In 1956, a guaranteed job affected a minority of the population and benefited most poll respondents only as a public good. The high and rising support for government jobs in the late 1950s—i.e., support for public jobs as a public good—is one piece of evidence in favor of a Hirschman cycle.

In 1964, when the question was next asked, the proportion favoring jobs provision was cut in half, falling to 31 percent. We shall see below that a small part of this "disappointment" is explicable even though the Great Society was barely under way. But the more direct cause of the decline was another change in wording. The 1964 question reads:

In general, some people feel that the government in Washington should see to it that every person has a job and a good standard of living. Others think the government should just let each person get ahead on his own. Have you been interested enough in this to favor one side over the other? (Bishop, Oldendick, and Tuchfarber 1978, p. 91)

[If the response is yes, the person is asked to give his opinions: government should do it; it depends; each person should get ahead on his own.]

Because the question poses the specific alternative of getting ahead on one's own, it can be expected to dilute sentiment in favor of government employment even without an actual shift in preference (Bishop, Oldendick, and Tuchfarber 1978). Thus it is not clear how much of the 1960–64

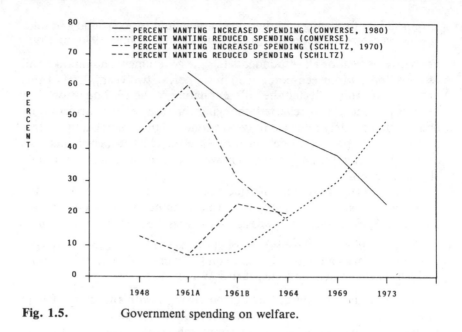

Fig. 1.5.   Government spending on welfare.

decline in support is real. But the same question is used for the remainder of the series, and the eroding support after 1968 (in response to the same question) also is consistent with Hirschman's argument.

Figure 1.5 charts the proportion of the population who say that welfare expenditures should be increased and the proportion who say that welfare expenditures should be decreased. (In all polls, people can respond that expenditures should remain the same.) Two researchers have constructed series on this question (Schiltz 1970, p. 152; Converse et al. 1980, p. 387). Since the two series cover largely different time periods and since they differ (in level but not in trend) where they do overlap, both series are displayed in figure 1.5.[2]

When asking questions on welfare, the element of wording involves a reference to the needy population. Ceteris parabus, "increased welfare expenditures to help the needy" elicits far greater support than "increased welfare expenditures" per se. In the case of the Schiltz series, the 1948 and 1960 questions both contain references to the needy. The rise in support favoring such increases from 45 percent in 1948 to 60 percent in 1960 is not an artifact of wording, and this growing positive attitude toward welfare is consistent with the Hirschman cycle's prediction (figure 1.5).

2. The difference between the series may arise from unreported differences in wording. While Schiltz explicitly gives the wording of the question used in each observation, Converse et al. 1980 uses one representative question per series, and the precise wording of each question cannot be readily ascertained. The impact of such changes in wording is explored in Bishop et al. 1978.

Questions in the Schiltz series drop references to the needy after 1960, undoubtedly accounting for much of the decline in support from 1960 (60 percent favoring increasing spending) to 1961 (35 percent). But the drop between 1961 and the next observation in 1964 is, as we shall see, consistent with Hirschman's conception of disappointment.

The few observations of the Converse series show a similar pattern involving a high level of support for increased welfare spending in 1960–61, a much lower level of support in 1969 (the next time the question was asked), and a still lower support in 1973.

Such data as exists, then, supports the development of a consensus for redistributive programs in the late 1950s and a deterioration of this consensus by the late 1960s. This pattern is consistent with a Hirschman cycle, but several points require further elaboration.

Beginning the development of consensus in the late 1960s did not mean that government initiatives immediately began to grow. Dwight Eisenhower felt strongly that he should hold down federal expenditures (Stein 1969, chaps. 11, 12); later John Kennedy assumed office with much rhetoric but little in the way of specific redistributive proposals. In one sense, the caution of these presidents amplified Hirschman's mechanism. Had Eisenhower or Kennedy tried an ambitious new intervention—say, a war against illiteracy—that failed, people might have become more skeptical about what the federal government could accomplish. But in fact, no such counterexamples were available, leaving the majority of the population amenable to Lyndon Johnson's description of his agenda.

A second amplifying factor was the nature of the 1960s economy. In section 1.2 we saw how the economy expanded continuously after 1961. The expansion created both rising real incomes and rising government revenues. Government programs could be financed with foregone tax cuts rather than new taxes. This meant that Lyndon Johnson's agenda apparently cost little, making it even more attractive.

But as the agenda unfolded, disappointment, in several varieties, ultimately set in. One unexpectedly early source of disappointment was the urban riots. Given the civil rights revolution a significant part of Johnson's agenda (including Head Start, etc.) was seen as a way to aid blacks. The urban riots of 1964 and 1965 were a first sign that any war on poverty would not be as easy or safe as it first appeared (at least to people outside the South). These riots are in part responsible for the rapid declines in support seen in figures 1.4 and 1.5.

A second source of disappointment, directly implied by Hirschman, came from boredom. The media—in particular, television—thrive on tragedy and movingly describe the hungry and the sick. This description is an important factor in the public good benefits that accompany programs of government assistance. But once a program is initiated, assistance becomes less interesting, particularly if it is successful and its recipients are in less dire straits. A hungry child receiving his first free school breakfast is, in television parlance, a "good visual." A well-fed child receiving his fiftieth school breakfast is not. Through this process, even the best redistributive programs lose support over time.

A final source of disappointment was expense. In section 1.1 we noted that Johnson administration officials were aware that their initiatives might become increasingly costly in future years. The reality was worse, in several ways, than they had anticipated. Medicare (for the elderly) and Medicaid (for the poor) together substantially increased medical cost inflation and program expense. In the early 1970s, Congress tied food stamps, Social Security, and other benefits to consumer prices, just before the 1973 food price explosion and the first major oil price increase. While wages failed to keep pace with this inflation, these benefits did (by law). This meant that the program costs became more expensive absolutely and took a greater relative share of output.

These varieties of disappointment had real consequences because while some programs were tied to consumer prices, others including Aid to Families with Dependent Children, required specific legislation for any increases. This legislation was more responsive to public attitudes. Thus Peter Gottschalk has shown that all cash transfers (including Social Security, etc.) generally rose as a percentage of national income during the 1970s. But income-tested cash transfers began the decade at 1.11 percent of national income, peaked at 1.34 percent in 1975, and declined thereafter until they equaled 1.05 percent in 1980 (Gottschalk 1982).

In retrospect, much of the disappointment in public goods appears unavoidable. A public highway continuously provides services to a large constituency. But a redistributive program reaches a broad constituency only as a public good and so, as we have argued, attains its highest support when it is initiated. Put simply, no such program could be as consistently exciting as Lyndon Johnson said it would be.

But although the disappointment was partially unavoidable, it was also due to bad luck. The most obvious element of bad luck was the food and oil price inflation of 1972–74 and the subsequent collapse of productivity. Without these events, real incomes in 1979 would have been 25 to 30 percent higher (about $29,000 rather than $24,000 for the thirty-five- to fifty-four-year-old men in table 1.2). The burden of government expenditures would have been lighter. And perhaps more important, people would have been more secure about their personal economic situation.

At the end of section 1.2 we argued that if during the Hirschman cycle such insecurity arose, it would only reinforce the return to private well-being. We close this section with a piece of evidence on this point drawn from the attitudes of college freshmen. These attitudes have been measured annually since 1966 in polls conducted under the auspices of the American Council on Education (*The American Freshman* 1967). Every poll includes a set of questions about life goals, which the respondent is to

rate on a four-point scale running from "essential" to "not important."
One of these goals is "being very well off financially" and a second is
"helping people in need." Figures 1.6 and 1.7 show the proportion of
male and female students, respectively, who rated each goal "essential" or
"very important" (the second-highest rating).

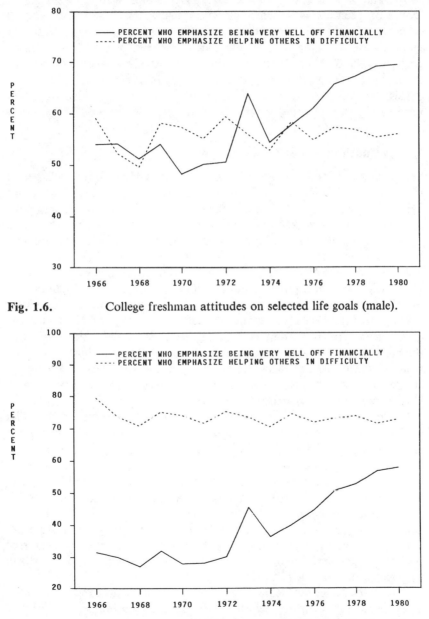

Fig. 1.6.   College freshman attitudes on selected life goals (male).

Fig. 1.7.   College freshman attitudes on selected life goals (female).

Because the polls begin in 1966, we would expect that the sentiment in favor of helping the needy to have already peaked. This is in fact the case—the series for both sexes shows a slight downward trend over the period. Conversely, the emphasis on doing well financially shows a dramatic turn-around in 1973. For men, this proportion had shown a slightly downward trend over the late 1960s and early 1970s; but in 1973 alone it jumped from 51 percent to 64 percent and, with one dip, continued increasing to 69 percent by the end of the decade. The corresponding proportions for women show a similar pattern with a jump from 30 percent in 1972 to 46 percent in 1973. These freshmen did not massively disavow the goal of helping people in need, but the dramatic drop in its relative importance is consistent with the idea that Hirschman's cycle was amplified by a bad economy.

1.4   A Conclusion and Reconciliation

The data reviewed in section 1.3 suggest that a Hirschman cycle began in the late 1950s and extended through the 1970s. The cycle's shift from private material gain to public goods helped motivate the opening in public opinion that was seized upon by Lyndon Johnson. The subsequent disappointment with many of the Great Society programs helps explain why this consensus ended.

Beyond explaining the mid-1960s period the Hirschman cycle also provides insight into how government could look so good in the 1960s and so bad thereafter. Part of the reason, of course, was economic. We have seen that most of the 1960s was spent in a sustained expansion for which the government took more than its share of credit. But equally important was the brief popular romance with public goods. People had high hopes for what government might accomplish, and the government was able to respond with new initiatives. The government, in short, was in a particularly good position to give people what they wanted.

Government's situation in the 1970s was an almost mirror image. The decade was spent in economic stagnation for which government took a disproportionate share of blame. The 1960s enthusiasm over (yet-to-be-initiated) public goods had been replaced with disappointment. But in response to this disappointment, there was little government could do. Government, of course, has a harder time reducing programs than letting them grow. And in the case of the United States in the 1970s, the indexation of many program benefits made reductions nearly impossible because they would require reneging on highly visible promises to keep real benefits intact. Here, then, government was in a particularly bad position to give people what they wanted.

Thus Hirschman's cycle helps us to understand the preconditions of the Great Society and, more generally, the shifting sentiments toward and away from government over the postwar period. But if Hirschman's analysis is useful, there remains the question of whether Easterlin's description of the postwar period is wrong.

The answer, it appears, is not that Easterlin's theory is wrong but that it is too cryptic, a comparative static argument that ignores the movement from one equilibrium to another. Consider again Easterlin's argument. Happiness depends upon one's relative income. If incomes rise throughout society, average happiness should remain unchanged.

The argument may hold for (static or dynamic) equilibrium but when incomes are changing in unexpected ways other standards may come into play. For example, one may judge one's current income by one's past income or by what one expected to be making in the current period. We have argued that the growth of real income over the 1950s was much better than what people expected at the end of World War II. This performance in excess of expectations can explain the rising trend of happiness during the period (which a pure relative income interpretation cannot). In this interpretation, only after economic growth was taken for granted did the growth of happiness slow.

When viewed in this light, the Easterlin argument and our interpretation of the Hirschman cycle are quite similar. It is well known that within any sample, richer individuals are more "public regarding" and have a greater taste for public goods as we have defined the term (e.g., Schiltz 1970, chap. 6).

In Hirschman's argument, as the population grows richer, it becomes, on average, more public regarding. But this attitude lasts only for a certain period of time, after which the population returns to its prior emphasis on private consumption. Here, too, one can argue that people temporarily confuse a rise in absolute income with a rise in relative status and modify their behavior as long as the confusion persists.

This consideration of dynamics does not completely reconcile the two theories, but it moves them toward a common message: Economic growth may not induce permanent changes in either the average level of society's happiness or society's attitudes toward public goods. But permanent changes are not the only test of importance: If economic growth can induce temporary changes in these attitudes, the consequences for society can still be profound.

References

The American freshman: National norms. 1967 and subsequent editions. Cooperative Institutional Research Program. American Council on Education: Washington, D.C.

Bishop, George F., Robert W. Oldendick and Alfred J. Tuchfarber. 1978. Effects of wording and format on political attitude consistency. *Public Opinion Quarterly* 42, no. 1: 81–92.

Blinder, Alan S. 1979. *Economic policy and the great stagflation*. New York: Academic Press.

Cantril, Harley. 1965. *The pattern of human concerns*. New Brunswick, N.J.: Rutgers University Press.

Converse, Phillip E., Jean D. Datsun, Wendy J. Haas and William H. McGee III. 1980. *American social attitudes data sourcebook, 1947–1978*. Cambridge: Harvard University Press.

Denison, Edward D. 1983. The interruption of productivity growth in the United States. *Economic Journal* 93, no. 369: 56–57.

Duesenberry, James S. 1952. *Income saving and the theory of consumer behavior*. Cambridge: Harvard University Press.

Easterlin, Richard A. 1974. Does economic growth impugn the human lot? In *Nations and households in economic growth*, ed. Paul A. David and Melvin W. Reder, 89–125. New York: Academic Press.

Gottschalk, Peter. 1982. Have we lost the war on poverty? *Challenge* 25, no. 2: 57–58.

Hirschman, Albert O. 1979. *Shifting involvements*. Princeton: Princeton University Press.

Key, V. O., Jr. 1961. *Public opinion and American democracy*. New York: Alfred A. Knopf.

Leuchtenberg, William E. 1963. *Franklin Roosevelt and the New Deal*. New York: Harper and Row.

Levy, Frank, and Richard Michel. 1983. The way we'll be in 1984: Recent changes in the distribution of disposible income. Urban Institute. Mimeo.

Miller, Warren E., Arthur H. Miller, and Edward J. Schneider. 1980. *American national election studies data sourcebook*. Cambridge: Harvard University Press.

Moynihan, Daniel P. 1967. The president and the Negro: The moment lost. *Commentary Magazine*, Feb., 31–45.

Rainwater, Lee, and William L. Yancey. 1967. *The Moynihan Report and the politics of controversy*. Cambridge: MIT Press.

Schiltz, Michael. 1970. *Public attitudes toward Social Security, 1935–1965*. Office of Research, Social Security Administration, Research Report #33. Washington, D.C.: GPO.

Smith, Tom W. 1980. America's most important problem: A trend analysis, 1946–1976. *Public Opinion Quarterly* 44, no. 2: 164–80.

Stein, Herbert. 1969. *The fiscal revolution in America*. Chicago: University of Chicago Press.

Sundquist, James L. 1968. *Politics and policy: The Eisenhower, Kennedy, and Johnson years*. Washington, D.C.: Brookings Institution.

U.S. Department of Commerce. Bureau of the Census. *Census of Population*. Various editions.
_____. *Current Population Reports*. Various editions.

Comment   Lee Rainwater

Frank Levy's chapter opens for exploration an important area at the borderline between the social psychology of well-being and the macroeconomics of growth. He explores the trade-off between public and private goods, between politics and markets, in the determination and the distribution of resources for well-being.

This is relatively uncharted territory. As one explores the empirical basis for assessing relative levels of subjective well-being it becomes apparent how extremely mushy these variables are and how ambiguous must be any effort to test a model such as the one Levy develops. Indeed a model of the abstractness of the Hirschman (HM) cycle is perhaps impossible to test empirically given the validity and the reliability of the data-gathering techniques available to us. But nevertheless an effort to array systematically the evidence, such as it is, can open the way hopefully to more successful efforts in the future.

In this discussion I would like to deal with only three of the many interesting issues raised by the chapter. First, the question of happiness measures and Easterlin's law. Next, I will raise some alternative possibilities for explaining the decline in support for government initiatives which the paper charts. And finally, I will raise some questions about the utility of the Hirschman cycle for helping us understand the pattern of government expenditures over the past two decades.

So far, systematic analyses of responses to happiness questions confirm Easterlin's assertions that economic growth does not seem to increase the expressed happiness of the general public. In the most intensive examination of this issue by James Davis, the author summarizes his findings as follows:

Data from 17 U.S. national surveys (1948–1975) are analyzed to resolve Easterlin's paradox—reported happiness is correlated with socio-economic status, but there seems to be no secular increase in happiness despite great socio-economic progress since World War II. A four variable (race, education, marital status, and happiness) categorical flow graph model is estimated for the period 1952–1975 with these conclusions: blacks and the non-married are distinctly less happy, the better-educated are slightly more happy. The increase in levels of education is

Lee Rainwater is professor of sociology at Harvard University.

shown to produce a statistically significant increase in happiness but the increase is (1) offset by negative trends from greater proportions of ex-married and blacks, (2) is diluted by erratic residual fluctuation and (3) is very small, something like 0.0005 per year. (Davis 1975)

Davis comments that one might say that in the entire post–World War II period a little over two million more Americans have been made happy.

Davis was not able to use income as a variable because of problems of missing data and different categorizations of the variable so he uses education as a proxy. The results, however, suggest that the sameness we see can be a result of compensating changes in the population. We know that something like that has happened with respect to income distribution with changes in family arrangements, pushing the distribution in a more unequal direction while other forces have created greater equality within the dominant family type of married couples.

Thus it may not really make too much sense to use a happiness measure for the total population as an aggregate measure for any kind of refined analysis. The stability of the proportion of the population that is happy over a long period of time and across countries is a striking finding; Easterlin was right to call our attention to how it challenges a lot of assumptions about relationships of affluence and happiness. I think that to go further than that one will have to mess around with the details of exactly who is happy, and changing patterns over time in who is happy. This is particularly the case in connection with the ideas behind the HM cycle because the reality of the welfare state is not one in which the same individuals trade off between public and private goods but rather one in which some individuals give up private goods in order that others may have public transfer income. Thus, it would be very interesting to look at changes over time in happiness measures for wage receivers versus transfer receivers, as this interacts with age.

A great deal of the work on satisfaction with life seems to suggest that individuals evaluate their life situations primarily in terms of the social situation close at hand. Thus satisfaction with family, with neighborhood, with social contacts are crucial in determining overall life satisfaction, as is satisfaction with job. Satisfaction with more distant aspects of life, like local and national politics, takes very much a back seat (see Andrews and Withy 1976; Campbell, Converse, and Rogers 1976). Thus any theory will be incomplete if it cannot specify the connections between macroevents and people's experiences in their daily lives with family, friends, neighborhood, and jobs.

There is the further worrying fact that no objective characteristics seem to have a strong causal relationship with happiness and satisfaction measures. The best predictors of overall satisfaction are other attitudinal factors about specific aspects of one's life situation. Easterlin's theory does not run into problems with this complexity because it simply asserts that people evaluate their situations comparatively with reference to the world they know, and that so long as one's relative standing in society does not change, one's reasons for being satisfied or unsatisfied are not likely to change.

The second set of concerns I would raise about the HM cycle theory as a historical explanation of public attitudes toward government during this period has to do with the possible powerful effect of noneconomic factors on public perceptions and the role of government. The HM cycle theory predicts support for public spending through the 1960s and then a decline in support in the 1970s due to both satiation and the end of the Golden Age. However, public attitudes toward government initiatives in the 1960s were extremely mixed. While there was strong support for expansion of some kinds of programs like Social Security from a fairly early time after their initiation there was strong opposition to other kinds of spending. The War on Poverty had a very mixed reception from its very beginning.

It seems to me that disenchantment with the Great Society can be better understood as a reaction to the massive social changes instituted during the 1960s by a variety of forces, than as a redressing of the balance in the trade-off between public and private goods. The centuries-old system of race relations was shattered by the civil rights revolution of the early 1960s. That left a lot of white people very unhappy, as anyone who remembers the broad support for George Wallace knows. The life-style revolution that followed rapidly on the civil rights revolution and was symbolized in different ways by the flower children and the new kinds of political activism similarly challenged traditional views concerning what was right and proper in society. Since all of these changes were reinterpreted as in some sense a product of government activity, or at least as encouraged by liberal government, it is not surprising that already by the mid-1960s one found resistance building to government-engineered social change. We know that there was an extremely rapid change in the perception of what government was doing for blacks during the mid-1960s.

I think this rapid buildup of negative views during the 1960s is difficult to rationalize in terms of the HM cycle because it comes much too early for satiation to have set in.

The Hirschman cycle is presented as a theory of welfare backlash. But Hirschman himself doesn't seem to have thought of his model of shifting involvement that way. He discusses government services in his section on consumer disappointment, relates backlash to frustration with services generally, and seems to reserve the idea of the public for "public life" rather than public consumption (Hirschman 1982, pp. 34–45).

There has of course been a great deal of comparative research in this area in the past decade by people like Harold Wilensky, Peter Flora, and Walter Korpi, and Gosta Esping-Andersen. Thus Hirschman's cyclic theory, as stated, applies to all of the advanced industrial democracies. In evaluating the theory, one needs to look at the phenomenon of public goods satiation comparatively.

I must say I do not find the theory particularly attractive. It is extremely abstract. I do not believe that political actors react to the abstract categories of public versus private goods except in a rhetorical or ideological sense and that is not at all what the HM cycle model is talking about. It deals with behavioral responses to the experience of a greater or lesser rate of growth in public expenditures. Most of the work on the growth of the welfare state (which is the principal element in the growth of government expenditure in all of the advanced industrial democracies) suggests that political actors think in terms of particular programs and make decisions to expand or contract particular kinds of programs. After all, the major components of growth in the post–World War II period are pensions, health care, and education. To support a theory like the HM cycle one would have to demonstrate its operation concretely with respect to these kinds of programs. In other words, to talk of trade-off between public and private consumption expenditure pushes one toward treating these two as relatively homogeneous categories, while the nitty-gritty of the political-economic development of programs suggests that that is not the case.

To the extent that the Hirschman cycle responds to patterns of economic growth then one would expect a great deal of similarity in patterns of welfare state growth in these countries. What we find however is a great deal of diversity. There is no strong correlation between the endpoint and the starting point. The welfare state leaders of 1950 or 1960 are not necessarily the same as those of 1970 or 1980. Countries have experienced government expenditure growth at vastly different rates, and the timing of the periods of greater or lesser growth have been different in different countries.

As soon as one focuses on a number of countries rather than just on the United States, numerous contradictions to the theory appear. For example, if satiation with public consumption is produced by higher spending levels, how can it be that opposition to spending seems strongest in the United States, with the lowest level of social program coverage and spending, and less strong in Germany and France with very high levels of spending and program coverage (Coughlin 1982, p. 152; Wilensky 1976)?

If there is an HM cycle, it has a very different history in each of the advanced industrial nations despite the fact that their economic histories up until the mid-1970s have shown remarkable similarities. We do know that within the range of some eighteen advanced industrial democracies no strong relationship exists between the rate of economic growth and the growth of government expenditures.

The slowing down of the rate of growth, which has affected almost all countries, began in roughly 1975, but I think this is much more easily explained by the economic crisis than by a more complicated theory of satiation. It should be noted also that if one takes the end of the Golden Age as 1973, over some fifteen nations for which there is complete data on average government expenditures grew twice as fast as a proportion of GNP in the period 1974–80 as in the period 1960–73. On average, over half the growth of government expenditures as a proportion of GNP between 1960 and 1980 took place after 1973. And this was true of such diverse countries as Great Britain, Sweden, France, Australia, and Japan. By 1980 only two countries, the United States and Germany, had actually reduced government expenditures as a proportion of GNP from the 1975 level.

For these various reasons therefore, I think the HM cycle theory will not survive as an explanation for changes in public support for public goods, or as a hidden factor sustaining happiness at its constant level.

On the other hand, the kinds of explorations that the chapter makes in the murky borderland between economics and social psychology are important because only if efforts are made to move beyond theory to empirical testing can we hope to improve our understanding of how social and economic forces form preferences, and how those preferences in turn play back into the political economy.

References

Andrews, Frank M., and Steven B. Withy. 1976. *Social indicators of well-being: Americans' perceptions of life quality*. New York: Plenum Press.

Campbell, Angus, Philip E. Converse, and Willard L. Rogers. 1976. *The quality of American life: Perceptions, evaluation, and satisfaction*. New York: Russell Sage Foundation.

Coughlin, Richard M. 1980. *Ideology, public opinion, and welfare policy*. Institute of International Studies. Berkeley: University of California Press.

Davis, James A. 1975. Does economic growth improve the human lot? Paper presented Sept. 8 at the International Conference on Subjective Indicators of the Quality of Life, Fitzwilliam College, Cambridge, England.

Hirschman, Albert O. 1982. *Shifting involvements: Private interest and public action*. Princeton: Princeton University Press.

Wilensky, Harold L. 1976. *The "new corporatism," centralization, and the welfare state*. London and Beverly Hills: Russell Sage Foundation.

2 The Impact of Changes in Income and Family Composition on Subjective Measures of Well-Being

Arie Kapteyn
Sara van de Geer
Huib van de Stadt

2.1 Introduction

Consider two families with different reference groups—a rich one and a poor one, let us say. Most likely the family with the rich reference group will feel that it needs more income to make ends meet than the family with the poor reference group. Suppose the income earners in both families lose their jobs and consequently apply for welfare benefits. Should the welfare benefits for the two families differ because they have different needs?

Probably many people will answer no to this question, but in a slightly different context they might answer yes. In the European Community, people from different countries require different incomes (in real terms) to make ends meet. Part of these differences are due to the different standards of living in the various countries. In other words, people from different countries have different reference groups. If we would choose to ignore these variations in need and set one poverty line for the entire European Community, an income maintenance policy based on it would probably turn the welfare recipients in the poor member countries into sudden "nouveau riche."

Next consider two families with different income histories, who both apply for welfare benefits. Is the family that used to be rich, and therefore

Arie Kapteyn is professor of econometrics at Tilburg University; Sara van de Geer is research associate at the Center for Mathematics and Computer Science (CWI), Amsterdam. Huib van de Stadt is research associate at the Netherlands Central Bureau of Statistics.

The authors gratefully acknowledge financial support from the Netherlands Organization for the Advancement of Pure Research. The views expressed in this paper are those of the authors and do not necessarily reflect those of the Netherlands Central Bureau of Statistics. Thanks go to Harold Watts and the editors of this volume for their comments and to Rob Alessie and Cees-Jan de Wolf for their capable research assistance.

needs more money to make ends meet, entitled to a higher level of benefits than the family that has always been poor?

Again, many people may initially answer no to this question. But unemployment benefits in a number of Western countries are related to previous earnings and decrease over time. At least one explanation for such a setup (apart from the insurance component in unemployment compensation) is that it gives people time to adjust their needs.

These two examples suggest that sometimes policymakers acknowledge that poverty is a relative concept, in that it is related to the standard of living of one's society and to one's previous income. If one takes for granted that poverty is at least partly relative, the question naturally arises *how* a poverty line (or an income maintenance policy built on it) should be related to the standard of living in society and *how* account should be taken of previous income.

In this chapter we employ a model that assumes poverty to be entirely relative. We present evidence on the empirical validity of the model, which explains variations across families and over time of two subjective measures of well-being. One measure is the individual welfare function of income developed by van Praag (1968, 1971). The second is a measure of how much an individual believes he (or she) needs to make ends meet, introduced by Goedhart et al. (1977). Based on both subjective measures is a definition of a poverty line. Using the model for the explanation of the subjective measures, one can trace out the effects of various forms of income maintenance policy on individual well-being. Conversely, using the model and the corresponding poverty line definitions, one can devise income maintenance policies that are in some sense optimal. Both avenues are pursued in this chapter.

In section 2.2 we present the subjective measures and the poverty line definitions based on them. In section 2.3 we present the model that explains the variations of these measures over time as a consequence of variations in family size, own-household income, and incomes in one's reference group. The model is estimated on the basis of a longitudinal household survey in the Netherlands. The estimation results are presented in section 2.4. Taking the model for granted, we explore in section 2.5 the optimality and consequences of different forms of income maintenance policies. Section 2.6 contains some concluding remarks.

As always, the analysis in the chapter is subject to various qualifications and limitations. Two of them are worth mentioning at the start. First, although we use words like *utility, well-being, welfare,* and *satisfaction* freely and interchangeably, these words have the very restrictive meanings implied by the two subjective measures used. Second, the only source of well-being considered is cash-after-tax family income. The limitations of such a narrow concept of economic resources are well-enough known (cf., e.g., Moon and Smolensky 1978) and future work should use more elaborate concepts.

2.2 Two Poverty Line Definitions

2.2.1 The Subjective Poverty Line

The respondents to the survey used in this paper were asked the following question (in Dutch; *Dfl.* stands for Dutch florin):

> Which after-tax family income would you, in your circumstances, consider to be absolutely minimal? That is to say that you would not be able to make ends meet with less.
> Absolutely minimal: Dfl. _____ per _____.

We shall refer to this question as the *minimum income question* (MIQ). A respondent's answer to the MIQ is referred to as his (or her) *minimum income, y_{min}*. This minimum income is a subjective quantity that will probably depend on the respondent's characteristics, like his income, family composition,[1] income in the reference group,[2] etc. We write

$$(1) \qquad y_{min} = y_{min}(y, x),$$

where y is the respondent's income and x is a vector of other characteristics influencing y_{min}. Relation (1) is illustrated in figure 2.1.

The lines labeled I, II, and III represent three versions of equation (1), corresponding to three different x vectors. Generally, if x changes, the relation between y_{min} and y will change, as illustrated. Let us concentrate on one particular value of x, say the value of x that leads to the solid line I. Note the special role played by the intersection point, A, of line I and the 45° line. At point A, $y_{min} = y$. Let us call that income y_{min}^*, so that y_{min}^* satisfies

$$(2) \qquad y_{min}^* = y_{min}(y_{min}^*, x).$$

Any individual with characteristics vector x whose income y is below y_{min}^* is not able to make ends meet; any individual with the same vector of characteristics and an income in excess of y_{min}^* is. If $y = y_{min}^*$, income is just enough to make ends meet. All this makes y_{min}^* a natural candidate for a definition of a poverty line for any individual with characteristics vector x (cf. van Praag, Goedhart, and Kapteyn 1980).

---

1. *Income* is defined in this paper as after-tax family income. *Family* and *household* are used as synonyms. When we talk about *individuals* or *respondents* these are usually family heads. The words *he* and *she* are used indiscriminately.
2. This dependence follows immediately if we view y_{min} as an indicator of a respondent's aspiration level. See, e.g., Katona 1960, chap. 3.

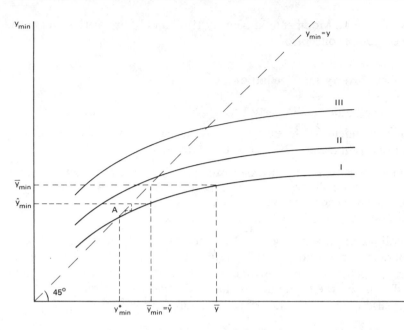

Fig. 2.1.   The relation between minimum income and actual income for different values of x.

There is an alternative motivation to take y_{min}^* as a definition of a poverty line. Consider an individual with income $\bar{y}$. His reponse to the MIQ is $\bar{y}_{min}$, representing what he feels to be the minimum amount that will allow him to just make ends meet. Now imagine that we take $\bar{y} - \bar{y}_{min}$ away from him. At first he will consider $\bar{y}_{min} = \hat{y}$ as minimal, but after a while he will become used to the income level $\hat{y}$ and, according to equation (1), he will now consider $\hat{y}_{min}$ as minimal. If we next take $\hat{y} - \hat{y}_{min}$ away from him, he will first consider his new income to be minimal, but after a while his minimum income will be below his actual income. We can continue to take away income from this individual, and his y_{min} will keep adjusting until we have reached y_{min}^*. (Later on we will have more to say about the dynamics of the adjustment of y_{min}). We may describe this adaptation process by saying that the individual makes mistakes about his minimum income because his actual income differs from his minimum. Only at y_{min}^* are no errors made because the respondent's actual income is equal to his minimum income. It is this interpretation that originally led Goedhart ct al. (1977) to adopt y_{min}^* as their definition of a poverty line.

Because y_{min}^* depends on x, we can have as many different poverty lines as there are different values of x. Thus we have implicitly defined poverty equivalence scales for different values of x. Both Danziger et al. (1984) and Colasanto, Kapteyn, and van der Gaag (1984) have used this approach to derive poverty lines with equivalence scales accounting for differences in family size, sex of the family head, age of the family head (under or over sixty-five), and whether or not a household lives on a farm. Below, x will be specified to include past income, reference group income, and family size.

It is worth noting that y^*_{min} depends only on what people *themselves* consider to be minimal. No interpersonal utility comparisons are involved. The approach is subjective in the sense that a poverty line is not defined in terms of some prespecified commodity bundle that a household should be able to afford. It is only the respondent's own opinion of what is minimally needed that is the basis for this definition. This puts a heavy burden on the wording of the question and involves the assumption that somehow *make ends meet* has the same meaning to everyone, at least approximately. Although this is an important issue that merits more research, it will not be pursued in this paper.

2.2.2 The Leyden Poverty Line

In the panel survey used in this paper, respondents have been asked the following so-called *income evaluation question* (IEQ):

What after-tax family income would	very bad	Dfl. _____
you consider, in your circumstances,	bad	Dfl. _____
to be very bad? And bad, insufficient,	insufficient	Dfl. _____
sufficient, good, and very good?	sufficient	Dfl. _____
	good	Dfl. _____
Please enter an amount on each line.	very good	Dfl. _____

Care has been taken that before answering the MIQ and the IEQ, the respondent has gained a good understanding of the notion of after-tax family income. Actually the respondent has been asked to compute his own after-tax family income.

A hypothetical response has been plotted in figure 2.2. The verbal labels "very good," "good," etc. have been associated with the midpoints of six equal intervals that partition the $[0,1]$ interval. Thus the verbal scale "very bad, bad, . . . very good" is transformed into a numerical scale $1/12$, $3/12, . . . , 11/12$. Given this procedure, one can fit a smooth function through the six points. According to a theory advanced by van Praag (1968), the points should lie approximately on a lognormal distribution function $\Lambda(.;\mu,\sigma)$. Tests by van Herwaarden and Kapteyn (1981) indicate a good fit for the lognormal function.

The lognormal function, dubbed the individual *welfare function of income* (WFI) (van Praag 1971), describes a relation between income levels (on the horizontal axis) and welfare levels (on the vertical axis). Our use of the term *welfare levels* means no more and no less than the numbers between zero and one that have been associated with the verbal labels in the IEQ. Whether respondents themselves associate the verbal labels with equal intervals on a numerical scale has been investigated by Buyze (1982)

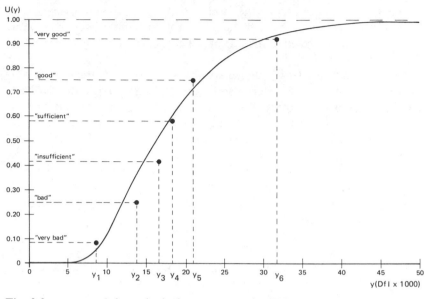

Fig. 2.2.   A hypothetical response to the IEQ.

and Antonides, Kapteyn, and Wansbeek (1980). Their conclusion is that the intervals are not exactly equal, but that they are not dramatically different. For the present paper, both lognormality and the equal interval assumption are maintained hypotheses.

The lognormal function is completely determined by its parameters μ and σ. The parameter μ is a location parameter; $\exp(\mu)$ is the income level evaluated by 0.5. Thus, the larger μ (or $\exp(\mu)$, for that matter) is, the more income one needs to attain a certain welfare level. The parameter σ determines the slope of someone's WFI. The larger σ is, the flatter a WFI will be. The parameters μ and σ are easily estimated per respondent by fitting a lognormal function through the scatter of points in figure 2.2 (see, e.g., van Herwaarden and Kapteyn 1981, for details).

Once WFIs are measured per respondent, poverty lines can be derived from them on the basis of the following argument: poverty is a situation with a low level of welfare. Setting a poverty line amounts to a choice of a point on a welfare scale such that everyone with a welfare level below that point is called poor and everyone with a higher welfare level is called nonpoor. Which welfare level should be the dividing line between a state of poverty and nonpoverty is a political decision. Suppose that politicians decide that α is the welfare level (measured on a [0,1] scale) defining the poverty line (e.g., $\alpha = 0.45$) and let $U(y)$ be the WFI of a particular individual, whose WFI parameters are μ and σ. Then this individual is poor or nonpoor depending on whether or not

(3) $$U(y) < \alpha .$$

Given the lognormal specification of $U(y)$, equation (3) is equivalent with

(4) $$\Lambda(y\,;\mu,\sigma) < \alpha\,,$$

where $\Lambda(.;\mu,\sigma)$ is the lognormal distribution function with parameters μ and σ. Equation (4) is in turn equivalent with

(5) $$N([\ln y - \mu]/\sigma\,;0,1) < \alpha\,,$$

where $N(.;0,1)$ is the standard normal distribution function.

Define u_α by

(6) $$\alpha = N(u_\alpha\,;0,1)\,,$$

i.e., u_α is the α quantile of the normal distribution. Then equation (5) is equivalent with

(7) $$[\ln y - \mu]/\sigma < u_\alpha\,.$$

Given μ and σ, it is easy to determine which income is required to make an individual nonpoor. The poverty line is simply

(8) $$\hat{y} \equiv \exp[\mu + \sigma \cdot u_\alpha]\,.$$

It turns out, however, that both μ and σ depend on income y and on other characteristics x, in a way to be specified in the next section. So this poverty line becomes dependent on x, just like the subjective poverty line.

A concluding word on terminology is in order here. In Goedhart et al. (1977) where the subjective poverty line was introduced, the definition above was only mentioned in passing as "an alternative method." Since the choice of α has to be a political one, van Praag, Goedhart, and Kapteyn (1980) dubbed this poverty line a "politically determined poverty line," which terminology was also adopted by Colasanto, Kapteyn, and van der Gaag (1984). Since, in the end, the adoption of any poverty line involves political decisions, the term *politically determined* is unfortunate. Van Praag, Spit and Van de Stadt (1982) call this the Leyden poverty line, referring to the fact that at the time of writing all four authors of Goedhart et al. (1977) were working in Leyden. Of course, this term does not distinguish it from the subjective poverty line, but at least the name is sufficiently uninformative to avoid confusion with other approaches. Hence we adopt this name here.

2.3   Determinants of μ, σ, and y_{min}

2.3.1   Determinants of μ and σ

The model for the explanation of μ and σ follows straightforwardly from a theory of preference formation put forward by Kapteyn (1977). Recent investigations into the theory's validity are by Kapteyn, Wansbeek, and Buyze (1980) and van de Stadt, Kapteyn, and van de Geer (1985).

Specialized to the present context, the theory amounts to the hypothesis that an individual's WFI is nothing other than a perceived income distribution. That is, an individual evaluates any income level by its ranking in the income distribution he perceives. The idea is that in order to evaluate incomes, an individual needs a frame of reference. This frame of reference is formed by his perceived income distribution. This perceived income distribution summarizes the incomes the individual has perceived over his lifetime. These incomes may be his own past or present income, or they may be past or present incomes in his reference group. The idea of a perceived income distribution can be somewhat formalized as follows.

Let there be N individuals in society. Time is measured in years, $t = -\infty, \ldots, 0$, where $t = 0$ represents the present. At each moment of time an individual n ($n = 1, \ldots, N$) is assumed to assign nonnegative *reference weights* $w_{nk}(t)$ to any individual k in society ($k = 1, \ldots, N$), $\Sigma_{k=1}^{N}$ $w_{nk}(t) = 1$. The reference weights indicate the importance individual n attaches to the income of individual k at time t. Obviously, quite a few of the $w_{nk}(t)$ will be zero. On the other hand, $w_{nn}(t)$, i.e., the weight that individual n attaches to his own income at time t, may be substantial. The set of individuals with $w_{nk}(t) > 0$, $k \neq n$, will sometimes be referred to as n's *social reference group* at time t. For notational simplicity, we adopt the convention (in sections 2.3 and 2.4 only) that arguments equal to zero are suppressed, e.g., $w_{nk} \equiv w_{nk}(0)$.

Furthermore, let $y_k(t)$ be the income of individual k at time t. The reference weights now allow for the definition of a *perceived income distribution at time t*. Denote this function by $G_n(y|t)$, then its definition is

$$(9) \qquad G_n(y|t) \equiv \sum_{\{k; y_k(t) \leq y\}} w_{nk}(t).$$

The $G_n(y|t)$ for any t can be aggregated to one *presently perceived income distribution, $G_n(y)$*. To that end a nonnegative *memory function* $a_n(t)$ is introduced, which describes individual n's weighting of perceived income over time,

$$(10) \qquad \sum_{t=-\infty}^{0} a_n(t) = 1, \quad n = 1, \ldots, N.$$

The idea behind the introduction of a memory function is that events that took place a long time ago will have less influence on a person's present frame of reference than more recent experiences. Hence, in building up a person's presently perceived income distribution out of income distributions in each time period we weigh each of these income distributions with a time-dependent weight $a_n(t)$.

The presently perceived distribution function $G_n(y)$ can now be defined as

(11)
$$G_n(y) \equiv \sum_{t=-\infty}^{0} a_n(t)\, G_n(y|t).$$

As indicated above, the preference formation theory claims that this perceived income distribution equals the utility function $U_n(y)$ of the individual.

The development of the argument so far has been in terms of individual incomes, whereas our data refer to family income (cf. the wording of the survey questions above). It may be expected that a family with children needs more income than a single person to reach the same utility level, so it stands to reason to reformulate the preference formation theory in terms of income per *equivalent adult* (or *per capita* as we will often say). Let $f_k(t)$ be the number of equivalent adults in family k at time t. The income per equivalent adult in this family at time t is denoted by

(12)
$$\tilde{y}_k(t) \equiv y_k(t)/f_k(t).$$

The reformulation of $U_n(y)$ in terms of per capita incomes amounts to a transformation of the income scale: y is replaced by $\tilde{y} \equiv y/f_n$ and e^{μ_n} by e^{μ_n}/f_n. Consequently,

$$U_n(y) = N(\ln y; \mu_n, \sigma_n) = N\left(\ln\left(\frac{y}{f_n}\right); \mu_n - \ln f_n, \sigma_n\right)$$

(13)
$$\equiv N(\ln y; \tilde{\mu}_n, \tilde{\sigma}_n) = \tilde{U}_n(y).$$

Replacing $y_k(t)$ and y in equations (9) and (11) by $\tilde{y}_k(t)$ and $\tilde{y}$, we obtain the perceived distribution of per capita incomes $\tilde{G}_n(y)$.

The theory of preference formation now states

(14)
$$\tilde{U}_n(\tilde{y}) = \tilde{G}_n(\tilde{y})\,;\, n = 1, \ldots, N; \tilde{y} = [0, \infty).$$

Equation (14) implies that utility is a completely relative concept. The utility of a certain income per equivalent adult is obtained by comparing it with the perceived distribution of incomes per equivalent adult.

As it stands, equation (14) is hardly operational, because $\tilde{G}_n$ has not been specified. Also for the purpose of policy simulations—the main goal of this chapter—we have to be more specific, altogether we will have to introduce quite a few new symbols before the model is in a form suitable for estimation and simulation.

Denote the first log moment of $\tilde{G}_n(\tilde{y})$ by $\tilde{m}_n$.

(15)
$$\tilde{m}_n = \int_0^\infty \ln \tilde{y}\, d\tilde{G}_n(\tilde{y}) = \sum_{t=-\infty}^{0} a_n(t) \sum_{k=1}^{N} w_{nk}(t) \ln \tilde{y}_k(t).$$

The equality of the two distribution functions $\tilde{U}_n$ and $\tilde{G}_n$ implies the equality of the first log moments:

(16)
$$\mu_n = \ln f_n + \tilde{m}_n + \epsilon_n$$
$$= \ln f_n + \sum_{t=-\infty}^{0} a_n(t) \sum_{k=1}^{N} w_{nk}(t) \ln \tilde{y}_k(t) + \epsilon_n .$$

Also the second log moments of $\tilde{U}_n$ and $\tilde{G}_n$ have to be equal:

(17)
$$\sigma_n^2 = \sum_{t=-\infty}^{0} a_n(t) \sum_{k=1}^{N} w_{nk}(t) [\ln \tilde{y}_k(t) - \tilde{m}_n]^2 + \delta_n .$$

The measurement errors in μ_n and σ_n^2 and errors in the equations are taken into account by means of the independently identically distributed disturbance terms ϵ_n and δ_n, with zero means and variances σ_ϵ^2 and σ_δ^2.

Although equations (16) and (17) relate observable variables on the left-hand side to observable variables on the right-hand side, there are still far too many parameters, in particular the reference weights $w_{nk}(t)$, that would have to be estimated. So we need further simplifications. First we assume that $w_{nn}(t)$ is the same for all individuals and constant over time, i.e., all individuals give themselves the same constant weight. We write $\beta_2 = w_{nn}(t)$ and $\beta_3 = \sum_{k \neq n} w_{nk}(t) = 1 - \beta_2$. The function $\ln f_k(t)$ is specified as $\beta_0 + \beta_1 \ln fs_k(t)$ where $fs_k(t)$ is the number of members of family k at time t. The memory function $a_n(t)$ is assumed to be the same for everyone and is specified as $a_n(t) = (1-a)a^{-t}$. Furthermore, we define

(18)
$$q_{nk}(t) \equiv w_{nk}(t)/\beta_3 , k \neq n$$
$$\equiv 0 \qquad , k = n ,$$

(19)
$$\overline{m}_n(t) \equiv \sum_k q_{nk}(t) \ln y_k(t) ,$$

(20)
$$\overline{h}_n(t) \equiv \sum_k q_{nk}(t) \ln f_k(t) = \beta_0 + \beta_1 \left\{ \sum_k q_{nk}(t) \ln fs_k(t) \right\}$$
$$\equiv \beta_0 + \beta_1 \overline{hs}_n(t) ,$$

where $\overline{hs}_n(t)$ is defined implicitly. So, $\overline{m}_n(t)$ and $\overline{hs}_n(t)$ are the log means of incomes and family sizes in family n's social reference group at time t.

All this makes it possible to rewrite equation (16) as

(21)
$$\mu_n = \ln f_n + (1-a) \sum_{t=-\infty}^{0} a^{-t} [\beta_2 \{\ln y_n(t) - \ln f_n(t)\}$$
$$+ \beta_3 \{\overline{m}_n(t) - \overline{h}_n(t)\}] + \epsilon_n .$$

Next we apply the Koyck transformation and use the expression for $\ln f_n$ to write equation (21) in lagged form as follows:

$$\text{(22)} \quad \begin{aligned} \mu_n &= [1 - \beta_2(1 - a)]\beta_1 \ln fs_n - a\beta_1 \ln fs_n(-1) + \beta_2(1 - a)\ln y_n \\ &+ \beta_3(1 - a)\overline{m}_n - \beta_3(1 - a)\beta_1\overline{hs}_n + a\mu_n(-1) + \epsilon_n - a\epsilon_n(-1). \end{aligned}$$

Going through a similar derivation regarding equation (17) we can derive an expression for σ_n^2 analogous to equation (12). This more complicated expression is given in Appendix A.

Some details of the maximum likelihood estimation of equation (22) are given in Appendix B.[3] Here we mention one aspect that will play a role in the simulations. In equation (22) there are still various quantities that involve the unknown reference weights. Consider, for example, $\overline{m}_n$ defined by equation (19). We have constructed a proxy for $\overline{m}_n$ as follows. The sample is partitioned into groups of individuals who share certain characteristics, i.e., within a group individuals have the same education level, are of about the same age, and have a similar employment status (see the next section for the exact definition of the characteristics). We call such groups *social groups*. Let the unweighted mean log-income in the social group to which individual n belongs be equal to y_n^*. Then we assume that we can write

$$\text{(23)} \quad \overline{m}_n = \kappa\cdot\eta + (1 - \kappa)y_n^* + u_n,$$

where η is mean log-income in society, u_n is an error term independent of y_n^*, and κ an unknown parameter that is to be estimated along with the other parameters in the model.

The parameter κ measures what share of the reference group of individual n lies within his social group. If $\kappa = 0$, the social group comprises the reference group; if $\kappa = 1$, the social group is irrelevant for the determination of the reference group of the individual. In van de Stadt, Kapteyn, and van de Geer (1985) explicit assumptions are made that justify the approximation equation (23). For $\overline{hs}_n$, which also involves q_{nk}, an approximation similar to equation (23) has been employed.

2.3.2   Determinants of y_{min}

A theory does not exist from which a model for the explanation of y_{min} is readily derived. One tempting approach is to assume that y_{min} corresponds to a point on the welfare scale, i.e., any respondent associates "making ends meet" with, say, a utility level $\overline{u}$.[4] Analogous to equation (8) we would find for the minimum income of individual n, $y_{min,n}$:

$$\text{(24)} \quad \ln y_{min,n} = \mu_n + \sigma_n\cdot\overline{z},$$

where $\overline{z}$ satisfies $\overline{u} = N(\overline{z}; 0,1)$. Equation (22) could be combined with equation (24), and we could estimate the two equations jointly. Because

---

3. Available from the authors on request.
4. This would make the subjective poverty line and the Leyden poverty line equivalent, except for the fact that in the subjective approach the welfare level associated with the poverty line would not be determined by politicians, but by the respondents themselves.

equation (24) would add further nonlinearities to an already complicated model we prefer the simpler assumption,

$$(25) \qquad \ln y_{\min,n} = \mu_n - \gamma_0,$$

with γ_0 an unknown constant to be estimated; equation (25) implies that $y_{\min,n}$ is a constant fraction of $\exp(\mu_n)$. This immediately allows us to derive for $\ln y_{\min,n}$ a relation like that in equation (22), with μ_n and $\mu_n(-1)$ replaced by $\ln y_{\min,n}$ and $\ln y_{\min,n}(-1)$ respectively. We will estimate this equation jointly with equation (22), but we also test equation (25) by testing whether the parameters in the $y_{\min}$ equation have the same value as in the μ equation.

2.4 Data and Estimation Results

The data consist of the first three waves of a panel of 616 households in the Netherlands (drawn randomly from the Dutch population). The main breadwinner of each household was interviewed in March 1980, and the same person was reinterviewed in March of 1981 and 1982. The items in the questionnaire included the IEQ, the MIQ, after-tax family income, family composition, and a number of demographic and socioeconomic characteristics. Three of the characteristics were used to construct the social groups mentioned in the previous section: education, employment status, age. Five education levels are distinguished, three states of employment (self-employed, employee, not employed), and five age brackets (less than 30, 30–39, 40–49, 50–65, over 65). This leads to a maximum of $5 \cdot 3 \cdot 5 = 75$ social groups, 51 of which are represented in the sample.

On the basis of this information, equation (22) and the $y_{\min}$ equation analogous to equation (22) have been estimated by means of the LISREL program (see Appendix B for details). A test has been carried out of the hypothesis that the parameters β_1, β_2, a, κ are the same for the $y_{\min}$ equation and equation (22). This equality of parameters implies equation (25). The results of the estimations with and without imposition of equality of parameters are given in table 2.1.

The first two columns of table 2.1 contain the parameter estimates for the case where equation (22) and the $y_{\min}$ equation are estimated jointly, but without imposition of equality restrictions on the parameters in equation (22), on the one hand, and the $y_{\min}$ equation on the other hand. The last column contains parameter estimates under the restriction that a, β_1, β_2, β_3, κ_1 are identical in equation (22) and the $y_{\min}$ equation. According to the χ^2 statistic the restrictions are not rejected by the data at any reasonable level of significance. Hence we will use the numbers in this last column for the policy simulations. Moreover, we maintain equation (25).

Although the meaning of the parameters will probably become clearer when we turn to policy analysis, a few interpretative comments may be en-

Table 2.1   **Estimation Results**

Parameter	Equation (22)	y^{min} Equation	Equations (22) and y^{min} Combined
a	0.36	0.36	0.37
	(0.05)	(0.06)	(0.05)
β_1	0.17	0.21	0.17
	(0.04)	(0.05)	(0.04)
β_2	0.67	0.70	0.67
	(0.10)	(0.12)	(0.10)
β_3	0.33	0.30	0.33
	(0.10)	(0.12)	(0.10)
κ	0.79	0.89	0.81
	(0.15)	(0.18)	(0.15)
Number of observations	616		616
Degrees of freedom	28		32
χ^2	33.96		37.89

Note: Asymptotic standard errors are in parentheses.

lightening. The estimate of the memory parameter a implies that the weights given to years 0, -1, -2, etc., are 0.64, 0.23, 0.08, 0.02, 0.01, 0.003, etc. Roughly speaking, the horizon is about five years.

The estimates of β_2 and β_3 suggest that one's own past incomes have about twice as much influence on one's present needs (as reflected by μ and y_{min}) than the incomes of others. Referring back to equation (23), the estimate of κ indicates that the social groups as we define them are rather poor proxies of the reference groups of individuals; we cannot reject the hypothesis that $\kappa = 1$. Although we would have liked to have better proxies, the standard errors of the other parameter estimates indicate that these parameters have been estimated with acceptable reliability. Ideally, of course, one would like to have information on the reference group of a respondent. Hence, this is one of our priorities for future data-collecting activities.

To conclude our brief discussion of the parameter estimates, consider β_1. Remember that the number of equivalent adults in a family, f_n, is specified as

$$(26) \qquad \ln f_n = \beta_0 + \beta_1 \ln fs_n.$$

This means that if the size of a family changes, say, from fs_1 to fs_2, its cost of living increases by a factor $(fs_2/fs_1)^{\beta_1}$. The equivalence scale implied by this is given in table 2.2.

These equivalence scales are very flat. Obviously, specification (26) is rather primitive and perhaps too restrictive, as it implies that the cost of

Table 2.2   Estimated Equivalence Scale

Family Size	Equivalence Scale
1	0.79
2	0.89
3	0.95
4	1
5	1.04
6	1.07
7	1.10
8	1.13

an additional child is a fixed percentage of family income, for any level of family income. In addition, the definition of family size in the survey questionnaire was ambiguous because children away from home, still partly supported by their parents, were counted as part of the family. On the other hand, it should be mentioned that the cost of children in the Netherlands is considerably less than, for instance, the cost of children in the United States, due to various government programs that provide among other things, free education and subsidized housing. Results by Danziger et al. (1984) and Colasanto, Kapteyn, and van der Gaag (1984) for the United States, based on the same subjective measures, show substantially steeper equivalence scales.

As was mentioned before, our model implies that welfare and poverty are entirely relative. In their well-known analyses of Gallup poll data, Rainwater (1974) and Kilpatrick (1973) come to somewhat contrasting conclusions. Rainwater finds that the Gallup measure ("How much does it take a family of four in your community to get along?") is completely relative, i.e., it rises in proportion to median family income in society. Kilpatrick finds that its elasticity with respect to median family income is less than one. The difference between the two authors' results is partly due to differences in method and data. But it is worth noticing that both studies are static. The Gallup measure in a given year is related to median family income in society in the same year, so no allowance is made for the effect of past incomes as in our model. As will be seen in the next section, our model predicts that y_{min} (which has a rather close relation with the Gallup measure) will tend to be a smaller proportion of median family income, the faster incomes grow. Thus, Kilpatrick's result that the income elasticity of the poverty line falls to a lower level sometime after the war could possibly be explained by a change in the pace of economic growth.

Finally, it should be noted that in the model we have ignored differences in cost of living due to causes other than family size differences. This implies for instance that people in Mississippi and Wisconsin are predicted to have similar responses, as long as their reference groups show a similar income distribution, even though the cost of living may differ substantially between both regions. In contrast, people in Ireland would be predicted to have very different responses than people in West Germany, even though the cost of living might be similar in both countries. For a homogenous country like Holland we did not consider it necessary to account for regional differences in the cost of living. Were the same analysis applied to the United States, for example, then the model should be extended to incorporate regional cost differences similar to the way the effect of family composition has been incorporated. If it were true, however, that people in a region only refer to other people within the same region, then our completely relativistic model would imply that the regional cost differences will come out insignificant.

2.5 Simulations

Given the empirical results reported in the previous section, the two poverty line definitions in section 2.2, and some additional political assumptions, one can derive various income maintenance schemes. In this section we take both the empirical results and the two poverty line definitions for granted and explore the effect of various policy decisions. We first consider some long-term (steady-state) implications; then we turn to some dynamic aspects of the two poverty line definitions.

As far as policy decisions are concerned we consider three possibilities:

1. In the computation of the poverty line, the actual reference group and the actual income history are taken into account, i.e., equations (22) and (A1), and the analogous equation for y_{min} is used without adaptations.

2. Politicians do not want to honor differences in reference groups, so income maintenance schemes are based on a hypothetical reference group, identical for everybody (e.g., the whole society serves as a reference group for everyone).

3. Politicians, in addition, ignore income histories, thus welfare benefits vary only with family composition. In this case, both the incomes in the reference group and an individual's income history are set at a hypothetical level.

We study the implications of these different policy principles for the two poverty line definitions introduced in section 2.2. We also pay attention to the role played by the rate of economic growth (or decline).

Generally, the analysis will be carried out in per capita terms, i.e., in terms of family income per equivalent adult. This greatly simplifies the algebra and implies that poverty lines always compensate fully for differences in family size. When appropriate, we pay some attention to the welfare effects of not fully compensating for variations in family composition. We ignore the error terms in the estimated equations and the uncertainty in the parameter estimates.

2.5.1   Poverty Lines in a Steady State

The Subjective Definition

By hypothesis (not rejected by the data) there holds

(27)
$$\ln y_{min,n} = \mu_n - \gamma_0 ,$$

where γ_0 has been estimated to be equal to 0.12, implying that $y_{min,n}$ equals approximately 88 percent of $\exp(\mu)$. Combining equations (22) and (27), and indicating per capita variables by a tilde on top, one finds

(28)
$$\ln \tilde{y}_{min,n} = -\gamma_0(1 - a) + \beta_2(1 - a)\ln \tilde{y}_n \\ + \beta_3(1 - a)\bar{\tilde{m}}_n + a \ln \tilde{y}_{min,n}(-1).$$

We define an income maintenance scheme based on the subjective definition as one where $\tilde{y}_n(t) = \tilde{y}_{min,n}(t - 1)$. An alternative approach would be to set $\tilde{y}_n(t)$ equal to $\tilde{y}_{min,n}(t)$. However, in the data, family income y_n refers to the past period, whereas the MIQ (see beginning of section 2.2) asks for y_{min} in the present period. So one is able to just make ends meet if $\tilde{y}_n(t) = \tilde{y}_{min,n}(t - 1)$, since in that case actual family income and stated minimum income refer to the same period and are equal. Whenever $\tilde{y}_n(t) = \tilde{y}_{min,n}(t - 1)$, we shall so indicate by an asterisk.

To incorporate the possible effect of economic growth, let us assume that median income in the reference group of individual n grows at a constant rate δ. Setting $\tilde{y}_n(t) = y_{min,n}(t - 1)$ in equation (28), it is easy to show that $\tilde{y}_{min,n}(t)$ and $\tilde{y}_n(t)$ converge to a steady state in which both grow at the same rate δ, provided that $0 < a < 1$ and $0 < \beta_2 < 1$. In the steady state there holds in each period:

(29)
$$\ln \tilde{y}_n^* = \bar{\tilde{m}}_n - \frac{1}{\beta_3} \left\{ \gamma_0 + \frac{\delta}{1 - a} \right\}$$

and

$$\ln \tilde{y}_{min,n}^* = \ln \tilde{y}_n^* + \delta .$$

The poverty line is simply a certain fraction of median income in the reference group of individual n.[5] If politicians do not accept that different people have different reference groups, but substitute, for instance $\tilde{\eta}$ (median per capita income in society) for $\bar{\tilde{m}}_n$, then the poverty line is a certain fraction of median income in society. In either case differences in family size are fully compensated. The distance of y_{min}^* to median income depends on β_3. The more weight one gives to other people, the closer $y_{min,n}^*$ will be to $\bar{\tilde{m}}_n$ (or $\tilde{\eta}$). To get an idea of what the number may look like in practice, let $\delta = 0$, and use our estimate for β_3 ($= 0.33$). Then $\gamma_0/\beta_3 = 0.36$. The poverty

---

5.   We call $\exp(\bar{\tilde{m}}_n)$ median per capita income in the reference group. Strictly speaking this terminology is only correct if the geometric mean of incomes, $\bar{\tilde{m}}_n$, coincide with the median, as in the case where incomes are lognormally distributed.

line is then $\exp(-0.36)$, 70 percent of median income. In the Netherlands the official poverty line is also approximately 70 percent of median income (again, after tax).

If there is economic growth, $\delta > 0$, the poverty line becomes a smaller fraction of median income. The faster incomes grow, the greater the relative distance between median income and the poverty line can be. (For instance, if $\delta = 0.02$, m_n^* is approximately 63 percent of median income; if $\delta = 0.05$, m_n^* is about 55 percent of median income.) If incomes go down ($\delta < 0$), the poverty line tends to be closer to the median; in fact if $\delta < -\gamma_0$ $(1 - a)$, the poverty line will even exceed the median. For our parameter estimates this happens if $\delta < -0.08$. In view of the model, this makes perfect sense, because previous incomes codetermine one's minimal needs. If incomes fall quickly enough, not even a median income earner will be able to make ends meet.

It is of interest to contrast this with political practice in the Netherlands, where in times of rising incomes the poverty line was moved closer to the national median income, and where in the present stagnation the poverty line appears to fall slightly faster than median income.

Politicians might decide that neither $\bar{m}_n$ nor $\bar{\eta}$ is the appropriate anchoring point in equation (29). It might be argued that poor people mainly refer to other people who are poor as well, so that $\bar{m}_n$ in equation (29) should be replaced by $\ln \bar{y}_n^*$. Obviously in that case the poverty line is not defined. This is according to expectation, because the model for the explanation of y_{min} is relativistic, i.e., the reference group incomes serve as an anchoring point. If these reference group incomes are themselves dependent on y_{min}, a well-defined equilibrium no longer exists.

The Leyden Poverty Line

In order not to burden the exposition with too many technicalities, most of the mathematics for this section are given in Appendix A. The same assumptions are made here as in the "Subjective Definition" section, but in addition it is assumed that the log variance of per capita incomes in the reference group remains constant. As with y_{min}, we assume that a measured WFI pertains to the present period, whereas $\bar{y}_n$ and $\bar{m}_n$ pertain to the previous period. A Leyden poverty line at time t is then defined as an income $\bar{y}_n(t)$ satisifying $\ln \bar{y}_n(t) = \bar{\mu}_n(t-1) + u_\alpha \cdot \bar{\sigma}_n(t-1)$, with u_α chosen by the policymakers (cf. equation (8)).

The steady-state behavior of the Leyden poverty line is derived in Appendix A. We mention the following characteristics of the steady state:

1. $\ln \bar{y}_n$ is monotonically increasing in u_α, as long as $0 < \beta_2 < 1$ and $0 < a < 1$.

2. There are vertical asymptotes for $\ln \bar{y}_n$ at $u_\alpha = (\beta_3/\beta_2)^{1/2}$ and $u_\alpha = -(\beta_3/\beta_2)^{1/2}$. In other words, we can let $\ln \bar{y}_n$ vary from $-\infty$ to $+\infty$ and u_α will vary only from $-(\beta_3/\beta_2)^{1/2}$ to $(\beta_3/\beta_2)^{1/2}$. In view of our estimates of β_2

and β_3, this means that u_α has to lie in the interval $(-1/2 \sqrt{2}, 1/2 \sqrt{2})$, which corresponds to a range of welfare levels between 0.24 and 0.76. Thus it is impossible to create a steady state in which someone is completely satisfied or completely dissatisfied with his income!

The higher β_2 is relative to β_3, the smaller the range of attainable welfare levels will be. The reason for this is that if the habit formation parameter β_2 is high, an individual adjusts her WFI strongly to own income, so no matter how high (or low) her income is, the WFI always catches up with it. It is doubtful, of course, whether the model still holds true for extremely low values of $\tilde{y}_n$, simply because below some point, $\tilde{y}_n$ will be insufficient to purchase enough food to sustain a biological minimum, which makes the notion of a steady state itself illusive. In any case, the results illustrate an important phenomenon: The stronger habit formation is, the less scope there is for socioeconomic policy to influence welfare permanently.

3. Similar to the subjective poverty line, the Leyden poverty line will be closer to the median (of either the reference group or society as a whole if politicians replace $\tilde{m}_n$ by $\tilde{\eta}$) if economic stagnation, rather than economic growth, occurs.

4. For $\alpha = 0.5$, (so $u_\alpha = 0$), the Leyden poverty line is given by

$$(30) \qquad \ln \tilde{y}_n = \tilde{m}_n - \frac{\delta \cdot a}{\beta_3 (1-a)} ,$$

which is equivalent to equation (29) for $\gamma_0 = 0$.

5. For $\delta = 0$ (no economic growth) the Leyden poverty line is

$$(31) \qquad \ln \tilde{y}_n = \tilde{m}_n + \frac{u_\alpha \tilde{\tau}_n}{(\beta_3 - \beta_2 u_\alpha^2)^{1/2}} ,$$

where $\tilde{\tau}_n^2$ is the log variance of per capita incomes in the reference group. In this case the poverty line is a certain fraction of median reference group income, where the fraction is smaller if u_α is smaller (assuming $u_\alpha < 0$), $\tilde{\tau}_n$ is larger, and habit formation is stronger. So the poverty line is lower if politicians pick a lower welfare level as a cutoff point, or if incomes in society (or reference group) are more dispersed, or if people pay less attention to the incomes of others.

2.5.2 Dynamics

Let us now investigate some dynamic aspects of income maintenance policies, maintaining the assumptions made above. The analysis in this section is purely numerical. We consider three representative families. The first family comes from a social group with a high median income; the second family comes from a social group with median income equal to median income in the sample (we take the sample median as a proxy for the median in the population); the third family belongs to a social group with a low median income.

For each family eight income paths are considered. The income paths correspond to eight different income maintenance policies. These policies are characterized by three traits.

1. The policy is either based on the Leyden poverty line, based on a welfare level equal to 0.4, or on the subjective poverty line.

2. In setting the poverty line, either the actual reference group of a family is taken into account or the family is assigned the whole society as a reference group (we call that a *hypothetical reference group*).

3. Either the income maintenance policy is only based on steady-state values of all variables, or benefits also depend on one's income history (we call the latter case *smooth adaptation*).

These three traits define a complete design of eight different income maintenance policies. For each policy we also consider the satisfaction with income in each period. All analyses are in per capita terms. For some selected cases we will also present the effects of not compensating for differences in family size. The rate of economic growth, δ, is set at 0.02.

The eight different income maintenance policies can be presented by means of four sets of diagrams. The first two sets refer to the Leyden poverty line and the last two sets refer to the subjective poverty line. For reasons of space only the first two sets are given here. The labels on the figures are self-explanatory.

In figure 2.3a the income paths of the three families converge to identical trajectories. The corresponding utility levels, drawn in figure 2.3b, each converge to a constant, but this constant is highest for the family with the poorest reference group and lowest for the family with the richest reference group. The only family that actually attains the prescribed welfare level of 0.4 is the middle family, for which actual and hypothetical reference groups coincide.

In figure 2.3c the income paths do not converge to the same trajectory, but now the welfare paths in figure 2.3d do. Apparently we are faced with a choice between equity in income terms (figs. 2.3a and 2.3b) or equity in welfare terms (figs. 2.3c and 2.3d), but in the latter case we have to accept that different families receive different amounts of benefits simply because they happen to have different reference groups.[6]

The families in figures 2.4a and 2.4b are not given time to adjust to their new income situation after they become eligible for benefits. The benefit level is set at the steady-state level (with a hypothetical reference group). Figure 2.4b shows that the first few years are hard on the previously well-to-do family. The poorest of the three families enjoys an increase in income and welfare by entering the income maintenance program.

Figures 2.4c and 2.4d are similar to figures 2.4a and 2.4b. The first-year welfare dips of the well-to-do and median family are somewhat mitigated

---

6. We have equated equity with equality here, which is not necessarily the best thing to do.

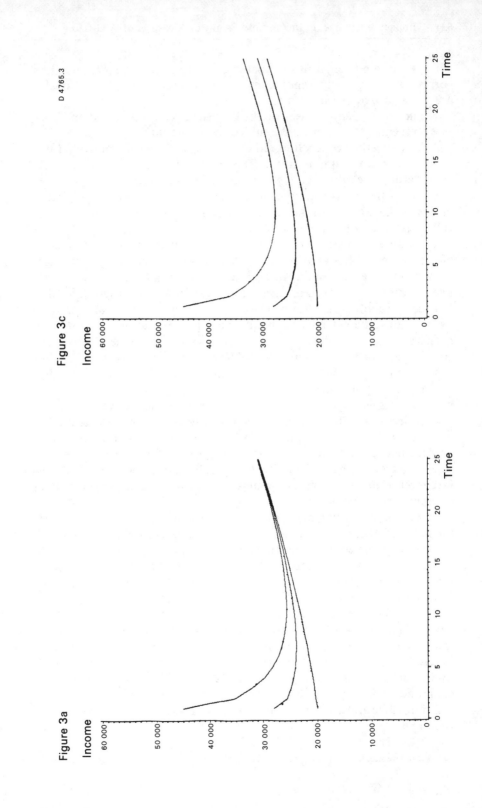

Figure 3a

Figure 3c

D 4765.3

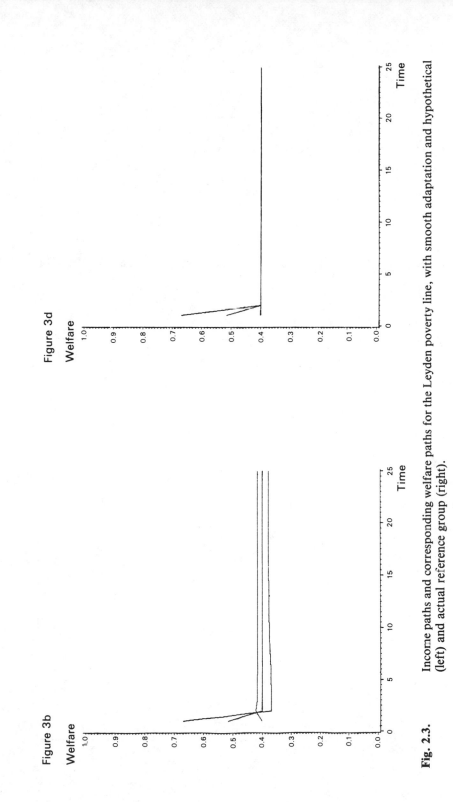

Fig. 2.3. Income paths and corresponding welfare paths for the Leyden poverty line, with smooth adaptation and hypothetical (left) and actual reference group (right).

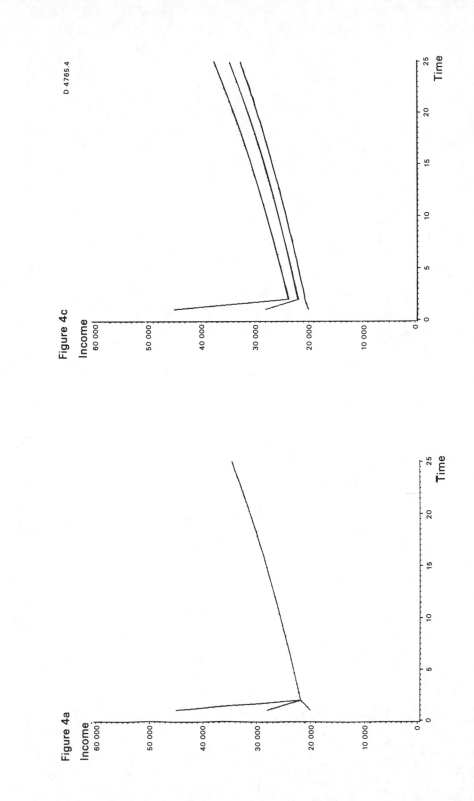

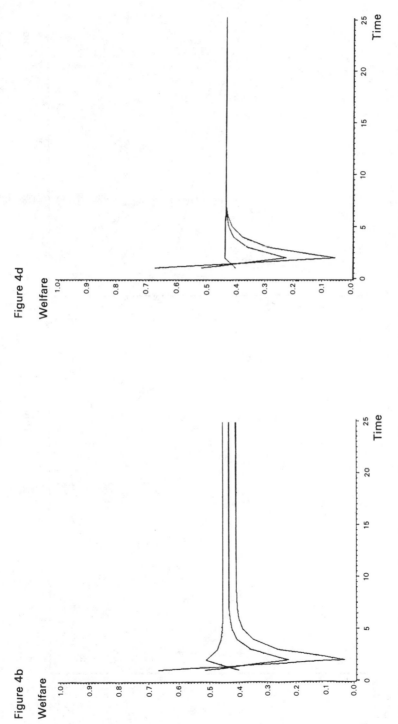

Figure 4b

Figure 4d

Fig. 2.4.   Income paths and corresponding welfare paths for the Leyden poverty line, with prompt adaptation and hypothetical (left) and actual reference group (right).

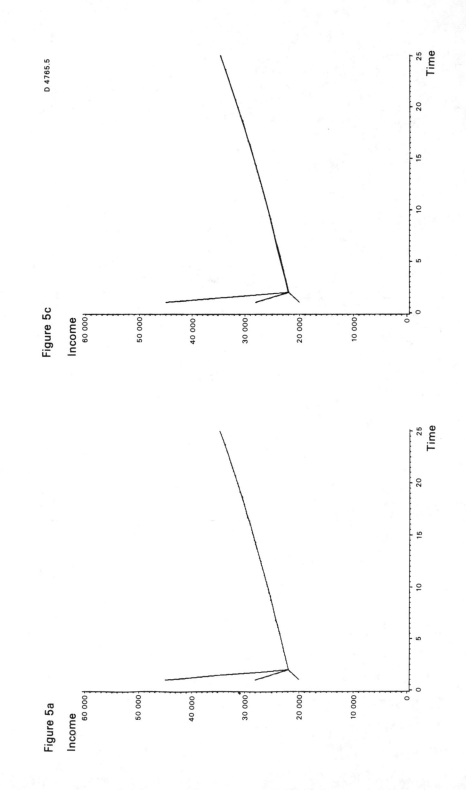

Figure 5c

D 4765.5

Figure 5a

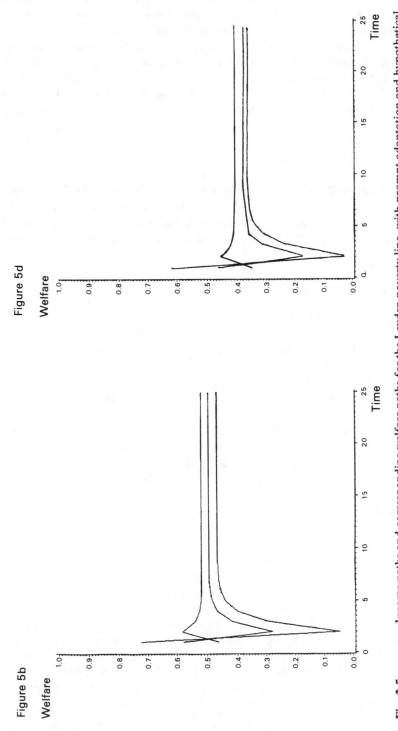

Figure 5b

Welfare

Figure 5d

Welfare

Fig. 2.5. Income paths and corresponding welfare paths for the Leyden poverty line, with prompt adaptation and hypothetical reference group, for family size = 1 (left) and family size = 8 (right).

in this case. After approximately five years the three families enjoy the same welfare level. This equality of welfare levels is achieved by allotting different amounts of benefits to the three families.

It so happens that, in the steady state, the subjective poverty line corresponds to a utility level of only slightly less than 0.4, so numerically the Leyden poverty line and the subjective poverty line are close together. As a consequence, the time paths for the subjective poverty line in the various cases are very similar to those of the Leyden poverty line. For reasons of space we do not present these graphs.

Finally, figures 2.5a and 2.5b give income and utility paths for the same cases as considered in figures 2.4a and 2.4b, but now the income compensation is based on a family size of three for every family, irrespective of its size. In figures 2.5a and 2.5b we see what this means for a family of size 1, whilst figures 2.5c and 2.5d tell the story for a family of size 8. The drawings are very much according to expectation. The one-person household gets a bonus and the eight-person family will have a hard time making ends meet.

2.6 Concluding Remarks

Given the model, one can simulate the effects of a variety of income maintenance programs on the distribution of well-being (as measured by our two subjective measures) of program participants. At the present stage, that would seem far too pretentious. The model is based on a rather small longitudinal data set for one country, and the specification of family composition effects is primitive. More importantly, the model does not have any behavioral relations.

However, the policy simulations have revealed a number of issues that have to be dealt with in the design of income maintenance policies. These issues do not depend heavily on the correctness of the model, but they do rest on the assumption that poverty is at least partly relative. Let us briefly summarize some of the issues.

Habit formation. The policy principles embodied in the two poverty line definitions require families to be able to make ends meet or to attain some prescribed minimum welfare level. To be consistent with these principles, we may have to pay very high initial compensations to, for instance, a former top executive of a firm that went bankrupt (leaving aside the possibility that this man can draw from savings accumulated in more prosperous times or from some kind of insurance policy). Politically, such high initial compensations will probably be considered absurd. Yet not paying these large sums amounts to a policy that is inconsistent in that the basic principle is not applied to all citizens. Former top executives of bankrupt firms apparently get a very small weight in the social welfare function.

Reference groups. We have seen various instances where consistent application of the policy principles leads to different benefit levels for people with different reference groups. If you have rich friends you are entitled to more support. Politically, this is once again hard to accept. It might mean, for example, that blacks would in general receive less income support than whites. But not taking reference groups into account means that differences in utility persist (cf. figs. 2.3a and 2.3b, 2.4a and 2.4b). If one conceives of a social welfare function as defined in terms of individual utilities, this means that people get less weight the richer their reference group is.

Which poverty line? Our analysis has been based on only two, perhaps rather special, definitions of poverty. We believe that other definitions, as long as they allow for a relativistic component in poverty, would yield similar conclusions. As the Leyden poverty line and the subjective poverty line lead to such similar results, not much of a choice exists between the two. The main difference between them is that, with the Leyden poverty line, a degree of freedom is left for politicians, since they bear the responsibility of choosing the utility cutoff point α. Whether politicians will appreciate having this responsibility remains to be seen.

Family size. In the policy simulations we have paid little attention to the effect of family size, because we took it for granted that most people would agree that differences in the cost of living caused by differences in family composition should be compensated for. Still one could argue that habit formation, reference groups, and family size all play the same role in that each influences parameters of the utility function. What sets family size apart is probably the term *cost of living,* which lends itself an objective nature. For the same reason distinctions according to region or farm/nonfarm are often accepted as a basis for differentiating benefit levels.

Of course *cost of living* is a rather arbitrary expression. It refers to the income compensation necessary to allow families of different composition to attain the same level of well-being. Precisely according to this definition, we can say that a person faces a high cost of living because he or she has rich friends.

References

Antonides, G., A. Kapteyn, and T. J. Wansbeek. 1980. Reliability and validity assessment of ten methods for the measurement of individual welfare functions of income. MRG working paper. University of Southern California.

Buyze, J. 1982. The estimation of welfare levels of a cardinal utility function. *European Economic Review* 17: 325-32.

Colasanto, D., A. Kapteyn, and J. van der Gaag. 1984. Two subjective definitions of poverty: Results from the Wisconsin Basic Needs Study. *Journal of Human Resources* 19: 127-38.

Danziger, S., J. van der Gaag, E. Smolensky, and M. Taussig. 1984. The direct measurement of welfare levels: How much does it take to make ends meet? *Review of Economics and Statistics* 66: 500–505.

Goedhart, T., V. Halberstadt, A. Kapteyn, and B. M. S. van Praag. 1977. The poverty line: Concept and measurement. *Journal of Human Resources* 12: 503–20.

Kapteyn, A. 1977. A theory of preference formation. Ph.D. diss., Leyden University.

Kapteyn, A., T. J. Wansbeek, and J. Buyze. 1980. The dynamics of preference formation. *Journal of Economic Behavior and Organization* 1: 123–57.

Katona, G. 1960. *The powerful consumer.* New York: McGraw-Hill.

Kilpatrick, R. W. 1973. The income elasticity of the poverty line. *Review of Economics and Statistics* 55: 327–32.

Moon, M., and E. Smolensky, eds. 1978. *Improving measures of well-being.* New York: Academic Press.

Rainwater, L. 1974. *What money buys: Inequality and the social meanings of income.* New York: Basic Books.

van de Stadt, H., A. Kapteyn, and S. van de Geer. 1985. The relativity of utility: Evidence from panel data. *Review of Economics and Statistics* 67.

van Herwaarden, F. G., and A. Kapteyn. 1981. Empirical comparison of the shape of welfare functions. *European Economic Review* 15: 261–86.

van Praag, B. M. S. 1968. *Individual welfare functions and consumer behavior.* Amsterdam: North-Holland.

———. 1971. The welfare function of income in Belgium: An empirical investigation. *European Economic Review* 2: 337–69.

van Praag, B. M. S., T. Goedhart, and A. Kapteyn. 1980. The poverty line: A pilot survey in Europe. *Review of Economics and Statistics* 62: 461–65.

Van Pragg, B.M.S., J. S. Spit, and H. van de Stadt. 1982. A comparison of the food ratio poverty line and the Leyden poverty line. *Review of Economics and Statistics* 64:691–94.

Appendix A
Steady-State Analysis of the Leyden Poverty Line

Analogous to equation (22) the following expression for σ_n^2 can be derived:

$$
\begin{aligned}
\text{(A1)} \quad \sigma_n^2 = {}& \beta_2(1 - a)d_n^2 + \beta_3(1 - a)s_n^2 \\
& + \beta_3\beta_1^2(1 - a)r_n^2 - 2\beta_3\beta_1(1 - a)c_n \\
& + al_n^2 + a\beta_1^2 p_n^2 - 2a\,\beta_1\,\omega_n + a\sigma_n^2(-1) + \delta_n - a\delta_n(-1),
\end{aligned}
$$

where

(A2) $$d_n^2 = (\ln y_n - \xi_n)^2,$$

(A3) $$\xi_n = \mu_n - \epsilon_n,$$

(A4) $$s_n^2 = \sum_k q_{nk}(\ln y_k - \xi_n)^2,$$

(A5) $$r_n^2 = \sum_k q_{nk}(\ln fs_k - \ln fs_n)^2,$$

(A6) $$c_n = \sum_k q_{nk}(\ln y_k - \xi_n)(\ln fs_k - \ln fs_n),$$

(A7) $$l_n^2 = [\xi_n - \xi_n(-1)]^2,$$

(A8) $$\xi_n(-1) = \mu_n(-1) - \epsilon_n(-1),$$

(A9) $$p_n^2 = [\ln fs_n - \ln fs_n(-1)]^2,$$

(A10) $$\omega_n = [\xi_n - \xi_n(-1)][\ln fs_n - \ln fs_n(-1)].$$

In principle, we can estimate equations (22) and (A1) jointly, by means of maximum likelihood, assuming that ϵ_n and δ_n are jointly normally distributed. Equation (A1) is substantially more difficult to estimate than equation (22), because it contains quadratic terms like c_n, s_n^2 and l_n^2 that involve the unobservables ξ_n and $\xi_n(-1)$. Since equation (22) contains the same parameters as equation (A1), the parameters can also be estimated by just using equation (22). This neglect of equation (A1) may cause loss of accuracy of the estimates, but it does not cause inconsistency. For the sake of simplicity we have chosen to use only equation (22) in estimation. In the simulations, equations (22) and (A1) are both used.

Rewrite equations (22) and (A1) in per capita terms:

(A11) $$\tilde{\mu}_n = \beta_2(1 - a) \ln \tilde{y}_n + \beta_3(1 - a) \tilde{\bar{m}}_n + a\tilde{\mu}_n(-1),$$

(A12) $$\tilde{\sigma}_n^2 = \beta_2(1 - a) \tilde{d}_n^2 + \beta_3(1 - a) \tilde{s}_n^2 + a \tilde{l}_n^2 + a\tilde{\sigma}_n^2(-1).$$

Under the assumptions of the section "Leyden Poverty Line," the steady-state solutions for $\ln \tilde{y}_n$, $\tilde{\mu}_n$, and $\tilde{\sigma}_n^2$ have to satisfy the following three equations:

(A13) $$\tilde{\mu}_n = \beta_2 \ln \tilde{y}_n + \beta_3 \tilde{\bar{m}}_n - \frac{a}{1 - a} \delta,$$

(A14) $$\tilde{\sigma}_n^2 = \beta_2(\ln \tilde{y}_n - \tilde{\mu}_n)^2 + \beta_3(\tilde{\bar{m}}_n - \tilde{\mu}_n)^2 + \beta_3 \tilde{\tau}_n^2 + \frac{a}{1 - a} \delta^2,$$

(A15) $$\ln \tilde{y}_n = \tilde{\mu}_n - \delta + u_\alpha \cdot \tilde{\sigma}_n,$$

where

$$\tilde{\tau}_n^2 \equiv \sum_k q_{nk}(\ln \tilde{y}_k - \tilde{\bar{m}}_n)^2.$$

Elimination of $\tilde{\mu}_n$ and $\tilde{\sigma}_n^2$ from this system yields the following quadratic equation in $(\ln \tilde{y}_n - \bar{m}_n)$:

(A16)
$$x^2 \beta_3(\beta_3 - \beta_2 u_\alpha^2) + 2\beta_3 xz + (1 - u_\alpha^2 a^2)z^2 \\ - u_\alpha^2(\beta_3 \tilde{\tau}_n^2 + a.\delta.z) = 0,$$

where

$$x \equiv (\ln \tilde{y}_n - \bar{m}_n) \text{ and } z = \delta/(1 - a).$$

The solution for $\ln \tilde{y}_n$ is:

(A17) $\ln \tilde{y}_n = \bar{m}_n$
$$+ \frac{-\beta_3 z + u_\alpha[\beta_3\{(\beta_3 a^2 - \beta_2 u_\alpha^2 a^2 + \beta_2)z^2 + (\beta_3 - \beta_2 u_\alpha^2)(\beta_3 \tilde{\tau}_n^2 + a.\delta.z)\}]^{1/2}}{\beta_3(\beta_3 - \beta_2 u_\alpha^2)}.$$

Note that there are vertical asymptotes at $u_\alpha = (\beta_3/\beta_2)^{1/2}$ and $u_\alpha = -(\beta_3/\beta_2)^{1/2}$ as claimed in section 2.5.1. The condition that u_α is between those extreme values guarantees convergence of the system to the steady state. The various characteristics of the steady state reported in section 2.5.1 follow from equation (A17).

Comment   Harold W. Watts

This chapter develops a theory about how individuals' subjective evaluation of their income status depends on social context and accumulated experience. The framework the authors present lends itself to two alternate approaches to the definition of poverty thresholds. An empirical section provides estimates of a particular specification of this model, and from these estimates illustrative examples show how income support targets would adapt for families with differing starting points in a world of steady growth.

As a part of the growing literature on subjective measures of utility, the first part of this chapter is very interesting and valuable. There are some interesting empirical regularities in the data from subjective questions such as the MIQ and IEQ; they must mean something. I am not yet fully convinced that we have figured out what question is really being answered, but the structure spelled out in this paper is a welcome addition to the conjectures. I fully share the notion that normative standards of some sort are formed in some way for some set of social groupings. I see a major challenge in eliciting and understanding their more precise meaning.

The process postulated by the authors for forming the perceived income distribution places familiar strains on the "as if" method of theorizing

Harold W. Watts is professor of economics at Columbia University.

about complex data-processing problems. The expressions presented in the paper are formidable for a person not yet familiar with household computers, so the typical individual must simply act "as if" he or she had evaluated such expressions. Aside from that, however, where do people get quantitative perceptions about money income levels? If television is as pervasive as it seems, and if the life-styles observed there can influence individual perceptions, then a very important societywide influence should be recognized. But I still have trouble understanding how money income (adjusted to a per-adult-equivalent basis of course) is estimated by everyone for everyone on the basis of every-day observations. People do not directly advertise their (normalized) income levels and may even try to deceive. Neither are such levels to be found as part of the documentation presented at the end of films and television programs. I would like to see more attention given to the problem of data gathering and processing, which must provide some plausible counterpart to the elaborate structure devised by the authors.

On a more basic level I have a problem with the identification of the empirical measures as "utility." Our training as economists may make utility a useful metaphor in this case, but repetition of the term may lead to taking the idea too seriously. In fact, we have some empirical regularities in search of a concept and, in utility, a concept in search of empirical realization. They have found each other, but I am not sure it is a stable union. The authors acknowledge that the proposed utility is partial—it is based only on income status, and at least a few other aspects of one's life and circumstances would have to be considered in a comprehensive measure. But this partial utility is expressed by a single member of a household, and whether that one is a despot, dependent, or something else, some question remains about how well that person can represent all family members. A parent who enjoys his or her large family may have a very different view about income adequacy than the children who were never canvassed about their preferred number of siblings. How, indeed, does one aggregate this "utility"? Is it assumed that each member of the family enjoys the same, undiminished common level of utility indicated by the respondent, or is the answer a measure of a total that must be shared out among all persons (and not just the "equivalent adults")?

When the model is specified for purposes of estimation, the double-log specification for the adult equivalent function was introduced. That specification was not tested, or at least the tests are not reported, but the elasticity seems extreme enough to suggest further examination. The implied economies of scale—12 to 15 percent more income provides the same utility for twice as many persons—would seem to have enormous policy implications if it could be believed. A campaign to raise real income by forming confederations of households would seem irresistable. Otherwise the estimates are not very remarkable, nor are they strongly inconsistent with the convenient approximations involved in ignoring reference groups smaller than nations and assuming that most adjustments to changed circumstances take place within a year or so. The strong influence of personal experience relative to perceptions of others leaves a need for careful modeling of relative income status, but places a definite limit on the homogeneity of income utility scales among individual respondents. The minimum or "ends meet" income appears to be at about 88 percent of the median of individual perceived income distributions, which seems rather high on an intuitive basis, but there may be reasons in the particulars of Dutch society or policies that can explain this finding.

The attempt to apply the utility model to public policy issues is what I find least persuasive. This part of the chapter seems naïve at least and may well be misleading. First, the simulated policy is a simplistic and generally discredited form of policy—that of "filling the gap" by granting whatever is the shortfall from some guarantee level stated either in income per adult equivalent or in terms of a prescribed dose of "utility" as defined in the theory. Such a policy is appropriate only if households are behaviorally inert. They must be subject only to exogenous determination of income flows, wealth accumulation, and family composition, making no decisions on their own that influence these matters. The authors recognize the absence of any behavioral response, but they do not indicate that features sensitive to such responses might largely dominate the choice of policies.

Even if the problem of incentives is ignored, it is doubtful that the objectives of public policy are well captured by seeking to maximize or equalize the narrowly defined utility (of money income only) as perceived through the eyes of one household "spokesperson." Indeed it seems quite likely that the purpose and justification of policy intervention is based on considerations that are *not* well reflected in the sort of additive and separable (by family) social welfare function (or fragment of one) that is represented here. In particular, the social objective may be more closely related to the external consequences of the household's investment and production activities than to its self-evaluated consumption. Certainly the impact of child-rearing activities on the productivity of future generations carries part of the justification for antipoverty transfers. Just how that issue is reflected in answers to survey questions about the level of a "good" income is far from clear.

We might ask what levels of deprivation or adequacy impair or enhance the next generation's capacity to support itself and the dependents it will inherit and produce. This form of the question may also have important relative aspects and may even be evoked from responses to survey questions. But it is not likely that this notion is the same as the more hedonistic assessment suggested by the IEQ and by the utility metaphor presented here.

Again, even if the consumption flow is given high priority in the social purpose, the current money income measure is a very weak proxy, and it certainly is not uniformly related to consumption among different low-income (or low-consumption) groups. Hence policies that contemplate giving higher public grants to those who have experienced higher consumption (either directly or vicariously) should consider whether that same history of well-being is reflected in wealth, credit, and access to private transfers. If so, the paradox of giving more to the formerly rich is not likely to occur.

The things not considered in the specimen policies examined in this paper will generally outweigh the weak influences of reference group and lagged response of perceptions on any realistic policy. In most cases I can think of, real policies would probably tilt in the opposite direction. Those with rich friends and family connections would get less so as to maintain rough equity with those whose family and friends cannot provide access to private resources of various kinds. Similarly, a loss of income for a low-earning person cannot plausibly be supplemented by drawing on past savings or credit lines. Those in low-cost and low-income areas might sometimes receive higher benefits as an attempt to "catch up" in development of that human capital that had suffered from prior deprivation. Effects on the incentive to migrate are likely to receive the most intense political attention, and some of that is deserved. All of these considerations are more important and more directly related to public policy than the issues introduced in this paper. There is little danger that well-formed policies will give bigger benefits to the formerly rich, even if full allowance is made for the influences discussed by the authors.

In the matter of making utility or happiness a direct focus of policy, I am inclined to demur. I remain more comfortable with the notion of happiness as something to be pursued, not something that the government catches and presumes to dole out. I think public policy has more urgent and more feasible tasks.

So where are we? The chapter presents an interesting rationale for a fascinating empirical regularity. The resulting model, when implemented, yields plausible or at least interpretable estimates that give a definite but limited role to lagged adjustments and to the influence of prevailing general income levels in forming perceptions and income standards. The leap to policy prescriptions is very premature and ill considered in my view. The issues raised by the model are among the least important for income maintenance policies, and considered alone, as they are, lead to apparently paradoxical results that probably would not be noted in realistic policies. Whether the subjective and relative approaches can give real guidance to policy in this area remains to be seen, but a much more sophisticated specification of public (and private) objectives is a clear prerequisite.

3 Estimating Changes in Well-Being Across Life: A Realized vs. Comprehensive Income Approach

Richard V. Burkhauser
J. S. Butler
James T. Wilkinson

Fear of living too long is paradoxically one of the major concerns of old age. This, together with the fear that a serious and prolonged illness or some unanticipated economic disaster could turn a life-style of independent retirement into one of dependence on children or other relatives, are real concerns to all of us as we think about retirement. They no doubt are responsible for the widespread support of government programs to lessen this uncertainty—i.e., Social Security retirement and health insurance.

In making a decision to retire, a worker is concerned not only with income in the next year but with income in all future years of expected life.[1] Yet in anticipating future retirement income many factors are unclear. Changes in health and in the real value of Social Security, pension benefits, and other assets are all factors that can affect future income and economic well-being but that cannot be anticipated with certainty.

In this chapter we look at the long-term consequences of retirement on the relative well-being of a group of workers who retired in the 1970s. We first develop a theoretically superior measure of well-being—comprehensive income—and using this measure compare and then predict how well-being changes over a ten-year period for our sample of men as they move from work to retirement. Finally, we look at the effect of initial levels of

Richard V. Burkhauser is senior research associate with the Institute for Public Policy Study and associate professor of economics at Vanderbilt University. J. S. Butler is assistant professor of economics at Vanderbilt University. James T. Wilkinson is assistant professor of economics at the University of Missouri.

This research was supported in part by funds granted to the Institute for Research on Poverty, University of Wisconsin, Madison, by the Department of Health and Human Services under the Small Grants program. The opinions expressed in this paper are solely those of the authors.

1. A wide literature now exists that incorporates life-cycle values of Social Security and pensions into the retirement decision. See Mitchell and Fields 1982 for a review of this literature.

income on the percentage change in that income over time in a model that incorporates unexpected changes into a standard human capital model of income distribution.

3.1 Realized versus Comprehensive Measures of Well-Being

In the United States and elsewhere economic well-being is defined almost exclusively in terms of income. Yet it is a person's ability to reach a given consumption level, not his or her income, that determines "well-being." Realized income is at best only an imperfect measure of consumption power. Much of the recent criticism of empirical measures of poverty has centered on the degree that different sources of income (in-kind versus money transfers) should be included in measures of well-being.[2] We raise an additional problem. A single-year realized income measure of well-being is misleading because it does not include important wealth effects generated over the life cycle.

Wealth, accumulated savings from previous time periods, can provide an important source of consumption ability. Two persons with the same realized income but different wealth holdings command different potential consumption bundles. For example, the ability to obtain a mortgage on a home can be used to generate funds for current consumption or unexpected health problems. A comprehensive measure of economic well-being must include both wealth and income components. Thus a more accurate measure of economic well-being not only includes the usual sources of income (wage earnings, realized flows from wealth—rents, interest, dividends, etc.), but also the potential consumption ability generated by accumulated wealth.[3]

Here using multiperiod data we construct a comprehensive measure of economic well-being and compare it with a more traditional realized income measure by examining income distributions for a sample of working males before and after retirement.[4] Because it incorporates the potential consumption ability generated by wealth, our comprehensive measure is a theoretically superior measure of well-being. Furthermore, we show that it provides significantly different predictions of future well-being from those occurring in retirement. In the next section we show that our measure also leads to different results with regard to unanticipated changes over the decade.

2. For example, see Smeeding 1984.
3. Intrafamily transfers are undoubtedly an important source of well-being for many of the aged. Unfortunately quantifying the extent of these income and in-kind transfers was beyond the scope of our data and was not included in our comprehensive measure of economic well-being.

An ideal measure of well-being would also include the value of leisure. Quantification of this value creates many formidable problems.
4. For studies that have used panel study data to look at issues related to single versus multiperiod measures of well-being, see for example, Benus and Morgan 1975 and Steuerle and McClung 1977.

Our analysis is conducted within a life-cycle framework.[5] Moon (1977) was the first to use a life-cycle concept of income that was specifically designed for application to the elderly. A life-cycle framework emphasizes the importance of using a comprehensive measure when evaluating the well-being of the aged population. First, life-cycle consumption theories suggest that people build up a stock of wealth during working years. At older ages it is expected that consumption expenditures will exceed income and that the difference will be financed out of wealth. Thus realized income measures will in general underestimate potential consumption. For this reason comparisons of pre- and postretirement income levels are likely to overstate the fall in well-being of the retired population. Second, in looking at the effect of unexpected changes, our comprehensive measure gives a more accurate measure of their true effect on well-being across the income distribution.

Standard measures of well-being are usually composed only of realized income variables as seen in equation (1).

(1) $RI = Y + RA + GT.$

Realized income (RI) includes wage and salary earnings (Y), income from privately held assets such as interest, rents, dividends, and pension payments (RA), and government transfers (GT)—Social Security and other income transfers. Note that in preretirement years, pension payments and Social Security are not received and thus not counted by this measure.

Our comprehensive measure of income will include the annuitized value of all wealth currently held.[6] In equation (2) we estimate the stock value,

(2) $SW = NR + NF + NS,$

of wealth (SW), which includes the present value of real assets minus debt of business, farm, house, and real estate (NR); net financial assets (NF)

---

5. Life-cycle consumption models argue that consumption and hence well-being in any one period is based on total expected lifetime income rather than income in that single period. In fact under the strong assumption of homotheticity with respect to time, lifetime utility can be shown to be maximized by equalizing consumption in each time period over the life cycle. While consumption is expected to be relatively constant over time under such assumptions, income flows for most people arc not. Given perfect foresight and information, a person's stock is just depleted on the last day of his life. Life-cycle hypotheses suggest that some decreases in consumption later in life are attributable to uncertainty and imperfect information. See Kotlikoff 1979 and Kotlikoff, Spivak, and Summers 1982 for recent discussions of this point.

6. It is important to note that the annuitized wealth flow we construct used the same technique as Weisbrod and Hansen 1968. It does not take into consideration whether people do or can convert wealth into an income flow. We want to derive a measure of economic well-being, and there are strong theoretical reasons for including a wealth component. To the extent that people do not convert wealth to flows, then there is evidence that people prefer the stock to the flow it can generate, or there are imperfections in capital markets that make the transformation of stocks to flows difficult or impossible. Some evidence on which of these hypotheses are valid may come from the reverse mortgage experiment now underway in Wisconsin.

composed of the stock value of annuities, bonds, stock certificates, saving and checking accounts; and the net present value of Social Security and pension benefits (*NS*). Note that like other forms of wealth, Social Security and pensions have a stock value regardless of whether workers are currently receiving a flow of realized income from them.

For most older workers two major sources of wealth are private pension and Social Security retirement benefits. For those actually receiving benefits these sources of wealth are already annuitized since this income includes the interest on principal as well as consumption of the principal. But other sources of wealth are not annuitized. Rents, interest, and dividends do not include consumption of the principal. This is also true of housing. Therefore for all wealth currently held we estimate an annuitized value that includes both interest and total consumption at death. Wealth is converted into an income measure through equation (3):

$$(3) \qquad FV = \frac{PV}{\sum_{i=1}^{n} \frac{P_i}{(1 + r)^i}},$$

where *PV* is the present value of the wealth variable. *FV* is the annuitized value. *P* is the probability of living through the *i*th period; *r* is the real rate of interest and *n* is the last period considered.[7]

Equation (4) combines the value of accumulated stocks, as measured by equation (2), with the value of current income measured in equation (1) to equal comprehensive income (*CI*).

$$(4) \qquad CI = RI + SW' - RF - SS.$$

For accounting purposes it is necessary to transform current stock values (*SW*) into flow units (*SW'*). This was done using equation (3). To avoid double counting we subtracted realized income from assets (*RF*) and pensions and Social Security (*SS*) because *SW'* includes both realized and unrealized income from these sources.

3.1.1 Empirical Results

This research is based on data from the Retirement History Study (RHS), a ten-year longitudinal survey of the retirement process by the Social Security Administration. The RHS began in 1969 with a sample of 11,153 men and nonmarried women aged fifty-eight through sixty-three, who were then reinterviewed at two-year intervals through 1979. Attrition occurred at the time of each reinterview because respondents had died,

---

7. We are discounting by a real interest rate of 5 percent. No inflation premium is added because all calculations use constant 1979 dollars. Life expectancy is based on data from *Vital Statistics of the United States,* vol. 2, 1973. All workers were assumed to live no longer than age ninety-five.

been institutionalized, disappeared, or refused to respond. This study is based on the male respondents for whom complete data are available from all waves. We look at a subsample of 1,782 married men who were working in 1969 but had retired by 1979 and whose spouse was present in the household.[8]

We calculated the realized and comprehensive income of each household in 1969 and repeated the calculation for the household ten years later. We use these measures to look at changes in income distributions across the transition from work to retirement and to determine how well income and wealth levels in 1969 predict subsequent income in 1979.

Tables 3.1 and 3.2 show the degree of movement across realized and comprehensive income quintiles as individuals move from working in 1969 to retirement in 1979. The diagonal cells contain those workers who remain in the same income quintile over the period. The off-diagonal cells show the degree of movement.

A comparison of the tables reveals that the two distributions are similar. In fact, a chi-square test does not reject the hypothesis of no difference ($\chi^2_{24} = 22.97$). However, this finding is not too surprising at this level of aggregation. For most respondents a relatively large change would be required to change quintiles. A test of diagonal versus off-diagonal cells is

Table 3.1   **Percentage Distribution of Workers by Realized Income Quintiles, 1969 and 1979**

Distribution of Workers by Realized Income Quintiles, 1979	Distribution of Workers by Realized Income Quintiles, 1969				
	0–20	21–40	41–60	61–80	81–100
0–20	56	21	14	5	3
21–40	20	35	23	15	7
41–60	14	26	28	22	10
61–80	6	13	24	33	24
81–100	4	5	11	23	56

Source: Data are from The Retirement History Study, a longitudinal survey developed by the Social Security Administration. The subsample used here contains 1,782 observations.

8. As a first use of our new methodology we choose to look at the most common group of recently retired workers, those in marriages that remained intact over the period. In choosing this group we avoided the complications related to measuring the well-being of households of different sizes. Our analysis does not look at the effect of death or divorce of a spouse, which may be unexpected and could have important effects on the well-being of surviving members of the family. However we believe the influence of the economic variables we do test does not differ substantially across marital status groups. In our RHS sample 87 percent of the male population was married in 1969. In our initial sample of married couples in which the husband was working in 1969, 25 percent of marriages ended in the death of one spouse over the ten-year period and 8 percent ended in divorce or separation. A more complete study of the effect of unexpected changes on well-being should incorporate changes in marital status into the analysis.

Table 3.2   Percentage Distribution of Workers by Comprehensive Income
                   Quintiles, 1969 and 1979

Distribution of Workers by Comprehensive Income Quintiles, 1979	Distribution of Workers by Comprehensive Income Quintiles, 1969				
	0–21	21–40	41–60	61–80	81–100
0–20	60	24	12	3	1
21–40	23	34	24	16	4
41–60	10	23	33	25	9
61–80	5	15	22	36	23
81–100	2	5	9	20	63

Source: See table 3.1.

significant at 5 percent ($\chi^2_1 = 4.68$), indicating that there are significantly fewer people moving into a new quintile when a comprehensive income measure is used.

We next examine smaller changes in the relative position of workers in the income distribution with a rank-order test. The coefficient for the Spearman rank-correlation test between single-year realized income for men working in 1969 and realized income in 1979 when the men have all retired is .56. Those with a higher income when working tend to have higher income when retired. This relationship is significant at the 1 percent level. The correlation for the same sample of workers using comprehensive income in 1969 and 1979 is .70. Once again the rank correlation between the two years is positive and significant at the 1 percent level. Notice that when this fuller measure of income is used the correlation improves over 25 percent. The neglect of unrealized wealth indicates a much greater fluctuation of well-being in retirement than is the case using our more sensitive measure of comprehensive income.

Now we test whether the two measures yield different results when we look at the effect of initial income and wealth in 1969 on predicted well-being in 1979. The dependent variables in these equations are realized income and comprehensive income respectively. The independent variables used to predict income level in 1979 consist of 1969 income variables, 1969 wealth variables, and demographic variables that capture changes in the worker's life between 1969 and 1979. Income variables include earnings, transfer payments, and interest income. Wealth variables account for physical wealth, financial assets, Social Security, and pension wealth. We expect that the higher a respondent's income and wealth in 1969, the higher his predicted income in 1979. The demographic variables are the respondent's age, the number of years retired, and his health status. The older a person is and the longer he has been retired, the larger the constraints on his optimal consumption path should it have to be changed due to unforeseen expenditures. Health status is based on the respondent's subjective belief about his health relative to his peers in each of the six interview years. Because we are interested in changes in health, this binary variable takes the value of one when health is good in 1969 and deteriorates in any of the later years. The exact definition of all variables can be found in the appendix.

Table 3.3 contains the summary statistics and coefficients for the two equations. In both equations all the income and wealth variables except Social Security wealth are significant at the 5 percent level or better and have the expected sign. But of special interest to us is whether these two equations are significantly different. To test this we estimated the two equations using ordinary least squares. The equations are seemingly unrelated (i.e., the equations appear to be independent but their residuals are correlated). We expect the residuals will be correlated because there are many factors such as ability, motivation, and luck that affect the level of future income that cannot be included in the equations. These factors will affect both comprehensive and realized income measures, yet their effect may not be picked up by the independent variables. To the extent their effects are captured by the residuals, the residuals will be correlated. In fact the correlation between the residuals is .532.

The covariance between the residuals should be taken into account because we wish to test hypotheses concerning the coefficients of the two equations, and when the residuals are correlated, the correct standard errors and t-values involve the covariance. Usually the equations would have to be estimated by generalized least squares (Zellner 1962), but the regressions have the same regressors, and it is well known that in such a case ordinary least squares is algebraically identical to generalized least squares except where the covariance between residuals is concerned. To estimate the covariance, the sample covariance between the residuals of the two equations was estimated separately. This information was then used in the calculation of t-statistics.

3.1.2 Tests of Model Differences

We want to see if these equations represent different models, i.e., do our comprehensive and realized income equations yield different results with regard to predictions about people's well-being. We test for model differences in two ways: first, we test for statistically significant differences between individual coefficients, and second, we use an F-test to look for significant differences between the models as a whole.

In the final column of table 3.3 we report the t-statistics for the null hypotheses that the individual regression coefficients are equal. The null hypothesis is rejected for all but two variables (Social Security wealth and age). The other coefficients are significantly different from each other. This strongly suggests that the models are different.

Table 3.3   Regression Coefficients and Summary Statistics

Variable	Realized Income Regression		Comprehensive Income Regression		Test of Differences H_0: $\beta_{1i} - \beta_{2i} = 0$
	Coefficient	t-statistic	Coefficient	t-statistic	t-statistic[a]
Constant	9,934.444	1.90*	8,597.380	0.84	.154
Resp. income	.139	9.28*	.237	8.15*	-3.99*
Spouse income	.283	11.20*	.407	8.27*	-2.98*
Asset income	.452	15.57*	.783	13.83*	-6.89*
Asset wealth	.024	8.28*	.075	13.15*	-10.49*
Physical wealth	.015	11.59*	.046	18.09*	-14.31*
Soc. Sec. wealth	.008	1.36	.018	1.54	-0.99
Pension wealth	.050	14.76*	.062	9.36*	-2.11*
Age (in 1969)	-67.410	0.76	19.946	0.11	-0.59
Years retired	-364.140	5.83*	-600.279	4.93*	2.28*
Health	-123.197	0.43	-826.198	1.48	1.48
R^2	.578		.583		
$F_{11,1771}$	242.87*		248.11*		H_0: $[I_1 - I_2]\begin{bmatrix}\beta_1\\\beta_2\end{bmatrix} = \underline{0}$[b] $F_{11,1770} = 214.20^*$

Source: See table 3.1

*Indicates significant at 5 percent level or smaller.

[a]Test of differences between individual coefficients.

[b]Joint test of coefficient differences.

The second test of model differences jointly tests for differences between coefficients. The null hypothesis is

$$[I_1 - I_2] \begin{bmatrix} \beta_1 \\ \beta_2 \end{bmatrix} = \underline{0}.$$

The actual F with 11 and 1,770 degrees of freedom is 214.2. The F-test confirms that the null hypothesis of no differences is rejected. These two tests provide convincing evidence that the two measures of income provide different information about an individual's level of well-being.[9]

3.2   The Influence of Unexpected Events on Future Well-Being

Table 3.4 shows the realized income distribution and the composition of income sources by decile of our sample in 1969. It then shows the mean and income composition of these same deciles in 1979. Table 3.5 does the same using a comprehensive income measure. Observe that the income of men in our sample, measured in either realized or comprehensive terms, fell in real terms over the period. Given that the men in our sample retired and that the average age increased from fifty-nine to sixty-nine over the period, this result is not surprising. However, what is not clear is how the distribution of income changed over the period and to what degree unexpected changes in that distribution are related to the initial level of income.

In order to estimate that dependence while avoiding biases related to the time-series nature of the data, we develop here a theory of the determination of the percentage change in income, consistent with the usual theory of human capital. Further, we develop a test of the responsiveness of the percentage change in income over the period 1969–79 to the initial level of comprehensive income to answer the question: Does the inclusion of the omitted (unrealized) asset income that differentiates comprehensive income from realized income affect the stability of measured income?

The following subsections briefly sketch the model of the determination of income and the stochastic process that determines unexpected changes in income. Our final specification is then presented, and its hypotheses are tested.

3.2.1   Human Capital Model

We assume a model of income as follows:

(5) $\ln y_t = \underline{X}'_t \underline{\beta} + \epsilon_t,$

where t indexes time, and $\underline{X}_t$ is the current value of the explanatory variables at t. They include the usual variables used to represent sources of human capital, such as education, experience, health, etc., and variables

9. Burkhauser and Wilkinson 1983 establishes a poverty line in comprehensive income terms and shows that the use of official poverty statistics will overestimate the dangers of falling into poverty in old age.

Table 3.4   Composition of Realized Income for 1969 and 1979 by 1969 Income Deciles

1969 Income Decile	Income Shares in 1969					Income Shares in 1979					
	Average[a] Income 1969	Social[b] Security	Private[c] Pension	Wages[d]	Other[e]	Average[a] Income 1979	Social[b] Security	Private[c] Pension	Wage[d]	Other[f]	n
0–10	4,504	3	1	94	2	5,442	60	5	15	20	181
11–20	9,555	1	1	96	2	7,570	56	8	23	13	176
21–30	12,228	*	2	94	3	7,877	59	22	9	10	178
31–40	14,466	*	2	95	2	8,925	55	20	14	11	178
41–50	16,637	*	2	94	4	9,592	51	22	13	14	182
51–60	19,008	*	1	96	3	9,718	53	26	10	10	178
61–70	21,649	*	1	95	3	11,486	46	28	12	14	176
71–80	25,003	*	1	94	5	12,634	42	25	13	19	176
81–90	31,152	*	1	92	7	15,341	37	32	10	21	180
91–100	53,353	*	2	84	14	23,614	24	27	11	39	177
TOTAL	20,719	*	1	92	7	11,207	43	24	14	21	1,782

Source: See table 3.1.

Note: Due to rounding, shares may not add up to 100.

*Indicates share of less than 1 percent.

[a]Realized income is equal to the sum of Social Security income, private pension income, wage income, and other income. All income figures are in 1979 dollars.

[b]Social Security income consists of Old-Age, Survivors, and Disability Health Insurance (OASDHI) payments.

[c]Pension income includes payments from railroad, military, government, and private pensions in 1969.

[d]Wage income includes respondent's and spouse's wage and self-employed earnings, paid sick leave, unemployment benefits, and workman's compensation payments.

[e]Other income in 1969 includes income from assets (stocks, bonds, savings accounts, and rental property), insurance payments, and annuity income.

[f]Other income in 1979 includes the same sources of income as in 1969 plus Social Security Income (SSI).

Table 3.5   Composition of Comprehensive Income for 1969 and 1979 by 1969 Income Deciles

1969 Income Decile	Income Shares in 1969					Income Shares in 1979					
	Average[a] Income 1969	Social[b] Security	Private[c] Pension	Wages[d]	Other[e]	Average[a] Income 1979	Social[f] Security	Private[g] Pension	Wage[d]	Other[e]	n
0–10	10,174	34	2	50	14	8,325	37	3	11	49	178
11–20	17,532	28	5	56	11	10,078	38	11	12	39	178
21–30	20,053	30	7	59	14	13,323	35	10	10	44	178
31–40	25,755	25	7	54	14	15,115	32	11	7	50	178
41–50	29,031	22	9	56	13	16,528	30	13	7	50	178
51–60	32,567	21	8	55	16	17,662	29	13	5	52	178
61–70	36,014	19	9	56	16	19,985	26	14	8	51	178
71–80	40,801	17	10	56	17	21,492	26	16	7	50	178
81–90	49,562	14	11	57	18	27,627	20	16	7	58	178
91–100	86,690	8	10	49	33	47,302	12	14	5	69	178
TOTAL	35,076	17	9	54	20	19,875	25	13	7	55	1,780

Source: See table 3.1.

Note: Due to rounding, shares may not add up to 100.

[a]Comprehensive income is equal to the sum of Social Security income, private pension income, wage income, and other income. All income figures are in 1979 dollars.

[b]Social Security income in 1969 is the annuitized value of Social Security wealth. Social Security wealth was calculated from Social Security Administration data by Quinn 1981.

[c]Private pension income in 1969 is the annuitized value of private pension income estimated by Quinn 1981.

[d]Wage income consists of respondent's and spouse's wage and self-employed earnings, paid sick leave, unemployment benefits, and Worker's Compensation payments.

[e]Other income includes the annuitized value of asset wealth (stock value of stocks, bonds, savings and checking accounts, and net loans) and physical wealth (net value of home, farm, business, and real estate, minus auto and medical debts).

[f]Social Security income in 1979 includes actual payments from OASDHI.

[g]Private pension income in 1979 includes payments from railroad, military, government, and private pensions.

used to represent tastes or discrimination, such as race, but not sex, because the sample contains only men. The logarithmic form of income is
justified primarily by the facts that income tends to be distributed lognormally and that the logarithm tends to stabilize the variance. That is, persons with more human capital tend to show more variation in income,
while showing more homogeneous levels of variation in log income. The
log form is standard in labor economics.

3.2.2   Percentage Changes

By differentiating each side of equation (5), we get

$$(6) \qquad d(\ln y_t) = dy_t/y_t = (d\underline{X}'_t)\underline{\beta} + d\epsilon_t,$$

where the disturbance can change over time. We consider equation (6) in
some detail here, but first let us consider the problems caused by t's not being observed in an infinitesimal change, but rather in a finite change. Then
we should integrate equation (6) from t_0 to t_1 to obtain:

$$(7) \qquad \int_{t_0}^{t_1} d(\ln y_t) = \sum_{k=1}^{K} \beta_k \int_{t_0}^{t_1} X_{tk} dt + \int_{t_0}^{t_1} \epsilon_t \, dt.$$

The left side of equation (7) can be expressed as

$$\ln(y_{t_1}) - \ln(y_{t_2}) = \ln(y_{t_1}/y_{t_2}).$$

The right side is still a function of the changes in the values of the explanatory variables and the disturbance, so the only important effect of the in-
tegral form of the problem is to change the dependent variable.

If we wanted to estimate the coefficients of the human capital model,
we could do so in a conventional regression. That would not, however,
permit a discussion of whether the percentage change in income over the
period 1969–79 is related to the initial distribution of income, and it is this
change, which is coincident with retirement, that is of interest here. Another alternative would be to use the sort of equation specified in the first
part of this chapter, with base-year income among the regressors. Such an
equation is perfectly adequate, indeed, may be preferable, for purposes of
predicting end-year income, because as we have shown, base-year income
is highly correlated with end-year income. However, for purposes of estimating coefficients, such as a coefficient relating base-year income to percentage changes in income, such an equation is seriously flawed. This
must be the case since base-year income is almost certainly correlated with
the disturbance in end-year income. We exploit such a relationship in the
next section to construct a model that avoids the bias caused by the correlation of disturbance and regressor (usually characterized as simultaneous
equations or measurement error bias), and therefore estimate unbiased
coefficient estimates. Thus neither the basic equation (5) nor the type of

equation found in the first part of the paper is suitable for our purposes, and we require a different model, which is presented next.

3.2.3   The Stochastic Process

The first term on the right side of equation (6) or (7) is $\Sigma \beta_k \Delta X_k$, that is, the changes in the explanatory variables over the period 1969–79 weighted by the regression coefficients from a model of income. The changes in the Xs are directly measurable.

The second term is $\Delta \epsilon_t$, which requires some explanation. We assume that ϵ_t basically follows a white noise process, but not necessarily with a mean of zero, because of unexpected but nonrandom drift in the macro-economic or policy variables affecting the income of the men in our sample. Therefore, it may have a drift component α^*. However, all the persons in the RHS sample are observed for ten years, so all have a drift of $10\alpha^*$, which is replaced with a single parameter α.

Our model is formally similar to models of stock prices, which are also assumed to be distributed lognormally and to have a time-dependent error term. Note, however, that those models usually assume $\Delta \epsilon_t$ to be pure white noise. That is, it has no systematic motion up or down over time but drifts randomly. The modification here is that, with regard to income, systematic drifting is possible.

Over the period 1969–79 unexpected changes occurred in the levels of benefits under the Social Security program and in the real returns to private pensions as well as to other assets such as houses or stocks.[10] Certainly different rates of increase in the various sources of income were observed over this period. Consequently, we hypothesize that the level of income may be correlated with the unexpected change in income, because persons at different levels of income may have had systematically different portfolios of income sources. As can be seen in table 3.5 the portfolio of upper comprehensive income decile varies substantially from those of lower decile with respect to Social Security and private pensions. If the unexpected drift in income is positively correlated with income in 1969, then the rich became relatively richer. Conversely if the unexpected drift is negatively correlated with 1969 income, then the reverse is true. Note that in absolute terms an increase equal to a constant percentage gives the rich more income, while a decrease equal to a constant percentage takes more away from the rich. Thus, we parameterize the disturbance as:

$$(8) \qquad\qquad d\epsilon_t = \alpha + \delta \ln y_t + \eta_t,$$

where α is the effect of macroeconomic policy on the drift in individuals' incomes; δ links individuals' initial levels of comprehensive income to the

---

10. For a discussion of the unexpected nature of the change in Social Security benefits in the 1970s see Anderson, Burkhauser, and Quinn 1983.

unexpected changes in income; and η is a random, pure-white-noise error term.[11]

The point is that ϵ_t, the unexpected change in income, is correlated through time because slowly changing unobservable variables, such as motivation, are presumably correlated through time, and because of systematic but unexpected factors related to the level of income.

3.2.4   The Final Specification

The equation to be estimated is:

$$(9) \qquad \ln(y_{t_1}/y_{t_0}) = (d\underline{X_t})\underline{\beta} + \alpha + \delta \ln y_{t_0} + \eta_t.$$

Our only changing explanatory variable is health. As in the previous section, health is a binary variable equaling one if self-reported health goes from good to bad over the period. The other two regressors are time (the constant) and initial income.

For a regression to be free of bias, the explanatory variables must be uncorrelated with the disturbance. We assume that the Xs and the changes in the Xs are uncorrelated with the disturbance. The dependent variable is, however, correlated with the disturbance at and before time t. But most important for our analysis, the dependent variable at t is uncorrelated with future additions to the disturbance. In that case our regressions are appropriate, since the 1969 level of income is one of the regressors, but the disturbance includes only the addition over the period 1969 to 1979. This assumption is seriously flawed if future changes were expected and taken into account in 1969. If this were the case the dependent variable, log income at time t, would be correlated with future disturbances as well. However, in that event, all attempts to model income without variables representing expectations of the future would be misspecified. We argue that the changes were unexpected, so our modeling is appropriate. It represents an intermediate position between the conventional ignoring of expectations and a full-blown attempt to respecify human capital models with endogenous expectational variables.

3.2.5   Expected Signs of Coefficients

We have three independent variables in our equation. The first is the time trend. Because real income tended to fall during the period, α is ex-

---

11. That the changes were unexpected implies that they should be in the disturbance. Alternatively, one could postulate a rational expectations model in which these changes are anticipated. In such a case, expectations are present in the model determining income, since future conditions help to determine present decisions. All conventional human capital models are misspecified in that case, since they omit expectations. Even in a rational expectation model, unexpected changes will still not affect present decisions. The importance of this matter to the question of whether regressors and disturbance are uncorrelated is discussed later.

pected to be negative. This need not be the case since α represents the trend in *unexpected* income changes, not actual income changes.

Our second coefficient is most important with regard to measured inequality. If the unexpected changes during the period had a greater proportionate effect on upper-income workers, then δ should be negative. Conversely a positive sign would indicate unexpected changes had a greater effect on lower-income groups. We have no a priori judgment on the direction this term will take. The 1970s saw a major increase in Social Security retirement and health benefits which make up a larger share of the comprehensive income portfolio of lower-income workers. But the ability of higher-income workers to protect against uncertainties by adjusting their portfolios may offset that change. Our only other variable measures health deterioration over the period, and we expect that such a fall in health should decrease income.[12]

We have argued that comprehensive income is a theoretically superior measure of well-being. In measuring the effect of unexpected changes on well-being we use this measure. Nevertheless, it is still useful to compare these results with those using other income measures. Comprehensive income is divisible into two components—realized and unrealized income. It is the omitted income from unrealized assets that is the difference between our comprehensive and realized measures.

Comprehensive income and its unrealized component should be more stable than realized income, in the sense that the percentage change in unrealized income should be less responsive to the prior level of comprehensive income than the percentage change in realized income is. Complete stability would be present in an income distribution in which all changes were equal percentage increases or decreases. As to the time trend α, we do not have strong prior convictions about which components should rise or fall more, but we can compare them. Finally, with regard to health, we expect that serious medical problems would eat into wealth and substantially affect unrealized income.

3.2.6   Results

Table 3.6 displays the results of the estimation. We find that income tended to decline over the period at an annual rate of 5.0 percent for comprehensive income, 3.8 percent for realized income, and 9.2 percent for unrealized (omitted) income.[13] Thus, the sources of income not normally included in flow income fell more rapidly as far as the trend in the disturbance is concerned. However, they fell more if the initial level of income

---

12. Because we are considering a group of men who are retired over most of the period of analysis, we do not expect income to be reduced because of lost work. Rather we expect the loss to come because of increased consumption of wealth. This loss should be offset to the degree that these men have medical insurance.

13. The annual rate of change is $\exp(-\alpha/10) - 1.0$.

Table 3.6   Regressions on Changes in Income, 1969–79

Independent Variables	Comprehensive Income[a]		Realized Income[b]		Unrealized Income[c]	
	Coefficient	t-statistic	Coefficient	t-statistic	Coefficient	t-statistic
Constant	-.517	-22.25*	-.375	-12.45*	-.853	-18.74*
Comprehensive income, 1969[d]	-.301	-6.29*	-.572	-9.15*	.287	3.06*
Health change	-.038	-1.58	.016	0.51	-.108	-2.03*
R^2	.022		.046		.009	
$F_{2,\,1979}$	20.15*		43.16*		8.30*	

Source: See table 3.1.

*Indicates significance at 5 percent level.

[a]$\log\left(\dfrac{\text{comprehensive income 1979}}{\text{comprehensive income 1969}}\right)$, comprehensive income in both periods is the sum of realized and unrealized income.

[b]$\log\left(\dfrac{\text{realized income 1979}}{\text{realized income 1969}}\right)$, realized income in both periods includes wages and salary, income received from assets, and any pension and Social Security received.

[c]$\log\left(\dfrac{\text{unrealized income 1979}}{\text{unrealized income 1969}}\right)$, unrealized income in 1969 includes annuitized values of Social Security wealth, pension wealth, asset wealth and physical wealth minus asset income, Social Security and pension income received. Unrealized income in 1979 includes annuitized values of physical and asset wealth minus asset income received.

[d]Income is measured in units of $1,000s.

were higher, so they tended to move in an equalizing manner. Realized income moved strongly in an equalizing direction, and strongly enough that the same was true for comprehensive income. For each increase of $1,000 in 1969 comprehensive income, there is an estimated decrease of 0.003 in the change of log income, or a decrease of about 0.3 percent. Loosely speaking, 0.3 percent of one's income was "given back" for each increase in the base level of $1,000. This is not a large effect in absolute terms (average comprehensive income was $35,000 in 1969), and one can regard it as not important in terms of redistribution, but the direction of effect is clearly established for these data.

With reference to the comparison between realized and unrealized income, we observe that, in fact, the unrealized component was absolutely less responsive to the prior level of income, and the net result is that comprehensive income is only about half as responsive as realized income is to the prior level of income (0.572 versus 0.301). The effect is quite significant, since the signs are opposite, and each is significantly different from zero.

Health has a strong negative effect on the omitted or unrealized portion of income, a slight positive effect on realized income, and on net a negative effect on comprehensive income. The coefficient is comparable to the effect of a $13,000 rise in income. Thus, the effect is quite large relative to that of comprehensive income; a change in health for the worse has an effect equivalent to that of 37 percent of the average level of comprehensive income. However, the t-statistic is only signficant at the 85 percent level. A change of this magnitude is somewhat surprising given that the great majority of these workers were eligible for medicare or medicaid.

Two inferences can be drawn from the regressions. First, they are statistically significant; second, they explain very little of the variation. We interpret this to indicate that the disturbance in the equation for log income is primarily a standard error term, unrelated to any systematic factors. Nevertheless, the significant relationships indicate a slight but meaningful effect of the prior level of income via unexpected changes in policies and returns on assets, and of health via systematic changes in health. We consider the low R^2 as positive support for our underlying assumptions. A higher R^2 might suggest that the relationships were too strong to be "unexpected." This point is best brought out by comparing our results with those of stock price models since it is from them that our model springs. Because stocks tend to follow a random walk, a regression of the type used here to estimate their future prices would be expected to have an R^2 close to 0.0. Any systematic factors would be ferreted out by profit seekers. Thus, all systematic factors should be incorporated into expectations. In the RHS sample, however, the men could not profit much from a better prediction of the future, would have had difficulty obtaining better information, and might not have been able to change their portfolios in any case. Thus, a small but significant effect such as that found here is unlikely to have been fully anticipated.

3.3 Conclusion

Comprehensive income offers a theoretically superior method of measuring well-being and of asking questions with regard to how and why it changes over time. Those using traditional realized measures of income are likely to overstate the fall in well-being associated with retirement and to predict future income incorrectly. Finally our measure of comprehensive income was useful in showing that unexpected events appear to be "income equalizing" at least over the last decade. It also appears that a deterioration in health, even in the face of substantial government insurance protection, has an important unexpected negative effect on well-being.

Appendix

Variable	Definition
Respondent income	All wages and salary earned by respondent in 1969 in 1979 dollars.
Spouse income	All wages and salary earned by respondent's spouse in 1969 in 1979 dollars.
Asset income	Income from interest, dividends, rent, and pension payments in 1969 in 1979 dollars.
Physical wealth	Net value of house, farm, business, and real estate in 1969 in 1979 dollars.
Asset wealth	Net wealth of bonds, stock certificates, savings and checking accounts, and stock value of annuities in 1969 in 1979 dollars.
Social Security wealth	Net present value of Social Security benefit stream at 5 percent in 1969 in 1979 dollars.
Pension wealth	Net present value of pension benefit stream at 5 percent in 1969 in 1979 dollars.
Age	Respondent's age in 1969 in years.
Years retired	Number of years respondent has been retired as of 1979.
Health	Health binary that equals 1 if the respondent was in good health relative to his peers in 1969 and his health subsequently deteriorated over the period. Otherwise health equals 0.

References

Anderson, Kathryn H., Richard V. Burkhauser, and Joseph H. Quinn. 1983. Do retirement dreams come true? A rational expectations approach to the retirement decision. Vanderbilt University Working Paper Series, 83–W16.

Benus, Jacob, and James N. Morgan. 1975. Time period, unit of analysis, and income concept in the analysis of income distribution. In *The personal distribution of wealth,* ed. James D. Smith, 209–27. New York: Columbia University Press.

Burkhauser, Richard V., and James T. Wilkinson. 1983. The effect of retirement on income distribution: A comprehensive income approach. *Review of Economics and Statistics* 65:653–58.

Kotlikoff, Lawrence J. 1979. Testing the theory of Social Security and life-cycle accumulation. *American Economic Review* 69:396–410.

Kotlikoff, Lawrence J., Avia Spivak, and Lawrence H. Summers. 1982. The adequacy of savings. *American Economic Review* 72:1056–69.

Mitchell, Olivia S., and Gary S. Fields. 1982. The effects of pensions and earnings on retirement: A review essay. In *Research in Labor Economics* 5, ed. R. Ehrenberg. Greenwich, Conn.: JAI Press.

Moon, Marilyn. 1977. *The measurement of economic welfare.* New York: Academic Press.

Quinn, Joseph. 1981. The importance of Social Security and pension rights in wealth portfolios of older Americans. Paper presented at the International Association for Research on Income and Wealth Conference, Gouvieux, France.

Smeeding, Timothy. 1984. Approaches to measuring and valuing in-kind subsidies and the distribution of their benefits. In *Social Accounting for Transfers,* ed. M. Moon. NBER Studies in Income and Wealth 48. Chicago: University of Chicago Press.

Steuerle, Eugene, and Nelson McClung. 1977. Wealth and the accounting period in the measurement of means. Technical paper 6. In *The Measure of Poverty.* U.S. Department of Health, Education, and Welfare. Washington, D.C.: GPO.

Taussig, Michael. 1973. *Alternative measures of the distribution of economic welfare.* Princeton: Princeton University Press.

U.S. Department of Health, Education, and Welfare. 1973. *Vital Statistics of the United States.* Vol. 2. Washington, D.C.: GPO.

Weisbrod, Burton A., and W. Lee Hansen. 1968. An income net-worth approach to measuring economic welfare. *American Economic Review* 58:1315–29.

Zellner, Arnold. 1962. An efficient method of estimating seemingly unrelated regressions and test of aggregation bias. *Journal of the American Statistical Association* 57:348–68.

Comment   Lee A. Lillard

Burkhauser, Butler, and Wilkinson provide us with new evidence on the consequences of retirement for financial well-being. In particular they compare estimates of changes and of stability based on realized income and on their concept of comprehensive income. Realized income includes wage and salary income, income from financial assets, and government transfers. Comprehensive income is essentially the sustainable annuity income flow from the stock value of current assets. Current assets include real assets less debts, financial assets, and Social Security wealth.

Using data from the Retirement History Survey (RHS) for men working in 1969 but retired in 1979, they find that comprehensive income is more stable than realized income, in terms of position in each distribution over time or rank correlation between periods a decade apart, that the two measures of well-being are related in significantly different ways to the composition of assets, income, age, time retired, and health, and that both measures decline in real terms over the period. These results provide us with a better understanding of the effect of retirement on financial well-being by acknowledging the presence of assets available to finance consumption, whether the potential is realized or not.

In the remainder of this discussion I will suggest some areas where improvements in the current study might be realized and some areas for further study.

Some additional calculations would improve our understanding of the current study. Are the current results sensitive to assumed parameters in the calculation of the stock value of assets and the sustainable annuity flow value, in particular the discount rate and the pattern of survival probabilities? These assumptions may interact with the composition of wealth holdings, e.g., current financial assets relative to Social Security wealth, which depends crucially on survival. In addition, it would be informative to learn more about the composition of assets between relatively liquid forms such as real and financial assets that may be used (or borrowed against) to finance realized consumption and relatively illiquid assets such as the expected stream of Social Security benefits. Are the observed relationships due more to liquid or illiquid assets? To the extent these assets are liquid, and potentially available to finance current consumption, the comprehensive income measure is more relevant.

More complete use could be made of the data. First, rather than using a simple comparison of two periods a decade apart, the full panel of data on interviewing periods could be introduced to study the path of events leading to the 1969–79 comparisons and to assess the degree of period-to-peri-

Lee A. Lillard is senior economist at Rand Corporation and adjunct associate professor of economics at the University of Southern California.

od variability in these measures at the individual level. That is, to what extent are the decade differences due to systematic developments of the financial position versus more transitory variation and errors of measurement of assets and income. These notions may be formalized and their effects estimated using more periods of observation. Use of the full panel would necessitate the fuller use of the time of retirement and age of retirement, which may influence the income measures in ways not considered in this study.

Second, selection of the sample used for this study may be systematically related to the behavior under study. The sample includes men who worked in 1969 and were retired in 1979, who were married with spouse present in both years and who were not institutionalized in either period. This is a nontrivial selection criteria, even though it makes analysis simpler. The selected individuals survived a decade, their spouses survived a decade, and their financial and health status was such that they need not be institutionalized. Since survival and health, and particularly being placed in a nursing home, are major concerns of the elderly, this selection is potentially an important one. Comparisons of the survivors with those less fortunate may provide substantial additional information about the behavioral interpretation of their findings.

The stock of assets at preretirement is endogenous in that it is the result of prior labor supply and consumption choices. The change in assets over the next decade is similarly endogenous in that it results in part from the consumption (and time-of-retirement) choices of the individuals. Individuals differ in their rate of time preference, in their probability of survival over time, and in their expected health status and need for institutionalization over time. Differences in the time path of assets or comprehensive income available from it, as well as realized income, may depend crucially on these individual differences. Individuals may anticipate events that the researcher cannot. A reduction in assets or reduced comprehensive income over time may not be "bad" in the sense that it may be optimal behavior given the expected situation, time preference, and attitudes toward risk.

Burkhauser, Butler, and Wilkinson begin their paper with an interesting and relevant declaration: "Fear of living too long is paradoxically one of the major concerns of old age." This proposition is central to the issues surrounding the well-being of the elderly and changes in well-being over time. If individuals anticipate their own future—their mortality, health, and institutionalization—better than the assumed aggregate probabilities used in the analysis, then we may learn more by comparing the behavior of the healthy survivors (the sample) with the "less healthy" survivors (institutionalized) and with those not surviving (including length of survival). If individuals have informed expectations, their behavior with respect to financial matters should be systematically different. Changes in financial position occurring in the first few years of the panel (for survivors of a shorter period) may be considered in relation to forthcoming changes in health or survival status. While this is clearly beyond the scope of the current study, it may provide further insights into the relevant issues.

This chapter is suggestive of the substantial gain to be realized by analysis going beyond current realized income measures. I look forward to their further work.

4 Wealth, Realized Income, and the Measure of Well-Being

Eugene Steuerle

4.1 Introduction

All modern societies attempt to measure well-being of their people for both policy and research purposes. Government must explicitly define well-being for purposes of designing tax and welfare policies, while researchers must explicitly choose classifications by which to compare data and perform statistical analyses.

Measures of well-being involve a contrast of means with needs. This chapter falls within that set of studies that deal with the measurement of means (Steuerle and McClung 1977; Smeeding 1982; and several chapters in this volume). Changing the measure of means does not necessarily imply that households are better or worse off, nor that the government should collect less or spend more for any particular type of program. Given any standard of needs, however, it will be possible to assert that the distribution of means, and therefore of well-being, changes significantly as the measurement of means is changed.

Attention will be directed toward the measure of well-being used most widely today—realized income—and its relationship to wealth and economic income. Using a unique national sample of income tax returns matched with estate tax returns, this chapter will compare the realized property income of individuals with the associated amount of wealth that generates that income.

Eugene Steuerle is deputy director (domestic taxation) of the Office of Tax Analysis, U.S. Department of the Treasury, and economic staff coordinator for the Treasury Department Project for Fundamental Tax Reform. At the time of presentation, he was a Federal Executive Fellow at the Brookings Institution.

The author is grateful to Keith Gilmour for assistance in the design and review of tabular material. He is also indebted to Millard Munger for programming assistance, to Harvey Galper for helpful comments, and to Kirk Kimmell for help in the preparation of the manuscript.

91

The purpose of this study is twofold. First, with respect to wealth holders, realized income (with emphasis on the word *realized*) is demonstrated to be an extremely poor measure of well-being. As a consequence, substantial inequity is introduced into tax and welfare programs. If the goal of these programs is to measure real economic income, that purpose may be better served by first obtaining measures of property or wealth than realized income. Second, in reporting the initial findings of the first national estate-income collation, this chapter shows the promise of this approach to research on the relationship between wealth and income. Whatever the problems, and they are not few, this estate-income collation may provide the best national data ever assembled for studying the wealth-income relationship for persons with significant amounts of wealth.

4.1.1   Source of Data

This study uses a collation of estate tax returns, income tax returns of decedents in years before death, and income tax returns of heirs in years both prior to and following the death of the persons granting the bequests. The estate tax returns were filed in 1977 (for deaths generally in 1976 or 1977), while income tax returns were collected for years 1974 through 1980. Each estate in the sample had a gross estate of $60,000 or more ($120,000 or more for decedents dying in 1977). The collation sample was a one-in-ten subsample of the sample of over 41,000 estate tax returns used for purposes of the *Statistics of Income—Estate Tax Returns* (U.S. Department of the Treasury, Internal Revenue Service 1979) and for related wealth studies (Schwartz 1983).

While the collation sample began with 4,143 estate tax returns, in many cases there was an absence of accurate reporting of bequests made, and many income tax returns could not be found or were not filed for both decedents and heirs. For purposes of this study, therefore, two subsamples were used: decedents with income tax returns in the year prior to death (sample size, 2,924); and nonspousal heirs for whom a bequest of $50,000 or more could be determined, while income tax returns were filed in a year prior to and a year following receipt of inheritance (sample size, 1,451).

The match of a decedent's estate tax return with the previous year's income tax return allowed a direct comparison of the realized or reported income from capital with the value of capital that produced that income. Similarly, the match of a bequest amount with income tax returns of an heir in years both prior to and after receiving the inheritance allowed comparison of the change in realized or reported income with a change in wealth.

Both types of comparisons suffer from the inexact match of income with wealth. Under ideal conditions, one would want to compare income on an instantaneous flow basis with the stock of wealth at a given point in time. The estate-income collation falls short of that ideal in two respects.

First, only annual flows of income are reported. Second, accounting for wealth takes place in a period different from that in which income is measured. Because partial-year returns are often filed on behalf of decedents in year of death, obtaining an annual measure of income requires the use of an income tax return in a year prior to death. In measuring change in income for heirs, on the other hand, it was necessary to allow a sufficient time to elapse so that income from inheritances would be reflected in their income tax returns rather than returns of estates. For both decedents and heirs, therefore, the comparison of income with wealth is inexact to the extent that any wealth transfer (not reported on estate tax returns), consumption out of wealth, or wealth accumulation out of income took place between the points in time at which measurements were made. Those problems are believed to be minor for the vast majority of returns, although important in a small number of cases.

For tax accounting reasons, a net upward bias exists in the measure of realized rates of return. Valuations for estate tax purposes are typically low for reported assets, especially businesses, farms, houses, and other illiquid or infrequently traded assets. Estimates must be reasonable, but there is a strong incentive to provide the lowest among available estimates. In addition, much wealth from life insurance and pensions does not pass through estates, so estimates of value of estates and inheritances are understated. Observations are also excluded from each subsample when income tax returns of decedents or heirs could not be found; in some of these cases, the decedent or heir did not file a return because of low amounts of realized income.[1]

Finally, the collation file has not yet been merged to obtain estate tax weights; therefore, the reported data are unweighted. Fortunately, estate tax filers were sampled according to size of gross estate. Weighted results in each wealth or similar class therefore would differ little from unweighted results, and most issues of within- or between-class differences can be addressed either way.

While these problems mean that the data must be interpreted with caution, the estate-income match still offers the possibility of vast improvement in our understanding of the wealth-income relationship for persons with significant wealth holdings. An analogy might be provided by the improvement in our understanding of the wealth distribution first obtained through the efforts of Lampman (1962) and Smith and Franklin (1974). Both then and now, the advantage of using administrative data stems in part from the considerable underreporting of wealth and income from property in survey data, even surveys dedicated to the measurement of

---

1. It was not possible to distinguish between cases in which an income tax return was not filed and cases in which the return could not be found because of an invalid Social Security number.

such items. The evidence is fairly conclusive: even though there is some bias to underreport for tax purposes, population estimates of income from property or of wealth are much higher when using tax return data than survey data. As will be seen, the variation in realized rates of return is so great across taxpayers that our qualitative conclusions with respect to horizontal equity would hold even in the presence of significant bias and limitations of data.

4.2   Why Realized Income Is Used as a Measure of Well-Being

The most common measure of well-being used for both statistical and policy purposes is realized income. Realized income is used to define income tax burdens, eligibility for various tax expenditures such as deductions for cost of health care and property tax relief, amount of assistance in various welfare programs, and distributions of income by class in many, if not most, census and survey analyses. The reason for this dominance is partly the result of historical circumstances. Originally, both in England and America, ability to pay was measured by property ownership (Musgrave 1959). In modern times, however, income has come to dominate other measures such as property as the prime measure of ability to pay and eligibility to receive. A major explanation for this shift is the increasing importance of wage income to most households' well-being. When labor income for most households was thought to equal only subsistence income, was derived in the form of self-employment income, or was paid in the form of in-kind benefits such as crop sharing, it was largely treated as both nontaxable and nonmeasurable.

With the development of the modern firm and the rise of the middle class, the problems of nontaxability and nonmeasurability dwindled enormously. Wage income now was large, varied markedly from one individual to the next, and could no longer be treated merely as subsistence income. In addition, there was a significant improvement in the availability and accuracy of measures of income because wage payments were entered in two different sets of accounts: those of employers and employees. Increasingly, therefore, the measure of ability to pay or eligibility to receive has come to be defined as wage-plus-property income. This measure of means is often compared to a measure of needs such as a subsistence level of income, with income taxes being imposed principally above that level, and income-conditioned grants or subsidies targeted mainly below that level.

Property is still used today to measure well-being for certain purposes, and debates do take place over such issues as asset tests in welfare programs and methods of valuation for wealth subject to property tax and estate tax. Income has become the dominant measure of well-being for most tax and welfare purposes, nonetheless, and property-related issues have declined in relative importance. Moreover, since wage income is the major source of total income, the accuracy of the measure of wage income has tended to make income itself appear to be accurately reported or measured, at least in aggregate terms.

In recent years, there also has been increasing emphasis on providing incentives for investment and savings, perhaps even replacing an income tax with a consumption tax. This new emphasis has had an impact upon attempts to reflect more accurately property income or other current measures of wealth in the measure of well-being, especially for tax purposes. Inaccuracy of the measure of well-being, whether on an income or consumption basis, is viewed by some as an insignificant issue. Although theoretically one can argue that improvement in the measure of property or property income need have no impact on marginal tax rates paid on returns to capital, it is sometimes feared that improvements in the measure of property income will not result simply in a more uniform treatment of such income, but also in an increase in the taxes paid on returns to capital. As one example, the accelerated cost recovery system (ACRS) was designed with little concern over the actual rates of depreciation of assets. The word *depreciation* was deliberately omitted in 1981 tax changes in favor of the term *cost recovery* to make clear that the accurate measure of income was no longer a policy goal. We will return in section 4.5 to the question of whether it is possible to move closer to the goal of horizontal equity regardless of the choice between consumption and income taxes.

4.2.1 The Realization Base

In one sense the switch to income as a measure of well-being was as much a result of, as a cause of, prevalent accounting practices. Accounting practices were also extremely influential in determining that the measure of income to be used for most policy, as well as statistical purposes would be based primarily upon realizations. Accounting for income, with a number of exceptions, has been associated with the realized payment and receipt of cash. The exceptions apply primarily at the business level, where accrual accounting is applied to such items as inventories and accounts receivable, and investment in plant, equipment, and buildings is treated differently from other expenses.[2] At the household level, however, measures of income for tax, welfare, and other purposes have tended to be recognized only when they show up in the form of cash. (This cash flow logic by the way, also helps explain the reluctance to count payments of in-kind benefits in the measure of income.)

It is well known that measuring income only when it shows up as household cash flow falls short in several respects of a Haig-Simons definition

---

2. Even at the business level, major items of income such as accrued capital gains and nominal interest payments and receipts are measured essentially by a cash flow criterion.

of economic income. The measure ignores implicit flows of services from housing and durables, accruals (less realizations) of gains and losses on assets, and often accruals of rights and services provided through insurance and pension plans. In addition, in an inflationary environment, a cash-flow-based measure tends to reflect nominal returns from assets, not real returns. Real payments and receipts of interest, for instance, are overstated by the inflationary component of the interest rate. Traditional measures of income of households are distorted, therefore, by nonrealizations of service flows, gains on assets, and accruals of benefits in certain institutional accounts, as well as by the failure to make proper adjustments for inflation.

In 1979 the income from over 80 percent of assets was found to benefit from one tax preference or another. Most of these preferences were a direct result of the tendency to recognize property income only when it showed up in the form of cash flow. As a result, only about 30 percent of the net real returns from capital were found to be reported on individual tax returns (Steuerle 1982). In addition, although most private payments of interest are deducted on tax returns, only about one-half of all interest receipts are taxed (Steuerle 1983c). These findings help support the view that at the individual level, the recognition of income from capital is in many ways a voluntary event for both tax and other purposes.

The voluntariness of the tax is actually a function of consumption needs (relative to income), risk, and knowledge. Put another way, the individual tax (and loss of benefits or implicit tax in welfare systems) on capital income is in part a tax on liquidity, risk reduction and diversification, simplicity, and ignorance. More than half of all interest and dividend receipts reported on individual tax returns are reported by taxpayers aged sixty-five and over. The elderly realize a greater percentage of their income than other wealth holders, although as a group they do not appear to draw down their wealth (Menchik and David 1983). Persons recognizing income from property are often in need of current receipts or liquid assets to cover consumption needs in the near future. For the person anticipating that savings may be needed soon, risk can also be reduced substantially by increasing the percentage of interest-bearing assets and by reducing the percentage of other assets in the portfolio. Those who realize capital gains or interest income also have greater opportunity for diversification relative to those who hold onto unrealized gains.

For many taxpayers, however, the tax is hardly paid after elaborate calculations of some optimally designed portfolio that achieves the maximum-expected after-tax rate of return. For these taxpayers, and to some extent for all taxpayers, the tax is merely a tax on simplicity and ignorance.

It is not hard to find examples. Many persons fail to achieve tax savings obtainable by switching to assets of equal yield and equal risk, but with greater tax preference. Employer contributions to pensions can substitute for employee contributions; annuities with withdrawal rights can replace savings accounts; direct shareownership can replace ownership of mutual funds that recognize capital gains frequently, and so forth. Ownership can also be transferred among family members, a practice used less frequently than possible both by taxpayers and certain welfare (principally elderly Medicaid) recipients. The persons paying the additional direct or implicit taxes may find their time too valuable to search out alternative mechanisms for achieving tax savings and government benefits; they may find it distasteful to play socially unproductive games; or they may simply be ignorant of the laws.[3]

The voluntary nature of capital income realization does not imply that the total tax paid on returns from capital is too high or too low, nor that total welfare payments should be larger or smaller. Such issues are not addressed here and, to be treated properly, would require consideration of measures of needs, as well as the ways in which the various tax and welfare systems combine or stack on top of each other. What the voluntary nature of capital income recognition will imply, however, is that the taxes paid and benefits received will vary tremendously among persons in fairly identical circumstances, and that income classifiers in statistical analyses will be inaccurate for many purposes.

4.3   A Comparison of Realized Income and Wealth

Aggregate data on income recognition lends support to the notion that substantial horizontal inequity is created when tax and welfare systems base the measure of well-being in part on recognized property income. To reinforce this view, we now turn to microdata on households.

Our first comparison of wealth and income is between wealth in estates of decedents and their reported income in the year prior to death. Table 4.1 summarizes the sources of income and wealth for this sample. As is immediately apparent, by far the most important sources of recognized capital income are dividends and interest. Realized rates of return on farms and business assets are especially low, especially when it is noted that reported farm and business income represents returns to labor as well as capital.[4]

Table 4.2 narrows our focus to a comparison of gross capital income subject to tax (GCIST) and wealth. The realized rate of return declines significantly as wealth increases, reaching a low of 2.2 percent for decedents

---

3. One can model ignorance as a cost of acquiring information. If we assume that the cost of acquiring information rises with one's ignorance of the tax and welfare laws, however, then the tax and welfare systems still impose taxes that rise with ignorance. These taxes can be paid directly to the government or indirectly to advisors.

4. For a separate analysis of the returns to owners of farms and closely held businesses, see Steuerle 1983a.

Table 4.1   **All Decedents: Average Income and Wealth by Source**

Income by Source	Average Amount of Item	Item as a Percentage of	
		Net Income Subject to Tax	Net Worth
Salaries and wages	$8,496	25.51	1.63
Dividends	10,425	31.30	2.00
Interest	6,951	20.87	1.33
Business (nonfarm)	1,460	4.38	.28
Farm	−122	−.37	−.02
Partnership	644	1.93	.12
Small business corporations	44	.13	.01
Capital gain distributions	11	.03	—
Net capital gain	2,725	8.18	.52
Supplemental gain	22	.07	—
Pensions and annuities	1,220	3.66	.23
Rents	1,751	5.26	.34
Royalties	771	2.32	.15
Estate and trusts	879	2.64	.17
Alimony	34	.10	.01
Other	−744	−2.23	−.14
Gross income subject to tax	34,339	103.10	6.59
Less: Interest deductions	1,032	3.10	.20
Net income subject to tax	33,308	100.00	6.39
Plus: State income tax returns	51	.15	.01
Less: Exemptions	2,196	6.59	.42
Other deductions	9,224	27.69	1.77
Adjustments	227	.68	.04
Taxable income	22,970	68.96	4.41

Wealth by Source	Average Amount of Item	Item as a Percentage of Total Wealth
Corporate stock	$228,813	40.7
Real estate	125,337	22.3
Cash, bonds, notes and mortgages	153,925	27.4
Noncorporate business assets	15,371	2.7
Other assets	39,185	7.0
Total wealth (total estate)	562,632	100.0
Less: Debts	41,208	7.3
Net worth (economic estate)	521,424	92.7

Note: Measures of income are from decedent's individual income tax return filed for year prior to death. Measures of wealth are from decedent's estate tax return.

with assets of $2.5 million or more. What is equally interesting is the large variation in realized rates of return in every wealth class. At least 5 percent of each wealth class report zero or negative returns from capital, while at least 23 percent of each class report rates of return between 0 percent and 3 percent.

Table 4.2 All Decedents: Gross Capital Income Subject to Tax as a Percentage of Wealth (amounts in thousands of dollars)

Size of Wealth	Total Number	Average Wealth	Average Gross Capital Income	Gross Capital Income as a Percentage of Wealth	Gross Capital Income Subject to Tax as a Percentage of Wealth					
					Zero or Negative			Under 3 Percent		
					Number	Wealth	Gross Capital Income	Number	Wealth	Gross Capital Income
Under $100,000	519	72	9	12.4	41	3,269	−43	120	9,620	140
$100,000 under $250,000	980	164	10	6.1	66	10,460	−140	263	42,429	547
$250,000 under $500,000	445	344	20	5.9	22	7,597	−139	102	35,261	532
$500,000 under $1,000,000	668	675	34	5.1	39	25,608	−775	168	114,206	1,273
$1,000,000 under $2,500,000	255	1,458	70	4.8	18	25,638	−144	75	110,868	1,656
$2,500,000 or more	57	8,272	183	2.2	9	48,197	−578	23	314,916	1,211
All decedents	2,924	563	26	4.5	195	120,770	−2,116	751	627,302	5,361

Gross Capital Income Subject to Tax as a Percentage of Wealth (continued)

Size of Wealth	3 Percent under 5 Percent			5 Percent under 7 Percent			7 Percent under 10 Percent		
	Number	Wealth	Gross Capital Income	Number	Wealth	Gross Capital Income	Number	Wealth	Gross Capital Income
Under $100,000	99	7,930	315	57	4,340	260	48	3,850	331
$100,000 under $250,000	235	39,291	1,541	161	27,583	1,623	98	15,943	1,360
$250,000 under $500,000	109	37,055	1,487	92	31,282	1,808	54	18,931	1,575
$500,000 under $1,000,000	204	139,757	5,692	119	78,818	4,628	70	47,243	3,852
$1,000,000 under $2,500,000	93	134,038	5,337	29	41,848	2,436	22	32,441	2,618
$2,500,000 or more	14	71,788	2,591	7	24,838	1,462	2	6,128	507
All decedents	754	429,860	16,964	465	208,707	12,216	294	124,534	10,244

Table 4.2 (continued)

| | Gross Capital Income Subject to Tax as a Percentage of Wealth (continued) | | | | | |
| | 10 Percent under 15 Percent | | | 15 Percent or More | | |
Size of Wealth	Number	Wealth	Gross Capital Income	Number	Wealth	Gross Capital Income
Under $100,000	42	2,968	358	112	5,192	3,237
$100,000 under $250,000	81	13,338	1,579	76	11,969	3,232
$250,000 under $500,000	40	14,490	1,716	26	8,398	1,916
$500,000 under $1,000,000	39	25,314	3,059	29	19,720	4,627
$1,000,000 under $2,500,000	11	17,137	1,925	7	9,790	3,999
$2,500,000 or more	—	—	—	2	5,645	1,751
All decedents	213	73,247	8,636	252	60,716	18,761

Rates of return of 10 percent or more are reported by 30 percent of the lowest-wealth class, with the proportion dropping to 4 percent for those with assets of $2.5 million or more. A separate analysis (not shown in the tables) was made on persons reporting unusually high rates of return. Capital gains were only a minor factor in explaining these rates; dividend and interest income, on the other hand, were implausibly high relative to total assets. Problems of accounting period differences or estate tax valuation are probably most significant for this group. That is, either many of these persons underreport wealth, or they transfer or consume wealth between accounting periods.

In table 4.3 we turn to a sample of beneficiaries other than surviving spouses, and compare the change in reported capital income between 1975 and 1978 to the amount of inheritance received in 1976 or 1977. Table 4.3 does not show any strong relationship between amount of inheritance and realized rate of return, but it does show striking differences within inheritance classes. In each class (except one class with a sample size of three), between 17 percent and 32 percent of all inheritors actually show a negative or zero change in gross capital income subject to tax. On the other hand, about 12 percent of those with inheritances under $250,000 and 7 percent of those with inheritances over $250,000 show a change in capital income that was equal to 20 percent or more of the recorded change in wealth.

Since reported capital income would normally increase over time regardless of inheritances, the number of inheritors reporting low or negative amounts of change becomes even more striking. Between 1975 and 1978, the average individual income tax return showed an increase of about 27 percent (from $1,752 to $2,218) in reported capital income, as contrasted with a 69 percent increase (from $12,792 to $21,562) for our sample (see table 4.4). If the change in interest rates, dividend rates, and growth in wealth in the economy were to have approximately equal effect on realized returns for both groups, capital income of inheritors also would have grown by 27 percent in absence of the inheritances. Thirty-nine percent (27 percent/69 percent) of the increase in reported capital income would then be attributable to factors other than the inheritances themselves.

Although table 4.3 shows little difference in realized rates of return across inheritors by size of inheritance, table 4.5 provides some explanation. The ratio of the change in income to change in wealth is shown to decline significantly with an increase in the amount of capital income reported prior to the receipt of the inheritance. That is, beneficiaries with substantial amounts of realized income from wealth prior to the receipt of their inheritances were much quicker to convert their inheritances into assets for which the rate of income recognition would be low. Three consistent explanations can be offered for such behavior: (1) those with more capital

Table 4.3   Change in Gross Capital Income Subject to Tax as a Percentage of Inheritance Received (amounts in dollars)

Size of Inheritance	Number of Beneficiaries	Gross Capital Income Subject to Tax		Change in		Income Change as a Percentage of Inheritance
		1975	1978	Income 1975–78	Inheritance Received	
Under $100,000	751	7,427,011	10,161,407	2,734,396	52,935,141	5.17
$100,000 under $250,000	521	7,693,609	11,823,199	4,129,590	80,309,871	5.14
$250,000 under $500,000	134	1,615,962	5,603,513	3,987,551	45,671,922	8.73
$500,000 under $1,000,000	42	1,506,610	2,874,181	1,367,571	28,563,514	4.79
$1,000,000 under $2,500,000	3	318,062	823,375	505,313	3,603,179	14.02
$2,500,000 or more	—	—	—	—	—	—
TOTAL	1,451	18,561,254	31,285,675	12,724,421	211,083,627	6.03

Change in Gross Capital Income Subject to Tax as a Percentage of Inheritance

Size of Inheritance	Zero or Negative			Under 5 Percent		
	Number of Beneficiaries	Change in Income	Inheritance Received	Number of Beneficiaries	Change in Income	Inheritance Received
Under $100,000	242	−2,854,798	16,997,682	148	294,188	10,248,779
$100,000 under $250,000	157	−2,079,446	23,213,559	122	573,490	19,487,771
$250,000 under $500,000	31	−371,890	10,784,633	44	434,550	14,924,315
$500,000 under $1,000,000	7	−43,158	5,002,242	21	363,306	14,293,016
$1,000,000 under $2,500,000	—	—	—	—	—	—
$2,500,000 or more	—	—	—	—	—	—
TOTAL	437	−5,349,292	55,998,116	335	1,665,534	58,953,881

Change in Gross Capital Income Subject to Tax as a Percentage of Inheritance (continued)

Size of Inheritance	5 Percent under 10 Percent			10 Percent under 15 Percent		
	Number of Beneficiaries	Change in Income	Inheritance Received	Number of Beneficiaries	Change in Income	Inheritance Received
Under $100,000	139	759,489	10,184,132	75	659,587	5,436,714
$100,000 under $250,000	110	1,314,997	17,805,773	56	1,050,233	8,529,982
$250,000 under $500,000	34	801,092	11,374,375	10	378,947	3,435,351
$500,000 under $1,000,000	8	364,623	5,392,852	3	211,936	1,879,189
$1,000,000 under $2,500,000	2	152,494	2,465,985	—	—	—
$2,500,000 or more	—	—	—	—	—	—
TOTAL	293	3,392,695	47,223,117	144	2,300,703	19,281,236

Change in Gross Capital Income Subject to Tax as a Percentage of Inheritance (continued)

Size of Inheritance	15 Percent under 20 Percent			20 Percent under 30 Percent		
	Number of Beneficiaries	Change in Income	Inheritance Received	Number of Beneficiaries	Change in Income	Inheritance Received
Under $100,000	34	405,801	2,355,276	43	755,138	3,085,816
$100,000 under $250,000	34	908,818	5,262,143	18	630,784	2,618,485
$250,000 under 500,000	6	317,876	1,821,144	3	223,257	1,022,271
$500,000 under $1,000,000	—	—	—	3	314,545	1,468,956
$1,000,000 under $2,500,000	—	—	—	—	—	—
$2,500,000 or more	—	—	—	—	—	—
TOTAL	74	1,632,495	9,438,563	66	1,923,724	8,205,528

Table 4.3 (continued)

Change in Gross Capital Income Subject to Tax as a Percentage of Inheritance (continued)

| | 30 Percent or More | | |
	Number of Beneficiaries	Change in Income	Inheritance Received
Size of Inheritance			
Under $100,000	70	2,714,991	4,626,742
$100,000 under $250,000	24	1,730,714	3,392,158
$250,000 under $500,000	6	2,203,719	2,309,833
$500,000 under $1,000,000	2	509,138	1,654,453
$1,000,000 under $2,500,000			
$2,500,000 or more	—	—	—
TOTAL	102	7,158,562	11,983,186

Note: Table includes beneficiaries other than surviving spouses.

Table 4.4   **Average Net Capital Income Subject to Tax, 1975 and 1978**

Item	All Individual Income Tax Returns		Beneficiaries Other Than Surviving Spouses	
	1975	1978	1975	1978
Dividends	266	336	3,807	7,344
Interest	528	682	2,427	4,810
Business	679	829	2,627	3,767
Capital and other gains	185	273	1,748	2,493
Rents and royalties	63	64	1,566	1,587
Estates and trusts	31	34	617	1,560
Gross capital income subject to tax	1,752	2,218	12,792	21,561
Less: Interest deductions	473	676	1,675	2,357
Net capital income subject to tax	1,279	1,542	11,117	19,205

Sources: For all returns, Statistics of Income, Individual Income Tax Returns for 1975 and 1978. For beneficiaries, all identifiable beneficiaries (included in the subject study) who received benefits of $50,000 or more and who filed income tax returns for *both* 1975 and 1978.

income in 1975 faced higher marginal tax rates and therefore had more of an incentive to convert or hold their inheritances in the form of preferred assets; (2) those with greater amounts of capital income were more likely to be savers and accumulators and, in any case, would be less likely to need the income from their inheritances for near-term consumption purposes; (3) many of those owning substantial amounts of capital would already be engaged in tax-induced portfolio shifting and have access to investment advice, whereas inheritors without previous wealth accumulation more likely would react only with a significant time lag to the tax incentives to hold preferred assets.

Since the realized rate of return declines with an increase in 1975 capital income, it should not surprise us that the percentage of returns showing a negative or zero change in capital income would actually rise with an increase in 1975 capital income. In fact, if one calculates returns reporting negative or zero changes in income as a percentage of total returns with similar amounts of 1975 capital income, a type of U-shaped curve emerges. At the bottom, 40 percent of those reporting zero or negative 1975 capital income show even more negative capital income by 1978 after receiving inheritances of $50,000 or more. In the middle, those with $5,000 to $7,500 in 1975 capital income have the smallest percentage of returns, 17 percent, showing a negative change after receiving their inheritance. At the top, 49 percent of those with $100,000 or more of 1975 capital income show less (or the same) capital income in 1978.

Table 4.5 Change in Gross Capital Income Subject to Tax as a Percentage of Inheritance Received by Size of Gross Capital Income Subject to Tax (amounts in dollars)

Size of Gross Capital Income Subject to Tax in 1975	Number of Beneficiaries	Change in Income 1975–78	Inheritance Received	Income Change as a Percentage of Inheritance	Change in Gross Capital Income Subject to Tax as a Percentage of Inheritance — Zero or Negative		
					Number of Beneficiaries	Change in Income	Inheritance
Zero or negative	200	3,564,235	25,426,276	14.02	79	−316,980	8,468,557
$1 under $2,500	473	2,716,533	56,089,179	4.84	132	−271,430	15,089,443
$2,500 under $5,000	157	1,393,149	21,812,321	6.39	32	−138,315	4,426,021
$5,000 under $7,500	99	1,470,276	16,256,501	9.04	17	−13,640	1,883,314
$7,500 under $10,000	72	593,570	9,403,363	6.31	17	−74,386	1,776,119
$10,000 under $15,000	100	955,851	14,614,693	6.54	26	−279,450	3,622,226
$15,000 under $20,000	71	687,683	12,707,604	5.41	18	−246,667	3,157,892
$20,000 under $30,000	88	606,954	16,417,317	3.70	33	−610,026	5,549,910
$30,000 under $50,000	78	74,003	12,597,643	.59	35	−752,210	4,469,510
$50,000 under $100,000	76	740,300	14,293,421	5.18	30	−1,086,604	3,856,196
$100,000 or more	37	−78,133	11,465,309	−.68	18	−1,559,584	3,968,928
TOTAL	1,451	12,724,421	211,083,627	6.03	437	−5,349,929	55,998,116

Change in Gross Capital Income Subject to Tax as a Percentage of Inheritance

Size of Gross Capital Income Subject to Tax in 1975	Under 5 Percent			5 Percent under 10 Percent		
	Number of Beneficiaries	Change in Income	Inheritance	Number of Beneficiaries	Change in Income	Inheritance
Zero or negative	33	208,051	6,138,233	24	226,315	3,204,985
$1 under $2,500	150	537,712	19,387,097	113	939,439	13,784,498

$2,500 under $5,000	48	217,505	7,286,223	41	395,684	5,383,093
$5,000 under $7,500	27	150,513	5,308,098	30	432,486	6,122,792
$7,500 under $10,000	17	81,559	2,987,902	13	140,136	1,181,693
$10,000 under $15,000	19	116,850	4,030,581	21	215,045	2,975,436
$15,000 under $20,000	13	119,533	3,880,828	15	247,900	3,342,123
$20,000 under $30,000	13	127,667	4,995,503	11	139,487	1,676,855
$30,000 under $50,000	9	40,151	2,309,102	13	267,703	3,577,919
$50,000 under $100,000	3	24,356	826,337	12	388,500	5,273,723
$100,000 or more	3	41,637	1,803,977			
TOTAL	335	1,665,534	58,953,881	293	3,392,695	47,223,117

Change in Gross Capital Income Subject to Tax as a Percentage of Inheritance (continued)

Size of Gross Capital Income Subject to Tax in 1975	10 Percent under 15 Percent			15 Percent under 20 Percent		
	Number of Beneficiaries	Change in Income	Inheritance	Number of Beneficiaries	Change in Income	Inheritance
Zero or negative	19	204,710	1,687,495	17	379,479	5,173,664
$1 under $2,500	37	481,917	3,993,123	14	264,787	1,537,155
$2,500 under $5,000	18	351,585	3,107,855	4	96,429	581,104
$5,000 under $7,500	11	143,625	1,196,516	6	101,321	569,838
$7,500 under $10,000	11	226,457	1,757,583	8	100,420	579,802
$10,000 under $15,000	12	157,298	1,378,723	5	113,922	641,633
$15,000 under $20,000	7	82,745	726,400	5	107,443	571,237
$20,000 under $30,000	12	247,563	2,036,655	5	147,587	899,864
$30,000 under $50,000	5	82,683	689,505	5	122,043	736,769
$50,000 under $100,000	7	184,108	1,541,160	5	199,064	1,147,497
$100,000 or more	5	138,012	1,166,221			
TOTAL	144	2,300,703	19,281,236	74	1,632,495	9,438,563

Table 4.5 (continued)

Size of Gross Capital Income Subject to Tax in 1975	Change in Gross Capital Income Subject to Tax as a Percentage of Inheritance (continued)					
	20 Percent under 30 Percent			30 Percent or More		
	Number of Beneficiaries	Change in Income	Inheritance	Number of Beneficiaries	Change in Income	Inheritance
Zero or negative	10	218,827	933,155	18	2,643,833	2,820,187
$1 under $2,500	14	295,789	1,250,384	13	468,319	1,047,479
$2,500 under $5,000	5	122,746	478,890	9	347,515	729,135
$5,000 under $7,500	2	45,482	186,458	6	610,489	989,485
$7,500 under $10,000	4	76,600	308,113	2	42,784	112,151
$10,000 under $15,000	8	277,136	1,235,791	9	355,050	730,303
$15,000 under $20,000	4	83,809	304,938	9	292,920	724,186
$20,000 under $30,000	7	195,190	836,729	7	359,486	511,801
$30,000 under $50,000	3	80,009	293,482	8	233,624	521,356
$50,000 under $100,000	7	213,591	898,632	14	907,080	1,654,220
$100,000 or more	2	314,545	1,478,956	7	897,462	2,142,873
TOTAL	66	1,923,724	8,205,528	102	7,158,562	11,983,176

Note: Table includes beneficiaries other than surviving spouses.

This finding is consistent with the observation that there are many wealthy taxpayers who report low or negative amounts of capital income because of substantial investment in tax-preferred assets or tax shelters of various sorts. They probably invest their inheritances in a similar manner. Those with significant amounts of reported capital income, on the other hand, include the wealthiest of taxpayers; they are also quite capable of limiting their increase in taxable income through sophisticated portfolio shifting. Those in the middle, however, often fall into neither category and include many whose experience of owning financial assets is confined principally to holding deposits in financial institutions. While this last group of individuals may also be likely to invest in owner-occupied housing—one of the best shelters of all—housing purchases are likely to take place only in discrete intervals and occur infrequently within a year or two after receiving an inheritance.

In summary, at least for persons receiving significant inheritances ($50,000 or more) and for persons who eventually leave sizeable estates ($60,000 or more), the measure of realized income from capital is likely to have only a small relationship to their economic rate of return from assets or any other accepted measure of well-being based on property income or property. Differences among households in realized rates of return are quite large in all wealth classes.

4.4   Horizontal Equity: Some Theoretical Considerations

We have argued that the recognition of income from capital is partly a voluntary event and, therefore, that the realized return from capital will vary across persons of equal circumstance, whether measured by equal economic income, equal wealth, or similar classifier of well-being. Our data showed such large variations in realized rates of return across taxpayers that using realized property income as a basis for measuring equals in statistical analyses, as well as tax and welfare programs, must be called into serious question.

One cannot address this topic, however, without turning to some of the theoretical arguments against the existence of horizontal inequity. "With multiple abilities or different tastes," as Feldstein notes, "any feasible tax on income or consumption will violate horizontal equity" (1976b, p. 129). Abstracting from the general case, however, it is then argued that if persons differ only in their endowment of a single type of ability, but have the same tastes, there will be no horizontal inequity. In the extreme case, of course, this argument would be hard to refute if it were assumed that equals were so alike in every respect—abilities, tastes, and outcomes—that there was no difference among them, including taxes paid and transfers received.

The first qualification to the argument must therefore come when persons with equal abilities and equal tastes are at least allowed to have different outcomes because of luck, uncertainty, and risk. Persons with equal abilities and tastes, for instance, might still purchase different assets with equal expected returns and equal risk. Once we introduce some degree of randomness to the returns from engaging in various forms of (investment) behavior, ex post results will start to deviate from ex ante expectations.

If tax and welfare systems, as well as statistical analyses, were to be designed on the basis of ex ante conditions, there would be much less need for many of them. In simplest terms, if all persons start out with equal opportunities in life, and several flips of the coin determine eventual well-being, a horizontally equitable tax or welfare system designed on an ex ante basis would tax everyone equally and grant everyone an equal amount of transfers. In that sense, except for required governmental goods and services such as defense, much of the tax-transfer system would be redundant and unnecessary. If, however, taxes, transfers, and statistical analyses are directed at ex post results, then they cannot ignore the issues of luck, risk, and uncertainty, nor can they treat those who have gambled and won the same as those who have gambled and lost.

Part of the argument against horizontal inequity also relies on what will be labeled here the *market compensation effect*. Even if persons purchase assets with different degrees of preference in tax or welfare systems, under certain assumptions (sometimes implicit), they will receive the same after-tax rewards from those purchases. The market compensates purchasers of nonpreferred assets by equilibrating after-tax rates of return across assets, while differentials in tax rates are then reflected in different before-tax rates of return on assets.[5]

A second qualification must therefore be made if the assumptions of the model do not hold in practice. Suppose that taxpayers are taxed under a progressive tax system or one in which there are substantial numbers of investors (such as tax-exempt institutions or foreign investors). Then it is not at all clear that after-tax rates of return will equilibrate across assets with different degrees of tax preference. Any movement up in the price of an asset A or asset B to equalize after-tax rates of return for a given group of taxpayers will give an incentive for arbitrage between A and B by tax-exempt investors (or investors in other tax brackets). For instance, foreign investors may turn to future markets, short sales, and other financial mechanisms to arbitrage between the assets whenever before-tax rates of

5. For an excellent model of the extent to which such market compensation might take place in a progressive tax system, as well as the implicit taxes paid and transfers received under certain conditions, see Galper and Toder 1984. For other portfolio effects, see Bailey 1974 and Blume, Crockett, and Friend 1974.

return begin to diverge. Theory alone cannot determine whether this financial arbitrage dominates the tax-induced tendency for before-tax rates of return to differ according to the preferences given various assets, and one must resort in part to studies of institutions and empirical data to try to find an answer.[6]

What the data show rather conclusively is that preferred assets generally have higher economic rates of return than nonpreferred assets (e.g., for corporate stock, see Ibbotson and Sinquefield 1982; for farms, see U.S. Department of Agriculture 1981).[7] In contradiction to the simple market compensation argument, interest-bearing assets usually have offered the lowest economic rate of return, yet at the same time are accompanied (for each investor) by the highest tax rate because of the inclusion of the entire inflationary component of the interest rate in income subject to tax. Even if the reasons for this result are partly institutional—statutory limitations of interest rates or the habitual tendency of many lenders and borrowers to require a higher before-tax rate of return on business investment than on loans financing that investment—the designer of a tax or welfare program or the statistical observer cannot assume away such differences.

Our own data also support the notion that those with lower realized rates of return have generally achieved higher economic rates of return. The very presence of large amounts of wealth means that the top wealth holders are likely to have been persons who were successful, rather than unsuccessful, in their investment. Yet at the same time, these are the same individuals holding the assets with the greatest amount of tax preference at the household level.

A further complication is added, however, once it is recognized that the assets with the greatest amount of tax preference are often the most risky, at least over a short period of time. One might argue that the compensation to holders of nonpreferred assets is hidden by this risk adjustment. Indeed, once account is made for risk, it is hard to deny that some compensation may have taken place through the lowering of economic rates of

6. A related issue is the effect of taxes on interest rates, especially in a period of inflation. Because inflation raises the effective tax rate on real income from interest-bearing assets, and because income from these assets is more vulnerable than other assets to this inflation-induced tax, one might initially expect the interest rate to rise by a multiple of the increase in the inflation rate. In almost all attempts to explain the effect of inflation and taxes on observed interest rates (e.g., Darby 1975; Tanzi 1980; Peek 1982), however, it is assumed incorrectly that the tax system is proportional or, through use of average marginal tax rates, effectively proportional for all investors, both domestic and foreign. This assumption prevents the type of financial arbitrage discussed above from working to reduce the increase in the interest rate. In addition, the failure to take into account the extent to which interest is deducted at a higher tax rate than it is included in income, as well as the extent to which receipts are never counted at all (Steuerle 1984), leads to a misestimation of average marginal rate.

7. An exception, of course, is provided by tax-exempt bonds, but even wealthy individuals generally hold only a small percentage of their assets in tax-exempt bonds. See Schwartz 1983.

return on risky, but tax-preferred, assets relative to the rates paid on other assets; however, there is no evidence, either theoretical or empirical, that this compensation is complete. Partly because of financial arbitrage and partly because of institutional factors, for instance, it would be quite difficult to provide full compensation to holders of interest-bearing assets if interest rates had to rise above the rate of return on other financial assets such as stock.

In deciding whether compensation for taxes paid takes place through equalization of after-tax rates of return, the obvious voluntary nature of the tax system also must be taken into account. It is simply not possible to argue that two persons owning the same stock receive a different economic rate of return or face a different risk because one recognizes capital gains and the other does not, nor that a person who finds a way to deposit and withdraw money from an annuity account faces a different risk or return than a person who engages in the same behavior at a bank. The greater the voluntariness of the tax, the less there can be any compensation through market adjustments to those who pay a higher rate of tax on the same income.

In summary, horizontal inequity is unimportant in a world in which tastes are so similar among equals that they purchase exactly the same assets and one is concerned with ex ante rather than ex post distributions of welfare. By the same token, all tax and welfare systems can be shown to have some degree of horizontal inequity under real-world assumptions of several abilities or different tastes. Between these two worlds lies the world of the designer of a tax or welfare system and the statistical analyst, both of whom must classify individuals in categories of equals primarily on the basis of means relative to needs, but not tastes. This designer or analyst must take into account luck, risk and uncertainty, ex post results, the inability of the financial markets to fully compensate holders of non-tax-preferred assets, and differences in taxes or benefits among individuals holding essentially the same assets, but having different patterns of recognition of income from those assets.

4.5   Implications for Research and Policy

There are several research and policy implications to the poor relationship between the realized rate of return and the economic income, wealth, or similar measure of well-being of the household. The first of the research implications is in many ways the most obvious, but in other ways the most difficult to handle. A statistical analysis of household characteristics, government payments, or taxes can be very misleading when it uses realized income as a variable or classifier. The researcher may be aware of the misleading nature of the data, but in few cases will his readers have a similar level of understanding. The problem is difficult because the correction often can be made only by imputation of other information. Because imputation is statistically imprecise, it often reduces bias only by adding errors of measurement to a file.

Studies such as the estate-income match help us to make the imputations that are necessary. Because we can obtain fairly good information on the relationship between realized income and wealth, we can enhance our ability to take files with only reported income from property and make imputations of wealth onto those files through the investment income approach to wealth estimation (Atkinson and Harrison 1978, p. 171). Imputations of economic income will be more difficult, but, once wealth is estimated, independent studies of returns to ownership of stock, land, housing, and other assets can also be used.

Information on the ratio of realized income to asset value can also help to correct measures of the degree of inequality in society or the count of those in poverty (e.g., U.S. Bureau of the Census 1981). From the type of data reported here, one can get an idea of the number of persons with substantial wealth who report low amounts of realized income from capital. This data must be supplemented at the bottom end of the distribution. Here survey data have a better chance of filling the void, both because wage income will tend to dominate property income no matter what the error and because there are usually fewer types of assets held and, except for homes and pensions, lesser amounts of unrealized income for which to account.

Proper measurement of property and property income is crucial for policy purposes as well. Welfare programs using realized income as a measure of means would probably be better off abandoning altogether the measure of realized income (except as a compliance check of actual property ownership) and turning instead to a measure of ability based upon wage income and property. For instance, an estimate of expected economic income from net worth, a fraction of net worth, or the annuity value of net worth could be added to wage income. Any of these measures would appear to be a more accurate, and less horizontally inequitable, measure of means than wage income plus realized income from property. Such a shift would redistribute welfare benefits more toward the longer-term poor and those with lesser amounts of wealth (Steuerle and McClung 1977). This approach also would have the advantage of no longer separating homes from other assets, and it could eliminate the need for separate asset tests with arbitrary cutoff or notch points. In addition, it would solve the problem of treating interest income as real income no matter what the rate of inflation, thus requiring welfare recipients to spend down their wealth at different rates in different years. These corrections need not add nor subtract to total welfare payments, but can be done in a way to make more equal the distribution of such payments across households of equal means relative to needs.

As for the tax system, better measurement of property or property income is certainly necessary if the base of the tax is meant to be economic income. Better measurement would require some substantial changes in the tax laws, including accurate measurement of economic depreciation, indexing or approximate indexing of different types of returns from capital, and movement toward an accrual rather than a realization base. By the same token, corporate, individual, and property taxes would need to be better integrated. One tax could be meant as a substitute for another tax, but an integrated design would need to eliminate conditions whereby some persons paid double taxes, while others with equal incomes paid no tax at all. Some of these steps would tend to raise taxes and some would lower them, but that should not be allowed to detract from the fact that it is possible to move toward greater horizontal equity in the income tax without necessarily raising or lowering the taxes on income from capital.

If our capability of taxing uniformly income from wealth continues to prove so poor, it raises the distinct possibility that a solution to the problem may come from the measurement of property value rather than of realized income. Such a solution is readily feasible when considering corporate wealth in publicly traded stock. Even the normal property tax on real estate, despite the variation in effective rates because of poor administration, may prove to provide less horizontal inequity with respect to property owners than does the income tax.[8] Its potential to provide more horizontal equity than a realized property income base is even greater. Better integration of property taxes with realized income taxes again may provide a back-door way of moving toward more uniform treatment of income from all assets.

If horizontal equity is the goal, better measurement of property and property income in required regardless of whether society moves further in the direction of a consumption tax or maintains an income tax. Horizontal equity requires at a minimum that, if two persons have equal incomes and equal savings, they should pay the same amount of taxes regardless of whether the ideal tax base is income or consumption.

The current policy approach of using realized income, adjusted by various piecemeal savings and investment incentives, unequivocally fails the standard of horizontal equity. Although the focus of this chapter has been on equity issues, the efficiency costs of existing failures to provide uniform treatment of different sources of capital income may be quite substantial and are caused by the same measurement problems that create horizontal inequity (Steuerle 1983b; Galper and Steuerle 1983).

Obviously, if no societal consensus exists on whether to move toward an income or a consumption standard, the steps that can be agreed upon will be less. All of the following, however, at least move in the direction of

8. See Aaron 1975 for an argument that the property tax may also be progressive.

meeting the common standard of imposing the same tax on those who have both equal incomes and equal savings: uniform measurement and taxation of real economic income from property, regardless of source;[9] unification of savings and investment incentives to measure total savings and investment; and uniform reciprocal treatment of interest paid and received, or borrowing (dissavings) and savings.

In summary, both for research and policy purposes, reliance upon realized income from capital as part of a measure of well-being has led to misleading analyses and poorly designed programs. The standard of horizontal equity in tax and welfare programs is violated whether the measure of equals is on the basis of economic income or consumption. Accounting for economic income may be difficult, but there are approximate methods that would allow greater accuracy in statistical analyses and a fairer distribution of benefits and taxes in government programs.

References

Aaron, Henry J. 1975. *Who pays the property tax?* Washington, D.C.: Brookings Institution.

Atkinson, A. B., and A. J. Harrison. 1978. *Distribution of personal wealth in Britain.* Cambridge: Cambridge University Press.

Bailey, Martin J. 1974. Progressivity and investment yields under U.S. income taxation. *Journal of Political Economy* 82: 1157–75.

Blume, Marshall E., Jean Crockett, and Irwin Friend. 1974. Stockownership in the United States: Characteristics and trends. *Survey of Current Business,* Nov., 16–40.

Brittain, John A. 1978. *Inheritance and the inequality of material wealth.* Washington, D.C.: Brookings Institution.

Bussman, Wynn V. 1972. Estimation of household corporate stock portfolios and a model of rate of return from a sample of Wisconsin income tax returns, 1946–64. Ph.D. diss., University of Wisconsin.

Cordes, Joseph J., and Steven M. Sheffrin. 1981. Taxation and the sectoral allocation of capital in the U.S. *National Tax Journal* 34: 419–32.

Darby, Michael R. 1975. The financial and tax effects of monetary policy on interest rates. *Economic Inquiry* 13:266–76.

Feldstein, Martin S. 1976a. On the theory of tax reform. *Journal of Public Economics* 84:77–104.

---

9. Strictly speaking, if one were to move all the way to a consumption tax, economic income would not have to be measured. However, a consumption tax would require wealth accounting, or, to be more precise, at least a measure of withdrawals and deposits in qualified (wealth) accounts. In addition, during a transition period, wealth accounting of existing assets would be required to insure that trillions of dollars worth of consumption were not allowed to go tax free for current holders of wealth.

_____. 1976b. Compensation in tax reform. *National Tax Journal* 29:123–30.

Galper, Harvey, and Eugene Steuerle. 1983. The design of tax incentives to encourage savings. Discussion paper, Brookings Institution.

Galper, Harvey, and Eric Toder. 1984. Transfer elements in the taxation of income from capital. In *Economic transfer in the United States,* 87–135. Studies in Income and Wealth. Chicago: University of Chicago Press.

Greenwood, Daphne. 1983. Age, income, and household size: Their relationship to wealth distribution in the United States. Paper read at the Conference on International Comparisons of the Distribution of Household Wealth, 11 November, at New York University.

Ibbotson, Roger, and Rex Sinquefield. 1982. *Stocks, bonds, and inflation: The past and the future.* Charlottesville, Va.: Financial Analysts Research Foundation.

Lampman, Robert J. 1962. *The share of top wealthholders in national wealth, 1922–56.* Princeton: Princeton University Press.

Menchik, Paul L., and Martin David. 1983. Income distribution, lifetime savings, and bequests. *American Economic Review* 83:672–90.

Musgrave, Richard. 1959. *The theory of public finance.* New York: McGraw-Hill.

Pechman, Joseph A., and Benjamin A. Okner. 1974. *Who bears the tax burden?* Washington, D.C.: Brookings Institution.

Peek, Joe. 1982. Interest rates, income taxes, and anticipated inflation. *American Economic Review* 72:980–91.

Schwartz, Marvin. 1983. Trends in personal wealth, 1976–81. *Statistics of Income Bulletin* 3:1–26.

Smeeding, Timothy. 1982. Alternative methods for valuing selected in-kind transfer benefits and measuring their effect on poverty. Technical paper no. 50. U.S. Bureau of the Census. Washington, D.C.: GPO.

Smith, James D., and Stephen D. Franklin. 1974. The concentration of personal wealth, 1922–69. *American Economic Review* 64:162–67.

Steuerle, Eugene. 1982. Is income from capital subject to individual income taxation? *Public Finance Quarterly* 10:283–303.

_____. 1983a. The relationship between realized income and wealth: A report from a select sample of estates containing farms or businesses. *Statistics of Income Bulletin* 2:29–34.

_____. 1983b. Building new wealth by preserving old wealth: Savings and investment tax incentives in the postwar era. *National Tax Journal* 36:307–19.

_____. 1984. Tax arbitrage, inflation, and the taxation of interest payments and receipts. In *Symposium: Canadian and American perspectives on the deduction for interest payments.* Special edition of *Wayne State Law Review* 30: 991–1014.

Steuerle, Eugene, and Nelson McClung. 1977. Wealth and the accounting period in the measurement of means. Technical paper no. 6. In *The measure of poverty*. U.S. Department of Health, Education, and Welfare. Washington, D.C.: GPO.

Tait, Alan A. 1983. Net wealth, gift and transfer taxes. In *Comparative tax studies,* ed. S. Cnossen. New York: North-Holland.

Tanzi, Vito. 1980. Inflationary expectations, economic activity, taxes and interest rates. *American Economic Review* 70:12–21.

U.S. Bureau of the Census. 1981. *Characteristics of the population below the poverty level, 1980*. Washington, D.C.: GPO.

U.S. Department of Agriculture. Various years. *Balance sheets of the farming sector*. Washington, D.C.: GPO.

U.S. Department of the Treasury. Internal Revenue Service. 1979. *Statistics of Income—1976 Estate Tax Returns*. Washington, D.C.: GPO.

Weisbrod, Burton A., and W. Lee Hansen. 1968. An income–net worth approach to measuring economic welfare. *American Economic Review* 58:1315–29.

Comment   James D. Smith

All societies have both political and functional imparities to define well-being. It is inevitably a topic of political debate, but beyond the realm of campaign rhetoric. The political process is the mechanism by which measures of well-being are translated into policies for sharing the burden of public goods, one of which is the distribution of well-being itself. The term *well-being* has a ring to it that endears it to those charged with ennobling entrances to public edifices, drafting political tracts, or engaging in pure theory—all endeavors where the felicity of language transcends understanding. For public policy a more analytically tractable concept is necessary. The most widely applied proxy for well-being is realized income. Steuerle suggests that the use of realized income derives from historic accident, convenience, and ideology. Whatever the reasons for the use, it is not Steuerle's chosen burden to explicate them, but rather to disabuse the reader of any notion that it is a wise use. He does this in a minor way by the didactics of public finance texts, but in a more compelling way by putting on display a new data base, indeed, a data base that is not yet quite finished. In its present state it is like the product of the consummate designer of women's fashion: in good taste, but revealing just enough to maximize speculation and interest on the part of the viewer. Steuerle spec-

James D. Smith is program director and research scientist in the Economic Behavior Program, Institute for Social Research, University of Michigan.

ulates a great deal about what is behind his data, and I will turn to his speculations and some of my own in a moment, but first let me describe its nature.

For routine statistical processing in its Statistics of Income (SOI) program, the Internal Revenue Service drew a sample of about 41,000 federal estate tax returns filed in 1977. These returns were for decedents who died in 1977 or before (the majority of them being for decedents in 1976 and 1977). A one-in-ten subsample, or about 4,100 estate tax returns, was selected for Steuerle from the initial IRS sample with the intent that for each of these, the income tax return of the decedent in the year preceding his death would be located as well as the income tax return of the decedent's nonspousal legatees in the year prior to and the year following inheritance. For reasons that are not obvious, but troubling, tax returns from the year preceding death were not found for over one-quarter of the decedents for whom an estate tax return had been selected. The about 2,900 decedents for whom an income tax return could be found were used for part of the analysis presented in Steuerle's paper.

Estate tax returns require filers to list legatees along with their Social Security number and amount bequeathed them. Steuerle formed a second analysis file consisting of all nonspousal legatees who received $50,000 or more and for whom an income tax return could be found for 1975 and 1978. Thus, he has a set of legatees for whom he knows taxable income shortly before and shortly after the receipt of a bequest of $50,000 or more. The size of this sample is 1,451 legatees.

Thus, he has two sets of data, one relating decedent's wealth to income in the year preceding death and another relating the income in the years preceding and following an inheritance to that inheritance.

I applaud the kind of administrative record matching Steuerle is doing; we need a lot more of it. In its present state the data are not representative of any meaningful population, however, and our uses of them should keep this in mind. Steuerle notes that the SOI file was stratified according to size of gross estate. He argues that because his analysis deals primarily with issues of within- and between-wealth classes that the unweighted form of his file will not be biased.

Although I agree with this proposition so far as he wishes to make statements about rich decedents and draw some inferences about income/wealth relationships, it does not follow, that one can safely make inferences about the importance of income/wealth relationships for the living population, which is the relevant one. The estate tax returns are a sample of wealthy, living persons stratified by age, sex, race, and marital status. The stratification occurs because the sample is drawn by death, and factors that influence mortality rates make it unrepresentative of the living population. For instance, his sample overrepresents older persons who have a higher probability of dying than do younger ones.

The sample can be unbiased by weighting the observations by the reciprocals of mortality rates applicable to decedent characteristics. In table C4.1, I compare the asset composition in Steuerle's sample of decedents to the asset composition of the SOI file after it was weighted to represent the living population sufficiently wealthy to file estate tax returns were they to die. The weighting reverses the relative importance of real estate and corporate stock—the two largest asset types, and ones that have quite different income realization potentials because real estate is dominated by owner-occupied residential structures.

To the extent that behavior related to age, sex, and other mortality-related variables bear upon realization rates or portfolio composition, properly weighted data would give different results. Steuerle's main point, that the variance of realization rates is so high as to render realized income an inappropriate measure of well-being, is so obvious in the data that it will likely hold when the sample is weighted, but the observed dispersion of the realization rates will be compressed some. His findings also pose considerable challenge to researchers who would link income and wealth either by capitalizing income flows or by converting asset value to yield. I will return to these research issues later. First, let me comment further on Steuerle's findings.

In table 4.1 Steuerle provides an overall view of the composition of the income of these relatively affluent individuals and of the proportion that each income type represents of total net worth. On first glance the percentages that incomes represent of total net worth seem too small. But when one remembers that these income flows are essentially for 1975, when the average yield of stocks traded on the New York Stock Exchange was 4.1 percent and treasury bills were yielding about 6 percent, the aggregate taxable income of this group which represented about 4.4 percent of its net worth certainly does not seem implausible. Keep in mind that not

Table C4.1   **Comparison of Asset Composition from Weighted SOI File and Unweighted Collation File**

	Percentage of Total Wealth	
Asset	Weighted SOI	Unweighted Collation
Corporate stock	23.9	40.7
Real estate	34.8	22.3
Cash, bonds, notes, and mortgages	22.5	27.4
Noncorporate business	4.5	2.7
Other assets	14.2	7.0
Total assets	100.0	100.0
Debts	15.5	7.3
Net worth	84.5	92.7

Source: Schwartz 1983.

only is this group rich, but it is made up of considerably more women and older persons than would be found in a random selection of equally rich individuals. This accounts for the relatively small share, 25.5 percent, of total income represented by wages and salaries. The interpretation of the percentage that a particular income flow, such as dividends, represents of total net worth is not obvious. But Steuerle is pushed to such comparisons because in the period between the income tax return and death one can convert assets—stock into cash for instance. For treasury bills the opportunity for conversion to cash would be automatic with the maturity of the bill.

Steuerle goes on, making the point quite strongly in table 4.2 that considerable variability exists in realized income from capital. He compares the gross capital income reported on income tax returns in the year before decedents' deaths with the value of assets reported on their estate tax returns. He notes that the average rate of realization declines with size of wealth. Decedents with under $100,000 in gross assets had a realization rate of 12.4 percent, while those with $2.5 million or more of wealth had a realization rate of 2.2 percent. He points out that an examination was undertaken of cases with unusually high rates of realization; it was found that dividend and interest income were implausibly high relative to total assets. He speculates that the time interval between the reporting of income and the recording of assets may have permitted people to transfer or consume wealth. Thus the high rates of realization observed for some decedents may, in fact, be a problem of intertemporal misalignment of accounting points and periods. I agree with the general speculation, but let me pursue it a bit.

First, it is known from estate tax data that costs of last illness can be substantial. The population with which he is dealing is quite old: the mean age is seventy-two. One can easily imagine prolonged illnesses. If the cost of these illnesses is less variable across individuals than is the value of their assets, the relatively higher medical cost for the less affluent of these rich folks diminishes their assets relatively more than it does the assets of the more affluent, and the ratio of their taxable income in the year before death to their wealth reported in their estate tax return is consequently higher. Steuerle can pursue this issue by examining the cost-of-last-illness value reported on the estate tax returns. He can also, with greater effort, locate decedents' death certificates, which provide information on cause of death and duration of last illness. Both of these might serve as proxies for the consumption of medical services.

In addition to consuming medical services, it is reasonable to expect that some of this decedent population was drawing down its assets for general consumption expenditures prior to death. If this drawing down involved the liquidation of bills, notes, and bonds as they matured, interest income will show up in the income tax returns, but some portion of the face value of the instruments will have been used for consumption and will not show up in the estate tax returns. If one hypothesizes, as I do, that consumption expenditures will not be proportional to wealth for this population, then the liquidation of assets will be relatively more important for the less affluent than for the more affluent. Thus the proportion of wealth represented by capital income would appear to be larger than for the more affluent in the Steuerle file.

There is also the problem that bearer bonds may generate an interest flow but can be "informally" distributed among the heirs, hence escaping taxation and not appearing in the estate tax return. Finally, there is the problem of the tax-paying unit represented on the estate tax return versus the tax-paying unit represented on the income tax return. It is not clear from Steuerle's discussion how income reported on a joint income tax return is related to the assets on an estate tax return, which is always filed for a sole decedent. There is not an easy solution to the problem of ascribing ownership of income on joint returns to the person owning assets on the estate tax return. Although the income tax return in 1976 requested that dividend income be designated as joint or as belonging to the husband or wife, taxpayer compliance with this request is believed to have been very poor. Furthermore, large amounts of dividend income were frequently reported as from street accounts without differentiation among different street accounts or the ownership thereof. For other types of property income no designation of ownership was required on the return. Some insight into the joint return problem could be provided by analyzing separately joint returns and all other returns. It is suspected that if Steuerle were able to make corrections for the temporal misalignment of the income-reporting period and the asset evaluation point as well as for assets that are informally distributed, the variation of rates of return across wealth-size classes would be considerably compressed. There still would remain substantial within-class variation of rates of realization, however. Steuerle notes with respect to table 4.2 that at least 5 percent of each wealth class has zero or negative realization rates. Because the denominator for the realization rate is gross assets, negative rates must come about because of negative income. This suggests that significant numbers of farm and business losses are present on the income tax returns. Since farms and business assets are more likely to be held by men than women, when the file is weighted the proportion of negative and zero rates of return can be expected to increase.

Thirty percent of the decedent population had realization rates of 10 percent or more as calculated by Steuerle. However, 20 percent of the decedent population with assets of $100,000 or less reported realization rates of 15 percent or more. I suggest that the factors offered in explanation for the overall high average realization rate (12.4 percent) for the group are at work to generate these unusually high rates of realization.

There is another factor that can generate artificially high realization rates. Professional practices and some small business assets are frequently identified with the owner. The value of the business for estate tax purposes may come down to an evaluation of accounts receivable and physical property, but the business income reported on tax returns reflects the owner's marketability. In purely economic terms, there would be a large factor payment to labor, but on the tax return it would all appear as business income. Thus we have a confounded problem of misconceptualization of income and asset devaluation induced by death.

Next Steuerle looks at the change in capital income from 1975 to 1978 for legatees other than spouses who inherited $50,000 or more. In the upper-right-hand portion of table 4.3 Steuerle calculates the change in gross capital income between 1975 and 1978 as a percentage of the amount of inheritance received. For the 1,451 inheritors, the change in gross capital income amounted to approximately 6 percent. Because these inheritors were nonspouses, it is reasonable to speculate that assets such as residential housing, consumer durables, works of art, and other non-yield-producing forms were less important in these inheritances than they would have been in the inheritances of spouses. Given this and the fact that one might reasonably expect some increment in legatees' asset holdings to have occurred quite independent of any inheritance, a change in gross capital income that amounted to 6 percent of the inheritance does not seem unreasonable at all. Steuerle notes there is relatively little difference in the realization rate by size of inheritance. This is also plausible for the same reasons. When one looks at the percentage that change in gross capital income represents of the value of inheritance within inheritance-size classes, however, one finds a substantial variability. For instance, nearly one-third of those inheriting between $50,000 and $100,000 have negative changes in gross capital income between 1975 and 1978. It is difficult, however, to tease much understanding out of the table because so many unobservable things are going on. For instance, we know little about the age of the inheritors and to what extent they might be selling off assets. We do not know the value of the assets they held prior to inheritance. For inheritors with substantial preinheritance wealth, small fluctuations in the rate of return of their prior wealth could swamp percentage changes in income due to inherited wealth. For inheritors who are farm and business proprietors, normal year-to-year variability in income could be substantially greater than any variability induced by the newly inherited assets. If the inheritance was itself a farm or business asset, then the variability in the asset yield on the inheritance itself could be quite large. In this particular instance the data has revealed too little to us to excite much speculation.

Finally, in table 4.5 Steuerle looks at changes in gross capital income over the period 1975 to 1978 by size of 1975 gross capital income. This is somewhat of a proxy for preinheritance wealth, but the whole thrust of

Steuerle's argument on realization rates qualifies this use of it. When he does this he finds that individuals with zero or negative capital income in 1975 were much more likely to have zero or negative changes in their capital income from 1975 to 1978 as were individuals with relatively high 1975 capital income. He speculates that persons with zero or negative capital income in 1975 and those with high capital income in 1975 are, in fact, similar individuals, the implication being that those with zero or negative capital income really were holding substantial amounts of assets but were effectively using tax shelters, as were very wealthy persons in 1975. It was, he argues, the petty rich, those with capital incomes between $2,500 and $20,000, who had high realization rates and consequently were taxed on their lack of tax sophistication. He speculates that legatees with large 1975 capital incomes were sensitive to high marginal tax rates and had strong incentives to convert their inheritances into preferred asset forms since they were likely to be savers and had already accumulated large amounts of wealth. Their propensity to consume out of their inheritances would be low. He also speculates that the owners of substantial capital would have a higher probability of having already engaged in tax-induced portfolio shifting and have access to investment advice. Legatees without previous wealth accumulations would have a tendency to engage in tax minimization efforts only after a time lapse. Again, Steuerle's speculations are plausible and the evidence is suggestive, but the reader is left with a terrible sense of urgency to examine the files in detail to understand what is really going on behind the tabulated results.

Conclusions and Research Implications

Steuerle, without a doubt, demonstrates that realized income is an inappropriate measure of well-being. To the extent that it is used as a basis for allocating tax burdens and transfers, it introduces substantial horizontal and vertical inequities. Although the collation file will provide substantial insight into the equity issues posed by the use of realized income, even after it is weighted and much more is understood about the file, we will have done only the necessary preliminary work to exploit the rich body of data he has assembled.

Although I encourage Steuerle to continue examining the relationship between income tax returns and assets on estate tax returns, I suggest that once he has completed this task that he consider a slightly different strategy.

Given the information he has available from the collation file plus some additional information he could obtain or may already have, I would argue for reconstructing a balance sheet for each individual decedent as it existed at some point within the year of the income tax return in the collation file. This would not necessarily be an easy task. It will require using information income tax returns filed by the decedent prior to his death and by executors of the estate for periods during which the decedent was alive but did not file. It might also require searching for gift tax returns. The central issue is that of entering into the balance sheet the value of assets that disappeared because they were consumed or transferred between the income tax observation and the estate tax observation in the collation file. Schedule C will be of some value in this endeavor as will information on medical costs that appear in the estate tax return as well as in the income tax return. Once one has such a file, not only can one make judgments about equity distortion introduced by the utilization of realized income but one can move a considerable distance the derivation of economic income for relatively affluent individuals. Such a file could be the basis for simulating a variety of tax policies.

References

Schwartz, Marvin. 1983. Trends in personal wealth, 1976–81. *Statistics of Income Bulletin* 3:1–26.

5 Inflation Vulnerability, Income, and Wealth of the Elderly, 1969–1979

Michael D. Hurd
John B. Shoven

5.1 Introduction

The welfare of the elderly in the United States is a major social and political concern for a number of reasons. First, the fraction of the population over sixty-five years of age has increased and is projected to increase dramatically. Second, because of a limited ability to participate in the labor market, the elderly may be particularly harmed by fluctuations in real asset values. Erosion in the financial position of the elderly may have occurred in the 1970s due to the poor performance of stock and bond markets and the unexpected, rapid rate of inflation. Third, the elderly are the beneficiaries of a number of large and growing federal transfer programs. Chief among these is Social Security, Medicare, and Supplemental Security Income (SSI). In combination, these programs are designed to put a floor under the income available to the retired population.

In two previous papers we began to examine how the elderly have fared with the combination of inflation, poor financial market returns, and massive federal programs (Hurd and Shoven 1982b, 1983). In those papers we found the following:

1. The cost of living increased the same percentage for the elderly as for the general population in the 1960s and 1970s. The Consumer Price Index (CPI) exaggerated the increase in the price level for all groups (because of an inappropriately high weight on housing), but the effect of the different consumption bundles of people in different age categories proves to be negligible.

Michael Hurd is professor of economics at the State University of New York at Stony Brook. John Shoven is professor of economics at Stanford University. Professors Hurd and Shoven are both research associates of the National Bureau of Economic Research, Inc.

2. The real income of the elderly rose faster than that of the nonelderly during the 1970s, whether income is measured on a per person or per household basis. This occurred despite the decreased labor force participation of the elderly and the increased labor force participation of the nonelderly.

3. Related to 2 above, even the poor among the elderly improved their position in the last two decades. The percent of elderly below the official poverty line had decreased from 1960 levels by well over half by 1977.

4. The composition of income of the elderly has changed markedly over the period. The biggest changes are the decline in the importance of labor income and the increase in the government-provided health care insurance (income in kind). Old Age Survivors Insurance (OASI) and private pensions have grown somewhat in their share of the elderly's income.

We began a detailed examination of the income and wealth of the elderly and their inflation vulnerability by analyzing the Social Security Administration's Retirement History Survey (RHS). Our earlier work used the 1969–75 waves of that longitudinal survey, as they were the only ones available. This chapter is very much an extension of our earlier work: it uses the full 1969–79 RHS data and explores in depth some of the results we found interesting from the earlier work. In particular, we now tabulate detailed income statements (as well as balance sheets) for the RHS population and subpopulations for 1969, 1975, and 1979. We emphasize these three years, but we use the 1971, 1973, and 1977 files to fill in values that are missing in the three years under examination. In preparing this material, we have changed our use of the data from our earlier papers. While in the past we only examined households that survived in the sample through 1975, we now include all households in each wave (regardless of whether they appear in subsequent surveys). This both expands our sample in 1969 and eliminates a possible bias in our numbers. The extension of the data to 1979 is interesting because by that time the RHS population was sixty-eight to seventy-four years of age and predominately retired. Also, our sample period now encompasses the majority of the inflationary episode of the 1970s. Further, the extension of the data allows us to examine whether elderly households adjusted their portfolios to the inflationary experience of the early part of the decade.

We examine in this paper a number of alternative measures of the vulnerability of the wealth of the RHS population to unexpected changes in inflation and price level. We compute how inflation vulnerability varies across time, by wealth level, and by marital status. Further, we ask how vulnerable the elderly would be if Social Security retirement annuities were not indexed (either implicitly or explicitly). Other measures of how much inflation protection government programs offer are presented. We examine the entire distribution of inflation vulnerability among the elderly. This gives us a picture of how risky the situation is for those whose wealth is the most affected by inflation.

5.2 Data

Our primary data source is the Longitudinal Retirement History Survey. In 1969, 11,153 heads of households who were born in the years 1906 through 1911 were interviewed. The surviving households were reinterviewed every two years through 1979. In this paper we report results for 1969, 1975, and 1979; thus the original heads of the households were ages fifty-eight through sixty-four, sixty-four through seventy, and sixty-eight through seventy-four during these years. Because the original household was reinterviewed even though the original head may have died after 1969, the age of the actual head often falls outside the standard age range. Our results cover all the surviving households regardless of the age of the actual head.

Many income and wealth figures are reported in the RHS. We use comprehensive measures of income and wealth, which we finally aggregate into thirty-seven income categories and forty-two wealth categories. At this level of disaggregation, there will invariably be many invalid responses and missing data items. Had we eliminated observations with missing values in any of the income or wealth categories, the sample would have been reduced until it was almost useless. Therefore, a substantial amount of work and care was devoted to filling in missing values. Our basic operating principle was to use data from other survey years to infer the value in the year of interest. For example, if the respondent indicated he owned a house in 1969, but the value of the house was missing, we inferred the value from the value reported in 1971 with an adjustment for housing inflation. If the 1971 value was missing, we used data from later years. Thus, we used all six surveys even though we only report results for three years. A complete description of the process is given in the appendix. Our aim was to estimate not only the mean values of the income and wealth variables, but the distribution as well; thus, it is important to retain the individual component. If the individual component is stable over time, our procedure will do this.

In some wealth or income categories, only the wealth component or only the income component is given in the RHS. Examples would be the value of a house and the income from an annuity. Wealth was converted to income at a 3 percent real rate of interest, and income was annuitized according to life tables and whether the income was inflation protected or not. Inflation-protected income was discounted at 3 percent. Other income was discounted at 6 percent in 1969, 7.75 percent in 1975, and 9.5 percent in 1979.

Observations are classified according to family type—married, single, or widowed—and in the case of singles, by sex. We report results for each family type.

We used one other source of data: we wanted to account for the implicit income from Medicare and Medicaid, and we did this by finding in official data average per elderly Medicare and Medicaid expenditures. The procedure is described in the appendix.

5.3 Income, Wealth, and Inflation

In this section we present the basic results on income, wealth, and inflation vulnerability from the RHS data. Table 5.1 gives the distribution of income for 1969, 1975, and 1979 for all households and for different marital status groups. Income is comprehensively defined to include the insurance value of government-provided health care or insurance and the real implicit return on owner-occupied housing. This latter was simply taken as 3 percent of the market value of the house. The first thing that is apparent in the distributions of table 5.1 is that mean incomes significantly exceed median incomes, indicating that the distribution is skewed towards high incomes. In real terms both mean and median incomes declined for the population over the period. In 1968 dollars, using the Boskin-Hurd (1982) cost of living estimates, the median income for all households was $6,529 in 1968, $5,428 in 1974, and $5,237 in 1978. The average income is $8,246 for 1968, $7,230 for 1974, and $6,768 for 1978. The decline in real income is due solely to the reduced labor force participation of this population as they age. This occurs most dramatically between 1968 when their ages range from fifty-eight to sixty-four and 1974 when they range from sixty-four to seventy. Despite the fall in mean and median real income, the real income of the lower tail of the distribution has increased. This is due to the sharp increase in SSI, Medicare, and Social Security for this population as most of them become age eligible for the programs. In general, the distributions become tighter through time. Another fact displayed in table 5.1 is that the distribution of income of single women is lower than for single men. This was particularly true in 1968, when earnings differentials contributed towards the income differences.

Table 5.2 presents a detailed breakdown of income composition of the RHS sample in 1968. The first striking fact is that earnings are still the major source of income for these people. For all households in the RHS survey in 1969 (while the survey took place in 1969, the income reported is from 1968), labor earnings amount to 76 percent of total income. Pensions and Social Security income are relatively unimportant and, as might be expected, property and capital income are quite concentrated. For instance, while the income of those in the upper 10 percent of the wealth distribution is three times the average, they receive nearly fifty times as much interest and dividends. The poorest 10 percent of the population in terms of wealth have incomes that average only $732; they have little labor income, only $160 for the year on average. This compares with an overall mean labor income of $6,304. The income of single females is less than that of single males, and the difference is more than accounted for in their

Table 5.1 Income Distribution of Retirement History Survey Population, Ages 58–63 in 1968, 1974, 1978

Percentile Points	Households			Nonfarm			Couples			Single Males			Single Females		
	1968	1974	1978	1968	1974	1978	1968	1974	1978	1968	1974	1978	1968	1974	1978
5%	793	2,007	3,295	807	1,985	3,266	1,869	3,685	5,710	419	1,732	3,344	266	1,338	2,454
10	1,362	2,711	3,954	1,376	2,698	3,933	3,106	4,801	6,964	882	2,402	3,742	666	1,897	3,308
25	3,745	4,314	5,714	3,358	4,240	5,634	5,546	6,992	9,667	1,753	3,505	4,873	1,435	2,893	4,274
50	6,529	7,494	9,501	6,678	7,450	9,379	8,740	10,270	13,250	4,120	5,405	7,167	3,068	4,312	5,932
75	10,595	12,044	14,608	10,718	11,980	14,443	12,590	15,208	18,682	7,145	8,361	10,704	5,254	6,852	8,902
90	15,689	18,340	22,228	15,736	18,650	21,657	18,447	22,974	28,910	10,697	12,724	15,386	7,841	10,670	13,468
95	21,062	25,483	30,257	21,089	25,129	29,568	25,038.	31,426	39,953	13,629	16,879	20,024	9,752	13,506	17,604
Mean	8,246	9,381	12,280	8,325	9,909	12,091	10,569	13,176	16,751	5,270	6,967	9,210	3,829	5,562	7,493
Observations	10,715	8,370	7,137	9,799	7,483	6,610	6,804	4,535	3,552	1,018	805	745	2,893	2,730	2,840

Table 5.2   Income Statements of the RHS Sample, 1968 (means in current dollars)

	All	Nonfarm	10% Wealth Tail	90% Wealth Tail	Couples	Singles	Single Males	Single Females
Income from								
1. House	344	310	95	881	433	340	315	347
2. Farm	140	54	8	618	192	49	77	39
3. Business	111	134	3	824	165	18	29	14
4. Other real property	325	329	80	1,455	400	194	175	200
5. Interest received	410	419	30	2,191	494	263	246	268
6. Interest paid	11	11	5	36	15	4	8	3
Income from								
7. Pensions and annuities	292	311	53	505	328	230	282	212
8. SSI	0	0	0	0	0	0	0	0
9. Welfare and other transfers	107	111	113	209	98	123	106	129
10. Insurance value of Medicare-Medicaid	0	0	0	0	0	0	0	0
11. Social Security	216	220	183	84	199	246	164	275
12. Transfers from relatives	7	7	12	1	4	13	2	17
13. Labor earnings	6,304	6,459	160	19,301	8,270	2,884	4,039	2,477
14. Total income	8,246	8,325	732	26,034	10,567	4,204	5,270	3,829
Observations	10,715	9,799	1,072	1,072	6,804	3,911	1,018	2,893

respective labor earnings. The mean 1968 labor earnings of the single females in the RHS sample is 63 percent of the males, a figure that is approximately the female/male average wage ratio for any date on record. It might be noted that Social Security is higher on average for single women than single men. This is probably because widows can begin collecting retirement annuities at age sixty and, therefore, more of them are age eligible than the rest of the singles.

Table 5.3 contains the same information for 1974 income. Earnings account for only 37 percent of income for the sample as a whole. As before, labor earnings form a lower fraction of income for the poor than the wealthy. It appears that people who are wealthy tend to work longer. Even in the age range sixty-four to seventy years, over half the income of those in the upper 10 percent wealth tail is derived from labor earnings. The income flows from pensions and Social Security are much larger in 1974 than 1968 because of greater eligibility and retirement. By 1974 single women no longer receive more Social Security than single males. This is presumably because both are now age eligible for the program. The income of those in the lowest wealth tail is still very low ($1,820 on average), but has increased significantly relative to the mean income level. This is because of the large government transfer programs that are age tested.

Table 5.4 shows the 1978 income statements. Earnings continue to decline in importance, accounting for 17 percent of income on average. Earnings are much more important for the wealthy, producing 28 percent of their income. Single male incomes, which at younger ages exceeded female incomes because of labor earnings, are, by 1978, greater than incomes of women due in large part to larger pensions. The combination of income from Social Security, SSI, and Medicare is much more evenly distributed than other income. Therefore, one does get the impression that these programs in combination somewhat reduce inequality among the elderly. Private pensions on the other hand seem at least as concentrated as total income. Those in the upper tail get 15 percent of their income from pensions and annuities, while this source accounts for only 4 percent of the income of those in the lowest 10 percent wealth tail.

Table 5.5 begins to present the wealth data. It shows the mean wealth and income levels for those reporting positive values and the percentage of those reporting positive values. This permits us to separate the change in mean value into a change in "participation" and a change in mean value of those participating. The table indicates that the RHS population did not sell their homes as they aged. Roughly 70 percent of the households own their own homes for the full ten years. The mean value of their homes increased faster than the general price level, as is well known. The homes of the elderly increased in value at about the same rate as the increase in the home ownership index of the CPI: from table 5.5 we find that market values of houses increased by 123 percent between 1969 and 1979; the

Table 5.3   Income Statements of the RHS Sample, 1974 (means in current dollars)

	All	Nonfarm	10% Wealth Tail	90% Wealth Tail	Couples	Singles	Single Males	Single Females
Income from								
1. House	565	503	137	1,372	740	340	315	347
2. Farm	139	66	−6	746	190	74	115	61
3. Business	75	76	2	561	121	16	18	15
4. Other real property	475	454	33	2,549	682	209	155	225
5. Interest received	956	973	43	4,725	1,261	565	639	543
6. Interest paid	16	16	28	52	22	8	10	7
Income from								
7. Pensions and annuities	1,290	1,351	91	3,388	1,670	801	1,174	691
8. SSI	63	65	226	19	31	105	82	112
9. Welfare and other transfers	156	157	95	231	171	136	122	95
10. Insurance value of Medicare-Medicaid	536	533	270	427	640	402	430	394
11. Social Security	2,033	2,048	834	1,620	2,415	1,543	1,660	1,509
12. Transfers from relatives	12	12	12	10	6	20	3	25
13. Labor earnings	3,697	3,687	112	16,208	5,270	1,679	2,198	1,526
14. Total income	9,981	9,909	1,820	31,804	13,176	5,882	6,967	5,562
Observations	8,070	7,483	807	807	4,535	3,535	805	2,730

Note: Convert 1974 dollars to 1968 dollars by multiplying by .724 (Boskin-Hurd index).

Table 5.4 Income Statements of the RHS Sample, 1978 (means in current dollars)

	All	Nonfarm	10% Wealth Tail	90% Wealth Tail	Couples	Singles	Single	
							Males	Females
Income from								
1. House	894	801	166	2,388	1,194	596	566	604
2. Farm	229	102	5	1,391	299	159	334	113
3. Business	73	77	−10	605	111	34	57	29
4. Other real property	558	534	99	2,867	813	305	308	305
5. Interest received	1,456	1,476	55	7,890	2,082	836	922	814
6. Interest paid	12	12	5	67	19	5	9	4
Income from								
7. Pensions and annuities	1,790	1,874	110	5,785	2,478	1,107	1,650	965
8. SSI	102	100	467	36	58	145	102	156
9. Welfare and other transfers	151	152	83	458	173	129	176	117
10. Insurance value of Medicare-Medicaid	1,388	1,375	703	1,580	1,813	967	1,054	944
11. Social Security	3,590	3,618	1,203	4,191	4,579	2,610	2,833	2,551
12. Transfers from relatives	12	13	8	15	5	19	2	23
13. Labor earnings	2,050	1,981	70	10,690	3,164	947	1,212	878
14. Total income	12,280	12,091	2,954	37,830	16,751	7,850	9,210	7,493
Observations	7,137	6,610	714	714	3,552	3,585	745	2,840

Note: Convert 1978 dollars to 1968 dollars by multiplying by .551 (Boskin-Hurd index).

Table 5.5   Mean Wealth and Income over Households with Positive Values, RHS Sample (current dollars)

	1969		1975[a]		1979[b]	
	% with Positive Values	Mean	% with Positive Values	Mean	% with Positive Values	Mean
A. Wealth Components						
House, market value	67.3	19,754	70.7	28,640	70.6	43,972
House, mortgage	20.8	7,168	15.9	8,694	11.8	10,522
Farm, market value	10.1	50,106	7.6	69,632	6.8	120,082
Farm, mortgage	2.7	12,558	1.5	23,336	0.9	51,181
Business, market value	8.7	50,595	5.3	62,810	3.6	87,229
Other property, market value	17.5	22,950	15.8	33,034	12.9	44,497
U.S. bonds	25.6	3,017	21.6	4,308	17.9	5,006
Stocks/bonds/shares	21.5	21,605	23.4	25,110	21.9	30,401
Loan assets	9.4	8,242	10.8	14,713	10.1	19,912
Checking accounts	61.9	1,042	70.2	1,212	75.2	1,383
B. Income Components						
Government pensions	8.1	1,992	13.6	4,212	15.5	5,574
Private pensions	5.4	1,970	23.8	2,450	26.6	2,823

[a]Convert to 1969 dollars by multiplying by .696 (Boskin-Hurd index).
[b]Convert to 1969 dollars by multiplying by .523 (Boskin-Hurd index).

home ownership index in the CPI increased by 126 percent over that period. The percentage of the households holding a mortgage declined, as did the percentage owning farms and businesses. The rapid rise in farm values between 1975 and 1979 is clearly shown. There was a decrease in the fraction of the RHS population who owned U.S. bonds. A number of reasons could account for this. First, savings bonds may have been accumulated during the working period and decumulated during retirement in accordance with life-cycle theory. Second, the real rates of return on government securities were very low in both absolute terms and in comparison with other instruments. Finally, this was a period of financial deregulation. Banks, savings and loans, and other financial organizations offered a wide variety of new accounts which made direct participation in U.S. security markets less attractive. Participation in the stock and bond markets stayed roughly constant with just over one-fifth of the elderly being involved. Those who did participate, however, had substantial investments, averaging over $30,000 in 1979. The participation in checking accounts is high and increasing. One theory would be that people open checking accounts to facilitate the automatic deposit of federal transfer checks. This practice is actively advocated by Social Security. The average balance in checking accounts is relatively modest and actually falls in real terms.

Part B of table 5.5 shows participation and average values (flows) conditional on participation in government and private pensions. Naturally, participation increases as this population ages and retires. By 1979, 26.6 percent of the population is receiving a private pension and 15.5 percent a government pension. Note that the amount of government pensions increases far more than private pensions. For example, between the figures reported in 1975 and 1979 (for 1974 and 1978 income, respectively) the average government pension grows 32.3 percent, while inflation was 31.4 percent. Private pensions, on the other hand, go up only 15 percent. In both the cases of private and public pensions, some of the increase is due to those who retired relatively late (between 1975 and 1979) receiving above-average pension amounts. This occurs because these people have a longer tenure on the job, and their pensions are for the most part inflation protected while they continue to work. The evidence of table 5.5 seems completely consistent with the findings of Clark, Allen, and Sumner (1983) that postretirement increases in private pension benefits offset two-fifths of the rise in the Consumer Price Index from 1973 to 1979. Later, when we examine the inflation vulnerability of the elderly, we will assume that private pensions do not adjust to inflation at all. It should be noted that this assumption exaggerates the inflation vulnerability of the elderly.

In table 5.6 we present average asset and liability holdings in 1969 over one entire sample and over a number of subsamples. The pensions and annuities figures are the capitalized value of the flow either reported as actu-

Table 5.6   Balance Sheet of the RHS Sample, 1969 (mean values in current dollars)

	All	Nonfarm	10% Wealth Tail	90% Wealth Tail	Couples	Singles	Single Males	Single Females
1. Net house	11,481	10,342	685	35,052	14,460	6,298	5,238	6,671
2. Net farm	4,655	1,795	−18	31,814	6,402	1,617	2,560	1,286
3. Net business	3,704	3,787	−941	30,980	5,485	606	973	477
4. Net other property	5,233	5,354	1,241	24,115	6,383	3,233	3,176	3,253
5. U.S. bonds	765	798	35	3,168	890	547	789	462
6. Corporate stocks and bonds	4,694	4,961	56	35,449	6,266	1,959	2,083	1,915
7. Loan assets	781	743	35	5,047	954	479	631	425
8. Bank accounts	4,417	4,414	318	15,975	5,054	3,309	3,226	3,338
9. Nonproperty debts	(366)	(355)	(237)	(1,492)	(492)	(148)	(276)	(103)
10. Pensions and annuities	13,663	14,523	318	55,924	14,023	13,038	13,730	12,795
11. SSI	0	0	0	0	0	0	0	0
12. Welfare and other transfers	935	976	492	3,032	758	1,243	863	1,376
13. Medicare-Medicaid	7,795	7,752	5,520	8,878	9,194	5,360	4,301	5,733
14. Social Security	18,485	18,769	6,605	23,027	23,021	10,595	9,994	10,807
15. Transfers from relatives	331	352	136	308	28	858	716	908
16. Total nonhuman wealth	76,573	74,211	14,243	271,275	92,426	48,993	48,003	49,341
17. Total human wealth	28,440	28,848	9,312	54,632	38,177	11,500	18,599	9,002
18. Total wealth	105,013	103,059	23,555	325,907	130,602	60,492	66,602	58,343
Observations	10,715	9,799	1,072	1,072	6,804	3,911	1,018	2,893

ally received or anticipated. The SSI number is zero since the program was not yet in effect. Social Security and Medicare wealth are again the capitalized flows for which households qualify based on their work history to date. Human wealth is the capitalized value of future labor earnings discounted for time, mortality, and labor force participation. The details of these calculations are described in the appendix. The mean wealth is $105,013 of which $28,440 is the present value of future earnings and $26,280 is Social Security and Medicare. The most striking information in the table, however, may be the distribution of wealth. The average wealth of the poorest 10 percent of the population is $23,555 and, of that, $9,312 is human wealth. Fully 89 percent of their nonhuman wealth is composed of Social Security, Medicare and Medicaid, and welfare and other transfers. On average, all other assets sum to only $1,626 for this group. The level of human wealth is very low: the poor in nonhuman wealth are also poor in future labor earnings. Apparently there is a persistent pattern of low lifetime income that results, naturally, in very little wealth. In contrast, the transfer programs just listed amount to 36 percent of the wealth of the whole population and only 13 percent of the wealth of those in the upper 10 percent of the wealth distribution.

Those in the wealthiest 10 percent of the RHS sample in 1969 have an average 3.1 times as much wealth as the entire population. Their average housing wealth is the same multiple of the overall average housing wealth, but they have farms and businesses that are 7.5 times as valuable as the population average, and have 7.6 times as much invested in stocks and bonds. Private pension wealth is roughly as concentrated in the upper wealth tail as is wealth in general. In absolute terms, the wealthy get more welfare and other transfers than the population as a whole. This is probably due to their receipt of more unemployment compensation and disability payments. The table indicates that couples are roughly twice as wealthy as singles, and that among singles, males and females have about the same nonhuman wealth. Males, on average, can expect more labor earnings (human capital). Even if females had the same wealth figures, they would in some sense be financially worse off since they must use this money to finance a longer expected lifetime.

Table 5.7 contains the balance sheets for the same subpopulations of the RHS sample as table 5.6, but the figures are for 1975. We should note that the composition of the subpopulations changed between 1969 and 1975; in particular, there was a growing number of singles because of the death of a spouse. Perhaps the first thing one notices about this table is that human wealth becomes small. On average, the present value of expected labor earnings amounts to only 6 percent of total wealth. Nonhuman wealth increases slightly faster than the CPI. Using that index to deflate the 1975 total nonhuman wealth figure to 1969 dollars results in a $78,900 figure, some 3 percent higher than nonhuman wealth in

Table 5.7   Balance Sheet of the RHS Sample, 1975 (mean values in current dollars)

	All	Nonfarm	10% Wealth Tail	90% Wealth Tail	Couples	Singles	Single Males	Single Females
1. Net house	18,828	16,775	1,232	56,031	24,680	11,321	10,494	11,565
2. Net farm	4,631	2,203	−636	34,329	6,326	2,457	3,845	2,048
3. Net business	2,494	2,524	−216	20,866	4,033	518	612	490
4. Net other property	5,807	5,828	299	33,171	8,314	2,591	2,667	2,566
5. U.S. bonds	931	940	40	3,255	1,120	689	880	633
6. Corporate stocks and bonds	5,878	6,197	44	44,303	8,366	2,686	3,199	2,535
7. Loan assets	1,586	1,555	45	9,024	2,205	792	850	775
8. Bank accounts	9,270	9,243	621	32,793	11,326	6,632	6,922	6,546
9. Nonproperty debts	(519)	(533)	(719)	(262)	(335)	(241)	(1,341)	(1,593)
10. Pensions and annuities	16,842	17,362	1,439	61,814	22,619	9,430	12,813	8,433
11. SSI	816	841	2,154	165	461	1,271	805	1,409
12. Welfare and other transfers	1,140	1,148	625	1,933	1,158	1,117	1,350	1,048
13. Medicare-Medicaid	11,985	11,895	8,362	14,270	14,961	8,167	6,878	8,547
14. Social Security	36,144	36,365	11,755	49,783	47,700	21,319	20,295	21,621
15. Transfers from relatives	103	102	126	181	49	172	20	217
16. Total nonhuman wealth	115,935	112,425	25,171	361,656	152,983	68,921	71,289	66,840
17. Total human wealth	7,340	7,232	1,804	19,936	10,396	3,419	3,755	3,319
18. Total wealth	123,275	119,657	26,975	381,592	163,379	72,348	75,044	70,159
Observations	8,070	7,483	807	807	4,535	3,535	805	2,730

Note: Convert 1975 dollars to 1969 dollars by multiplying by .969 (Boskin-Hurd index).

1969. Pension wealth drops in real terms (partly due, of course, to shorter remaining life expectancy), but Social Security wealth more than off-sets this decline. Bank accounts grow, perhaps due to the aforemen-tioned easing of regulations and automatic deposit of federal transfer payments.

The poorest group still has very little nontransfer wealth. Social Secur-ity, SSI, Medicare and Medicaid, and welfare amount to 91 percent of their nonhuman wealth. Other assets amount to only $2,275, of which $1,232 is house equity. The richest 10 percent continue to have a dispro-portionate amount of farm, business, and stock and bond wealth. The in-stitution of SSI equalizes wealth somewhat, since unlike other transfer programs, the wealthy seem to be effectively excluded from this program. Couples now have slightly more than twice as much as singles, and among the singles, the men have a little more wealth than the women.

Table 5.8 gives the analogous numbers for 1979. By this time, human wealth is trivial, barely accounting for 2 percent of total wealth. Social Se-curity accounts for 28 percent of total wealth, about the same percentage as in 1975 and sharply up from the 18 percent figure of 1969. The fact that government transfer programs make up the vast majority of the wealth of the poor amongst the elderly continues to be true. In 1979, SSI, Social Se-curity, Medicare and Medicaid, and welfare total 86 percent of the nonhu-man wealth of those in the lowest 10 percent of the wealth distribution. The same programs amount to 19 percent of the nonhuman wealth of those in the upper 10 percent tail. The patterns reamin roughly the same. The mean real value of nonhuman wealth declines, though very little. The 1979 figure expressed in 1975 dollars would be $113,000 versus the 1975 figure of almost $116,000. Such a trivial decline seems inconsistent with the life-cycle theory since these people have "consumed" at least 20 per-cent of their life expectancy between 1975 and 1979. In fact, the decline in Social Security wealth (due exclusively to the aging of the population) more than accounts for the decline in total wealth. Other assets that de-cline in real value are pensions and annuities, and stocks and bonds. Houses, bank account balances, and Medicare wealth all grow at rates fas-ter than inflation.

Tables 5.9 and 5.10 give a more complete picture of the wealth distribu-tions in 1969, 1975, and 1979. The former shows the distributions of total wealth (including human capital) and the latter includes only nonhuman wealth. The first point is that the wealth distributions changed far less from 1969 to 1979 than did the income distributions in table 5.1. This is because the 1969 wealth figures include the capitalized expected value of assets (such as Social Security and Medicare), which generated no current income in 1969. Further, there is only a weak link between human capital and 1969 labor income because retirement age varies widely and a six-year age difference occurs between some of the households in the sample. One

Table 5.8   Balance Sheet of the RHS Sample, 1979 (mean values in current dollars)

	All	Nonfarm	10% Wealth Tail	90% Wealth Tail	Couples	Singles	Single Males	Single Females
1. Net house	29,784	26,704	1,418	94,819	39,792	19,868	18,864	20,131
2. Net farm	7,619	3,389	46	59,715	9,969	5,292	11,147	3,756
3. Net business	2,418	2,559	−836	22,505	3,699	1,149	1,901	951
4. Net other property	8,969	9,005	1,974	41,961	12,409	5,561	5,099	5,683
5. U.S. bonds	897	920	32	2,963	1,131	665	924	597
6. Corporate stocks and bonds	6,654	6,975	92	46,756	10,330	3,010	3,848	2,791
7. Loan assets	2,020	2,028	35	12,689	2,925	1,123	1,211	1,100
8. Bank accounts	13,214	13,026	775	49,455	17,769	8,701	9,675	8,446
9. Nonproperty debts	(388)	(411)	(230)	(2,192)	(621)	(157)	(300)	(120)
10. Pensions and annuities	17,304	18,017	1,552	57,327	24,839	9,838	14,115	8,716
11. SSI	1,157	1,138	3,503	439	777	1,534	853	1,713
12. Welfare and other transfers	1,093	1,099	522	3,037	1,192	996	1,320	911
13. Medicare-Medicaid	17,836	17,717	11,919	21,760	23,429	12,294	9,875	12,929
14. Social Security	43,767	44,008	14,240	64,131	60,886	26,805	25,346	27,188
15. Transfers from relatives	93	99	51	12	46	140	15	173
16. Total nonhuman wealth	152,437	146,273	35,094	475,378	208,571	96,820	103,894	94,964
17. Total human wealth	3,876	3,850	982	14,320	6,095	1,677	1,228	1,795
18. Total wealth	156,313	150,124	36,076	489,698	214,666	98,497	105,122	96,759
Observations	7,137	6,610	714	714	3,552	3,585	745	2,840

Note: Convert 1979 dollars to 1969 dollars by multiplying by .523 (Boskin-Hurd index).

Table 5.9   Total Wealth Distribution of RHS Sample (current dollars)

Percentile Points	All Households	Nonfarm	Couples	Singles	Single	
					Males	Females
				1969		
5%	20,262	20,511	37,563	14,483	12,779	14,792
10	27,605	27,626	48,584	18,176	17,011	18,648
25	47,261	46,911	71,420	27,719	27,489	27,756
50	82,512	81,793	102,684	45,088	51,889	42,901
75	124,969	122,889	146,107	75,155	85,527	71,018
90	180,363	175,591	210,156	107,705	120,700	103,133
95	239,950	232,945	287,589	132,828	156,118	129,131
Mean	105,012	103,059	130,602	60,492	66,602	58,343
				1975[a]		
5%	28,247	28,061	57,993	21,640	19,876	21,942
10	35,065	34,664	68,978	27,228	25,014	27,949
25	55,931	54,329	94,035	36,702	36,003	36,909
50	96,674	94,528	130,140	54,650	55,402	54,527
75	148,093	144,572	179,729	86,580	92,078	85,603
90	217,507	208,472	264,715	130,659	133,682	128,779
95	294,769	279,378	365,962	170,862	178,758	169,714
Mean	123,275	119,657	163,379	72,340	75,044	70,159

Table 5.9 (continued)

| Percentile Points | All Households | Nonfarm | 1979[b] | | | Single | |
			Couples	Singles	Males	Females
5%	37,584	37,361	78,933	32,776	30,743	33,211
10	45,386	44,848	94,739	37,880	35,377	38,838
25	69,327	67,576	124,680	49,186	46,012	49,941
50	121,241	118,254	170,707	72,897	69,547	73,558
75	185,760	180,403	233,645	117,259	120,099	116,833
90	279,654	263,573	357,247	172,804	174,121	170,692
95	388,594	353,695	499,112	236,479	258,972	232,869
Mean	156,313	150,124	214,666	98,497	105,122	96,789

[a]Convert to 1969 dollars by multiplying by .696 (Boskin-Hurd index).

[b]Convert to 1969 dollars by multiplying by .523 (Boskin-Hurd index).

Table 5.10   Nonhuman Wealth Distribution of RHS Sample
(current dollars)

Percentile Points	All Households	Nonfarm	Couples	Singles	Single	
					Males	Females
				1969		
5%	15,982	16,171	27,282	11,835	10,793	12,357
10	21,169	21,116	33,139	14,747	13,431	15,494
25	33,527	33,239	45,780	21,413	19,154	22,305
50	54,741	53,730	65,808	33,340	31,108	33,715
75	86,361	84,396	99,586	57,412	64,872	55,101
90	131,994	126,522	152,874	92,056	90,406	92,385
95	177,749	167,687	211,976	114,857	114,702	115,161
Mean	76,573	74,211	92,426	48,993	48,003	49,341
				1975[a]		
5%	26,759	26,727	53,944	20,828	19,581	21,091
10	33,977	33,533	64,986	25,970	24,422	26,744
25	52,591	51,097	88,194	35,532	34,554	35,815
50	90,604	88,488	121,753	51,577	52,918	51,147
75	139,102	136,022	168,309	81,328	82,960	80,769
90	204,432	196,808	247,111	125,958	131,425	122,620
95	274,016	259,235	340,658	162,816	169,453	162,073
Mean	115,935	112,425	152,983	68,921	71,289	66,840

Table 5.10 (continued)

Percentile Points	All Households	Nonfarm	Couples	Singles	Single	
					Males	Females
			1979[b]			
5%	37,089	36,736	76,629	31,895	30,560	32,787
10	44,982	44,283	91,592	37,306	35,115	38,122
25	68,247	66,308	121,814	48,414	45,493	49,363
50	118,579	115,946	166,879	71,866	68,885	72,356
75	181,608	176,269	228,197	115,149	116,982	114,667
90	272,437	257,016	347,480	167,104	173,301	165,947
95	380,039	341,956	480,873	233,451	257,920	229,946
Mean	152,437	146,274	208,571	96,820	103,894	94,964

[a]Convert to 1969 dollars by multiplying by .696 (Boskin-Hurd index).
[b]Convert to 1969 dollars by multiplying by .523 (Boskin-Hurd index).

notices in both tables 5.9 and 5.10 that median wealth figures are far below the mean. There is a large dispersion in the wealth distribution, slightly more so with singles than with couples. Among singles, the female wealth distribution is slightly more compact than that for males. All the total wealth distributions of table 5.9 become more compact in real terms through time. For instance, the lower five percentile points remain about constant whereas the median and ninty-five percentile points fall considerably in real terms. The fall of these higher percentile points in real terms is partly due to the decline in human capital wealth. The big change occurs between 1969 and 1975 when average human wealth falls from $28,440 to $7,340. By 1979 female singles have a higher median wealth than males, although a lower mean wealth. This, of course, is just another reflection of the somewhat more compact wealth distribution of single women. By 1979 it would seem that a substantial fraction of the RHS population, whose ages range from sixty-eight to seventy-four years at that time, are reasonably well-off financially. This is particularly true for couples where the top half has more than $170,707 in wealth and the top 10 percent more than $357,247.

Table 5.10 also shows that the real nonhuman wealth position of each family type improves over time for the entire wealth distribution. That is, not only does median real wealth of couples increase, but the five percentage and ninety-five percentage points of the distribution increase in real terms. The same is true of the wealth distributions of single males and single females. Considering the shorter life expectancy required to be financed by nonhuman assets, it appears that people in all parts of the wealth distribution gain between 1969 and 1975 and between 1975 and 1979.

Table 5.11 shows median nonhuman wealth by age for 1969, 1975, and 1979 for the entire sample and particular subsamples. The numbers are weakly supportive of the life-cycle theory. First, notice that wealth generally increases with age in 1969, where the oldest are closest to retirement, and decreases with age in 1979, where almost all are retired but the oldest have lower wealth. This effect in 1979 is partly or perhaps solely due to the reduced annuity value of Social Security, other transfers, and private pensions for the older members of the cohort because of their shorter expected remaining life. Nonetheless, this is the pattern the life-cycle theory predicts. Also consistent is the fact that the youngest members of each cohort had the largest real wealth gain between 1969 and 1975 and also between 1975 and 1979. This is partly due to the fact that they were more likely to be working during this period and hence more likely to benefit from the double indexing of Social Security.

Table 5.12 provides information regarding the correlation of income and wealth for each of the three years. The numbers shown are cross-tabulations of income and wealth quartiles in absolute frequencies; for example, the upper-left-hand-corner number indicates that 18.3 percent of

Table 5.11	Median Nonhuman Wealth by Age and Marital Status						
Age in 1969	58	59	60	61	62	63	64
All							
1969	49,874	53,352	53,367	54,138	55,920	56,913	59,929
1975	92,732	94,095	97,081	93,409	91,857	87,374	89,027
1979	126,155	129,497	129,958	121,519	114,805	114,888	106,672
Couples							
1969	61,451	63,166	63,285	65,626	67,247	70,282	68,405
1975	119,579	119,531	123,262	123,811	123,762	118,463	120,596
1979	170,611	172,411	171,060	168,131	165,077	161,450	154,020
Singles							
1969	28,966	31,113	30,457	34,629	34,839	34,594	34,363
1975	57,711	52,188	49,607	49,499	50,488	48,744	48,318
1979	80,609	73,784	65,989	69,607	66,587	64,917	61,617
Single males							
1969	24,630	31,116	29,553	29,382	32,536	35,815	29,649
1975	46,043	58,801	52,800	49,437	55,973	50,240	55,879
1979	76,098	84,656	69,829	61,084	75,468	65,176	75,456
Single females							
1969	30,262	31,109	31,063	35,637	35,634	34,238	34,768
1975	60,880	51,005	48,811	49,507	50,084	47,616	47,027
1979	83,730	70,440	63,869	72,770	65,989	64,658	60,050

Table 5.12   Cross-Tabulation of Income Quartiles by Total Wealth Quartiles, 1969, 1975, 1979 RHS Sample

Wealth Quartiles	Income Quartiles			
	0–25%	25–50%	50–75%	75–100%
	1969			
0–25%	18.3	6.2	0.5	0.1
25–50%	3.9	13.6	6.8	0.7
50–75%	2.2	3.6	13.0	6.0
75–100%	0.6	1.4	4.7	18.2
	1975			
0–25%	18.8	5.2	0.8	0.2
25–50%	5.0	13.5	5.4	1.1
50–75%	0.9	5.4	13.5	5.3
75–100%	0.3	1.0	5.4	18.4
	1979			
0–25%	19.2	5.2	0.5	0.1
25–50%	4.8	14.0	5.6	0.7
50–75%	0.9	5.2	14.0	5.0
75–100%	0.2	0.6	5.0	19.3

Note: Entries are percentage of total population in each cell.

the population in 1969 is in both the lower-income and -wealth quartile. Another way of saying the same thing is that 73.2 (or four times 18.3) percent of those in the lowest-income quartile are also in the lowest-wealth quartile. One can see from the tables that income is a good predictor of wealth at the extremes. That is, those with high income are likely to have high wealth, and those with low incomes, low wealth. The off-diagonal corners are almost nonexistent; for example, almost no one in the top income quartile is in the bottom wealth quartile. The concentration along the diagonal is high (63.1 percent in 1969 are in the same income and wealth quartiles, 64.2 in 1975, and 66.5 in 1979) and increases with time. The reason that income becomes a better proxy for wealth is that nonpaying retirement assets are fewer in 1979 and labor force participation has greatly declined.

We next investigate the vulnerability of the wealth position of the elderly to unanticipated changes in the price level and the inflation rate. As we mentioned in the introduction, the elderly may be particularly harmed by inflation because of their inflexibility in not being able to work. Further, a common and lasting impression is that the elderly often have to make do on fixed nominal incomes. To investigate the inflation vulnerability of the RHS population, we have constructed a number of measures. All of them classify assets and liabilities into three categories: those that offer a real or indexed return and are therefore protected from unanticipated price changes or inflation; those that offer fixed nominal returns and hence whose real value is reduced by inflation; and those whose real values increase (or real liabilities decrease) with inflation. Our basic classification is shown in table 5.13, although we do investigate the vulnerability of the wealth of the elderly when common stocks and even Social Security are fixed nominal assets. If someone has a nominal asset and prices take an unexpected and once-and-for-all 1 percent jump, the real value of that asset will be 1 percent lower. However, the effect of a 1 percent change in inflation and nominal interest rates (via a Fisher effect) on real wealth values depends on the maturity of the nominal asset. A long-term bond may easily and immediately lose 6 to 8 percent of its value if interest rates climb 1 percent. In table 5.13 we list the sensitivity of the value of nominal assets and liabilities to an unexpected 1 percent change in the long-term nominal interest rate. The numbers differ by year because of differences in the base interest rate and the duration of the assets. For example, private pensions become a shorter asset with the passage of time as remaining life expectancy falls. Table 5.13 indicates that in 1969, a 1 percent increase in the nominal interest rate would have reduced the value of a nominal pension claim for the RHS population by 9.4 percent. This sensitivity to nominal interest rates is only 4.2 percent by 1979. A detailed explanation of table 5.13 is given in the fourth section, "Calculation of Inflation Vulnerability," of the appendix.

Our first measure of vulnerability (V_1) measures the percentage loss in real wealth per percentage of unanticipated increase in the price level. It is simply defined as nominal assets less nominal liabilities (the sum of category B entries in table 5.13 less those in category C) divided by total non-human capital net worth. The idea is that the real value of nominal assets and liabilities declines point for point with unanticipated jumps in the price level. A V_1 value of zero would mean that the household is completely protected against price level jumps, whereas an index of one would indicate that the household's real wealth declines 1 percent for each 1 percent rise in the price level. V_2, our second measure, differs only in that it treats common stocks as nominal assets and, therefore, places them in category B. Theoretically, stocks represent a claim to the income flows of real capital, and unanticipated increases in the price level should increase their real value to the extent the company is leveraged. That is, it is the stockholders who should gain at the expense of the bondholders. The performance of the U.S. stock market in the past seventeen years is such that one would not want to carry this argument too far, and hence the calculation of V_2.

The third measure, V_3, differs from the first two in that it attempts to measure the sensitivity of the wealth position of the elderly to an unex-

Table 5.13   **Inflation Vulnerability of Assets and Liabilities**

A. Protected from Price Level Shocks and Inflation

Social Security
Medicare-Medicaid
Transfer payment benefits
Houses[a]
Other physical assets
Common stocks[b]

B. Vulnerable to Price Changes and Inflation (Financial Assets)

	Price Sensitivity to Inflation Change		
	1969	1975	1979
U.S. bonds	3.5	2.4	3.4
Corporate bonds	8.0	6.1	5.9
Private pensions	9.4	5.0	4.2
Loan assets	1.0	1.0	1.0
Bank accounts	1.0	1.0	1.0

C. Gain from Price Changes and Inflation (Financial Liabilities)

	Price Sensitivity to Inflation Change		
	1969	1975	1979
Mortgage liabilities	6.4	6.1	4.2
Other debts	2.5	2.5	2.5

[a]There is a theoretical reason for thinking that houses are overindexed—the value of houses will rise faster than inflation due to their tax treatment. Thus, our vulnerability measures may overstate true vulnerability.

[b]We examine some inflation vulnerability statistics where common stocks are considered in class B, i.e., vulnerable to unexpected price changes.

pected increase in the inflation rate and the long-term nominal interest rates. We assume a strict point-for-point Fisher effect. The difference between this vulnerability and V_1 and V_2 is that for V_3 the maturity of assets is important. For example, a 1 percent price level increase would depress the real value of a consol by 1 percent. However, a 1 percent increase in inflation that drove interest rates from 7 to 8 percent would immediately reduce the value of a consol by 12.5 percent. We attempt to calculate in V_3 the immediate fall in real wealth as a fraction of total nonhuman wealth for an unexpected one point increase in inflation.

The vulnerability of assets listed in table 5.13 to price level shocks is zero for those in category A, plus one for those in category B, and minus one for category C. Their vulnerability to inflation rate shocks is again zero for assets in category A, the numbers shown in the table for category B, and minus the numbers shown for category C. The vulnerability of a portfolio is the weighted average of the vulnerability of the assets in the portfolio where the weights are the relative importance of the assets. Vulnerability will be low if either assets in category A are relatively large or if those in category C offset those in category B.

Table 5.14 displays the median vulnerability figures for the three measures with respect to three different wealth bases. Each measure is the ratio of the loss in real wealth caused by a 1 percent change in price level (V_1 and V_2) or inflation (V_3) to a particular wealth measure (total nonhuman wealth, nonhuman, non–Social Security wealth, and nonhuman, nontransfer wealth). We also calculate what the price and inflation vulnerability of the nonhuman wealth of the elderly would be if Social Security were not indexed. This presumes that households would not adjust their portfolios to such a change in regimes. If the government simply announced that Social Security were no longer indexed, the possibilities for the existing elderly to alter greatly their wealth portfolio is probably limited, so our assumption may not be too far off the mark.

Concentrating first on the vulnerability of total nonhuman wealth (the first set of measures in table 5.14), we see that median vulnerability is low by all measures. For example, both V_1 and V_3 measure .034 for 1969, meaning that a 1 percent inflation or price shock would reduce real wealth only 0.34 percent. V_2, which treats the stock market as vulnerable to price shocks, still only has a median value of .042. The measures' increase over time may be due to the decrease in mortgage liabilities in the population. Among singles, men are more vulnerable than women. This is due to the higher private pension wealth of men and their lower Social Security and Medicare-Medicaid wealth figures. The vulnerability measures are, thus, consistent with the wealth composition figures of tables 5.6–5.8. The median vulnerability within the lowest 10 percent wealth tail is zero, while the richest 10 percent of the RHS population is far more vulnerable than average. The poor simply have zero or trivial nominal financial assets. They have nothing to lose. The rich, on the other hand, hold bonds and have substantial pension wealth, both of which make them more vulnerable to price or inflation shocks. Even for the wealthy, the vulnerability medians are not large: a 10 percent jump in prices would cause them to lose 1.1 percent in real wealth in 1969, and a 10 percent permanent increase in the rate of inflation would cause them to lose 3.2 percent of their wealth in 1969.

All the numbers in the first part of the table lead us to conclude that the popular notion of inflation vulnerability of the elderly is wrong: the elderly do not live on fixed incomes derived from assets that depreciate when inflation increases. Rather, a substantial fraction of the elderly have an index of inflation vulnerability that is so low that inflation has no appreciable effect on their wealth. To the extent that the elderly are vulnerable, the vulnerability is concentrated in the class that is of least social concern—the wealthy elderly. Of course, these statistics do not imply that

Table 5.14 Measures of Vulnerability of Wealth to Inflation of RHS Sample (medians)

	All Households	Couples	Singles	Single Male	Single Female	Wealth Tails 10%	Wealth Tails 90%
A. Vulnerability of Total Nonhuman Wealth							
V_1							
1969	.034	.035	.031	.044	.027	.000	.110
1975	.057	.066	.042	.057	.037	.000	.130
1979	.065	.083	.042	.063	.036	.000	.120
V_2							
1969	.042	.045	.038	.053	.033	.000	.160
1975	.065	.075	.045	.062	.041	.000	.200
1979	.074	.094	.046	.073	.041	.000	.210
V_3							
1969	.034	.036	.030	.045	.027	.000	.320
1975	.063	.079	.041	.056	.038	.000	.230
1979	.085	.122	.046	.075	.040	.000	.230
B. Vulnerability of Non-Social Security, Nonhuman Wealth							
V_1							
1969	.053	.054	.051	.070	.045	.000	.120
1975	.098	.115	.075	.098	.069	.000	.160
1979	.108	.137	.066	.097	.058	.000	.250
V_2							
1969	.069	.074	.062	.083	.055	.000	.190
1975	.114	.133	.080	.103	.074	.000	.250
1979	.122	.155	.075	.108	.065	.000	.280
V_3							
1969	.057	.059	.053	.080	.045	.000	.360
1975	.111	.137	.074	.099	.069	.000	.280
1979	.138	.196	.074	.112	.065	.000	.350

Table 5.14 (continued)

		All Households	Couples	Singles	Single		Wealth Tails	
					Male	Female	10%	90%
		C. Vulnerability of Private (Nontransfer) Wealth						
V_1	1969	.087	.084	.091	.107	.085	.000	.130
	1975	.178	.168	.198	.245	.187	.090	.170
	1979	.165	.188	.125	.173	.113	.000	.180
V_2	1969	.114	.116	.109	.132	.102	.000	.200
	1975	.211	.200	.228	.282	.216	.090	.270
	1979	.188	.220	.143	.196	.129	.000	.280
V_3	1969	.107	.104	.114	.181	.098	.000	.380
	1975	.224	.214	.231	.325	.220	.050	.290
	1979	.217	.274	.152	.212	.136	.000	.300
		D. Vulnerability of Total Nonhuman Wealth with Social Security Treated Like a Nonindexed Pension Annuity						
V_1	1969	.447	.459	.412	.465	.399	.490	.230
	1975	.524	.527	.517	.565	.499	.530	.300
	1979	.482	.497	.457	.511	.445	.450	.310
V_2	1969	.471	.485	.436	.490	.423	.490	.300
	1975	.543	.548	.532	.580	.517	.530	.390
	1979	.502	.519	.475	.520	.461	.460	.390
V_3	1969	3.714	3.932	3.211	3.648	3.130	4.52	1.41
	1975	2.251	2.298	2.167	2.341	2.119	2.56	1.08
	1979	1.749	1.821	1.662	1.828	1.623	1.86	.960

the poor elderly are well-off: to the contrary, as we have seen, the lowest 10 percent of the wealth distribution has very little wealth. The statistics simply show that they are not made worse off by price or inflation shocks.

The second part of the table answers the question What would inflation vulnerability be if there were no Social Security wealth, yet everything else were the same? The price shock index, V_1, is about 60 percent higher with no Social Security wealth because Social Security significantly increases wealth, and it is inflation protected. The differential is greater for females than for males; it is small for the wealthy in 1969. V_3 changes in about the same way as V_1 in going from part A to part B of table 5.14. One interesting finding is that by 1979 excluding Social Security wealth, as was done for part B, causes V_1 and V_3 to increase substantially for the wealthy. This happens because the importance of Social Security in the portfolios of the wealthy increases between 1969 and 1979: in 1969 Social Security is about 8 percent of the wealth of those in the upper 10 percent tail of the wealth distribution; by 1979 it accounts for about 13 percent of their wealth.

Part C of table 5.14 gives the inflation vulnerability indexes over private wealth, that is, SSI, welfare, Medicare, Medicaid, and Social Security wealth are excluded. A comparison of parts A and C shows that the government programs are very important in reducing vulnerability: overall household price shock vulnerability, V_1 in 1969 changes from .034 to .087. Over some groups the changes are much greater: V_1 of single males in 1975 changes from .057 to .245. The changes in inflation vulnerability, V_3, are even greater. For example, for all households in 1975 V_3 changes from .063 to .224; for single males, it goes from .056 to .325. We conclude that the government programs included in our wealth calculation, all of which are roughly inflation protected, make an important contribution to protecting the elderly from inflation.

The last part of table 5.14 gives the vulnerability measures when Social Security is not indexed. Thus, Social Security is treated like the usual private sector annuity. The changes in the indexes are large and make the elderly at the median substantially vulnerable to inflation. For example, V_1 in 1969 changes from .034 to .447; with Social Security indexed, a price jump would have caused a trivial change in real wealth; without indexing of Social Security, a 1 percent price jump causes almost a 0.5 percent loss in real wealth. Even more startling are the changes in V_3: with indexed Social Security, inflation rate changes are not a serious problem at the median; without indexing a 1 percent change in the inflation rate would have caused in 1969 a 3.7 percent drop in real wealth at the median. But perhaps the most important finding is what the change would do to the poor elderly. It would change them from a group that at the median is completely insulated from inflation shocks to one that is highly vulnerable. In 1969 their V_3 changes from zero to 4.52 when Social Security is taken to be not indexed. This means, of course, that the household with the median vulnerability among the poor would suffer nearly a 23 percent loss in real wealth if inflation and interest rates unexpectedly increased 5 percent.

The wealthy elderly also gain from indexing Social Security, but the gain in inflation protection is not nearly as great as the gain of the poor elderly. We conclude, therefore, that indexing Social Security has been an important tool in protecting the poor elderly from inflation, and without its protection they would have suffered considerable wealth losses in the inflation of the 1970s.

Part D of the table also shows that the importance of indexing Social Security declines with time. This is because the RHS population is aging, so the importance of Social Security in their wealth portfolios declines as life expectancy decreases. Also, since Social Security is a shorter asset, it is less vulnerable to inflation shocks even if it is unindexed. Nevertheless, even by 1979 when the RHS population is sixty-eight to seventy-four years of age, our elderly sample would have substantial inflation risk without the indexing of Social Security. For example, the median person would lose about 1.7 percent of his real wealth if the inflation rate permanently and unexpectedly increased by 1 percent.

Our overall conclusion from this table is that as a group the elderly are not especially vulnerable to either price jumps or increases in the rate of inflation. At the median, the poor elderly are completely unaffected by inflation; the wealthy are somewhat vulnerable, but from a social policy point of view that vulnerability may not be important. The impression one has from the popular press and from casual observation is that the elderly suffer greater wealth losses than the young when inflation increases. In fact, if there are no real wealth consequences of increases in inflation and only distributional consequences, a loss by the elderly would be a gain by the young. Our findings indicate that although some elderly may gain and some may lose through inflation, as a group the losses are slight. Thus, inflation does not cause any substantial transfer of wealth from the elderly to the young, and the popular impression is false.

We have alluded to the fact that some elderly may actually gain when an increase occurs in the inflation rate. This can happen to people whose assets are inflation protected but whose liabilities are nominal with a long maturity. Home mortgages are a good example of the latter. In table 5.15 we give the distributions of V_1 and V_3 by age and year in two situations: when all nonhuman wealth is included and when Social Security is treated like a nominal annuity. The two sets of distributions correspond, therefore, to parts A and D of table 5.14.

We see that in 1969, 5 percent of the fifty-eight-year-olds have a V_1 index less than − .24. That is, among fifty-eight-year-olds in 1969, a 1 percent increase in the price level would cause at least a .24 percent gain in real wealth in 5 percent of that population. At the upper end, 5 percent of that same group would have at least a .43 percent loss in real wealth in response to a 1 percent jump in the price level. This seems to us to be a substantial spread in the distribution of inflation vulnerabilities. For example, as reported in table 5.14, the median of V_1 in the upper-wealth tail is .11, which is much smaller than ninetieth percentile point of about .32. This means that many people who are not in the upper-wealth tail still have high-inflation vulnerability. One may conclude from table 5.14 that as a group the elderly are not particularly vulnerable to inflation, but table 5.15 shows that there is a wide spread in the vulnerability, and that some individuals have considerable inflation vulnerability.

The distribution seems to become more compact as people age. For example, in 1969 the 5 percent point rises from $-.24$ at age fifty-eight to $-.16$ at age sixty-four; yet the 95 percent point falls as age increases. This is probably caused by a decrease in the fraction of the RHS population with mortgage liabilities: people holding mortgages tend to be in the lower part of the vulnerability distribution in 1969, whereas people in the upper part of the distribution are not mortgage holders. Thus, when mortgages decrease, the lower part of the distribution changes, but the upper remains the same.

It is hard to see any time trend in the distribution. We can roughly check this by comparing the index of sixty-four-year-olds in 1969 with the index of sixty-four-year-olds in 1975. These are, of course, different cohorts. Similarly, we can compare sixty-eight-, sixty-nine-, and seventy-year-olds in 1975 and 1979. Such a comparison gives little evidence of a change in the distribution over time. For example, the 10 percent points of sixty-four-year-olds in 1969 and 1975 are $-.07$ and $-.05$ respectively. The 10 percent point of sixty-eight-year-olds is $-.02$ in both 1975 and 1979. Our overall reading of these and other comparisons is that little change occurs in the distribution of V_1 over time, holding age constant.

The distribution of V_3 is even more wide spread than the distribution of V_1. For example, the 5 percent point in 1969 of fifty-eight-year-olds is -1.42, and the 95 percent point is 3.26. Thus 5 percent of that group gains at least 1.42 percent of their wealth for an increase in the inflation rate of 1 percent, yet 5 percent of the group loses at least 3.26 percent of its wealth for each 1 percent jump in the inflation rate. These are much bigger variations in the vulnerability index than we found across the groups given in table 5.14. The impression is that although at the median the RHS population in 1969 is not especially vulnerable to jumps in the inflation rate, substantial numbers of people gained or lost significant fractions of their wealth in the inflation of the 1970s.

As with V_1, aging seems to make the V_3 distribution more compact: the 5 percent point rises and the 95 percent point falls in 1969 as age increases. An interesting finding that does not appear in the distribution of V_1 is the large decrease in the 95 percent point over time: its average over all the age groups declines from about 2.95 in 1969 to about .85 in 1979, yet the medians remain roughly the same. It is not easy to say what caused this change because we do not have the distribution of the composition of wealth. One might speculate that the high inflation of the 1970s induced people who were particularly vulnerable to inflation rate increases to change their portfolio composition to gain some inflation protection.

The large decline in the 95 percent point is symptomatic of the compacting of the distribution of V_3 over time, holding age constant. Again, making the same kind of comparisons that were outlined for V_1, we find, holding age constant, a tighter distribution. For example, the 10 percent points of sixty-four-year-olds in 1969 and 1975 are -1.51 and $-.42$ respectively; the 90 percent points are 1.48 and .70.

The second part of table 5.15 gives the distributions of V_1 and V_3 when Social Security is treated like a nominal annuity. A comparison with the first part of the table shows that for V_1 the whole distribution is shifted to the right and substantial numbers of people are highly vulnerable to price jumps. For example, about 10 percent of the people in each year have V_1 indexes above .70. Their losses would be at least 70 cents for each dollar or price jump. There does not seem to be a time trend in the shape of the distribution, nor any systematic variation in the distribution by age.

The distribution of V_3 under nominal Social Security shows the importance of indexing Social Security in protecting some of the elderly from inflation. In 1969 fully 25 percent of the RHS population have a V_3 index of more than five. Permanent increases in the rate of inflation would have wiped out substantial fractions of their wealth. For example, if we take the inflation rate of 1968, 4.7 percent, to be the initial permanent rate, this group would have lost about 37 percent of its real wealth with the inflation that occurred in the 1970s. With nominal Social Security, this group would conform to the popular stereotype of an inflation-vulnerable elderly population. The V_3 distribution becomes somewhat more compact over time, due in large part to the fall in the upper 5 percent point. That fall is mainly caused by the declining importance of annuities in the portfolios.

We conclude from the distributions given in table 5.15 that there is great variation in the elderly's vulnerability to price jumps and inflation increases. Substantial numbers of the RHS are completely protected or even gain from inflation, while substantial numbers are hurt. If Social Security were not indexed, the distribution would be much wider and many elderly would be badly hurt by inflation increases. Indexing seems both to protect the elderly as a group and to reduce the variation in the risk.

5.4   Conclusion

Our overall impression from the RHS data is that as a group the elderly maintained their economic position quite well during the 1970s. Their in-

Table 5.15 Vulnerability of Nonhuman Wealth for 1969, 1975, and 1979

A. Total Nonhuman Wealth, Distribution by V_1

Percentile Points		Age in 1969						
		58	59	60	61	62	63	64
5%	1969	-.24	-.22	-.22	-.21	-.16	-.15	-.16
	1975	-.11	-.16	-.11	-.09	-.07	-.05	-.08
	1979	-.08	-.08	-.05	-.05	-.05	-.02	-.03
10	1969	-.13	-.13	-.13	-.11	-.08	-.07	-.07
	1975	-.05	-.06	-.04	-.02	-.02	-.01	-.02
	1979	-.02	-.02	-.01	-.01	-.01	-.00	-.00
25	1969	-.02	-.02	-.02	-.01	-.00	.00	.00
	1975	.00	.00	.00	.00	.00	.00	.00
	1979	.00	.00	.00	.00	.00	.00	.01
50	1969	.02	.02	.03	.03	.04	.04	.04
	1975	.05	.04	.06	.06	.06	.07	.05
	1979	.06	.06	.07	.06	.06	.07	.07
75	1969	.17	.15	.16	.16	.17	.16	.15
	1975	.16	.16	.17	.17	.19	.18	.15
	1979	.17	.16	.17	.16	.17	.17	.17
90	1969	.33	.33	.33	.32	.33	.32	.31
	1975	.31	.28	.30	.29	.30	.32	.31
	1979	.30	.27	.29	.27	.28	.31	.30
95	1969	.43	.41	.42	.41	.42	.42	.40
	1975	.40	.35	.40	.36	.36	.40	.40
	1979	.37	.33	.37	.35	.36	.38	.37

Table 5.15 (continued)

B. Total Nonhuman Wealth, Distribution by V_3

Percentile Points		Age in 1969						
		58	59	60	61	62	63	64
5%	1969	-1.42	-1.38	-1.38	-1.23	-1.02	-.91	-.43
	1975	-.65	-1.01	-.68	-.69	-.49	-.40	-.49
	1979	-.33	-.33	-.24	-.23	-.30	-.12	-.18
10	1969	-.83	-.81	-.74	-.69	-.50	-.44	-.51
	1975	-.42	-.42	-.26	-.22	-.16	-.12	-.18
	1979	-.08	-.10	-.05	-.04	-.05	-.01	-.02
25	1969	-.12	-.11	-.10	-.04	-.02	-.01	-.02
	1975	-.01	-.01	.00	.00	.00	.00	.00
	1979	.00	.00	.00	.00	.00	.00	.00
50	1969	.02	.02	.02	.03	.04	.05	.04
	1975	.05	.04	.07	.06	.08	.08	.06
	1979	.07	.08	.09	.08	.08	.10	.09
75	1969	.54	.49	.49	.50	.63	.65	.45
	1975	.27	.24	.36	.36	.38	.40	.32
	1979	.33	.32	.39	.32	.34	.37	.30
90	1969	2.02	2.15	2.10	2.03	2.01	1.98	1.48
	1975	.77	.75	.82	.86	.89	.83	.70
	1979	.67	.64	.67	.65	.64	.70	.64
95	1969	3.26	3.20	3.00	2.96	2.90	2.79	2.51
	1975	1.14	1.07	1.25	1.16	1.16	1.23	1.14
	1979	.88	.84	.85	.84	.85	.84	.85

C. Social Security Treated as a Nonindexed Pension Annuity, Distribution by V_1

Percentile Points		58	59	60	61	62	63	64
					Age in 1969			
5%	1969	.00	−.01	.00	.00	.00	.00	.00
	1975	.04	.00	.06	.01	.07	.02	.03
	1979	.06	.03	.09	.05	.06	.08	.03
10	1969	.06	.05	.10	.08	.12	.10	.10
	1975	.17	.12	.18	.17	.21	.17	.14
	1979	.19	.13	.20	.16	.18	.18	.15
25	1969	.24	.21	.25	.26	.27	.28	.26
	1975	.36	.31	.35	.34	.36	.37	.33
	1979	.35	.31	.35	.32	.32	.34	.31
50	1969	.42	.41	.45	.45	.47	.46	.45
	1975	.52	.50	.54	.52	.53	.53	.52
	1979	.49	.48	.49	.47	.47	.49	.47
75	1969	.59	.58	.60	.60	.62	.61	.60
	1975	.65	.63	.66	.65	.65	.66	.64
	1979	.60	.59	.60	.59	.60	.61	.59
90	1969	.71	.70	.70	.71	.72	.72	.70
	1975	.73	.72	.74	.73	.75	.76	.74
	1979	.68	.69	.68	.68	.70	.71	.70
95	1969	.76	.76	.75	.76	.77	.77	.75
	1975	.78	.76	.78	.79	.79	.80	.78
	1979	.72	.73	.73	.73	.75	.76	.75

Table 5.15 (continued)

				Age in 1969				
Percentile Points		58	59	60	61	62	63	64
5%	1969	.00	.00	.06	.01	.07	.03	.00
	1975	.04	.00	.09	.01	.11	.03	.02
	1979	.15	.07	.26	.04	.15	.17	.03
10	1969	.52	.47	.87	.75	.91	.85	.65
	1975	.58	.32	.73	.55	.73	.64	.48
	1979	.46	.45	.70	.51	.63	.61	.38
25	1969	1.84	1.73	2.13	2.09	2.21	2.29	2.11
	1975	1.42	1.25	1.45	1.45	1.52	1.50	1.36
	1979	1.24	1.10	1.21	1.13	1.17	1.22	1.10
50	1969	3.50	3.46	3.76	3.76	3.84	3.83	3.74
	1975	2.26	2.16	2.34	2.30	2.25	2.26	2.22
	1979	1.81	1.74	1.80	1.77	1.72	1.75	1.69
75	1969	5.11	5.03	5.26	5.23	5.25	5.23	5.07
	1975	2.94	2.83	2.99	2.92	2.93	2.94	2.85
	1979	2.27	2.27	2.28	2.23	2.22	2.26	2.18
90	1969	6.20	6.18	6.19	6.25	6.34	6.29	6.03
	1975	3.40	3.36	3.42	3.44	3.48	3.51	3.40
	1979	2.66	2.70	2.70	2.64	2.67	2.72	2.61
95	1969	6.68	6.69	6.62	6.76	6.79	6.82	6.49
	1975	3.62	3.56	3.63	3.64	3.76	3.77	3.60
	1979	2.85	2.87	2.85	2.87	2.93	2.93	2.84

D. Social Security Treated as a Nonindexed Pension Annuity, Distribution by V_3

comes held up in the face of growing inflation, and their nonhuman wealth actually increased slightly in real terms. Furthermore, their portfolios were such that at the median they were substantially protected from inflation. We found that government programs can take credit for much of the inflation protection in the sense that private wealth is much more inflation vulnerable than the sum of private and public wealth. Indexing Social Security is largely responsible for this fact in that if Social Security were not indexed, the elderly would be highly vulnerable to inflation. This is especially true of the poor elderly, a group that under indexing is, at the median, completely protected from inflation; without indexing, the poor elderly would lose large fractions of their small wealth, were the rate of inflation to rise. They would change from being the least vulnerable group among the elderly, to being the most vulnerable. We also found, however, from our study of the distributions of income, wealth, and inflation vulnerability, that to speak of the median or mean of the elderly obscures the wide diversity of economic positions among them. Many elderly are well-off with adequate holdings of private wealth augmented with Social Security and Medicare, while at the same time many elderly have almost no wealth beyond that supplied by government programs. Similarly, the median elderly person is not particularly vulnerable to inflation, yet many elderly actually gain from increases in the rate of inflation, and many others lose significant amounts. The findings that the elderly's wealth positions were not harmed during the 1970s and that they were not particularly vulnerable to inflation are not, of course, independent findings. Rather, they complement each other and ought to increase our confidence that both findings are correct.

Appendix

Description of the Data

The Retirement History Survey (RHS) is a national longitudinal survey of 11,153 households whose heads were born in 1906 through 1911. The surviving households were reinterviewed every two years through 1979. Detailed data on financial characteristics, work behavior, and health were obtained. The file is especially useful for this study because the RHS data were matched to Social Security earnings records, which give contributions to Social Security throughout the working life through 1974. Therefore, it is possible to calculate exactly the Social Security benefits a worker would receive were he to retire in 1975 or before. We construct from the RHS the earnings records for 1975 through 1979, so that Social Security benefits can be calculated for workers not yet retired by 1975.

For a variety of reasons, missing values occurred on the data tape. If we had eliminated households on the basis of missing values, the resulting sample would have been small because of the large number of components of income and wealth. Therefore, we imputed missing values after carefully examining the raw data. Where an item was missing in the particular wave of the RHS, its value was imputed if possible from the previous wave of the RHS by multiplying the answer given for the same item by the same respondent from the previous wave by the growth rate in the median value of such assets for all nonmissing respondents between the previous wave of the RHS and the particular wave. Imputation used the latest wave of the RHS that had a valid value, but could reach as far back as the 1969 (first) wave or as far forward as 1979. If a datum could not be imputed by reference to the same question in another year for the same respondent, the datum was set equal to the median of all nonmissing answers for other respondents in the particular wave.

The raw data yielded fifty-two data items for each year. Several of these items are aggregates of even more finely defined variables. For 1971, 1973, 1975, 1977, and 1979, a list of fifty-two corresponding completion codes precedes the list of data items. The data items are:

1. Market value of house
2. Outstanding mortgage debt on house
3. Other debt on house
4. Market value of farm
5. Outstanding mortgage debt on farm
6. Other debt on farm
7. Market value of business
8. Business debt
9. Market value of other real property
10. Outstanding mortgage debt on other real property
11. Other debt on other real property
12. Market value of motor vehicles
13. Debt on motor vehicles
14. Face value of U.S. savings bonds
15. Value of U.S. corporate stocks and bonds
16. Value of loans owned by respondent
17. Money in checking accounts
18. Money in savings accounts
19. Face value of life insurance
20. Face value of annuities
21. Medical bills outstanding
22. Store debts outstanding
23. Outstanding debts to banks and savings institutions
24. Outstanding debts to private individuals

25. Actual annual pension income, railroad retirement
26. Actual annual pension income, military service
27. Actual annual pension income, government employment
28. Actual annual pension income, private employment
29. Annual income from SSI program
30. Annual benefits from AFDC program
31. Annual benefits from other public assistance programs
32. Annual state cash sickness benefits
33. Annual workmen's compensation benefits
34. Annual benefits from unemployment insurance
35. Annual income from private insurance and annuities
36. Annual benefits from private welfare agencies
37. Annual benefits from disability programs, other than Social Security
38. Annual income from relatives
39. Annual income from other private individuals outside the household
40. Annual interest income from stocks, bonds, dividends, and savings
41. Annual rental income
42. Annual income from Social Security
43. Expected annual income from AFDC
44. Expected annual pension income, railroad retirement
45. Expected annual pension income, military service
46. Expected annual pension income, government employment
47. Expected annual interest income
48. Expected annual income from private insurance and annuities
49. Expected annual rental income
50. Expected annual income from relatives
51. Expected annual income from other private individuals outside the household
52. Expected annual income from other public assistance programs.

After each of the fifty-two data items are imputed (this process is repeated for the survey years 1969, 1975, and 1979), a vector of incomes and a vector of wealth components are created. Responses to questions regarding flows are capitalized to yield wealth figures if corresponding wealth data were not available. Where possible, expected rather than actual flows were capitalized to yield wealth. Incomes were obtained directly from the RHS questions if possible. Otherwise, corresponding wealth figures were converted to flows by assuming a 3 percent service flow from the stock figure. Items that are capitalized to create wealth stocks are capitalized at either a nominal interest rate (nominal rate = 6 percent in 1969, 7.5 percent in 1975, and 9.5 percent in 1979) or a real rate of 3 percent depending on the particular income. Flows that were not expected to grow with inflation were capitalized at the nominal rate, while flows that were expected to grow (such as income from government programs) were capitalized at the real rate. Flows were capitalized for a term consisting of the expected value of the life expectancy (assuming person is midway between birthdays) of the respondent or his spouse (if present, and greater than respondent's), depending upon whether the income flow was assumed to continue to the spouse after the death of the respondent. The assumptions on length of flow were:

Railroad pension—respondent's life expectancy
Military pension—respondent's life expectancy
Government pension—respondent's life expectancy
Private pension—respondent's life expectancy
Income from SSI—maximum of respondent's or spouse's life expectancy
Benefits from AFDC—three years only, or respondent's life expectancy if less
Benefits from other public assistance—maximum of respondent's or spouse's life expectancy
Income from private insurance and annuities—maximum of respondent's or spouse's life expectancy
Benefits from private welfare agencies—maximum of respondent's or spouse's life expectancy
Benefits from non–Social Security disability—respondent's life expectancy
Income from relatives—maximum of respondent's or spouse's life expectancy
Income from other private persons outside household—maximum of respondent's or spouse's life expectancy.

A capitalized value of Medicare and Medicaid payments is computed by applying the average per person benefits to the life expectancy (appropriately discounted) of the respondent, plus benefits over the life expectancy of respondent's spouse, if married. For survey year 1969, the mean 1975 Medicare-Medicaid value was used, adjusted by change in price index between 1968 and 1975. The figures were obtained from the 1981 Social Security annual statistical supplement. Of course, actual payments will vary from individual to individual, and the insurance value will vary somewhat from state to state. Furthermore, the utility value to someone in a payment-in-kind program is overstated by the cash value of the program. Our numbers, therefore, overstate the actual insurance value, and they do not capture the variation from individual to individual.

In computing income for the sample, we took a broad view of the components of income. In addition to such conventional income sources as Social Security, wage, rent, interest, pensions, government transfers, annuities, and contributions from relatives, we imputed income from owner-occupied housing and Medicare-Medicaid.

The imputations and conversion of stocks to flows and the reverse where necessary produced the basic data used in the analysis. These variables are:

1. House services
2. Mortgage service
3. Other debt on house service
4. Farm services
5. Mortgage on farm service
6. Other debt on farm service
7. Business services
8. Debt on business service
9. Other real property services
10. Other real property mortgage service
11. Other real property debt service
12. Car services
13. Car debt service
14. Interest income
15. Income from life insurance and annuities
16. Medical bills service
17. Store debt service
18. Bank debt service
19. Private debt service
20. Rental income (this actually should be ignored, as rental income is already included in income from real property)
21. Pension income, railroad retirement
22. Pension income, military
23. Pension income, government
24. Pension income, private
25. Income from relatives
26. State cash sickness benefits
27. Workmen's compensation
28. Unemployment insurance
29. SSI
30. AFDC
31. Income from other public assistance (non-AFDC)
32. Income from non–Social Security disability
33. Income from private welfare
34. Income from other private individuals
35. Medicare-Medicaid
36. Income from Social Security (from RHS)
37. Wage income (computed in phase 1 and phase 2)
38. Market value of house
39. Mortgage on house

40. Other debt on house
41. Market value of farm
42. Mortgage on farm
43. Other debt on farm
44. Market value of business
45. Debt on business
46. Market value of real property
47. Mortgage on real property
48. Other debt on real property
49. Market value of motor vehicles
50. Debt on motor vehicles
51. U.S. savings bonds, face value
52. U.S. corporate stocks and bonds, face value
53. Loans owned
54. Checking accounts
55. Savings accounts
56. Life insurance, face value
57. Annuities, face value
58. Medical bills
59. Store debts
60. Debts to banks
61. Debts to private individuals
62. Rental wealth (should ignore)
63. Pension wealth, railroad
64. Pension wealth, military
65. Pension wealth, government
66. Pension wealth, private
67. Wealth from relatives

Variables 68 through 70 are not capitalized. It is assumed that the household only received these benefits for the year prior to the evaluation year and in the evaluation year.

68. Wealth from state cash sickness benefits
69. Wealth from workmen's compensation
70. Wealth from unemployment insurance
71. Wealth from SSI
72. Wealth from AFDC
73. Wealth, other public assistance
74. Wealth, non–Social Security disability
75. Wealth, private welfare
76. Wealth, from other source (private individuals)
77. Wealth, Medicare-Medicaid
78. Wealth, Social Security
79. Human capital.

Calculation of Social Security Variables

The input data set is a matched file of responses to the 1969, 1971, 1973, 1975, 1977, and 1979 Retirement History Surveys, plus matched Social Security Administration earnings records through 1974. From these data we calculate Social Security benefits were the worker to retire; Social Security wealth—the expected present value of benefits were the worker to retire; and Social Security taxes—the present value of taxes paid in with an adjustment for probabilities of death. For most observations the calculations, while not routine, are reasonably straightforward. Here we mainly concentrate our discussion on the difficulties that arise due to the complexity of the law and peculiarities of the data. In particular, the treatment of widows is very complicated.

Because of differences between SSA earnings record year-of-birth information and year-of-birth derived from age in the 1969 RHS, the year-of-birth derived from RHS was used in the computation of Social Security wealth. Using the SSA earnings record year-of-birth would make some respondents as old as seventy years at the time of the RHS survey.

The Social Security Primary Insurance Account (PIA) is calculated for each person based on his earnings record, using the law in effect on 1 January of a particular year (the evaluation year) and assuming the individual retires as soon as possible (age sixty-two or as soon as sufficient quarters of covered employment are accumulated after age sixty-two for those not yet eligible by age sixty-two). If an individual's PIA is based on average monthly wage; if the year is later than 1970, then an individual who delays retirement past age sixty-five receives a bonus of 1 percent per year for each year of delayed retirement past age sixty-five. However, if PIA is based on either of the other methods (covered-years method or method using pre-1950 income), then no bonus is received for delayed retirement. Also, the bonus stops at age seventy-two. (See U.S. Department of Health and Human Services 1981, p. 19.) If an individual retires before reaching age sixty-five, PIA is reduced for early retirement.

We assumed that for married couples, the male's Social Security wealth is always simply based on his own PIA computed from his own earnings record. The female's Social Security wealth is taken as the maximum of her own PIA or her spouse or widow's benefit based on her husband's PIA. She is allowed to switch from her own benefit to her spouse or widow's benefit over time, or from spouse or death benefit to her own benefit. Single men and women have a Social Security wealth based on their own PIA only.

If the original 1969 respondent was a widow (and has not remarried by the evaluation year), then we calculate her benefits in a special way. The Social Security Administration Earnings file contains no information on the widow's deceased husband, so we utilize data from the RHS to obtain widows' benefits. If the widow has remarried since the 1969 survey year, she is treated the same as other married women (her new husband should have SSA records). If an original 1969 widow is still a widow in the evaluation year, then we calculate widows' benefits using information from RHS. We perform the calculation only if she has good tax records from the SSA file. We take the view that if a widow is found to receive Social Security benefits, those benefits are survivors' benefits. This approach was used because it is possible that true survivors' benefits were recorded in the retired worker's benefits slot. Note that this may not be true in practice and the woman may actually be drawing benefits based on her own PIA. Beginning with data from the 1971 survey, we calculate benefits either from the RHS (using old age or survivors' benefits) or from her own earnings records. If survivors' or old age benefits are not being drawn, then Social Security wealth is calculated based only on the widow's own PIA. If survivors' or old age benefits are drawn (as indicated in RHS), we assume that the individual began drawing those benefits at the earliest possible age (age sixty). That age is earlier than the earliest age at which the widow could draw benefits based on her own PIA (i.e., age sixty-two). Hence, we assume that if the widow is receiving survivors' or old age benefits, she never drew (and never will draw) benefits based on her own PIA.

We check whether the widow is drawing Social Security or survivors' benefits. If so, then we ask whether she is receiving Social Security in 1969 (note that in the 1969 survey, no distinction is made between survivors' and old age benefits). If so, then we assume the widow drew benefits at the earliest possible age. If she did not draw in 1969, then we assume she began to draw in 1970. If a widow did not draw in 1971, then we search forward to the other survey years. We assume she began to draw benefits (Social Security or survivors' benefits) in the year prior to the survey year where a positive response was elicited for receiving benefits. If a widow has not drawn benefits by the 1979 survey year, then we assume she never would draw widows' benefits. When we find a survey year in which a widow was found to receive benefits, we determine widows' benefits by taking the maximum of survivors' benefits and old age benefits. We then adjust the benefit back to the evaluation year (the adjustment allows for change in Social Security law).

For surviving widows of original 1969 male respondents, however, there is information on the deceased spouse. These widows are allowed to draw widows' benefits if they are greater than the benefits based on their own PIA. If the original husband was eligible for benefits by the time he died (i.e., had accumulated sufficient quarters of coverage by the year of death) but was not old enough to retire by the time of death, then we assume the person would not have retired until age sixty-five (thus, for a widow, she would not be penalized for her husband's "computed" early retirement in the calculation of her benefits). If the deceased husband was not eligible for benefits by the time of his death, then his widow would not be eligible for widow benefits.

If the deceased husband was older than age sixty-five at the time of his death, then we search the wage data to determine whether he retired at an age greater than sixty-five (the widow does not receive a bonus if her husband delayed retirement—but if he retired early, then his basic benefit would be reduced for purposes of computing widows' benefits. This reduction, however, only applies for evaluation years after 1972). Not that this is only important for female surviving spouses since for these individuals, death benefits are computed using the husband's PIA and any adjustment for early retirement.

If the husband was sixty-two years of age or younger at the time of his death, then we assume that he had not retired by the year of his death. For purposes of calculating widow benefits, we set retirement age of the deceased husband at sixty-five. If the husband was working in the year prior to his death, we assume he did not retire by the time he died. For purposes of computing widows' benefits, we set the husband's age at retirement at sixty-five. Male-surviving-spouse Social Security benefits are computed using own PIA information only.

If a respondent does not have sufficient covered quarters of employment by the evaluation year to be eligible for Social Security benefits, we use information on current employment, state of retirement, and expectations about future employment to determine the quarter of eligibility, if any.

Life tables by race and sex were used in all wealth calculations, and an interest rate of .03 was used to discount benefits.

Calculation of Human Capital

The basic idea is to find the actual flow of earnings during the years of the RHS, the expected flow during the years after 1979, and then calculate an expected present value of earnings using the life tables and a real interest rate of .03. We use conditional labor force participation rates (the probability of participating in year $t + 1$ given participation in year t) to estimate the probability of earnings in years after 1979 for those not yet retired in 1979. The extrapolation and imputation of earnings is now described.

We calculate human capital by extrapolating income in the evaluation year out to age eighty-three using labor force participation rates and life tables. Age eighty-three is the last age used in the calculations, because labor force participation is zero after age eighty-three for all individuals. If income is missing in the evaluation year, then it is first imputed from income data for other years. Both forward and backward (if possible) searches were made for the imputation, though backward searches were tried first. Imputed income is calculated by adjusting a valid income datum by the ratio of nominal wage indexes and then by adjusting for the price level. If income could not be imputed, it was set to zero (only two individuals on the full file had bad income data for all years). In addition, we impute income for the year prior to the evaluation year if that value was invalid.

We needed labor force participation rates for males, married females, and single females. The rates were computed by using figures in Bowen and Finegan for individuals age fifty-five plus. Those rates are from the 1960 census. These 1960 figures were adjusted by the change in the labor force participation in the population between 1960 and the evaluation year. Values for earlier ages were derived from the *Employment and Training Report of the President* (1981). If figures were not given for each age (as was the case for the figures for ages below fifty-five), values were interpolated by assigning the mean labor force participation rate to the mean age in each age category, and then joining each of those points to form a piecewise linear function. Values for each age were then taken from this derived function.

Calculation of Inflation Vulnerability

Table 5.13 classifies assets and liabilities into three categories: (1) those for which unexpected inflation or price shocks do not affect real value, (2) those whose real value is eroded, and (3) those whose real value is increased (or whose real liability is reduced). We distinguish between a one-shot price-level jump, which leaves all interest rates unaffected, and an unexpected increase in the (steady) rate of inflation, which causes nominal interest rates to rise. If the scenario is a one-shot, 1 percent jump in prices, then nominal assets that are vulnerable lose 1 percent of their real value (as do liabilities). However, if the circumstance is a change in the rate of inflation accompanied by a rise in nominal interest rates, then the erosion in real value of assets or liabilities depends on their maturity. We have assumed a strict Fisher point-for-point relationship between inflation and nominal interest rates. An unexpected 1 percent rise in interest rates would roughly reduce the value of a one-year asset by 1 percent, but could change the value of a twenty-year asset by 10 or 12 percent, depending on the initial interest rate. The sensitivity of the value of long-term nominal assets to interest rate fluctuations depends on both the maturity of the assets and on the basic interest rate. A change in the rate of interest from 4 to 5 percent affects value far more than a change from 10 to 11 percent, for example.

The numbers in parts A and B of table 5.13 were constructed using available published data where possible. The figure for U.S. bonds was calculated using the average maturity and interest rate figures published in the *Economic Report of the President* (1983). The corporate bond figures take ten years as the average maturity of long-term corporate bonds and use average Baa interest rates during 1969, 1975, and 1979, which were 7.8, 10.6, and 10.7 percent, respectively. The sensitivity of the value of bonds to a 1 percent increase in interest rates declined through time as interest rates rose between 1969 and 1979. We do not take into account that the elderly may hold shorter-than-average maturity issues of U.S. and corporate bonds.

The private pensions are valued as a nominal annuity lasting the average life expectancy of our sample in 1969, 1975, and 1979. These numbers are certainly not precisely estimated, given the range of ages in the sample and the inclusion of couples and both single males and females. The estimates are consistent with a seventeen-year annuity in 1969, thirteen years in 1975, and ten years in 1979, and probably capture inflation risk reasonably accurately. The final inflation vulnerability figures in this chapter are quite interesting to the precision of these assumptions. It is not clear what number to estimate for the average duration of bank accounts and loan assets. It depends on how fast the interest rate in these contracts adjusts. We have assumed that the loans and bank accounts remain outstanding at a fixed nominal interest rate for one year.

Households gain in their wealth position when inflation erodes the real value of their liabilities. Again, the extent of this gain depends on the existing interest rate and the maturity of the contract. We have gathered figures on average mortgage rates from the *Economic Report of the President* (1982) and have assumed the maturity of mortgages for this RHS population declines from fifteen years in 1969 to ten years in 1979. Other debts, including personal and automobile loans, have an assumed maturity of roughly three years.

Once we have estimated the vulnerability of the real value of each asset and liability to changes in the nominal interest rates, our computation of each household's vulnerability is straightforward. The vulnerability of a household's portfolio is simply the weighted average of the vulnerability of the assets in that portfolio, where the weights depend on the amount of each type of asset. Take, for example, someone who in 1975 had 75 percent of his net wealth in corporate bonds, 75 percent in bank accounts, and negative 50 percent in mortgages (that is, he had a mortgage liability of 50 percent of net worth). His vulnerability to inflation and interest rate changes would be

$$.75 \times 6.1 + .75 \times 1.0 - .5(6.1) = 2.25.$$

This would indicate that a 1 percent rise in inflation would reduce the value of his wealth by 2.25 percent.

Comparison with Previous Results

In an earlier paper (1982b) we calculated wealth and inflation vulnerability only over the sample that survived until 1975. It turns out that the basic conclusion holds whether we use the sample of survivors or the complete sample—the basis for the results of this chapter. For example, we previously reported mean wealth in 1969 to be $71,302; it is $76,573 in this chapter. The difference is almost entirely due to an increase in pension evaluation from $6,645 to $13,663. The change in pension evaluation is caused by a more elaborate imputation procedure employed in this chapter, not to the sample selection. Median inflation vulnerability, V_3, was .06 based on the old sample and .03 on the new sample. Both numbers are small and the difference is not important.

References

Boskin, M., and M. Hurd. 1982. Are inflation rates different for the elderly? National Bureau of Economic Research Working Paper No. 943.
Bowen, William G., and T. A. Finegan. 1969. *The economics of labor force participation.* Princeton: Princeton University Press.
Clark, R., S. Allen, and D. Sumner. 1983. Inflation and pension benefits. Final Report for Department of Labor, Contract No. J-9-p-10074.
Clark, R., G. Maddox, R. Schrimper, and D. Sumner. 1982. Inflation and economic well-being of the elderly. Final report for National Institute on Aging, Grant No. 1 RO AG 92345 01.
Economic report of the president. 1982. Washington, D.C.: GPO.
_____. 1983. Washington, D.C.: GPO.
Employment and training report of the president. 1981. Washington, D.C.: GPO.
Hurd, M., and J. Shoven. 1982a. Real income and wealth of the elderly. *American Economic Review* (May): 314–18.
_____. 1982b. The economic status of the elderly. National Bureau of Economic Research Working Paper No. 914. Also in *Financial aspects of the U.S. pension system,* ed. Z. Bodie and J. Shoven, 359–97. Chicago: University of Chicago Press, 1983.
_____. 1983. The distributional impact of Social Security. National Bureau of Economic Research Working Paper No. 1155. Also in *Pensions, labor, and individual choice,* ed. D. Wise. Chicago: University of Chicago Press, forthcoming.
U.S. Department of Health and Human Services. 1981. Social Security bulletin annual statistical supplement, 1977–79. Washington, D.C.: GPO.

Comment   Sheldon Danziger

Introduction

Hurd and Shoven have provided, in their own words, "a detailed examination of the income and wealth of the elderly and their inflation vulner-

Sheldon Danziger is professor of social work, Romnes Faculty Fellow, and director of the Institute for Research on Poverty at the University of Wisconsin, Madison.

ability by analyzing the . . . Retirement History Survey. . . . This chapter is very much an extension of our earlier work" (p. 126). The chapter contains a wealth of descriptive information, but the documentation is so sparse that the reader must accept much of what is presented on the basis of what the authors choose to reveal. As a result, my critique consists mainly of a list of questions whose answers could not be found in this chapter. These possible sources of bias would not necessarily alter the conclusions, although they would attenuate some of the results.

Two quotations illustrate the major conclusions of the two main parts of the paper:

> Our overall impression from the RHS data is that as a group the elderly maintained their economic position quite well during the 1970s. Their incomes held up in the face of growing inflation, and their nonhuman wealth actually increased slightly in real terms. (P. 156)

In this quotation the meaning of *quite well* is not entirely clear. For example, one can use the Boskin-Hurd price index and compare the change in incomes over the 1968–78 decade. The data in tables 5.2 and 5.4 show a decline in real income of 18 percent for all elderly households, a 13 percent decline for couples, and a 3 percent increase for singles. If we exclude the insurance value of Medicare-Medicaid (one of the authors' adjustments that is very ad hoc) from this calculation for both years, the result would be a decline of 22 percent for couples and a decline of 10 percent for singles.

Nonhuman wealth (table 5.6), however, increases by 2 percent for all the elderly over the 1969–79 decade even if Medicare-Medicaid is excluded. Also, the real income of the bottom 10 percent has increased because of increased expenditures on public transfer programs. While data on the nonelderly are not presented in this paper, it is in comparison to the nonelderly that the elderly do "quite well." That is, over this period the real incomes of the elderly fell by less than those of the nonelderly, even though most of the elderly had retired.

> We found that government programs can take credit for much of the inflation protection in the sense that private wealth is much more inflation vulnerable than the sum of private and public wealth. Indexing Social Security is largely responsible for this fact in that if Social Security were not indexed, the elderly would be highly vulnerable to inflation. This is especially true of the poor elderly, a group that under indexing is, at the median, completely protected from inflation; without indexing, the poor elderly would lose large fractions of their small wealth, were the rate of inflation to rise. They would change from being the least vulnerable group among the elderly to being the most vulnerable. (P. 161)

The latter part of the paper, from which this conclusion is derived, is better documented than the first because the authors show the sensitivity of the inflation-vulnerability results to some of their assumptions about the sources of income. Also, while there are several other recent studies of the relative economic status of the elderly, Hurd and Shoven are the first to focus on the distributional effects of inflation among the elderly.

Sample Selection

Let me begin my catalog of questions with reference to the sample selectivity issue. What difference does it make that in an earlier paper the authors analyzed survivors, including only those who were in the sample in both the initial and terminal years, while in this chapter they included anyone who was in the sample in any single year? Obviously this chapter uses a larger number of observations—but how much larger? Because sample size for some of the deciles is already small (e.g., about 75 for single males in 1978), comparisons of population subgroups over time could be misleading even if the means for the entire sample are not very sensitive to this issue.

Using the Current Population Survey computer tapes, I found that the cohort of couples who were fifty-five to sixty-four in 1967 and sixty-nine to seventy-eight in 1981 was 40 percent smaller for whites and 42 percent smaller for blacks in the later year. We know that mortality rates are higher for the poor and that the poor are more likely to leave the sample by moving in with others or into nursing homes. If more of the poor are excluded in the terminal year, then income growth over time is biased upward. In fact, in the earlier Hurd and Shoven paper they stated: "Because we study changes in economic position, we dropped from the 1969 sample households that did not survive until 1975. We were left with 8,244 households (a decline of 26 percent from the initial 11,153 heads)" (1982, p. 52). In this paper they defend their choice of all observations, because "This both expands our sample in 1969 and eliminates a possible bias in our numbers" (p. 126). To what bias are they referring? I accept the logic of the first paper.

The compositional change in the sample due to differential survivorship is probably largest for single women and couples. The typical case is one in which the husband dies and the widow remains in the sample. If poorer males are the most likely to die, then the trend in well-being is biased upward for couples, since the poor are not in the terminal-year sample. But if the recently widowed women are wealthier than the already-widowed or never-married women, then the change in well-being for single women is also biased upward.

Data Creation

Turning now to the data creation, I have several additional questions. The authors converted wealth to income at a 3 percent real rate of return. How sensitive are their results to this discount factor? What if they had used actual data on average rates of return that varied by year and by type of asset? What I have in mind is the range of actual rates of return shown in chapter 11 of this volume, by Farley and Wilensky. Hurd and Shoven specify some income as inflation protected when it may not be—for example, transfers other than Social Security and Medicaid. How sensitive are their results to this factor? While the inflation-vulnerability section considers alternative assumptions, the income and wealth tables do not.

The authors state: "Responses to questions regarding flows are capitalized to yield wealth figures if corresponding wealth data were not available. Where possible, expected rather than actual flows were capitalized" (p. 163). Why use expected flows when actual ones are observed? For example, how did the authors derive a value for expected income from AFDC? Why didn't they use actual data?

For how many observations did the authors impute income and wealth data? Was it done more for the poor than for the elderly? If so, the procedure would impart biases since "if a datum could not be imputed by reference to the same question in another year for the same respondent, the datum was set equal to the median of all nonmissing answers for other respondents" (p. 162). Thus, if the poor were most likely to have missing data in all the years, then the use of the median would raise well-being and reduce inequality relative to their "true" values.

Hurd and Shoven's use of a single value for real Medicare and Medicaid expenditures for every year for every elderly person is particularly troublesome. The authors are interested in differences across the income and wealth distributions, and these payments vary dramatically by state of residence, over time, and by income of the respondent. Since the real values of Medicare and Medicaid benefits have eroded in recent years, estimates of changes in well-being over time will be biased upward. And to the extent that residents of poorer states receive below-average Medicaid benefits, the results are again upward biased.

In addition, most Medicaid expenditures for the elderly subsidize nursing home residents who are not included in the RHS sample. The appropriate procedure to obtain a Medicare-Medicaid value for persons in the RHS is either to reduce the numerator to reflect the insurance value of Medicare and Medicaid for the noninstitutionalized or to increase the denominator to account for elderly persons in nursing homes. The latter procedure also requires an adjustment to the mean level of well-being of the cohort, since nursing home residents have below-average income and wealth.

Finally, the aged now spend a higher percentage of their income on medical care than they did in the mid-1960s. Could some portion of the large increase in Medicare-Medicaid income the authors assign to RHS respondents, not in a general equilibrium model, be more appropriately assigned to medical care providers? Of course, one would need to distinguish pure price gains to providers from quality and quantity increases. This problem is most relevant to comparisons of the relative economic well-being of the elderly and nonelderly, but also to differences over time for this cohort.

Life-Cycle Hypothesis

The authors examine the median nonhuman wealth data in table 5.11 and suggest that "the numbers are weakly supportive of the life-cycle theory" because wealth increases with age in 1969 and decreases with age in 1979.

But rather than read across the rows (age groups) as the authors do, I suggest reading down the columns (years) and focusing on how the wealth of a single-year age cohort changes over the ten-year period. Consider couples, for example. In each age group, real wealth is much higher in 1979 than in 1969. For example, among those couples whose head was sixty in 1969, nonhuman wealth was $63,285 in 1969 and $171,060 in 1979. This latter figure, adjusted with the Boskin-Hurd index (see table 5.8), is about $90,000 in 1969 dollars. Thus, as these couples aged from 60 to 70, and as most retired, their nonhuman wealth increased by over 40 percent. I view this failure of wealth to decline as a weak rejection of the life-cycle hypothesis. I suggested above that the authors' choices of sample, data, and valuation techniques probably overstated the growth in well-being over time. However, I do not think that the alternatives I discussed would turn a 40 percent increase in wealth into a decline.

Conclusion

I am confident that the adjustments and data concerns I suggested would not affect the authors' strong conclusion that government programs substantially increase the well-being of the elderly, reduce inequality among them, and make them less vulnerable to inflation. Nor do I doubt that the most important contributor to these results in recent years has been the indexation of government benefits, particularly Social Security.

For example, consider the relative economic well-being of two successive cohorts of the elderly, one of which is similar to the RHS cohort. Using Current Population Survey data, I found that between 1967 and 1981, the real-money income of couples whose head was fifty-five to sixty-four in 1967 and sixty-nine to seventy-eight in 1981 declined by about 25 percent. This is consistent with the Hurd-Shoven change in real-money income. But couples whose head was sixty-nine to seventy-eight in 1981 had real incomes about 25 percent above those of couples who were sixty-nine to seventy-eight in 1967. The major source of improvement for the younger cohort was that its real Social Security income was more than 50 percent higher.

Hurd and Shoven have provided a detailed picture of the progress of the elderly over the 1969–79 decade. Although they do not draw policy implications, one point is clear. The taxation of Social Security benefits, such as the method enacted in the 1983 Social Security Amendments, will have much less adverse distributional impacts on the distribution of well-being among the elderly than will any change in benefit indexation.

Reference

Hurd, M. and J. Shoven. 1982. The economic status of the elderly. National Bureau of Economic Research Working Paper No. 914. Also in *Financial aspects of the U.S. pension system,* ed. Z. Bodie and J. Shoven, 359–97. Chicago: University of Chicago Press, 1983.

6 The Horizontal and Vertical Equity Characteristics of the Federal Individual Income Tax, 1966–1977

Marcus C. Berliant
Robert P. Strauss

6.1 Introduction

The purpose of this paper is twofold: to compare and contrast traditional and recent theoretical constructs of horizontal and vertical equity through the use of a general, theoretical framework; and to measure the horizontal and vertical equity of the federal individual income tax,[1] over a significant period of time, through the use of large, microdata files of federal individual income tax returns, and through the use of certain summary index numbers developed earlier by the authors and based on Wertz (1975).[2]

In terms of our major theoretical results, we find that the traditional principle of equity, taken to mean "equal treatment of equals," is logically separate from the more recent notion of horizontal equity which suggests

Marcus C. Berliant is assistant professor of economics at the University of Rochester. Robert P. Strauss is professor of economics and public policy at Carnegie-Mellon University.

Initial funding for this research was provided by the Office of Research and Statistics, Social Security Administration, under grant 10-P-98082-3-01. The authors would like to thank Martin David, Kenneth Wertz, Fritz Scheuren, and Carsten Kowalczyk for comments. They also wish to acknowledge the forbearance and general assistance provided by the Carnegie-Mellon Computation Center where all computer work was performed. Responsibility for errors rests with the authors.

1. Throughout this study we examine the ratio of net taxes to measured, economic income and interpret this ratio to reflect the equity of the tax system. Much of this chapter addresses the issue of what *equity* may be defined to mean. These measures are ex post measures of the relationship between individual taxes and their pretax income. It is therefore unnecessary to account separately for behavioral responses of taxpayers to tax rules that lead them to rearrange their sources of income and ultimately affect their taxes as well. Because we are examining various ex post measures over time, we are able to see if stability exists in the observed pattern of vertical and horizontal equity in the system. A disadvantage with examining just one year of data is that the observed, ex post distribution may reflect transitory reactions to a particular event.

2. See Berliant and Strauss 1983.

that the relative positions of individuals' before-and after-tax income be maintained for horizontal equity to be achieved. While several authors have stated that the classical criteria of equals-treated-equally implies this no-rank-reversal criterion,[3] we demonstrate through two simple counter-examples that this is not true. Also, we suggest that the analysis of a tax system's equity is inherently a two-variable problem (the economic position of taxpayers without regard to the tax system, and the taxpayers' effective tax rates), rather than a single variable problem (the distribution of before- or after-tax income).

Generally, our framework permits the distinction between measures of income inequality, and vertical and horizontal equity. The new notion of horizontal equity that requires maintenance of relative rank position may be viewed in this framework, according to our nomenclature, to be a vertical rather than a horizontal equity concept, while inequality measures are found to be income distribution concepts.

In terms of our major empirical results, we find a number of interesting regularities in the pattern of horizontal and vertical equity of the U.S. personal income tax. Over the period 1966-77 we find that the overall vertical progressivity of the federal personal income tax has remained at a high level—that is, comparisons of pairs of taxpayers in each of the twelve years suggests that at least 80 percent of the comparisons are progressive; that is, those with higher incomes experienced higher effective tax rates than those with lower incomes. By contrast, there is substantial evidence of horizontal inequity. Those taxpayers classified as being in the same economic position were found in 80 percent of the comparisons to experience different effective tax rates; we interpret this to be evidence of horizontal inequity.

While the level of progressivity was generally high, evidence indicates that it has declined somewhat over the sample period (1966-77). Also, we find that the progressivity of the tax system for single taxpayers and married-filing-jointly taxpayers has been declining over the study period. We do not, by contrast, find significant trends in horizontal equity over time for any subgroups.

If we characterize the impact of taxation through the use of the Gini coefficient of after-tax income, an income inequality measure, we find that it is declining over time in a significant fashion generally and for single and married-filing-jointly taxpayers. Thus, the Gini coefficient tells us that the distribution of after-tax income became more egalitarian or equal, while the vertical and horizontal index numbers indicate that a more complex process has been at work, since there has been a decline in progressive components in the system and in increase in regressive components in the tax system over the period 1966-77.

3. For example, Feldstein 1976, Atkinson 1980, Plotnick 1981, and King 1983.

If we examine the overall level of progressivity and horizontal equity by type of filing unit, we find that there are much greater differences among these strata, in the extent to which the tax system creates horizontal inequity, in comparison to the differences in the overall level of progressivity. That is, the tax system tends to be progressive at the same rate, but fails to achieve horizontal equity at the same rate for different types of filing units. Generally, horizontal equity tends to be greatest for single taxpayers and smallest for married-filing-jointly taxpayers. This appears to be related to the high degree of itemization among married taxpayers filing jointly.

The body of this chapter is organized as follows: section 6.2 provides a general conceptual framework within which various equity concepts may be analyzed, and provides a comparison of traditional concepts and measures with others in the literature. The intuition behind the index numbers developed by the authors is also discussed. Section 6.3 describes the microdata files used in the empirical section of the paper, and compares the empirical measures of income with notions of theoretically desired, economic income. Section 6.3 also discusses a number of technical, related issues of how one implements the index numbers developed in section 6.2. Section 6.4 provides the empirical results for our measures of horizontal and vertical equity along with those found in the literature. Section 6.5 concludes.

6.2   Concepts of Horizontal and Vertical Equity

6.2.1   A Framework for Analyzing Alternative Concepts of Equity

We provide here a discussion of alternative horizontal and vertical equity concepts and a rationale for the use of our index numbers, which are relatively novel. Since the emphasis in this paper is primarily empirical, we omit formal proofs of the central propositions here; a more complete study is Berliant and Strauss (1984), where proofs of the propositions stated below may be found.

Summary measures of income and other distributions have long interested economists and statisticians. In a number of related papers Atkinson (1970), Blackorby and Donaldson (1976), Sen (1973), Kondor (1975), Rosen (1978), Fields and Fei (1978), and King (1983) have pointed out that index measures of the income distribution should be consistent with a social welfare function. Atkinson (1970), for example, develops on the basis of certain characteristics, or postulates concerning an underlying social welfare function, a particular index of vertical income inequality, while Fields and Fei (1978) examine a number of commonly used index measures (coefficent of variation, Gini coefficient, Atkinson's index, and

Theil's index) to see if they are consistent with three axioms that they recommend for vertical measures of income inequality.[4]

Related to the broad area of income distribution has been a literature in public finance concerned with the measurement of the progressivity of a tax system. For example, Musgrave and Thin (1948) examined a variety of formulas for calculating the degree of progression of a personal income tax system. Much earlier, Mill (1921) sought to ascertain whether one could produce a progressive income tax regime if one knew consumers' marginal utilities of income; Samuelson (1947) made this approach more precise.

Most recently, Feldstein (1976), Atkinson (1980), and Plotnick (1981) have rekindled interest in horizontal equity. In an important recent paper, King (1983) unified consideration of the vertical and horizontal characteristics of tax systems by using a social welfare function approach suggested by these earlier papers.

In this recent literature, the term *vertical equity* refers to any comparison of the after-tax income distributions generated by tax systems. Measures of vertical equity (or inequity) are essentially measures of after-tax income inequality. The term horizontal equity in this literature refers to the measurement of any characteristic of a tax system that requires the use of the prior- or pretax positions of taxpayers. For example, a measure of horizontal equity or inequity might require the use of the pretax income of each consumer.

It is possible to construct a general framework that incorporates this scheme as well as others. A set of pretax attributes is postulated to be a vector space of variables such as location, income, and marital status parameterized in Euclidean space. There is a vector of pretax attributes associated with each consumer. If a tax system is defined to be a map from any vector of pretax attributes of a consumer to after-tax income, then it is impossible to separate the ranking of tax systems from the distribution of pretax attributes. This is due to the idea that a tax system that has an inequitable feature that applies to no consumer should not be ranked differently from a tax system without this feature. Hence, an equity concept (of any type) is defined to be any ordering over the product of tax systems and attribute distributions; a tax system–attribute distribution pair is our basic construct. The measures of vertical and horizontal equity discussed above are all equity concepts in the sense just defined.

In the literature described above, a restriction placed on horizontal equity concepts is that there should be no rank reversals in moving from pretax to posttax income. In other words, if a tax system–attribute distribution pair, (reflected, for example, by an effective tax rate and before-tax

---

4. Whether or not such index numbers indeed have all the desirable properties of their parent social welfare functions is discussed by Berliant and Strauss 1983. It should also be noted in this regard that if the operational measure of equity is a multivariate index number, it generally cannot be uniquely deduced from a social welfare function.

income pair of values) satisfies a no-rank-reversal condition, then this tax system–attribute distribution pair ought to be placed in the highest equivalence class of the ordering associated with a horizontal equity concept (or the *lowest* equivalence class of the ordering associated with a horizontal *in*equity concept). We call the highest and lowest equivalence classes of an ordering the extreme equivalence classes generated by that ordering.

Is the no-rank-reversal condition sufficient, necessary, or both, for placement of a tax system–attribute distribution pair in an extreme equivalence class? It can be easily shown that such a condition is in fact only sufficient for placement in an extreme equivalence class. For example, this condition is only sufficient for the measures in King (1983). More generally, any condition that is postulated to be sufficient to assign a tax system–attribute distribution pair satisfying the condition to an extreme equivalence class of an equity concept is called an *equity principle*. An example of an equity principle is the no-rank-reversal condition. It is obvious that some equity principles are stronger than others and that the weaker equity principles have larger extreme equivalence classes.

The more traditional scheme that we employ below differs substantially from the horizontal-vertical scheme used by the authors listed above. The traditional ideas about equity with which we are concerned seem to divide equity measures into three categories rather than the two noted above, while at the same time using a similar nomenclature. Indeed, we believe that this has been the source of some confusion. Therefore, we use three terms—income inequality, a concept of horizontal equity that we label HE, and a concept of vertical equity that we label VE—in specific ways which we define below. These three concepts of equity correspond, in our view, to precise definitions of older (or classical) notions of income inequality, and vertical and horizontal equity.

These three categories of equity concepts are used, for example, by Musgrave (1959). By creating a distinction between the distributive and allocative functions of government, Musgrave makes a distinction between income redistribution (a distributive idea), and the determination of the method of taxation for providing public goods (an allocative idea). The latter includes, as a partial solution, the use of taxes based on ability to pay, which in turn includes as considerations vertical and horizontal equity. It is in this sense that we shall develop three equity concept classifications.

The first category of equity concepts that we call *income inequality* is the same as the term *vertical equity* as used by the recent literature; it consists of all equity concepts that are functions of only the after-tax income distribution generated by a tax system–attribute distribution pair.

The second category of equity concepts, *HE,* derives from the view, stated, for example, by Musgrave and Musgrave (1980): "Perhaps the most widely accepted principle of equity in taxation is that people in equal positions should be treated equally."

Of course, this statement is only an equity principle, not an equity concept. It requires that a tax system–attribute distribution pair that treats equals in the same manner be placed in an extreme equivalence class of an equity concept. However, the principle does indicate that one must be able to say who are equals and who are not equals in order to evaluate a tax system–attribute distribution pair. Hence, we divide the space of attributes into cells, where those in each cell are considered to be equals by the policy analyst. This may seem arbitrary, but must be done in order to use the traditional notion of equity, and, from a pragmatic point of view, must be done in order to evaluate any index measure since data are always provided in aggregates.

Once this classification is accomplished, an HE equity concept is an ordering such that if the posttax income distribution for each cell of equals for two tax system–attribute distribution pairs is the same, then the two pairs are equivalent under the ordering. In this way only changes in the comparisons of equals can alter the ranking of a pair. In other words, equals are treated in the same manner by both pairs without regard to how unequals are treated. Examples of such measures can be found in Wertz (1975, 1978) and Berliant and Strauss (1983). Also, Pechman and Okner (1974) study empirically variations in effective tax rates by income class; this is essentially an example of a measure of HE as well.

Our development of the third equity concept, *VE,* is complementary to the concepts of HE and distributional equity presented above. A measure of VE is defined to be an equity concept that is neither an HE equity concept nor an income inequality equity concept. That is, measures of VE do not depend solely on the posttax income distribution (they depend on some pretax variables), nor do they depend solely on the posttax position of equals. Thus, they involve pre- and posttax positions as well as comparisons of taxpayers who are not equals.

This completes the development of the two schemes for categorizing equity concepts. Note that the second, traditional classification scheme yields a finer, and, in our opinion, more natural partition of equity concepts. One can say more precisely what an index number is measuring when it is classified using the second scheme. The index numbers implemented empirically below to evaluate progressivity and equity are respectively VE, and HE satisfying the principle of treating equals equally.

Moving now to an examination of the two equity principles used most frequently in the recent literature—those principles dealing with no-rank-reversal and equals-treated-equally—it can be shown using two counterexamples that neither one implies the other. That is, equals-treated-equally is neither necessary nor sufficent for a tax system–attribute distribution pair to satisfy the no-rank-reversal criterion.

For the first counterexample, taxpaying units are evenly divided between two narrow pretax income brackets—one high and one low—where the brackets have the same width and the same internal distribution within each bracket. The brackets also have substantial space between them without any taxpaying units (see fig. 6.1). Further, suppose the tax-transfer system maintains the overall distribution of these units, but is such that the corresponding units in each band switch places. Certainly, given that these units *within* each band are considered to be equals, this tax system conforms to the classical notion of equity, that of equals being treated equally. However, this tax system also plays havoc with the rank ordering of *all* of the units. Thus, changes in the rank ordering do not imply that there are horizontal inequities present in the tax system.

Two obvious objections may be raised to the structure of this example. First, the term *equals* is never defined; but this is not needed since the bands can be made as narrow as necessary (even degenerate). Second, no real-income distribution looks like this one. However, it is equally obvious that this example may be embedded in a larger distribution while maintaining its purpose and conclusion.

The second counterexample postulates a pretax regime with one narrow income bracket in which the entire population is concentrated (see fig. 6.2). Suppose the tax-transfer system spreads the distribution proportionally over a much wider range (i.e., its support becomes larger). Certainly the rank ordering of all individuals does not change under this tax scheme. Also, if the pretax income band is narrow enough to allow all taxpaying units to be considered equals, then the tax system is not horizontally equitable in the classical or HE sense; some taxpayers receive windfalls while others experience huge losses through imposition of the tax system. Thus, tax systems characterized by horizontal inequities do not necessarily change the rank order of taxpaying units.

These counterexamples have demonstrated that each equity principle must be justified *independent* of the other if one is used as an underlying assumption for the measurement of horizontal equity. Of course, they

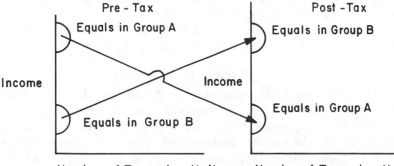

Fig. 6.1.

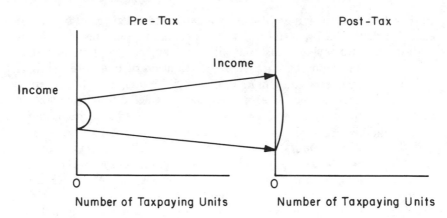

Fig. 6.2.

might also enter as constraints in other models. However, the following result relates the two principles in a different way:

PROPOSITION: If cells of equals are singletons in the space of attributes,[5] and equals are not treated equally by a tax system–distribution pair, then there exists a ranking of taxpayers so that the tax system reverses some ranks. If a tax system–attribute distribution pair generates a rank reversal, then there exists a set of cells of equals in the space of attributes such that equals are not treated equally.

In summary, we have treated classification schemes for equity concepts or measures of vertical and horizontal equity to clarify some semantic problems and to uncover the assumptions behind various measures. We have also examined the relationships between two commonly used equity principles. To develop a specific measure, one must not only decide on a classification scheme and category along with perhaps an equity principle, but must make other assumptions as well. We have indicated where the measures that we favor fit in; a more complete mathematical development of them may be found in Berliant and Strauss (1984).

To compare a variety of other approaches, a broad selection of index numbers are calculated in the empirical work that follows. Their algebraic statements in consistent notation may be found in Appendix A.

6.2.2 Classifications of Vertical and Horizontal Equity

We now turn to the matter of providing operational criteria that permit us to make distinctions between horizontal and vertical equity in the sense of HE and VE; we provide here the criteria used to classify pairs of attributes. To describe the vertical characteristics of the tax system, we follow Wertz (1978) and partition taxpayers into three parts: the fraction of taxpayers whose tax liability is progressively distributed, ϕ; the fraction of

---

5. A singleton is a set consisting of a point.

taxpayers whose tax liability is proportionately distributed, θ; and, the fraction of taxpayers whose tax liability is regressively distributed, γ. Note that by construction, $\phi + \theta + \gamma = 1.0$. Also, note that the concepts employed are relative concepts obtained by making pairwise comparisons of relative income and effective tax rate positions. A comparison of two taxpayers shows progressivity when both the income and effective tax rate of one taxpayer are greater than the income and tax rate of another taxpayer. Proportionality occurs when the incomes of the two taxpayers being compared are different, but the effective tax rates are the same. Finally, regressivity is said to occur when one taxpayer has a larger income but a lower effective tax rate than the other in the comparison.

To ascertain the extent to which taxes are distributed progressively, proportionately, and regressively, we take into account not only the number of occurrences of each type of comparison, but also the degree of income and tax rate disparities. Our subjective judgment is that it matters when scoring such comparisons whether person A with tax rate of 28 percent and person B with tax rate of 20 percent have similar or very different incomes. Thus, actual measurement involves the weighting of each comparison count by the absolute difference in income of each pair of taxpayers.

Similarly, it would seem to matter whether the tax rates of A and B are similar or very different. If A has an income of $30,000 and B an income of $15,000, it would seem important to observe whether the respective tax rates were 28 percent and 20 percent, or 32 percent and 18 percent. The former would seem to be less progressive than the latter comparison. When we account for differences in tax rates, however, we weight by the ratio of tax rates rather than the difference in tax rates. We do this for several reasons. First, using the ratio distinguishes more effectively between a paired comparison of tax rates of 14 percent and 10 percent, and 54 percent and 50 percent. While the differences are both 4 percent, the former pair of tax rates are clearly more disparate. Second, using the ratio of rates deals with proportional comparisons. Recall that if the tax rates in a paired comparison were the same, the difference in rates would yield a weight of zero, while the ratio would yield a weight of one. In the second case the property of the three types of comparisons adding to 1.0 is maintained, whereas under the first weighting scheme, proportional comparisons, because of zero weights, drop out.

It should be noted that our analysis of tax rate/income positions is based on effective rates of taxation and pretax income as classification criteria. Another approach would be to compare individuals in terms of how much income they retain after taxation, or their after-tax income. The two are obviously related. If the effective tax rate is t, then the after-tax-income approach to measuring vertical equity involves making comparisons of the quantity $(1 - t)$ among pairs of taxpayers. The scoring of comparisons in terms of progressivity, regressivity, and porportionality would be the same in both instances, except that progressivity would be deemed to occur when the fraction of retained or after-tax income declined as income rose. It can be shown,[6] however, that using the after-tax-income approach results in index numbers that are not invariant to scalar multiplication. Because such invariance is generally viewed as a desirable property of index numbers, and the after-tax approach fails to maintain it, we shall use the effective tax rates calculated as the ratio of net taxes to pretax income.

Horizontal equity in the sense of HE, unlike vertical equity, does not admit of progressive, proportional, or regressive distinctions in our framework, but a disparity in treatment of those in the same position. Accordingly, we shall measure the extent to which effective rates are different—instances of inequity—and instances in which effective rates are the same—instances of equity—for pairs of taxpayers. As with our measure of vertical equity, we shall weight the count of such comparisons by the ratio of effective tax rates, since greater disparities in ratios of tax rates are taken to reflect greater horizontal inequity.

Both the horizontal and vertical measures are obtained by making all possible comparisons among pairs of taxpayers and accumulating the weighted counts of each type of classification. Note that in case of the vertical comparisons, a tax system may be said to have, simultaneously, progressive, regressive, and proportional components. This occurs because the comparisons are relative, and the number of comparisons are numerous; for n individuals, there are $n(n - 1)$ comparisons. Normalization of the accumulation of each of the three possible weighted, vertical counts by the sum of the three components provides a description of the fraction of comparisons that are progressive, proportional, and regressive, and as such, provides a simple index score that can be compared over time for various possible tax schemes. Normalization of the weighted counts of horizontal equity and inequity by their sum provides the same sort of information.[7] See Appendix A for a presentation, in tabular form, of the algebra of various index numbers implemented below.[8]

6.3   Data, Measurement Considerations, and Other Index Numbers

6.3.1   Data Sources and Limitations

In order to measure repeatedly the distribution of federal personal income taxes, we use the publicly available samples of individual income tax

---

6. See Berliant and Strauss 1983.

7. A more complete development of the intuition and mathematics of these and related, multiperiod index numbers may be found in Appendix 1 of Berliant and Strauss 1983.

8. The index numbers considered throughout this paper relate ex post effective tax rates to pretax economic income. Often it is of interest to compare ex ante effective tax rates under different tax regimes. For an analagous set of index numbers that keep track of the relative position of taxpayers under different tax regimes, see Berliant and Strauss 1983.

returns maintained by the National Archives. Each year, the Statistics of Income (SOI) Division of the Internal Revenue Service creates a random, stratified sample of several hundred thousand individual tax returns which are used for the annual publication *Statistics of Income Individual Income Tax Returns*. A sample of this file is typically drawn by the U.S. Treasury Department for revenue-estimating purposes in support of tax legislation. This sample is used in conjunction with the department's microsimulation model of the individual income tax,[9] and is usually described as the tax model data file.

Also, SOI creates a sample from its large SOI sample and provides it annually to the National Archives. This public-use sample of anonymous individual income tax returns is usually at least twice the size of the sample provided to the Treasury Department, though it is less complete than the Treasury sample in that the Office of Tax Analysis usually synthetically adds additional income information to the sample and creates new weighting schemes to permit the sample to forecast for more recent periods. At the time this project was initiated (1980), annual files for 1966 through 1977 were available from the National Archives and are accordingly the focus of this study.

As is well known, information on the income and tax position of individuals and families is available from a variety of sources; each source has certain strengths and weaknesses. The files used in this study reflect the income and individual income taxes of taxpayers. Other files such as the Current Population Survey (CPS) are much richer sources of demographic information and information about nonwage income. The CPS data base contains the richest information about nonwage income, but does not have actual data on taxes paid. Researchers interested in using this broad definition of income have had to either match tax information synthetically or simulate personal taxes to examine effective tax rates. The SOI data base contains actual tax information, but does not have as broad a definition of income as these other sources. Thus, the SOI does not have information about low-income individuals, neither are they in the file nor are their sources of income given. Various cash and noncash sources of transfer income are not recorded for federal tax purposes and are thus unavailable to this study. Since variations in effective tax rates over time is the primary subject matter of our research, we have chosen to utilize the richer source of information on taxes actually paid by individuals and sacrificed access to a broader definition of income.

Both the SOI and CPS information fail to reflect nonmarket income captured by the personal income concept in the national income accounts. Personal income, as defined in the national income and product accounts,

---

9. See Wyscarver 1978 for a description of the simulation model and techniques used to extrapolate historical data to more current time periods.

is substantially broader than adjusted gross income, total money income, or the concept of economic income we were able to construct from the available data files. Our income concepts do not capture, for example, interest on state and local bonds, which is tax exempt for federal purposes and therefore not reported on tax forms.

Table 6.1 displays the components of economic income available for this study. Such items as wages and salaries, interest and dividend income (return to capital), and types of business income from farming, sole proprietorships, rents, and royalties are contained in our measure, as are such items as long- and short-term capital gains, gains from installment sales, and pension income.

Table 6.1   Components of Economic Income Used in Analysis by Year

Component of Income	66	67	68	69	70	71	72	73	74	75	76	77
Wages and salaries	X	X	X	X	X	X	X	X	X	X	X	X
Interest income	X	X	X	X	X	X	X	X	X	X	X	X
Gross dividends	X	X	X	X	X	X	X	X	X	X	X	X
Interest income	X	X	X	X	X	X	X	X	X	X	X	X
Gross business or profession income	X	X	X	X	X	X	X	X	X	X	X	X
Short-term capital gains	X	X	X	X	X	X	X	X	X	X	X	X
Long-term net capital gains	X	X	X	X	X	X	X	X	X	X	X	X
Farm income	X	X	X	X	X	X	X	X	X	X	X	X
Rental income	X	X	X	X	X	X	X	X	X	X	X	X
Royalty income	X	X	X	X	X	X	X	X	X	X	X	X
Partnership income	X	X	X	X	X	X	X	X	X	X	X	X
Small business corporation income	X	X	X	X	X	X	X	X	X	X	X	X
Estate and trust income	X	X	X	X	X	X	X	X	X	X	X	X
Capital gain distributions							X	X	X	X	X	X
Taxable portion of pensions	X	X				X	X	X	X	1	1	1
Fully taxable pensions							X	X	X	X	X	X
Gross pensions			X	X	X					X	X	X
Alimony	2	2	2	2	2	X	X	X	X	X	X	X
State income tax refunds	2	2	2	2	2	X	X	X	X	X	X	X
Premature distribution from IRAs and Keogh plans	2	2	2	2	2	2	2	2	2	2	X	2
Miscellaneous income	X	X	X	X	X	X	X	X	X	X	X	X
Supplemental schedule gains							X	X	X	X	X	X
Ordinary gains	X	X	X	X	X	X						
Other gains	X	X	X	X	X	X						

Sources: SOI files.
Notes: (1) Shown separately but also included in gross pension; (2) included in miscellaneous income.

Table 6.2   **Comparison of Income Concept Used in Study to Adjusted Gross Income and BEA Personal Income Concepts ($ in billions)**

Year	Sample Count[a]	Economic Income[b]	AGI	BEA Pers. Income	Sample Wages	BEA Wages	Sample/ BEA Wages %
1966	86,610	482.8	468.5	588.2	379.9	398.4	95.4
1967	87,160	524.4	504.8	629.9	411.3	426.9	96.3
1968	91,484	581.8	555.5	690.6	451.6	469.6	96.2
1969	93,065	623.6	603.2	754.7	497.2	515.7	96.4
1970	95,316	653.5	631.9	811.1	531.9	548.7	96.9
1971	99,137	696.0	672.6	868.4	565.2	581.5	97.2
1972	106,581	775.9	746.8	951.4	621.1	635.2	97.8
1973	112,440	853.4	828.1	1065.2	687.3	702.6	97.8
1974	98,645	924.6	909.9	1168.6	759.9	765.2	99.3
1975	100,851	964.3	947.0	1265.0	794.5	806.3	98.5
1976	164,137	1105.9	1054.6	1391.2	881.0	889.9	99.0
1977	155,212	1173.5	1159.4	1540.4	969.9	983.2	98.6

[a]Number of returns on SOI data file.
[b]See text for definition.

Table 6.2 displays the number of (unweighted) observations used by year in the analysis below, along with the total economic income and adjusted gross income (AGI) that were on the annual tapes.[10] Our measure of economic income was typically 1 to 3 percent larger than adjusted gross income each year, though considerably smaller than the personal income measure estimated by the Bureau of Economic Analysis (BEA). A sizeable portion of the difference between either AGI or our measure of economic income and personal income is due to various types of transfer payments. Since many of these transfer payments accrue to nontaxable, low-income individuals and families and do not affect their tax status (they simply are not in the tax system and are not taxable), part of the discrepancy between personal income and our measure of income is not problematical for our purpose. That is, since the purpose of this study is to measure the vertical and horizontal characteristics of the tax system, the fact that some types of income are not in our measure is not problematical to the extent that such income accrues to those outside the tax system.

The last columns in table 6.2 indicate wages and salaries in our data files in comparison to those estimated by BEA. Of interest here is that the coverage ratio is quite high—between 95 and 99 percent. Thus, at least for wage and salary income, our estimates of the vertical and horizontal equity of the tax system should be reliable.

10. It should be noted that our control totals of weighted, adjusted gross income compared favorably with published totals in the pertinent *Statistics of Income* publication or that displayed in table 8.13 of the 1981 supplement to the *Survey of Current Business,* U.S. Department of Commerce 1981.

6.3.2   Other Index Numbers, and Computational and Related Considerations

As noted earlier, there is a substantial index-number literature devoted to ascertaining the structure of income inequality. Since this project involved the repeated computer analysis of better than 1.29 million (anonymous) tax returns,[11] we implemented, in addition to the vertical and horizontal measures developed above, seventeen other measures of the vertical distribution of after-tax income, and one additional measure of the horizontal distribution of taxes which we gleaned from the literature. Appendix A provides in a consistent mathematical form these index numbers and the appropriate reference. Of interest is that sometimes various students of index numbers have different definitions of what is purportedly the same index number.[12]

With roughly 100,000 observations per year, calculation of each independent vertical measure, say γ and ϕ, would require 1×10^{10} calculations each per year, which was clearly too burdensome computationally. In order to make the computations tractable, we elected to classify returns into 25 income classes, and 114 tax rate classes.[13] This dimensionality was used in our earlier study, and thus permits comparison of results from the Treasury and public-use SOI data bases. The finer division of tax rates is justified by our interest in the extent of progressivity in the system. Because we performed the analysis over time, we created income intervals that corresponded to 4 percent of the weighted number of tax returns each year.[14]

11. For each year under study, substantial effort was involved in converting and checking, against published tables, the twelve data files from the National Archives. Their files provided to the project were in IBM packed decimal format. We then converted them to Dec ASCII, extracted the relevant variables for the analysis, constructed control totals of AGI and the cumulative distributions in $500 intervals to choose proper income intervals, and performed the index number calculations per se. On average, each file was passed four times. Even using high-density storage formats, many years required the use of multireel data files.

12. Compare Theil 1967 with Bourguignon 1979, for example.

13. Even this reduction in the size of the computation problem results in many calculations. Using a 25X114 matrix creates 2,850 cells which need to be compared to 2,849 cells or 8.1 million potential comparisons. Of course, many cells are empty (low-income taxpayers do not face high effective rates (and vice versa), so initial identification of nonzero cells can reduce materially the computational burden. Generally, under 1,000 cells needed to be considered. Copies of the algorithms developed for this project are available from the authors upon request.

As is apparent from the mathematics of our vertical and horizontal index numbers, the dimensionality of the income classes and tax rate classes will affect the overall level of results obtained. In our earlier study, Berliant and Strauss 1983, we experimented with widening the tax rate intervals from single percentage points, as implemented in this paper, to intervals of four percentage points. The vertical equity scores remained essentially the same, while horizontal equity levels rose. In particular, this fourfold widening in the tax rate classification was accompanied by a twofold improvement in the measured level of horizontal equity.

14. It is worth noting here that the income intervals we used are rather different than those used routinely over the years by the Treasury Department in their policy analysis. Generally, our income classes are much finer in the lower and middle ranges of the income distri-

In our earlier study we found that stratifying the analysis by type of filing unit (single, married filing jointly, married filing separately, and head of household) revealed the greatest differences in horizontal and vertical equity, as contrasted with other strata such as those who itemized and those who did not. Accordingly, we stratified our analysis by filing type, and, in 1974, by whether or not a spouse with wage and salary income was present. Unfortunately, limitations of funding for computer resources prevented the complete exploitation of this very rich set of data.[15]

6.4 Empirical Results

We present here the empirical results of applying the index numbers developed above, and detailed in Appendix A, to the data for 1966–77, in terms of overall measures of vertical and horizontal equity and stratified by filing status.

6.4.1 Overall Results, 1966–77

Panel A of table 6.3 presents the overall results for all filers and indicates that the extent of overall progressivity in the U.S. personal income tax was high. In 1968, 97.7 percent of the weighted vertical comparisons displayed progressivity. This represents the highest progressivity score recorded over the study period. The lowest progressivity score recorded was in 1966 when only 87.5 percent of the vertical comparisons displayed progressivity. Our vertical results with the public-use SOI data correspond to those obtained with the Treasury tax model sample and reported in Berliant and Strauss (1983). The latter data source recorded vertical progressivity scores of .882 in 1973 and .891 in 1975 while the public data source recorded scores of .890 in 1973 and .871 in 1975. As noted earlier, the Treasury tax model sample contains certain income imputations not available in the public samples, and, in the years in question, contained only 50,000.[16]

Since the vast majority of vertical comparisons display progressivity, it is not surprising that relatively small amounts of regressivity and proportionality are observed. Generally, between 8 to 11 percent of the comparisons display regressivity, and between 1 to 2 percent of the comparisons display proportionality.

---

bution compared to their classifications; the Treasury income groupings tend to focus attention on higher-income taxpayers. For general, statistical purposes, use of the four percentage point intervals is the more appropriate methodology.

15. Also due to resource limitations, we have been unable to analyze in a parallel manner the panel of matched personal tax returns jointly provided to the project by the Statistics Division of the Internal Revenue Service, Social Security Administration, and the Office of Tax Analysis, U.S. Treasury Department.

16. Horizontal equity scores are, however, notably different. Those obtained using Treasury data suggest greater inequity.

Table 6.3   **Vertical and Horizontal Index Values**

A. All Filers

Year	Prog %	Regr %	Prop %	Equity %	Ineq %	Avg Rate	Gini
1966	0.875	0.101	0.024	0.181	0.819	0.302	0.452
1967	0.877	0.099	0.024	0.170	0.830	0.289	0.457
1968	0.977	0.000	0.023	0.157	0.843	0.310	0.463
1969	0.878	0.102	0.020	0.150	0.850	0.323	0.459
1970	0.877	0.100	0.023	0.159	0.841	0.292	0.441
1971	0.892	0.087	0.021	0.164	0.836	0.310	0.448
1972	0.902	0.077	0.021	0.172	0.828	0.298	0.450
1973	0.890	0.091	0.020	0.166	0.834	0.357	0.457
1974	0.874	0.108	0.018	0.154	0.846	0.415	0.462
1975	0.871	0.108	0.021	0.163	0.837	0.471	0.465
1976	0.901	0.078	0.020	0.211	0.789	0.318	0.455
1977	0.864	0.119	0.017	0.183	0.817	0.498	0.471

B. Head of Household

Year	Prog %	Regr %	Prop %	Equity %	Ineq %	Avg Rate	Gini
1966	0.881	0.096	0.023	0.149	0.851	0.243	0.354
1967	0.854	0.123	0.023	0.126	0.874	0.241	0.332
1968	0.977	0.000	0.023	0.130	0.870	0.238	0.331
1969	0.910	0.069	0.021	0.180	0.820	0.285	0.373
1970	0.875	0.101	0.024	0.167	0.833	0.257	0.348
1971	0.879	0.098	0.023	0.145	0.855	0.312	0.341
1972	0.899	0.077	0.024	0.135	0.865	0.318	0.339
1973	0.889	0.085	0.026	0.140	0.860	0.238	0.355
1974	0.866	0.110	0.023	0.123	0.877	0.329	0.338
1975	0.880	0.087	0.033	0.212	0.788	0.351	0.351
1976	0.891	0.072	0.037	0.332	0.668	0.344	0.366
1977	0.857	0.119	0.024	0.241	0.759	0.413	0.382

C. Married Filing Separately

Year	Prog %	Regr %	Prop %	Equity %	Ineq %	Avg Rate	Gini
1966	0.849	0.115	0.036	0.217	0.783	0.343	0.421
1967	0.843	0.124	0.034	0.204	0.796	0.286	0.416
1968	0.974	0.000	0.026	0.172	0.828	0.284	0.417
1969	0.804	0.177	0.019	0.199	0.801	0.287	0.464
1970	0.859	0.115	0.026	0.169	0.831	0.325	0.407
1971	0.885	0.089	0.026	0.232	0.768	0.261	0.417
1972	0.866	0.105	0.029	0.183	0.817	0.294	0.394
1973	0.863	0.115	0.022	0.200	0.800	0.315	0.420
1974	0.783	0.189	0.028	0.173	0.827	0.349	0.422
1975	0.821	0.151	0.028	0.211	0.789	0.413	0.453
1976	0.872	0.108	0.020	0.212	0.788	0.341	0.405
1977	0.809	0.170	0.021	0.200	0.800	0.438	0.476

Table 6.3 (continued)

D. Married Filing Jointly

Year	Prog %	Regr %	Prop %	Equity %	Ineq %	Avg Rate	Gini
1966	0.887	0.092	0.021	0.097	0.903	0.253	0.343
1967	0.894	0.085	0.021	0.093	0.907	0.250	0.348
1968	0.980	0.000	0.020	0.087	0.913	0.255	0.353
1969	0.890	0.092	0.018	0.085	0.915	0.271	0.344
1970	0.883	0.096	0.021	0.086	0.914	0.255	0.337
1971	0.884	0.096	0.020	0.090	0.910	0.253	0.346
1972	0.900	0.080	0.019	0.091	0.909	0.250	0.343
1973	0.878	0.104	0.019	0.088	0.912	0.282	0.346
1974	0.862	0.121	0.017	0.082	0.918	0.314	0.354
1975	0.859	0.124	0.017	0.091	0.909	0.369	0.360
1976	0.901	0.083	0.016	0.106	0.894	0.252	0.349
1977	0.843	0.144	0.013	0.097	0.903	0.382	0.360

E. Single

Year	Prog %	Regr %	Prop %	Equity %	Ineq %	Avg Rate	Gini
1966	0.942	0.038	0.020	0.467	0.533	0.241	0.486
1967	0.937	0.043	0.020	0.465	0.535	0.220	0.497
1968	0.981	0.000	0.019	0.443	0.557	0.261	0.497
1969	0.944	0.041	0.015	0.433	0.567	0.244	0.487
1970	0.934	0.041	0.025	0.522	0.478	0.224	0.476
1971	0.945	0.032	0.023	0.556	0.444	0.258	0.489
1972	0.939	0.037	0.025	0.564	0.436	0.227	0.496
1973	0.934	0.046	0.020	0.516	0.484	0.365	0.482
1974	0.912	0.071	0.017	0.458	0.542	0.437	0.468
1975	0.915	0.063	0.022	0.457	0.543	0.507	0.480
1976	0.926	0.050	0.024	0.530	0.530	0.266	0.470
1977	0.895	0.085	0.020	0.448	0.552	0.511	0.476

Over time there is evidence of a decline in progressivity; the Pearson correlation between progressivity and time is − .74 (see table 6.4). There is also a modest corresponding upward drift in the fraction of comparisons displaying proportionately over time.[17] When there are increases in progressivity, they are accompanied by decreases in observed regressivity in the system, and vice versa.[18]

While the U.S. tax system displays substantial progressivity over the period 1966–77, it also displays very substantial horizontal inequity. No more than 21 percent of the weighted comparisons of taxpayers in the

17. The simple correlation between time and the fraction of comparisons displaying proportionality is .7067. See table 6.4 for various bivariate correlation coefficients.

18. The simple correlation between progressivity and regressivity over the study period is − .9901. Since the VE index numbers have two degrees of freedom, any bivariate correlation among pairs of VE scores is nontautological.

Table 6.4   Correlations among Index Numbers

	YR	PROG%	REGR%	PROP%	EQUITY%	INEQ%	AVINC	VAR	CO	MD	GINI	AG
YR	1.0000	-0.7388	0.7067	0.2196	0.1604	-0.1604	0.9820	0.9622	-0.6425	0.9807	-0.6776	-0.6748
PROG%		1.0000	-0.9901	-0.0548	0.0647	-0.0647	-0.7390	-0.7225	0.5874	-0.7223	0.7057	0.7035
REGR%			1.0000	-0.0854	-0.1748	0.1748	0.7002	0.6983	-0.5170	0.6817	-0.6974	-0.6947
PROP%				1.0000	0.8029	-0.8029	0.2640	0.1633	-0.4776	0.2806	-0.0165	-0.0197
EQUITY%					1.0000	-1.0000	0.1549	0.1062	-0.2251	0.1716	0.0331	0.0496
INEQ%						1.0000	-0.1549	-0.1062	0.2251	-0.1716	-0.0331	-0.0496
AVINC							1.0000	0.9789	-0.6769	0.9980	-0.6726	-0.6740
VAR								1.0000	-0.5205	0.9732	-0.6832	-0.6880
CO									1.0000	-0.6773	0.4941	0.4815
MD										1.0000	-0.6259	-0.6270
GINI											1.0000	0.9983
AG												1.0000
COCON												
AT1												
AT2												
KOLM												
RMD1												
RMD2												
THEIL1												
THEIL2												
THEIL3												
SDL												
LV												
HIND												

	COCON	AT.1	AT.2	KOLM	RMD1	RMD2	THEIL1	THEIL2	THEIL3	SDL	LV	HIND
YR	-0.2710	-0.6832	-0.3504	0.7111	-0.8229	-0.8332	-0.9181	0.9619	0.9872	-0.2255	0.7503	0.7307
PROG%	0.3717	0.7427	0.4240	-0.5067	0.7031	0.7034	0.8473	-0.7586	-0.7226	0.3997	-0.7893	-0.7214
REGR%	-0.4235	-0.6930	-0.4044	0.4140	-0.6422	-0.6399	-0.8163	0.7357	0.6806	-0.4399	0.7831	0.7489
PROP%	0.3688	-0.3238	-0.1110	0.6754	-0.4003	-0.4198	-0.2235	0.1504	0.2875	0.3028	0.0406	-0.2155
EQUITY%	0.1987	-0.3100	-0.2692	0.6837	-0.2719	-0.2908	-0.1508	0.0224	0.2408	0.1831	-0.1965	-0.3819
INEQ%	-0.1987	0.3100	0.2692	-0.6837	0.2719	0.2908	0.1508	-0.0224	-0.2408	-0.1831	0.1965	0.3819
AVINC	-0.1955	-0.6693	-0.3196	0.7196	-0.8506	-0.8597	-0.8977	0.9888	0.9847	-0.1706	0.7310	0.6859
VAR	-0.3466	-0.6543	-0.3817	0.6879	-0.7826	-0.7922	-0.9014	0.9728	0.9728	-0.3120	0.7098	0.6866
CO	-0.3555	0.5654	0.0928	-0.5216	0.8292	0.8279	0.5254	-0.6393	-0.6335	-0.3085	-0.5013	-0.3855
MD	-0.1589	-0.6337	-0.2720	0.7346	-0.8281	-0.8385	-0.8991	0.9846	0.9789	-0.1272	0.7376	0.6815
GINI	0.5588	0.8985	0.7778	-0.3248	0.8468	0.8384	0.5978	-0.6763	-0.7187	0.6129	-0.4463	-0.5351
AG	0.5654	0.8892	0.7719	-0.3155	0.8411	0.8333	0.5971	-0.6812	-0.7177	0.6179	-0.4478	-0.5412
COCON	1.0000	0.4597	0.6771	-0.0339	0.1251	0.1258	0.3770	-0.2235	-0.2868	0.9626	-0.2563	-0.3820
AT1		1.0000	0.8505	-0.6225	0.8558	0.8565	0.6963	-0.6260	-0.7422	0.5419	-0.4163	-0.3721
AT2			1.0000	-0.3718	0.5299	0.5281	0.3851	-0.2831	-0.4434	0.7611	-0.0160	-0.0624
KOLM				1.0000	-0.6126	-0.6345	-0.7796	0.6380	0.7563	-0.0503	0.4260	0.1807
RMD1					1.0000	0.9994	0.6905	-0.8155	-0.8620	0.1717	-0.5191	-0.4901
RMD2						1.0000	0.7048	-0.8222	-0.8726	0.1689	-0.5254	-0.4907
THEIL1							1.0000	-0.8865	-0.9034	0.3536	-0.8254	-0.7118
THEIL2								1.0000	0.9582	-0.1952	0.7560	0.7304
THEIL3									1.0000	-0.2583	0.6730	0.6439
SDL										1.0000	-0.2388	-0.3365
LV											1.0000	0.9102
HIND												1.0000

same economic circumstance demonstrate similar effective tax rates. In 1969, measured horizontal equity was at its low point with only 15 percent of the weighted comparisons of taxpayers in the same economic circumstance demonstrating similar effective tax rates. We may conclude then that the federal personal income tax is both progressive and horizontally *in*equitable.

In our earlier study we conjectured that increases in vertical progressivity might be accompanied by reductions in horizontal equity. However, examination of the overall pattern of progressivity and horizontal equity fails to reveal any systematic relationship. The correlation between the fractions of observed progressive comparisons and horizontally equitable comparisons is − .05.

If we use the weighted coefficient of variation in effective tax rates as our measure of horizontal inequity, then we observe several regularities. Recall that this measure is the (weighted) sum of coefficients of variation in effective tax rates within each income bracket, and thus reflects the relative amount of within-income bracket dispersion in effective tax rates. This measure of horizontal inequity suggests that there has been, over the period 1966–77, between 30 to 50 percent variation in effective tax rates within income classes—a substantial amount of variation. Also, it appears that this variation is increasing over time; the simple correlation between it and time is .73. Since 1973 the coefficient of variation exceeded 40 percent in three of the four years under study.

We also display in table 6.3 the Gini coefficient of income inequality. Interestingly, some evidence exists that the equality in after-tax income is increasing over time; the simple correlation between the Gini and time is − .67. More intriguing, however, is the relationship between income inequality as captured by the Gini and horizontal inequity as captured by the weighted coefficient of variation in effective tax rates. The simple correlation between the two measures is − .531, which is statistically significant at the 95 percent confidence level. This suggests that when the distribution of after-tax income becomes more equal, the increased equality is accompanied by greater horizontal inequity.

6.4.2   Results by Filing Type, 1966–77

The results of the calculated index numbers by filing type are contained in panels B through E of table 6.3. The high levels of progressivity found in panel A, the overall results, are evident for head-of-household, married-filing-separately, married-filing-jointly, and single taxpayers. Among these four types of taxpayers, single taxpayers display the greatest progressivity. Single taxpayers displayed progressivity in better than 91 percent of the weighted comparisons in all but one of the years under study, while none of the other types of taxpayers displayed such progressivity more than twice in the study period.

Not only does the federal tax system achieve its vertical objective most effectively with single taxpayers, it achieves its horizontal equity objective most effectively with them as well. Single taxpayers demonstrated horizontal equity from 43 percent to 56 percent of the comparisons, depending on the year in question. By contrast, married-filing-jointly taxpayers displayed horizontal equity in only 9 to 10 percent of the weighted comparisons. Undoubtedly the absence of significant variation in exemptions for single taxpayers and the fact that the vast majority of single taxpayers do not itemize explain these two results.

Both single and married filing jointly taxpayers display a downward drift in the degree of progressivity in their vertical comparisons over time. The simple correlations between time and the progressivity scores are $-.74$ and $-.53$ respectively.[19] Thus, while there is no apparent overall movement in the extent of progressivity in the tax system, there appears to be a modest downward trend in the cases of single and married-filing-jointly taxpayers.[20]

6.4.3 Other Filing Strata

In addition to stratifying the analysis by type of tax schedule, we performed analyses for single and itemized returns over the period 1966–72, and for strata of returns in 1974 corresponding to the presence or absence of wage and salary by sex.

Table 6.5 displays our horizontal and vertical measures for itemizers and non-itemizers. Again, we see that progressivity is substantial for both types of filers, perhaps contradicting the notion of some that itemized deductions reduce the progressivity of the system. In two of the seven years for which the analysis was performed, itemized returns actually displayed somewhat greater progressivity. However, substantial differences can be seen in the horizontal equity scores between itemizers and nonitemizers, as might be expected. Generally, equity is apparent in only 7 to 8 percent of the comparisons among taxpayers who itemized during the study period, while comparable figures for nonitemizers are 29 to 37 percent. These results compare favorably with those obtained in our earlier study. As with the earlier overall results, there are no apparent temporal relations for itemizers and nonitemizers, nor is there any apparent relationship between equity and progressivity scores.

Stratification by the presence or absence in wage and salary earnings by sex provides some interesting comparisons (see table 6.6). For example,

19. Detailed tables supporting these findings are available from the authors upon request and are omitted here due to space limitations.

20. If one estimates simple regressions of the natural log of the progressivity score on the natural log of time for single and married-filing-jointly taxpayers from the data in table 6.3, one obtains elasticities of $-.3$ in the case of single taxpayers and $-.28$ in the case of married-filing-jointly taxpayers with t-ratios in excess of 2.7.

Table 6.5   Horizontal and Vertical Scores
                   for Itemizers and Standard Filers, 1966–72

A. Itemizers

Year	Prog %	Regr %	Prop %	Equity %	Inequity %
1966	.877	.102	.021	.084	.916
1967	.880	.099	.021	.079	.921
1968	.978	.000	.022	.0706	.924
1969	.868	.114	.019	.074	.926
1970	.862	.115	.023	.072	.928
1971	.874	.105	.021	.075	.925
1972	.889	.092	.019	.074	.926

B. Standard

Prog %	Regr %	Prop %	Equity %	Inequity %
.879	.090	.032	.316	.684
.876	.091	.032	.311	.689
.969	.000	.031	.301	.699
.895	.079	.026	.311	.689
.884	.082	.034	.366	.634
.894	.076	.030	.316	.684
.903	.068	.029	.293	.707

Table 6.6   Horizontal and Vertical Scores by Number of Wage and Salary
                   Earners (1974 data)

Filing Unit	Prog %	Regr %	Prop %	Equity %	Inequity %	Gini	Av Rate
Male W&S >0	.899	.082	.018	.181	.819	.452	.292
Female W&S >0	.926	.052	.022	.339	.661	.441	.257
Male, Female W&S =0	.770	.212	.018	.097	.903	.652	.677
Male, Female W&S>0	.885	.089	.027	.099	.901	.244	.199
Total	.874	.108	.018	.154	.846	.462	.415

when female wage and salary payments are the only earnings present, horizontal equity is much greater than in any other strata. In this case, 34 percent of the comparisons display equity, compared to, for example, the overall figure of 15.4 percent. For returns that contained wage and salary for both men and women, the situation of working couples, we find that progressivity is high at 88.5 percent, and horizontal inequity is also high at 90.1 percent. Here, however, we also find that the after-tax distribution of income is equal as measured by the Gini coefficient. The Gini for working couples is .244, almost half of the overall Gini of .462. This suggests that working couples found themselves in similar after-tax-income positions, and may reflect that wage rates in 1974 for working couples were comparable when viewed in terms of family units.

The case in which neither male nor female wages and salaries are present displays the least amount of progressivity and equity of the strata examined. These, of course, would be individuals who receive only non-labor income or retirement or capital income. Note too that these taxpayers have the most unequal distribution of after-tax income; their Gini is .652 compared to the overall figure of .462.

6.4.4   Relations among All Index Numbers

As noted earlier, table 6.4 contains the simple correlations among the twenty-three index numbers (and time) investigated for all filers. There is much information that we will not attempt to summarize here; however, several general comments are in order. First, there is a high intercorrelation among the various income inequality measures. For example, the Gini is highly correlated with a wide variety of measures such as the variance in income, the coefficient of income concentration, Atkinson's three measures (his Gini, and his I evaluated at .3 and .7), the measures of the relative mean deviation, and so forth. Thus, while many of these measures have different numerical values, when compared for a moment in time, or across time, they tend to move closely together and in effect contain similar information.

While the inequality measures are generally highly correlated with each other, they are not always correlated with our measures of progressivity or regressivity. Thus, to the extent one wishes to measure VE in the sense used above, some of the income inequality measures can fail to capture VE type effects. Simple correlations between our progressivity measure and Atkinson's I (.7) were only .42, while the analagous correlation with Theil's measure was .85. This is not surprising, of course, since the inequality measures are not expected to capture the VE effects. This suggests, in turn, that if progressivity or regressivity is of interest to the analyst and the VE concept is persuasive, then some form of progressivity measure as we suggest is appropriate to the task, not an inequality measure. Conversely, if one is interested in the extent to which income inequality changes over time or as a result of proposed changes, then our VE measures are inappropriate measures of such effects.

6.5   Conclusion

We have sought in this paper to create a theoretical framework that allows the comparison of traditional and more recent concepts of horizontal and vertical equity, and to characterize empirically the horizontal and vertical distribution of federal individual income taxes over a significant period of time. Theoretically, we have shown that the recent concept of horizontal equity, which requires that the pre- and posttax ranks of individuals' income positions be unchanged, is logically divorced from the traditional horizontal equity concept, which requires that the tax system impose identical effective tax rates on individuals in the same (pretax) economic position.

Using carefully defined equity concepts and publicly available data for the period 1966–77, we have found what appears to be substantial and continuing evidence of progressivity in the U.S. personal income tax. However, we also have found substantial and continuing horizontal inequity in the federal personal tax system.

Stratification of our empirical analysis by type of tax schedule reveals that single persons experience the greatest progressivity and horizontal equity in the system, while married-filing-jointly taxpayers experience the least amount of horizontal equity in the system.

Examination of a wide variety of measures of after-tax income inequality reveals that they do not often capture the same information as the proposed vertical and horizontal equity measures, although they are highly related to each other in the sense of being highly correlated. This empirical information is consistent with the above theoretical results.

We have not sought in this chapter to "explain" the extent of measured vertical and horizontal equity, partly due to the size of the task and partly because the initial characterization of equity in the federal individual income tax over time seemed to be the proper point of departure. The extent of observed horizontal inequity is worthy of further study, as the observed discrepancies from some sort of norm of "acceptable" levels of horizontal inequity, compared to observed discrepancies between observed levels of progressivity and what is theoretically possible, would appear to be large. That is, observed progressivity appears to be at least 80 percent of what could be attained, whereas observed horizontal equity is only 10 percent of what could be attained. One may argue that the observed horizontal inequities are the peculiarity of our tax system which provides for exemptions and beneficial tax treatment for various types of activity. However, it is remarkable that units with the same economic position, broadly defined, find themselves facing comparable tax rates in only 10 percent of possible comparisons.

References

Atkinson, A. B. 1970. On the measurement of inequality. *Journal of Economic Theory* 2:244–63.

_____. 1980. Horizontal equity and the distribution of the tax burden. In *The economics of taxation,* ed. H. Aaron and M. J. Boskin. Washington, D.C.: Brookings Institution.

Berliant, M. C., and R. P. Strauss. 1983. Measuring the distribution of personal taxes. In *What role for government? Lessons from policy research,* ed. R. Zeckhauser and D. Leebaert, 97–115. Durham, N.C.: Duke University Press.

_____. 1984. On recent expositions of vertical and horizontal equity. Carnegie-Mellon University. Mimeo.

Blackorby, D., and D. Donaldson. 1976. Measures of equality and their meanings in terms of social welfare. University of British Columbia discussion paper, no. 76-20.

Bourguignon, F. 1979. Decomposable income inequality measures. *Econometrica* 47, no. 4: 901–20.

Bridges, B., Jr. 1978. *Intertemporal changes in tax rates.* Studies in Income Distribution, 11. Washington, D.C.: GPO. Social Security Administration, Office of Research and Statistics.

Feldstein, M. S. 1976. On the theory of tax reform. *Journal of Public Economics* 6, nos. 1–2: 77–104.

Fields, G. S., and J. C. H. Fei. 1978. On inequality comparisons. *Econometrica* 46, no. 2: 303–16.

Kendall, M. 1947. *The advanced theory of statistics.* London: Griffin and Co.

Kiefer, Donald W. 1983. The characteristics of the distributional tax progressivity measures. Congressional Research Service, Library of Congress. Mimeo.

King, M. A. 1983. An index of inequality: With applications to horizontal equity and social mobility. *Econometrica* 51, no. 1: 99–115.

Kolm, S. C. 1976. Unequal inequalities. *Journal of Economic Theory* 12/13: 82–112.

Kondor, Y. 1975. Value judgements implied by the use of various measures of income inequality. *Review of Income and Wealth* 21: 309–21.

Mill, J. S. 1921. *Principles of political economy.* Ed. W. J. Ashley. London: Longmans.

Musgrave, R. A. 1959. *The theory of public finance.* New York: McGraw-Hill.

Musgrave, R. A., and P. B. Musgrave. 1980. *Public finance in theory and practice.* New York: McGraw-Hill.

Musgrave, R. A., and T. Thin. 1948. Income tax progression, 1928–48. *Journal of Political Economy* 56, no. 6: 498–514.

Okner, B. A. 1979. Distributional aspects of tax reform during the past fifteen years. *National Tax Journal* 32, no. 1: 11–28.

Pechman, J. A., and B. A. Okner. 1974. *Who bears the tax burden?* Washington, D.C.: Brookings Institution.

Plotnick, R. 1981. A measure of horizontal inequity. *Review of Economics and Statistics* 63, no. 2: 283–88.

_____. 1982. The concept and measurement of horizontal inequity. *Journal of Public Economics* 17: 373–91.

Pyatt, G. 1976. On the interpretation and the disaggregation of Gini coefficient. *Economics Journal* 86: 243–55.

Rosen, H. 1978. An approach to the study of income, utility, and horizontal equity. *Quarterly Journal of Economics* 92: 307–22.

Samuelson, Paul A. 1947. *Foundations of economic analysis*. Cambridge: Harvard University Press.

Sen, A. 1973. *On economic inequality.* Oxford: Clarendon Press.

Shorrocks, A. F. 1980. The class of additively decomposable inequality measures. *Econometrica* 48, no. 3: 613–25.

Suits, D. B. 1975. Measurement of tax progressivity. *American Economic Review* 67, no. 4: 747–52.

Theil, H. 1967. *Economics and information theory*. Amsterdam: North-Holland.

U.S. Department of Commerce. Bureau of Economic Analysis. 1981. *The national income and products account of the United States, 1929–76: Statistical tables*. Washington, D.C.: GPO.

U.S. Department of Treasury. Internal Revenue Service. 1966–77. *Statistics of Income: Individual Income Tax Returns*. Washington, D.C.: GPO.

Wertz, K. L. 1975. Empirical studies of tax burdens: Design and interpretation. *Proceedings* of the National Tax Association, Houston, 115–22.

_____. 1978. A method of measuring the relative taxation of families. *Review of Economics and Statistics* 60: 145–60.

Wyscarver, R. 1978. The Treasury personal individual income tax simulation model. OTA Paper 32. U.S. Department of the Treasury, Office of the Assistant Secretary for Tax Policy. Washington, D.C.: GPO.

Appendix A
Algebraic Statement of Various Index Numbers

Key to symbols:

I = # of economic income classes

A = # of after-tax income classes

R = # of effective rate classes

N^J = population in economic income class i, rate class J

Y_i^J = average income in economic income class i, rate class J

Z_i = average income in after-tax income class i

P_i = population in after-tax income class i

$T_i = Z_i{*}P_i$ = total income in after-tax income class i

POP = total population

INC = total after-tax income

D_i^J = population in income class i, change in effective rate class J

Q = # of change in rate classes (difference between old and new effective rates)

$$VSUM = \sum_{i=1}^{I} \ \sum_{k=i+1}^{I} \ \sum_{J=1}^{R} \sum_{L=1}^{R} \ N_i^{J}{*}N_k^{J}{*}|Y_i^{J} - Y_k^{L}|{*}MAX(J/L, L/J)$$

$$HSUM = \left[\sum_{i=1}^{I} \sum_{J=1}^{R} \ \sum_{L=J+1}^{R} \ N_i^{J}{*}N_i^{L}L/J \right] + \left[\frac{1}{2} \sum_{i=1}^{I} \sum_{J=1}^{R} \ N_i^{J}{*}(N_i^{J} - 1) \right]$$

$$DVSUM = \sum_{i=1}^{I} \ \sum_{k=i+1}^{I} \ \sum_{J=1}^{Q} \sum_{L=1}^{Q} \ D_i^{J}{*}D_k^{L}$$

Table 6.A.1 Algebraic Statements for Alternative Vertical and Horizontal Index Numbers

Index Number	Variable Name	Expression	Reference
Progressive (%)	PROG	$\dfrac{1}{VSUM}\displaystyle\sum_{J=1}^{R}\sum_{L=J+1}^{R}\sum_{i=1}^{J}\sum_{k=i+1}^{J} N_i^J * N_k^L *\left|Y_i^J - Y_k^L\right| * L/J$	Berliant and Strauss 1983
Regressive (%)	REGR	$\dfrac{1}{VSUM}\displaystyle\sum_{J=1}^{R}\sum_{L=1}^{J-1}\sum_{i=1}^{J}\sum_{k=i+1}^{J} N_i^J * N_k^L *\left|Y_i^J - Y_k^L\right| * L/J$	"
Proportional (%)	PROP	$\dfrac{1}{VSUM}\displaystyle\sum_{J=1}^{R}\sum_{L=1}^{R}\sum_{i=1}^{J}\sum_{k=i+1}^{J} N_i^J * N_k^L *\left|Y_i^J - Y_k^L\right|$	"
Equity (%)	HGO	$\dfrac{1}{2*HSUM}\displaystyle\sum_{i=1}^{J}\sum_{J=1}^{R} N_i^J * (N_i^J - 1)$	"
Dispersion	HBAD	$\dfrac{1}{HSUM}\displaystyle\sum_{i=1}^{J}\sum_{L=J+1}^{R} N_i^J * N_i^L * L/J$	"
Average after-tax income	AVINC	INC/POP	
Variance	VAR	$\dfrac{1}{POP}\displaystyle\sum_{i=1}^{A}(Z_i - AVINC)^2 * P_i$	Kondor 1975
Coefficient of variation	CO	$\sqrt{VAR}/AVINC$	Atkinson 1970; Fields and Fei 1978
Mean difference	MD	$\dfrac{1}{POP^2}\displaystyle\sum_{i=1}^{A}\sum_{j=1}^{i-1} P_i * P_j *\left|Z_i - Z_j\right|$	Kendall 1947
Gini coefficient	GINI	MD/AVINC	Pyatt 1976
Atkinson Gini	AG	GINI/2	Atkinson 1970
Coefficient of concentration	COCON	$\dfrac{1}{AVINC*POP*(POP-1)}\displaystyle\sum_{i=1}^{A}\sum_{j=1}^{i-1}\left|Z_i - Z\right| * P_i * P_j$	Kondor 1975
Atkinson	AT1, AT2	$1-\left(\displaystyle\sum_{i=1}^{A}\left(\dfrac{1}{AVINC}\right)^{1-\epsilon}\dfrac{1}{POP}\right)^{\frac{1}{1-\epsilon}}$	Atkinson 1970 AT1: $\epsilon=.3$ AT2: $\epsilon=.7$

Kolm	KOLM	$1000*\log\left(\sum_{\substack{i=1\\R\neq 0}}^{A}\exp\left[(AVINC\text{-}Z_i)*\frac{1}{1000}\right]\frac{P_i}{POP}\right)$	Kolm 1976
Relative mean deviation #1	RMD1	$\frac{1}{POP}\sum_{i=1}^{R}\left|\frac{Z_i}{AVINC}-1\right|*P_i$	Atkinson 1970
Relative mean deviation #2	RMD2	$RMD1/2$	Kondor 1975
Theil #1	THEIL1	$X_i = Z_i/INC$ $\sum_{i=1}^{A}P_i*X_i*\log(X_i)$	Bourguignon 1979
Theil #2	THEIL2	$\sum_{i=1}^{A}P_i*Z_i\log(POP*Z_i)$	Fields and Fei 1978; Theil 1967
Theil #3	THEIL3	$\frac{1}{POP}\sum_{i=1}^{A}Sign(Z_i)*P_i*\log(|Z_i|)$	Theil 1967
Standard deviation of logarithms	SDL	$\frac{1}{POP}\sum_{i=1}^{A}P_i*(\log(|Z_i/AVINC|))^2$	Atkinson 1970
Logarithmic variance	LV	$\frac{1}{POP}\sum_{i=1}^{A}(Sign(Z_i)*\log(|Z_i|)-THEIL3)^{2}*P_i$	Kondor 1975
Kuznets ratio	XKUZ	$\sum_{i=1}^{A}P_i*\left|\frac{Z_i}{INC}-\frac{1}{POP}\right| = RMD1$	Fields and Fei 1978
Average coefficient of variation of effective rates	HIND	$\frac{1}{POP}\sum_{i=1}^{I}\left[\dfrac{\sum_{j=1}^{R}N_j^{i2}}{\sum_{j=1}^{R}N_j^i*J}\right]*\left[\dfrac{\sum_{J=1}^{R}\sum_{K=J+1}^{R}(J\text{-}K)^{2}*N_K^i*N_J^i}{\sum_{J=1}^{R}\sum_{K=J+1}^{R}(N_K^i*N_J^i)+\frac{1}{2}\sum_{j=1}^{R}N_J^i*(N_J^i-1)}\right]^{1/2}$	Fields and Fei 1978

Table 6.A.2   **Appendix B Other Index Numbers**

Panel A. All Filers

YR	(1)	(2)	(3)	(4)	(5)	(6)	(7)	(8)	(9)
66	6060.	0.3211E + 08	0.935	2741.	0.452	0.226	0.452	0.108	0.261
67	6421.	0.3759E + 08	0.955	2932.	0.457	0.228	0.457	0.109	0.264
68	6822.	0.4444E + 08	0.977	3161.	0.463	0.232	0.463	0.113	0.271
69	7056.	0.4245E + 08	0.923	3241.	0.459	0.230	0.459	0.109	0.266
70	7643.	0.4476E + 08	0.875	3374.	0.441	0.221	0.441	0.100	0.247
71	8166.	0.5523E + 08	0.910	3657.	0.448	0.224	0.448	0.104	0.254
72	8758.	0.6278E + 08	0.905	3941.	0.450	0.225	0.450	0.105	0.255
73	9195.	0.7252E + 08	0.926	4198.	0.457	0.228	0.457	0.108	0.265
74	9549.	0.1017E + 09	1.056	4415.	0.462	0.231	0.462	0.111	0.266
75	10170.	0.8626E + 08	0.913	4725.	0.465	0.232	0.465	0.111	0.278
76	11340.	0.1046E + 09	0.902	5155.	0.455	0.227	0.455	0.105	0.257
77	11650.	0.1157E + 09	0.923	5485.	0.471	0.235	0.471	0.112	0.284

Panel B. Head of Household

YR	(1)	(2)	(3)	(4)	(5)	(6)	(7)	(8)	(9)
66	5222.	0.1922E + 08	0.840	1847.	0.354	0.177	0.354	0.069	0.163
67	5381.	0.1851E + 08	0.799	1788.	0.332	0.166	0.332	0.062	0.142
68	5681.	0.2061E + 08	0.799	1881.	0.331	0.166	0.331	0.062	0.143
69	5347.	0.2157E + 08	0.869	1996.	0.373	0.187	0.373	0.076	0.180
70	5567.	0.1779E + 08	0.758	1937.	0.348	0.174	0.348	0.066	0.164
71	5962.	0.2239E + 08	0.794	2036.	0.341	0.171	0.341	0.065	0.157
72	6519.	0.2506E + 08	0.768	2211.	0.339	0.170	0.339	0.063	0.151
73	6830.	0.3408E + 08	0.855	2423.	0.355	0.177	0.355	0.071	0.170
74	7121.	0.3667E + 08	0.850	2408.	0.338	0.169	0.338	0.062	0.148
75	7741.	0.3427E + 08	0.756	2715.	0.351	0.175	0.351	0.066	0.164
76	8082.	0.4235E + 08	0.805	2957.	0.366	0.183	0.366	0.072	0.178
77	8392.	0.4610E + 08	0.809	3205.	0.382	0.191	0.382	0.079	0.201

Panel C. Married Filing Separately

YR	(1)	(2)	(3)	(4)	(5)	(6)	(7)	(8)	(9)
66	3331.	0.1125E + 08	1.007	1401.	0.421	0.210	0.421	0.093	0.221
67	3584.	0.1354E + 08	1.027	1492.	0.416	0.208	0.416	0.093	0.225
68	3784.	0.2037E + 08	1.193	1580.	0.417	0.209	0.417	0.098	0.224
69	4041.	0.1837E + 08	1.061	1874.	0.464	0.232	0.464	0.105	0.253
70	4445.	0.1791E + 08	0.952	1807.	0.407	0.203	0.407	0.087	0.210
71	4770.	0.2155E + 08	0.973	1988.	0.417	0.208	0.417	0.090	0.212
72	5099.	0.1944E + 08	0.865	2012.	0.394	0.197	0.394	0.081	0.194
73	5326.	0.2647E + 08	0.966	2234.	0.420	0.210	0.420	0.094	0.230
74	5563.	0.4450E + 08	1.199	2350.	0.422	0.211	0.422	0.090	0.223
75	5873.	0.3467E + 08	1.003	2662.	0.453	0.227	0.453	0.103	0.265
76	6891.	0.3746E + 08	0.888	2789.	0.405	0.202	0.405	0.083	0.207
77	7197.	0.5809E + 08	1.059	3428.	0.476	0.238	0.476	0.106	0.276

Panel A. All Filers

(10)	(11)	(12)	(13)	(14)	(15)	(16)	(17)	(18)
0.6071E+04	0.639	0.320	−17.880	0.1154E+14	8.201	1.231	2.670	0.302
0.7311E+04	0.643	0.321	−17.910	0.1252E+14	8.255	1.247	2.670	0.289
0.7639E+04	0.654	0.327	−17.910	0.1374E+14	8.301	1.294	2.689	0.310
0.1041E+05	0.652	0.326	−18.030	0.1464E+14	8.340	1.294	2.819	0.323
0.1123E+05	0.625	0.312	−18.030	0.1555E+14	8.459	1.155	2.745	0.292
0.1200E+05	0.633	0.317	−18.020	0.1673E+14	8.507	1.180	2.915	0.310
0.1364E+05	0.638	0.319	−18.020	0.1875E+14	8.581	1.257	2.619	0.298
0.1279E+05	0.651	0.325	−18.050	0.2054E+14	8.601	1.288	2.966	0.357
0.1477E+05	0.659	0.330	−18.180	0.2212E+14	8.636	1.016	3.547	0.415
0.1482E+05	0.665	0.332	−18.170	0.2326E+14	8.643	1.314	4.030	0.471
0.1984E+05	0.650	0.325	−18.156	0.2682E+14	8.827	1.227	2.989	0.318
0.2058E+05	0.673	0.337	−18.350	0.2826E+14	8.754	1.310	4.667	0.498

Panel B. Head of Household

(10)	(11)	(12)	(13)	(14)	(15)	(16)	(17)	(18)
0.4391E+04	0.482	0.241	−14.490	0.2679E+12	8.266	0.478	1.879	0.243
0.3814E+04	0.454	0.227	−14.510	0.2970E+12	8.351	0.438	1.160	0.241
0.3673E+04	0.456	0.228	−14.640	0.3543E+12	8.394	0.410	1.455	0.238
0.4460E+04	0.514	0.257	−14.790	0.3897E+12	8.257	0.610	1.903	0.285
0.4456E+04	0.483	0.242	−15.090	0.5210E+12	8.311	0.535	2.242	0.257
0.4281E+04	0.473	0.236	−15.050	0.5615E+12	8.401	0.479	1.960	0.312
0.6712E+04	0.471	0.235	−15.180	0.7018E+12	8.514	0.549	1.450	0.318
0.5196E+04	0.490	0.245	−15.220	0.7932E+12	8.508	0.554	2.136	0.238
0.7352E+04	0.477	0.238	−15.350	0.8883E+12	8.599	0.418	1.873	0.329
0.7772E+04	0.490	0.245	−15.320	0.9610E+12	8.645	0.576	2.051	0.351
0.1253E+05	0.505	0.253	−15.455	0.1096E+13	8.659	0.707	2.214	0.344
0.1171E+05	0.529	0.265	−15.610	0.1252E+13	8.618	0.755	3.452	0.413

Panel C. Married Filing Separately

(10)	(11)	(12)	(13)	(14)	(15)	(16)	(17)	(18)
0.3328E+04	0.591	0.295	−14.850	0.2286E+12	7.699	0.821	2.449	0.343
0.4055E+04	0.576	0.288	−14.820	0.2209E+12	7.749	0.815	2.984	0.286
0.2813E+04	0.582	0.291	−14.660	0.2467E+12	7.830	0.796	2.227	0.284
0.7335E+04	0.648	0.324	−15.050	0.2671E+12	7.805	0.897	3.683	0.287
0.4364E+04	0.572	0.286	−14.540	0.2351E+12	8.004	0.744	2.495	0.325
0.9628E+04	0.589	0.294	−14.380	0.2191E+12	8.091	0.891	1.727	0.261
0.6129E+04	0.554	0.277	−14.540	0.2767E+12	8.183	0.722	1.968	0.294
0.7127E+04	0.588	0.294	−14.630	0.3014E+12	8.132	0.930	2.900	0.315
0.1151E+05	0.595	0.298	−14.950	0.2904E+12	8.163	0.631	4.387	0.349
0.1193E+05	0.626	0.313	−14.790	0.2587E+12	8.101	1.039	5.219	0.413
0.1484E+05	0.574	0.287	−14.540	0.3051E+12	8.429	0.815	3.040	0.341
0.1755E+05	0.666	0.333	−14.740	0.2172E+12	8.241	0.940	7.012	0.438

Table 6.A.2 (continued)

Panel D. Married Filing Jointly									
YR	(1)	(2)	(3)	(4)	(5)	(6)	(7)	(8)	(9)
66	8339.	0.3575E + 08	0.717	2859.	0.343	0.171	0.343	0.064	0.158
67	8847.	0.4221E + 08	0.734	3076.	0.348	0.174	0.348	0.066	0.163
68	9483.	0.5065E + 08	0.751	3351.	0.353	0.177	0.353	0.068	0.167
69	9842.	0.4663E + 08	0.694	3388.	0.344	0.172	0.344	0.062	0.159
70	10430.	0.4861E + 08	0.668	3516.	0.337	0.169	0.337	0.060	0.153
71	11070.	0.6086E + 08	0.705	3833.	0.346	0.173	0.346	0.064	0.163
72	12140.	0.6937E + 08	0.686	4158.	0.343	0.171	0.343	0.062	0.154
73	12950.	0.8204E + 08	0.699	4475.	0.346	0.173	0.346	0.064	0.163
74	13590.	0.1285E + 09	0.834	4806.	0.354	0.177	0.354	0.070	0.176
75	14320.	0.9955E + 08	0.697	5161.	0.360	0.180	0.360	0.069	0.185
76	16007.	0.1190E + 09	0.682	5584.	0.349	0.174	0.349	0.063	0.163
77	16780.	0.1361E + 09	0.695	6040.	0.360	0.180	0.360	0.069	0.189

Panel E. Single									
YR	(1)	(2)	(3)	(4)	(5)	(6)	(7)	(8)	(9)
66	2832.	0.1054E + 08	1.146	1375.	0.486	0.243	0.486	0.123	0.283
67	2981.	0.1264E + 08	1.193	1480.	0.497	0.248	0.497	0.125	0.283
68	3169.	0.1486E + 08	1.216	1575.	0.497	0.248	0.497	0.130	0.292
69	3250.	0.1346E + 08	1.129	1584.	0.487	0.244	0.487	0.123	0.281
70	3651.	0.1502E + 08	1.062	1739.	0.476	0.238	0.476	0.113	0.264
71	3878.	0.1951E + 08	1.139	1897.	0.489	0.245	0.489	0.119	0.274
72	4245.	0.2276E + 08	1.124	2104.	0.496	0.248	0.496	0.122	0.285
73	4440.	0.2390E + 08	1.101	2140.	0.482	0.241	0.482	0.120	0.279
74	4630.	0.3121E + 08	1.207	2167.	0.468	0.234	0.113	0.113	0.256
75	5022.	0.2717E + 08	1.038	2411.	0.480	0.240	0.480	0.119	0.286
76	5829.	0.3729E + 08	1.048	2737.	0.470	0.235	0.470	0.113	0.265
77	5980.	0.3800E + 08	1.031	2847.	0.476	0.238	0.476	0.116	0.281

Notes:

Column	Index Number	Appendix A Definition
Col. (1)	Average income	(AVINC)
Col. (2)	Variance	(VAR)
Col. (3)	Coefficient of variation	(CO)
Col. (4)	Mean difference	(MD)
Col. (5)	Gini	(GINI)
Col. (6)	Atkinson Gini	(AG)
Col. (7)	Coefficient of concentration	(COCON)
Col. (8)	Atkinson I (.3)	(AT1)
Col. (9)	Atkinson I (.7)	(AT2)

Panel D. Married Filing Jointly

(10)	(11)	(12)	(13)	(14)	(15)	(16)	(17)	(18)
0.9878E + 04	0.467	0.233	− 17.460	0.8900E + 13	8.724	0.506	2.314	0.253
0.9890E + 04	0.474	0.237	− 17.460	0.9681E + 13	8.769	0.507	2.491	0.250
0.1200E + 05	0.480	0.240	− 17.490	0.1056E + 14	8.833	0.529	2.510	0.255
0.1546E + 05	0.470	0.235	− 17.600	0.1127E + 14	8.880	0.515	2.632	0.271
0.1520E + 05	0.463	0.232	− 17.580	0.1194E + 14	8.948	0.490	2.566	0.255
0.1543E + 05	0.476	0.238	− 17.580	0.1293E + 14	8.982	0.538	2.818	0.253
0.1765E + 05	0.473	0.237	− 17.520	0.1413E + 14	9.109	0.534	2.162	0.250
0.1888E + 05	0.473	0.236	− 17.580	0.1536E + 14	9.139	0.549	2.818	0.282
0.2214E + 05	0.478	0.239	− 17.670	0.1640E + 14	9.150	0.514	3.548	0.314
0.2224E + 05	0.495	0.248	− 17.680	0.1721E + 14	9.163	0.670	3.999	0.369
0.2763E + 05	0.481	0.241	− 17.652	0.1956E + 14	9.346	0.557	3.016	0.252
0.3064E + 05	0.493	0.247	− 17.820	0.2034E + 14	9.291	0.667	4.895	0.382

Panel E. Single

(10)	(11)	(12)	(13)	(14)	(15)	(16)	(17)	(18)
0.1569E + 04	0.705	0.353	− 16.760	0.1808E + 13	7.426	1.201	2.213	0.241
0.3852E + 04	0.720	0.360	− 16.900	0.1967E + 13	7.487	1.225	2.025	0.220
0.1913E + 04	0.720	0.360	− 16.780	0.2191E + 13	7.528	1.266	2.035	0.261
0.2254E + 04	0.709	0.355	− 16.860	0.2290E + 13	7.571	1.253	2.005	0.244
0.6025E + 04	0.688	0.344	− 16.970	0.2413E + 13	7.716	1.170	2.156	0.224
0.7442E + 04	0.702	0.351	− 17.000	0.2553E + 13	7.756	1.180	2.349	0.258
0.8952E + 04	0.705	0.352	− 17.110	0.3082E + 13	7.816	1.306	2.528	0.227
0.4551E + 04	0.692	0.346	− 16.990	0.3473E + 13	7.875	1.274	2.315	0.365
0.5294E + 04	0.696	0.348	− 17.200	0.3865E + 13	7.965	0.783	2.867	0.437
0.4986E + 04	0.688	0.344	− 17.130	0.4133E + 13	7.952	1.238	3.365	0.507
0.8359E + 04	0.672	0.336	− 17.117	0.5052E + 13	8.177	1.196	2.253	0.266
0.7933E + 04	0.682	0.341	− 17.340	0.5594E + 13	8.129	1.197	3.650	0.511

Notes:

Column	Index Number	Appendix A Definition
Col. (10)	Kolm's index	(KOLM)
Col. (11)	Relative mean deviation #1	(RMD1)
Col. (12)	Relative mean deviation #2	(RMD2)
Col. (13)	Theil inequality measure #1	(THEIL1)
Col. (14)	Theil inequality measure #2	(THEIL2)
Col. (15)	Theil inequality measure #3	(THEIL3)
Col. (16)	Standard deviation of log of income	(SDL)
Col. (17)	Log of variance of income	(LV)
Col. (18)	Average rate index	(HIND)

Comment   T. N. Srinivasan

I have several criticisms of this very interesting chapter.

Not only can taxpayers respond behaviorally to tax systems by rearranging their sources of income as the authors acknowledge in footnote 2 (only to emphasize what they have ignored), but taxpayers can determine their filing status as well. As such, the analysis of various equity measures by filing status could be potentially affected by self-selection biases. Second, taxpayers can *evade* as well as *avoid* taxes—tax systems and sources of income affect the feasibility as well as the probability of evasion and avoidance. In particular, a more equitable tax system compared to another may be less equitable once allowance for possible evasion and avoidance is made.

The literature on income inequality measures that is based on social welfare rankings identifies individual income with individual welfare levels. Problems arise when one employs this literature to analyze the equity of tax systems—e.g., a tax return, even in the case of a single taxpayer, may represent not only that person but others dependent on that person as well. It is not enough that deductions are allowed based on the numbers of dependents, even if we ignore the fact that by law, some categories of taxpayers such as nonresident aliens are not allowed deductions. Since such deductions do not depend on the level of income of the taxpayer, they need not equal the true "cost" of dependents to the taxpayer if such costs depend on income. Since more than one member of a household whose members pool their incomes and expenditures may file separate returns, posttax income associated with one of these returns is an indadequate indicator of household welfare. As long as society is organized in the form of households, it is household welfare that should enter as an argument in the social welfare function.

Yet another dimension in assessing equity of tax systems should be their treatment of identifiably transitory and permanent components of income (a tax system based on consumption expenditure rather than measured income will implicitly tax permanent income only, if it is the case that all transitory incomes are saved), of income streams of differing riskiness, etc. Most tax systems distinguish, however imperfectly, between safer and risky incomes, but their differential treatments of these incomes do not usually depend on the level and composition of the income of taxpayers. Since attitudes towards risk (as well as perception of risk) may depend on income, once again from a welfare point of view, assessments of tax systems that look only at effective tax rates and post- or pretax incomes are unsatisfactory.

T. N. Srinivasan is the Samuel C. Park, Jr., Professor of Economics at the Economic Growth Center, Yale University.

Comparisons over time and space of equity measures are subject to well-known problems arising from price variations across space and time; the same posttax nominal income may correspond to different real-income levels depending on the location of taxpayers in the relevant income distribution. (After all, because of various differences in quality, convenience, frequency of purchase, volume of purchase, etc., the same broadly defined commodity may not cost the same for the poor and the rich!) There is no reason to believe that inflation or, for that matter, cost-of-living difference between Alaska and Alabama affects all taxpayers "equally" so that equity measures are unaffected by these differences. In addition, to some extent taxpayers can choose to shift income over time, and certainly can choose to change their places of residence. For all these reasons and more, I would not place too much welfare significance on the equity indexes. I would treat them as yet another set of statistics describing tax systems.

Before turning to some specific comments let me raise one general conceptual issue: is it appropriate to look only at the tax system's treatment of identified or named individual returns in assessing its equity? Shouldn't one characterize a tax system as satisfying a horizontal equity principle if it treats equals equally by randomly assigning tax rates? For instance, if there are one hundred individuals, all equal in some well-defined sense, and if the tax system assigns a random tax independently drawn from some distribution of tax rates to each of the one hundred individuals, it is indeed treating them equally, even though *observed* ranks of pre- and posttax incomes of any two individuals can be reversed by this process. More generally, is there an argument for applying Rawlsian concepts of justice rather than vertical and horizontal equity in some narrow sense in assessing tax systems?

Some specific comments:

Page 180. It is well known that the Gini coefficient is a rather insensitive measure of inequality.

Page 182. Is it correct to draw an analogy from Arrow's general possibility theorem and argue that if the domains of tax systems and pretax attributes are unrestricted, then it is impossible to define equity concepts that are applicable over the entire domain?

Page 182. Are there any taxes other than lump-sum taxes that are purely distributive? Are there any purely allocative taxes?

Which is the relevant measure of horizontal equity—the policy analyst's characterization of who are equal and who are not or the taxpayers' perception of equality as it relates to themselves?

Page 186 Proposition. By "cells of equals are singletons" do the authors mean that all members of a given cell have identical pretax incomes, while members of different cells have different incomes?

Page 188. The arguments for introducing income difference and tax-rate-ratio weights in making paired comparisons are essentially ad hoc.

They do not seem to have any identifiable connection with the conceptual discussion in section 6.2.1. At least some sensitivity analysis with alternative weighting schemes would be appropriate.

Page 188. Since t is a tax *rate,* its unit is defined once one chooses to measure rates in proportions, percentages, mills, etc. As such, it does not make sense to require that scoring of comparisons be invariant with respect to scalar multiplication of t.

Page 189. To the extent that one is attempting to draw welfare inferences from equity measures, the facts are bothersome that some incomes are excluded from the data and that the extent of such exclusion may depend on the levels of included income.

Page 198. In respect of vertical equity measures, 1968 (and to a lesser extent, 1977) numbers seem to be out of line with those for other years. Is there any explanation?

Page 196. Since the progressivity, proportionality, and regressivity measures add to 1, if one of them (proportionality) is negligible, the other two by definition must be highly and negatively correlated.

Page 199. For reasons of selectivity bias mentioned earlier, I will be more cautious in interpreting the results by filing type and filing strata (except perhaps by sex).

7 Measuring the Benefits of Income Maintenance Programs

David Betson
Jacques van der Gaag

7.1 Introduction

This chapter addresses the following question: To what extent do the payments that households receive from an income maintenance program, such as Aid to Families with Dependent Children (AFDC) or food stamps, measure the benefit or the value of these programs to the household? In a world where households can always achieve their desired levels of work and consumption and where all the relevant economic constraints are known with certainty, it can be shown that these payments will overestimate or be equal to the value of the program to the household as measured by either the equivalent or compensating measure of variation. This result is due to the manner in which all income maintenance schemes compute their payments. Since the payment is designed to decline as the household income rises, the price of leisure (work) is distorted from its market price (the gross wage rate). This distortion, not unlike the effects of the tax rate in the theory of positive taxation, produces a "wedge" between the value the household places on the program and the payment the government makes to the household. This wedge, which could be considered the deadweight loss to society (to borrow a concept from the evaluation of the positive taxation), measures the excess payment that the government makes to the household over the payment the government would have to make if the payment was given in a lump-sum manner.

David Betson is assistant professor of economics at the University of Notre Dame. Jacques van der Gaag is an economist in the Development Research Department of the World Bank.

The views expressed in this chapter are the authors' and do not necessarily reflect those of the institutions with which they are affiliated. The authors wish to thank Thomas Juster, A. Myrick Freeman, and participants of the NBER Conference on Income and Wealth for valuable comments on an earlier draft.

The purpose of this chapter is to examine how this conclusion stands up when we abandon the assumption that the household possesses perfect knowledge about its employment prospects and potential standard of living. Thus we are interested in the measurement not only of the value of the income transfer to the household, but also of the insurance value of the program to the household. When factors that reflect uncertainty in the household's future potential standard of living are taken into account, the payment or expected payments from an income maintenance scheme will tend to underestimate the value of the program to the household.

Section 7.2 will present the methodology underlying the measurement of the value of an income maintenance program under the assumptions of certainty. Section 7.3 extends the methodology to the situation where the household faces an uncertain future, the major factor of uncertainty being the possible limitation placed on the availability of work (unemployment). In this section we evaluate the benefits of a hypothetical income maintenance program that pays benefits only to unemployed individuals. In section 7.4 we extend the analysis to consider how the valuation of an income maintenance program would be affected due to uncertainty in the real-wage rate. Here we also introduce a more realistic program that allows transfers to the household as long as its income does not exceed a given level, regardless of the household's employment. In both sections 7.3 and 7.4 we will calculate the value of an income maintenance program, using as an example a female-headed household with children. The final section of the chapter offers a summary and discusses the implications of our findings for the evaluation of income maintenance and transfer schemes in general.

7.2 Measurement of the Value to a Household of an Income Maintenance Program: The Certainty Case

To clarify the various issues in the measurement of the value of an income maintenance program to a household and to simplify the exposition, we abstract from the many complexities of income transfer schemes as they exist today and consider an income maintenance program that can be described by the following relationship:

$$(1) \qquad P = \begin{cases} G - tI & \text{if } I < G/t, \\ \\ 0 & \text{if } I \geq G/t, \end{cases}$$

where
P = the payment the household would receive if it had I amount of income,
G = the maximum payment or income guarantee to the household,
t = the program's benefit reduction rate, and,

I = the household's income from earnings and other nontransfer sources.

In order to further simplify the analysis, we consider female-headed households with children only, thus eliminating the complication of multiple earners. Thus the household's income is equal to

$$I = wh + Y,$$

where
w = the woman's real-wage rate,
h = the hours of work, and,
Y = the amount of nontransfer nonemployment income she receives.

We will also assume that the woman possesses a complete preference ordering over consumption of goods and services purchased in the market (X) and the amount of nonmarket time, leisure (l). This preference ordering will be represented by a real-value utility function;

$$U = U(X, l),$$

where U is concave in X and l, and the marginal utility of X and l is positive for all values of X and l. Let T be equal to the time available to the woman to either work in the market or "consume" leisure, (i.e., $T = h + l$). We will need the following concepts to develop the methodology to measure the value of the program to the household:

$h(w, Y)$ = the woman's labor supply function,
     = {h such that $U(wh + Y, T - h)$ is maximized},
$V(w, Y)$ = the indirect utility function,
     = {the maximum value of U given $X + wl = wT + Y$},
$E(w, U)$ = the expenditure (cost) function,
     = {the minimum Y such that $U(X, l) = U$
       and $X + wl = wT + Y$}.[1]

In a world without uncertainty about wages and with a complete choice of hours of work, the woman will participate in the income maintenance program (i.e., work a number of hours so that her income will qualify her for a payment) if her utility level as a participant exceeds her utility level as a nonparticipant. Formally, she will not participate if

$$V((1 - t)w, G + (1 - t)Y) < V(w, Y);$$

she will participate, and receives a payment P, if

$$V((1 - t)w, G + (1 - t)Y) > V(w, Y),$$

---

1. Note that our definition of the expenditure function differs slightly from the standard textbook presentation. It is more common to define $E(w, U)$ as the minimum $wT + Y$ needed to achieve μ if the woman faces a real wage of w. But since we will be more concerned with the amount of nonemployment income, we use this definition of the expenditure function.

where

$$P = G - t(Y + wh)$$

and

$$h = h((1 - t)w, G + (1 - t)Y).$$

Thus, a woman who does not participate should give the program a value zero, otherwise she would have participated. However, a woman who receives a payment must value the program positively, since, by participating, she is better off in utility terms. The question we address is: Is the payment she receives an appropriate measure of the value she places upon the existence of the program?

Traditional benefit analysis would address this issue by asking the woman two alternative questions. First, what would be the maximum lump-sum payment she would be willing to make in order to keep the program in existence? This monetary measure of the program's value is denoted in the literature as the compensating variation (CV), which can be expressed in our notation as

CV such that $V((1 - t)w, G + (1 - t)Y - CV) = V(w, Y)$.

Or equivalently as

(2) $$CV = (G - tY) + E(w, V_0) - E((1 - t)w, V_0)$$

(3) $$= E((1 - t)w, V_1) - E((1 - t)w, V_0),$$

where

$$V_0 = V(w, Y),$$

$$V_1 = V((1 - t)w, G + (1 - t)Y).$$

Alternatively, we could ask the woman the question: What is the minimum lump-sum payment the government would have to make, so that she feels indifferent about the program's existence? This equivalent variation (EV) can be defined using our notation as

EV such that $V(w, Y + EV) = V((1 - t)w, G + (1 - t)Y)$.

Or,

(4) $$EV = (G - tY) + E(w, V_1) - E((1 - t)w, V_1),$$

(5) $$= E(w, V_1) - E(w, V_0).$$

As can be seen from equations (3) and (4), these two approaches attempt to measure, in monetary terms, the distance between the maximum utility achievable with the program (V_1) and the maximum utility achievable without the program (V_0). Each measure utilizes a different price of leisure to measure this distance. The compensating variation uses $(1 - t)w$ while the equivalent variation measure uses the wage rate, w.

Given that the compensating and equivalent variations represent the monetary value of the program to the individual, how does the payment the woman actually receives compare to these other "true" measures of the welfare gain due to the program? Intuition would lead one to conclude that, since the payment, P, reflects a labor supply reduction due to both income and substitution effects of the program, this payment would tend to overestimate the value of the program to the woman. On the other hand, if one computes the payment the woman would receive if she had chosen to work the same number of hours as she did in the absence of the program, then this hypothetical payment, P_0, would underestimate the true welfare measures. In Appendix A we demonstrate that the above intuition is correct and that the four measures can be ranked in the following manner:

$$P_0 \le CV \le EV \le P .$$

In the above discussion we have assumed that the woman is free to work her desired level of hours and that she is not limited in her choice, except by budget constraints. We showed that, in this case, the transfer payment serves as an upper bound of the value of the program to the household. We also obtained a lower bound, thus defining a range within which the true value of the program lies. How would these results change if the woman suffers a spell of involuntary unemployment? If she still decides not to participate, her evaluation of the program does not change, i.e., it remains zero. If, however, she participates, the woman will place a value on the program which is exactly equal to the payment she receives. For example, consider a woman who is participating in the program, becomes unemployed, and can only find $\bar{h} \le h_1$ hours of work at the gross wage rate, w.[2] Her payment, P, will now equal $G - tY - tw\bar{h}$. In the absence of a program the woman would also work only $\bar{h}$ hours, so the hypothetical payment P_0 also equals $G - tY - tw\bar{h}$. Hence, it follows that

$$P_0 = CV = EV = P .$$

Thus, in this case, the benefit value of the program to the involuntarily unemployed woman is exactly equal to the transfer.

7.3 The Value of the Income Maintenance Program When the Household Faces Unemployment Uncertainty

In the previous section we explored how a woman would value the existence of an income maintenance program when all the relevant economic

---

2. A woman who, in the absence of involuntary unemployment, chooses not to participate may opt for participation if her working hours are restricted ($\bar{h} < h_0$). If her optimal working hours under participation, h_1, are less than $\bar{h}$, her evaluation would be equal to the certainty case in section 7.2. If $\bar{h} < h_1$, the value of the benefit again equals the payment.

constraints, including the occurrence of a spell of unemployment, are known to her. To a large extent this analysis should be considered an ex post evaluation of the program on the part of the woman. This ex post evaluation ignores an important feature of income maintenance programs: it insures the eligible population against reductions in their real standard of living. In the previous section, we concluded that when a woman suffers a reduction in her standard of living due to a spell of unemployment, she places an ex post value on the income maintenance program equal to the payment she receives.

However, if the woman could have found sufficient employment that made her ineligible for payments, ex post she would not place a value on the program. Obviously, ex post evaluations of income maintenance programs do not capture the insurance aspects that an income maintenance program possesses.

In order to capture this insurance aspect, it is necessary to introduce uncertainty in the decision-making process of the woman. The question now becomes: What is the value the woman places on the existence of the program if she has a probability of becoming unemployed, even though she is currently employed and not receiving a payment? One possibility is to use the expected payment, i.e., the payment she would receive if she became unemployed times the probability of becoming unemployed.[3] In this section we will show that this measure is likely to underestimate the value of the program to the woman.

In order to analyze this proposition, we first need to introduce the concept of unemployment uncertainty into the above framework. We will assume that the woman with a probability, π, will not be able to work any hours at wage rate, w. She will, with a probability $(1 - \pi)$, be able to work as many hours as she wishes at this same wage rate. Further, in order to simplify the analysis in this section, we assume a fairly restricted type of income maintenance program. If the woman is unable to work, she will receive a payment of P dollars from the government. However, she will receive nothing if she is employed.[4] Finally, we assume that she has no sources of income other than earnings, i.e., Y will be equal to zero.

The woman chooses her hours of work, h^*, so as to maximize her expected level of well-being. Formally, she chooses h^* so as to maximize:

$$EU = \pi U(P, T) + (1 - \pi)U(wh, T - h) \ .$$

---

3. See Long 1967 for an example. See also Smeeding 1982 for alternative approaches to valuing in-kind transfers.

4. The structure of this program resembles the unemployment insurance program; it could also be considered a description of the program seen in equation (1) where the tax rate (t) is set high enough so that the individual would not participate in the program if she were employed.

As Sjoquist (1976) has shown, the optimal choice of labor supply to the above problem is the same as the optimal solution to the labor supply decision under certainty, i.e., h^* will maximize $U(wh, T - h)$. Thus the optimal amount of labor supply for this problem will be solely a function of the wage rate (i.e., $h^* = h(w)$).

Now let the expected utility in the absence of the income maintenance program be denoted by:

$$EU_0 = \pi U(O, T) + (1 - \pi)U(wh^*, T - h^*) ;$$

and with the program be denoted by:

$$EU_1 = \pi U(P, T) + (1 - \pi)U(wh^*, T - h^*).$$

The question we now raise is how does the woman value the gain in her expected utility that the income maintenance program provides her?

Burton Weisbrod, in a pathbreaking article (Weisbrod 1964; see also Cicchetti and Freeman 1971; Graham 1981) argued that the appropriate measure of the woman's valuation of the program could be constructed by asking for the maximum certainty payment the woman would be willing to make to have the program in existence. He denoted this amount as the option price (OP). Using our notation, the option price can be defined such that

(6) $\pi U(P - OP, T) + (1 - \pi)U(wh^* - OP, T - h^*) = EU_0 .$

As Graham (1981) has shown, the option price is just one of many measures one can utilize to measure the value of a program that insures the individual against some risk.[5] An alternative benefit measure is the expected surplus that the program yields. That is, if a given state occurs, the program yields a given amount of surplus to the individual. For each state this surplus can be measured by either the compensating variation or the equivalent variation discussed in the previous section. The expected surplus is then obtained by weighting the state-contingent surplus values by the probability that the state occurs. For example, in this section the woman receives no surplus if she is employed because she will not receive a payment in this state. However, her surplus will be P dollars if she is unem-

---

5. In this paper we have adopted as a measure of value the maximum certainty payment the individual would wish to make in order to have the program in existence. The use of the measure—the option price—is in keeping with the literature. However, upon further reflection, we have concluded that a more appropriate measure in the case of an income maintenance program would be the minimum certainty lump-sum payment the individual would require in order to be indifferent to the program's existence. When stated in this manner, we see that the option price is the uncertainty equivalent of the compensating variation measure, while the above alternative measure would have the equivalent variation as its certainty counterpart. If the relationship that exists between the compensating and equivalent variation holds up in the uncertainty case, then the option price would underestimate the value of the income maintenance program to the individual. Exploration of this issue represents our future work in this area.

ployed. Hence her expected surplus is πP, which in this simple case is equal to her expected payments from the program.

Following the literature, we will define the risk premium a woman places upon an income maintenance program as the difference between the option price and the expected surplus, i.e., the risk premium, RP, is equal to

$$RP = OP - ES,$$

where ES is the expected surplus. Thus in the above example the risk premium is equal to $(OP - \pi P)$.

7.3.1 Numerical Example

If we adopt the option price as our ex ante measure of the woman's valuation of the program, then it remains to explore whether or not the option price will exceed the woman's expected payment (expected surplus) from the program (πP). As Schmalensee (1972) and Henry (1974) have shown, the option price depends upon the individual's preferences and may or may not exceed the expected payment.[6]

Thus, first we have to specify the woman's preferences for income and leisure. One approach would be to specify a direct utility function, $U(X, l)$, and then to make some assumptions about the parameters of the function. Our approach is different. We will assume a given labor supply function and derive the implicit utility function from it. By doing so we can take empirical estimates of labor supply functions that appear in the literature as statements about the "average" woman's preferences for income and leisure. In particular, we assume the linear labor supply function

(7) $$h = \delta + \alpha w + \beta Y,$$

where δ, α, and β are all constant parameters that may depend upon the individual's demographic characteristics. If the labor supply function takes the above functional form, the expenditure function can be written as (Sheppard's lemma):

(8) $$E(w, U) = (\alpha - \beta(\delta + \alpha w))/\beta^2 + U \exp(-\beta w);$$

or in terms of the direct utility function:

(9) $$U(X, h) = ((\beta h - \alpha)/\beta^2) \exp(\beta(\delta + \beta X - h)/(\beta h - \alpha)).[7]$$

For the purposes of this paper, we chose to utilize the estimates of the linear labor supply function from the Hausman study (Hausman 1981). In

---

6. In Appendix B, we derive a sufficient condition for the option price to exceed the expected value of the payment.

7. It should be noted that the utility function for the linear labor supply function meets our sufficient conditions for OP to exceed the expected payments from the program for all payments P that are less than an amount roughly equal to $15,000 per year.

Table 7.1   **Values of Option Price (OP) and Risk Premium (RP)
                        Computed from Equation (6)**

Probability of Unemployment	Wage Rate					
	$3.00		$4.00		$5.00	
	OP	RP	OP	RP	OP	RP
0.90	$3,786	$186	$3,794	$194	$3,798	$198
0.75	3,404	404	3,440	440	3,449	449
0.50	2,680	610	2,680	701	2,698	698
0.25	1,530	530	1,606	606	1,625	625
0.10	681	281	727	327	738	338

Source: Calculations by authors.

Notes: Figures computed for a female head under forty-five years of age who has one child aged six. $P = \$4,000$.

this study, Hausman has estimated that for female-headed households (i.e., households with children present and only one, female, adult), α equals 0.3509 while an average β is equal to -0.122. The intercept term (δ) in the Hausman study was made a function of several demographic characteristics such as age and family composition. For the numerical example in this paper, we chose a female who is less than forty-five-years-old and has one child under six years of age. A woman with these characteristics has a value of δ of 1.0563. It should be noted that hours of work are measured in the Hausman study in terms of annual hours of work (in thousands), while Y is also measured in thousands of dollars per year.

Finally, we chose to simulate a value of $4,000 for P—the payment the woman would receive if she became unemployed. In order to examine how the risk premium and option price would vary for other parameters of the problem, we computed these variables utilizing various wage rates ($3.00, $4.00, and $5.00) and for various probabilities of becoming unemployed (0.10, 0.25, 0.50, 0.75, and 0.90). The results of these computations, using equation (6) and the above assumptions, appear in table 7.1.

As the numbers in table 7.1 illustrate, the risk premium that a woman places upon an unemployment contingent payment of $4,000 can be quite large. As one would expect, the option price declines as the probability of unemployment declines. However the risk premium does not possess this same monotonic behavior. First, we note that the risk premium actually rises initially with a decline in the probability of unemployment and then starts to decline when the probability of unemployment falls below 50 percent.[8] Second, reading across table 7.1 we see that the risk premium rises with the wage rate of the woman holding the probability of unemployment constant.

8. While the risk premium shows an inverted U-shape pattern, the ratio of the risk premium to the expected surplus is monotonically increasing with the probability of employment. For a similar result, see Freeman 1984.

Maybe the most important result of table 7.1 is that it illustrates the magnitude of the potential error one makes by using either the actual payments received (ex post analysis), or the use of expected payment from the program as the program's value to the household. To illustrate this, consider two women, one with a wage rate of $3.00 and 90 percent probability of becoming unemployed (ex ante) and the other with a $5.00 wage rate and a 10 percent chance of becoming unemployed. For the sake of argument let us assume that the low-wage woman becomes unemployed and the high-wage woman does not. Ex post considerations would indicate that the low-wage woman benefited by $4,000 from the program while the high-wage woman did not benefit at all. Using the expected payments from the program as a measure of the program's benefits we would be led to say that the low-wage woman values the program at $3,600 and the high-wage woman at $400. However, as the calculations in table 7.1 indicate, either one of these measures will tend to impart different kinds of biases into the measure of the value of the program to the individual women. For the low-wage woman who receives a payment, the use of the actual payment received ($4,000) overstates the value of the program to her ($3,786), while the use of the expected payment ($3,600) underestimates the value of the program because it ignores the risk premium. For the high-wage woman a different relationship emerges. Both the actual payment (zero) and the expected payment ($400) underestimate the value of the program to her ($738).

While there are differential effects on the two women, the results in the aggregate are clear. The total value the two women place upon the existence of the program ($4,524) is 13 percent higher than the actual payments (or the sum of the expected payments). The implications for the distributional effects of the program are also quite clear. The use of the actual payments would indicate that 100 percent of the total benefits are received by the low-wage woman, while the use of the expected payments would indicate that 90 percent of the benefits of the program went to her. However, the use of the option price measure of value indicates that only 84 percent of the total benefits would accrue to the low-wage woman. If the results of our example are indicative for the population as a whole, we have to conclude that the use of either the actual or the expected payment would overestimate the redistributive effects of income maintenance programs such as the one we simulated in the above example, and will serve to underestimate the total benefits the group receives from the program.

7.4   An Expanded Notion of Uncertainty

In the previous section we examined the extent to which a woman would place a risk premium on her expected payments from a specific unemployment contingent program. To clarify the issues and presentation we made some admittedly simplifying assumptions. The most crucial one was the way in which we characterized employment uncertainty: Previously, we assumed the woman faced only two states—employment and the ability to work as much as she wishes at a prespecified wage rate that was known to her in advance, or unemployment. In this section we shall expand our concept of uncertainty by treating the real wage as a random variable.[9] This implies a continuum of employment states with hours worked (and corresponding earnings) dependent upon this stochastic wage rate. We shall also introduce a somewhat more realistic income maintenance program: the woman is now assumed to be eligible for payments as long as her income does not exceed a given level, regardless of her state of employment. Thus, this income maintenance program insures the women against a drop in her level of well-being due to unemployment or due to an unlucky draw from the distribution of wages.

In order to measure the value that the woman places upon this insurance protection, we will need to modify equation (6) to reflect the uncertainty about the wage rate. First, let us assume that the woman possesses a subjective probability function over real wages, $f(w)$. Given that we will continue to characterize employment uncertainty as a two-state occurrence (employment at hours desired, given the stochastic wage rate, or no employment at all), we can modify equation (6) to define the option price, OP, such that

(10) $$EU_1 = EU_0,$$

where

$$EU_0 = \pi U(O, T) + (1 - \pi) \int_0^\infty U(wh_0^*, T - h_0^*)f(w)dw$$

with

h_0^* = the hours that maximize the expected utility when there is no program,

and

$$EU_1 = \pi U(G - OP, T) + (1 - \pi) \int_0^\infty U(wh_1^* + P^* - OP, T - h_1^*)f(w)dw$$

with

h_1^* = the hours that maximize the expected utility when there is an income maintenance program,

---

9. See Block and Heineke 1973 and Cowell 1981 for the treatment of wage uncertainty in the absence and presence of income maintenance programs respectively.

where
$$P^* = \begin{cases} G - twh_1^* & \text{if} \quad h_1^* < G/tw, \\ 0 & \text{if} \quad h_1^* \geq G/tw. \end{cases}$$

Before turning to some numerical calculations of the value that a woman might place upon an income maintenance program given the above characterization of the environment, we wish to remind the reader that two important distinctions must be made between the numerical calculations below and the previous ones. First, in the previous example we considered only unemployment contingent payments. In the current example the woman will be eligible for a payment not only if she is unemployed but also if she is employed and her earnings are less than G/t. This "extension" of the income maintenance program is, of course, likely to increase the option price significantly. Second, in the previous example the labor supply decision is made with no regard to the payment she would receive if she became unemployed. However, in the current example her decision of how much labor to supply will depend not only on the distribution of wages, but also on G and t, since she may be eligible for a payment if her real earnings fall below G/t.

7.4.1   Numerical Example

In order to compute numerical values for the option price and other variables of interest, the only additional concept that needs to be quantified from our previous example is the distribution of real wage rates. We have assumed that wages are distributed normally. Note that the symmetry of the normal distribution implies that we implicitly assume that the woman expects her potential real wage rate to remain unchanged. We choose three values for the mean of the distribution, corresponding to the wage rates utilized earlier: $3.00, $4.00 and $5.00. In all cases, we utilize a standard deviation of $.25.

Table 7.2 presents the numerical values for the option value, expected surplus, expected payment, and risk premium a woman with one child would place upon an income maintenance program as described by equation (1), where G is equal to $4,000 and t is equal to 0.50. The expected surplus presented in table 7.2 is defined to be the expected compensating variation, i.e.,

$$ES = \pi G + (1 - \pi) \int_0^\infty CV(w) f(w) \, dw,$$

where $CV(w)$ is such that

$$U(wh_1^* + P^* - CV(w), T - h_1^*) = U(wh_0^*, T - h_0^*)$$

for all w. From the above definition of the expected surplus, we note that if h_0^* is equal to h_1^*, the compensating variation given a specific wage rate will be equal to the payment the woman receives. Hence if this condition is met, the expected surplus will be equal to the expected payment the woman

Table 7.2   **Values of Option Price and Risk Premium**
                       Computed Using Equation (10)

Probability of Unemployment	$3.00 Wage Rate			
	OP	ES	EP	RP
0.90	$3,834	$3,761	$3,830	$ 73
0.75	3,565	3,403	3,590	155
0.50	3,014	2,807	3,179	207
0.25	2,333	2,210	2,769	123
0.10	1,831	1,803	2,522	28
Probability of Unemployment	$4.00 Wage Rate			
	OP	ES	EP	RP
0.90	$3,795	$3,602	$3,602	$193
0.75	3,441	3,006	3,006	435
0.50	3,682	2,012	2,012	670
0.25	1,607	1,018	1,018	589
0.10	728	403	403	325
Probability of Unemployment	$5.00 Wage Rate			
	OP	ES	EP	RP
0.90	$3,798	$3,600	$3,600	$198
0.75	3,449	3,000	3,000	449
0.50	2,690	2,000	2,000	698
0.25	1,625	1,000	1,000	625
0.10	738	400	400	338

Source: Calculations made by authors.
Notes: Figures computed for a female head under forty-five years of age who has one child aged six. $G = \$4,000$; $t = 0.50$.

receives. However, if h_1^* is less than h_0^* as we would expect in this example, then, as has been shown in section 7.2, the payment the woman receives will always exceed the compensating variation for all wage rates. Hence in the case where there is a labor supply reduction in response to the program, the expected payment will always exceed the expected surplus. Finally, we would like to remind the reader that the risk premium is defined to be equal to the difference between the option price and the expected surplus.

Let us begin by comparing the numerical values of the option price computed here with the ones in our previous example. As expected, the option prices in table 7.2 are much larger than those in table 7.1. For instance, the option prices rose from $681 to $1,831 for a woman with an (expected) wage rate of $3.00 and a 10 percent probability of becoming unemployed. The main cause of the increase in the value of the option price is the extension of the program, which now provides a real-income floor even when employed. This, of course, is especially valuable for a woman with a low expected wage rate, since given her distribution of real wage rates she is most likely to be eligible for payments from the program. For the women with a higher expected wage rate, the option prices calculated in tables 7.1 and 7.2 are essentially the same because if these women are employed they have only a very small probability of receiving a payment, due to their distribution of wages.

As noted above, if a labor supply reduction occurs due to the program, the expected payments will exceed the expected surplus the woman receives from the program. For the low-wage woman (the $3.00 expected wage rate case), the difference between the two concepts is significant and reflects the effects of a large labor supply reduction in the order of 30 percent. However, for the higher wage women there is no difference between these two concepts, reflecting the fact that for these women a reduction in their labor supply does not occur due to the program.

From table 7.2 we note that the expected surplus never exceeds the option price. Consequently, the risk premium is always positive. Also, the U-shaped pattern of risk premiums that was present in the earlier example is present in this example.

While in general the calculations indicate that the relationships between the various concepts in this example are similar to those in the previous example, one major difference does appear. This difference is between the value of the option price and the expected payments. In the previous example, the option price always exceeded the expected payments to the women in all cases. However, for the low-wage woman, the expected payment exceeds the option price in all cases except when the probability of unemployment is high. A rational for why this reversal occurs and why the difference widens as the probability of employment increases, eludes us at this time and is an area for further examination.

The possibility that the expected payments exceed the option price for some cases in table 7.2 causes us to soften some of our conclusions presented in the previous example. Since the option price always exceeds the expected payments, we could conclude that use of either the actual payments or expected payments would underestimate the aggregate value of the program. Further, either of these methods would tend to overestimate the redistribution that was accomplished by the program. While the second conclusion will remain, it should be noted that since it is possible that the expected payment exceeds the option price for low-wage-rate women, it is possible in the aggregate that the payments made to individuals exceed the sum of individual option prices.

7.5   Conclusions

In this chapter we have examined the relationship between the payment the household receives and the value the household would place upon the program that either transfers or potentially transfers income to the household. In the case of certainty and with benefit payments only in the case of unemployment, we concluded that the payment the household receives provides an upper bound to the value the household places upon the program. Using the option price as the "correct" measure of the value of the program, we showed that the expected value of the payment, i.e., the payment times the probability of being unemployed, tends to underestimate the value of the program to the population in general and to each household individually. In the numerical examples presented, the risk premium, i.e., the difference between the expected value and the option price, ranged from $186 for a low-wage/high-probability-of-unemployment woman, to $698 for a high-wage woman with a 50 percent probability of unemployment. The corresponding values of the expected payments of the program were $3,600 and $2,000 respectively. Consequently, the use of expected payments as the value of the program to the households will overestimate the distributional impact of the program.

We then discussed a more realistic case with wage rate uncertainty, where the program made payments to a woman as long as her earned income did not exceed a certain amount. Given that the program now insures against erosions in a household's real income even when a woman is employed, it came as no surprise to find that for a woman with a low expected wage rate, the option prices were even larger than in the first case. This was almost entirely the result of the extension of the program. For a woman facing a higher wage rate this extension had no effect on the option price. To summarize our results somewhat differently: the difference between the value of expected payments and the option price is large for those cases where large behavioral responses to the program can be expected.

The methodology to measure the value of welfare programs, as developed in this chapter, has a wide range of applications. In principle it is straightforward, once the option price is accepted as the value of the program. In order to calculate this option price, one needs information not only on what benefits are potentially available to the individual, but also on the distribution of real-wage rates, probability of unemployment, and the individual's preferences over the various alternatives, i.e., a utility function. While in principle the first three elements needed to compute the option price can be inferred from various data sources, the individual's preferences are conceptually more difficult to specify. What we have demonstrated in this paper is that observations on labor supply behavior can—through Sheppard's lemma—yield such a utility function.

We should stress, however, that our results are based on one labor supply function (and thus one particular income-leisure preference ordering) only, as applied to a selected set of hypothetical households. As a next step in our research we need to analyze a "real" sample of household data (like a CPS), estimate various specifications of the labor supply function for

female heads, and use the observed distributions of the probability of unemployment and the wage rate to estimate the value of, say, AFDC or
food stamp programs. As our examples indicate, the differences between
the option price on the one hand and such commonly used measures as
payment received or expected benefits on the other hand, are large enough
to warrant such a study, especially when the focus is on the distributional
aspects of the program.

References

Block, M. K., and J. M. Heineke. 1973. The allocation of effort under
    uncertainty: The case of risk-adverse behavior. *Journal of Political
    Economy* 81:376–85.
Cicchetti, C. J., and A. M. Freeman. 1971. Option demand and con-
    sumer surplus: Further comment. *Quarterly Journal of Economics*
    85:528–39.
Cowell, F. 1981. Income maintenance schemes under wage rate uncer-
    tainty. *American Economic Review* 71:692–703.
Freeman, A. M. 1984. The sign and size of option value. *Land Economics*
    60, no. 1:1–13.
Graham, D. A. 1981. Cost-benefit analysis under uncertainty. *American
    Economic Review* 71:715–25.
Hausman, J. A. 1981. Labor supply. In *How taxes affect economic be-
    havior*, ed. H. J. Aaron and J. A. Pechman, 27–83. Washington, D.C.:
    Brookings Institution.
Henry, C. 1974. Option values in the economies of irreplacable assets. *Re-
    view of Economic Studies* 64:89–104.
Lindsay, C. M. 1969. Option demand and consumer's surplus. *Quarterly
    Journal of Economics* 83:344–46.
Long, M. L. 1967. Collective-consumption services of individual-
    consumption goods: Comment. *Quarterly Journal of Economics*
    81:351–52.
Schmalensee, R. 1972. Option demand and consumer surplus: Valuing
    price changes under uncertainty. *American Economic Review* 62:813–
    24.
Sjoquist, D. L. 1976. Labor supply under uncertainty: Note. *American
    Economic Review* 66:929–30.
Smeeding, Timothy M. 1982. Alternative methods of valuing selected in-
    kind benefits and measuring their effect on poverty. Technical paper
    no. 50, Bureau of the Census.
Weisbrod, B. A. 1964. Collective consumption services of individual con-
    sumption goods. *Quarterly Journal of Economics* 78:71–77.

Appendix A

Demonstration That the Income Maintenance Payment Will Exceed the Traditional Benefit Measures

In order to show that the payment a woman receives from the program exceeds either of the two benefit measures, we will first show that EV will always be as great as CV. Using equations (3) and (5) for EV and CV, we can state that

$$CV \gtreqless EV$$

if and only if

$$E((1 - t)w, V_1) - E((1 - t)w, V_0) \gtreqless E(w, V_1) - E(w, V_0);$$

or equivalently,

$$E((1 - t)w, V_1) - E(w, V_1) \gtreqless E((1 - t)w, V_0) - E(w, V_0).$$

Because the woman is participating in the program, V_1 will exceed V_0. If leisure is a normal good (i.e., the marginal utility of leisure is decreasing in l), then

$$E((1 - t)w, V_1) - E(w, V_1) \leq E((1 - t)w, V_0) - E(w, V_0).$$

Hence

$$CV \leq EV.$$

Now we will demonstrate that the transfer the household receives from the program will exceed EV. First, let the transfer be equal to P, i.e.,

$$P = G - tY - twh_1,$$

where

$$h_1 = h((1 - t)w, G + (1 - t)Y).$$

Furthermore, from equation (4),

$$EV \gtreqless P$$

if and only if

$$G - tY + E(w, V_1) - E((1 - t)w, V_1) \gtreqless G - tY - twh_1,$$

or equivalently,

$$E(w, V_1) \gtreqless E((1 - t)w, V_1) - twh_1.$$

In order to determine which condition will hold, first note that if $\tilde{h}(w, U)$ is the Hicksian labor supply function, then

$$h_1 = \bar{h}((1 - t)w, V_1).$$

Next note that due to the derivative property of the expenditure function (Sheppard's lemma), the derivation of the expenditure function with respect to the wage is equal to minus the Hicksian labor supply function,

$$\partial E(w, U)/\partial w = -\bar{h}(w, U) .$$

Because the expenditure function is concave in w,

$$E(w, V_1) \leq E((1 - t)w, V_1) + tw (\partial E((1 - t)w, V_1)/\partial w)$$

(this inequality is known as the Könus inequality), or equivalently,

$$E(w, U_1) \leq E((1 - t)w, U_1) - twh_1.$$

Hence the payment P exceeds the equivalent variation measure of a woman's gain in well-being caused by the existence of the income maintenance program. Since we have shown that EV will always exceed CV, this payment will also exceed the compensating variation measure.

Let us now define an alternative payment, P_0, which is the (hypothetical) payment a woman would receive if she worked the same number of hours under the program as she would in the absence of the program. Let

$$P_0 = G - tY - twh_0$$

where

$$h_0 = h(w, Y) .$$

Now by the same line of argument as used above, we can demonstrate that

$$P_0 \leq CV .$$

Hence we can use the two payments, P_0 and P, to bound the appropriate benefit measures, i.e.,

$$P_0 \leq CV \leq EV \leq P .$$

Appendix B
A Sufficient Condition for the Option Value to Exceed the Expected Payments from a Program

While we have not been able to establish necessary and sufficient conditions for OP to exceed πP, we have been able to establish a sufficient condition that we believe is likely and plausible. Formally, for the risk premium to be positive, the marginal utility of income at $(1 - \pi)P$ dollars of income and T hours of leisure must exceed the marginal utility of income at $wh^* - \pi P$ dollars of income and $T - h^*$ hours of leisure.

In order to demonstrate this, note (from equation 6) that if the marginal utility of income (U_X) is positive for all X and l, then

$$OP > \pi P \text{ if and only if}$$

$$\pi U((1 - \pi)P, T) + (1 - \pi)U(wh^* - \pi P, T - h^*) > EU_0,$$

which can be rewritten as

$$OP > \pi P \text{ if and only if}$$

$$\frac{\pi}{1 \quad \pi} > \frac{U(wh^*, T - h^*) - U(wh^* - \pi P, T - h^*)}{U((1 \quad \pi)P, T) \quad U(O, T)}$$

Now due to the concavity of U

$$\pi P\, U_X(wh^* - \pi P, T - h^*) > U(wh^*, T - h^*) \\ - U(wh^* - \pi P, T - h^*)$$

and

$$(1 - \pi)P\, U_X((1 - \pi)P, T) < U((1 - \pi)P, T) - U(O, T) .$$

Thus

$$\frac{U(wh^*, T - h^*) - U(wh^* - \pi P, T - h^*)}{U((1 - \pi)P, T) - U(O, T)}$$

$$< \frac{\pi\, U_X(wh^* - \pi P, T - h^*)}{(1 - \pi)\, U_X((1 - \pi)P, T)} .$$

Hence if $U_X(wh^* - \pi P, T - h^*)$ is less than $U_X((1 - \pi)P, T)$ then the option price will exceed the expected payment to a woman, πP. While concavity of the utility function is not enough to guarantee that the above sufficient condition will hold (note that concavity of the utility function is the same assumption as risk aversion), the examples in section 7.4 indicate that this condition is likely to be met for reasonable values of P, w, and π.

It might prove useful to amplify the significance of the above result. Let us consider a population of N female-headed households each facing a prospect of becoming unemployed with probability π. In any given year we would observe that πN of the women were unemployed and receiving P dollars; as presented above, each woman in the population would be willing to pay up to OP dollars each year to have the program in existence. This means that $N(OP)$ dollars can be collected from the population. Thus if our sufficient condition is met, the women in the population will collectively value the program in excess of the payments that are made to the group.

Comment   F. Thomas Juster

The Betson/van der Gaag chapter is concerned with assessing the consequences for the evaluation of income maintenance programs of introducing uncertainty both about hours of work and real-wage rates. The chapter has five sections: the first is an introduction, the second examines valuation issues under conventional assumptions of no uncertainty, the third extends the valuation analysis to uncertainty about hours of work, the fourth extends the analysis further to uncertainty about real-wage rates, and the fifth and last section provides a summary and discussion of policy implications.

In section 7.2 the authors demonstrate that alternative measures of program benefits can be derived from a household utility function in which consumption and leisure are the arguments, and that these welfare-oriented benefit measures can be shown to lie between two observable benefit measures. One observable measure is the actual payments received by a female head of household who participates in an income maintenance program, such as AFDC or food stamps, which is shown to be an upper bound. The other is the payment that the woman would receive if she worked the same number of hours in the absence of the program as she chose to work, given the incentive structure contained by the program, which is the lower bound.

Two features of this analysis are worth noting. First, the two alternative welfare-oriented benefit measures, discussed in the literature as the compensating variation and the equivalent variation, require valuation measures based on questions that are not likely to be answerable in any straightforward manner. The welfare measures are obtained from the answers to questions concerning counterfactual situations, and there is no reason to believe that people can provide useful answers to questions of that sort. Second, the analysis makes the conventional assumptions about utility functions—that the arguments are consumption and leisure and that both are decreasing and positive throughout.

In section 7.3 the analysis is extended to a situation where hours of work are uncertain because some probability, π, of unemployment exists. Thus hours of work equal either the preferred amount given the utility function and the opportunity set, or equal zero because of unemployment. It is further assumed that those who become unemployed will participate in the program, while those who do not become unemployed will not be eligible for the program (it ensures only against uncertainty with respect to hours of work, not real income).

F. Thomas Juster is director of the Institute for Social Research and professor of economics at the University of Michigan.

Given that model, the authors argue that the program can be evaluated by finding the maximum payment that those potentially eligible for the program would be willing to make to have the program in existence—this amount is defined as the option price (*OP*). The remainder of this section explores the circumstances under which the option price can be expected to exceed the expected value of the payments to potential participants. The difference between the option price and the expected payment is defined as the risk premium—the value of the hedge against uncertain hours represented by the program's existence.

Numerical estimates of the risk premium are derived in the paper by specifying the parameters of a particular labor supply function, originally estimated for female-headed households with children present. The basic purpose of this exercise is to calculate the distributional consequences of the program by comparing the distribution of option prices (which includes risk premiums) with the distribution of expected payments. The conclusion is that existence of a program that hedges against uncertainty in work hours provides relatively more benefits to higher-wage workers with low probabilities of becoming unemployed than would be inferred from observing the actual distribution of program payments. That is, the distribution of program benefits as measured by the option price suggests that more benefits would go to high-wage workers than would appear to be true from simply observing the distribution of actual payments. Thus a program that hedges against hours uncertainty will be less redistributive than a program in which hours uncertainty is absent.

In the next section, the analysis of uncertainty effects is extended to cover uncertainty about real-wage rates. For this analysis the authors assume a normal distribution of real-wage expectations, with a standard deviation of $1.00 per hour at alternative specified levels of the mean of that distribution.

Working through the same kinds of numerical example as used in the earlier section, the value of the program to potential participants as measured by the estimated option price is substantially greater, especially for low-wage workers with relatively low probability of becoming unemployed. The reason is not that the hedge against real-wage uncertainty is especially valuable for these workers, but that the basic structure of the program is modified so that people who are employed at low-wage rates become eligible. Thus the substantial increase in the value of the program for some categories of workers is not a consequence of wage-rate uncertainty, but occurs because low-wage workers are covered by the program even if they are employed, while in the analysis in the previous section, coverage was contingent on becoming unemployed.

It should be noted that the higher option prices for most workers in the hypothetical examples provided are seriously overstated because of the assumptions about real-wage uncertainty. A standard deviation of $1.00 with an expected mean of $3.00, $5.00, or $7.00 implies an enormous amount of real-wage uncertainty relative to what one would expect to find in the real world. The authors are not talking here about real-wage uncertainty as reflected by what kind of job people might be able to obtain, but simply about uncertainty as reflected by the difference between rates of price inflation and rates of inflation in nominal wage rates. Uncertainty of this sort is in fact trivial in quantitative terms: under extreme conditions one might visualize a rate of price inflation of 10 percent associated with stability in nominal wages, hence a real wage cut of 10 percent. But that would imply a standard deviation of expected real-wage rates that would be much smaller than any of the numerical examples used in the paper, hence the real-wage effect is seriously exaggerated in the calculations that are shown by the authors.

The principal difficulties with the paper are twofold. First, the calculations are not carried out on a real sample of the U.S. population, thus providing the reader with an assessment of the distributional consequences of these uncertainty considerations by using data that represent the right proportions of individuals with different wage rates, different employment/unemployment experiences, different serial correlation properties in the incidence of unemployment, and so on. In the real world, just how much consideration of the uncertainty issue would modify the distribution of benefits as reflected by the distribution of actual payments is not at all clear from the paper, although I would guess that the two distributions would not differ very much from each other. Since the main concern of the paper is the effect on the benefit distribution of taking account of both hours and wage-rate uncertainty, the importance of these considerations cannot really be assessed without applying the model to real distributions. There are of course numerous bodies of data on which such a calculation could be made.

The more serious problems with the paper are less easily fixed. The authors use a conventional welfare function in which utility is a function of income and leisure. Unemployment affects that welfare function in two ways: by increasing the amount of (valuable) leisure time, which in the model augments welfare, and by reducing income, which lowers welfare. The latter effect is stronger, hence welfare is reduced on balance. While there may be population elements where the increased leisure resulting from unemployment is a welfare-enhancing element, substantial evidence exists in the psychological literature that there are population elements where increased leisure of this form does not create any welfare enhancement at all, and in fact may reduce the value of leisure time generally. Aside from the long-term consequences of unemployment for conventional human capital theory, parts of the population probably assess unemployment-induced increases in their leisure time as a net disbenefit, over and above the real income loss. The principal point I would make is that imposing the same utility function on everyone may not be very good social science, and may be seriously misleading when it comes to analysis of the utility attached to various programs.

The notion that the utility from being unemployed cannot be well represented by seeing it as simply an increase in leisure time is reflective of a more general issue related to the usual form of utility functions in the economic literature. Specifying the utility function as a combination of income plus leisure really amounts to the view that utility is produced by the combination of *ex*trinsic rewards from one kind of activity (work for pay in the market), plus *in*trinsic rewards from other activities (leisure). But work for pay may also carry intrinsic rewards, and the conventional model simply suggests that they are fully accounted for in the equilibrium choice between work and leisure—the marginal intrinsic rewards attached to work being part of the utility obtained from the last hour worked.

The available literature here is concerned with the existence of compensating wage differentials, which equate the mixture of extrinsic and intrinsic rewards from various types of work by providing monetary offsets to any intrinsic rewards differential. Attempts to test that idea have not been notably successful (see Duncan and Holmlund 1983), although some evidence exists that particular kinds of intrinsic differences in work situations are associated with monetary wage differentials.

More generally, recent data obtained in conjunction with research on nonmarket activities have turned up some results that may be fundamentally inconsistent with much of the conventional utility function literature (see Juster, forthcoming; Dow and Juster, forthcoming). As part of a data base focused on the nonmarket activities of households, we obtained direct measurements of intrinsic rewards (not at the margin, but on average), for a variety of activities that included leisure, work for pay, and work in the home. Conventional utility theory would suggest that these intrinsic satisfaction data should show that leisure outranks work and that interesting, challenging, and pleasant jobs outrank dull, routine, and distasteful jobs. But the data do not show these patterns: work outranks leisure with respect to intrinsic satisfactions, and that result is not due to the fact that the intrinsic satisfaction measures for work represent a mixture of intrinsic and extrinsic rewards. Jobs of all sorts appear to provide about the same level of intrinsic satisfactions.

References

Duncan, Greg J., and Bertil Holmlund. 1983. Was Adam Smith right, after all? Another test of the theory of compensating wage differentials. Working paper no. 93. Industrial Institute for Economic and Social Research, Stockholm.

Dow, Greg, and F. T. Juster. Forthcoming. Goods, time, and well-being: The joint dependence problem. In *Time, goods, and well-being,* ed. F. T. Juster and F. P. Stafford, chap. 16. Ann Arbor, Mich.: Institute for Social Research.

Juster, F. T. Forthcoming. Preferences for work and leisure. In *Time, goods, and well-being,* ed. F. T. Juster and F. P. Stafford, chaps. 1 and 3. Ann Arbor, Mich.,: Institute for Social Research.

8   A Comparison of Measures of Horizontal Inequity

Robert Plotnick

8.1 Introduction

The principle of horizontal equity is usually stated as "equal treatment of equals." Policies that redistribute should levy identical taxes or provide identical transfers to all units with the same level of well-being. In recent years several researchers have argued that, if this classic definition is to be analytically useful and intuitively reasonable, it must be amended to include the more general condition that a redistribution of well-being must not alter the rank order of units (Atkinson 1980; Feldstein 1976; King 1983; Plotnick 1982).[1]

As attention to the concept of horizontal equity has grown, methods for appropriately measuring the extent of horizontal inequity have also received increased scrutiny (Atkinson 1980; Berliant and Strauss 1983; Cowell 1980, 1982; King 1983; Plotnick 1981, 1982; Rosen 1978). Empirical work on this issue, however, has been meager and unsystematic.[2] Pa-

Robert Plotnick is associate professor of public affairs and social work, Graduate School of Public Affairs and School of Social Work, University of Washington.

The author wishes to thank Stephan Chase and William Epstein for research assistance. This research was supported in part by a contract to the Institute for Research on Poverty from the U.S. Department of Health and Human Services. The views expressed in this paper are those of the author and do not necessarily reflect the views of either DHHS or the Institute for Research on Poverty.

1. While Berliant and Strauss 1982 have taken issue with this amendment, it is adopted in this study. See part 8.2 for further discussion.

2. Here is a quick but nearly complete review of the empirical literature: Plotnick and Skidmore 1975, (pp. 156, 234–36) offered tabular evidence for cash transfers but no summary measure. Atkinson 1980 used aggregate data on the U.S. income tax and one measure. Berliant and Strauss 1983 also examined this tax using a measure they developed. Rosen 1978 analyzed the U.S. income and payroll tax with two measures. King 1983 applied the index he derived to a simulated reform of housing subsidies in England and Wales. Plotnick 1981 adopted the same index as Atkinson, but used microdata and two measures of well-being to examine several redistributions involving taxes and cash and in-kind transfers. Still different

pers with empirical sections have simply illustrated a particular measure (or measures) using a convenient data set. Comparisons of different measures applied to the same data and measure of economic welfare, and differences resulting from using the same measure of horizontal inequity and same data but alternative definitions of economic well-being, have not been explored.

This chapter seeks to fill this gap in the literature. Such an exercise is needed to give analysts a better "feel" for the meaning of different values of an inequity index and for how various indexes differ in their sensitivity to changes in the definition of well-being.[3]

Aside from whatever intrinsic scholarly interest it may hold, advancing our understanding of the measurement of horizontal inequity may contribute to better informed policy analyses and decisions. It is evident that the horizontal inequity generated by public policies that explicitly or implicitly redistribute economic welfare concerns decision makers. Analyses of proposed tax and welfare reforms and changes in entitlement programs prepared by the Congressional Budget Office or the U.S. Treasury Department routinely include simple "gainers and losers" tables. Such information provides a crude assessment of the extent of reordering. Examples of situations in which a nonworking welfare mother's cash and in-kind transfer income exceeds the take-home pay of a working poor family have featured prominently in welfare reform debates since 1969. So, too, have examples of differences in public assistance provided to equally needy families caused by state-by-state variation in eligibility rules and benefit schedules. Waiting lists for subsidized public housing or other benefits with limited availability have been viewed as unfair since some equally deserving persons are denied access. Special provisions in the tax code are frequently defended or attacked by claiming they reduce or induce unequal treatment of equals.

There are sound reasons for this concern. Unequal treatment of equals and rank reversals are likely sources of social tension in a society that tends to view incomes (and, hence, ranking in the distribution) generated by market processes as deserved. Knowledge that some persons with lower market incomes than oneself attain greater disposable incomes by receiving some public benefit or avoiding their "fair share" of taxes may well breed resentment.

---

indexes are implemented in the specialized studies by Chernick and Reschovsky 1982 and Menchik and David 1982. See Plotnick 1982 for citations to earlier studies and criticisms of many of the horizontal inequity indexes used in them.

3. In contrast, analysts appear to have a better intuitive sense of, for example, what a Gini coefficient of .3 means relative to one of .6. In addition, substantial work has been done on the sensitivity of measures of inequality to changes in the reporting unit or measure of well-being (Beach, Card, and Flatters 1981; Benus and Morgan 1975; Danziger and Taussig 1979; Taussig 1973).

Because public policies may create horizontal inequity in accomplishing their primary objectives, decision makers should be aware of the extent of this negative effect. They may also be interested in possible trade-offs between it and the likely efficiency and conventional distributional impacts (i.e., effects on poverty or inequality independent of any reordering) of policy options. But to do so, they require useful indicators of the magnitude of horizontal inequity. This chapter, then, takes a necessary step towards enabling us to sensibly evaluate the implications for horizontal inequity of specific policy proposals.

The balance of this chapter has four parts. Part 8.2 more carefully examines the concept of horizontal inequity and develops the implications for properly measuring it. The third section describes the measures of horizontal inequity and well-being used and the data set. Part 8.4 contains the empirical findings. The final section is a summary and conclusion. A word of warning: The conclusion will not identify the best index on the basis of the empirical results. Such a judgment, as argued in part 8.3, is normative to an important degree and cannot be reached solely from the evidence provided here.

8.2 The Concept of Horizontal Inequity

While the classic notion of horizontal equity as equal treatment of equals expresses an important principle of policy design, it is conceptually incomplete. King (1983, p. 101) observes:

> In practice, of course, no two individuals are ever identical, and the principle of equal treatment of equals has little empirical significance unless it can be usefully extended to include "and unequals treated accordingly." To do this we are led naturally to a comparison of the ordering of utility levels before and after a tax change.

Following this logic, a horizontally equitable redistribution is one that preserves the initial rank order of the units. This conception encompasses the classic definition but is more general.

The requirement of rank preservation has raised objections from some quarters (Berliant and Strauss 1982). I believe it is essential for two reasons. First, though one is always free to require that the term *horizontal inequity* only concern unequal treatment of equals, the concept will then have little practical application, as King noted. Arbitrarily grouping "similar" units together and examining whether their treatments were equal appears to be an artificial way to salvage empirical applicability. Broadening the definition to cover rank reversals makes empirical analysis more feasible.[4]

---

4. If one wants to label rank-order requirements something other than horizontal inequity, so be it. Semantics aside, my interest in this study is in understanding and quantifying the extent of such reversals.

The second is more fundamental and is rooted in the view that, ceteris paribus, horizontal inequity diminishes social welfare. Consider an economy characterized by competitive markets and equal opportunity.[5] As many have observed, the distribution of marginal revenue products and rents generated in such an economy is not necessarily just. Consequently, transforming the distribution of market income into one that better conforms to society's preferred distribution will raise social welfare. The degree to which differences in initial well-being should be narrowed is debatable, but once this is resolved, what social purpose would be promoted by reversing ranks during the transformation? None—if the economic game is regarded as a fair process. (And such an economy, I believe, would likely be a U.S. choice by consensus for a fair system.) Unless the socially optimal distribution is one of full equality, those earning more initial well-being should surely have greater final well-being than those earning less. What logic could justify otherwise? Thus, any reversals incidental to the redistributive process would seem to lower social welfare.[6]

A reranking causes a unit's actual level of final well-being to diverge from its rank-preserving final level. It is this divergence, rather than the rank reversal per se, that is the real source of the problem and that lowers social welfare. A useful measure of horizontal inequity, therefore, must be a function of such differences in economic well-being.[7]

In the dense portions of the income distribution, a modest cardinal difference in well-being would translate into a large difference between the actual ordinal rank and the rank-preserving one. The same difference in well-being for a unit in the upper tail would lead to a much smaller difference in ranks. A measure that examines differences in well-being, therefore, is probably superior to one based on rank differences.

If this perspective on horizontal inequity is accepted, the implications for the narrower equal-treatment-of-equals approach are serious. Suppose that distinct groups of equals could somehow be identified. And assume that all members within any specific group received identical treatment. Then according to the equal treatment view, no horizontal inequity exists. Yet the final levels of well-being of two groups could well be in reverse order of their initial levels. The unfairness of such a situation would never be recognized by focusing on equal treatment.[8]

5. I.e., no discrimination in any market or social institution based on ascriptive characteristics such as race or sex. See Rae et al. 1981 for extended discussion of the concept of equal opportunity.

6. I am using *social welfare* in a broader sense than usual. Typically, overall social welfare is a function only of individual utility levels. Here, though, I am suggesting that reordering has an effect on social welfare independent of the utility levels at each rank. The social welfare function, then, incorporates nonutility information and rejects "welfarism" (Sen 1979).

7. Useful measures will *not* be concerned with comparisons between initial and actual final levels of well-being, nor between initial and final rank-preserving levels. These comparisons may also be of interest, but they are not appropriate for assessing horizontal inequity.

8. See the remarks in footnote 4 also.

The view that rank reversals reduce social welfare rests, ultimately, on an intuitive appeal to notions of fairness and deservingness in the distribution and redistribution of economic resources. This judgment cannot be derived from either the principle of welfare maximization nor that of Pareto optimality (Atkinson 1980; Stiglitz 1982). It appears to be an independent principle of tax and transfer policy. (Hence, complete criteria for evaluating alternative redistributive policies must allow for trade-offs among their horizontal inequities, vertical inequities, inefficiencies, administrative costs, and other attributes.)

As should now be clear, I interpret the principle of horizontal equity as one concerned with fairness in the *process* of redistribution. The principle offers no guidance on whether the initial or final distribution is optimal or just, nor on whether the redistributive instruments made the distribution more or less just. Instead, given the initial and final distributions, it poses a criterion to judge the fairness of the means used to alter the distribution. Conceivably, one could argue that a particular final distribution was not just, but agree that it was obtained by a horizontally equitable process.

The emphasis on process brings out an important implicit assumption in the interpretation of horizontal inequity—the initial ranking is accepted as fair. Yet in real economies, unlike the ideal one posited above, there are many reasons to reject this assumption. For example, the influence of racial discrimination, monopoly rents, or bribes on setting the initial ranking would lead one to question its fairness. Nonetheless, on pragmatic grounds this assumption may not be too bad. If, despite the contrary arguments that can be offered, most persons tacitly accept the initial ranking as reasonably fair when making judgments on redistributive equity, a useful measure of horizontal inequity (useful in the sense that it measures a phenomenon of public concern, even if the concern is partly based on "faulty" perception of what constitutes the fair ranking) must also accept this ranking.

If no normative value attaches to the initial ranking, a reranking need not, of course, be inequitable. In the empirical section of the paper, I necessarily assume that the initial ranking deserves to be preserved.[9]

8.2.1 Horizontal versus Vertical Equity

The rank condition may appear to be a principle of vertical equity. Carefully distinguishing between the concepts of vertical and horizontal equity shows that this interpretation does not follow, however. Vertical equity is perhaps best interpreted, in Nozick's (1974) terms, as an "end state principle." One compares an observed distribution of economic

---

9. If the fairness of the initial ranking is questionable, the analyst may, in principle, specify what the fair initial ranking should be. This can be compared to the actual final ranking to assess horizontal inequity.

well-being to an optimal one. (How the optimum is derived is immaterial for this discussion.) If they differ, vertical inequity exists—the relative incomes of some or all of the units are too large or too small. A redistribution reduces the extent of vertical inequity if it moves the actual distribution "closer" to the optimum.[10]

This notion of vertical equity does not include a rank-order condition. Measures of inequality that satisfy the widely accepted anonymity principle are independent of which unit occupies each position in the distribution.

Conflict and confusion have arisen over terminology among researchers who analyze changes in the income distribution. This semantic problem leads to disagreement about how to properly measure various effects of redistributive activity. One can ask if a redistributive policy (1) alters the level of inequality, (2) reranks units, and (3) requires those with greater ability to pay, in fact, to pay more taxes or receive lower benefits. I view these as questions of vertical equity, horizontal equity, and progressivity, respectively. Others may choose different terms to label these three issues or use these three terms to refer to different issues. It would be useful to reach consensus on terminology.

8.3   Empirical Procedures

8.3.1   Five Measures of Horizontal Inequity

Economists have proposed a large variety of indexes for measuring horizontal inequity. Many are unsatisfactory, however, because they mistakenly fold norms of vertical equity into the index formula or do not adequately deal with reranking (Plotnick 1982, pp. 386–90).

This study provides empirical results only for the five "good" measures that I have found in the literature. "Good" measures satisfy three properties (Plotnick 1982, p. 384). First, their values are independent of the mean of the final distribution of well-being. Second, they satisfy a simple anonymity condition. Last, if one redistribution differs from a second solely because some units' actual final levels of welfare are closer to what their rank-preserving (i.e., their horizontally equitable) final levels are, the index must show less horizontal inequity for the first redistribution. This third property is crucial, for it forces measures to embody the loss-of-social-welfare interpretation of horizontal inequity offered in part 8.2.

Denote unit i's actual observed level of welfare in the final distribution by oy_i. Unit i's final level of welfare, if its rank in the initial and final distribution were identical, is denoted fy_i. That is, fy_i is the level of well-being

---

10. The term *vertical equity* as used here is not equivalent to *progressivity*. Kakwani 1982 establishes the conceptual distinction between progressivity and changes in inequality (i.e., changes in vertical inequity) due to taxes and transfers.

that would have been attained in a rank-preserving, completely horizontally equitable redistribution. The observed rank in the final distribution and the rank in the initial distribution are, respectively, or_i and fr_i. Assume N units with mean final welfare of Y. The first of the five measures is

(1)
$$A - P = \frac{\sum_i fr_i (fy_i - oy_i)}{N^2 YG},$$

where G = Gini coefficient of final well-being.

This index has a familiar geometric interpretation (Atkinson 1980; Plotnick 1981). Construct a concentration curve by ordering units according to their initial rank and plotting cumulative shares of *final* well-being. The curve will always lie above and to the left of the conventional Lorenz curve for final well-being. The area between these two curves, divided by the maximum possible area between them (which has the same value as G), equals $A - P$.

The second measure is

(2) $$K_{h,t} = 1 - \left[\frac{\sum_i [oy_i \exp(- h| oy_i - fy_i|/Y)]^t}{\sum_i (oy_i)^t} \right]^{1/t}, \quad t \neq 0;$$

$$= 1 - \exp \left(\frac{-h}{N} \sum_i |oy_i - fy_i|/Y \right), \quad t = 0.$$

In this index h is a nonnegative number chosen by the analyst and indicates the degree of aversion to horizontal inequity (King 1983). King notes that the social value of the level of economic well-being, oy_i, of a unit that is reranked equals the social value of a level of well being, $oy_i e^{-hs}$, where $s = |oy_i - fy_i|/Y$. If $h = 1.0\ (5.0)$, $s = 0.05$ is equivalent in terms of social evaluation to a reduction in well- being of about 5 (22) percent. Parameter $t = 1 - e$, where e is the coefficient of inequality aversion (Atkinson 1970). Since e may be any nonnegative number, t may have any value less than or equal to one. I obtained results for twenty combinations of h and t: $h = 0.5, 1, 2$, or 5; $t = -1, -0.5, 0, 0.5$, or 1.

Indexes (3) and (4) are special cases of a family of one-parameter measures (Cowell 1980) with the parameter equal to zero or -1:[11]

(3)
$$C_0 = \frac{\sum_i oy_i \ln(oy_i/fy_i)}{NY}.$$

---

11. While Cowell developed measures of distributional change, they are readily adapted as measures of horizontal inequity, which are less general. To do so, interpret his distributions of "old" x_i and "new" y_i as the distributions of fy_i and oy_i, respectively. See Cowell 1980, p. 151. Since the means of fy and oy are identical, expressions 5 and 7 in his paper simplify to what I have presented.

$$(4) \qquad C_{-1} = \frac{- \sum_i fy_i \ln(oy_i/fy_i)}{NY}.$$

Of the infinite set of possible indexes, only these two yield useful decompositions of total horizontal inequity into within and between subgroup components.

Measure (5) is defined as

$$(5) \qquad P_h = \left[\frac{\sum_i |oy_i - fy_i|^h}{max} \right]^{1/h}, \qquad h \geq 1,$$

where max = the maximum value possible for the expression in the numerator and $h \geq 1$. P_h is a slight modification of the index suggested by Plotnick (1982, p. 385). As in King's index, P_h is an increasing function of h. The calculations set $h = 1, 1.5, 2, 2.5, 3$, and 4.

Last,

$$(6) \qquad S = \frac{3 \sum_i (or_i - fr_i)^2}{N^3 - N}.$$

This measure is half of one minus the Spearman rank correlation coefficient. (The subtraction is a needed formality if S is to satisfy the third property listed earlier.)

$A - P$, $K_{h,t}, P_h$, and S range between zero and one. C_0 and C_{-1} have a lower bound of zero, but indeterminate upper bound.

These measures vary along two general dimensions. First, different functional forms are used to cardinalize the "amount of horizontal inequity" produced by a gap between oy_i and fy_i. For example, $K_{h,t}$ exponentiates the product of h and the absolute value of the difference between oy_i and fy_i, while C_0 and C_{-1} use the logarithm of the income ratio. For all measures except $K_{h,t}$ with a nonzero t, if $oy_i = fy_i$ (which implies $or_i = fr_i$), the functions give the value zero for unit i, as one would expect.[12] Second, different weights are assigned to each unit in the income distribution when summing the amount of horizontal inequity. For example, $A - P$ uses the rank of the unit in the initial distribution. P_h assigns equal weights. Thus, like inequality indexes, measures of horizontal inequity necessarily contain implicit judgments or require explicit ones, and are not objective.[13]

8.3.2 Measures of Well-Being

To compute indexes of horizontal inequity, one must define the initial and final measures of economic well-being. The precise characteristics of

---

12. If t is nonzero and $oy_i = fy_i$, exp $\{-h(oy_i - fy_i)\}$ attains its largest value and, thus, lowers the index as much as possible. If $oy_i = fy_i$ for all i, $K_{h,t} = 0$.

13. Note that S uses rank differences instead of differences in well-being. For this reason it is probably the least satisfactory index. See also Plotnick 1982, pp. 383, 388.

the distribution of initial well-being (such as its level of inequality) are not important. Rather, it is important for establishing the fair ranking of units that a horizontally equitable redistribution would preserve.[14] The vector of actual final levels of well-being, in which element j is the level of final well-being of the unit with rank j in the initial distribution, is then compared to what the rank-preserving vector of levels of final well-being would have been, and the differences summarized by an index.

The concept of horizontal inequity itself offers no guidance on how equals are to be identified and the appropriate ranking established. Instead, the choice of initial and final concepts of well-being necessarily varies with the interests of the analyst. For example, if the horizontal inequity of the cash transfer system were at issue, initial well-being might be pretax, pretransfer income. Final well-being would then be pretax, post–cash transfer income. (Or one might use a posttax variant.) If the inequity of only cash public assistance were under scrutiny, initial and final well-being might be pretax, post–social insurance income (since social insurance income helps define eligibility) and pretax, post-all-cash-transfer income, respectively. And if one wanted to know whether food stamps reduce horizontal inequities created by interstate variation in cash public assistance, one would compare the index resulting from the preceding definition of initial and final well being to one based upon the same initial income, but final well-being equal to income after taxes, all cash transfers, *and* food stamps.[15] Adjustments for needs, cost-of-living differences, leisure, net assets, etc. may also be incorporated if the analyst regards them as important "admissible distinctions" (Stiglitz 1982, pp. 25–28) for determining the initial ranking that serves as the benchmark.

This exploratory exercise examines a variety of redistributions. Table 8.1 lists the measures of initial and final income that define each redis-

14. For example, the two redistributions A and B below are equally inequitable because the pattern of reranking is identical:

	Initial Well-Being		Final Well-Being	
	A	B	A	B
Unit x	12	9	6	6
Unit y	5	7	9	9
Unit z	3	4	5	5

The differences between initial and final levels of well-being at each position in the distribution vary in A and B. However, attention to this distinction between A and B reflects *vertical* equity judgments on the appropriate pattern for altering relative levels of welfare via redistribution.

15. Similarly, to see if a program reform affects horizontal inequity, one would compare the horizontal inequity of the current situation to that with the reformed program in place, using the pre–current program distribution as the initial measure of well-being in both cases. Note that whatever the initial measure selected by the analyst, he or she is implicitly assuming that the initial ranking is fair.

Table 8.1   Concepts of Initial and Final Income Used in the Analysis

	Initial Income Concept	Final Income Concept	Assesses Horizontal Inequity Of
A. Comprehensive Redistributions			
1. *CASHT*	pretax, pretransfer[a]	pretax, post–cash transfers	all cash transfers[b]
2. *ALLT*	pretax, pretransfer	pretax, post–all transfers	all cash transfers, food stamps, Medicare, Medicaid
3. *CASHT+FS*	pretax, pretransfer	pretax, post–cash transfers and –food stamps	all cash transfers, food stamps
4. *CASHT+TAX*	pretax, pretransfer	posttax, post–cash transfers	as in row 1, plus federal income and payroll tax
5. *ALLT+TAX*	pretax, pretransfer	posttax, post–all transfers	as in row 2, plus federal income and payroll tax
6. *CASHT+FS +TAX*	pretax, pretransfer	posttax, post–cash transfers and –food stamps	as in row 3, plus federal income and payroll tax
B. Redistribution by Income-Tested Programs			
7. *WELF*	pretax, post–cash social insurance	pretax, post–cash transfers	public assistance
8. *WELF+FS*	pretax, post–cash social insurance	pretax, post–cash transfers and –food stamps	public assistance, food stamps
9. *WELF+FS +MCAID*	pretax, post–cash social insurance	pretax, post–all transfers	public assistance, food stamps, Medicaid
C. Redistribution by Explicitly Redistributive Instruments			
10. *INCTX +INCTEST*	post–payroll tax, –social insurance, and –Medicare	post–all taxes and –transfers	income tax, public assistance, food stamps, Medicaid
D. Redistribution by Taxes			
11. *TAX*	pretax, pretransfer	posttax, pretransfer	federal income and payroll tax

[a]Includes labor, property, and miscellaneous market income and private transfers.
[b]OASDI, unemployment insurance, workers' compensation, veterans' compensation and pensions, government pensions, and all forms of cash public assistance.

tribution. In some, the horizontal inequity of a wide set of tax and transfer instruments is assessed. *CASHT* considers all cash transfers. *ALLT* examines cash transfers plus the major in-kind programs—food stamps, Medicare, and Medicaid. Since the appropriate method for assigning benefits from medical care transfers is uncertain (Smeeding and Moon, 1980), *CASHT + FS* includes only cash and food stamp benefits. The next three redistributions cover the same sets of transfers but also include federal income and payroll taxes. With others, the difference between the concepts of well-being involves three or fewer transfer programs or taxes. *WELF* looks at cash public assistance; *WELF + FS* adds food stamps, and *WELF + FS + MCAID* examines Medicaid as well. Redistribution 10 assesses these three income-tested transfers and the federal income tax, all of which have explicit redistributive purposes. Finally, *TAX* isolates just the federal income and payroll taxes for analysis. I also computed all index values for each redistribution using welfare ratios based on the federal poverty lines and income per family member to check the indexes' sensitivity to alternative needs adjustments.

Redistributions 1 through 6 and 10 have substantial impacts on income inequality. The Gini coefficient is reduced by between 15 and 26 percent. The other four redistributions exert much smaller equalizing effects since they are less comprehensive. The Gini coefficient falls by 3 to 6 percent. (Table 8.A.1 contains initial and final Gini coefficients for all rows in table 8.1.)

8.3.3 Data

The data set is a modified March 1975 Current Population Survey. Income information is for 1974 and has been adjusted for underreporting of all types of money income. Estimated federal income and payroll taxes and imputed benefits from food stamps, Medicare, and Medicaid have been added to the data. Both medical transfers are imputed on an insurance value basis. In-kind benefits are counted at taxpayer cost, not cash equivalent values.[16] Expressions (1) through (6) are suitably modified to account for the data's population weights. To reduce computational burdens, one-quarter of the observations ($N = 11,495$) were used in the calculations.

8.4 Empirical Results

Table 8.2 presents a representative set of ten index values for the eleven redistributions listed in table 8.1, using income as the indicator of well-

---

16. I thank Tim Smeeding for sharing the data. Procedures for correcting and augmenting the CPS data are in Smeeding 1975. Using Smeeding's cash equivalent values gave similar results.

Table 8.2   Values of Selected Indexes of Horizontal Inequity

					Index of Horizontal Inequity					
Redistribution	$A-P$ (1)	$K_{1,.5}$ (2)	$K_{1,0}$ (3)	$K_{5,0}$ (4)	$K_{2,-.5}$ (5)	P_1 (6)	P_4 (7)	C_{-1} (8)	C_0 (9)	S (10)
1. CASHT	.0194	.110	.112	.448	.215	.106	.181	.0336	.0426	.0238
2. ALLT	.0245	.119	.122	.481	.244	.122	.182	.0329	.0386	.0310
3. CASHT + FS	.0195	.109	.111	.455	.220	.106	.181	.0293	.0354	.0239
4. CASHT + TAX	.0333	.146	.144	.542	.264	.150	.293	.0442	.0557	.0354
5. ALLT + TAX	.0423	.157	.156	.573	.297	.173	.298	.0435	.0511	.0471
6. CASHT + FS + TAX	.0337	.145	.143	.538	.272	.151	.295	.0390	.0468	.0361
7. WELF	.0018	.013	.019	.093	.065	.017	.054	.0078	.0164	.0026
8. WELF + FS	.0022	.014	.022	.104	.081	.020	.056	.0075	.0129	.0032
9. WELF + FS + MCAID	.0045	.025	.034	.159	.096	.032	.075	.0097	.0158	.0067
10. INCTX + INCTEST	.0095	.073	.072	.310	.142	.075	.197	.0140	.0210	.0110
11. TAX	.0009	.044	.030	.141	.005	.024	.084	.0012	.0006	.0004

Note: Computed using income as the measure of well-being.

Table 8.3   Ordinal Rankings of Redistributions in Terms of Horizontal Inequity

	Index of Horizontal Inequity					
Redistribution	$A - P$ (1)	$K_{1,.5}$ (2)	$K_{2,-.5}$ (3)	P_1 (4)	C_0 (5)	S (6)
1. CASHT	7	7	6	6.5	8	6
2. ALLT	8	8	8	8	7	8
3. CASHT + FS	6	6	7	6.5	6	7
4. CASHT + TAX	9	10	9	9	11	9
5. ALLT + TAX	11	11	11	11	10	11
6. CASHT + FS + TAX	10	9	10	10	9	10
7. WELF	2	1	2	1	4	2
8. WELF + FS	3	2	3	2	2	3
9. WELF + FS + MCAID	4	3	4	4	3	4
10. INCTX + INCTEST	5	5	5	5	5	5
11. TAX	1	4	1	3	1	1

Note: This table based on table 8.2.

being.[17] All indexes clearly are sensitive to the choice of initial and final income since, as a glance down the columns shows, their values vary by factors of 5 or more. Columns (3) and (4) show that increasing the degree of aversion to horizontal inequity (holding t constant) can significantly raise that index's value. Columns (6) and (7) suggest somewhat less sensitivity of P_h to the size of h. Differences across a row cannot be meaningfully compared (just as one would not cardinally compare the Gini coefficient, coefficient of variation, and Atkinson's index for the same distribution).

More interesting is a comparison of how the indexes order the extent of horizontal inequity of the various redistributions. Table 8.3 shows the ordinal ranking according to six of the indexes presented in table 8.2. For the same six indexes, table 8.4 normalizes the figures in table 8.2 by setting the top value in each column at 100. (For completeness, parallel computations for the other four are in tables 8.A.2 and 8.A.3.) The columns, then, display the relative changes in the cardinal values of each index as the redistribution varies. Every index (except P_4, as seen in tables 8.A.2 and 8.A.3) separates the redistributions into three strata. Redistributions 7 through 11 create the least horizontal inequity. The top three fall in a middle range. Rows 4 through 6 show the most inequity.

The rankings and normalized values are surprisingly similar among the $A-P$, $K_{h,t}$, P_h, and S measures. Each shows its largest value for $ALLT + TAX$. In table 8.4, each records very small differences between rows 4 and 6, though $K_{1,.5}$ ordinally ranks 4 higher than 6 and the others

---

17. For $K_{h,t}$ and P_h, results for other choices of h and t were similar to one of the four columns shown here and in later tables.

Table 8.4   Normalized Index Values as the Redistribution Varies

	Index of Horizontal Inequity					
Redistribution	$A-P$ (1)	$K_{1,.5}$ (2)	$K_{2,-.5}$ (3)	P_1 (4)	C_0 (5)	S (6)
1. CASHT	100	100	100	100	100	100
2. ALLT	126	109	113	115	91	130
3. CASHT + FS	101	99	102	100	83	101
4. CASHT + TAX	172	133	122	142	131	149
5. ALLT + TAX	218	143	138	164	120	198
6. CASHT + FS + TAX	173	132	126	142	110	152
7. WELF	9	12	30	16	39	11
8. WELF + FS	11	13	38	19	30	13
9. WELF + FS + MCAID	23	23	45	30	37	28
10. INCTX + INCTEST	49	67	66	71	49	46
11. TAX	5	40	3	23	1	2

give the reverse order. These five indexes all rank *ALLT* eighth and place *INCTX + INCTEST* fifth. All five exhibit trivial normalized differences between *CASHT* and *CASHT + FS*. Only for rows 7, 8, 9, and 11 do the rankings and relative values differ noticeably. Though all five measures rank *WELF, WELF + FS,* and *WELF + FS + MCAID* in ascending order, they disagree on where the horizontal inequity of *TAX* stands in relation to the inequity of these three redistributions.

The ranking of C_0 differs substantially from those of the other measures (though it is nearly identical to that of C_{-1} shown in table 8.A.2). For example, C_0 indicates that *CASHT + TAX* (not *ALLT + TAX*) is most inequitable, that *CASHT + FS* is sharply less inequitable than *CASHT* (instead of being almost equal), that *WELF + FS* is less inequitable than *WELF* (instead of being more inequitable), and that *ALLT* clearly ranks seventh instead of eighth. Thus, the choice of index may well affect one's perceptions of the relative amount of horizontal inequity created by different redistributions.

To examine the effect of needs adjustments, tables like 8.2 were prepared using welfare ratios and income per family member in the computations. (See tables 8.A.4 and 8.A.5.) For each of redistributions 1 through 6, 10, and 11, the index values were usually smallest when income was used and largest with the per capita adjustment. (This was true in 85 percent of the comparisons.) For redistributions 7 through 9, though, results based on welfare ratios were lowest in twenty-three of the thirty cells. Since a major component of these three redistributions is cash welfare, which, like the poverty lines, increases with family size but at a decreasing rate, this difference is understandable. Thus, for a given set of tax and transfer programs, the particular measure of well-being defined by the needs adjustment does affect the absolute values of the indexes.

The sensitivity to needs adjustment varies across the measures. In redistributions 1 through 6, for example, values of $A-P$ based on income and welfare ratios were about 54 and 82 percent, respectively, of the corresponding values based on income per member. For $K_{5,0}$ the same calculations were about 82 and 91 percent.

At the same time, the choice of needs adjustment tends to have little effect on how each index scales the relative degree of horizontal inequity of various redistributions. Compare table 8.3 to table 8.5, which contains the ordinal rankings of each index when welfare ratios were used in the calculations. The rankings in both tables are identical for columns (2), (5), and (6), and similar in the other three columns. With income per family member as the indicator of economic well-being, rankings again were very similar to those in tables 8.3 and 8.5. When rankings differed, the source was often small differences in cardinal index values. Tables of relative values for indexes calculated with welfare ratios and income per member (not shown) generally resembled table 8.4, as well.

While the figures in tables 8.2 through 8.5 provide evidence on how different measures behave, they do not inform us whether they signal a "lot" or a "little" horizontal inequity. The indexes with an upper bound of 1.0 are generally well below this value.

The following calculations may help decide if redistributions generate high, moderate, or low levels of horizontal inequity. Compute conventional inequality indexes for the initial and final distributions. For each redistribution divide its horizontal inequity index by the decline in inequality it produced as measured by initial inequality minus final inequality,

Table 8.5   **Ordinal Rankings of Redistributions in Terms of Horizontal Inequity**

	Index of Horizontal Inequity					
Redistribution	$A-P$ (1)	$K_{1,5}$ (2)	$K_{2,-.5}$ (3)	P_1 (4)	C_0 (5)	S (6)
1. *CASHT*	6.5	7	7	7	8	6
2. *ALLT*	8	8	8	8	7	8
3. *CASHT + FS*	6.5	6	6	6	6	7
4. *CASHT + TAX*	9	10	10	10	11	9
5. *ALLT + TAX*	11	11	11	11	10	11
6. *CASHT + FS + TAX*	10	9	9	9	9	10
7. *WELF*	2	1	2	1	4	2
8. *WELF + FS*	3	2	3	2	2	3
9. *WELF + FS + MCAID*	4	3	4	4	3	4
10. *INCTX + INCTEST*	5	5	5	5	5	5
11. *TAX*	1	4	1	3	1	1

Note: This table is based on table 8.A.4, which uses income/poverty line as the indicator of well-being.

Table 8.6   **Redistributions' Horizontal Inequity Relative to Percentage Decline in Inequality**

Redistribution	Index of Horizontal Inequity				
	$A - P$ (1)	$K_{1,0}$ (2)	$K_{5,0}$ (3)	P_1 (4)	C_0 (5)
1. *CASHT*	.131	.205	.821	.815	.137
2. *ALLT*	.133	.196	.769	.763	.104
3. *CASHT + FS*	.125	.190	.762	.779	.109
4. *CASHT + TAX*	.151	.239	.899	.600	.127
5. *ALLT + TAX*	.163	.230	.840	.612	.102
6. *CASHT + FS + TAX*	.146	.223	.838	.585	.103
7. *WELF*	.059	.068	.327	.766	.214
8. *WELF + FS*	.055	.063	.301	.672	.134
9. *WELF + FS + MCAID*	.077	.091	.425	.713	.119
10. *INCTX + INCTEST*	.062	.152	.660	.379	.066
11. *TAX*	.016	.657	.310	.217	.005

Note: This table is computed from results in table 8.2, divided by (initial inequality–final inequality)/initial inequality.

divided by initial inequality. The quotients are indicative of the amount of horizontal inequity generated per unit reduction in vertical inequity.

In addition, some redistributions might show relatively little horizontal inequity but have a minor effect on inequality (e.g., cash welfare), while another might create more horizontal inequity but reduce inequality substantially (e.g., all cash transfers). The quotients are simple attempts to adjust for these differences and might be a useful alternative way to compare redistributions.[18]

Four of the horizontal inequity indexes have natural analogs among the inequality measures. For $A - P$, I used the Gini coefficient. For $K_{h,t}$, Atkinson's index with $e = 1 - t$ is the obvious choice. The coefficient of variation pairs with P_h. Theil's two entropy measures, which are special cases of a one-parameter family with the parameter set to zero or $- 1$ (Cowell 1980), correspond to C_0 and C_{-1}. The fifth index, S, has no clear mate among inequality measures and is omitted from this analysis.

Table 8.6 contains the quotients for five of the indexes. Results for the other four are in table 8.A.6. They give widely varying readings. $K_{5,0}$ and P_1 suggest that most of the eleven redistributions create major horizontal inequities relative to the net vertical equalization. $A - P$ and Cowell's index, in contrast, suggest relatively small horizontal inequities, while $K_{1,0}$ falls in the moderate range. If these figures can be reasonably compared across a row (unlike those in table 8.2), the choice of index will strongly

18. A more rigorously derived method for balancing vertical and horizontal equity effects of a redistribution would be welcome.

Table 8.7   Ordinal Rankings of Redistributions

| | Index of Horizontal Inequity | | | | |
Redistribution	$A-P$ (1)	$K_{1,0}$ (2)	$K_{5,0}$ (3)	P_1 (4)	C_0 (5)
1. *CASHT*	7	7	7	11	10
2. *ALLT*	8	6	6	8	5
3. *CASHT+FS*	6	5	5	10	6
4. *CASHT+TAX*	10	10	10	4	8
5. *ALLT+TAX*	11	9	9	5	3
6. *CASHT+FS+TAX*	9	8	8	3	4
7. *WELF*	3	2	2	9	11
8. *WELF+FS*	2	1	1	6	9
9. *WELF+FS+MCAID*	5	3	3	7	7
10. *INCTX+INCTEST*	4	4	4	2	2
11. *TAX*	1	11	11	1	1

Note: This table is based on table 8.6.

influence one's perception of the degree of horizontal inequity of a given redistribution.

Table 8.7 presents the ordinal ranking, by column, of the figures in table 8.6. Every index assigns a small rank to *INCTX + INCTEST* (row 10), which had a low rank in table 8.3 as well, where no adjustment for changes in inequality had been made. But this is the extent of any uniformity in the ordering and of any congruence with the rankings in tables 8.3 or 8.A.3. Only three indexes rank *WELF, WELF+FS,* and *WELF+FS+MCAID* low in table 8.7. Three rank *TAX* low, but two place it eleventh! Yet these four redistributions had consistently low ordinal values in table 8.3.[19] There is little agreement on the ranks of redistributions 1 through 6. So, in line with an earlier conclusion, the choice of measure will affect the relative amount of horizontal inequity observed among redistributions.

Finally, turn from this analysis of the anatomy of measures to the policy-oriented question: Do food stamps reduce the horizontal inequities created by the categorical nature of most cash welfare programs and state differences in their benefit levels? Since food stamp benefits are greater for families with lower incomes, unequal treatment of equally poor families by the cash welfare programs would tend to be reduced. But welfare recipients tend to be channeled to the food stamp program and are probably better informed of it than families who are ineligible for AFDC or SSI. If participation rates in the program are higher for welfare recipients, food stamps will tend to promote unequal treatment. The net effect is unclear a priori.

19. Normalized values derived from table 8.6 reveal similar disagreement with table 8.4.

From table 8.2 one concludes that the second effect probably dominates. Comparing rows 7 and 8 shows that every index except C_0 and C_{-1} has a larger value when the inequity of cash welfare and food stamps is assessed relative to the inequity of only cash welfare.[20] At the same time, food stamps reduce inequality. Thus, whether food stamps, on balance, are equitable overall depends on one's willingness to trade off more horizontal inequity for less inequality. Table 8.6 suggests that the trade-off is favorable, for all the numbers in row 7 exceed those in row 8. Different methods of evaluating this trade-off might reverse this finding. (Indexes computed using welfare ratios and income per person yield the same results.)

8.5 Summary and Conclusion

This chapter has sought to explore in a systematic fashion the behavior of five measures of horizontal inequity. The five were selected from many proposed in the literature because they possessed characteristics consistent with an interpretation of horizontal equity that emphasizes the social welfare costs due to reversals of rank in the distribution of economic well-being. These measures can be used to assess any actual redistributive program(s) or to see if a proposed reform or new program would change the extent of horizontal inequity. Their sensitivity to different types of redistributions and needs adjustments was examined using microdata for 1974. Three main findings emerged:

1. The choice of index may well affect one's perceptions of the relative amount of horizontal inequity of different redistributions.

2. The particular needs adjustment does affect the absolute values of the indexes. Sensitivity to such adjustments varies among the indexes.

3. The choice of needs adjustment tends to have little effect on how each index scales the relative degree of horizontal inequity of various redistributions.

---

20. This result may also be partly caused by the food stamp asset test. Suppose some low-income families are declared ineligible for food stamps because their assets are too large. Then it will appear in these data, which have no asset information, that food stamps create rank reversals and that living units with roughly equal levels of well-being are receiving different benefits from the program. The lack of asset data prevents analysis of the role of asset tests in producing horizontal inequity. Similarly, asset tests for cash public assistance and Medicaid may also be responsible for part of the measured horizontal inequity in the tables.

If the data were suitable, one might wish to incorporate assets into one's measure of well-being before determining initial and final rankings and measuring horizontal inequity. Even with such an adjustment, asset tests would lead to horizontal inequity. For example, consider two units with equal cash incomes that would qualify them both for $1,000 in food stamp assistance. Assume that one has assets $100 above the limit for benefit eligibility, while the other has assets $100 below. Although the latter's economic well-being before the in-kind transfer is less, it is not much less, and a $1,000 benefit would reverse ranks.

To improve the usefulness of the measures for policy applications, several steps might be taken. Better data sets such as the Survey on Income and Program Participation (SIPP), with information on more transfer programs and assets, and actual rather than imputed values for taxes and in-kind transfers, should be used. Such data would permit examination of the horizontal inequity of more varied combinations of transfers (and taxes) and the possible horizontal inequities created by asset tests. The calculations would be more accurate than those based on imputed benefits (as in this chapter) since variation within the imputed variables tends to be suppressed. Further development of methods for judging the magnitude of horizontal inequity in relation to redistributions' impacts on inequality or poverty is needed.[21] Behavioral responses to redistributive policies, and to possible changes in them, should be incorporated via simulation techniques developed in recent years. Exploration of horizontal inequity within demographic groups (e.g., the aged or families with female householders) remains on the research agenda. Last, detailed analysis of how the interaction between program rules and persons' economic and demographic circumstances creates horizontal inequity is needed for policy analysis and reform to reduce such inequity.

These exploratory findings provide no support for preferring one measure over the others because, as noted in part 8.3, all measures embody normative judgments. It would have simplified matters if all indexes had produced similar ordinal rankings. Since this did not occur, analysts must be sensitive to the normative issues.

Appendix Tables

(tables follow on pp. 258–62.)

21. On the other hand, instead of seeking an explicit formula, analysts perhaps should simply compute the level of horizontal inequity and changes in inequality and poverty, and let policymakers draw their own conclusions about the right balance.

Table 8.A.1   **Gini Coefficients of Initial and Final Economic Well-Being**

	Measure of Well-Being					
	Income		Welfare Ratio		Income Per Family Member	
Redistribution	Initial	Final	Initial	Final	Initial	Final
1. CASHT	.474	.403	.465	.386	.494	.412
2. ALLT	.474	.386	.465	.367	.494	.393
3. CASHT+FS	.474	.400	.465	.382	.494	.408
4. CASHT+TAX	.474	.367	.465	.351	.494	.380
5. ALLT+TAX	.474	.350	.465	.331	.494	.361
6. CASHT+FS+TAX	.474	.365	.465	.346	.494	.375
7. WELF	.416	.403	.400	.386	.426	.412
8. WELF+FS	.416	.400	.400	.382	.426	.408
9. WELF+FS+MCAID	.411	.386	.394	.367	.420	.393
10. INCTX+INCTEST	.414	.350	.397	.331	.423	.361
11. TAX	.474	.446	.465	.434	.494	.466

Table 8.A.2   **Ordinal Rankings of Redistributions in Terms of Horizontal Inequity**

	Index of Horizontal Inequity			
Redistribution	$K_{1,0}$ (1)	$K_{5,0}$ (2)	P_4 (3)	C_{-1} (4)
1. CASHT	7	7	5.5	8
2. ALLT	8	8	7	7
3. CASHT + FS	6	6	5.5	6
4. CASHT + TAX	10	10	9	11
5. ALLT + TAX	11	11	11	10
6. CASHT + FS + TAX	9	9	10	9
7. WELF	1	1	1	3
8. WELF + FS	2	2	2	2
9. WELF + FS + MCAID	4	4	3	4
10. INCTX + INCTEST	5	5	8	5
11. TAX	3	3	4	1

Note: This table based on table 8.2.

Table 8.A.3   **Normalized Index Values as the Redistribution Varies**

	Index of Horizontal Inequity			
Redistribution	$K_{1,0}$ (1)	$K_{5,0}$ (2)	P_4 (3)	C_{-1} (4)
1. CASHT	100	100	100	100
2. ALLT	110	107	101	98
3. CASHT + FS	99	99	100	87
4. CASHT + TAX	129	121	162	132
5. ALLT + TAX	140	128	165	130
6. CASHT + FS + TAX	128	120	163	116
7. WELF	17	21	30	23
8. WELF + FS	19	23	31	22
9. WELF + FS + MCAID	30	35	42	29
10. INCTX + INCTEST	64	69	109	42
11. TAX	27	31	46	4

Note: The figures are computed from unrounded values of the indexes, thus they may differ slightly from those calculated using the rounded values in table 8.2.

Table 8.A.4 Values of Selected Indexes of Horizontal Inequity, Welfare Ratio as the Measure of Well-Being

Redistribution	$A-P$ (1)	$K_{1,.5}$ (2)	$K_{1,0}$ (3)	$K_{5,0}$ (4)	$K_{2,-.5}$ (5)	P_1 (6)	P_4 (7)	C_{-1} (8)	C_0 (9)	S (10)
					Index of Horizontal Inequity					
1. CASHT	.0290	.131	.132	.508	.264	.134	.177	.0404	.0506	.0352
2. ALLT	.0374	.143	.145	.543	.289	.157	.179	.0399	.0477	.0479
3. CASHT+FS	.0290	.130	.130	.502	.262	.133	.177	.0349	.0421	.0356
4. CASHT+TAX	.0503	.172	.169	.604	.322	.191	.298	.0532	.0670	.0542
5. ALLT+TAX	.0652	.186	.184	.638	.351	.223	.302	.0528	.0638	.0749
6. CASHT+FS+TAX	.0506	.170	.166	.597	.323	.191	.303	.0457	.0564	.0547
7. WELF	.0015	.011	.018	.086	.070	.017	.040	.0078	.0149	.0020
8. WELF+FS	.0017	.012	.019	.091	.077	.018	.040	.0071	.0110	.0024
9. WELF+FS+MCAID	.0047	.024	.033	.157	.098	.034	.058	.0092	.0133	.0071
10. INCTX+INCTEST	.0107	.082	.079	.336	.157	.090	.175	.0138	.0184	.0132
11. TAX	.0007	.049	.032	.151	.010	.027	.073	.0011	.0008	.0004

Table 8.A.5 Values of Selected Indexes of Horizontal Inequity, Income per Family Member as the Measure of Well-Being

Redistribution	$A-P$ (1)	$K_{1,.5}$ (2)	$K_{1,0}$ (3)	$K_{5,0}$ (4)	$K_{2,-.5}$ (5)	P_1 (6)	P_4 (7)	C_{-1} (8)	C_0 (9)	S (10)
				Index of Horizontal Inequity						
1. CASHT	.0354	.151	.150	.556	.273	.146	.148	.0492	.0688	.0478
2. ALLT	.0478	.168	.168	.601	.308	.174	.150	.0503	.0666	.0695
3. CASHT+FS	.0357	.150	.148	.552	.281	.145	.148	.0430	.0569	.0489
4. CASHT+TAX	.0590	.196	.191	.653	.330	.205	.267	.0646	.0915	.0713
5. ALLT+TAX	.0795	.217	.212	.696	.371	.243	.272	.0666	.0898	.1026
6. CASHT+FS+TAX	.0597	.195	.189	.649	.341	.205	.267	.0573	.0770	.0735
7. WELF	.0019	.012	.019	.093	.073	.017	.039	.0086	.0200	.0033
8. WELF+FS	.0023	.014	.021	.101	.084	.019	.040	.0078	.0144	.0041
9. WELF+FS+MCAID	.0069	.030	.039	.179	.101	.037	.057	.0104	.0171	.0124
10. INCTX+INCTEST	.0138	.086	.083	.353	.152	.089	.122	.0156	.0243	.0211
11. TAX	.00002	.054	.037	.172	.006	.030	.083	.0010	.0018	.0007

Table 8.A.6   Redistributions' Horizontal Inequity Relative to Percentage Decline in Inequality

	Index of Horizontal Inequity			
Redistribution	$K_{1,.5}$ (1)	$K_{2,-.5}$ (2)	P_4 (3)	C_{-1} (4)
1. CASHT	.255	.413	1.39	.050
2. ALLT	.240	.335	1.14	.044
3. CASHT + FS	.242	.336	1.34	.041
4. CASHT + TAX	.276	.503	1.17	.061
5. ALLT + TAX	.264	.410	1.05	.055
6. CASHT + FS + TAX	.264	.414	1.15	.052
7. WELF	.098	.073	2.40	.024
8. WELF + FS	.090	.058	1.92	.019
9. WELF + FS + MCAID	.126	.092	1.67	.023
10. INCTX + INCTEST	.204	.243	.99	.027
11. TAX	.466	3.66	.76	.018

Note: This table is computed from results in table 8.2, divided by (initial inequality–final inequality)/initial inequality.

References

Atkinson, Anthony. 1970. On the measurement of inequality. *Journal of Economic Theory* 2: 244–63.

_____. 1980. Horizontal equity and the distribution of the tax burden. In *The economics of taxation,* ed. Henry Aaron and Michael Boskin. Washington D.C.: Brookings Institution.

Beach, Charles, David Card, and Frank Flatters. 1981. *Distribution of income and wealth in Ontario: Theory and evidence.* Toronto: University of Toronto Press.

Benus, Jacob, and James Morgan. 1975. Time period, unit of analysis, and income concept in the analysis of income distribution. In *The personal distribution of income and wealth,* ed. James D. Smith. National Bureau of Economic Research Studies in Income and Wealth, no. 39. New York: Columbia University Press.

Berliant, Marcus, and Robert Strauss. 1982. On recent expositions of the concept of horizontal equity. Mimeo.

_____. 1983. Measuring the distribution of personal taxes. In *What role for government?* ed. Richard Zeckhauser and Derek Leebaert. Durham, N.C.: Duke University Press.

Chernick, Howard, and Andrew Reschovsky. 1982. The distributional impact of Proposition 13: A microsimulation approach. *National Tax Journal* 35: 149–70.

Cowell, Frank. 1980. Generalized entropy and the measurement of distributional change. *European Economic Review* 13: 147–59.

_____. 1982. Measures of distributional change: An axiomatic approach. London School of Economics. Mimeo.

Danziger, Sheldon, and Michael Taussig. 1979. The income unit and the anatomy of income distribution. *Review of Income and Wealth* 25: 365–75.

Feldstein, Martin. 1976. On the theory of tax reform. *Journal of Public Economics* 6: 77–104.

Kakwani, Nanak. 1982. On the measurement of tax progressivity and redistributive effect of taxes with applications to horizontal and vertical equity. Mimeo.

King, Mervyn. 1983. An index of inequality with applications to horizontal inequity and social mobility. *Econometrica* 51: 99–115.

Menchik, Paul, and Martin David. 1982. The incidence of a lifetime consumption tax. *National Tax Journal* 35: 189–204.

Nozick, Robert. 1974. *Anarchy, state, and utopia*. New York: Basic Books.

Plotnick, Robert. 1981. A measure of horizontal inequity. *Review of Economics and Statistics* 63: 283–88.

_____. 1982. The concept and measurement of horizontal inequity. *Journal of Public Economics* 17: 373–91.

Plotnick, Robert, and Felicity Skidmore. 1975. *Progress against poverty: A review of the 1964–1974 decade*. New York: Academic Press.

Rae, Douglas, Douglas Yates, Jennifer Hochschild, Joseph Morone, and Carol Fessler. 1981. *Equalities*. Cambridge: Harvard University Press.

Rosen, Harvey. 1978. An approach to the study of income, utility, and horizontal inequity. *Quarterly Journal of Economics* 92: 306–22.

Sen, Amartya. 1979. Personal utilities and public judgements: Or what's wrong with welfare economics? *Economic Journal* 89: 537–58.

Smeeding, Timothy. 1975. Measuring the economic welfare of low-income households, and the anti-poverty effectiveness of cash and non-cash transfer programs. Ph.D. diss., University of Wisconsin, Madison.

Smeeding, Timothy, and Marilyn Moon. 1980. Valuing government expenditures: The case of medical transfers and poverty. *Review of Income and Wealth* 26: 305–24.

Stiglitz, Joseph. 1982. Utilitarianism and horizontal equity. *Journal of Public Economics* 18: 1–33.

Taussig, Michael. 1973. *Alternative measures of the distribution of economic welfare*. Princeton: Princeton University Press.

Comment   Edward M. Gramlich

Robert Plotnick attempts to compute several newly developed measures of the horizontal inequity of tax- transfer changes in the distribution of income with real live data. The work is done with great care, comprehensiveness, and skill. However, one must read the chapter with more than the usual amount of discrimination to figure out what it is really saying. While the chapter has a good deal of promise and much useful material, the conclusions are shown in ways that are fairly awkward to think about and the results can easily be misunderstood. In these remarks I will show what Plotnick has done, mention some pitfalls, and suggest how such calculations can be better done in the future.

To begin with Plotnick's argument, he defines horizontal inequity in terms of rank reversals. A horizontally equitable redistribution of income is one that preserves the initial rank order of the units; an inequitable redistribution is one that does not. To measure rank reversals (the higher the score, the greater the inequity), Plotnick introduces five different measures of horizontal inequity:

1. An Atkinson-Plotnick measure that is roughly related to the impact of rank reversals on the Gini coefficient. It compares the actual Lorenz curve with a concentration curve that plots a unit's final level of well-being on its initial rank.

2. A measure developed by King that exponentiates the product of some prespecified measure of aversion to horizontal inequity and the difference in well-being due to rank reversals, then combines with another prespecified measure of aversion to inequality.

3. A measure developed by Cowell that weights percentage changes in well-being due to rank reversals by either the rank-preserving or final level of well-being.

4. A measure developed by Plotnick that appears to be similar to the weighted coefficient by variation of income due to rank reversals, with a prespecified weight.

5. A measure based on the Spearman rank correlation coefficient.

But these five soon become ten. To compute King's measure, the analyst must assign two parameters, so Plotnick uses four combinations. To compute Cowell's, Plotnick must use either the rank-preserving or final level of well-being, and he does both. To compute his own measure, Plotnick must assign one parameter, for which he tries two values.

And then the ten become thirty. This is because each measure could in principle be computed on rank reversals in the family income distribution, the per-family-member income distribution, or the welfare ratio (income

Edward M. Gramlich is professor of economics and public policy and chairman of the Department of Economics, University of Michigan.

over family needs) distribution. And then the thirty become sixty because each measure could either be examined in gross form, or computed in terms of the horizontal inequity generated by a given decline in overall inequality. When there are sixty ways of answering what you thought was a straightforward question, the reader begins to be overwhelmed.

Unfortunately the complexities do not end there. Because a variety of policy measures either try to or unintendedly do bring about redistribution, Plotnick can use his measures to answer various questions. He focuses on eleven, based on the rank reversals implicit in various packages of cash and in-kind transfers and income and payroll taxes. With sixty possible answers to each of eleven questions, it is no wonder that Plotnick's overall conclusion is a resounding "it all depends."

But Plotnick's chapter does have both promise and useful results. He is right that rank reversals are generally to be avoided, and it is helpful to compute measures of their importance. With this many questions asked and answered, there must be some useful information. Let us sort through his results to see what we can learn.

First I focus on the concept of rank reversals. Plotnick is on firm ground in stressing that a rank reversal is only undesirable if the pre-policy change ranking was desirable. If not, this whole approach has little merit. Using this reasoning, several types of rank reversals might be ignored. One class is based on the fact that what should be ranked is utility and what is ranked is income. If some relatively well-off poor person received a transfer and reduced labor supply, while some poorer person did not, we would observe an income rank reversal but not a utility rank reversal. This type of rank reversal should not bother redistributors, and measures showing it have little value. More broadly, if the income tax altered differentially propensities to invest in either human or physical capital, it could cause income but not utility rank reversals that should also be ignored. This theoretical point does *not* denigrate Plotnick's work because he simply assumes away endogenous behavioral responses. Late in the chapter he says he should not have assumed them away, and perhaps will not in his next paper. But if he does redo the analysis, he should be careful to rank utility, not income.

There is another type of not undesirable rank reversal that he should ignore but does not. Often a government policy, passed by duly elected representatives of the people, will explicitly try to bring about rank reversals. It makes little sense to criticize the policy by saying that people do not want rank reversals. In general that may be true, but they presumably do want these particular ones.

Barring the caveats listed above, it seems to me that the rank reversals to be avoided are the large ones. I would not be particularly bothered if, as a result of some general income redistribution, my neighbor's disposable income rose from one dollar below mine to one dollar above mine; I would be bothered if the one dollar above mine became ten thousand. Hence, what is to be avoided is not rank reversals per se, but ones that entail sizeable changes in welfare. Plotnick recognizes this problem and adopts criteria for selecting horizontal equity measures that can be zero when either rank reversals are zero or the dollar changes in welfare due to rank reversals are small. But he does include one measure, based on the Spearman rank correlation unadjusted for the size of the cardinal change, that is not weighted by size of change and hence is not as meaningful as the others.

In like manner, just as nobody seems to worry about (or even compute) poverty statistics based on the unadjusted distribution of family income, Plotnick's measures that focus on the welfare ratio seem to be superior to the others. I also prefer his admittedly ad hoc calculation of horizontal inequity generated per unit of overall reduction in inequality. We do not want to make horizontal inequity comparisons between programs that bring about a lot or a little overall redistribution; this adjustment is one way to avoid them.

With these comments, I have pruned away a lot of Plotnick's numbers. The most important of his results are those that use his appropriate rank reversal measures on interesting questions. These numbers are summarized in table C8.1 (a subset of numbers given in table 8.A.6).

Even with all the weeding out of Plotnick's less meaningful results, the remaining results must be interpreted with great care. As an example, in the first row Plotnick compares the ranking of families before all taxes

Table C8.1   Horizontal Inequity per Unit Decline in Overall Inequality

Policy Measure	Ranking in Counterfactual Case	Measure of Horizontal Inequity			
		King 1	King 2	Plotnick	Cowell
Cash transfers	Pretax, pretransfer	.255	.413	1.39	.050
Cash transfers and food stamps	Pretax, pretransfer	.242	.336	1.34	.041
Cash transfers, food stamps, and taxes	Pretax, pretransfer	.264	.414	1.15	.052
Public assistance	Pretax, post–social insurance	.098	.073	2.40	.024
Public assistance and food stamps	Pretax, post–social insurance	.090	.058	1.92	.019

Source: Based on rankings of family welfare ratio, 1974 data, Current Population Survey.

and transfers with the ranking after all cash transfers (public assistance and social insurance payments). Using Plotnick's own measure with a pre-specified high exponent of 4 on rank reversal welfare changes, a large degree of horizontal inequity appears to be created per unit reduction in overall inequality. The George Gilders of the world might well conclude from this 1.39 number that income redistribution is not worth the bother—a great deal of horizontal inequity is created in the process of reducing inequality. But there are several reasons why this conclusion would not necessarily be warranted. For one thing, it hinges on the arbitrarily specified high weight—all other measures show a moderate degree of horizontal inequity per unit of inequality reduction. For another, the units of horizontal inequity and inequality reduction are not comparable. Thirdly, part of the policy change dealt with here—social insurance transfers—intends to bring about rank reversals by favoring the aged and unemployed at the expense of the nonaged and employed. Even with all my pruning, what we are to make of this number of Plotnick's is still not clear.

But we can get closer if we take rows in pairs. Suppose we despair of knowing how to weight horizontal inequity and inequality reduction and focus just on food stamps. There are three reasons why food stamps should improve Plotnick's balance between horizontal inequity and inequality reduction. First, food stamps are available on a roughly standard basis across the country—inequality reduction without large rank reversals. Second, food stamps are taxed in the public assistance program—in states where AFDC benefits are high (implying potential rank reversals), benefits are lowered when recipients receive food stamps. Third, AFDC benefits are taxed by the food stamp program, again implying that food stamps will boost overall support levels in low-AFDC states more than in high-AFDC states. Food stamps, then, ought to lower all of the Plotnick horizontal inequity measures. Indeed they do that, as a comparison of the numbers in rows 1 and 2 of Table 8.1 indicate. The same is true if social insurance is taken as given, as in rows 4 and 5. The indication is that the food stamp program is doing a job in reducing horizontal inequity per degree of inequality reduction, and we need something like this calculation to show that. We are finally beginning to find some way of using Plotnick's numbers. But we are still not all the way home. The numbers do not say *how much* food stamps reduce horizontal inequity or increase inequality reduction.

As a final illustration of my point, compare rows 2 and 3 of table 8.1. Here Plotnick focuses on the differences in rank reversal made by income taxes; the suggestion is that incomes taxes go the wrong way—by all but one measure they increase horizontal inequity per unit of inequality reduction. Why is this? Plotnick gives no clue. Perhaps this strange result is based entirely on the impact of the income tax on high-income people and has little to do with the redistribution policy for low-income people, which seems to receive more attention. Perhaps this result is due to the congressional mandate that various types of income should be taxed at different rates, or not taxed at all, leading to all manner of intended rank reversals (to say nothing of loopholes). Or perhaps the result is not even true. We should be focusing on the Plotnick measure and not on other measures. No doubt a great many possibilities exist; until we know more about why results are coming out the way they do, we will not know how seriously to take Plotnick's calculations.

All of this suggests how calculations of this sort might be better done. To a large extent my frustration with Plotnick's numbers can be explained by the fact that he has summarized too much material in one simple number. There is so much material that the summary begs as many questions as it answers. If Plotnick had taken the other tack and given appendix table after appendix table without any summary measure, I would chastise him for lacking a summary. However, we need both the summary and the underlying numbers to determine why the summary measure is doing what it is doing. The summary measure is a red flag indicating that the rank reversals in certain tax-transfer programs should be investigated. But it can do no more than motivate our search through the detailed tables—the summary measure alone is not very helpful.

9   Rewards for Continued Work: The Economic Incentives for Postponing Retirement

Olivia S. Mitchell
Gary S. Fields

This chapter develops empirical measures of the economic incentives for deferred retirement among older workers. Using a new data file on pay and pensions, we construct intertemporal budget sets reflecting income available to workers at alternative retirement ages. The analysis explores how continued labor force attachment is rewarded in terms of net earnings, Social Security benefits, and private pension income.

Two motivations guide the research. First, it is important to understand how workers' income opportunities change with age. Studies of retirement patterns, including our own and others',[1] have demonstrated that these economic rewards influence the choice of retirement age. Savings decisions, consumption paths, and other economic outcomes are also responsive to the budget set at older ages. Unfortunately, data limitations have made it difficult for previous authors to explore the range of income opportunities available to older individuals. This paper presents and discusses new empirical evidence on how older workers' income opportunities change as the workers age.

Olivia S. Mitchell is a faculty research associate of the National Bureau of Economic Research and associate professor of labor economics at Cornell University. Gary S. Fields is professor of economics and labor economics at Cornell University. Both authors are equally responsible for the contents of this paper; first mention is determined randomly.

The authors wish to thank Joseph Quinn for helpful comments, Vivian Fields for careful computer programming, and Rebecca Luzadis for capable research assistance. Research support was received from the U.S. Department of Labor, Cornell University, and the National Bureau of Economic Research. The research reported here is part of the NBER's research program in labor studies and pensions. Any opinions expressed are those of the authors.

1. Mitchell and Fields 1984; Fields and Mitchell 1984; Boskin and Hurd 1978; Burkhauser and Quinn 1983; Burtless and Hausman 1982; Gordon and Blinder 1980; Gustman and Steinmeier 1984.

Exploring how companies differ in the compensation packages they offer to older workers is important as well. Some authors, e.g., Lazear (1982), have suggested that firms use their pension plans to encourage early retirement, though data on this phenomenon are difficult to obtain. The present chapter develops a detailed description of private pension structures and the ways in which they treat prolonged job attachment.

Two main conclusions arise from the analysis. First, the data show that total net income rises as people defer retirement, but the size of the income increment varies with age. Second, the data show that some pension plans encourage early retirement among older workers but others penalize it. Thus differences in private pension structures prove to be an important source of variation in income opportunities among older workers. Our results have implications for researchers interested in older workers' income patterns and for policymakers who propose mandating actuarial neutrality in private pension plans.

Section 9.1 of this chapter reviews briefly the most important theoretical features of older workers' income opportunities and discusses some general considerations when building an empirical counterpart of the theoretical budget set. Section 9.2 presents our methodology and data, and section 9.3 presents the findings. Conclusions are collected in section 9.4.

9.1   Theoretical Considerations

We consider the rewards for continued work in the context of older persons' retirement decisions. Previous theoretical studies of retirement behavior have identified the individual's problem as selecting the optimal amount of work to do over the remaining lifetime, subject to income and time constraints.[2] *Optimal* is defined as the labor supply path that maximizes intertemporal utility; accordingly, the goal is to select the retirement age that provides a worker with his most preferred combination of leisure time and income from among available options. The worker's income constraints are determined by net earnings available from market work, and net Social Security and private pension benefits available during retirement. His time constraint consists of time remaining until death; this time may be allocated between work and leisure.[3]

More formally, the worker is postulated to select the retirement age (R) that maximizes intertemporal utility, the arguments of which are lifetime consumption (C) and lifetime leisure (RET):

2. For a review of studies of retirement behavior, see Mitchell and Fields 1982.

3. We abstract here from retirement options involving part-time work or gradual withdrawal from the labor force; Gustman and Steinmeier 1984 and Burtless and Moffitt 1982 consider these alternatives in some detail. For the sample of older workers described below, retirement may be best described as accepting the pension and leaving the firm since only a tiny minority ever worked after becoming pensioners.

$$U = U(C, RET); \; U \text{ concave,}$$

subject to an intertemporal budget constraint with the following structure:

$$C = PDVY(R) + W_0 - B_0.$$

In other words, planned consumption equals the present value of discounted income over the remainder of the individual's life ($PDVY$), plus wealth at the time of retirement decision (W_0), minus planned bequests (B_0). Survival probabilities and pure time preference are incorporated via a discount factor (r). Both the lifetime utility function and the income constraint are viewed as stationary over time.

The $PDVY$ component of the older worker's budget constraint depends on the retirement age chosen. This is because $PDVY$ is composed of three elements, each of which is a function of R. The present value of earnings ($PDVE$) is computed from the age at which the worker begins planning for retirement (normalized to 0) until R:

$$PDVE = \int_0^R E_t e^{-rt} dt.$$

The other two components of $PDVY$—the discounted values of Social Security and pension benefits—also depend on R since they are computed from R to the end of the planning horizon (T):

$$PDVSS = \int_R^T SS_t e^{-rt} dt$$

and

$$PDVPP = \int_R^T PP_t e^{-rt} dt.$$

Annual retirement benefits are fairly complex functions of several factors including the worker's retirement age:

$$SS_t = f(R, t, F),$$
$$PP_t = g(R, t, F).$$

When the worker defers retirement, many firms raise annual pension benefits to acknowledge the shorter period over which benefits will be paid; when benefits are only sufficiently larger to offset increased mortality, the pension structure is termed actuarially neutral.[4] As with private pension formulas, Social Security rules also provide a positive credit as R

---

4. In the empirical analysis below, we focus on defined benefit plans, i.e., those in which benefit amounts are functions of years of service and/or pay rather than pension contributions. Benefits in such plans need not be actuarially neutral.

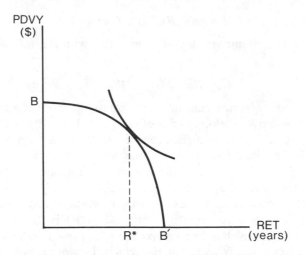

Fig. 9.1.   The intertemporal budget set (*BB'*) and the optimal retirement date (*R**).

increases. Social Security and private pension benefits depend upon two other variables as well. The year itself, *t*, enters the annual benefit computation because benefits often vary with time. This would occur in the case of negotiated benefit improvements in bargained plans, or legislated Social Security formula changes. Finally, the pension factor (*F*) is included to allow for interactions between benefits and other variables; for example, in some pension plans, preretirement earnings are used in the benefit formula.

In addition to the income constraint, an older worker faces a total time constraint. By definition, years of retirement leisure (*RET*) are equal to the difference between the individual's expected lifetime (*N*) and the age at which retirement occurs:[5]

$$RET = N - R.$$

Understanding the income-leisure trade-off facing older workers is facilitated by figure 9.1. This figure graphs the present value of income available to the older individual and the expected retirement period for all possible retirement ages; the diagram indicates that, for this hypothetical worker at least, his income is lowest if he chooses to retire as early as possible, while his income would rise substantially if he remained with the firm additional years. The figure presumes that deferring retirement is rewarded by even more income; below we show empirically that the intertemporal budget set in fact has such a shape.

5. Remaining lifetime may, of course, vary with health. The empirical work below uses standard life expectancies in computing the average value of future income streams; however, annuities are worth less to those with shorter remaining lifespans due to poor health, and benefits to such retirees should be adjusted accordingly.

Presenting the older worker's decision in this way highlights the similarities between this model and the conventional labor economics approach to the hours-of-work decision. Figure 9.1 also indicates that the optimal retirement date (R^*) is determined in a familiar way: R^* is the age at which the marginal utility of an additional increment to lifetime income is just offset by the loss in utility from leisure foregone. While we do not develop comparative dynamics for R^* here, they may be derived in much the same manner as in the cross-sectional framework (Fields and Mitchell 1984).

Some features of the intertemporal budget set should be underscored. First, the older worker's budget set is defined over all possible retirement dates rather than at just one moment in time. A complete understanding of the rewards for continued work therefore requires that one investigate not only one or two points on the budget surface, but all alternatives. Second, to be able to compute $PDVY$ at each age, one must understand the private pension and Social Security benefit formulas facing a given worker, since these institutional rules impart structure to the intertemporal budget set. Third, the income-leisure trade-off embodies expectations about future income streams and formulas, inflation rates, mortality rates, and a host of other variables. These must also be modeled in empirical work.

9.2 Building the Empirical Intertemporal Budget Set

To construct an intertemporal budget set, we require complete data on each worker's earnings, private pension benefits, and Social Security benefits. The data set used in the present empirical analysis is a subsample of the Benefit Amounts Survey (BAS) developed in 1978 by the U.S. Department of Labor's Pension and Welfare Benefits Program.[6] This survey consisted of a stratified random sample of private sector pension plans filing reports with the Labor Department as required under the Employee Retirement Income Security Act of 1974 (ERISA). The firms whose pension plans were selected for analysis were asked to provide a limited amount of information on the beneficiaries; data collected at the firms included birth year, year of retirement, and tenure with the firm for each sample worker. Individual records were then merged with administrative data from the Social Security Administration so that each worker's file also contained his earnings history from 1951 on.

The sample of workers available for analysis consists of 8,733 men born in 1909 or 1910. This limited age cohort was selected because, by the survey date (1978), virtually all would have been retired, yet relatively few would have died and therefore been excluded from the sample.

---

6. A data appendix describing empirical computations in more detail is available from the authors on request.

For the analysis at hand, we must know the rules determining pension benefits. We constructed such information from union contracts and summary plan descriptions on file with the U.S. Department of Labor for fourteen defined benefit plans. No larger data set with information on both pensions and their beneficiaries is now available; the present analysis thus extends our own previous efforts as well as those of other analysts who have generally been limited to an examination of a single pension plan.[7] On the other hand, our sample of pension plans is still small enough that findings reported here must be viewed as exploratory rather than representative of pension plans as a whole.

The plans represented here cannot be identified individually for confidentiality reasons. We may say, though, that our sample includes several blue collar plans negotiated with the United Auto Workers, several other plans in the manufacturing sector, a craft union plan, and one in the trade sector.

An example of the benefit rules used in one of the United Auto Workers plans is given in table 9.1. Even this apparently simple years-of-service formula turns out to be quite complex in practice.

The formula given in table 9.1 describes pension benefit rules in effect around 1970, at which time our sample workers were about sixty years of age. But the rules in 1970 would not necessarily have been appropriate for a worker who waited to retire until, say, 1975. In this company, and in the other companies in our study, the pension formulas were incremented several times during the 1960s. In evaluating what future retirement benefits would have been, workers in that company might reasonably have expected that benefits would rise in the future as much as they had in the past. Therefore we looked at prior union contracts, the Bureau of Labor Statistics *Pension Digest*, and other documents to determine what had occurred prior to 1970. Empirical analysis of changes in pension benefits over time for newly retiring workers, as well as for previously retired individuals, revealed that pension plans typically raised benefits in line with inflation for workers not yet retired, but held nominal benefits constant for those already retired. Therefore, the empirical model assumes that a prospective retiree would have expected nominal preretirement increases just short of the inflation rate, but probably zero postretirement increases.

The specific pension formula outlined in table 9.1 depends only on age and years of service. To compute pension amounts in plans where earnings are also used in the benefit formulas, it is necessary to know what a worker would have earned had he remained on his job. Earnings information is also needed, of course, in constructing the total lifetime income available from alternative retirement strategies.

7. See, for instance, the work of Burkhauser 1979 and Fields and Mitchell 1984 on the United Auto Workers, and Burtless and Hausman 1982 on federal government workers.

Table 9.1   Private Pension Structure in Company X

	Benefit until 62	Benefit until 65	Benefit at 65 and Beyond
Retire after 60[a]	$4,800	$5,400	$2,548
Retire after age 62[b]	—	$5,400	$2,944
Retire after age 65[c]	—	—	$3,214

Note: The pension structure in company X is negotiated every three years and written into a contract with the United Automobile Workers union (UAW). The plan is noncontributory. The benefit formula negotiated in the early 1970s, when the sample workers were about sixty years of age and were presumably deciding when to retire, varied depending on age and/or years of service. The above figures applied to an individual who started work at company X at age thirty.

[a]This benefit is available only after completing ten years of service. Calculated as ($90 × years of service less [.04 × the difference between the retirement age and 62]) + $63.60.

[b]This benefit is available only after completing ten years of service. Calculated as ($90 × years of service) + $63.60.

[c]Calculated as ($90 × years of service) + $63.60.

Information on earnings is available from the BAS–Social Security earnings data merged file. For the period prior to retirement, earnings in excess of the Social Security taxable maximum are imputed using a variant of a routine described in Fox (1976). Earnings a worker could anticipate if he did not retire are imputed from previous years' real earnings figures. Gross earnings are then reduced by income taxes and payroll taxes to obtain net earnings.

The other element of the intertemporal budget set is Social Security benefits. These are computed based on the Social Security rules in effect in 1972. We use 1972 benefit rules for retirement plans being devised in 1970, because future changes had been legislated two years in advance. The algorithm incorporates what the worker might have anticipated had he retired earlier and filed for benefits when first eligible at age sixty-two, and what he would have received if he had postponed retiring and filing for benefits until later ages. As with the projection of future private pension benefits, this requires an assumption about how benefits would have been expected to change over time. The algorithm incorporates the real growth rate in Social Security benefits experienced during the 1960s as the best estimate of how real benefits might have been expected to change during the 1970s.

One limitation of the Social Security computation should be noted. It is possible to estimate only the male's Social Security benefits, but not his spouse's benefits, since marital status information is not reliably reported in our file.

In moving from the annual budget set components (all of which are in nominal dollars) to present discounted values (which are much more informative if expressed in real dollars), several additional assumptions must be made. Standard practice is followed by discounting each year's benefits by the probability of mortality at each age, based on survival rate information for the cohort in question. In addition, future benefits are deflated by two factors—inflation and a real discount rate. Estimated future benefit streams assume continuation of the rate of price increases prevailing in the early 1970s; to discount benefits accruing in the future, the same nominal rate is used. In addition, a 2 percent real discount rate is used to reflect time preference. Confirmatory analysis with other discount rates produces results virtually identical to those reported below.

The foregoing describes the construction of the budget set in the BAS file. In the balance of the chapter we summarize this information by calculating the overall budget set and its components for a specific "illustrative worker."[8] We do this for purposes of comparison, since it is useful to derive benefits using the same basic earnings and job tenure characteristics, while holding constant other factors that might vary across plans. Nonetheless, this illustrative individual should be relatively similar to actual workers in the pension plan, since benefit structures are generally constructed with a relevant salary range in mind. The illustrative worker discussed below is assigned the mean net earnings and job tenure derived from the underlying sample described above. The average tenure figure, twenty-six years, is compatible with Hall's (1982) recent discussion of lifetime jobs among males in the U.S. labor force. Others who have computed pension benefits (e.g., Lazear 1982; Kotlikoff and Smith 1983) did not have this type of individual-level information and were thus required to use a range of tenure and salary assumptions to represent most possibilities.

9.3   The Economic Rewards for Deferring Retirement

As discussed earlier, two empirical questions guide our empirical explorations: (1) How do total income profiles change as workers age? and (2) How do pension plans reward continued work effort? Each question is investigated in turn in this section.[9]

9.3.1   The Shape of the Total Income Path (*PDVY*)

Table 9.2 displays the elements of the illustrative worker's intertemporal budget set, expressed in annual terms in the top panel and in present discounted value terms in the lower panel.[10] Expected income amounts are reported only until age sixty-five in this relatively aggregative table, since some firms prohibited employment after that age; disaggregated figures

8. Readers of our earlier work should be alerted to the fact that those papers use actual workers in a company, not the illustrative worker used here.

9. The calculations in this section assume that the illustrative worker is single. Alternative calculations assuming that he is married yield identical qualitative conclusions, except for one point noted below.

10. All present discounted value figures are reported in 1970 dollars.

Table 9.2   Earnings, Social Security, and Private Pension Income at Alternative Retirement Ages, for the Illustrative Worker

	If Retirement Occurred at Age					
	60	61	62	63	64	65
A. Annual Amounts (nominal dollars)						
1. Net earnings (E_t)	$ 0	8,254	8,717	9,185	9,563	9,760
2. Social Security (SS_t)[a]	1,858	1,916	1,973	2,333	2,749	3,209
3. Net private pension (PP_t)	2,190	2,350	2,322	2,513	2,724	2,634
B. Present Values of Streams (real dollars)						
1. Net earnings ($PDVE$)	$ 0	7,677	15,203	22,549	29,618	36,269
2. Social Security ($PDVSS$)	27,887	28,755	29,614	31,013	32,288	33,191
3. Net private pension ($PDVPP$)	15,071	18,960	19,953	19,493	19,029	18,542
4. Total PDVY	$45,958	55,392	64,770	73,055	80,935	88,002
5. Marginal Increases		8,434	9,378	8,285	7,880	7,067
		(18%)	(17%)	(13%)	(11%)	(9%)

Note: These computations are based on pension algorithms devised for fourteen pension plans and illustrative worker; see text.
[a]Assumes worker retires at that age and files then or at age sixty-two, whichever is later.

for later ages are provided below for those plans in which continued work beyond age sixty-five was possible.

Of most interest for the present discussion are the last two lines on table 9.2 (lines B.4 and B.5), which report total *PDVY* and marginal changes as retirement is deferred. The following features of the expected *PDVY* stream are noteworthy:

1. *PDVY rises monotonically as retirement is deferred.* At each age, earnings plus (or minus) pension and Social Security accruals exceed the pension and Social Security benefits foregone. In real terms, a worker postponing retirement from age sixty to sixty-five would roughly double his real income stream.

2. *PDVY rises nonlinearly with age of retirement.* The payoff to working one additional year is highest in both dollar and percentage terms between ages sixty and sixty-one; if the same worker deferred retiring between sixty-four and sixty-five, his dollar gain would be about $1,400 less, for a marginal percentage gain only half as large.

Therefore, the data show that the economic rewards for postponing retirement are positive but that the gains vary across ages. Previous studies have not discerned these patterns because they used data containing less detail on the components of *PDVY*.

The fact that the intertemporal budget set for older workers rewards deferred retirement implies that observed income for any particular retiree is a function of when he chooses to retire, rather than being exogenously given. If one wishes to assess income opportunities that would have been available to a retired worker prior to his retirement, it is necessary to develop an intertemporal budget set such as the one in table 9.2 indicating the magnitudes of contingent income flows at alternative retirement dates.

The observed pattern of the budget set for the BAS sample also implies that the value of *PDVY* (or its component parts) at any one particular age will not be very informative about the overall shape of workers' intertemporal income paths. Unfortunately, most data sets other than the BAS contain insufficient detail on earnings, Social Security, and private pension benefits, making it difficult to develop a *PDVY* path in as much detail as here.[11]

On average, workers in the fourteen plans have very similar earnings and Social Security streams. The main source of variation arises in the private pension streams. These differences are elaborated below.

9.3.2   The Shape of Private Pension Income Paths

Pension benefits constitute a fairly significant source of income for older workers who participate in these plans. The top panel of table 9.2

---

11. Approximations are possible using the Longitudinal Retirement History Survey; see Fields and Mitchell 1984.

shows that annual (first-year) benefits from private pensions are sizeable, equaling or exceeding the single worker's Social Security payments for all ages but sixty-five, where they are only slightly less.[12] Net private pension benefits amount to one-quarter to one-third of after-tax earnings for individuals in the sample.[13]

Still focusing on annual benefits, line A.3 indicates large differences in benefits depending on when the worker retires. On average, an age-sixty retiree would have received private pension income of about $2,200 in the year he retired. If he deferred retirement by one year, the addition to (nominal) benefits would be on the order of 7 percent. However, the marginal pension payoff to an additional year's work is by no means uniform across retirement ages; for example, benefits at age sixty-two are *lower* than for age sixty-one. This benefit decline is attributable to pension plan supplements provided until a retiree attains age sixty-two, the age of eligibility for Social Security. A reduction is again evident between the ages of sixty-four and sixty-five; the pension rules thus acknowledge that workers can file for full Social Security retirement income at age sixty-five and provide a bridge for individuals retiring earlier. In general, the marginal pension payoff to retiring one year later varies a lot across retirement ages, a fact not immediately evident from a cursory review of benefit rules.

Line B.3 of table 9.2 converts the annual pension benefit figures into present discounted values in real dollars. Again it is evident that the reward structure built into private pensions varies for different retirement ages. The illustrative worker would receive *more* in lifetime benefits if he left the firm at age sixty than if he postponed retirement to age sixty-one, despite the fact that annual benefits are higher at age sixty-one than at sixty. In fact, the annual pension benefits are increased at less than actuarially neutral rates at several ages, as is evident from computed changes in the present values of lifetime benefits:

	Change in Retirement Age				
	60–61	61–62	62–63	63–64	64–65
Change in *PDVPP*	0%	+ 5%	− 2%	− 2%	− 2%

Clearly the structure of lifetime pension income flows very much affects the economic rewards for continued work.

12. For a married worker, the sum of the worker's plus spouse's Social Security benefits exceeds private pension benefits.

13. Previous studies have not computed after-tax replacement rates both for private pensions and Social Security, so these figures cannot be directly compared with others in the literature. We find that the overall replacement rate including both pensions and a single retiree's Social Security benefit is between 50 and 60 percent on average, though in some cases individuals received as much as 95 percent of preretirement net earnings. Replacement rates would be higher if spouse benefits were included.

Present values in table 9.2 are averages across fourteen pension plans, so they conceal potentially interesting differences in company pension structures. Table 9.3 splits the sample into two groups: *pattern* and *conventional* plans. Pattern plans are pensions where benefits are based almost exclusively on years of service with the firm (or occupation, if a craft union). Conventional plans, more common among nonunion firms, determine benefits based both on final salary and tenure with the firm.

It is evident from table 9.3 that the overall means obscure some key differences between the two kinds of benefit structures. Pattern plans tend to structure their first-year benefits so that they rise more or less smoothly, reaching a peak at age sixty-four; annual benefits typically fall for workers deferring benefits beyond that point. First-year benefits in conventional plans operate differently; in this case, benefits for the age-sixty-two retiree are lower than for the worker leaving one year earlier. It is this subgroup of plans that produces the dip in annual benefits found in the overall mean. However, after age sixty-two, conventional plans tend to provide ever-increasing benefit amounts for workers postponing retirement up to age sixty-five.

An examination of discounted pension values in these two types of plans suggests even sharper contrasts. Pattern plans (line B.2) actively discourage work beyond age sixty.[14] An employee in a pattern plan who defers retirement until age sixty-five will in fact receive lifetime benefits that are about 18 percent *lower* than he would have received had he retired at age sixty! On the other hand, present value streams in conventional plans are structured so that a worker deferring retirement until age sixty-five receives about 17 percent *higher* benefits than if he retired at age sixty. Thus between ages sixty and sixty-five, conventional pension plans appear to improve benefits by about the same amount that pattern plans reduce them.

Clearly, the overall incentives differ between the two types of plans. To see whether marginal incentives are smooth or erratic, changes in pension present values are computed for each additional year of work:

	Change in Retirement Age				
	60–61	61–62	62–63	63–64	64–65
Pattern plans change in *PDVPP*	−2%	−2%	−5%	−5%	−5%
Conventional plans change in *PDVPP*	+2%	+14%	+0%	+0%	+0%

Evidently, pattern plans actively encourage early retirement, whereas conventional plans strongly encourage work up to age sixty-two. After age

14. This is similar to the finding reported by Lazear 1982.

Table 9.3   **Net Private Pension Amounts at Alternative Retirement Ages in Pattern and Conventional Plans**

			If Retirement Occurred at Age			
	60	61	62	63	64	65
	A. Annual Net Pension Benefits[a]					
1. Overall mean	$ 2,190	2,350	2,322	2,513	2,742	2,634
2. Pattern plan mean	2,653	2,760	2,907	3,059	3,214	2,626
3. Conventional plan mean	1,728	1,939	1,883	2,103	2,356	2,639
	B. Present Value of Net Pension Benefits[b]					
1. Overall mean	$19,070	18,960	19,953	19,493	19,029	18,542
2. Pattern plan mean	24,795	24,192	23,787	22,617	21,432	20,275
3. Conventional plan mean	14,777	15,036	17,078	17,150	17,227	17,243

Note: This table is based on pension algorithms of fourteen plans as applied to the illustrative worker (see text).

[a]Nominal dollars.

[b]Real dollars.

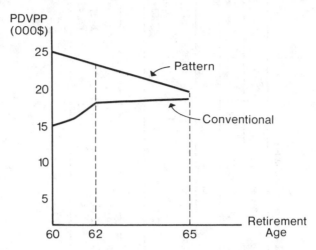

Fig. 9.2.   Present value of private pension benefits in pattern plans and conventional plans.

sixty-two, conventional plans provide a flat payoff schedule for additional years of work; in pattern plans, the slope becomes strongly negative (see figure 9.2).

Table 9.4 disaggregates to the level of the individual plan. This breakdown of pension plan benefit structures reveals even more variability in economic rewards for continued work. These plan-specific data permit the computation of benefit streams for ages beyond sixty-five in cases where continued work was permitted; firms with mandatory retirement are indicated with a dash.

This disaggregative investigation of pension plan rules suggests two conclusions:

1. *Pension plans reward deferred retirement differently from one company to the next.* Pattern plans as a whole, and the UAW plans in particular, encourage early retirement by structuring benefits so that they attain a maximum between ages sixty and sixty-two. Conventional plans are more complex, but as a rule structure their benefit flows to reward continued work well beyond age sixty.

2. *Marginal payoffs to deferred retirement are uneven; actuarial neutrality across retirement ages is rare.* In our sample, a worker deferring retirement by one year could have increased his lifetime pension income flow by as much as 14 percent, or reduced it by 5 percent, depending on the pension plan in which he worked.

In overview, then, some private pensions reward prolonged work and others penalize it, both in overall and marginal terms. It is *not* true that pensions always discourage work beyond age sixty.

Table 9.4 Present Values of Net Private Pension Benefits for Alternative Retirement Ages: Plan-Level Data

	If Retirement Age Occurs at Age								
	60	61	62	63	64	65	66	67	68
A. Pattern Plans									
UAW plans									
Plan A	$28,181	27,586	27,189	25,455	23,787	22,195	21,706	21,140	20,500
Plan B	36,030	36,146	36,599	36,341	35,730	34,987	34,081	—	—
Plan C	28,176	27,571	27,189	25,455	23,787	22,195	—	—	—
Plan D	28,176	27,571	27,189	25,455	23,787	22,195	21,706	21,140	20,500
Non-UAW plans									
Plan E	21,858	19,814	17,912	16,147	14,512	13,001	11,608	10,328	9,153
Plan F	6,351	6,464	6,641	6,850	6,986	7,079	6,620	6,156	5,692
B. Conventional Plans									
Plan G	0	0	9,300	10,027	10,087	10,497	9,461	8,891	7,951
Plan H	13,527	14,176	20,471	19,364	18,173	16,869	—	—	—
Plan I	16,410	16,709	16,841	16,977	17,028	16,893	—	—	—
Plan J	20,012	20,256	20,270	19,335	18,359	17,246	16,190	15,081	13,841
Plan K	14,851	15,079	15,290	15,504	16,318	17,174	16,563	15,866	15,109
Plan L	17,671	19,669	21,594	23,468	25,295	26,981	—	—	—
Plan M	16,526	17,042	17,668	18,291	18,810	19,084	—	—	—
Plan N	19,491	17,254	15,193	14,230	13,742	13,198	12,605	11,592	10,950

Note: This table is based on pension algorithms as applied to illustrative worker; see text. Underlined numbers are row maxima. Dashes indicate retirement is mandatory in that plan at that age.

9.4   Conclusion

The notion of an intertemporal budget set facing older workers flows from an economic model of choice of retirement age subject to income and time constraints. Measuring the budget set empirically requires that total discounted income be computed for each possible retirement age. In so doing, it is important to model Social Security and private pension rules defining benefits available at each age, and in addition to determine how workers would have expected these rules to change in the future.

Using a unique new data set known as the Benefit Amounts Survey, we develop empirical answers to two questions: (1) How do workers' total incomes change as they defer retirement? and (2) Do private pension structures reward or penalize continued work at older ages?

The data suggest two important features of the discounted total income streams *(PDVY)* facing older workers, which have not been noted in previous studies. *First, PDVY rises monotonically as retirement is deferred.* This is the result of rising Social Security and earnings streams balanced against flat or declining private pension streams. *Second, PDVY rises nonlinearly with age.* In general the economic rewards to postponing retirement are always positive but the gains vary depending on the age in question.

The data also point to two new conclusions about the incentive structures of private pension plans. *First, pension plans reward deferred retirement differently across companies. Second, marginal payoffs to deferred retirement are uneven; actuarial neutrality across retirement ages is uncommon.* Some private pensions reward prolonged work but others penalize it.

The patterns just noted have implications for both researchers and policymakers. Analysts interested in modeling and estimating the determinants of retirement, savings, and other economic behavior among older workers must build and examine the intertemporal budget sets anticipated by individuals as they age. Similarly, income distribution studies should recognize that actual retirement income among retirees is determined to a significant degree by workers' retirement behavior. These considerations highlight the importance of developing new data sets containing more complete information on workers, their earnings histories, and their company records, including pension system rules. In particular this chapter has shown that evaluating older individuals' incomes requires devising data sets quite different from those used by social scientists in the past. Conventional worker-level or even household-level surveys collected over short periods of time cannot provide detail sufficient to compute accurate measures of Social Security benefits and private pension opportunities. Instead what is required is a new and more creative matching of data on workers, their entire work histories, and characteristics of the firms employing them throughout their lifetimes. Ideally such data would also incorporate other needed measures on employee health, wealth, and demographic traits especially important for the study of income and aging.

The observed differences in pension patterns also have an interesting policy implication. One proposal that has received some attention of late in policy circles is the idea that the federal government should mandate pension benefit neutrality. This proposal is motivated by the belief that pension structures currently encourage early retirement. It is thought that mandatory pension neutrality would result in higher benefits for those continuing to work beyond age sixty, thereby encouraging longer workforce commitment. However, our analysis shows that the actual result depends on the benefit structure presently available to the covered employee. In pattern plans, the effect of mandatory neutrality would probably be to cut early benefits rather than to increase later ones. Though this would affect retirement ages in the anticipated direction, retirement benefits would be lower than at present, not higher.

In conventional plans, on the other hand, mandatory neutrality could conceivably remove the desired incentives currently in place to defer retirement; such a result would not be consistent with federal efforts to encourage later retirement. Altering pension reward structures currently in place could produce other undesirable results as well. If the current pension benefits patterns are structured in accordance with firms' perceptions of the relative efficiency of older workers compared to younger ones, imposing regulatory restrictions would be expected to increase firms' costs, some part of which would probably be passed on to workers in the form of lower wages or lower pension benefits. Both the welfare and the efficiency costs of mandating pension neutrality should be analyzed much more carefully before concluding that such a policy is desirable.

References

Boskin, Michael J., and Michael D. Hurd. 1978. The effect of Social Security on early retirement. *Journal of Public Economics* (Dec.): 261–77.

Burkhauser, Richard V. 1979. The pension acceptance decision of older workers. *Journal of Human Resources* (Winter): 63–75.

Burkhauser, Richard V., and Joseph F. Quinn. 1983. Is mandatory retirement overrated? Evidence from the 1970s. *Journal of Human Resources* (Summer): 358–77.

Burtless, Gary, and Jerry Hausman. 1982. Double dipping: The combined effects of Social Security and civil service pensions on employee retirement. *Journal of Public Economics* (July): 139–59.

Burtless, Gary, and Robert Moffitt. 1982. The effect of Social Security on labor supply of the aged: The joint choice of retirement date and post-retirement hours of work. Paper presented at the American Economic Association meetings, New York.

Fields, Gary S., and Olivia S. Mitchell. 1984. The effects of Social Security reforms on retirement ages and retirement incomes. *Journal of Public Economics* (Nov.): 143–159.

————.1984. Economic determinants of optimal retirement age: An empirical investigation. *Journal of Human Resources* (Winter): 245–62.

Fox, Alan. 1976. Alternative means of earnings replacement rates for Social Security benefits. In *Reaching Retirement Age*. Office of Research and Statistics. Social Security Administration report no. 47. Washington, D.C.: GPO.

Gordon, Roger H., and Alan S. Blinder. 1980. Market wages, reservation wages, and retirement decisions. *Journal of Public Economics* (Oct.): 277–308.

Gustman, Alan L., and Thomas L. Steinmeier. 1984. Partial retirement and the analysis of retirement behavior. *Industrial and Labor Relations Review* (Apr.): 403–15.

Hall, Robert. 1982. The importance of lifetime jobs in the U.S. economy. *American Economic Review* (Sept.): 716–24.

Kotlikoff, Larry, and Daniel Smith. 1983. *Pensions and the American Economy*. Chicago: University of Chicago Press.

Lazear, Edward P. 1982. Severence pay, pensions, mobility, and the efficiency of work incentives. Working paper no. 854. National Bureau of Economic Research.

Mitchell, Olivia S., and Gary S. Fields. 1982. The effects of pensions and earnings on retirement: A review essay. In *Research in Labor Economics*, ed. Ronald G. Ehrenberg, vol 5. Greenwich, Conn.: JAI Press.

————. 1984. The economics of retirement behavior. *Journal of Labor Economics*, 84–105.

Quinn, Joseph F. 1977. Micro-economic determinants of early retirement: A cross-sectional view of white married men. *Journal of Human Resources* (Summer): 329–45.

Comment   Joseph F. Quinn

As it was with Gaul, so shall it be with my remarks. I will divide them into three parts: a brief introduction to put this chapter by Olivia Mitchell and Gary Fields (or vice versa) into perspective within the retirement litera-

Joseph F. Quinn is professor of economics at Boston College.

ture, a summary of what they have attempted and discovered, and some comments and suggestions for further improvement.

The retirement decision is a research area of considerable recent progress. The traditional view of the retirement decision was that it was usually imposed on an individual by an outside event such as mandatory retirement, a layoff, or a health problem. Once retired, the individual then turned to whatever retirement income sources were available and was grateful for them. The idea that these income sources might have *induced* the retirement behavior was given little currency. The support for this view came from surveys in which recent retirees were asked why they retired. The most common answer was always health, and the existence of Social Security or pension benefits was only rarely mentioned. Today, on the other hand, nearly everyone agrees that there are financial incentives in our retirement income plans, that they play an important role in individual retirement decisions, and that these incentives can be used as policy instruments to alter aggregate behavior.

Until recently, analysts tended to describe the magnitude of retirement income rights by the size of the annual benefit, or by its close relative, the replacement rate. Though useful summary statistics, these annual flow concepts ignore key aspects of the retirement incentives—how annual benefits change with continued work or with inflation after retirement. It is now generally agreed that a superior summary statistic is a pension's asset or stock equivalent—the present discounted value (PDV) of future benefits. This new view, emphasizing retirement *wealth*, has become a mainstay of modern retirement research.

These new views on the quantification of complex retirement income arrangements and on their behavioral impact are the result of a decade of intense research activity by economists, including Mitchell and Fields (and vice versa). Some have tried to quantify the magnitude of the incentives; others to measure their impact on individual behavior. To do so, analysts have taken one of two approaches—extensive or intensive. The extensive approach, which has characterized Richard Burkhauser's and my work, utilizes large microdata sets, such as the Retirement History Study or the National Longitudinal Surveys. The advantages are a large representative sample and extensive demographic, social, and economic data on the respondents. The disadvantage is very spotty information on the details of the individuals' pension plans. The latter is particularly unfortunate for at least two reasons. A key incentive derives from how pension wealth changes with continued work—details unavailable on the large microdata sets. And, as we will see below, much of the interpersonal variation in incentives comes from pension plans. Most of this is lost to the extensive researchers.

Mitchell and Fields, on the other hand, have taken the intensive route— to analyze in great detail the specifics of a small number of pension plans and their recipients. The advantages are obvious—they can (and do) calculate the actual financial consequences of individuals retiring at various ages. The big disadvantage is that they can do so for only a small sample. It is impossible to extrapolate to the economy and to know how general, and important, their findings are.

This chapter is descriptive. It describes what the work incentives looked like around 1970 for a representative individual in fourteen actual pension plans. It does not ask whether their incentives influenced retirement behavior.

The chapter begins with a theoretical section describing how an individual chooses a retirement age to maximize intertemporal utility. The decision affects three components of wealth—the present discounted values of future earnings, pension benefits, and Social Security receipts. The last two are complex, because delayed retirement after eligibility implies foregone pension benefits today, but higher benefits in the future. Whether the individual gains or loses retirement income wealth depends on the person's work history and on the details of the pension plan—precisely the details that Mitchell and Fields (and few others) have mastered. Frankly, I think the theoretical section adds little to our understanding. It ignores issues of uncertainty concerning the length of life or the size or likelihood of future benefits. It ignores hours of work, the possibility of partial retirement, or retirement and later reemployment. But it does emphasize the importance of analyzing the financial implications of retirement at *all* possible ages (not just the current one or sixty-two or sixty-five), and it leads nicely into the empirical section of the chapter where the real contribution lies.

The data set includes all the relevant details on fourteen pension plans in the 1978 Benefit Amounts Survey (BAS) of the Department of Labor. Also included are sparse descriptions of the plans' 1978 beneficiaries (year of birth, year of retirement, and tenure with the firm) and their Social Security earnings records since 1951. These individual data are not used in the paper except to define an "illustrative worker." (And it is not completely clear whether this worker is the same for all firms, or if one is invented for each. I suspect the former.) The authors then back up to 1970, when this worker was sixty years old and presumably contemplating retirement. With these data, they ask two questions for this same worker in each of the fourteen pension plans: (1) How does the *total* income profile (the PDV of future after-tax earnings *plus* pensions *plus* Social Security) fare with retirement at each age from sixty to sixty-five? and (2) How do the pension plans *alone* reward continued work? Does the size of pension wealth rise or fall with later and later retirement?

The first question is addressed only in table 9.2, where the results from all fourteen defined benefit plans are aggregated and averaged. The authors find that the PDV of total future income always rises with delayed retirement, because a year's earnings plus future benefit increments always outweigh a year's benefits lost. This is no surprise. Work pays more than retirement. But what is interesting is the magnitude of the increment in each subsequent year of work. Though positive, it declines for each year after sixty-two, the age of earliest Social Security eligibility. This means that even if paychecks grow, true compensation is falling because of losses in private pension wealth. This representative worker keeps getting his pay cut if he works beyond sixty-two—surreptitiously cut, but cut nonetheless. And the magnitude of the change is large. His net compensation drops from $9,378 at age sixty-one to sixty-two to only $7,067 at sixty-four to sixty-five, a decrement of 25 percent.

What is impressive about table 9.2 is that it includes the three major streams of income that depend on the retirement age chosen, expresses them in PDV form, and adds them together. The profiles of the sum are potentially interesting and important in understanding behavior. The problem is that there is too much averaging in the table—across individuals (since only an illustrative person is considered) and then across fourteen diverse plans. This averaging has eliminated much of the variation that the chapter is about.

I do not know how to interpret these numbers because an "average plan" makes no sense to me. My first suggestion is that table 9.2 would be more interesting if the two key rows (the PDV of total future income by retirement age (B.4) and the incremental changes in this sum (B.5) were repeated for *each* of the plans. For reasons described below, this would be the best part of the paper.

The authors do proceed to disaggregate, but only for the pension component. Future earnings and Social Security benefits are ignored after table 9.2. They first disaggregate the fourteen plans into two categories, depending on whether earnings (or just years of service) enter the pension benefit formula. They then analyze the fourteen plans separately.

The key finding, which is very interesting, is diversity. Does pension wealth rise or fall with continued work? It depends. Pattern plans (in which benefits depend solely on years of service) tend to have falling profiles. Of the six studied, four peaked at age sixty, and one peaked at sixty-two. On the other hand, pension wealth in conventional plans (which also consider terminal earnings in the benefit calculation) tend to rise with delayed retirement, at least until age sixty-five. Of the eight studied, four peaked at sixty-five, and one at sixty-four. Pattern plans encourage early retirement by penalizing continued work; conventional plans do just the opposite. But all plans, it should be noted, drop in value after age sixty-five. This combines with the actuarially unfair Social Security adjustment after sixty-five to create a substantial work disincentive for workers over that age.

This information, found in table 9.4, is fascinating. It is precisely the detail that other researchers have had to do without or invent. It illustrates the rich diversity that exists within the pension sphere. We always knew there was considerable diversity (relative to Social Security, for example) with respect to pension coverage and benefit levels. Now we see that the implicit work incentives vary greatly as well. This is precisely what is needed to understand retirement behavior.

Unfortunately, it is only part of the story, and here is where the chapter could be dramatically improved. Pension plans are frequently integrated with Social Security as the authors note. The benefits often decrease when one becomes eligible for Social Security. This is observed in table 9.2, where the average pension benefit drops at age sixty-two and again at sixty-five. But this is being offset, according to their same table 9.2, by higher Social Security benefits, and earnings as well. What sense does it make to isolate one component (pensions), especially when it is specifically integrated with another (Social Security)? Whether pensions encourage or discourage early retirement is much less important than whether pensions *and* Social Security in tandem do. This joint impact is discussed in table 9.2, but only as the average of fourteen dissimilar plans. What this chapter lacks is the methodology of table 9.2 and the disaggregation of table 9.4. Can this not be done? It would be a useful contribution to the field.

My second major suggestion concerns expectations. Mitchell and Fields turn back the clock, returning their representative individuals to the days of yesteryear—to 1970, to be exact. They then "forecast" real earnings and pension and Social Security benefits for the next five or more years. How should this be done? Should they use the experiences that actually occurred, which, of course, we now know? Or should they use what a reasonable person might have *expected* if planning to retire in 1970? What if the retirement decision was not made until 1975? Should they use 1970 expectations or those appropriate for 1975? In either case, upon what would the expectations be based?

There is a great deal of mystery about what was done, because the details are never spelled out. For example, in forecasting real pension benefits, the authors looked into the 1960s and found

> that pension plans typically raised benefits in line with inflation for workers not yet retired, but held nominal benefits constant for those already retired. Therefore, the empirical model assumes that a prospective retiree would have expected nominal preretirement increases *just short of* the inflation rate, but *probably* zero postretirement increases. (P. 274, emphasis mine)

Why "just short of"? How much "short of"? Why "probably"? What was actually done? The reader should know.

Concerning prospective earnings, the hints are sparser. "Earnings a worker could anticipate if he did not retire are imputed from previous years' real earnings figures" (p. 275). How? What real growth rate was assumed? And what methods were used to compute income and payroll taxes to obtain net earnings?

For Social Security, Mitchell and Fields use the 1972 rules, and "the real growth rate in Social Security benefits experienced during the 1960s as the best estimate of how real benefits might have been expected to change during the 1970s" (p. 275). What is this growth rate? How was it obtained? Would this not have dramatically underestimated what actually happened beginning in 1969? Does it make sense to apply the 1972 rules to someone who works through 1975 and then decides to retire?

Finally, future benefits are deflated by inflation and a real discount rate (2 percent). The authors assume continuation of the inflation rates observed in the early 1970s, but we are not told what the assumed inflation rate is or why expectations are based on early 1970s inflation, but on 1960s experiences with Social Security and pension benefits.

I harp on these problems because the numbers generated by these assumptions are the heart and soul of this chapter—what it is all about. The chapter should include a statement of the general expectations philosophy being used, details on how this philosophy is applied in each case, and some indication of how sensitive the results are to the expectations assumptions made. Only then can the reader adequately evaluate the interesting conclusions that are drawn.

Let me summarize and conclude. This chapter differs from most of the recent literature on retirement incentives in three important ways. Mitchell and Fields use a small number of actual pension plans for which they know the benefit calculation rules. They calculate the present discounted value of future earnings, pension, and Social Security benefits, and they do so for every possible retirement age within the range of interest. It is nice work, and I appreciate the complexity of what they have done. The resulting chapter is good and interesting. But, it could be better and more interesting. Here is how.

I would reduce the theory section and eliminate figure 9.1. I would eliminate table 9.2, which contains too much averaging—across eight thousand individuals and fourteen pension plans—to be interesting. I would then combine the methodology of table 9.2 (combining all three future income flows, not just pensions) and the degree of disaggregation of table 9.4 (individual plans). Finally, I would add a detailed appendix explaining exactly what assumptions and figures the authors used to forecast the subsequent decade from their 1970 vantage point, and how much difference they made.

I end with two suggestions for future research. These are topics well beyond the scope of this chapter. First, how have these incentive structures changed since the 1977 elimination of mandatory retirement at sixty-five? Have firms, deprived of the stick, augmented the carrot to *induce* workers to do what they could previously force them to. It would be fascinating to know if they have. And second, what explains the wide diversity in incentive structures—the fact that some firms encourage early retirement while others discourage it. Mitchell and Fields disaggregate by type of plan—

pattern versus conventional—which is an uninteresting dimension from an economics point of view. Are there other aspects of the firm or industry—growth in product demand, importance of new technology, worker-training requirements—that seem to explain why employees are induced to leave in one case and to stay in another. This information would shed valuable insight on whether these plans are *designed* to induce specific behavior, which I suspect they are, or whether they have evolved by historical accident.

10   Income, Inequality, and Uncertainty: Differences between the Disabled and Nondisabled

Robert H. Haveman
Barbara L. Wolfe

It is no surprise that disabled individuals of working age fare poorly in the labor market relative to individuals without impairments. The earnings of the disabled will tend to be lower not only because of their impairments, but also because, as a group, they tend to have a higher incidence of older people, minorities, and those with low levels of education. Individuals with long-standing impairments may also receive smaller amounts of non-earned income, due to relatively constrained opportunities for asset accumulation. While average income levels of the disabled are likely to be below those of the nondisabled population, it is not known whether the variation in expected income within the groups at a point in time and in actual income over time will be greater for the disabled than the nondisabled.

To the extent that the health status of the disabled is likely to fluctuate over time more than that of the nondisabled, there is reason to believe that the level of intertemporal variation in the income of a disabled person will exceed that of a nondisabled person with the same nonhealth personal characteristics. Moreover, the effect of disability—i.e., deviations from an unimpaired state of physical and mental health—on earnings capacity

Robert H. Haveman is John Bascom Professor of Economics, University of Wisconsin, Madison, and research associate at the Institute for Research on Poverty. Barbara L. Wolfe is associate professor of economics and preventive medicine at the University of Wisconsin, Madison, and research associate at the Institute for Research on Poverty.

Dan Usher's original comments on this chapter helped clarify the conceptual difference between inequality and uncertainty, and led to additional statistical analysis and a reinterpretation of the cross-sectional findings. The authors are indebted to him for his contribution. Martin David, Irwin Garfinkel, Lee Lillard, Timothy Smeeding, and Eugene Smolensky also provided helpful comments on the earlier draft. The authors would like to thank Michael Przybylski and Shee Ham as well for their assistance. This research was supported in part by the Department of Health and Human Services, Office of the Assistant Secretary for Planning and Evaluation.

293

would seem to be highly variable, depending on the nature of specific job skills and the effect of impairments on them. Some people with severe impairments (e.g., Itzak Perlman) seem to experience little if any loss of earnings capacity; others who share a particular physical or mental problem (and identical other relevant characteristics) seem to be unable to work at all. Still further, there is evidence of substantial variability in the attitudes toward and response to the disabled by potential employers. The economic discrimination faced by the disabled is not of a radically different sort than that facing racial and sexual minorities; conversely, some with physical and mental impairments are favored in the labor market precisely because of their handicap. On the other hand, given the truncation of earned income at zero, the lower mean income of the disabled might suggest a concomitant lower variation about that mean.

Interpreting the degree of variation in the income of an individual over time or in the incomes of a group of individuals at a point in time is not straightforward. Some of the variation may reflect uncertainty facing an individual. On the other hand, much of it might simply reflect inequality in outcomes among people. Indicators of both uncertainty and inequality are of interest. Because the bearing of uncertainty entails real economic losses, differences in the uncertainty facing disabled relative to nondisabled individuals is relevant to appraising the differences in economic status between the two groups. Similarly, public decision-makers may well respond if the level of income inequality among a fairly homogeneous group of the disabled (and, hence, the level of relative income poverty) is substantially greater than that for a similarly defined group of the nondisabled.

Our focus in this chapter is on the differences between the disabled and nondisabled populations both in expected income and the variation in income. We take two approaches to investigating these differences. In section 10.1 we employ longitudinal data and investigate how the *mean income* of the disabled and nondisabled groups in a particular age cohort differs through time. We also analyze the extent of *inequality in incomes* between the two groups over time. Finally, we decompose the variation in income, defining uncertainty to be the variation in income remaining after accounting for differences between individuals in relevant permanent characteristics. We then compare the average level of *uncertainty in income* faced by individuals in the disabled group through time relative to that faced by the nondisabled. Two income definitions are employed— pretax, pretransfer income (PTY) and posttax, posttransfer (or disposable) income (DY)—so that the differential effects of the tax and cash transfer systems on income levels, income inequality, and income uncertainty in the two groups can be investigated. In section 10.2 a cross-sectional analysis is presented for both 1968 and 1980. For each of these years, the differences between the two groups in mean incomes, income inequality, and income uncertainty are again investigated. Again, two income measures are employed—PTY and DY. Section 10.3 concludes.

10.1 Mean Income, Income Inequality, and Income Uncertainty Differences between the Disabled and Nondisabled, 1969–81

In this section we ask the following questions: How does a single age-cohort of individuals—some of whom are disabled and others nondisabled at a point in time—fare over time? As the cohort reaches retirement age, do the differences in income expectations between the disabled and nondisabled narrow? Is the inequality in income among individuals who are disabled greater than that for the nondisabled, and does the disparity in inequality increase or decrease over time? Does a disparity in uncertainty of income exist between the two groups, and does that disparity decrease through time (reflecting the growth of public transfer programs) or increase (because of unequal access to private pensions and previously accumulated assets)?

10.1.1   Data and Definitions

To answer these questions we constructed a longitudinal cohort sample from the Michigan Panel Study of Income Dynamics. Men fifty-one to sixty-two years of age as of 1969 were identified and followed for thirteen years—to 1981.[1] In the early years of the analysis, this sample is of working age; by the end of the period its members are of retirement (or early retirement) age. In 1981, the age of the sample ranges from sixty-two to seventy-three years. We begin with 515 persons in 1974 and track all of those who remain in the sample over the thirteen-year period. Individuals entering the sample after 1974 are not included. Persons leave the sample after 1974 because of death, geographic mobility without a forwarding address, or institutionalization along with incapacity to answer survey-type questions. In 1981, 367 of the 515 remain in the sample.

The base population is classified as either disabled or nondisabled in 1974. Those included in the disabled group either report they are disabled in each of three years prior to 1974, or report they are severely disabled in two or more of these years. All of the disability measures are self-report measures.[2]

---

1. Owing to the need to track specific individuals in the sample and to the identification system used for each year, the earliest date from which we could follow individuals was 1974. The two groups are identified in this base year and then followed backward to 1969 and forward to 1981.

2. The survey questions on which the disabled-nondisabled designation is based are: "Do you have a physical or nervous condition that limits the type of work, or the amount of work you can do?" (Asked in all years.) "Does your health limit the work you can do around the house?" (Asked in three years.)

Table 10.1   **Mean (Standard Deviation) of Demographic and Socioeconomic Variables for Male Cohort, 1969, 1974, and 1981**

	Disabled		Nondisabled	
1969				
Number	112		403	
Age	56.4	(3.19)	55.1	(3.69)
No. of adults in household	2.15	(0.70)	2.43	(0.94)
Education	8.5	(10.2)	9.7	(7.42)
Nonwhite	.36	(0.48)	.31	(0.46)
Spouse present	.86	(0.35)	.90	(0.30)
1974				
Number	112		403	
Age	61.2	(3.83)	60.2	(3.59)
No. of adults in household	2.13	(0.70)	2.34	(0.85)
Education	8.5	(10.2)	9.7	(7.42)
Nonwhite	.35	(0.48)	.31	(0.46)
Spouse present	.80	(0.40)	.89	(0.31)
1981				
Number	61		306	
Age	68.0	(3.77)	67.1	(3.39)
No. of adults in household	2.18	(0.81)	2.17	(0.73)
Education	9.1	(12.59)	10.1	(6.42)
Nonwhite	.38	(0.49)	.29	(0.45)
Spouse present	.84	(0.37)	.86	(0.34)

Note: Ages in cohort were fifty-one to sixty-two as of 1969.

Of the initial 1974 sample, 112 (22 percent) are tagged as disabled, 403 (78 percent) as nondisabled. Forty-five percent of the disabled group and 24 percent of the nondisabled group dropped out of the sample from 1974 to 1981. The higher dropout rate of the disabled may reflect higher mortality (in part associated with higher average age), more institutionalization, or greater geographic mobility (to the South and Southwest, for example) than among the nondisabled.

Table 10.1 reports the mean and standard deviation of certain demographic and socioeconomic characteristics of the two groups as of 1969, 1974, and 1981.[3] These data indicate that the groups became more alike over the time period analyzed in terms of age and number of adults in the household—two factors that might influence the income measures used below. The difference in age is statistically significant in each of the years; from 1975 on, the difference in the number of adults is not significant. The samples also differ by at least one year of education—a difference likely to be associated with income differences.

3. Even though the sample is the same, the mean and standard deviation of age may differ between 1969 and 1974 because respondents were interviewed in different months of the year.

Table 10.2   **Average Weighted Income of Disabled and Nondisabled, 1969–81 (in 1967 dollars)**

	Pretax Pretransfer Income			Disposable Income		
	Disabled (1)	Nondisabled (2)	(1) ÷ (2)	Disabled (4)	Nondisabled (5)	(4) ÷ (5)
1969	$6,514	$11,397	.572	$6,285	$10,020	.627
1970	5,824	11,443	.509	5,917	10,043	.589
1971	6,155	11,442	.538	6,252	10,190	.614
1972	6,642	11,593	.573	6,773	10,506	.643
1973	6,025	11,270	.535	6,415	10,361	.619
1974	4,753	10,337	.460	5,939	9,651	.615
1975	4,644	9,242	.502	5,542	9,121	.608
1976	4,104	8,524	.481	5,573	9,000	.619
1977	4,169	8,029	.523	5,287	8,837	.598
1978	3,236	7,358	.440	5,722	8,359	.685
1980	3,809	5,417	.703	5,916	7,343	.806
1981	3,083	4,967	.620	5,326	7,294	.730

Note: 1979 is not included due to missing information on the available PSID tape.

10.1.2 Income Status of Older Disabled and Nondisabled Cohorts over Time

Table 10.2 indicates that, throughout the period, the PTY of the disabled members of the cohort is substantially below that of the nondisabled. In all but one year prior to 1980 (when nearly everyone is retired), the expected PTY of the disabled is less than 58 percent of that of the nondisabled and averages about 50 percent. Those classified as disabled have somewhat higher relative income in 1969 (when some of the group may not yet be disabled), but then face generally declining PTY through the rest of the years studied, both absolutely and relative to the nondisabled. Their relative position improves somewhat in the post-1979 period, when the mean PTY of the disabled rises to about 65 percent of that of the nondisabled. This change, however, is due largely to a relative deterioration in the PTY position of the nondisabled as retirement occurs. In constant dollars, the expected PTY of the disabled generally declines as they become older; that of the nondisabled is relatively stable through 1973, and then declines steadily through 1981, but at an accelerating rate after 1979.

Table 10.2 also shows the mean posttax, posttransfer (or disposable) income (DY) of the two groups from 1969–81.[4] The mean DY of the disabled is greater than their PTY in all of the years except 1969, and a ratio between the two measures rises steadily through time. Average DY of the

---

4. In the PSID data, both transfer income and federal income taxes for the family unit are reported in the survey instrument.

disabled group is relatively stable over the entire period, in contrast to that of the nondisabled group. For the nondisabled, mean DY is below mean PTY through 1974, when some of the cohort reaches retirement age. Beyond 1975, and especially in the retirement years after 1979, the mean DY of the nondisabled is above their PTY. Nevertheless, the mean DY of the nondisabled group is lower during postretirement years than during the preretirement years prior to 1979, as the sum of both public and private pensions does not fully offset the decline in earned income.

As a result of this pattern of changes, the ratio of the expected DY of the disabled to that of the nondisabled is substantially greater than the PTY ratio. The DY ratio ranges from .59 to .64 in the preretirement years, and from .73 to .81 in the years after 1979. The PTY ratio decreases from .57 to .44 in the years prior to 1979 and then increases to .70 and .62 in the postretirement period after 1979.

How, then, do each of the cohorts fare, as they move from preretirement to postretirement ages? In terms of PTY, the disabled face a slow and continuing drop from the early 1970s; the nondisabled maintain their higher average income through 1973 and then face a more severe drop in income than do the disabled, as both cohorts pass into retirement years. This pattern does not exist for DY. In preretirement years, the disabled are helped more by the transfer system than are the nondisabled, and their DY is quite stable over the entire period. As retirement occurs, the nondisabled receive increased pension income, and the two groups become more alike in terms of DY.

The important role of federal taxes and transfers in altering the relative DY position of the disabled and the nondisabled is highlighted in table 10.3. In each of the eleven years after 1969, the continued effect of taxes and transfers increases the DY of the disabled, and by increased amounts with time. In contrast, the net effect of federal taxes and transfers on the nondisabled is negative through 1975, when the cohort is fifty-six to sixty-seven years of age. In subsequent years, the combined effect of taxes and transfers on the nondisabled population is positive and steadily increasing. Only in 1981 is the net effect of taxes plus transfers greater for the nondisabled than for the disabled, and then only slightly. Hence, except for the final year, the joint effect of federal taxes and transfers increases the DY of the disabled relative to that of the nondisabled.

The pattern of transfers alone is shown in the last two columns of table 10.3. It is as expected, and consistent with the joint transfer-tax series in the first two columns: (1) transfers to the disabled group increase over time until 1978, (2) transfers to the disabled exceed those to the nondisabled prior to 1980, (3) after 1979, when most individuals in both groups are over sixty-five, transfers to the nondisabled are greater than those to the disabled, reflecting the higher earnings base of retirement pensions of the nondisabled due to both higher earnings during working age and a longer work history.

Table 10.3   **Average Transfers Received and Taxes Paid, Disabled and Nondisabled, 1969–81 (in 1967 dollars)**

	Transfers plus Taxes		Transfers Only	
	Disabled	Nondisabled	Disabled	Nondisabled
1969	$ − 229	$ − 1,377	$ 803	$ 280
1970	+ 93	− 1,400	883	304
1971	+ 97	− 1,252	1,157	377
1972	+ 131	− 1,087	1,232	496
1973	+ 390	− 909	1,436	716
1974	+ 1,186	− 686	1,753	908
1975	+ 898	− 121	1,851	1,215
1976	+ 1,469	+ 476	2,027	1,735
1977	+ 1,091	+ 808	2,570	1,994
1978	+ 2,486	+ 1,001	2,849	2,221
1980	+ 2,107	+ 1,926	2,634	2,655
1981	+ 2,243	+ 2,327	2,726	3,036

Note: 1979 is not included due to missing information on the available PSID tape.

10.1.3   Income Inequality and Uncertainty before and after Retirement: Disabled and Nondisabled

In addition to differences in the average income status of the disabled and the nondisabled, there are important differences between the two groups in (1) the degree of inequality within the two groups and (2) the uncertainty with regard to income expectations faced by individuals in the two groups. We first discuss the concepts of inequality and uncertainty that we use, and then describe our results on inequality and uncertainty for the two groups.

Income Inequality and Income Uncertainty: Definitions

Individuals within any group have differences in their permanent characteristics, which will result in differences in their observed incomes. In addition, some individuals in a group may be lucky during some time period; others may be unlucky. Luck also accounts for variations in income. We refer to the total variation in incomes observed for a group as income *inequality;* it reflects the outcome of all of the factors that contribute to income differences among people—differences in permanent characteristics whether observed or not, and luck.

Uncertainty in expected income is a more limited concept. It refers to the variation in income that individuals face, given their knowledge about all of their relevant permanent characteristics. It is akin to luck. For example, assume that an individual knows the trend of his or her expected income over time, which trend reflects all of his or her relevant permanent characteristics. This trend could be called the "permanent" income trend. Because all of the individual's permanent characteristics are built into the permanent income trend, any remaining variation is stochastic, depending on unexpected changes over time in "permanent" characteristics (e.g., motivation), intertemporal fluctuations in labor market conditions, or simply "luck." Clearly, this remaining variation can be called uncertainty, with no violence done to the term. At any time during the period, the individual may well know the trend value of his or her income, but be quite uncertain regarding whether or not actual income in the next time period will fall above or below that value.

Under certain circumstances, the income inequality within a group and the income uncertainty faced by individuals in the group may closely approximate each other. Consider a particular group, say twenty- to thirty-year-old, white, male, college graduates. The variation in their incomes during a year depicts the prevailing level of income inequality among them. The extent to which that variation is also uncertainty is far less clear. Some of this observed variation may be caused by differences in permanent characteristics among individuals in the group that are not captured by the race, sex, age, and educational characteristics of the group. Differences in such characteristics as tastes for work (motivation), appearance, religion, "connections," or health status will likely account for some of this variation. In addition, transitory labor market vagaries, accidents, or other luck-type variables will also contribute to this variation. Indeed, only if the delineation of the group is very precise and detailed, so that all of the permanent characteristics of the individuals in the group relevant to income are captured by the definition of the group, can observed inequality also be called uncertainty.

Utilizing these definitions, we can measure both the inequality in income within the disabled and nondisabled groups and the level of income uncertainty that individuals in each group face. In the following discussion, the measure of inequality will be based on the deviation of an individual's observed income in a period of time from the mean income of the individuals in the group to which he belongs. If Y_{it}^k = measured income in year t of individual i in group k, $i = 1, N$, this deviation is equal to

$$R_{it}^k = |Y_{it}^k - \sum_{}^{N} Y_{it}^k/N|.$$

The magnitude of these deviations among individuals within a group is summarized in the Atkinson index of inequality, $I = 1 - Y_E/Y_M$, where Y_E is equally distributed income defined as the level of income that, if received by each of the members of the group, would provide the same level of social welfare as the actual distributions of income. The assumed utility function is additive and takes the form $U(Y_i) = \alpha + \beta Y_i^{(1 - \epsilon)}(1 - \epsilon)^{-1}$, Y_M is observed mean income, and ϵ, the degree of aversion to inequality, is set equal to 1.5 (Atkinson 1970). (See Appendix A.)

The summary measure of uncertainty is also based on the variation in individual incomes about some expected value. However, in this case the deviation used is substantially different from that employed in measuring inequality; it is the difference between an individual's observed income at a point in time from the trend value of the individual's own-income stream for that year. Because this trend value is based on the individual's permanent characteristics related to income, it can be considered to be the individual's own evaluation of his permanent income at a point in time. This trend value for year t, then, can be expressed as:

$$\tilde{Y}^k_{it} = \sum_{t=0}^{T} Y^k_{it} - \frac{Y^k_{iT} - Y^k_{i0}}{T-1} (t - T/2),$$

where: $t = 0, \ldots, T,$
and the deviation from the trend value in year t can be expressed as

$$R^k_{it} = | Y^k_{it} - \tilde{Y}^k_{it}|.$$

The measure we will use to compare the uncertainty faced by the disabled and nondisabled groups is also the Atkinson index. In this case we adjust the index by adding the subgroup's matched mean income to the base deviation in order to capture the appropriate uncertainty—uncertainty around the group's expected income. We check it against an alternative measure of uncertainty, relative mean deviation (U), where

$$U = \sum_{i=1}^{N} R^k_{it}/N \Big/ \sum_{i=1}^{N} Y^k_{it}/N = \sum_{i=1}^{N} R^k_{it} \Big/ \sum_{i=1}^{N} Y^k_{it}.[5]$$

Inequality among the Disabled and Nondisabled before and after Retirement

Table 10.4 presents the Atkinson measure of income inequality for both PTY and DY for the disabled and nondisabled cohorts over time. Four primary patterns are present in the data: First, irrespective of the income concept used and the year, the disabled group has greater income inequality than does the nondisabled group. The year-specific ratio of the Atkinson index of the disabled group to that of the nondisabled group is greater than one throughout the period, and for both income concepts. Second, the inequality in the distribution of PTY generally increases as the cohort ages, particularly for the nondisabled. For the nondisabled, the PTY inequality index more than doubles during the preretirement period and continues rising after 1979. Indeed, in the post-1975 period, the index is quite similar for the disabled and nondisabled. Third, the tax-transfer sys-

---

5. We use the relative mean deviation $\left(\sum_{i=1}^{N} R^k_{it} \div \sum_{i=1}^{N} Y^k_{it} \right)$ rather than the mean deviation $\left(\sum_{i=1}^{N} R^k_{it} \right)$ since a \$1,000 deviation from an expected income of \$10,000 is quite different from a \$1,000 deviation from an expected income of \$50,000. To reflect this difference, a percentage formulation is appropriate.

Table 10.4   Atkinson Index of Income Inequality, Disabled and Nondisabled, 1969–81

	Pretax Pretransfer Income			Disposable Income		
	Disabled (1)	Nondisabled (2)	(1) ÷ (2)	Disabled (4)	Nondisabled (5)	(4) ÷ (5)
1969	.822	.367	2.24	.467	.275	1.70
1970	.843	.330	2.55	.443	.241	1.84
1971	.865	.390	2.22	.417	.244	1.71
1972	.844	.488	1.73	.387	.251	1.54
1973	.877	.570	1.54	.400	.254	1.57
1974	.853	.625	1.36	.334	.249	1.34
1975	.870	.681	1.28	.343	.285	1.20
1976	.850	.767	1.11	.306	.268	1.14
1977	.843	.783	1.08	.427	.284	1.50
1978	.868	.769	1.13	.360	.264	1.36
1980	.877	.801	1.09	.347	.287	1.21
1981	.865	.813	1.06	.410	.267	1.54

Note: 1979 is not included due to missing information on the available PSID tape. In Atkinson index, $\epsilon = 1.5$.

tem contributes significantly to a reduction in inequality for both the disabled and the nondisabled groups over the entire period of analysis. Indeed, for the nondisabled, the tax-transfer system reduces income inequality in the retirement years to a level well below that estimated for PTY in the working years. However, inequality of DY for the disabled continues to be above that of the nondisabled, even though they are the primary recipients of transfers. Thus, the disabled group has more income inequality than does its nondisabled counterpart during the entire twelve-year period, irrespective of the income definition used. Finally, during the early part of the twelve-year period—1969–75—the effect of taxes and transfers is to reduce the relative income inequality between the disabled and the nondisabled; the DY ratio lies below that of the PTY ratio. However, as the nondisabled move into retirement and receive retirement pensions, the pattern is reversed. From 1976 on, the disparity in relative income inequality between the two groups is increased by the tax-transfer system.

Income Uncertainty Facing the Disabled and the Nondisabled before and after Retirement

Table 10.5 presents the Atkinson index measuring income uncertainty for the disabled and the nondisabled populations for 1969 to 1981. As indicated above, this statistic reflects the average level of uncertainty facing individuals in each of the two groups over the period 1969–81. This evi-

Table 10.5   **Atkinson Index of Income Uncertainty, Disabled and Nondisabled, 1969–81**

	Pretax Pretransfer Income			Disposable Income		
	Disabled (1)	Nondisabled (2)	(1) ÷ (2)	Disabled (4)	Nondisabled (5)	(4) ÷ (5)
1969	.489	.272	1.80	.251	.204	1.23
1970	.639	.230	2.78	.287	.177	1.62
1971	.704	.265	2.66	.306	.164	1.87
1972	.586	.356	1.65	.237	.121	1.96
1973	.719	.451	1.59	.294	.131	2.24
1974	.683	.535	1.28	.235	.162	1.45
1975	.732	.614	1.20	.282	.223	1.26
1976	.677	.718	0.94	.247	.197	1.25
1977	.635	.709	0.90	.376	.178	2.11
1978	.691	.645	1.07	.222	.110	2.02
1980	.710	.649	1.09	.258	.244	1.06
1981	.693	.588	1.18	.306	.145	2.11

Note: 1979 is not included due to missing information on the available PSID tape. In Atkinson index, $\epsilon = 1.5$.

dence on income uncertainty is complementary to that on income inequality. The typical person in the disabled group faced a higher level of income uncertainty than that faced by the typical nondisabled individual throughout the period using DY and, for all but two years, using PTY. For PTY, the level of uncertainty faced by the disabled was about 190 percent of that faced by the nondisabled in the early part of the period (1969 to 1974); in the latter part of the period, the disabled-nondisabled uncertainty ratio fell to about 1.06. Hence, during the postretirement period, the relative levels of uncertainty were about equal between the groups. The intertemporal pattern for DY was quite different from that of PTY. The ratio fluctuates erratically, reaching a high of 2.24 in 1973 and a low of 1.06 in 1980, but is generally above that measured for PTY. Across the years, the average PTY uncertainty ratio is 1.48; for DY the average ratio is 1.68.

The indicator of income inequality for pretax, pretransfer income (table 10.4) shows increased variation for the nondisabled and relatively constant variation for the disabled as the cohort aged. The corresponding uncertainty indicator suggests the same pattern. Indeed, the ratios comparing income inequality and income uncertainty of the disabled to the nondisabled for PTY follow a similar steadily decreasing pattern from 1970 through 1980, with a slight deviation in pattern in 1981. For both groups, the PTY uncertainty is greater than that of DY, providing evidence that taxes and transfers reduce uncertainty within each of the groups.

If, instead of measuring income uncertainty by the Atkinson index, we use the relative mean deviation (U), we again find that for most years and for both PTY and DY, the typical person in the disabled group faced greater uncertainty than that faced by the typical nondisabled individual. For PTY, the level of uncertainty faced by the disabled was about 140 percent of that faced by the nondisabled, while for DY the income uncertainty faced by the disabled was about 133 percent of that faced by the nondisabled.

Thus, irrespective of the measure of uncertainty used, the conclusion remains the same: the average disabled person faced greater income uncertainty than the average nondisabled person. For both groups, uncertainty is greater using PTY than DY, indicating that taxes and transfers reduce income uncertainty within both of the groups.

10.2   Mean Income, Income Inequality, and Income Uncertainty, 1968–80

In this section we focus on the entire working-age population at two points in time—1968 and 1980—inquiring into the levels of income, income inequality, and income uncertainty among the disabled and nondisabled in these years and the changes in these indicators over the period. First, we will describe the data bases that we will employ, and define the two population groups, the income concept, and the index of inequality and uncertainty. Second, we will present the tabulations of differences in incomes, inequality, and uncertainty between the disabled and nondisabled, based on these definitions.

10.2.1   Data, Definitions, and Concepts

The data used in this analysis are the microdata of the 1969 and 1981 Current Population Survey (CPS), pertaining to income years 1968 and 1980, respectively. The sample is restricted to households in which both a head and spouse are present; single individuals, with or without dependents, are excluded. The weighted number of households is 42.9 million (48.5 million) in 1968 (1980); 69.3 percent (58.8 percent) of the total. This sample was chosen to enable comparison of income, inequality, and uncertainty levels for living units in which (at least) two adults are potential labor market participants.

A determination of the disability status was made for both the head and the spouse in each household. This determination was made on the basis of individual information in the CPS on (1) participation in programs designed for the disabled, (2) nonwork or limited work due to illness or disability, and (3) wage and occupational characteristics consistent with shel-

Table 10.6   Composition of the Disabled and Nondisabled Population in 1968 and 1980, by Age, Education, and Race (in percentages)

	1968		1980	
	Nondisabled	Disabled	Nondisabled	Disabled
Age				
18–35	31.3%	16.2%	33.3%	23.1%
36–64	56.9	66.1	52.5	55.3
65 or more	11.8	17.1	14.2	21.6
	100.0	100.0	100.0	100.0
Education				
< 12 years	40.2	55.8	25.1	42.1
12 years	33.0	26.1	36.7	33.0
> 12 years	26.8	18.1	38.2	24.9
	100.0	100.0	100.0	100.0
Race				
White	92.9	90.4	91.7	89.1
Nonwhite	7.1	9.6	8.3	10.9
	100.0	100.0	100.0	100.0

tered workshop employment.[6] For family heads, 11.73 (12.12) percent were classified as disabled in 1968 (1980); 5.08 (8.24) percent of spouses were so classified in 1968 (1980).

On the basis of this classification, four household disability categories were established: (1) neither head nor spouse disabled, (2) head only disabled, (3) spouse only disabled, (4) both head and spouse disabled. In comparisons presented in the following section, group 1 is taken to be the nondisabled population and group 2 is taken to be the disabled population. The sum of the number of weighted households in these two categories is 94.9 (91.8) percent of the total number of weighted head-and-spouse households in 1968 (1980).

The households in the disabled and nondisabled populations were further subdivided into eighteen age, race, and education categories on the basis of the characteristics of the head. These categories and the percent of the weighted sample in each of the groups are shown in table 10.6.

For each of the eighteen disabled and nondisabled population subgroups, a variety of economic status indicators were calculated for both 1968 and 1980. These include: (1) mean pretax, pretransfer income (PTY), (2) mean posttax, posttransfer (disposable) income (DY),[7] (3) the

6. The criteria for classifying an individual as disabled or not are described in Appendix B. See Wolfe 1979 and 1980 for more detail.

7. The tax calculation adjusts for federal income taxes only. It is simulated using tax tables for the appropriate year (1968 or 1980) assuming (1) all families take the standard deduction appropriate for their family size and age of head and spouse, and (2) the minimum deduction is 10 percent.

Atkinson index of inequality (with $\epsilon = 1.5$) of
dex of inequality (with $\epsilon = 1.5$) of DY.

The first two of these indicators reflect the res
holds both before and after the impacts of a por
dicators for any of the eighteen subgroups of t
abled populations represent the expected va
households in the group. The difference betwee
for any group reflects the impact of those tran
here on the mean income of the group. Compar
mean income levels between the disabled and
(for any age-education-race category) indicates
and transfers in reducing the gap between the
disabled and nondisabled populations in access
taxes and transfers can also be measured over tin
race category.

The second two indicators reflect the inequal
before and after the impacts of transfers and taxe
categories of the disabled and nondisabled pop
the within-group inequality of income can be m
the disabled and the nondisabled, and between
abled with any set of characteristics. Again, co
this indicator for PTY and DY for any subgroup
and transfers in reducing income inequality for
comparison can be made between the disabled a
over time.

10.2.2 Income Status of the Disabled and Non

Table 10.7 presents the calculation of mean P
nondisabled populations for 1968 and 1980; tabl
lation for DY. Breakdowns by age and educatio
down by racial group is discussed in Appendix C

Comparing the total disabled and nondisabled
in PTY is observed for both 1968 and 1980.[8] Thi
While mean real income (in 1968 dollars) rose s
riod for the nondisabled (from $10,200 to $10,
for the disabled (from $7,500 to $6,400). As a res
tween the two groups fell from .74 to .59 over the

This fall in the mean real PTY of the disabled
ed in the middle-age group (36–64), and within th
with twelve years or more than twelve years of
those disabled and in the middle-age group with
education experienced a fall in income from $13

8. Earlier comparisons of the economic status of disable
are Lando and Krute 1976 and Wolfe 1979 and 1980.

Table 10.6   Composition of the Disabled and Nondisabled Population in 1968 and 1980, by Age, Education, and Race (in percentages)

	1968		1980	
	Nondisabled	Disabled	Nondisabled	Disabled
Age				
18–35	31.3%	16.2%	33.3%	23.1%
36–64	56.9	66.1	52.5	55.3
65 or more	11.8	17.1	14.2	21.6
	100.0	100.0	100.0	100.0
Education				
< 12 years	40.2	55.8	25.1	42.1
12 years	33.0	26.1	36.7	33.0
> 12 years	26.8	18.1	38.2	24.9
	100.0	100.0	100.0	100.0
Race				
White	92.9	90.4	91.7	89.1
Nonwhite	7.1	9.6	8.3	10.9
	100.0	100.0	100.0	100.0

tered workshop employment.[6] For family heads, 11.73 (12.12) percent were classified as disabled in 1968 (1980); 5.08 (8.24) percent of spouses were so classified in 1968 (1980).

On the basis of this classification, four household disability categories were established: (1) neither head nor spouse disabled, (2) head only disabled, (3) spouse only disabled, (4) both head and spouse disabled. In comparisons presented in the following section, group 1 is taken to be the nondisabled population and group 2 is taken to be the disabled population. The sum of the number of weighted households in these two categories is 94.9 (91.8) percent of the total number of weighted head-and-spouse households in 1968 (1980).

The households in the disabled and nondisabled populations were further subdivided into eighteen age, race, and education categories on the basis of the characteristics of the head. These categories and the percent of the weighted sample in each of the groups are shown in table 10.6.

For each of the eighteen disabled and nondisabled population subgroups, a variety of economic status indicators were calculated for both 1968 and 1980. These include: (1) mean pretax, pretransfer income (PTY), (2) mean posttax, posttransfer (disposable) income (DY),[7] (3) the

6. The criteria for classifying an individual as disabled or not are described in Appendix B. See Wolfe 1979 and 1980 for more detail.

7. The tax calculation adjusts for federal income taxes only. It is simulated using tax tables for the appropriate year (1968 or 1980) assuming (1) all families take the standard deduction appropriate for their family size and age of head and spouse, and (2) the minimum deduction is 10 percent.

Atkinson index of inequality (with $\epsilon = 1.5$) of PTY, (4) the Atkinson index of inequality (with $\epsilon = 1.5$) of DY.

The first two of these indicators reflect the resources available to households both before and after the impacts of a portion of the fisc. These indicators for any of the eighteen subgroups of the disabled and nondisabled populations represent the expected value of income for the households in the group. The difference between the first two indicators for any group reflects the impact of those transfers and taxes analyzed here on the mean income of the group. Comparison of this difference in mean income levels between the disabled and nondisabled populations (for any age-education-race category) indicates the effect of these taxes and transfers in reducing the gap between the specific categories of the disabled and nondisabled populations in access to income. This effect of taxes and transfers can also be measured over time for any age-education-race category.

The second two indicators reflect the inequality in income flows both before and after the impacts of transfers and taxes for each of the eighteen categories of the disabled and nondisabled populations. Comparison of the within-group inequality of income can be made among subgroups of the disabled and the nondisabled, and between the disabled and nondisabled with any set of characteristics. Again, comparing the difference in this indicator for PTY and DY for any subgroup shows the effect of taxes and transfers in reducing income inequality for that subgroup, and this comparison can be made between the disabled and the nondisabled, and over time.

10.2.2   Income Status of the Disabled and Nondisabled, 1968–80

Table 10.7 presents the calculation of mean PTY for the disabled and nondisabled populations for 1968 and 1980; table 10.8 presents the calculation for DY. Breakdowns by age and education are shown. The breakdown by racial group is discussed in Appendix C.

Comparing the total disabled and nondisabled populations, a wide gap in PTY is observed for both 1968 and 1980.[8] This is shown in table 10.7. While mean real income (in 1968 dollars) rose slightly over this time period for the nondisabled (from $10,200 to $10,800), it fell substantially for the disabled (from $7,500 to $6,400). As a result, the ratio of PTY between the two groups fell from .74 to .59 over the twelve-year period.

This fall in the mean real PTY of the disabled population is concentrated in the middle-age group (36–64), and within that group especially those with twelve years or more than twelve years of education. For example, those disabled and in the middle-age group with more than a high school education experienced a fall in income from $13,100 to $10,400 over the

8. Earlier comparisons of the economic status of disabled and nondisabled households are Lando and Krute 1976 and Wolfe 1979 and 1980.

Table 10.7   Mean Pretax, Pretransfer Income (PTY) of Disabled and Nondisabled Household Heads (in 1968 dollars)

	Disabled		Nondisabled		Ratio of Disabled to Nondisabled	
	1968	1980	1968	1980	1968	1980
Young head (18–35)						
Schooling:						
< 12 years	$ 5,512	$ 5,087	$ 7,282	$ 6,537	0.76	0.78
12 years	8,556	7,082	9,004	8,911	0.95	0.79
> 12 years	9,676	8,851	11,006	11,577	0.88	0.76
Middle-age head (36–64)						
Schooling:						
< 12 years	6,718	5,657	9,364	9,383	0.72	0.60
12 years	9,785	7,579	11,804	12,249	0.83	0.62
> 12 years	13,132	10,398	15,953	16,023	0.82	0.65
Older head (65 +)						
Schooling:						
< 12 years	2,169	2,006	3,668	3,153	0.59	0.64
12 years	3,614	3,400	5,370	4,876	0.67	0.70
> 12 years	4,559	4,887	9,007	8,376	0.51	0.58
TOTAL	7,514	6,397	10,182	10,752	0.74	0.59

Note: Presents disabled and nondisabled household heads, in head-spouse families, by head characteristic.

period. A similar pattern of reductions exists for the disabled in the younger group, although the falloff is not as substantial as for those in the middle-age group.

The pattern of PTY for the nondisabled group shows far less change over the period than for the disabled group. Some decrease in PTY is observed for the young group of nondisabled families with less education. Income for all of the education groups in the middle-age category of non-disabled workers showed some small increase; however, a sizable decrease in real PTY is observed for all education categories among the older group.

As a result of these income changes over the period, the pattern of intertemporal change in the disabled-nondisabled PTY income ratio varies substantially among the groups. For all of the groups with a head younger than sixty-five years of age (except one), the ratio falls substantially over the period. The greatest reductions are for the middle-age group, especially those with the most education (e.g., for the middle-age group with twelve years of education, the fall in the mean PTY ratio is from .83 to .62 over the period).

Table 10.8 presents the same comparisons, but using DY rather than PTY. For both groups, mean DY rose somewhat over the period, with the larger increase experienced by the nondisabled. The ratio of incomes be-

Table 10.8   Mean Disposable Income (DY) of Disabled and Nondisabled Household Heads (in 1968 dollars)

	Disabled		Nondisabled		Ratio of Disabled to Nondisabled	
	1968	1980	1968	1980	1968	1980
Young head (18–35)						
Schooling:						
< 12 years	$ 5,403	$ 5,334	$ 6,268	$ 6,033	0.86	0.88
12 years	7,560	7,043	7,589	7,768	1.00	0.91
> 12 years	8,279	8,525	9,082	9,502	0.91	0.90
Middle-age head (36–64)						
Schooling:						
< 12 years	6,673	6,630	7,964	8,342	0.84	0.79
12 years	8,782	8,645	9,886	10,490	0.89	0.82
> 12 years	11,104	10,876	12,967	12,967	0.86	0.84
Older head (65 +)						
Schooling:						
< 12 years	3,853	4,909	5,078	5,821	0.76	0.84
12 years	5,152	6,696	6,473	8,010	0.80	0.84
> 12 years	6,334	8,234	9,381	11,503	0.68	0.72
TOTAL	7,231	7,523	8,738	9,581	0.83	0.79

Note: Presents disabled and nondisabled household heads, in head-spouse families, by head characteristic.

tween the two groups fell slightly (from .83 to .79), in spite of the rapid growth in disability transfers over this period. By and large, the patterns are similar, although the changes are not as substantial as those observed using PTY.

For both the disabled and nondisabled groups, real DY remained virtually unchanged over the period for both the younger and middle-age groups, irrespective of educational level. For the older group, sizeable increases in mean real DY are recorded for all of the education groups, with the largest increases experienced by the highest education group. For example, for the older group with more than twelve years of education, real mean DY rose from $6,300 to $8,200 for the disabled population and from $9,400 to $11,500 for the nondisabled. Indeed, mean DY for the older nondisabled group with more than a high school education was the second highest of all of the groups, exceeded only by the middle-age nondisabled group with more than a high school education.

Some deterioration in the disabled-nondisabled DY ratio over the decade of the 1970s is seen for nearly all groups other than the oldest age group, where an increase is recorded for all of the education categories.

By comparing the data in tables 10.7 and 10.8, the changing role of the tax-transfer system can be observed. In 1968 the combination of taxes and

Table 10.9   **Atkinson Inequality Index of Pretax, Pretransfer Income (PTY) of Disabled and Nondisabled Household Heads (in 1968 dollars)**

	Disabled		Nondisabled		Ratio of Disabled to Nondisabled	
	1968	1980	1968	1980	1968	1980
Young head (18–35)						
Schooling:						
< 12 years	.631	.666	.227	.452	2.78	1.47
12 years	.246	.561	.154	.243	1.60	2.31
> 12 years	.237	.324	.201	.196	1.18	1.65
Middle-age head (36–64)						
Schooling:						
< 12 years	.715	.746	.300	.373	2.39	2.00
12 years	.537	.682	.210	.263	2.56	2.59
> 12 years	.559	.644	.244	.249	2.29	2.59
Older head (65 +)						
Schooling:						
< 12 years	.817	.766	.808	.760	1.01	1.01
12 years	.804	.743	.783	.716	1.03	1.04
> 12 years	.861	.776	.786	.716	1.10	1.08
TOTAL	.759	.751	.487	.515	1.56	1.46

Note: In Atkinson index, $\epsilon = 1.5$.

transfers increased the income ratio between the two groups from .74 (PTY) to .83 (DY). In 1980 the tax-transfer system had a substantially larger effect; the PTY ratio of .59 was increased to a DY ratio of .79.[9] In spite of this, the real DY gap between the disabled and nondisabled groups was larger in 1980 than in 1968.

10.2.3 Income Inequality between the Disabled and Nondisabled, 1968–80

Table 10.9 presents the calculation of the income inequality indicators based on PTY for each of the subgroups of the disabled and nondisabled populations for 1968 and 1980; Table 9.10 presents the within-group inequality calculations for DY.

Table 10.9 indicates that, irrespective of subgroup, inequality is larger for the disabled population than for the nondisabled. The index of within-group inequality for the entire disabled group was 156 percent of that for the nondisabled in 1968, and only a slightly smaller 146 percent in 1980. The ratio of the disabled-nondisabled indexes is substantially greater for

9. The growth in transfers targeted on the disabled grew rapidly during the decade of the 1970s. From 1965 to 1978, public expenditures (in current dollars) on programs targeted on the disabled grew from $8 billion to $82 billion. See Burkhauser and Haveman 1982.

the middle-age group than for either the younger or the older groups, and stands at 2.00 or more for all educational categories for this age group in both of the years. For the older group, the level of within-group inequality of PTY is only slightly larger for the disabled than for the nondisabled groups.

The stability in the disabled-nondisabled PTY inequality index ratio over time, however, disguises the fact that within-group inequality for both disabled and nondisabled groups rose from 1968 to 1980 for nearly all of the subgroups in the younger and middle-age ranges. However, for the group of families whose head is over sixty-five years, the income inequality index based on PTY fell for both the disabled and nondisabled from 1968 to 1980.

Table 10.10 presents the inequality indexes for both groups in 1968 and 1980, but in terms of DY, rather than PTY. All of the indexes are lower for both groups, and in both years, than those recorded for PTY. This is especially true for the disabled groups, irrespective of age, and for the above-sixty-five group of the nondisabled population. For both the disabled and nondisabled groups taken as a whole, the DY indexes are less than one-half the value of those based on PTY. The disabled-nondisabled ratio in 1968 was 1.39 based on DY; it fell to 1.30 by 1980.

Table 10.10   **Atkinson Inequality Index and Disposable Income (DY) of Disabled and Nondisabled Household Heads (in 1968 dollars)**

	Disabled		Nondisabled		Ratio of Disabled to Nondisabled	
	1968	1980	1968	1980	1968	1980
Young head (18–35)						
Schooling:						
< 12 years	.341	.309	.197	.264	1.73	1.17
12 years	.127	.219	.130	.165	0.98	1.33
> 12 years	.170	.148	.175	.145	0.97	1.02
Middle-age head (36–64)						
Schooling:						
< 12 years	.293	.305	.223	.202	1.31	1.51
12 years	.264	.240	.152	.150	1.74	1.60
> 12 years	.339	.239	.178	.146	1.90	1.64
Older head (65+)						
Schooling:						
< 12 years	.256	.239	.283	.250	0.90	0.96
12 years	.255	.225	.285	.243	0.89	0.93
> 12 years	.296	.386	.345	.379	0.86	1.02
TOTAL	.327	.288	.235	.221	1.39	1.30

Note: In Atkinson index, $\epsilon = 1.5$.

Again, the disabled-nondisabled ratio of the within-group inequality indexes is largest for the middle-age groups, ranging from 1.31 to 1.90 in 1968 and 1.51 to 1.64 in 1980. For the young group, the ratio of the inequality indexes was relatively close to one—ranging from .97 to 1.73 across the educational groups in 1968 and from 1.02 to 1.33 in 1980. The major change from the results on within-group inequality based on PTY occurs in the groups of aged heads. Using DY as the indicator of well-being, the level of inequality for the aged who are disabled is less than that for the aged nondisabled in both of the years. In 1968 the disabled-nondisabled inequality ratio for the older population group ranged from .86 to .90 across the education categories; in 1980, the ratio ranged from .93 to 1.02.

10.2.4 Uncertainty between the Disabled and Nondisabled, 1968–80

The previous section indicated that the disabled with almost any set of age-education-race characteristics tend to experience greater within-group income inequality than do the nondisabled with these same characteristics. Is this information in itself sufficient to claim that the disabled in general, or those in any subgroup, face greater income uncertainty than do their disabled counterparts? As indicated above, if the characteristics used to define a group composed the full set of permanent characteristics relevant to the income determination process, the income inequality within the group and the income uncertainty facing individuals within the group would be equivalent concepts. Somewhat more generally, the measured income inequality of each of two groups can be interpreted as differences in the levels of uncertainty facing individuals in the two groups only if the definition of the groups is sufficiently precise to capture all of the relevant permanent characteristics of the members of the groups. While age, education, race, and sex would appear to be among the most important determinants of income, the existence of other characteristics not captured in the definitions of our groups implies that our measures of income inequality may not, in themselves, be reliable indicators of income uncertainty.

However, this is not to say that the measure of income inequality can give no indication of the relative degrees of uncertainty among groups. Indeed, if for each group the contribution to inequality in incomes of permanent characteristics *not* used to define the groups is a constant proportion of the inequality attributable to *all* of the relevant permanent characteristics in the two groups, the ratio of income inequality between the groups also measures the relative extent of uncertainty facing individuals within the groups.

A crude measure of the extent to which income inequality proxies for income uncertainty can be obtained from calculations based on the longitudinal data analyzed in section 10.1. Using PTY, the ratio of income uncertainty to income inequality[10] in the sample over the twelve-year period is slightly greater for the nondisabled than for the disabled using the Atkinson index, and equal using the relative mean deviation measure of variation.[11] Using the DY concept, the uncertainty-to-inequality ratio is higher for the disabled than for the nondisabled using both measures of variation.[12] For both income concepts, then, the proportion of measured inequality that is attributable to uncertainty appears to be similar for the disabled and for the nondisabled. Hence, irrespective of income concept, the uncertainty of income facing the disabled appears to be substantially greater than that facing the nondisabled. In addition to the fact that those in the disabled population have lower and more unequally distributed incomes than the nondisabled, the disabled also confront greater uncertainty in income flows than do the nondisabled. Indeed, the differences in disposable income inequality between the disabled and nondisabled reported in table 10.10 would appear to understate the differences in income uncertainty faced by these two groups.

10.3 Conclusions

Disabled individuals fare worse in terms of PTY than do the nondisabled. The tax and transfer system reduces these differences so that DY of these two groups is less dissimilar than PTY. Nevertheless, the income available to the disabled is less than that available to the nondisabled. Moreover, both PTY and DY are more unequally distributed for the disabled than for the nondisabled, although again the tax and transfer system reduces this inequality of income for both groups.

The uncertainty of income, another aspect of economic well-being, is greater for the disabled than the nondisabled, also suggesting that the disabled are worse off than the nondisabled. The disparity between the disabled and the nondisabled in income uncertainty was found to persist over time for a single age cohort.

10. The uncertainty-to-inequality ratios measure the dispersion of an individual's income from the individual's own expected trend value based on individual observed incomes over the twelve-year period of observation, relative to the dispersion of an individual's income from the mean trend value of all observations in the individual's group. The groups are the disabled and the nondisabled. Using these ratios to implicitly measure differentials in uncertainty between the disabled and the nondisabled rests on two assumptions: (1) the uncertainty-to-inequality ratios measured for the group of older males in the longitudinal data accurately proxy the ratios for all males eighteen years or older (the sample used in the cross-sectional analysis); and (2) the uncertainty-to-inequality ratios of the disabled and nondisabled in the longitudinal data are applicable to the somewhat different definitions of these two groups in the cross-sectional data (see note 13).

11. For the Atkinson and relative mean deviation measures, the uncertainty-inequality ratios were .77 (disabled) versus .80 (nondisabled), and .44 for both, respectively.

12. For the Atkinson and relative mean deviation measures, the uncertainty-inequality ratios were .72 (disabled) versus .65 (nondisabled), and .41 versus .38, respectively.

Over the time period studied in the cross-sectional analysis, the expected income of the disabled deteriorated relative to the nondisabled. The deterioration was substantial using PTY, but was partially offset by the growth of the tax-transfer system. Hence, the deterioration in relative DY (and growth of the absolute dollar difference in DY between the two groups) was small. From 1968 to 1980 the average expected net transfer of income to the disabled increased by approximately $1,400 (in constant dollars).

Following a single age cohort through time shows a similar picture. Over the 1969–79 preretirement period, the expected PTY of the disabled deteriorated relative to that of the nondisabled. The tax-transfer system made up most of this deterioration, however, as the absolute amount of transfers (and transfers less taxes) to the disabled increased over time until 1979. During the postretirement period after 1979, however, the PTY of the nondisabled group deteriorated substantially owing to the reduction in labor force participation. At this time the transfers received by the nondisabled increased substantially and exceeded those received by the disabled.

For the disabled as well as the nondisabled, both income inequality and uncertainty in PTY increased over the period from 1968 to 1980. The exception is for those in the retirement years. The cross-sectional analysis shows that for older heads, the PTY inequality index declined from 1968 to 1980. For the cohort traced over time, the inequality index for PTY increased over the twelve years studied for the nondisabled but stayed constant for the disabled. The index of PTY uncertainty followed a similar pattern.

Inequality and uncertainty of expected income is reduced by the tax-transfer system. The indexes of inequality in DY are substantially lower than for PTY. In the cross-sectional results, the inequality in the distribution of DY for the disabled is generally greater than that for the nondisabled. The exception is among the sixty-five-or-older age group in both 1968 and 1980. This pattern does not hold in the longitudinal analysis. Here, even in the retirement years, the index of inequality of DY for the disabled is greater than that facing the nondisabled.[13]

Both of these approaches—cross-sectional and longitudinal—suggest that the nondisabled become more like the disabled in terms of PTY as they reach retirement age. This is largely due to a deterioration in the earnings of the nondisabled as they age. In the retirement years, the DY of the

13. This difference may be caused by differences in the definitions of the disabled and nondisabled groups in the two sections of the study. The CPS disabled post-sixty-five group is more homogeneous than that in the analysis based on the Michigan data. All of the CPS disabled older than sixty-five are disabled at each point in time and are part of intact head-spouse families. The longitudinal analysis defines men as disabled as of 1974, but some of them may not be disabled in the later years, and they may or may not be part of an intact family.

two groups also becomes less dissimilar, as both
reliant on transfers. Nevertheless, the relative posi
pears to have deteriorated over time in terms of
spective of the income concept used.

The implications of these results are important
transfer income below that of labor market income
centive grounds, the resulting income gap reflects
come inequality among the disabled nor the grea
that they face relative to the nondisabled. Indeed,
lying on transfers is often viewed as "guaranteed
that the substantial DY gap between the disabled
compounded by greater inequality within the disa
uncertainty in income expectations for the disable
the rapid growth of the transfer system, the relative
disabled is viewed as having improved over time
fact, it has not. Finally, the greater existing incom
tainty faced by the disabled relative to the nondis
upon current policy designed to remove from the
recipients through reexamination and applicatio
standards. Is it sound policy to increase income in
certainty for those already disadvantaged in this
more appropriate to look to reform in the current
for the disabled, a reform designed to integrate
grams—Social Security Disability Insurance tied t
totally and permanently disabled, earnings-condit
curity Income, workers' compensation, vocatio
training, labor market opportunities, private insu
may provide adequate incomes to many of the dis
to fall through the cracks?

References

Atkinson, Anthony. 1970. On the measurement o
    Economic Theory 2: 244–63.
Burkhauser, Richard, and Robert Haveman. 198
    The economics of American policy. Baltimore:
    sity Press.
Johnson, William R. 1977. Uncertainty and the d
    In The distribution of economic well-being, ed.
    York: National Bureau of Economic Research a

Over the time period studied in the cross-sectional analysis, the expected income of the disabled deteriorated relative to the nondisabled. The deterioration was substantial using PTY, but was partially offset by the growth of the tax-transfer system. Hence, the deterioration in relative DY (and growth of the absolute dollar difference in DY between the two groups) was small. From 1968 to 1980 the average expected net transfer of income to the disabled increased by approximately $1,400 (in constant dollars).

Following a single age cohort through time shows a similar picture. Over the 1969–79 preretirement period, the expected PTY of the disabled deteriorated relative to that of the nondisabled. The tax-transfer system made up most of this deterioration, however, as the absolute amount of transfers (and transfers less taxes) to the disabled increased over time until 1979. During the postretirement period after 1979, however, the PTY of the nondisabled group deteriorated substantially owing to the reduction in labor force participation. At this time the transfers received by the nondisabled increased substantially and exceeded those received by the disabled.

For the disabled as well as the nondisabled, both income inequality and uncertainty in PTY increased over the period from 1968 to 1980. The exception is for those in the retirement years. The cross-sectional analysis shows that for older heads, the PTY inequality index declined from 1968 to 1980. For the cohort traced over time, the inequality index for PTY increased over the twelve years studied for the nondisabled but stayed constant for the disabled. The index of PTY uncertainty followed a similar pattern.

Inequality and uncertainty of expected income is reduced by the tax-transfer system. The indexes of inequality in DY are substantially lower than for PTY. In the cross-sectional results, the inequality in the distribution of DY for the disabled is generally greater than that for the nondisabled. The exception is among the sixty-five-or-older age group in both 1968 and 1980. This pattern does not hold in the longitudinal analysis. Here, even in the retirement years, the index of inequality of DY for the disabled is greater than that facing the nondisabled.[13]

Both of these approaches—cross-sectional and longitudinal—suggest that the nondisabled become more like the disabled in terms of PTY as they reach retirement age. This is largely due to a deterioration in the earnings of the nondisabled as they age. In the retirement years, the DY of the

---

13. This difference may be caused by differences in the definitions of the disabled and nondisabled groups in the two sections of the study. The CPS disabled post-sixty-five group is more homogeneous than that in the analysis based on the Michigan data. All of the CPS disabled older than sixty-five are disabled at each point in time and are part of intact head-spouse families. The longitudinal analysis defines men as disabled as of 1974, but some of them may not be disabled in the later years, and they may or may not be part of an intact family.

two groups also becomes less dissimilar, as both groups become heavily reliant on transfers. Nevertheless, the relative position of the disabled appears to have deteriorated over time in terms of expected income, irrespective of the income concept used.

The implications of these results are important. First, while disability transfer income below that of labor market income is justified on work incentive grounds, the resulting income gap reflects neither the greater income inequality among the disabled nor the greater income uncertainty that they face relative to the nondisabled. Indeed, the income of those relying on transfers is often viewed as "guaranteed." Our results indicate that the substantial DY gap between the disabled and the nondisabled is compounded by greater inequality within the disabled group and greater uncertainty in income expectations for the disabled. Second, because of the rapid growth of the transfer system, the relative economic status of the disabled is viewed as having improved over time and through time. In fact, it has not. Finally, the greater existing income inequality and uncertainty faced by the disabled relative to the nondisabled should cast doubt upon current policy designed to remove from the rolls current disability recipients through reexamination and application of stricter eligibility standards. Is it sound policy to increase income inequality and income uncertainty for those already disadvantaged in this regard? Would it not be more appropriate to look to reform in the current income support system for the disabled, a reform designed to integrate a set of transfer programs—Social Security Disability Insurance tied to prior earnings for the totally and permanently disabled, earnings-conditioned Supplemental Security Income, workers' compensation, vocational rehabilitation and training, labor market opportunities, private insurance—that at present may provide adequate incomes to many of the disabled, but allows others to fall through the cracks?

References

Atkinson, Anthony. 1970. On the measurement of inequality. *Journal of Economic Theory* 2: 244–63.

Burkhauser, Richard, and Robert Haveman. 1982. *Disability and work: The economics of American policy.* Baltimore: Johns Hopkins University Press.

Johnson, William R. 1977. Uncertainty and the distribution of earnings. In *The distribution of economic well-being,* ed. F. Thomas Juster. New York: National Bureau of Economic Research and Ballinger Press.

Lando, Mordechai E., and Aaron Krute. 1976. Disability insurance: Program issues and research. *Social Security Bulletin* (Oct.): 3–17.

Projector, D. S., and E. G. Murray. 1978. *Eligibility for welfare and participation rates.* U.S. Department of Health, Education, and Welfare, Social Security Administration, HEW 78–11776.

Wolfe, Barbara L. 1979. Impacts of disability and some policy implications. Discussion paper no. 539–79. Institute for Research on Poverty, University of Wisconsin, Madison.

_____. 1980. How the disabled fare in the labor market. *Monthly Labor Review* (Sept.): 48–52.

Appendix A
Calculating the Atkinson Index

The Atkinson index of inequality is based on a concept of equally distributed income (Y_E) and reflects aversion to inequality of income. An additive (strictly concave) concept of social welfare is assumed where each individual's utility equals

$$U(Y_i) = \alpha + \beta Y_i^{(1 - \epsilon)} (1 - \epsilon)^{-1}.$$

The value of ϵ chosen reflects the degree of aversion to inequality.

In this analysis, α is set equal to 0 and β to 1. Y_E, the equally distributed income, is calculated by

$$\sum_{i=1}^{n} U(Y_i) = \sum_{i=1}^{n} [Y_i^{(1 - \epsilon)} (1 - \epsilon)^{-1}],$$

$$U(Y) = \frac{\sum_{i=1}^{n} U(Y_i)}{n}$$

$$Y_E = U(Y)(1 - \epsilon)^{\frac{1}{1-\epsilon}}.$$

Thus Y_E is the level of income that, if received by each of the n members of society, would provide the same level of social welfare as the actual distribution of income (the Y_is).

Then, the Atkinson index is calculated by the following formula:

$$I = 1 - \frac{Y_\epsilon}{\overline{Y}}, \text{ where } \overline{Y} \equiv \text{ mean of } Y_i \text{ or } \frac{\sum_{i=1}^{n} Y_i}{n}.$$

Appendix B
Definition of Disabled in Cross-Sectional Analysis

In the cross-sectional analysis reported here, a broad definition of long-term disability is used. The disabled are defined by three basic categories: program participation, work limitation, and low wage and participation in a sheltered workshop-type occupation. These categories reflect a goal of defining as disabled all those who are disabled in a long-term sense—not just those who are working part time or who are being served by a program for the disabled.

There are a number of programs designed specifically for the disabled. Included are Social Security Disability Insurance (SSDI); Supplemental Security Income (SSI), an income-tested program; railroad disability annuities; workers' compensation; and veterans' benefits.

Except for payments under the Social Security program and railroad retirement, individuals who receive any dollar benefits from one or more of these programs are designated as disabled. The exceptions include those who receive veterans' benefits only and who are veterans and nonstudents. Among Social Security recipients aged twenty to sixty-four, the following distinctions define the disabled: individuals nineteen to sixty-one who are not students, or students twenty-three to sixty-one, or widow(er)s nineteen to fifty-nine who have no dependent children under eighteen. These distinctions are based on program eligibility.

Individuals are also defined as disabled because they do not work or are limited in the amount of work they can perform. Individuals who do not work are so designated for one of the following two reasons: either the main reason they did not work last year is that they were ill or disabled (variable $P133 = 1$, 1980 CPS tape), or they are classified as unable to work on the employment status recode (variable $P12 = 6$). The latter variable is the one generally used by the Bureau of Labor Statistics.

Individuals are designated as "limited in amount of work" if personal illness is the reason they usually work less than thirty-five hours. This classification is given to two groups: one that worked some last week, but less than 35 hours, and another that did not work last week (variable $P18 = 2$ and $P19 = 10$, or $P23 = 2$ and $P21 = 1$). Alternatively, individuals are designated disabled if they work less than fifty weeks and most of the remaining weeks are ill or disabled ($P145 = 1$). The definitions for 1968 are analogous but the variable numbers differ. In a sense, this attempt to define an eligible population is similar to that used by Projector and Murray (1978), who use the 1971 CPS to attempt to identify those eligible for welfare.

Thus, this approach defines as disabled those who are unable to work or are ill for substantial periods of time, while excluding those who missed work for short periods of time because of short-term, acute illnesses.

Individuals who work in programs designed especially for the disabled are also included in the definition of disability. Many of these may not respond to inquiries directed at work limitations, so an additional definition is used. Individuals whose hourly wage rate is positive but less than $1.00 are included as disabled if their occupation is one that is included in sheltered workshops. These include services such as nonprivate housecleaning, food, health and personnel, certain laborers, some operatives, and certain sales and clerical workers. A total of 0.04 percent of heads in 1968 and 0.8 percent in 1980 are designated as disabled by this definition.

Using all three factors to define disability, the proportions of disabled are 14.6 percent in 1968 and 15.9 percent in 1980. In Wolfe (1980) this measure of disability is compared to the self-assessment designation used in the 1972 Survey of Disabled Adults (SDA). Using the 1977 CPS and our definition, 13.5 percent of men are defined as disabled; the comparable percentage is 14.0 for the SDA. In other respects, the two surveys (CPS and SDA) show similar disabled population patterns: more disabled in the South than in the other regions, fewer whites disabled than nonwhites, and a greater percentage of disabled among older age groups.

Appendix C

Income and Inequality Comparisons of White and Nonwhite Disabled and Nondisabled Populations, 1968–80

Table 10.A.1 indicates the changes in DY for white and nonwhite disabled and nondisabled households over the 1968–80 period. Looking first at the disabled groups in 1968, it is clear that black households fared far worse than their white disabled counterparts; black disabled households had but 72 percent of the DY of white disabled households. For the nondisabled population, the comparable 1968 figure was 80 percent. The relative status of nonwhite disabled households improved substantially from 1968 to 1980, however, and in the latter year nonwhite disabled families had 89 percent of the income of their white disabled counterparts. The relative nonwhite gains for the nondisabled population are much smaller—an increase from 80 to 90 percent. From the population subgroup comparison, it appears that the smallest nonwhite-white ratios are for the middle-age, less-educated populations.

This 1968–80 gain in DY for the nonwhite disabled relative to white disabled is due to both the improved relative status of disabled nonwhites in the labor market and the rapid expansion of the transfer system during this period. From 1968 to 1980, the ratio of nonwhite to white PTY for the disabled population increased from .62 to .91. For the same two years, the

Table 10.A.1   Nonwhite-White Ratio of Mean Disposable Income (DY)
                 (in 1968 dollars)

	Disabled		Nondisabled	
	1968	1980	1968	1980
Young head (*18–35*)				
Schooling:				
< 12 years	.82	—	.86	.87
12 years	—	.97	.87	.99
> 12 years	—	1.07	.98	1.00
Middle-age head (*36–64*)				
Schooling:				
< 12 years	.80	.88	.80	.91
12 years	.95	.99	.88	.98
> 12 years	—	.97	.92	.91
Older head (*65+*)				
Schooling:				
< 12 years	.75	.66	.92	.86
12 years	—	—	—	.97
> 12 years	—	—	—	.80
TOTAL	.72	.89	.80	.90

Note: Represents disabled and nondisabled household heads, in head-spouse families, by head characteristic.

tax-transfer system raised PTY of black disabled individuals by 11 and 15 percent, respectively (see table 10.A.2). The increased impact of the tax-transfer systems on the white disabled population is even more remarkable. The system actually lowered white disabled PTY by 5 percent in 1968, but raised it by 18 percent in 1980. Thus, over the period, disabled nonwhites improved their labor market performance relative to disabled whites, while the rapidly growing income transfer system appears to have concentrated its increased benefit flows on the white, relative to the nonwhite, disabled population. This comparison raises the conjecture that the transfer system in 1968 targeted benefits on nonwhite relative to white disabled households and that expansion in the system from 1968 to 1980 was

Table 10.A.2   Percentage Change in Income Due to the Tax-Transfer System
                 (in 1968 dollars)

	Disabled		Nondisabled	
	1968	1980	1968	1980
Nonwhites	.11	.15	−.13	−.09
Whites	−.05	.18	−.14	−.11

Note: Represents white and nonwhite, disabled and nondisabled household heads in head-spouse families.

Table 10.A.3   Atkinson Index of Disposable Income Inequality (in 1968 dollars)

	Disabled		Nondisabled	
	1968	1980	1968	1980
Whites	.319	.280	.230	.215
Nonwhites	.347	.343	.274	.278
Nonwhite-white ratio	1.09	1.23	1.19	1.29

Note: Represents white and nonwhite, disabled and nondisabled household heads in head-spouse families. In Atkinson index, $\epsilon = 1.5$.

focused on the white disabled population. In both 1968 and 1980 the tax-transfer system decreased the incomes of the nondisabled population—by about 13 percent in 1968 and 9 to 11 percent in 1980. The reduction in the negative impact is again due to the rapid expansion of the transfer system from 1968 to 1980.

The patterns of DY inequality between whites and nonwhites are shown in table 10.A.3. They indicate that, even after the effect of the tax-transfer system, inequality is higher among nonwhite families than among white disabled families in both years. Indeed, from 1968 to 1980 the nonwhite-white ratio for the disabled increased from 1.09 to 1.23. This change is also consistent with the conjecture that the growth in the transfer system from 1968 to 1980 was relatively targeted on the white disabled population. For nondisabled families, a similar nonwhite-white pattern holds with nonwhite, nondisabled families experiencing more inequality in DY than white nondisabled families. The 1968–80 increase in the ratio for nondisabled is not as severe as that for the disabled.

Comment   Dan Usher

1. Suppose for some group of people, the income of the i person in the t year is

$$Y_{it} = \overline{Y} + Y_t + Y_i + \eta,$$

where $\overline{Y}$ is the double mean of all incomes in all years, Y_t is the average deviation of income in the year t, Y_i is the average deviation of the income of the person i, and η is a random variable independent of i and t. By definition, the means of Y_t and Y_i are both zero. What Haveman and Wolfe call inequality would seem to correspond to the average of the variances of the series Y_{1t}, Y_{2t}, Y_{3t}, . . . for every year t. What Haveman and Wolfe call uncertainty would seem to correspond to the average of the variances of the

Dan Usher is professor of economics at Queen's University, Ontario.

detrended series Y_{i1}, Y_{i2}, Y_{i3}, . . . for every person i. Obviously both variances would in general be positive along with the variance of η. It follows that what appears as inequality in a given year may be nothing more than a reflection of uncertainty. Even if all the terms Y_i were equal to zero, some variation in the series Y_{1t}, Y_{2t}, Y_{3t}, . . . would still occur. This variation would not be indicative of a fundamental inequality because an above-average income this year would be no predictor that one's income would be above average next year as well. It should be possible to mix the time-series and cross-sectional data so as to yield an unbiased estimate of the variance of Y_i alone rather than of the sum of Y_i and η. Similarly it should be possible to construct an Atkinson inequality index that is not biased by the variance of η.

2. It might be interesting to experiment with different values of ϵ in the utility function $U = Y^{1-\epsilon}/(1 - \epsilon)$. A value of $\epsilon = 1.5$ means that an uncertain income consisting of a 50 percent chance of $100,000 and a 50 percent chance of $25,000 has a certainty equivalent of $44,000. That does not seem too far off the mark, but may be a little low for many people.

3. The great disparity between incomes of disabled and nondisabled among the highly educated may arise because disability destroys human capital acquired before the onset of the disability. Also, for educated and uneducated alike, variation of income among the disabled may reflect variation in the extent of the disability.

4. From the way the data are presented, it is difficult to tell whether the disabled are receiving transfers because they are disabled or because they are poor. Of two people with identical pretax and pretransfer incomes, one disabled and the other not, does the former get the higher posttax and posttransfer income? This question has some bearing on the finding that differences between disabled and nondisabled are closer for posttax and posttransfer income than for pretax and pretransfer income. It would be a simple matter to reconstruct tables to deal with this question, so as to be able to say, for example, that x cents out of every dollar of transfers to the disabled is because they are poor and $100 - x$ cents is an additional transfer because they are disabled. It would also be useful to make allowance for transfers in kind.

5. Little discussion takes place in this chapter of the social or political significance of the numbers. In particular, it is questionable whether inequality among the disabled ought to be a consideration of public policy. We are concerned as a society to reduce inequality in total. We are not concerned about inequality among academics, doctors, lawyers, or taxi drivers. Academics may be concerned about inequality among academics, but that is of little interest to anyone else. Similarly with the disabled. Suppose A and B are both disabled, and society has decided that A who is poor is to be assisted in some manner. Should it make any difference to that decision whether B is rich or very rich? Only if one can answer yes to this question is inequality among the disabled important. Nor is it evident

what to make of the data on uncertainty. One might expect the disabled to display considerable year-to-year variation in income because the severity of disabilities changes over time. Should evidence of uncertainty constitute a justification for supporting the disabled more generously than otherwise? Should payment to a disabled person this year take account of whether the disability was less severe last year, or of whether it will become less severe next year?

This brings us to the larger question of how to choose the proper compensation for the disabled. Nothing in the Haveman and Wolfe chapter enlightens us as to whether the transfers to the disabled are too small, too large, or just right. What I would like to see—though it would be unfair to fault Haveman and Wolfe on this account—is a theory, comparable to the theory of optimal progressivity of the income tax, that somehow organizes our perceptions of proper economic policy or enables us to deduce right policy by maximizing a social welfare function subject to constraints. I have no guidance to offer as to how this theory might be designed, and can only express regret that I have nothing but sentiment with which to construct policy on the basis of the numbers in this chapter.

11 Household Wealth and Health Insurance as Protection against Medical Risks

Pamela J. Farley
Gail R. Wilensky

11.1 Introduction

Accidents, major illnesses, and other health disasters can reduce to penury people who have been economically productive all of their lives. Even the cost of relatively common illnesses can create serious problems for a family's budget. The most obvious response to the risks and uncertainties posed by the threat of poor health or other calamities is to purchase insurance. But insurance is not the only means by which individuals in an uncertain world can protect themselves against an unacceptable reduction in their future standard of living. Savings and wealth are also protection against such risks.

Precautionary savings and insurance can be viewed as alternative components in a portfolio of assets that provide for a household's future (Mayers and Smith 1983). Savings, if there is some asset that offers a safe rate of return, guarantee an improved standard of living in all future circumstances. Insurance, by contrast, is a contingent asset that provides additional wealth only in the event of misfortune. In this chapter we develop a theory of household behavior that describes the choice between health insurance and wealth as protection against the uncertainty of medical expenses, and we show that the tax subsidy associated with the current ex-

Pamela J. Farley is an economist at the National Center for Health Services Research. Gail R. Wilensky is vice-president, Domestic Division, at Project Hope.

The authors are greatly indebted to Angelita Manuel of Social and Scientific Systems, Incorporated. Her hard work and quick, capable computer programming made this analysis possible. She was assisted by Ann Corrigan. Georgine Prokopik deserves thanks for her research assistance, as do John Carrick and Sandy Widmar for typing the manuscript. Dean Farley and Dan Walden made helpful suggestions that improved an earlier version.

The views expressed here are those of the authors and no official endorsement of the National Center for Health Services Research, the Department of Health and Human Services, or Project Hope is intended or should be inferred.

clusion of employer-paid insurance benefits from an employee's taxable income alters the choice in favor of insurance. Before making empirical estimates of this model we review the distribution of wealth and patterns of insurance coverage in the United States as described in our data source. We then analyze household insurance purchases and household wealth, testing in particular for evidence of substitution between the two. The final section discusses the implications of our findings.

11.2   Theoretical Model of Household Savings and Insurance

A simple, two-period model can be used to describe the relationship between a household's savings and its insurance purchases. The model calls attention to precautionary motives for saving by assuming that a household decides on its savings and insurance in the first period while confronting the risk of an uncertain loss in the second period. Either type of expenditure ensures a higher level of expected consumption in the future. The model assumes that precautionary savings can be invested in a safe asset that offers a certain rate of return. It also incorporates a life-cycle perspective on saving, by assuming that all of a household's income (except for interest) is earned in the first period.

Consumption in the second period is consequently uncertain. It can be described by the following expression:

$$(1) \qquad C_2 = S(1 + (1 - t)r) - iL.$$

S is the household's savings in the first period, r is the rate of interest, t is the tax rate on income, i is the coinsurance rate chosen by the household in the first period, and L is a random variable denoting its insured loss. Viewed as a model of health insurance purchases, L represents the household's medical expenses and i is the share of its medical expenses that its policy requires it to pay. For a fully insured household, $i = 0$.

Health insurance is generally purchased through employers who often pay all or part of the premium. The income earned by a household in the first period (Y) consequently consists of two types of compensation—wages (W) and health insurance benefits (equal to eP, if P is the total premium for the household's health insurance and e is the share paid by employers).

$$(2) \qquad Y = W + eP.$$

Unlike the wages paid to an employee, employer-paid health insurance premiums are not subject to income or Social Security taxes. Consumption in the first period is therefore equal to the difference between the household's disposable income from wages and whatever it chooses to allocate to savings and its own share of insurance expenditures.

(3) $$C_1 = (1 - t)W - S - (1 - e)P.$$

Substituting for W from equation (2) and rearranging terms,

(4) $$C_1 = (1 - t)Y - S - (1 - et)P.$$

The last term in this expression, $(1 - et)P$, is the implicit cost of health insurance to the household, taking into account the tax exclusion for health insurance benefits and assuming that Y is fixed, with the incidence of the subsidy falling entirely on the household. Health insurance premiums are implicitly subsidized at a rate equal to et.

To finish specifying the relationship in the first period between consumption and expenditures on insurance, it is necessary to describe the relationship between the household's insurance premiums and the quantity of insurance it buys as measured by i. Assume that premiums are set in proportion to expected benefit payments,

(5) $$P = (1 + f)E[(1 - i)L] = (1 + f)(1 - i)E[L]$$
$$= (1 + f)(1 - i)\bar{L},$$

where $E[\ ]$ is the expectation operator and $\bar{L} = E[L]$. The "loading fee," f, reflects the administrative and selling costs associated with insurance and insurance company profits. If $f = 0$, then premiums are actuarially fair. For the purposes of this analysis, the acknowledged effect of health insurance on health expenditures is usefully ignored; L is not treated as a function of i. (See Arrow 1976, Phelps 1973, or Feldstein and Friedman 1977 for models that take this effect into account).

Finally, the household is assumed to maximize the expected utility of its consumption in the two periods, where

(6) $$u[C_1, C_2] = u[C_1] + \frac{1}{1 + d} u[C_2].$$

It chooses S and i to maximize $U = E[u[C_1, C_2]]$, defining two first-order conditions:

(7) $$U_s = -u_1' + \frac{1 + (1 - t)r}{1 + d} E[u_2'] \le 0;$$

(8) $$U_i = u_1'(1 - et)(1 + f)\bar{L} - E[u_2'L] \le 0.$$

In the notation employed here, the subscripts of the utility function denote the period.

At an interior solution, the first of these two equations imposes a condition similar to one that is familiar from models without uncertainty:

(9) $$\frac{u_1'}{E[u_2']} = \frac{1 + (1 - t)r}{1 + d}.$$

The opportunity cost of an additional dollar of consumption in period one is $1 + (1 - t)r$ dollars in every state of the world in period two. An optimal savings plan consequently equates the marginal utility of a dollar in period one with the marginal utility of $1 + (1 - t)r$ dollars averaged over states of the world in period two. Subtracting 1 from both sides of equation (9) yields an expression in terms of the rate of return (measured in utility) from diverting a dollar of consumption in period two to period one.

$$(9') \qquad \frac{u_1' - E[u_2']}{E[u_2']} = \frac{1 + (1 - t)r}{1 + d} - 1.$$

This is equal to the discounted rate of return on savings. With a zero rate of time preference ($d = 0$) and no taxes ($t = 0$), this rate of return is the interest rate, r.

The intuition of equation (8) is more apparent after substituting for u_1' from equation (7), dividing by $E[u_2']\overline{L}$, and subtracting 1 from both sides of the equation. This yields an equation similar to equation (9').

$$(10) \qquad \frac{E[u_2'L] - E[u_2']\overline{L}}{E[u_2']L} = \frac{1 + (1 - t)r}{1 + d}(1 - et)(1 + f) - 1.$$

If premiums were actuarially fair ($f = 0$), then the denominator on the left side of equation (10) would represent the marginal cost of insurance in terms of period-two utility. That is to say, to buy a marginal increase in i would require a certain reduction in consumption in every state of the world in period two that was proportional to $\overline{L}$. The numerator of equation (10) is the expected gain in utility from spending the money on insurance rather than keeping it. The left side of equation (10) can consequently be viewed as the rate of return on insurance bought at actuarially fair rates. As in equation (9'), this rate of return is measured in expected period-two utility. Note that if the implicit subsidy were zero ($et = 0$) and premiums were actuarially fair ($f = 0$), the rate of return on insurance would equal the rate of return on first-period consumption. Without taxes and with a zero rate of time preference, this rate of return is the interest rate, r. With the tax subsidy, the rate of return on insurance is driven below the rate of interest and the rate of return on consumption.

In a single-period model of the demand for health insurance, complete insurance is optimal if it is available at actuarially fair rates (no loading fee) and does not alter expected losses (no moral hazard) (Arrow 1963; Pauly 1980). However, by calling attention to saving as an alternative to insurance, this model calls attention to another cost associated with insurance that must be ruled out if complete insurance is to be optimal, namely the opportunity cost of foregone interest. Equation (10) demonstrates that, in the absence of a tax subsidy, it is not optimal for a household to insure its medical expenses completely when the loading fee is zero, if the rate of return on precautionary savings is positive.

To see that complete insurance is not optimal, note that the numerator of the left-hand side of equation (10) is simply the covariance between L and the marginal utility of income in period two, $\text{cov}[u'_2, L]$. Letting $f = 0$, equation (10) can be written as

$$(11) \qquad \frac{\text{cov}[u'_2, L]}{E[u'_2]\overline{L}} = \frac{1 + (1 - t)r}{1 + d}(1 - et) - 1.$$

Complete insurance necessarily leads to a contradiction with this condition. Suppose that a household did fully insure. Then u'_2 would not be a random variable and $\text{cov}[u'_2, L]$ would be zero. However, without the subsidy ($et = 0$), the right side of equation (11) is the discounted rate of return on savings. Consequently, if the rate of return on savings is greater than zero, then the left-hand side cannot be zero. Some degree of risk, as measured by $\text{cov}[u_c^2, L] > 0$, remains. By contrast, with an implicit subsidy that is relatively large in relation to the rate of return on savings and offsets the opportunity cost of the foregone interest, it is indeed possible for the equality to hold when the left-hand side of equation (11) is zero. The subsidy may, in other words, make complete insurance optimal. Also, if insurance companies discount premiums in recognition of the time that elapses before benefits are paid, implicitly paying consumers the interest that they could have earned by saving, then all costs of insurance are eliminated and complete insurance is optimal.

We would generally expect a reduction in the relative price of insurance to lead to a substitution of insurance for savings in this model. However, the comparative statics are ambiguous if insurance and savings are assumed to be substitutes in the sense of $U_{si} > 0$. The key consideration is the shape of the utility function and, in particular, the household's risk aversion over the range of L in the second period. Consider, for example, the effect on i and S of an exogenous increase in disposal income in the first period. In general, because of the subsequent decrease in the marginal utility of income in the first period, one would expect both savings and insurance purchases to increase. However, either type of expenditure changes the uncertain prospects confronting the household in the future and results in a higher level of expected consumption that may alter its attitudes toward risk. In particular, by assumption, an increase in savings diminishes the value of insurance and vice versa. As a consequence, additional saving could conceivably be accompanied by a cutback in insurance purchases. Or an increase in insurance coverage could make a simultaneous reduction in saving desirable.

By the same token, the income affect of an exogenous increase in the price of insurance (an increase in the loading fee, for example, or a decrease in the employer share) could conceivably result in such a significant reduction in savings and increase in risk aversion that a compensating increase in insurance purchases would result.

11.3 Empirical Model of Household Savings and Insurance

11.3.1 Data on Savings and Insurance

To investigate the empirical significance of the factors outlined in this theory of savings and insurance, we draw upon data from the 1977 National Medical Care Expenditure Survey (NMCES). NMCES provides extensive information on the benefit provisions, premiums, and financing of the health insurance held by approximately ten-thousand households that are representative of the noninstitutionalized civilian population in the United States. It also includes data on each household's 1977 federal income tax return and the specific components of its income. In conjunction with information in the survey about home ownership, we capitalize these income flows to obtain an estimate of the household's stock of wealth. Our empirical analysis focuses on wealth rather than savings.

The details of this procedure are described in the appendix at the end of this chapter. Briefly, the definition of household wealth is based on the concept of net equity; debts associated with a particular asset are deducted from its gross value. Income received as interest, dividends, rent, from nonfarm businesses (including royalties), and from estates or trusts are capitalized at different rates of return to produce an estimate of income-producing assets. Farm and home equity are derived from responses to direct questions asked in the survey. Home equity is the only non-income-producing asset that is included in the wealth estimates. The data do not permit consideration of other consumer durables that amount to about 9 percent of household wealth in the aggregate. They also exclude the cash value of life insurance and employee contributions to pensions.

Tables 11.1 and 11.2 show the resulting estimates of household wealth in the United States in 1977. The figure for mean total assets per household is $61,499 and implies a national total of about $4.5 trillion. According to national balance sheets (Ruggles and Ruggles 1982), household net worth in 1977 was $5.3 trillion. This is a discrepancy of about 15 percent, much of which can be explained in terms of the exclusion of most consumer durables. Since estimates of national wealth based on household surveys tend to produce consistently lower estimates than are measured by the national aggregates (Greenwood 1983), our figures appear to be reasonable.

Moreover, these estimates are consistent with other published information. For example, homes represent 27 percent of household wealth according to the Federal Reserve's 1963 Survey of Consumer Finances (Projector and Weiss 1966) and 23 percent according to Wolff's (1980) estimates for 1969. Since the Federal Reserve's definition of wealth includes only automobiles among consumer durables and Wolff's estimates include all consumer durables, the 26 percent share of mean total assets re-

Table 11.1   Percentage of Families with Equity in Specified Assets

Family Characteristics	Number of Families (thousands)	All Assets	Interest Bearing	Stock	Home	Rental Property	Nonfarm Business	Farm	Estates/ Trusts
All families	73,873	79.1	52.5	15.5	58.5	8.6	9.4	4.0	2.3
Family income									
$8,000 or less	20,494	59.7	35.4	7.2	38.7	6.2	5.2	2.6	1.0
$8,001–15,000	18,583	76.0	49.0	12.6	51.4	6.5	7.4	3.9	1.8
$15,001–25,000	19,270	89.6	59.1	15.7	70.8	9.3	9.9	3.9	2.1
$25,001–50,000	12,329	94.8	68.4	27.4	78.5	11.0	13.9	5.1	4.1
Over $50,000	3,196	98.2	82.0	39.7	75.4	22.5	28.7	9.7	8.2
Age of head									
Under 35 years	23,340	65.0	44.5	8.9	37.9	3.8	7.9	2.0	1.6
35–54 years	24,462	84.0	51.5	16.1	69.3	10.0	12.4	4.6	2.9
55–64 years	11,191	88.4	59.3	21.4	69.3	9.9	11.5	6.5	2.7
65 years or older	14,880	86.3	61.7	20.6	65.0	12.8	5.5	4.3	2.2
Wealth of family									
Zero	15,424	0.0	0.0	0.0	0.0	0.0	0.0	0.0	0.0
Less than $5,000	8,419	100.0	70.3	9.5	29.1	1.3	3.3	1.1	(0.0)*
$5,000–9,999	4,751	100.0	48.9	8.1	68.7	4.9	2.9	1.6*	0.1*
$10,000–49,999	25,444	100.0	56.0	12.2	86.6	7.9	5.5	2.7	1.5
$50,000–99,999	9,431	100.0	80.5	25.0	81.7	17.6	15.1	7.5	3.5
$100,000–199,999	5,749	100.0	79.8	44.1	75.4	19.8	33.7	13.2	8.6
$200,000–849,999	3,921	100.0	87.8	50.3	73.5	26.6	41.2	13.7	8.6
$850,000 or more	734	100.0	95.1	44.8	76.8	21.3	26.0	10.8	23.7

Source: Estimates derived from the National Medical Care Expenditure Survey, National Center for Health Services Research.

*Standard error greater than 30 percent of estimate.

Table 11.2   **Mean Total Equity per Family and Percentage Distribution**

Family Characteristics	Mean Total Equity (dollars)	Interest Bearing	Stock	Home	Rental Property	Nonfarm Business	Farm	Estates/Trusts
All families	61,499	34.3	10.7	26.3	5.6	13.6	6.1	3.3
Family income								
$8,000 or less	17,655	21.9	5.2	47.0	5.0	8.5	10.5	1.8
$8,001–15,000	31,721	28.6	9.0	37.5	3.4	9.8	8.9	2.9
$15,001–25,000	47,237	24.4	10.7	40.1	4.2	12.0	5.8	2.8
$25,000–50,000	95,309	33.1	10.7	28.1	3.0	16.3	5.5	3.3
Over $50,000	471,307	46.4	12.8	7.3	9.4	15.3	4.7*	4.2
Age of head								
Under 35 years	27,347	38.0	2.7	24.2	6.0	19.8	6.2	3.1
35–54 years	75,504	27.9	9.2	27.8	8.1	17.3	5.3	4.4*
55–64 years	87,948	32.7	13.6	26.1	3.0	12.8	8.4	3.5
65 years or older	72,156	44.7	15.5	25.2	3.3	4.4	5.4	1.5
Wealth of family								
$1–$4,999	1,829	48.7	5.0	40.6	1.3	2.6	1.8*	(0.0)*
$5,000–9,999	7,313	28.2	2.4	62.7	3.0	2.1*	1.5	0.1*
$10,000–49,999	26,731	17.5	2.5	71.2	3.0	2.7	2.2	0.9
$50,000–99,999	70,220	25.5	4.2	45.9	6.3	9.9	6.3	1.8
$100,000–199,999	141,371	26.0	13.3	24.6	3.7	19.7	8.9	3.8
$200,000–849,999	373,859	31.8	14.9	10.5	9.7	23.3	6.8	3.1
$850,000 or more	1,187,536	66.0	13.2	3.0	2.1*	3.7*	5.6*	6.5*

Source: Estimates derived from the National Medical Care Expenditure Survey, National Center for Health Services Research.

*Standard error greater than 30 percent of estimate.

presented by mean home equity in table 11.2 is consistent with both estimates. Farms, nonfarm businesses, and rental property represent 6
percent, 14 percent, and 6 percent respectively of household wealth according to table 11.2. The Federal Reserve reports farms and nonfarm
businesses as 18 percent of household wealth; Lebergott (1976), who includes all consumer durables in his wealth definition, estimates that they
are 14 percent of household wealth; and Wolff puts the figure for farms,
businesses, and investment real estate at 25 percent.

The data shown in tables 11.1 and 11.2 on family wealth by age are
broadly consistent with life-cycle considerations. The positive relationship between income and wealth is also apparent. The probability of having a particular asset and mean equity per family increases with the age of
the head up to sixty-four, and then roughly levels off or declines as families dissave in their retirement. Interest-bearing assets, the type most
commonly held by families with little wealth, vary least with the age of the
head. The sharpest contrasts with respect to age occur between the youngest group and those thirty-five to fifty-four. Except for interest-bearing
assets, the latter age group is about twice as likely to have any particular
type of wealth as the youngest group. Its average holdings exceed the
youngest group's by an even greater factor.

The estimates of the number of families by wealth category that are
shown in table 11.1 describe the distribution of wealth in the United States
in 1977. Five thousand dollars corresponds approximately to the thirtieth
percentile; $10,000 is the median. The additional categories starting at
$50,000 that are shown in table 11.1 begin approximately at the seventy-
fifth, ninetieth, ninety-fifth, and ninety-ninth percentiles. Also, estimates
of the concentration of wealth can be derived by calculating each group's
total assets from the number of families in the category and the mean per
family shown in table 11.2. Such a calculation suggests that 1 percent of
the families in the United States have about 20 percent of household assets
and 5 percent of the families hold about 50 percent of the assets.

Table 11.3 shows the relationship between the depth or type of health
insurance coverage and assets. Our expectation is that families with considerable assets, particularly financial assets that are more liquid and are
most likely to be held as precautionary balances, are likely to have less
comprehensive insurance coverage and vice versa. However, in making
these comparisons it must be remembered that the self-employed are less
likely to have group coverage and will generally have less comprehensive
benefits. Yet they are by definition major holders of business assets included in household wealth. The first rows in table 11.3 show the relationship between family wealth and group versus nongroup enrollment. Nongroup enrollees have more total wealth than those with group insurance.
However, the difference is concentrated almost entirely in the "other"
category, which is dominated by business and farm property. In particu-

Table 11.3   **Average Wealth in 1977 of Privately Insured and Uninsured Families with Heads under Sixty-five, by Insurance Benefits**

	All Assets	Financial[a]	Home	Other[b]
All families[c]	$ 62,776	$25,472	$16,904	$20,400
Type of coverage				
Group	59,711	26,083	17,650	15,978
Nongroup	105,415	28,903	19,278	57,233
No private insurance	43,140	15,140*	6,472	21,528
Hospital benefits[d]				
Full semiprivate, generous limit	51,768	20,439	18,536	12,793
Full semiprivate, less-generous limit	70,256	29,764	16,501	23,991
Less than semiprivate	74,232	29,618	18,104	26,510
Physician office benefits[e]				
No deductible	58,793	24,303	18,579	15,910
Deductible, less than 20% coinsurance	55,155	22,331	18,805	14,019
Deductible, 20% or more coinsurance	62,946	26,713	17,274	18,959
No physician office coverage	79,970	31,841	17,464	30,665
Maximum major medical benefit				
Less than $250,000	58,962	23,089	18,085	17,787
$250,000 or more	64,422	27,208	17,845	19,369
Unlimited	65,683	29,173	17,274	19,236
No major medical	73,013	29,690	17,146	26,177
Out-of-pocket maximum				
$750 or less under major medical	60,788	21,764	18,105	20,919
Over $750 under major medical	68,289	35,955	16,966	15,368
No major medical limit, but comprehensive inpatient benefits[f]	53,040	18,215	18,742	16,083
Other privately insured	70,272	28,806	17,374	24,092
Dental coverage				
Yes	57,306	25,220	19,235	12,851
No	66,781	26,718	17,351	22,712

Source: Estimates derived from the 1977 National Medical Care Expenditure Survey, National Center for Health Services Research.

*Standard error greater than 30 percent of estimate.

[a]Includes interest-bearing assets and stock.

[b]Includes farm and nonfarm business, rental property, and estates or trusts.

[c]Excludes families with heads under sixty-five where only insurance is public. Includes those with unknown hospital or physician office benefits; dental coverage, maximum, or out-of-pocket limit not shown below.

[d]A generous limit is defined as 365 days or more of basic benefits, or $250,000 of major medical coverage for those with only major medical hospital coverage.

[e]Benefits stated in terms of a copayment or allowance per visit are converted to a coinsurance rate by assuming a cost of $20 per visit.

[f]Comprehensive inpatient benefits are defined as 120 days or more of full semiprivate basic benefits or full semiprivate major medical benefits, full coverage of a $1,000 UCR (usual, customary, reasonable) charge for surgery, and full coverage for physician inpatient visits.

lar, there is a much smaller and statistically insignificant difference between group and nongroup families with respect to financial assets. Thus, a comparison of financial assets across health insurance benefits is not greatly confounded by the different asset holdings of the nongroup self-employed; this is where a trade-off with health insurances seems most relevent.

In general, table 11.3 shows that families with less generous health insurance benefits seem to have more financial assets. Families with full semiprivate hospital benefits and a generous limit hold about $9,000 less in financial assets than families with less comprehensive coverage. Those with both a deductible and 20 percent or more coinsurance for office visits, or no coverage at all, hold more financial assets. Finally, families whose out-of-pocket expenses are limited to less than $750 by their major medical coverage or whose comprehensive inpatient benefits provide a similar safeguard against high out-of-pocket expenses have about $5,000 to $15,000 less in financial assets than families that are open to the risk of significant medical expenses. The differences for hospital benefits and out-of-pocket limits are statistically significant; the differences with respect to physician benefits are in the expected direction but are not significant.

These descriptive statistics on the wealth of families with different types of health insurance consequently suggest that families may indeed hold wealth, particularly in more liquid assets, as a substitute for more comprehensive insurance. To analyze this and other aspects of savings and insurance behavior more closely, we now present an econometric model estimated from the NMCES data.

11.3.2   Health Insurance Purchases

The theoretical model that was presented earlier calls attention to the significance of the tax subsidy associated with employer-paid premiums and the insurance company's loading fee in determining the effective price of health insurance. Both factors are closely related to whether or not a household has access to group insurance. Almost all group insurance is employment related (99 percent in the NMCES data), and the loading fees for group coverage average about 10 percent compared to 40 to 50 percent for nongroup coverage (Carroll and Arnett 1979). We treat enrollment in a group plan as exogenous and consequently divide the sample into families who did and families who did not have group coverage. For those with group coverage, the quantity of insurance is modeled as a function of the employer share, the marginal tax rate of the household head, and the size of the group (which also reduces the loading fee). For families without group coverage, we first model the decision to purchase health insurance and then the quantity purchased. Because of the peculiar benefits and private insurance needs of the Medicare population, families headed by people sixty-five and older are excluded from the analysis.

The equations are presented in tables 11.4 to 11.6. Two different measures of insurance coverage are analyzed—premiums and hospital room and board benefits. The premium equations in tables 11.4 and 11.6 follow a modified log-linear specification, implying constant elasticities with respect to nonzero continuous variables on the right-hand side of the equation. Room and board benefits are measured as the number of days of full semiprivate coverage per disability per year. Ignoring deductibles, which were relatively uncommon (Farley and Wilensky 1983), about 75 percent of the families in the group sample and a third of those in the nongroup sample were fully insured for a semiprivate hospital room. Because 25 percent of the group sample and 70 percent of the nongroup sample had zero days of full coverage, these equations are estimated with the Tobit procedure.

Recall that the theoretically appropriate measure of the implicit subsidy rate is the product of the employer share and the marginal tax rate (*et*). Other independent variables include the age, sex, and education of the family head, race, income, and the family's public insurance coverage. Dummy variables for region and for families living outside Standard Metropolitan Statistical Areas (SMSAs) and the average expense per day among hospitals in the county account for geographic differences in health insurance benefits and the price of medical care.

Each family's expected medical expenses ($\bar{L}$ in the theoretical model) are estimated from coefficients obtained by regressing the log of total expenses for all fourteen thousand households in the NMCES household survey on the log of family size, categories of income adjusted for family size, race, and the age, sex, and activity limitations of family members. The R^2 of this equation was 0.19.

Neither total family medical expenses nor family health insurance premiums are strictly proportional to family size. In the equation used to derive expected family expenses, the elasticity with respect to family size was 1.31. This figure was significantly greater than one, implying more than proportional increases in expenditures with increasing family size. The premium for a family policy is typically about 2.5 times the premium for an identical individual policy, but does not usually vary with the number of dependents. Large families consequently enjoy lower per person insurance costs. Given these considerations, the model is not specified with premiums, income, or expected expenditures in terms of dollars per family member. Instead, family size is entered separately and, in the premium equations, the elasticity is specified as a linear function of family size rather than a constant. (This is the effect of including both family size and the log of family size in the equation.)

Table 11.4   Health Insurance Purchased by Families with Group Coverage Headed by Persons under Sixty-five

		Premiums[a]		Days of Full Semiprivate Benefits[b]		Mean
		Coefficient × 10	t-statistic	Coefficient	t-statistic	
Dependent variables						
LOGPREM	Log total premiums					6.66
MAXHSP	Days of full semiprivate benefits per year					198
Independent variables						
	Intercept	40.91	14.67	4.93	0.12	1
AGE	Age of head	—	—	2.41	1.20	40.4
AGESQ	AGE squared	—	—	-0.02	-0.65	1,786
LAGE	Log AGE	2.27	7.12	—	—	3.65
HEADSEX	1 = female head	-2.30	-8.22	-10.83	-1.30	0.17
FAMSIZ	Family size	-1.24	-6.99	-1.80	-0.54	3.21
LFAMSIZ	Log FAMSIZ	6.06	9.04	—	—	1.02
FAMINC	Family Income	—	—	-0.50D-3	-2.33	22,181
LFAMINC	Log FAMINC	0.42	3.19	—	—	9.74
EXPDLR	Expected family medical expenses	—	—	0.01	0.88	562
LEXPDLR	Log EXPDLR	0.66	2.47	—	—	6.07
EDUC1	1 = head with less than 12 years education	-0.24	-1.00	-30.02	-3.96	0.25
EDUC2	1 = head with 13–15 years education	-0.56	-2.02	-1.55	-0.18	0.16
EDUC3	1 = head with 16+ years education	-0.05	-0.20	28.47	3.51	0.20
RACE	1 = nonwhite	-0.93	-2.97	18.84	2.03	0.10
REG1	1 = lives in Northeast	-0.26	-0.86	65.93	6.75	0.22

Table 11.4 (continued)

		Premiums[a]		Days of Full Semiprivate Benefits[b]		Mean
		Coefficient × 10	t-statistic	Coefficient	t-statistic	
REG2	1 = lives in North Central	0.89	3.06	66.63	7.19	0.31
REG3	1 = lives in South	−0.72	−2.34	−14.10	−1.43	0.29
NONSMSA	1 = not SMSA	−0.54	−2.10	3.88	0.49	0.27
GRPSIZ	Group size	—	—	0.10D-2	10.92	19,664
GRPSIZSQ	GRPSIZ squared	—	—	−0.20D-8	−7.32	5,380D6
LGRPSIZ	Log GRPSIZ	0.29	8.28	—	—	6.70
EMPMTR	Employer share × marginal tax rate	4.06	5.65	92.05	4.04	0.23
HSPCOST	Ave. expense per day in county hospitals	—	—	0.25	3.32	166.6
LHSPCOST	Log HSPCOST	1.02	2.36	—	—	5.08
PUBPCT	Percent of family publicly insured	−2.56	−5.54	—	—	0.06
PUBREF	1 = person with private benefit is publicly insured	—	—	−26.38	−1.59	0.03
Statistics						
Number of observations		5,411		4,508		
R- squared		0.20		—		
Prob(F)		0.0001		—		
Chi-square				455.3		

Note: D(integer) denotes figures to be multiplied by the indicated power of ten.

[a] Omitted category is a white family headed by a male with twelve years of education living in an SMSA in the West.

[b] Tobit estimates. Omitted category is a white family headed by a male with twelve years of education and no public insurance, living in an SMSA in the West.

Looking first at the equations in table 11.4 that represent families with group insurance, the price effects of the implicit tax subsidy and group size are clear. Group size is positive and highly significant in all three equations. The subsidy rate, *EMPMTR,* has a positive and significant effect on premiums and the number of fully insured hospital days. A family that spent the average amount on premiums ($987) with no employer contribution and was subject to the average tax rate, 31 percent, would spend another $132 if the employer were to pay the entire premium. The elasticity of premiums with respect to the subsidy is .09 at the mean; the elasticity for the number of fully insured hospital days is about .11.

Although income is positive and significant in the premium equation with an elasticity of .04, it is negatively related to the number of fully insured hospital days. The higher premium expenditures of high-income families apparently go towards other types of benefits. Age, too, has a significant effect on premiums but not on hospital benefits. The same pattern seems to apply to families with higher expected medical expenses; they have significantly more expensive coverage but not more comprehensive hospital benifits.

The premiums of families headed by women are about 20 percent lower than the premiums of families headed by men, but such families do not have significantly less comprehensive hospital coverage. Nonwhites have lower premiums, too, but are more likely to have full semiprivate coverage than whites.

Education seems to figure significantly only in the comprehensiveness of a family's hospital benefits. Families headed by someone without a high school degree have fewer days of complete coverage. Families headed by college graduates tend to be insured for more days of complete coverage. These patterns are not apparent in the premium equations.

Finally, there are significant geographic differences in health insurance purchases. The higher the local price of hospital care, the higher are premiums and the greater a family's semiprivate hospital benefits. Thus, there appears to be a mutually reinforcing relationship between medical care prices and more comprehensive health insurance that may, as Feldstein (1977) has warned, contribute to the escalation of health care costs. Other geographic differences include the higher level of premiums in North Central states and lower premiums in the South and outside of SMSAs. This may partly be a reflection of general cost-of-living differences. However, full semiprivate benefits are also less extensive in the South than in the Northeast and in North Central states.

For families not enrolled in a group plan, the major decision is whether or not to purchase health insurance on a nongroup basis. We show both OLS and Probit estimates in table 11.5, partly to note that there is little difference in the results. As with the premium expenditures of group enrollees, the sex of the family head, income, education, race, and the family's expected medical expenses are all associated with the decision to buy

Table 11.5   Decision to Purchase Private Health Insurance among Families without Group Coverage Headed by Persons under Sixty-five

		OLS[a]		Probit[a]			Mean
		Coefficient	t-statistic	Coefficient	t-statistic	Marginal Effect[b]	
Dependent variables							
1 = private coverage							0.346
Independent variables							
	Intercept	0.293	2.67	−0.751	−1.68	—	1
AGE	Age of head	−0.002	−0.45	0.009	0.44	0.003	40.7
AGESQ	AGE squared	0.100D-3	1.66	0.900D-4	0.39	0.300D-4	1850
HEADSEX	1 = female head	0.047	2.29	0.085	1.11	0.029	0.37
FAMSIZ	Family size	−0.032	−3.75	−0.168	−5.01	−0.057	2.76
FAMINC	Family income	0.300D-5	4.89	0.700D-5	3.03	0.200D-5	12,819
EXPDLR	Expected family medical expenses	0.200D-3	4.98	0.800D-3	5.49	0.300D-3	437
EDUC1	1 = head with less than 12 years education	−0.111	−5.28	−0.417	−5.36	−0.140	0.41
EDUC2	1 = head with 13–15 years education	−0.038	−1.29	0.019	0.17	0.006	0.12

EDUC3	1 = head with 16+ years education	0.060	1.82	0.202	1.60	0.068	0.09
REG1	1 = lives in Northeast	0.223	7.82	0.647	5.73	0.218	0.19
REG2	1 = lives in North Central	0.192	6.90	0.673	5.93	0.226	0.21
REG3	1 = lives in South	0.096	3.53	0.384	3.63	0.129	0.35
RACE	1 = nonwhite	-0.084	-3.34	-0.400	-4.25	-0.134	0.18
NONSMSA	1 = not SMSA	0.001	0.06	-0.004	-0.05	-0.001	0.32
HSPCOST	Ave. expense per day in county hospitals	-0.900D-4	-0.36	-0.184D-3	-0.19	-0.600D-4	165.9
PUBPCT	Percent of family publicly insured	-0.387	-18.08	-1.636	-16.67	-0.551	0.37
Statistics							
Number of observations		1991			1991		
R-squared		0.31			—		
Prob (F)		.0001			—		
Chi-square		—			774.2		

Note: D(integer) denotes figures to be multiplied by the indicated power of ten.

[a] Omitted category is a white family headed by a male with twelve years of education, living in an SMSA in the West.

[b] The marginal effect of X_i on the probability of private insurance is $f(X_i\beta)\beta$ where f is the normal density function. Here f is evaluated at the means of X and equals .3367.

Table 11.6   Health Insurance Purchased by Families with Nongroup Coverage Headed by Persons under Sixty-five

		Premiums[a]		Days of Full Semiprivate Benefits[b]		
		Coefficient × 10	t-statistic	Coefficient	t-statistic	Mean
Dependent variables						
LOGPREM	Log total premiums					5.83
MAXHSP	Days of full semiprivate benefits per year					52.8
Independent variables						
	Intercept	50.84	5.48	452.42	2.32	1
AGE	Age of head	—	—	−23.47	−2.51	45.7
AGESQ	AGE squared	—	—	0.24	2.17	2,280
LAGE	Log AGE	3.25	3.00	—	—	3.76
HEADSEX	1 = female head	−0.06	−0.08	17.46	0.56	0.31
FAMSIZ	Family size	0.09	0.13	13.74	0.94	2.62
LFAMSIZ	Log FAMSIZ	3.07	1.50	—	—	0.80
FAMINC	Family income	—	—	0.10D-3	0.13	18,175
LFAMINC	Log FAMINC	0.12	0.43	—	—	9.28
EXPDLR	Expected family medical expenses	—	—	0.01	0.20	460
LEXPDLR	Log EXPDLR	0.06	0.08	—	—	5.86
EDUC1	1 = head with less than 12 years education	−0.37	−0.49	−12.46	−0.36	0.31
EDUC2	1 = head with 13–15 years education	0.86	0.84	−11.21	−0.27	0.12

Variable		Coef.	t	Coef.	t	Mean
EDUC3	1 = head with 16+ years education	1.33	1.37	75.45	1.98	0.14
RACE	1 = nonwhite	-2.28	-1.90	55.98	1.06	0.08
REG1	1 = lives in Northeast	-1.20	-1.13	45.02	1.07	0.25
REG2	1 = lives in North Central	1.08	0.99	-104.33	-2.32	0.27
REG3	1 = lives in South	-1.50	-1.37	-156.62	-3.39	0.33
NONSMSA	1 = not SMSA	-1.64	-1.96	-62.76	-1.78	0.35
HSPCOST	Ave. expense per day in county hospitals	—	—	0.03	0.09	161.0
LHSPCOST	Log HSPCOST	-1.41	-0.94	—	—	5.04
PUBPCT	Percent of family publicly insured	-6.67	-4.93	—	—	0.11
PUBREF	1 = person with private benefit is publicly insured	—	—	-288.82	-3.56	0.09
Statistics						
Number of observations		671		511		
R-squared		0.14		—		
Prob(F)		.0001		—		
Chi-square		—		89.2		

Note: D(integer) denotes figures to be multiplied by the indicated power of ten.

[a]Omitted category is a white family headed by a male with twelve years of education living in an SMSA in the West.

[b]Tobit estimates. Omitted category is a white family headed by a male with twelve years of education and no public insurance, living in an SMSA in the West.

health insurance. Holding the family's total income and expected expenses constant, family size has a negative effect. This may be an indicator of the budgetary effect of stretching the same income over more people. Regional differences that roughly parallel the likelihood of comprehensive hospital coverage also emerge with respect to nongroup enrollment. Lastly, and not surprisingly, enrollment in public insurance programs drastically reduces the likelihood of private coverage.

With respect to the amount of insurance that a family purchases on a nongroup basis, there appear to be few consistent or significant behavioral relationships. Private insurance purchases are reduced by the availability of public insurance, and premiums again appear to be somewhat less in nonmetropolitan areas. Age is positively related to premium expenditures, but, from a joint test on *AGE* and *AGESQ,* is not significant in explaining semiprivate hospital benefits. This relationship may well reflect the higher rates that older persons are required to pay.

11.3.3   Household Wealth

Two types of assets are analyzed in the econometric model of household wealth described in table 11.7. First, all wealth (including home equity, stock, interest-bearing assets, farm and nonfarm businesses, rental property, and estates and trusts) are considered. A second equation examines only financial wealth (stock and interest-bearing assets). These more liquid assets are more likely to be held as a precaution against unexpected expenses. Both equations are estimated in a modified log-linear form, using the Tobit procedure. Families with zero wealth are arbitrarily assigned a value of zero for the dependent variable, corresponding to one dollar of wealth.

The equations are premised on the precautionary and life-cycle motives for savings that are assumed in the theory presented earlier. Like other empirical models of household assets that are derived from the life-cycle theory (Kotlikoff 1979; Feldstein and Pellechio 1979; Blinder, Gordon, and Wise 1981), the explanatory variables include age of the household head, family size, and marital status to account for the family's place in the life cycle, its retirement needs, and unforeseeable changes in family composition. As in the health insurance premium equations, family size is entered in both a log and linear form. The model also accounts for racial, educational, and regional differences in savings behavior. A cost-of-living index, derived by fitting 1977 figures available from the Bureau of Labor Statistics for a limited number of cities to secondary data available for all counties and SMSAs, is used to control for variations in the real value of asset holdings.

Recall that each household's wealth is defined from components of its income. The resulting tautological relationship between wealth and total family income makes the latter an inappropriate variable for measuring

Table 11.7   Wealth of Families Headed by Persons under Sixty-five

		Total Assets[a]		Financial Assets[a]		Mean
		Coefficient	t-statistic	Coefficient	t-statistic	
Dependent variables						
LASSET	Log total assets					7.81
LOGFIN	Log financial assets					4.56
Independent variables						
	Intercept	-6.60	-1.22	-47.40	-5.18	1
LAGE	Log AGE	5.63	30.04	5.74	18.51	3.65
HEADSEX	1 = female head	-1.17	-6.19	-1.10	-3.44	0.22
FAMSIZ	Family size	-0.29	-2.87	-0.37	-2.06	3.09
LFAMSIZ	Log FAMSIZ	1.72	5.22	0.03	0.05	0.97
NONVINC	Noninvestment income	0.40D-4	8.07	0.60D-4	6.61	16,646
LNONVINC	Log of NONVINC	-0.21	-4.80	-0.21	-2.96	9.23
EDUC1	1 = head with less than 12 years education	-1.29	-9.53	-1.95	-8.40	0.30
EDUC2	1 = head with 13–15 years education	0.40	2.46	0.58	2.15	0.15
EDUC3	1 = head with 16+ years education	0.77	4.93	2.27	8.92	0.17
MARST1	1 = married head	1.16	5.28	0.83	2.25	0.66
MARST2	1 = divorced, widowed, separated head	-0.49	-2.29	-2.37	-6.49	0.18
RACE	1 = nonwhite	-2.82	-15.96	-4.64	-14.36	0.13
REG1	1 = lives in Northeast	-0.27	-1.58	0.06	0.22	0.21
REG2	1 = lives in North Central	0.54	3.42	0.57	2.17	0.28
REG3	1 = lives in South	0.13	0.71	-0.30	-0.96	0.31
NONSMSA	1 = not SMSA	-0.10	-0.77	-0.55	-2.59	0.30

Table 11.7 (continued)

		Total Assets[a]		Financial Assets[a]		
		Coefficient	t-statistic	Coefficient	t-statistic	Mean
LCSTLIV	1 = log of cost-of-living index	−1.38	−1.18	6.84	3.48	4.58
SELFEM	1 = self-employed	2.07	10.32	0.72	2.18	0.09
GROUP	1 = group	0.17	0.72	0.45	1.16	0.75
LGRPSIZ	Log *GRPSIZ*	0.04	1.59	0.08	2.09	4.98
EMPPCT	Employer share of premiums	0.02	0.12	−0.65	−2.12	0.53
PUBPCT	Percent of family publicly insured	−3.24	−15.96	−3.10	−8.71	0.14
Statistics						
Number of observations		6,948		6,948		
Chi-square		3,372		1,718		

Note: D(integer) denotes figures to be multiplied by the indicated power of ten.

[a]Tobit estimates. Omitted category is a white family headed by a single, wage-earning male with twelve years of education without group coverage, living in an SMSA in the West.

the effect of income on asset holdings. Accordingly, only noninvestment income is considered. This variable largely corresponds to labor income, but also includes government transfers and pensions. Like the effects of family size, the income elasticity is assumed to be linear in income rather than a constant.

In addition to these variables, the precautionary savings theory suggests that the price of insurance—an alternative to holding precautionary balances—should also enter the wealth equations. That is, the significance of group enrollment and group size (as proxies for the loading fee) and the health insurance subsidy rate provides a test for substitution between wealth and health insurance in hedging against the risk of illness. If households do trade off between the two, then these variables that alter the price of insurance and have a demonstrably positive effect on insurance purchases will have a negative effect on wealth holdings.

Because the marginal tax rate increases with total family income and the latter is used to define family wealth, the tax rate is positively correlated with the error term in the wealth equations. Because its coefficient is consequently biased, the employer share is entered alone and our estimate of the effect of the subsidy is obtained from the elasticity with respect to the employer share.

The equations are estimated for all families headed by individuals under age sixty-five. Initially, because nongroup enrollment is correlated with self-employment and with several categories of business assets included in household wealth, we also estimated the equations for a sample restricted to group enrollees. The differences in the two sets of equations proved to be negligible, and we show only the equations for the entire sample.

Table 11.7 appears to be a reasonable model of household wealth, in terms of the signs and significance of the variables and the fit of the equations. There is also evidence, in the negative and significant sign on the employer's share of premiums, that households do indeed hold financial assets as a substitute for health insurance. The elasticity of financial assets with respect to the employer share is − .34. Negative and significant coefficients for group enrollment and group size would provide stronger support for the substitution hypothesis. However, these variables generally have the wrong sign, and group size is positive and significant in the financial assets equation.

Other findings worth noting include the great effect of age on asset holdings, as predicted by the life-cycle hypothesis for families who have not reached retirement. A 1 percent increase in the age of the family head is associated with almost a 6 percent increase in total wealth or financial assets. Also in keeping with the life-cycle hypothesis, more wealth is accumulated by families with married partners. The widowed, divorced, and separated hold less wealth, probably because they have less incentive and less income to save.

The generally positive effects of family size on total wealth can also be explained in terms of the life cycle, and in terms of the desirability of home ownership and the bequest motives among families with children. Note, however, that total asset holdings start to decline with increases in family size beyond about six members. After a certain point, the budgetary constraints imposed by having a larger family apparently outweigh the incentive to save. Financial assets decline in general with increased family size, holding marital status constant.

The income elasticity for total wealth evaluated at the mean is about .46. However, the elasticity increases by about .04 for every $1,000 increase in a family's noninvestment income. The elasticity for financial wealth is .79 at the mean and increases by .06 for every $1,000 increase in income. Because some families with very little noninvestment income have a lot of investment income and a lot of assets, the relationship between family wealth and noninvestment income less than about $4,000 to $5,000 is negative.

Finally, there are important sociodemographic factors in family wealth patterns. Holding other considerations constant, nonwhites have substantially less total or financial wealth per family than whites. Families headed by females have about 65 percent less total or financial wealth. The education of the family head also bears a strong positive relationship to wealth holdings.

11.4   Summary and Conclusions

Our two-period theoretical model demonstrates that savings and health insurance both serve as protection against medical risks. Within such a model, the expected rate of return (measured in utility) to be gained by diverting a dollar from savings to present consumption is the after-tax interest rate. The expected rate of return on insurance purchased at actuarially fair rates is also equal to the rate of interest. Given the subsidy implicit in the exclusion of health insurance benefits from an employee's taxable income, we have shown that the expected rate of return on an actuarially fair policy is driven below the rate of interest and the return on savings. We also demonstrate that complete insurance is not optimal, even at actuarially fair rates, if it is possible to earn a certain, positive rate of return on savings.

To estimate an empirical model of the behavior described by this theory, variables describing each household's wealth were constructed from detailed income components reported in a nationally representative household survey. Capitalizing these income flows and utilizing data on home and farm equity that are also available from the survey produce estimates of the wealth of U.S. households that are consistent with other sources. In a preliminary test for a trade-off between health insurance and wealth in household portfolios, these data on assets are compared among households with different types of insurance coverage. Even such gross comparisons suggest that there is a negative relationship between the level of insurance and holdings of relatively liquid assets. This relationship cannot be explained by the connection between self-employment, the lack of group coverage among the self-employed, and the less comprehensive insurance benefits available to nongroup enrollees.

The econometric model of household wealth and insurance purchases also suggests that precautionary balances are held in lieu of health insurance. The estimates imply that the group insurance premiums of a family whose premiums are paid entirely by employers and a family that pays all of its premiums differ by 12 percent. At the same time, the family with more insurance holds 48 percent less in financial assets. The findings on the substitution question are mixed, however, since group size also reduces the price of insurance but has a positive correlation with financial wealth.

The empirical model of insurance purchases does confirm, at any rate, that the tax subsidy encourages an increase in the quantity of health insurance. This effect is apparent with respect to premiums and the comprehensiveness of hospital benefits. Income, the family's expected medical expenses, and medical care prices also have a positive effect on the quantity of insurance. Among families not enrolled in health insurance groups, income and expected expenses mainly affect whether a family has any insurance at all. This decision seems to be the main issue for such families, rather than the quantity of insurance to purchase.

In addition to the findings with respect to the effect of employer-paid insurance benefits, the econometric estimates shed light on other aspects of household behavior in accumulating wealth. The elasticity of wealth with respect to noninvestment income appears to increase by four to six percentage points with every $1,000 increase in income. Family size is associated with greater holdings of wealth, but only up to a point. In general, the effects of age, family size, and marital status testify to the significance of life-cycle considerations. And the disparity in the wealth of families headed by educated white males compared to others is very evident.

In contrast to savings accumulated by a household for its use in any future circumstances, the wealth offered in the future by health insurance is contingent on future circumstances. From our estimates of the relative effect of the tax subsidy on premiums and financial assets, it is possible to make inferences about the value to households of this contingent asset in terms of its certain equivalent. Consider a family with median total assets for families headed by a person under sixty-five in 1977, in the range of $10,000–15,000. The average health insurance premiums of such a family were about $900, with employers paying about 60 percent and an implicit tax subsidy of $200. The average marginal tax rate was 27 percent, the average subsidy rate was 18 percent, average financial assets were $1,900, average total income was $17,400, and average noninvestment income was $17,000. Simultaneously compensating such a family for the $200 loss of income, elimination of the tax subsidy would reduce its expenditures on health insurance by $63. Its holdings of financial assets would increase by $933 to a total of $2,833. In sum, the contingent wealth represented by a marginal expenditure of $63 on health insurance is equivalent to holding about fifteen times that amount in tangible assets.

The subsidy implicit in the exclusion of employer-paid premiums from taxable income has a number of effects. It represents a loss in government revenues amounting to about $31 billion in 1983 (Taylor and Wilensky 1983). In this paper we have demonstrated that it encourages employees to choose more comprehensive health insurance. This in turn contributes to increased spending on health care. We have also called attention to the fact that spending more on health insurance necessarily means spending less on something else. In particular, we have argued, and evidence exists in our empirical findings, that precautionary savings may be one of the close substitutes for insurance where the reduction occurs.

Appendix

The National Medical Care Expenditure Survey

The National Medical Care Expenditure Survey (NMCES) provides detailed national estimates of personal and family characteristics, the use of health services, health expenditures, and health insurance for the civilian noninstitutionalized population in 1977. The survey was funded and undertaken by the National Center for Health Services Research with the cosponsorship of the National Center for Health Statistics, two agencies in the U.S. Department of Health and Human Services. NMCES consists of several different surveys—the main household survey and other follow-up surveys that complement the household data collection. In the household survey, data were obtained for a nationally representative sample of approximately fourteen thousand households (representing approximately forty thousand people) who were interviewed six times over an eighteen-month period during 1977–78. The complex, clustered sampling design of the household survey is described in Cohen and Kalsbeek (1981), and the survey instruments are described in Bonham and Corder (1981). All regressions and descriptive statics are estimated with weights that produce national estimates and account for the nonrandom sampling design of the survey and differential nonresponse.

The estimates of household wealth that are presented are derived from two types of information collected in the household survey. First, income-producing assets of each household are inferred by capitalizing various types of income derived from such assets. This part of a household's wealth is calculated from detailed components of each person's income that were reported, including the amount of interest, dividends, farm income, nonfarm business income, rental income, income from estates and trusts, and royalties.

Second, each household was asked a series of questions concerned with home ownership. These questions provide the only information on non-income-producing assets owned by a household that are included in the wealth estimates, namely home equity. Homeowners were asked the present value of the property and the amount remaining on the mortgage(s). Where applicable, the value of the property and mortgage were reported for the entire farm or multiunit dwelling owned by the homeowners who resided there.

The data on health insurance premiums and benefits are drawn from one of the follow-up surveys, the Health Insurance/Employer Survey (HIES). This was a survey of the employers, unions, insurance companies, and other organizations that were identified by NMCES households as the source of their private health insurance coverage. It was designed to verify the coverage reported in the household survey and to obtain information on benefit provisions, premiums, and premium payments by employers, employees, and others. A copy of the policy or certificate describing the benefits offered through each respondent was requested and subsequently abstracted onto forms suitable for computer analysis. Because of nonresponse in this additional phase of data collection, national estimates derived from the HIES survey are based on a sample of approximately 10,000 households and 24,000 individuals. This is the sample that underlies the data analyzed here. However, because premium data were often obtained when information about the policy was not, different weights are used to analyze benefits and premiums. About 9,100 households have benefit data. (See Cohen and Farley 1984 for a more detailed description of the Health Insurance/Employer Survey.)

In the data on family insurance benefits that are presented here, a family is characterized by the benefits of the head. Except, however, the benefits of a family member with group insurance were selected over the non-group benefits of a head without any group benefits.

Definition and Estimation of Household Wealth

The estimates of household wealth are based on the concept of net equity or net worth. To the extent possible, wealth is measured in these terms. Debts associated with a particular asset are either explicitly or implicitly deducted from its gross value.

Because of limitations of the data source, not all types of wealth are included. Most significantly, consumer durables (except for homes) are not considered. Both Wolff (1980) and Lebergott (1976) estimate that these other consumer durables represent about 9 percent of household wealth. Also excluded are equity in life insurance and annuities, and household contributions to pension funds. The measurement of household wealth also ignores debts that were not secured by one of the assets included in the definition. Thus, home mortgages are included, but automobile loans or installment credit are not.

Income-Producing Assets

Wealth in income-producing assets is estimated by capitalizing the specific types of income shown in table 11.A.1. A similar technique has been employed by Lebergott (1976), Wolff (1980), and Greenwood (1983) to estimate household wealth. As shown in table 11.A.1, different rates of return are applied to each type of income. A single figure is used for all households with a particular type of income—an apparently reasonable assumption according to Greenwood. She reports that rates of return do not appear to vary substantially or systematically by income class.

Ninety-eight of the 1,284 households that reported income or losses from a nonfarm business reported losses, and about 130 reported losses on rental property out of 1,242 with income or losses. An analysis of families reporting business losses in the 1967 Survey of Economic Opportunity suggested that their business equity followed a distribution similar to those with positive income; households in the NMCES survey with negative business income are consequently assigned the mean for households with positive income. In the Survey of Economic Opportunity, the mean equity in rental property of families with rental losses was about 1.5 times the mean for families with positive income, and such families in the NMCES survey are assigned a value equal to 1.5 times the comparable figure from NMCES.

As noted earlier, households that lived on farms or in multiunit dwellings were asked about their equity in the entire property. Equity thus reported for families with farm income or losses is categorized as farm equity. This is the primary basis for estimating farm equity. However, if a household was not able to report its equity in a farm, then its farm equity is capitalized from its farm income at a rate of 6.57 percent (Evans and Simunek 1978, p. 28). If a family did not report any rental income but lived in and owned a multiunit dwelling, then equity in the property not assigned to home equity (see below) was categorized as wealth in rental property.

Home Equity

The home equity of families that owned and lived in multiunit dwellings is defined as the net worth of the particular housing unit that they occu-

Table 11.A.1   Estimation of Income-Producing Assets

Type of Income	Rate of Return on Equity (capitalizing ratio)	Source
1. Interest	5.48%	Interest as a percentage of time and savings deposits in Federal Reserve member banks in 1977 (*Annual Statistical Digest* 1978, p. 307)
2. Dividends	4.56	Average dividend-price ratio for common stock in 1977 (*Annual Statistical Digest* 1978, p. 94)
3. Estates/trusts	4.56	Assumes rate of return comparable to stocks.
4. Nonfarm business and royalties	13.51	Aggregate proprietor's income received by households as a percentage of noncorporate, nonfarm equity in 1977 (Ruggles and Ruggles 1982, pp. 33 and 43)
5. Rental income	14.87	The average rate of return on equity in rental property reported by households in the 1967 Survey of Economic Opportunity was 15.55 percent. This figure was adjusted by the difference between the average rate of increase in household rental income and increase in gross assets in residential structures reported by Ruggles and Ruggles (1982) for the period 1969–77. This difference was −4.3 percent.

pied. If its value was not reported, then the value was calculated in equal proportion to the number of units in the dwelling. Homeowners who were not able to estimate the current market value of their property were asked its purchase price and year. For 587 such households, the value of the property was inflated from the Bureau of Labor Statistics' Consumer Price Index for home purchases and depreciated at a rate of 1.5 percent per year. The latter figure is the 1970–77 average annual rate of depreciation on the assets held by households in residential structures, calculated from Ruggles and Ruggles (1982, pp. 42–43).

Among the 10,045 households in the HIES sample, 945 did not respond to any of the questions concerning home ownership that were asked in the final round of the household survey. The weights utilized in the analysis of household wealth are adjusted to account for these nonrespondents by the age of the household head, income, family size, and location in an SMSA, allowing national estimates to be made from the remaining 9,100 households with data on home ownership. Among the 5,742 homeowners in the remaining sample, 799 households are imputed a value for home equity from partial information on the property's current value or mortgage, income, family size, location, and the age of the household head.

References

Annual statistical digest, 1973–1977. 1978. Washington, D.C.: Federal Reserve Board of Governors.

Arrow, Kenneth J. 1963. Uncertainty and the welfare economics of health care. *American Economic Review* 53, no. 5: 941–73.

_____. 1976. Welfare analysis of changes in health coinsurance rates. In *The role of health insurance in the health services sector,* ed. Richard N. Rosett. New York: National Bureau of Economic Research.

Blinder, Alan S., Roger Hall Gordon, and Donald E. Wise. 1981. Social Security, bequests, and the life cycle theory of saving: Cross-sectional tests. Working paper no. 619, NBER Working Paper Series. National Bureau of Economic Research.

Bonham, Gordon Scott, and Larry S. Corder. 1981. *NMCES household interview instruments.* National Health Care Expenditures Study, Instruments and Procedures 1. U.S. Department of Health and Human Services. Washington, D.C.: National Center for Health Services Research.

Carroll, Marjorie S., and Ross H. Arnett III. 1979. Private health insurance plans in 1977: Coverage enrollment and financial experience. *Health Care Financing Review* 1, no. 2: 3–22.

Cohen, Steven B., and Pamela J. Farley. 1984. *Estimation and sampling procedures in the insurance surveys of the National Medical Care Expenditure Survey.* National Health Care Expenditures Study, Instruments and Procedures 3. U.S. Department of Health and Human Services. Washington, D.C.: National Center for Health Services Research.

Cohen, Steven B., and William Kalsbeek. 1981. *NMCES estimation and sampling variances in the household survey.* National Health Care Expenditures Study, Instruments and Procedures 2. U.S. Department of Health and Human Services. Washington, D.C.: National Center for Health Services Research.

Daly, Michael J. 1982. The impact of public pensions on personal retirement saving in Canada: Some evidence from cross-sectional data. *Southern Economic Journal* 49, no. 2: 428–39.

Diamond, P., and J. Hausman. 1980. Individual savings behavior. Paper prepared for the National Commission on Social Security. Massachusetts Institute of Technology.

Dreze, J., and F. Modigliani. 1972. Consumption decisions under uncertainty. *Journal of Economic Theory* 5:308–55.

Evans, Carson D., and Richard W. Simunek. 1978. *Balance sheet of the farming sector, 1978.* Supplement no. 1, Agriculture Information Bulletin No. 416. Economics, Statistics, and Cooperative Services, U.S. Department of Agriculture. Washington, D.C.: GPO.

Farley, Pamela J., and Gail R. Wilensky. 1983. Private health insurance: What benefits do employees and their families have? *Health Affairs* 2, no. 1:92–101.

Feldstein, Martin. 1976. Social security and the distribution of wealth. *Journal of the American Statistical Association* 71, no. 356: 800–807.

———. 1977. Quality change and the demand for hospital care. *Econometrica* 45, no. 7:1681–702.

Feldstein, Martin, and Bernard Friedman. 1977. Tax subsidies, the rational demand for insurance, and the health care crisis. *Journal of Public Economics* 7:155–78.

Feldstein, Martin, and Anthony Pellechio. 1979. Social security and household wealth accumulation: New microeconometric evidence. *Review of Economics and Statistics* 61, no. 3:361–68.

Ferber, Robert. 1962. Research on household behavior. *American Economic Review* 52, no. 1:19–63.

Greenwood, Daphne. 1983. An estimation of U.S. family wealth and its distribution from microdata, 1973. *Review of Income and Wealth* 29, no. 1:23–44.

Kotlikoff, Laurence J. 1979. Testing the theory of Social Security and life cycle accumulation. *American Economic Review* 69, no 3:396–410.

Lebergott, Stanley. 1976. *The American economy: Income, wealth, and want.* Princeton: Princeton University Press.

Leland, H. E. 1968. Saving and uncertainty: The precautionary demand for saving. *Quarterly Journal of Economics* 82:465–73.

Mayers, David, and Clifford W. Smith, Jr. 1983. The interdependence of individual portfolio decisions and the demand for insurance. *Journal of Political Economy* 91, no. 2:304–11.

Pauly, Mark. 1980. Overinsurance: The conceptual issues. In *National health insurance: What now, what later, what never?* ed. Mark Pauly. Washington, D.C.: American Enterprise Institute.

Phelps, Charles E. 1973. *Demand for health insurance: A theoretical and empirical investigation.* Santa Monica, Calif.: Rand Corporation.

Projector, Dorothy S., and Gertrude S. Weiss. 1966. *Survey of financial characteristics of consumers.* Federal Reserve technical paper. Washington, D.C.: Board of Governors of the Federal Reserve System.

Ruggles, Richard, and Nancy D. Ruggles. 1982. Integrated economic accounts for the United States, 1947–1980. *Survey of Current Business* 62, no. 5:1–53.

Sandmo, A. 1970. The effect of uncertainty on saving decisions. *Review of Economic Studies* 37, no. 3:353–60.

Taylor, Amy K., and Gail R. Wilensky. 1983. The effect of tax policies on expenditures for private health insurance. In *Market reforms in health care,* ed. Jack A. Meyer. Washington, D.C.: American Enterprise Institute.

U.S. Department of Health, Education, and Welfare. Office of Economic Opportunity. 1967. *1967 survey of economic opportunity codebook.* Washington, D.C.: GPO.

Wolff, Edward N. 1980. Estimates of the 1969 size distribution of household wealth in the U.S. from a synthetic data base. In *Modeling the distribution and intergenerational transmission of wealth,* ed. James D. Smith. Studies in Income and Wealth, no. 46. Chicago: University of Chicago Press.

Comment   Joseph P. Newhouse

The chapter by Farley and Wilensky makes a contribution, but it is a different contribution than the authors think they have made. And the chapter contains some important theoretical and empirical problems. The most startling statement in the theoretical section is on page 326: "in the ab-

Joseph P. Newhouse is head of the economics department of the Rand Corporation.

sence of a tax subsidy, it is not optimal for a household to insure its medical expenses completely when the loading fee is zero, if the rate of return on precautionary savings is positive." This statement appears to overturn a basic result of Arrow (1963), who showed that if moral hazard was zero—an assumption Farley and Wilensky also make—a risk-averse consumer facing no loading charge would fully insure. (For generalizations of Arrow 1963, see Arrow 1973a, 1973b.)

The authors argue that Arrow ignored precautionary savings and therefore reached a different conclusion, but closer inspection reveals that the authors have made a strange assumption. If an individual saves in period one, he receives the after-tax rate of interest in period two; but if he buys a health insurance policy in period one that pays off in period two, the health insurer earns no interest. But insurers do, of course, earn interest on reserves. Thus, actuarially fair insurance in this context must extend to insurers passing on to consumers any interest that those reserves earn.

If we assume, for simplicity, that insurers earn the same after-tax rate of interest as consumers, then the right-hand side of equation (5) and the first term on the right-hand side of equation (8) should be divided by $1 + r(1 - t)$, a term that then comes into the first term of the denominator of the right-hand side of equations (10) and (11), canceling the same term in the numerator. Making this revision in equation (11), the authors reach Arrow's result: if d is equal to or exceeds zero (neutral or positive time preference), the subsidized consumer will fully insure. He would like to more than fully insure (given that et is positive), but as long as more than 100 percent reimbursement of costs is not permitted, the left-hand side of equation (11) cannot be negative; thus, he fully insures.

With this change of assumptions the inferred substitution between financial assets and health insurance, if there is no loading, vanishes. The presumed substitution of precautionary savings for insurance derives from the asymmetry in interest rates earned by the consumer (greater than zero) and the insurer (zero). Thus, insurance in this model has a price analogous to a loading (namely, foregone interest), and it is not surprising that under these conditions full insurance is generally not optimal. In actuality, the insurer may well be able to earn a higher return than the individual consumer, thereby favoring insurance, not precautionary saving.

Indeed, one can ask: Given that et is on the order of 0.2 if typical values are used, and given that f for hospital insurance is on the order of 0.1 or less in a standard group plan, why doesn't equation (10) imply full hospital insurance in all group plans? The authors tell us that 75 percent of those insured by group plans do in fact have full insurance (or a deductible, but the latter category is said to be "uncommon").

Why do not the other 25 + percent have full insurance? The explanation, I think, lies in heterogeneity. Those who have less than average probability of hospitalization face effectively higher loadings than 0.1. Why such higher loadings do not lead to a demand for deductibles rather than coinsurance is not clear, although it may well have to do with moral hazard.

If the authors' theory, when corrected to allow the insurer to earn interest, does not (without positive loading fees) yield a prediction of precautionary saving as a substitute for insurance, what about the empirical results in their table 11.7 that appear to support such a prediction? The authors find a negative and highly significant relationship between the employer share of family premiums and the log of a family's financial assets. This they take as evidence in support of their thesis that the two assets are substitutes.

Unfortunately, this evidence is marred by an econometric problem. As the authors note (p. 345), one explanatory variable, the marginal tax rate, is positively correlated with the error term. They go on to say, "Because [the coefficient of the marginal tax rate] is consequently biased, the employer share is entered alone and our estimate of the effect of the subsidy is obtained from the elasticity with respect to the employer share." But the coefficient of the employer share is inconsistent if the marginal tax rate and employer share are positively correlated, which theory would predict. In a simple two-variable model

$$(1) \qquad Y = a + bX + cf + e,$$

where X is the marginal tax rate and f is the employer share, it can be shown that plim $\hat{c} = c\,(D - m_{Xf}\,m_{Xe})/D)$, where D is the determinant of the asymptotic moment matrix $(m_{XX}m_{ff} - m_{Xf}m_{Xf})$ and m_{Xf} and m_{Xe} are the population moments toward which the sample moments tend asymptotically. (This assumes f is independent of e.) Because all the terms in the parentheses are positive, the entire expression may be positive or negative; hence, the negative sign on the employer's share in table 11.7 could be a statistical artifact.

Of course, the actual positive loading on insurance would make these two assets substitutes, so a negative relationship between insurance and financial assets is not surprising. But detecting the relationship does seem surprising because of the small amounts involved, the noise in the asset data, and the difficulty of portfolio adjustment for the fifth of the sample with zero assets. The authors have reestimated this equation omitting the marginal tax rate, and the employer's share is still negative and significant. On the other hand, access to group insurance is not significant and group size is marginally significant with the wrong sign. I take this as weak evidence in support of the substitution hypothesis, but for most of the nonaged population the amounts of probable out-of-pocket medical care expenditure is small relative to wealth.

What then is the chapter's contribution? I read it as presenting, in tables 11.4 through 11.6, estimates of the demand for insurance that are probably more reliable than any in the literature. The only remotely comparable study is Phelps (1973, 1976), and the present paper uses a larger, more recent sample and studies more measures of insurance.

The result on demand for insurance that I found most noteworthy was the positive sign on the average expense per day in county hospitals in table 11.4. (I assume the authors mean the average for all general hospitals in a county and not the average in hospitals operated by a county.) The authors note that this evidence is consistent with Feldstein's discussion of a vicious circle of more hospital insurance leading to higher hospital prices which leads to more hospital insurance.

I confess to some skepticism about this conclusion. Previous econometric evidence is certainly mixed. The authors' result with premiums as a dependent variable could be a reflection of cost-of-living differences (although the estimated coefficient seems large for that interpretation), especially if the hospital price index is a proxy for all medical input prices. There is also a higher demand (in group policies) for full semiprivate room benefits as hospital expense rise, which would not be explained by cost-of-living differences. But full semiprivate room benefits tend to be found in Blue Cross policies, and Blue Cross has quite different market shares across states. I would like to see the authors take account of the tax subsidies that Blue Cross receives; it may be that a tax subsidy leads to a high Blue Cross market share that leads to widespread full semiprivate coverage. Specifically, would the coefficient on hospital cost remain significant if subsidies to Blue Cross were accounted for? My reasons for raising this issue are that the vicious circle hypothesis is of some significance, evidence from other studies is sketchy, and Marquis and Phelps (1982) find the opposite result using a different approach.

Another result of some note in table 11.4 is the significance of the age variable. Although a number of interpretations of this result are possible, one is that older workers tend to have more complete coverage, indicating that group insurance should not be considered exogenous with respect to medical conditions.

In sum, the theoretical case that health insurance and financial assets are substitutes is true—almost by definition—but the empirical case that health insurance exerts an important influence on the makeup of families' asset portfolios is not one that I find compelling.

References

Arrow, Kenneth J. 1963. Uncertainty and the welfare economics of medical care. *American Economic Review* 53: 941–73.

_____. 1973a. *Optimal insurance and generalized deductibles.* Publication no. R-2208-OEO. Santa Monica: Rand Corporation.

————. 1973b. *Welfare analysis of changes in health coinsurance rates.* Publication no. R-1281-OEO. Santa Monica: Rand Corporation.

Marquis, M. Susan, and Charles E. Phelps. 1982. Demand for supplementary health insurance. Paper presented at the American Economic Association meetings, New York City.

Phelps, Charles E. 1973. *Demand for health insurance: A theoretical and empirical investigation.* Publication no. R-1054-OEO. Santa Monica: Rand Corporation.

————. 1976. Demand for reimbursement insurance. In *The role of health insurance in the health services sector,* ed. Richard N. Rosett. New York: National Bureau of Economic Research.

12 The Valuation of Environmental Risks Using Hedonic Wage Models

V. Kerry Smith
Carol C. S. Gilbert

12.1 Introduction

Whenever benefit-cost analysis is applied to evaluate policies intended to reduce the risks to life experienced by members of a community, the valuation of these risk changes is inevitable. This process has been a continuing source of controversy in areas with these types of policy-making responsibilities. Indeed, for nearly twenty years economists have been criticized on ethical grounds for attempting to "value human life." While there is unlikely to be an end to this philosophical debate, it would appear that progress has been made in recognizing the importance of addressing explicitly these valuation decisions. This has been especially true for environmental policy, since William Ruckelshaus returned to EPA. Ruckelshaus identified risk management as one of the most important issues facing environmental policy-making. In discussing before the National Academy of Sciences the difficulties associated with the current regulatory process at EPA, he observed that

> Science and the law are thus partners at EPA, but uneasy partners. . . .
> The main reason for the uneasiness lies, I think, in the conflict between
> the way science really works and the public's thirst for certitude that is
> written into EPA's laws. . . . EPA's laws often assume, indeed demand,
> a certainty of protection greater than science can provide at the current
> state of knowledge. (Ruckelshaus 1983, pp. 3–4)

V. Kerry Smith is the Centennial Professor of Economics at Vanderbilt University. Carol C. S. Gilbert is a senior research scientist at the General Motors Research Laboratories.

Thanks are due to Allen Basala for stimulating the authors' interest in this research and to Bill Desvousges, Ann Fisher, Tom Tietenberg, and to the editors of this volume, Martin David and Tim Smeeding, for helpful comments on an earlier draft. V. Kerry Smith's initial research was partially supported by the University of North Carolina's University Research Council while Smith was a member of that faculty.

The purpose of this chapter is to consider whether economic methods are currently capable of responding to the demands likely to be posed by an approach to environmental regulation that focuses on the changes in risk resulting from more stringent standards for one or more dimensions of environmental quality. It is reasonable to expect that there will be a corresponding demand for these risk changes to be valued.

Several methods exist for measuring an individual's valuations of nonmarketed goods or services, including changes in risks.[1] The specific focus of this chapter is on only one of these methodologies—the hedonic wage model. It has been the mainstay of most valuation estimates for the risk changes associated with life-threatening events, and plays an important role in the benefit estimates derived for the health effects associated with the primary national ambient air quality standards.[2]

To conduct our appraisal of this framework, consideration will be given to the strengths and the limitations of the conceptual model underlying the hedonic approach and to the most detailed set of empirical estimates for a hedonic wage model currently available. Finally, this evaluation will be used to interpret the range of estimates currently available for valuing a "statistical life." However, before turning to this evaluation, it is important to provide some perspective on what the policy-making needs are likely to be. Consequently, in section 12.2 we discuss the types of risk assessments that are a part of the standard-setting process for air pollutants, since they serve to define the nature of the valuation problems.

Section 12.3 develops the conventional conceptual framework for the hedonic model, focusing particular attention on the assumptions important to the use of empirical model estimates of an individual's willingness to pay for risk reduction.

Section 12.4 describes a detailed empirical analysis of real wages using the 1978 Current Population Survey, including both individual and site characteristics as determinants of wages, together with three types of risk variables: one of the conventional measures of on-the-job accidents, an air quality index as a measure of the risk of potential chronic and acute health effects resulting from exposure to these pollutants, and an index of

1. A variety of taxonomic frameworks are used in describing these methods (see, for example, Schulze, d'Arge, and Brookshire 1981, Desvousges, Smith, and McGivney 1983). The *indirect market methods* rely on market transactions to infer an individual's demand (and thereby willingness to pay) for a good or service. With nonmarketed goods, some linkage must be established between the marketed good and the nonmarketed commodity. This can be an a priori restriction to the utility function (as in weak complementarity), an assumption regarding how the marketed and nonmarketed goods are used in consumption (e.g., a restriction to the household production technology, see Bockstael and McConnell 1983), or a technical linkage caused by the physical delivery system for the nonmarket good (i.e., air pollution is "delivered" in different doses to different geographic locations).

The direct valuation methods rely on surveys to elicit individuals' willingness to pay for hypothetical changes in one or more dimensions of environmental quality.

2. See MathTech 1983 for the benefits analysis associated with the proposed new primary standards for particulate matter.

the prospects for exposure to carcinogenic substances in the workplace. Specific consideration is given to the sensitivity of the valuation estimates to decisions that cannot be resolved on an a priori basis using economic theory.

The last section summarizes the chapter and provides a prognosis for this method in valuing environmental risks.

12.2 The Nature of Policy Demands for Risk Valuation

It is common practice among economists to assume that the primary issue in valuing the risk changes associated with air and water pollution control policies involves selecting a value for a statistical life.[3] While there can be little doubt that this is an important component of these tasks, it is not the sole area where risk valuation is required. Indeed, this perspective can be misleading. It would seem to imply that estimates of individuals' valuations for risks to life in other contexts (such as industrial accidents) can be readily transferred to the valuation of environmental risks.

There is no a priori reason to accept this conclusion. Different types of activities that impose risks to an individual's life may well lead to quite disparate willingness-to-pay values for risk reductions. The correspondence between willingness-to-pay values across different types of risk is the result of an assumption in the economic model used to describe individual behavior, not a conclusion drawn from empirical analysis. Moreover, as we shall develop in the next section, analyses of individuals' risk-taking decisions suggest quite different conclusions.

A second reason for questioning this view of the valuation problem arises from the specific needs of environmental policy-making and the likely expansion in these needs under a regime of standard setting based on concepts of risk management.

In order to limit the scope of our summary of the policy-based needs for environmental risk valuation, we will consider only air quality regulations. Under section 109 of the Clean Air Act, EPA is required to establish ambient air quality standards for the criteria pollutants.[4] This section mandates that primary standards be set at a level necessary to protect public health with an adequate margin of safety. Based on the act and its legislative history, EPA has interpreted this mandate in defining primary ambient air quality standards to be based on protecting those individuals established to be most sensitive to each criteria pollutant (though not necessarily the most sensitive members of the group) against adverse health effects (see Richmond 1981, and Jordan, Richmond, and McCurdy 1983).

3. An explicit example of these practices can be found in EPA's guidelines for preparing the regulatory impact analyses required by Executive Order 12291. See especially U.S. Environmental Protection Agency 1982, Appendix A, pp. 10–12.

4. See Richmond 1981 and Jordan, Richmond, and McCurdy 1983 for further discussion.

In order to implement this approach, the activities associated with defining a standard for each pollutant must: (*a*) identify the types of health effects likely to result from alternative ambient concentrations of the pollutant under evaluation; (*b*) specify the groups within the population most likely to be susceptible to these health effects; and (*c*) judge the changes in likelihood of these health effects that would accompany changes in the ambient concentration of the relevant pollutant.

This process inevitably leads to a fairly detailed description of the health effects considered relevant to the standard-setting process. To illustrate the nature of these effects, we have considered a recent analysis of four criteria pollutants—carbon monoxide, sulfur dioxide, particulate matter, and lead. Table 12.1 describes the types of health effects considered in each case.[5] Three aspects of these risks are important from a valuation perspective.

The first arises in the definition of the group used to value statistical lives. A statistical life is an alternative measure of risk reduction. It is based on an ex ante welfare criterion and envisions the decision process as follows (see Hammond 1981 and Ulph 1982). The decision maker is confronted with a policy that will reduce the risk for a group of individuals by a certain amount, say Δr. Since this risk reduction is experienced equally by all individuals it is a type of public good. A common approach for reporting the valuations of risk reductions has been to form an aggregate by asking how large the group would need to be in order for the change of Δr to lead to a reduction of one in the expected number of deaths for the group (i.e., $N = 1/\Delta r$). If we have estimates of the willingness to pay for Δr for each member of the group, then their valuation of the risk change can be considered their collective willingness to pay (*AWTP*) for a statistical life (i.e., $AWTP = \Sigma w_i(\Delta r)$, where $w_i(.)$ is the *i*th individual's willingness to pay for risk reductions). This has been a common format used in reporting the valuations of risk reductions.

However, in interpreting these estimates it is important to recognize that the risks described in table 12.1 are not experienced by all members of society. Rather they are usually associated with specific groups (i.e., the sensitive members of the population). These groups will not, in general, correspond to the groups used in estimating (with hedonic wage models) the "representative" individual's willingness to pay for risk reductions.[6]

---

5. These health effects are not intended to provide an exhaustive summary of those identified in the criteria document for each pollutant. Rather, they are indicative of the level of detail required in specifying both the nature of the effects at risk.

6. See Smith 1979, Blomquist 1979, and Violette and Chestnut 1983 for reviews of the literature estimating the value of risk reductions using wage models. These analyses are confined to groups with available wage surveys and often to subsets of employed individuals involved in more hazardous work. This was the case for one of the first studies in the area by Thaler and Rosen 1975.

Table 12.1   **Selected Criteria Pollutants and Health Effects at Risk**

Pollutant	Health Effect	Threat to Life
Carbon monoxide[a]	aggravation of Angina[b]	no
	aggravation of peripheral vascular disease	no
	myocardial infarction	yes
	effects on fetuses (increases in late fetal and early neonatal mortality rates)	yes
Sulphur dioxide[c]	aggravation of asthma	no
	aggravation of emphysema	no (?)
	aggravation of chronic bronchitis	no
	aggravation of heart disease	yes
	aggravation of other forms of lung disease	yes (?)
Particulate matter[d]	aggravation of acute respiratory disease	no
	aggravation of chronic respiratory disease	yes
	aggravation of heart disease	yes
Lead[e]	impacts on the nervous system	no
	IQ detriment in children	no
	impacts on the circulatory system	yes (?)
	increased risks in childbirth	yes (?)
	aggravation of anemia	no

Notes: The judgments as to the threat to life resulting from the health effect are interpretations of discussions in the risk assessments used to develop this table. They are intended to convey an appraisal of whether the health effect noted would be the primary cause of death.

[a]The sources of this summary of health effects were Keeney et al. 1982, and Smith, McNomee, and Merkhofer, n.d.

[b]Some questions have been raised recently with respect to the statistical analysis undertaken to establish this effect. Therefore, it should be regarded as a potential impact but not as clearly established as the others.

[c]The health effects were not drawn directly from a risk assessment for sulphur dioxide. Rather they were taken from Merkhofer's 1981 summary of the principles involved in conducting such assessments.

[d]These health effects were not as specifically defined because the criteria document focused on epidemological studies rather than clinical studies in defining the health risks. See MathTech 1983, vol. 2 for more details.

[e]These health effects are based on the preliminary work currently underway in the development of a primary standard for lead and are based on private correspondence with Allen Basala, Chief Methods Development Section, OAQPS, U.S. Environmental Protection Agency.

To the extent that members of these groups have specific characteristics that affect their performance in the labor market, we can expect differences between their "true" *AWTP* and that estimated using the results from conventional hedonic wage models.

A second issue arises with the type of events at risk. They are different from those providing the risk estimates in the hedonic wage models. The latter are based on accidents within the workplace and are likely to involve immediate physical consequences including physical impairment and, in some cases, fatalities. These differences are important because a growing body of research suggests that attributes of the events at risk and the risks themselves affect individuals' valuations of risk.[7] Violette and Chestnut (1983) in their recent summary of the relevance of these findings to the economic methods for valuing statistical lives noted that

> The evidence accumulated by the studies that have researched this topic indicates that society may place different values on different types of risks . . . it may be the case that individuals value the flexibility associated with the acceptance of voluntary risks. Voluntary risks are usually associated with activities that could be discontinued in the future if the individual's risk preference structure were to change. This is not the case with many involuntary risks. (Violette and Chestnut 1983, pp. 5-18 to 5-19)

Equally important, the character and quality of an individual's life (Zeckhauser and Shepard 1976) are clearly affected by the types of health effects leading to fatalities.

Finally, many of the risk changes involve health effects that do not represent immediate (or indeed any) threats to life. They are changes in the likelihood of either chronic or acute health effects. While a willingness-to-pay criterion would also offer the most appropriate basis for valuing these risk changes, there has been no empirical basis for developing these estimates.[8]

Thus, the policy demands for risk valuation require more detailed and discriminating estimates of individuals' willingness to pay, accounting for both the nature of the health effects and the character of the risk than is generally available with hedonic models. Of course, it should also be acknowledged that these limitations are largely the result of the constraints imposed by the available information used in constructing these models. Consequently, it seems reasonable to consider the behavioral assumptions made in describing individual actions that function as a "partial" substitute for the more discriminating information. A risk management policy may well require transferring the available risk valuation estimates based on experience within the workplace to a wider range of environmental risks. An examination of the implications of these assumptions should

7. See Violette and Chestnut 1983 for a review of the research in this area that is most directly related to the economic estimates of the value of risk. Other related work in psychology is discussed in Fischhoff et al. 1981, chap. 5.

8. See Freeman's 1979 summary of practices in this area. Several authors have attempted to distinguish separate effects for the risks of fatal and nonfatal accidents. Olson 1981 is one notable example. However, this practice is also imperfect because of the heterogeneity in the nonfatal accidents.

also provide some basis for judging the desirability of these transfers of the willingness-to-pay estimates.

12.3 The Application of Hedonic Models to Represent Risk-Taking Decisions

The application of the hedonic framework to explain transactions in labor markets has been described as a formal statement of the theory of equalizing differences (see Thaler and Rosen 1975; Smith 1979). Hedonic wage functions are thus considered to be equilibrium relationships, representing a double envelope—the lower boundary of the individual worker's wage acceptance functions and the upper frontier of firms' wage offer functions.[9] Consequently, the specifications necessarily reflect both the demand and supply determinants of these tied transactions in labor markets. By maintaining that these functions describe the market equilibrium, it is possible to use them to estimate the representative individual's marginal willingness to pay for any attribute (or component) of the tied transaction. This conclusion follows from the nature of the equilibrium itself. Under ideal conditions, if the contribution made to the market-clearing price by an increment to any attribute was not simultaneously equal to the marginal willingness to pay and offer price for that attribute, then there would be scope for arbitrage behavior.

When this framework is applied to the analysis of job risks, these risks are treated in simplified terms. The events at risk are assumed identical and capable of being fully described by the probability of a homogeneous accident. Consequently, risk becomes similar to any other job attribute. To appreciate the implications of this framework, we need to consider, in specific terms, the model of individual behavior used to describe such choices.

Assume an individual seeks to maximize expected utility defined in terms of Von Neumann–Morgenstern utility functions over the states of nature. Each state has implications for the income stream an individual can expect to realize and therefore for the goods and services that can be consumed. The individual will be assumed to be risk averse (i.e., the utility function $\mu(x, y)$, is concave in x and y). For our purposes we maintain that there are two states—either the individual incurs an accident or he does not incur an accident. The accident is defined as equivalent to an income loss of L. An individual obtains income by working and can select jobs that deliver wages and some probability, r, of an accident. He also selects commodities x and y.

---

9. See Rosen 1974 for a general discussion of the hedonic framework and Thaler and Rosen 1975 for a derivation of the framework with job risks. Triplett 1983 has recently provided an overview of this literature, appraising the implications of recent theoretical developments for the practical use of hedonic models.

In this framework the individual's objective function can be written as equation (1):

(1) $$\text{Maximize } E = R \cdot \mu \left(\frac{w(r) - P_y y - L}{P_x}, y \right)$$

$$+ (1 - R)\mu \left(\frac{w(r) - P_y y}{P_x}, y \right),$$

where P_i = price of commodity i ($i = x, y$);
           R = probability of state involving loss of L (in this example $R = r$);
           $w(.)$ = wage function describing equilibrium locus of wages and risks, r.

If we assume that the individual cannot change jobs and, in the process, control the level of risk experienced (i.e., r is not a choice variable), then risk of the loss, L, is a given to the decision process. Under these circumstances the individual's marginal willingness to pay ($MWTP$) for risk reduction is given by equation (2).

(2) $$MWTP = P_x MRS_{rx} = P_x \frac{\mu^* - \bar{\mu}}{r\bar{\mu}_x + (1 - r)\mu_x^*},$$

$$\text{where } \bar{\mu} = \mu \left(\frac{w(r) - P_y y - L}{P_x}, y \right),$$

$$\mu^* = \mu \left(\frac{w(r) - P_y y}{P_x}, y \right),$$

$$\mu_i^*, \bar{\mu}_i = \text{first derivative of } \mu^*, \bar{\mu} \text{ with respect to } i.$$

Since equation (2) defines the individual's inverse demand for risk reduction, it provides the accepted economic basis for valuing changes in risk.

Once we acknowledge an individual's ability to select a job and assume that those selections are based on the wage–job risk combinations available in the market, then the model must be adapted. If we assume, in addition, that an individual correctly perceives job risks (so that $R = r$), then there is some basis for using behavioral actions to estimate an individual's valuation of risk changes. That is, the existence of $w(.)$ allows us to observe one point on this inverse demand function corresponding to the individual's equilibrium selection of the terms of work. The first-order conditions for a maximum of equation (1) with r a choice variable imply that $P_x \times MRS_{rx}$ will equal the slope of the hedonic wage function at the equilibrium selection of r, as given in equation (3).

(3) $$\frac{dw}{dr} = P_x \frac{\mu^* - \bar{\mu}}{r\bar{\mu}_x + (1 - r)\mu_x^*}.$$

This framework can be seen as an adaptation to that presented by Thaler and Rosen (1975) (see also Freeman 1979).

Nonetheless, several points are worthy of specific attention. First, the loss, L, is assumed capable of being expressed in monetary terms. As Thaler and Rosen observed, this simplification implies that if individuals can insure against the loss at actuarially fair rates, then this specification would imply an equalization of incomes between the two states.

To the extent we believe that the events at risk do not readily translate into monetary terms, then the utility function for the loss state may include a reduction in income, L (and the corresponding decreased consumption of x and y), as well as changes in other variables that are assumed to be associated with characteristics of the loss state, which are not purchased in markets but are "delivered" with the events at risk. These variables might reflect the nonmonetary dimensions of the events at risk. This case can be treated as implying state-dependent utility functions. With this specification the equalization of marginal utilities under fair insurance would not imply equal incomes.[10] Indeed, in such cases even with fair insurance an individual will nonetheless prefer one of the states over another (see Cook and Graham 1977).

These two assumptions (i.e., state dependency of the utility function and existence of fair markets for diversifying risk) have direct implications for the interpretation of the hedonic wage model. For example, if we assume that there are fair insurance and state-independent utility functions, then we can write dw/dr in terms of the loss experienced, as in equation (4) below.[11]

(4)
$$\frac{dw}{dr} = L.$$

By contrast with state-dependent utility functions, or an absence of actuarial fair insurance, the form of dw/dr is altered as given for the former in equation (5).

10. This conclusion follows because the utility functions for each state are assumed to be different. Consequently, the income certainty and utility certainty loci will be distinct and also different from locus of equilibrium choices in a contingent claims framework.

11. This result can be established by respecifying the objective function as:

$$EU = r\mu \left(\frac{w(r) - P_y y - L + I}{P_x}, y \right) + (1 - r)\mu \left(\frac{w(r) - P_y y - (r/1 - r)I}{P_x}, y \right),$$

where I = level of insurance. Differentiating with respect to the selection of I yields equality of the marginal utilities for x in both states. Consequently the income levels assigned to each state will be equal and $I - L$ must equal $-(r/1 - r)I$. Thus $I = (1 - r)L$. Given this result, the specification of the utility function implies equal marginal utilities with respect to y.

$$\frac{dw}{dr} = P_x \left[\frac{\tilde{\mu} - \overline{\mu}}{\mu_x} \right] + \frac{I}{(1 - r)},$$

where $\tilde{\mu}$ = total utility in no accident state and $\overline{\mu}$ = total utility in accident state. However, equal income implies $\tilde{\mu} - \mu = 0$. Substituting for I we have equation (4).

(5)
$$\frac{dw}{dr} = L + P_x \left(\frac{\tilde{\mu} - \hat{\mu}}{\tilde{\mu}_x} \right),$$

where $\tilde{\mu}$ = the total utility without the accident and $\hat{\mu}$ = the total utility with the accident. The existence of fair markets for insurance implies that $\tilde{\mu}_x = \hat{\mu}_x$.

Equation (5) implies that transferring the estimates of individuals' willingness to pay for risk reduction for one type of risk to the valuation of the incremental changes in another type of risk may not be possible. That is, even if the monetary losses at risk are identical, the nonmonetary may well be different, and therefore we can expect differences in the magnitude of $(\tilde{\mu} - \hat{\mu})$.

Thus, examining the behavior of a set of individuals facing one type of risk and using their behavioral responses to develop estimates of the same individuals' valuation of another type of risk will lead to incorrect estimates of the values of the risk change. The same conclusion can be drawn if there are differences in the extent to which individuals can diversify activities and reduce the impacts of each type of risk. In this case, dw/dr for the risks facing one individual would reflect that individual's risk distribution of income, which may not characterize the opportunities available to a second individual.[12]

It may be more reasonable to assume that the same individual faces risks from different activities and can select the risk level in each by either changing jobs or altering the mix of his activities. The conventional assumption for these models is to maintain that these risks lead to the same outcome (see Freeman 1979 as an example). The risk of death from any source has the same valuation. It is this assumption (i.e., R in equation (1) is simply $\sum_{j=1}^{n} r_j$, where n = the alternative mutually exclusive ways in which an individual might experience risks of fatalities) that assures that the marginal valuations of the alternative risks correspond.[13] However, if

12. See Cook and Graham 1977 for further discussion of this concept of inefficiency in the risk distribution of income.

13. In this case the objective function could be rewritten as

$$EU = (r + s)\mu \left(\frac{w(r) - P_y y(s) - L + I}{P_x}, y(s) \right)$$

$$+ (1 - (r + s))\mu \left(\frac{w(r) - P_y y(s) - \frac{(r + s)}{1 - (r + s)} I}{P_x}, y(s) \right),$$

where s = risk associated with consumption activity that is selected by the intensity of undertaking y (hence y is a function of s). Differentiating with respect to s we have a general expression for dy/ds that suggests the marginal valuations of risk are equated after adjustment to reflect their respective roles in consumption in relationship to relative prices. That is,

$$P_y \frac{dy}{ds} = \frac{1}{\left(\frac{P_x}{P_y} \cdot \frac{\mu_y}{\mu_x} - 1 \right)} \left[P_x \left[\frac{\tilde{\mu} - \mu}{\mu_x} \right] + \frac{I}{1 - (r + s)} \right].$$

it is believed that the attributes of the events at risk are important to an individual's evaluation, then the model must be amended to include new states and corresponding distinct utility functions for each. These amendments imply that the transfer of marginal valuations estimated from decisions on one type of risk to those of another type would not be warranted. It seems reasonable, therefore, to consider the nature of the evidence available for differences in how individuals respond to different types of risk.

As we noted earlier Violette and Chestnut (1983) used this literature in their review of the available estimates of the willingness to pay for risk reductions. Clearly one can use the differences in risk valuations between workplace (i.e., hedonic wage) and consumer market studies to provide informal evidence that individuals value different types of risk differently.[14] In 1982 dollars, the range of estimates for the values of a statistical life derived from the consumer market studies was confined to the lower end of the valuations from wage hedonic models based on workplace risks.[15] Of course, it should be acknowledged that each type of study is subject to many assumptions that might also account for this discrepancy. Nonetheless, when considered together with the policy and psychological analyses of risk-taking behavior, this interpretation cannot be dismissed as irrelevant.

The policy analyses of risk-taking behavior begin with the assumption that individual (and indeed social) preferences toward risk are revealed through individuals' behavior in accepting different types of risk. Starr (1969) appears to have been the first to use this framework to compare risks in an effort to identify the characteristics of risks that influence individuals' willingness to accept them. All of the studies in this area have been crude in their methodologies and should therefore be regarded as suggestive of the important characteristics of risk. Nonetheless, the characteristics identified by the most recent of these studies of Litai (1980) conform in several respects with the features found to affect the performance of the expected utility model in experimental tests (see Hershey, Kunreuther, and Schoemaker 1982). They include: volition, severity, origin, effect manifestation, exposure pattern, controllability, familiarity, benefit, and necessity.

Both sets of research seem to suggest that a state-dependent framework that recognizes the influence of the attributes of risk may be necessary for modeling individuals' responses to different types of risk. Furthermore, this would imply that valuation estimates derived for risks in one context may not be relevant to comparable risk reductions in another setting.

---

14. The consumer market studies are more limited and refer to such decisions as wearing seatbelts or purchasing smoke detectors. See Violette and Chestnut 1983 for a review.

15. These estimates were quite close to Portney's 1981 implicit valuations of risk derived using the results of a hedonic property value model.

Unfortunately, it is not possible to directly investigate this issue. Data limitations prevent specific consideration of how individuals' value different types of risks. It is, however, possible to consider the sources of some of these risks (e.g., exposure to air pollution and to carcinogenic materials) in a hedonic wage model and to consider how robust the model and its estimates of willingness to pay for risk reductions in the workplace are to the role of these environmental variables in the model.

12.4   Estimates of a Hedonic Wage Model and the Valuation of Risk

Our reviews both of the policy requirements for estimates of individuals' valuation of risk reductions and of the theoretical basis for valuing risk changes endorse the need for distinguishing different types of risks. From the perspective of environmental policy (especially air pollution policies), such distinctions are important because they arise from the nature of the effects of different pollutants. The theoretical analysis also focuses on these differing effects, but emphasizes the possibility that individuals might value them differently. Consequently, even though two different activities might yield the same risk to life, an individual may well value reductions in the risk posed by one of these activities more highly than the other.

In order to evaluate the practical significance of these policy needs and theoretical arguments, empirical estimates of the willingness to pay for risk reductions across a range of activities are needed. Moreover, these estimates must be derived from a consistent description of individual behavior if they are to be compared in a meaningful way. As we noted earlier, the present analysis will fall short of this goal. Data limitations remain the primary culprit. While the analysis that can be undertaken is more limited, it is, nonetheless, suggestive of the importance of refining our empirical models for estimating individuals' valuation of risk.

Our empirical analysis will consider two aspects of hedonic wage models. First, using a detailed wage model developed with microdata, we estimate individuals' willingness to pay for two types of risks—life-threatening accidents in the workplace and risks of death through exposure to air pollutants (i.e., total suspended particulates). Our results indicate under reasonable assumptions that these two sources imply quite different implicit valuations for comparable risk changes.

The second aspect of our empirical analysis considers the variation in estimates of these marginal valuations that would arise from plausible variations in the specification of the hedonic wage model. The objective of this appraisal is to gauge whether the discrepancy in the estimates of the marginal valuation of different types of risk reductions would be attributed to the imprecision of the hedonic model.

12.4.1 The Basic Model

Since the hedonic wage function is an equilibrium relationship, the model should include both demand and supply determinants of wage rates. Moreover, to the extent that the sample used in estimating this relationship includes individual wage rates in different geographic locations, we can expect that the equilibrium locus will reflect the marginal valuations of site amenities (see Rosen 1979). Equation (6) provides a general statement for the hedonic wage function.

$$(6) \qquad \left(\frac{w}{P}\right)_i = f(x_{I_i}, x_{J_i}, x_{S_i}) + \epsilon_i,$$

with ϵ_i a stochastic error. This specification maintains that the real wage rate (i.e., the nominal wage w divided by a cost-of-living index, P, for individual i) will be a function of individual characteristics (x_{I_i}), job characteristics (x_{J_i}), and geographic site characteristics (x_{S_i}).

Past hedonic models have tended to focus on a subset of these variables, with those arising from the wage differential literature emphasizing x_I and x_J (see Brown 1980, Lucas 1977, Thaler and Rosen 1975, and Viscusi 1978a as examples), while those from the environmental and urban applications focusing on x_I and x_S (see Hoch 1974, Cropper and Arriaga-Salinas 1980, and Rosen 1979 as examples). In order to avoid the possibility of specification errors, all three sets of variables must be included.

To meet this objective requires a merging of the information from conventional wage surveys with data on job and site characteristics. This task was undertaken using the individuals living in each of forty-four Standard Metropolitan Statistical Areas (SMSAs) for the May 1978 Current Population Survey. This locational attribute permitted the assignment of site characteristics to each sample respondent. In addition the available information on individuals' characteristics, including socioeconomic attributes, occupation, and industry, permitted the assignment of job characteristics.

Since the specific details of these assignments are discussed in Smith (1983), we will turn to a description of the variables included in the specification of the basic model used for the estimation of the marginal values for risk reductions from different sources. The sample after these assignments consisted of 16,199 observations.[16]

A wide array of variables describing site characteristics were considered. The final set of variables used in the model included: a crime rate measure (i.e., serious crimes per 100,000 inhabitants of the SMSA in 1975), *CRIME;* the average unemployment rate for the SMSA in 1978, *UN78;* the mean annual percentage of possible sunshine, *SUN;* and an air

---

16. For the specific details on the treatment of missing observations, consideration of alternative specifications and samples, and discussion of the implications of the selectivity bias for the model's results, see Smith 1983.

quality index, *TSP* (i.e., total suspended particulate matter in micrograms per cubic meter, measured as the annual geometric mean at sites with complete data).[17]

The job characteristics were confined to four variables that could be assigned based on translating the census identification of industries to the Standard Industrial Classification (SIC). They were as follows: the BLS occupational injury rate for 1975, *ACCIDENT RATE;* an index of exposures to carcinogens in the workplace,[18] *CANCER;* a measure of workers' knowledge of job hazards (defined as the number of workers in each industry covered by collective bargaining agreements with general provisions concerned with health and safety conditions relative to the total employment in that industry), *KNOW;* and a measure of the degree of price uncertainty in the product market for each industry, *OJT.*[19] Based on earlier theoretical research (i.e., Holtmann and Smith 1977, 1979), it was hypothesized that uncertain product market conditions would affect the availability of on-the-job training.

Finally, the individual characteristics provide the most extensive set of variables, including most of the factors mentioned in earlier studies of the determinants of wage rates including: education, *EDU;* experience (measured as age minus years of education minus six), *POTEXP;* race (white = 1); sex (male = 1); veteran status, *VET* (veteran = 1, and relevant only for males); union member (union = 1); head of household (head = 1), dual-job holder (if dual-job holder variable = 1); and qualitative variables for occupations (see table 12.2 for the specifics).

The wage rate measure was calculated as usual weekly earnings divided by usual hours worked. The local cost-of-living index was based on the 1977 BLS cost-of-living index for an intermediate budget (see Smith 1983).

The first columns in tables 12.2 and 12.3 report the ordinary least-squares estimates for the basic model with the full sample and a subsample composed only of males respectively. A semilog specification (with the log of real wages as the dependent variable) was used for these results. The overall estimates of the effects of individual characteristics are comparable to earlier studies. The site and job characteristics are also generally consistent with those earlier studies which included subsets of the set of variables included in this specification. Consequently, either model (i.e., that based on the full sample or that derived using only males) would be

17. A variety of other pollution measures were also considered. However, the measures are closely intercorrelated, suggesting that precise estimates for each one's effect on wages will be difficult to realize.

18. For more details and caveats with respect to these exposure estimates see Hickey and Kearney 1977.

19. See Smith 1983 for more details.

Table 12.2   **Hedonic Wage Models: Full Sample with Alternative Environmental Quality Measures**

Variable	Basic Model	EQ A	EQ B	EQ C
Intercept	.341	.767	.694	.668
	(6.15)	(9.13)	(8.72)	(8.69)
EDU	.024	.017	.018	.018
	(3.88)	(2.34)	(2.32)	(2.40)
EDU^2	.0013	.002	.0017	.0016
	(5.05)	(5.38)	(5.39)	(5.33)
POTEXP	.026	.026	.026	.026
	(32.44)	(26.94)	(27.05)	(26.88)
POTEXP^2	−.046	−.040	−.045	−.040
	(−26.62)	(−21.4)	(−21.54)	(−21.40)
Race	.056	.054	.056	.056
	(5.85)	(4.72)	(4.82)	(4.89)
Sex	.166	.163	.164	.163
	(17.59)	(14.51)	(14.56)	(14.48)
VET	.075	.083	.082	.083
	(7.80)	(7.20)	(7.17)	(7.20)
UN78	−.014	−0.014	−0.010	−0.014
	(−5.59)	(−4.39)	(−2.82)	(−4.61)
Professional	.347	.301	2.99	.300
	(16.67)	(11.86)	(11.80)	(11.81)
Manager	.374	.311	.311	.312
	(17.32)	(11.88)	(11.85)	(11.89)
Sales	.149	.099	.099	.100
	(6.52)	(3.54)	(3.55)	(3.56)
Clerical	.200	.147	.146	.147
	(10.15)	(6.09)	(6.05)	(6.07)
Craftsman	.265	.214	.214	.216
	(12.26)	(8.07)	(8.05)	(8.12)
Operative	.078	.023	.023	.025
	(3.62)	(.89)	(.85)	(.94)
Transport equip. operator	.123	.081	.081	.083
	(4.68)	(2.58)	(2.55)	(2.63)
Nonfarm labor	.078	.024	.023	.025
	(3.25)	(.81)	(.78)	(.84)
Service	−.0098	−.054	−.055	−.054
	(0.48)	(−2.16)	(−2.20)	(−2.13)
ACCIDENT RATE	.011	.010	.010	.010
	(12.87)	(9.71)	(9.67)	(9.89)
CANCER	.219	.105	.107	.096
	(2.757)	(1.03)	(1.05)	(.94)
TSP[a]	.0871	.175	.121	.201
	(3.88)	(5.92)	(4.62)	(5.85)
Household head	.157	.158	.157	.157
	(18.08)	(15.23)	(15.15)	(15.18)
SO$_2$ measure	—	−0.257	−0.118	−0.281
		(−5.33)	(−4.60)	(−4.56)

Table 12.2 (continued)

Variable	Basic Model	EQ A	EQ B	EQ C
Union member	.183	.184	.184	.185
	(22.32)	(19.131)	(19.103)	(19.159)
OJT*POTEXP	−.0012	−0.0016	−0.0017	−0.0017
	(−0.98)	(−1.12)	(−1.15)	(−1.16)
CRIME[b]	.094	−0.151	.262	.156
	(4.60)	(−0.40)	(.75)	(.43)
SUN	−.0015	−0.0056	−0.0049	−0.0052
	(−2.62)	(−6.12)	(−5.61)	(−5.66)
Dual job	−.0439	−0.0436	−0.042	−0.043
	(−2.28)	(−1.91)	(−1.86)	(−1.90)
KNOW*CANCER	4.303	4.374	4.347	4.589
	(6.01)	(5.19)	(5.16)	(5.46)
R^2	.460	0.463	0.426	0.463

Note: The numbers in parentheses below the estimated coefficients are the t-ratios for the null hypothesis of no association.

[a]Coefficient has been scaled by 100 (i.e., reported = estimated × 100).

[b]Coefficient has been scaled by 10,000.

Table 12.3   Hedonic Wage Models: Male Sample with Alternative Environmental Quality Measures

Variable	Basic Model	EQ A	EQ B	EQ C
Intercept	.651	1.031	1.006	0.847
	(8.98)	(9.68)	(9.91)	(8.69)
EDU	.031	0.035	0.035	0.035
	(4.06)	(3.94)	(3.92)	(3.90)
EDU^2	.0010	.0010	.0010	.0010
	(3.30)	(2.78)	(2.78)	(2.80)
POTEXP	.0309	0.0315	0.0316	0.0414
	(25.67)	(21.61)	(21.72)	(21.54)
$POTEXP^2$	−.053	−.053	−.053	−.053
	(−22.26)	(−18.20)	(−18.29)	(−18.15)
Race	.112	0.106	0.107	0.107
	(8.66)	(6.97)	(7.03)	(7.04)
VET	.036	0.042	0.041	0.042
	(3.60)	(3.56)	(3.51)	(3.56)
UN78	−.021	−0.020	−0.014	−0.023
	(−6.47)	(−5.028)	(−3.040)	(−5.73)
Professional	.087	0.044	0.041	0.043
	(2.79)	(1.17)	(1.11)	(1.13)
Manager	.141	0.077	0.074	0.077
	(4.45)	(2.02)	(1.94)	(2.02)
Sales	.0019	−0.0317	−0.0334	−0.0315
	(−0.05)	(−0.77)	(−0.81)	(−0.76)

Table 12.3 (continued)

Variable	Basic Model	EQ A	EQ B	EQ C
Clerical	−.101	−0.159	−0.162	−0.161
	(−3.06)	(−4.00)	(−4.08)	(−4.05)
Craftsman	.017	−0.026	−0.029	−0.025
	(0.54)	(−0.67)	(−0.74)	(−0.65)
Operative	−.147	−0.196	−0.200	−0.195
	(−4.40)	(−4.86)	(−4.96)	(−4.84)
Transport	−.118	−0.152	−0.155	−0.150
equip. operator	(−3.35)	(−3.60)	(−3.67)	(−3.55)
Nonfarm labor	−.129	−0.172	−0.175	−0.172
	(−3.81)	(−4.16)	(−4.23)	(−4.16)
Service	−.253	−0.285	−0.289	−0.286
	(−7.77)	(−7.24)	(−7.34)	(−7.24)
ACCIDENT RATE	.011	.00987	.00976	0.010
	(10.65)	(7.768)	(7.688)	(7.913)
CANCER	.028	0.0211	0.0211	0.0201
	(2.77)	(1.344)	(1.343)	(1.280)
TSP[a]	.112	.207	.155	.186
	(3.85)	(5.455)	(4.605)	(4.260)
Household head	.232	0.225	0.225	0.225
	(16.96)	(13.942)	(13.924)	(13.887)
SO_2 measure	—	−.00284	−.00160	−.00181
	—	(−4.603)	(−4.905)	(−2.319)
Union member	.173	0.177	0.176	0.177
	(17.09)	(14.956)	(14.896)	(14.916)
OJT*POTEXP	−.002	−.002	−.002	−.002
	(−1.60)	(−1.313)	(−1.301)	(−1.335)
CRIME[b]	.078	−.289	−.076	.490
	(2.94)	(−0.599)	(−0.170)	(1.0669)
SUN	−.0021	−.0067	−.0066	−.0050
	(−2.79)	(−5.813)	(−5.933)	(−4.401)
Dual job	−.041	−0.032	−0.031	−0.032
	(−1.71)	(−1.162)	(−1.119)	(−1.140)
KNOW*CANCER	3.879	3.261	3.148	3.560
	(4.70)	(3.294)	(3.175)	(3.601)
R^2	.462	0.481	0.481	0.479

Note: The numbers in parentheses below the estimated coefficients are the t-ratios for the null hypothesis of no association.
[a]Coefficient has been scaled by 100 (i.e., reported = estimated × 100).
[b]Coefficient has been scaled by 10,000.

regarded as a plausible framework for measuring the implicit valuation of job risk or the marginal willingness to pay for reductions in air pollution.

Equally important, these results indicate that it is possible to estimate separate, statistically significant effects on real wages for different sources of risk—accidents on the job, health risks that arise from exposure to air pollution, and the long-latency health risks associated with exposure to carcinogens in the workplace. It appears that the statistical significance and direction of these effects are stable for variations in sample composition (see Smith 1983). Consequently, at a general level these results confirm the earlier work of Hoch (1974), Rosen (1979), and Cropper and Arriaga-Salinas (1980).

What has not been undertaken, to date, is the development of a comparison of the implied valuations of risk changes. Unfortunately, we cannot include in this comparison the long-latency risks. Our index of carcinogenic exposures is based on a limited survey of experience with carcinogens in the workplace. The estimated exposures were extrapolated for each two-digit SIC code to the industry level. They do not take account of control methods that may be in place in each industry and should be treated as a crude measure of potential exposure, scaled by the estimated working hours from the BLS injury rate data. Given the limitations in the index, we have interpreted it as a proxy variable to account for this factor and not attempted to use it as an estimate of exposure risk. Consequently, in what follows we develop and compare the estimates of the willingness to pay for risk reductions implied by these models for two of the three sources of risk.

12.4.2   The Estimated Valuation of Risk Reductions

We have estimated two implicit valuations for risk changes from the hedonic wage models. The first follows directly from conventional practices. As we noted in section 12.2 above, the valuation estimates for "statistical lives" are simply transformations to the wage premiums required for small increments in the risk of fatal accidents. Rather than scale these estimates to correspond to the value implied by reducing the expected number of fatalities by one, we have simply reported the estimated marginal valuations for an incremental reduction in risk.

The second is derived by adapting an ingenious proposal by Portney (1981) to the wage-hedonic framework. Portney's suggestion was made using a hedonic property value model but is equally relevant for a wage model. It maintains that individuals seek to avoid exposure to air pollution because they recognize that such exposure increases mortality risks. Consequently, if we assume that individuals "know" the relationship between air pollution exposure and this increased risk, we can infer an implicit valuation for risk reductions using the wage premiums required to accept increased pollution.

For our particular application, both risk valuation estimates require some specific adjustments to the estimated parameters. The first valuation relates to the wage premiums for increased risk of fatal accidents, while the risk measure used in our hedonic wage model is for all accidents.[20] Consequently we must estimate the share of total accidents that are fatal. Following Viscusi (1978b) we maintain that fatalities are approximately .4 percent of all accidents. Our wage measure is the hourly rate. To convert our valuation estimate to an annual willingness to pay, we assume 2,000 hours are worked per year. Thus, the estimated marginal willingness to pay for a risk reduction is assumed to correspond to the acceptance wage in annual terms and is calculated by rescaling the estimated parameter for our risk measure to reflect the units of measure and proportion of fatal accidents. This coefficient is then multiplied by the relevant (depending on the sample) average hourly wage and by 2,000. Since our model corresponds to wages in 1978, the result is adjusted by the Consumer Price Index to provide the 1982 estimates of implicit marginal valuations of risk changes. The resulting estimate for our basic model is reported in the first column and row of table 12.4.

To translate the wage premium for incremental changes in TSP to a valuation of risk, we must postulate the mortality risk–TSP relationship that is assumed to be recognized by our sample respondents. This literature is fraught with problems and exhibits a diverse array of estimates (for discussion see Gerking and Schulze (1981), and Freeman (1982). Fortunately, as part of the benefit analysis conducted for its review of the current primary standard for particulate matter, the EPA sponsored research that attempted to provide consensus estimates of the total mortality risk–TSP relationship based on both micro- and macroepidemiological studies. We have selected three values, including the consensus point estimate from the macroepidemiological studies, for our analysis. The range of estimates was from 0 to .471 as the impact of a change of one microgram per cubic meter in TSP (measured as the annual geometric mean) on the total mortality rate (deaths per 100,000). Our three estimates span the range of possible impacts of particulates on mortality. Each has been considered in the calculations including what was judged to be the "best" estimate of .171 (see MathTech 1983, pp. 4-55–4-56). Using these estimates together with the wage premiums for increments to TSP we can impute values for fatality risks associated with air pollution exposures (i.e., $\partial w/\partial \beta = (\partial w/\partial TSP)/(\partial \beta/\partial TSP)$, where β = risk of death due to air pollution exposure). This scaling together with the use of the average hourly wage and assumption of 2,000 hours worked yields estimates for the implicit annual valuation of this risk. They are reported in 1982 dollars for the basic model in the second column (I) for the smallest impact, the intermediate value (II) in the third column, and the highest value (III) in the fourth. All estimates are for 1×10^{-5} increments in risk.

---

20. The BLS accident rate measure was scaled to a rate per hundred workers. Hence the parameter estimates must be adjusted to reflect this scaling.

Table 12.4   Estimated Marginal Valuations for Risk Reductions

| | | Source of Risk | | |
| | | Exposure to Air Pollution[a] | | |
Model	Workplace	I	II	III
1. *Basic model*				
Comparable treatment of fatal + nonfatal accidents	52.70	941.82	94.18	34.19
Proportional reduction in marginal valuation to reflect role of aesthetics[b]	—	659.27	65.93	23.94
2. *Alternative samples*				
Male[c]	61.02	2,419.45	241.95	51.36
3. *Alternative models/samples*				
Full sample, unrestricted[d]	51.78	508.22	50.82	18.45
Full sample, excluding air pollution	53.62	—	—	—
Male sample, unrestricted	59.41	871.67	87.17	31.92
4. *Expansions in air pollutants treated*				
SO_2 measured as annual arithmetic mean (A)	46.23	1,892.31	189.23	68.70
SO_2 measured as annual arithmetic mean of daily highs (B)	46.23	1,308.40	130.84	47.50
SO_2 measured as annual arithmetic mean of daily lows (C)	46.23	2,173.45	217.35	78.91

Note: These estimates are in 1982 dollars and were converted from 1978 dollars using the Consumer Price Index for December 1982.

[a]These estimates of the marginal willingness to pay for risk reduction relate to the increased risk of mortality based on exposure to total suspended particulates. I assumes a marginal effect of .017, II an effect of .171, and III an effect of .471.

[b]In a contingent valuation survey of individuals' willingness to pay for air quality improvements, Brookshire et al. 1979 asked respondents to allocate their total willingness to pay among aesthetic and health motivations. Their results indicated that 30 percent of the total willingness to pay was attributed to aesthetic motives. This estimate maintains that the same proportion can be applied to the willingness-to-pay estimates from the wage model.

[c]These estimates utilize the average wage for males of $7.22 rather than the overall sample average wage rate of $6.18.

[d]In the semilog specification of the hedonic wage model, the use of the log of the real wage is equivalent to a specification using the log of the nominal wage with the log of the cost of living as a determinant of wages whose coefficient is restricted to unity. The unrestricted form uses nominal wages and allows the parameter for the cost-of-living variable to be freely estimated.

Clearly these marginal valuations are quite different. The implicit valuation due to air pollution ranges from a value nearly twenty times to one that is about 60 percent of that associated with fatal accidents in the workplace. Since it might be argued that these estimates reflect other motives for valuing air quality, we have considered a variety of adjustments to this estimate.

The second row in the table uses the only available estimate of the portion of household's valuation of air quality due to health and aesthetics to adjust implicit risk valuation as a result of exposures to air pollution. The highest valuation (I) remains well outside the scope that might be attributed to random variation, while the intermediate case could well be considered within the range of estimates for risk valuations due to job risks. However, it is also fair to note that further adjustments are clearly warranted. Even after adjustment for aesthetics, this approach to valuation attributes all the wage premiums to mortality risk reductions. The wage differential may also reflect morbidity effects. Finally, within a simple general equilibrium description of household adjustment in the property and labor markets (i.e., selecting site amenities by changing location), we might also expect that these estimates of willingness to pay for air quality improvements would reflect the implications of these changes for all household members.

We have attempted two further adjustments to reflect these two considerations. Freeman's (1982) recent analysis of the benefits with the air quality improvements from 1970 to 1978 indicated that approximately 18 percent of the total benefits arose from morbidity effects. Using either this adjustment or the assumption of a three-person household, we can narrow the discrepancy between the valuation implied by the intermediate mortality/particulate association. For example, assuming the valuation is equal for all household members is below the workplace risks (i.e., $31.39 versus $52.50). Adjustment for morbidity effects alone reduces the valuation to $77.23. This is not true for either of the extreme assumptions concerning mortality/particulate associations. In both cases, these adjustments and the implicit valuations remain substantially different. In case I, they remain substantially greater than the implicit valuation of workplace risk, while in case III they become much smaller. These distinctions serve to highlight the importance of the individual's perception of the relationship between exposure to particulate matter and the associated risk of death.

The balance of the table repeats the calculations presented in the first row with a variety of alternative model or sample specifications including: (a) confining the sample to males (as frequently has been the case in the literature on valuing job risks); (b) changing the treatment of the local cost-of-living variable; (c) excluding air pollution completely; and (d) expanding the types of pollutants included in the model to include another pollutant—sulphur dioxide. The complete results for the wage models associated with the last of these variations are also reported in tables 12.2 and 12.3. The equation designations—A, B, and C—correspond to the various measures of sulphur dioxide identified in table 12.4.

These results clearly indicate that the implicit value of risk associated with air pollution exposure is sensitive to model specification, while that due to job fatalities is not. However, these variations do not serve to narrow greatly the discrepancy in marginal valuations of risk associated with these two sources. Accordingly, if we accept the theoretical premises of the hedonic model itself, these results provide indirect and tentative support for the need to distinguish estimates of the willingness to pay for risk based on the types of risk and of the effects involved. At the same time, they also indicate the significant limitations of the hedonic wage model as a method for precisely estimating distinct valuations for risk reductions from different sources.

12.5   Implications

There is growing evidence that the hedonic wage model can provide an empirical basis for isolating the site and job characteristics that influence equilibrium wage rates. Our analysis with a large microdata set and more extensive definitions for site characteristics is also clearly consistent with this conclusion. Equally important, it provides some evidence that indicates individuals may well value comparable risk changes differently. That is, we have considered risk increments that are of equivalent size and lead to the same ultimate outcome (a fatality). Of course the initial probabilities of the fatality and the avenues available for adjustment can be expected to be different in these two cases.

It should also be acknowledged that access to information and the corresponding perception of these risks are likely to be different in these cases. Work-related risks are more tangible. Many union contracts require not only wage adjustments to reflect such hazards, but also disseminate information on the risks. By contrast, the extent of general knowledge of the risks of exposure to air pollution, especially pollution associated with one particular pollutant, is much more limited. Indeed, the available technical information of the health risk exhibits considerable diversity of opinion on the severity of the risks. It would therefore not be too surprising to find that these estimates were subject to large errors. Nonetheless, to attribute all of the difference between these estimates of individual willingness to pay for risk to random error requires that we regard the effects of air pollution on wages as essentially noninformative. This is certainly not the position that has been taken in benefit cost analyses of air quality changes. Consequently, we must attempt to explain the discrepancy. One of the most important explanations is the role of perceptions in the valuation of risk changes. Clearly the sensitivity of the implicit valuation of risk derived from the wage-risk relationships illustrates the importance of this explanation.

In his discussion of the failure of the expected utility model as a description of individual behavior under uncertainty, Schoemaker (1982) identifies five aspects of decision making that have been established from psychological research. They deal with limitations in the simple economic description of individual choice, noting that: (1) most decisions are made by decomposing the problem involved and using relative comparisons; (2) the strategies used for decisions vary with the complexity of the task to be undertaken; (3) choices on one problem are often made in isolation from other decisions; (4) selections involving gains and losses are made with individual reference points; and (5) subjective perceptions of probabilities may not relate linearly to objective estimates.

While these are all interesting and potentially important reasons for amending economic models of individual behavior, they have been derived largely in frameworks that are purely experimental and therefore outside the domain of actual economic choices.

In order to advance our understanding of individual behavior under uncertainty and the role of perceptions for it, research must be directed to how individuals conceive of risks that are part of their everyday economic choices. Slovic, Fischhoff, and Lichtenstein's (1979) work began in inquiry in this direction, but did not go far enough. Research must examine tangible choices involving risk, how they would be (and are) made, the information acquired to judge risk, and how prior beliefs are changed with the availability of new information. In conducting such research there is an inevitable trade-off between the controlled, but unrealistic, environment of the laboratory versus the realistic, but hypothetical, setting of survey research. For real-world economic choices we see little alternative to the survey approach. However, such surveys must be paired with behavioral models where actual choices can be observed and used to gain insight into individuals' trade-offs. For example, surveys can attempt to elicit wage-acceptance functions for job risk and investigate how they change with new information. These responses could be compared with respondents' actual choices and with the results derived from empirically estimated hedonic wage models.

Comparative analyses of the perceptions of environmental risks versus other types of risks also might serve to identify the factors that influence individuals' understanding of these risks and the sources used for information on them.

One of the most important distinctions between these research efforts and those undertaken in psychology is a willingness to use behavioral models in conjunction with survey research to frame the research questions and analyze the findings. This should not be misconstrued as a call for blind acceptance of the current economic framework for describing individual behavior under uncertainty. Rather, it is a suggestion that we need not dispense with it entirely. Indeed, there appears to be a framework that is capable of explaining contradictions to the expected utility framework, but requires empirical research to facilitate our understanding of its implications. That is, our theoretical analysis suggests that if, following Cook and Graham, the effects at risk cannot simply be converted into equivalent income streams, state-dependent utility functions may be the most appropriate way of modeling individuals' valuation of risk changes. Within these models, differences in the willingness to pay for comparable risk changes can be expected. This poses significant problems for the transfer of willingness-to-pay estimates for one type of risk change to value a comparable change in another.

Finally, our analysis also suggests that the wage-hedonic framework based on secondary data cannot be regarded as a precise instrument for estimating the value of risk changes. It is simply incompatible with the degree of resolution and detail expected in environmental risk assessment. This incompatibility poses significant problems for the economic valuation of the estimates of risk changes available from the current structure of risk assessment practices in environmental policy-making.

References

Blomquist, Glenn. 1979. Value of life-saving: Implications of consumption activity. *Journal of Political Economy* 87:540–58.

Bockstael, Nancy E., and Kenneth E. McConnell. 1983. Welfare measurement in the household production framework. *American Economic Review* 83:806–14.

Brookshire, David S., Ralph C. d'Arge, William D. Schulze, and Mark A. Thayer. 1979. *Methods development for assessing air pollution control benefits, vol. 2: Experiments in valuing nonmarket goods.* Environmental Protection Agency. Washington, D.C.: GPO.

Brown, Charles. 1980. Equalizing differences in the labor market. *Quarterly Journal of Economics* 94:113–34.

Brown, J. N., and H. S. Rosen. 1982. On the estimation of structural hedonic price models. *Econometrica* 50:765–68.

Cook, Phillip J., and Daniel A. Graham. 1977. The demand for insurance and protection: The case of irreplaceable commodities. *Quarterly Journal of Economics* 91:143–56.

Cropper, Maureen L., and A. S. Arriaga-Salinas. 1980. Inter-city wage differentials and the value of air quality. *Journal of Urban Economics* 8:236, 254.

Desvousges, William H., V. Kerry Smith, and Matthew McGivney. 1983. *A comparison of alternative approaches for estimating recreation and related benefits of water quality improvements.* Environmental Benefits Analysis Series. Environmental Protection Agency. Washington, D.C.: GPO.

Dillingham, Alan E. 1979. The inquiry risk structure of occupations and wages. Ph.D. diss., Cornell University.

Freeman, A. Myrick, III. 1979. *The benefits of environmental improvement: Theory and practice.* Baltimore: John Hopkins University Press.

_____. 1982. *Air and water pollution control: A benefit-cost assessment.* New York: John Wiley & sons.

Fischhoff, Baruch, Sarah Lichtenstein, Paul Slovic, Stephen L. Derby, and Ralph L. Keeney. 1981. *Acceptable risk.* Cambridge: Cambridge University Press.

Gerking, Shelby, and William D. Schulze. 1981. What do we know about the benefits of reduced mortality from air pollution control? *American Economic Review* 71:228–34.

Hammond, Peter J. 1981. *Ex ante* and *ex post* welfare optimality under uncertainty. *Economica* 48:235–50.

Hershey, John C., Howard C. Kunreuther, and Paul J. H. Schoemaker. 1982. Sources of bias in assessment procedures for utility functions. *Management Science* 28:936–54.

Hickey, J. L. S., and J. J. Kearney. 1977. Engineering control research and development plan for carcinogenic materials. Report to National Institute for Occupational Safety and Health. Contract no. 210-76-0147.

Hoch, Irving. 1974. Wages, climate, and the quality of life. *Journal of Environmental Economics and Management* 1:268–95.

Holtmann, A. G., and V. K. Smith. 1977. Uncertainty and the durability of on-the-job training. *Southern Economic Journal* 44:36–42.

_____. 1979. Uncertainty and the durability of on-the-job training: An extension. *Southern Economic Journal* 45:855–57.

Jordan, Bruce C., Harvey M. Richmond, and Thomas McCurdy. 1983. The use of scientific information in setting ambient air standards. *Environmental Health Perspectives.*

Keeney, R. L., L. R. Keller, R. K. Sarin, A. Sicherman, and R. L. Winkler. 1982. *Development and application of a risk assessment methodology to study alternative national ambient carbon monoxide standards.* Final report to U.S. Environmental Protection Agency. Woodward-Clyde Consultants, San Francisco.

Litai, Dan. 1980. A risk comparison methodology for the assessment of acceptable risk. Ph.D. diss., Massachusetts Institute of Technology.

Lucas, Robert. 1977. Hedonic wage equations and psychic wages in the returns to schooling. *American Economic Review* 67:549–58.

MathTech. 1983. *Benefit and net benefit analysis of alternative national ambient air quality standards for particulate matter.* Vol. I-V. Final report to U.S. Environmental Protection Agency. Mathematica, Inc., Princeton.

Merkhofer, Miley W. 1981. Risk assessment: Quantifying uncertainty in health effects. *Environmental Professional* 3, no. 3/4:225–34.

Olson, C. A. 1981. An analysis of wage differentials received by workers on dangerous jobs. *Journal of Human Resources* 16:167–85.

Portney, Paul R. 1981. Housing prices, health effects, and valuing reductions in risk of death. *Journal of Environmental Economics and Management* 8:72–78.

Richmond, Harvey M. 1981. A framework for assessing health risks associated with national ambient air quality standards. *Environmental Professional* 3, no. 3/4:225–34.

Rosen, Sherwin. 1974. Hedonic prices and implicit markets. *Journal of Political Economy* 82:34–55.

———. 1979. Wage-based indexes of urban quality of life. In *Current issues in urban economics,* ed. P. Mieszkowski and M. Straszheim. Baltimore: John Hopkins University Press.

Ruckelshaus, William D. 1983. Science, risk, and public policy. Speech before the National Academy of Sciences, 22 June.

Schoemaker, Paul J. H. 1982. The expected utility model: Its variants, purposes, evidence, and limitations. *Journal of Economic Literature* 20:529–63.

Schulze, William D., Ralph C. d'Arge, and David Brookshire. 1981. Valuing environmental commodities: Some recent experiments. *Land Economics* 2:151–73.

Slovic, Paul, Bernard Fischhoff, and Sarah Lichtenstein. 1979. Rating the risks. *Environment* 21, no. 3:14–20, 36–39.

Smith, A. E., P. C. McNomee, and M. W. Merkhofer. No date. *Development of decision analysis methodology for health risk assessment.* Final report to U.S. Environmental Protection Agency. SRI International.

Smith, Robert S. 1979. Compensating wage differentials and public policy: A review. *Industrial and Labor Relations Review* 32:339–52.

Smith, V. Kerry. 1983. The role of site and job characteristics in hedonic wage models. *Journal of Urban Economics* 13:296–321.

Starr, C. 1969. Social benefit vs. technological risk. *Science* 165:1232–38.

Thaler, Richard, and Sherwin Rosen. 1975. The value of life saving. In *Household production and consumption,* ed. Nestor E. Terleckyj. New York: Columbia University Press.

Triplett, Jack E. 1983. Introduction: An essay on labor cost. In *The measurement of labor cost,* ed. Jack E. Triplett. NBER Studies in Income and Wealth, no. 48. Chicago: University of Chicago Press.

Ulph, Alistair. 1982. The role of ex ante and ex post decisions in the valuation of life. *Journal of Public Economics* 18:265–76.

U.S. Environmental Protection Agency, 1982. *Guidelines for performing regulatory impact analyses, Appendix A: Regulatory impact analysis guidance for benefits*. Draft.

Violette, Daniel M., and Lauraine G. Chestnut. 1983. *Valuing reductions in risks: A review of the empirical estimates*. Environmental Benefits series. Environmental Protection Agency. Washington, D.C.: GPO.

Viscusi, W. Kip. 1978a. Health effects and earnings premiums for job hazards. *Review of Economics and Statistics* 60:408–16.

——. 1978b. Labor market valuations of life and limb: Empirical evidence and policy implications. *Public Policy* 26:359–86.

Zeckhauser, Richard, and D. S. Shephard. 1976. Where now for saving lives? *Law and Contemporary Problems* 40:5–45.

Comment   T. H. Tietenberg

Risk management used to be a private affair. In these simpler times consumers were seen as holding producers and sellers accountable by refusing to purchase excessively risky products, while employees were seen as holding employers accountable by demanding higher wages in risky occupations. In the face of these market pressures producers and employers were expected to reduce their risk to acceptable levels or be driven out of business while consumers and workers were expected to insure against any remaining risk. Courts provided a vehicle for risk bearers to exert pressure on third-party risk creators (those with whom they held no contractual relationship and, therefore, were immune from direct market pressures).

Risk management is no longer a private affair. As a result of growth in the magnitude and complexity of risks, the government has become more heavily involved in the process of identifying and controlling these risks. Consumers and employees are increasingly seen as ill informed, particularly concerning those risks involving long latency periods. Even the courts are seen as impotent in dealing with disputes where the number of parties is large, such as in air pollution cases, or where the cause-and-effect relationship between a particular activity, such as producing pesticides, and the onset of cancer some thirty years later is hard to establish.

This transformation in public sector responsibilities has triggered a concurrent quantum increase in the need for analytical support both to

T. H. Tietenberg is professor of economics and codirector of the Public Policy Program at Colby College and a Gilbert White Fellow at Resources for the Future, Inc.

define an acceptable level of risk and to choose the most desirable ways of achieving it. Are the analytical concepts, the empirical methods, and the available data equal to the task?

Purpose

The Smith-Gilbert chapter attempts to provide a partial answer to this question by focusing on how reliably one kind of analytical technique (the hedonic wage model) values changes in one kind of risk (environmentally induced fatalities). They begin by analyzing the kinds of demands placed on the analysis by the policy process, proceed by developing a theoretical model to value state-dependent risks, continue by estimating a model based on a sample of 16,199 individuals, and conclude by computing alternative risk valuations based on this model for the purpose of evaluating the reliability of the state of the art.

Principal Conclusions

In their own words the principal conclusions of the authors are:

it is possible to estimate separate, statistically significant effects on real wages for different sources of risk—accidents on the job, health risks that arise from exposure to air pollution, and the long-latency health risks associated with exposure to carcinogens in the workplace. It appears that the statistical significance and direction of these effects are stable for variations in sample composition. (P. 375–76)

the implicit value of risk associated with air pollution exposure is sensitive to model specification, while that due to job fatalities is not. (P. 380)

these results provide indirect and tentative support for the need to distinguish estimates of the willingness to pay for risk based on the types of risk and of the effects involved. (P. 380)

the wage-hedonic framework based on secondary data cannot be regarded as a precise instrument for estimating the value of risk changes. It is simply incompatible with the degree of resolution and detail expected in environmental risk assessment. This incompatibility imposes significant problems for the economic valuation of the estimates of risk changes available from the current structure of risk assessment practices in environmental policy-making. (P. 382)

A Critique

I should say at the outset that I think this is an excellent chapter and, although I am by nature an optimist, I have no disagreement with its rather pessimistic conclusions. Indeed the thrust of my remarks will be to reinforce them. My differences with the authors will be more a question of degree than direction.

The Theoretical Model

Perhaps my strongest difference with the authors is the degree of faith they seem to have in the wage model as a method of valuing risks. They attribute most of the difficulties in interpreting and using the results for policy purposes to the lack of sufficiently rich data, whereas I believe the wage model itself has significant inherent limitations that could not completely be overcome even with the best data we could reasonably expect to derive from actual occupational situations.

At the most general level a basic inconsistency exists between the need to derive these valuations and the use of wage differentials as the means for derivation. The need for these estimates by the public sector has been driven by the conviction that markets do not adequately compensate workers for risk (i.e., that wages do not adequately reflect risk). This implies that actual wage valuations of risk will be biased (upward if the workers are unrealistically fearful or downward if they are unaware of the very real risks they face).

One possible answer to this problem is that those who lack knowledge are only a subset of workers, and the ill-perceived risks are only a subset of the risks workers face. With an appropriate knowledge variable the valuations of the most clearly perceived risks by the most informed workers could be extracted and applied to other cases. The Smith-Gilbert knowledge variable is certainly a step in the right direction, but, as I am sure the authors would readily admit, it is quite crude. This is neither the time nor the place to go into detail on information and uncertainty, but in brief the available empirical evidence seems to cast doubt on the ability of people to process information on low-probability, high-loss events, even when the information is available (see Schoemaker 1982, p. 544). Furthermore, the authors themselves cast doubt on the transferability of one set of risk valuations to a different set of circumstances.

In my opinion the problems with using the wage model to value risk are greater when it is used to value *general environmental* risks (such as exposure to ambient air pollution), than when it is used to value *specific occupational* risks. The compensation for occupational risk, to the extent it takes place in the market at all, will certainly take place in the labor market. The case is less clear for general environmental risks.

For general environmental risks there are other markets in which compensation can occur. Indeed the empirical literature suggests a considerable sensitivity of property values to pollution levels. If these results are valid, are victims receiving complete compensation in both property and labor markets (meaning they are overcompensated in total) or do they derive only partial compensation in each market? If the latter, then labor markets provide only a partial picture of risk valuation for general environmental risks. In any case it is not obvious that labor markets fully compensate for general environmental risks.

My final concern with using the wage model relates to the existence of nonwage forms of payment such as workmen's compensation. The existence of workmen's compensation triggers two rather different problems. First, when a workmen's compensation system exists, more dangerous industries may face higher compensation costs, but these will be borne as premiums paid into the system, not as higher wages. Therefore, wages will not reflect actual risk, though total compensation, correctly defined, would.

The second problem is with a possible bias introduced by workmen's compensation. Some type of accidents have a higher probability of coverage under workmen's compensation than others. For example, health effects with a long latency period and those for which the industrial cause is not obvious have a lower likelihood of coverage. In a perfect market wages would reflect the latter (lower-coverage) risk more accurately than the former (higher-coverage) risk. Unfortunately, however, the lower-coverage risks are precisely those about which the workers probably have the least information and, therefore, are precisely those risks where wage differentials are least likely to capture the "fully informed" risk premium.

The Data

The authors decry the lack of useful data, and I agree with their analysis of the situation. However, I want to add yet another concern about the kind of data that analysts are currently forced to use.

The Smith-Gilbert equations are based on 16,199 observations, but not all variables have that many individual observations. Many of the variables are not measured relative to the individual; they are measured relative to an occupation, an industry, or an SMSA. For these variables the measured intraoccupation, intraindustry or intra-SMSA variance is zero. The only measured variance occurs among occupations, industries, and SMSAs. Unfortunately all of the risk variables—the primary focus of their paper—fall within this category.

This would not be a problem if all workers within each of these categories faced the same risk, but clearly they do not. To take one example, all workers in a city do not face the same pollution level. Their exposure depends on where they live and work. Pollution levels are high in certain parts of the city and low in other (typically less-congested) parts.

This creates an errors-in-variables problem that has two dimensions. First, compared to a measure of actual exposure to risk, these measurements rob us of a significant amount of potentially information-rich variance. An intuitive feel for the importance of this point can be gained by considering an extreme, but nontheless revealing, example. Suppose that the average pollution levels in all cities were the same, although each city had a considerable variance in pollution levels within its boundaries. Suppose further that residents placed a high value on pollution reduction; therefore, those who were most exposed demanded a significant wage premium. In this case the regression model would find no relationship between wages and pollution level whereas, in fact, a significant relationship exists. The type of measurement of exposure to risk mandated by current data availability fails to capture a significant amount of the interesting variance. It also enhances the unpleasant prospect that these proxies may be picking up other determinants of wages that are correlated with the cross-industry, -occupation, or -SMSA variance but have no direct bearing on risk.

The second point to be made about this missing variance is that it applies to some, but not all, of the variables. This differential treatment of variables creates the potential for bias. To illustrate the point consider, as an example, the air pollution variable that varies only among SMSAs in the Smith-Gilbert analysis. All workers within an SMSA have the same measured value of air pollution, though in fact they may experience very different levels. It is probably the case that there is a correlation between the true (unobserved) value of within-city air pollution exposure and other variables in the model for which individual observations are available. The existing empirical air pollution literature (see, for example, Asch and Seneca 1978) suggests that such a correlation exists with race (blacks typically have higher exposures) and with education levels (the least educated tend to experience the highest exposure). If this is the case, some of the variance that would have been explained by the risk variables, had they been correctly measured, is mistakenly attributed to these correlated variables. Thus the coefficients on the risk variables may tend to be biased.

Applying the Data

The Smith-Gilbert chapter provides both theoretical and empirical reasons for believing that the value of lowering the probability of death from an environmental risk depends on the types of risk. Though this result accords well with common sense (the intensity and duration of pain as a factor, for example), it flies in the face of much common practice. It is easier, and of even more importance quicker, to transfer calculations among situations involving risks with some similar attributes than it is to derive separate estimates. Yet until we are able to obtain some firmly established set of propositions on how risk valuations vary systematically with identifiable risk attributes, separate estimates cannot be avoided if the valuations are to be meaningful.

Suggestions for Future Research

Improving the Data

The Smith-Gilbert chapter is helpful in calling our attention to limitations in the available data. Using their analysis and that in the preceding sections of this chapter it is possible to begin setting an agenda for future data collection efforts.

Perhaps one of the more intriguing avenues for further research comes out of the Smith-Gilbert finding that risks involving similar probabilities of fatality are valued differently by workers. This finding introduces a significant difficulty into risk management practices because separate risk valuations are required for each unique risk.

This difficulty could be reduced, however, if we could find identifiable attributes of risk that have a common valuation across various types of risk. In this framework, differences in risk valuations would arise from different bundles of common-valued attributes rather than from different valuations of the attributes themselves. Once the attributes and their values were determined, risk assessment would be rescued from the need for a unique empirical study for every conceivable kind of risk. To establish whether common-valued attributes can be identified and valued, a richer set of data is needed. Specifically *attribute* variables need to be included in the set of risk measures, not merely *exposure* variables. These could include, for example, the voluntariness of the risk, the potential intensity and duration of pain, other effects on the quality of life, and so forth.

Other, more immediate, steps are possible. Great strides could be undertaken if true *individual* risk measures were available for workers. The current use of grouped or common-risk measures opens the door to biased risk evaluation. Although it is not clear how much bias exists in the current estimates, the fact that we do not know is unsettling.

The availability of information on risk to workers is probably another important factor about which we need better measurements. Current variables that control for this are obviously crude. It would not be difficult to design better variables; the problem is going to be collecting this information from the same sample of workers as wage rate information is collected. The responsibilities for collecting wage rate information and for managing worker risk do not reside in the same organization.

Better Use of Existing Data

Though it is obviously easier to construct data wish lists than to confront the task of doing more with what we have, I do have a few modest suggestions. These concern developing a better understanding of the socioeconomic determinants of risk valuation and the role of unions in supplying information.

One question of interest concerns whether risk valuation varies among socioeconomic groups. The current model estimated by Smith and Gilbert controls for race and education, but presents no evidence on the possibility of interactions. It would be a simple matter to include interaction terms for education and risk as well as for race and risk as a point of departure. One could develop any number of scenarios that would lead one to expect differences to arise (e.g., information and income effects), but it remains an empirical question whether these differences are of sufficient magnitude to deserve special emphasis.

The Smith-Gilbert data set includes a binary variable that states whether the worker is a member of a union. Given their predisposition to believe that unions affect the amount of information available, an interaction variable constructed by multiplying union membership by measures of occupational risk would seem appropriate. It might further be possible to separate those unions that tend to make risk information available to their workers from those that do not.

Concluding Comments

This is a balanced and perceptive chapter that has improved our knowledge of the state of the art. The main message is a negative one—we have a long way to go. Yet this message should not obscure another, equally important, message—we have come a long way.

Two aspects of the empirical work in particular suggest that this line of research is worth pursuing. With the exception of the air pollution variables the results are stable across model specifications. Furthermore, again with the exception of one air pollution variable (SO_2), there is a remarkable agreement between those signs suggested by theory and those signs estimated from the data. Though I have qualms about the bias of the estimated coefficients, it does appear that the general approach has validity.

References

Asch, Peter, and Joseph J. Seneca. 1978. Some evidence on the distribution of air quality. *Land Economics* 54:278–97.

Schoemaker, Paul J. H. 1982. The expected utility model: Its variants, purposes, evidence, and limitations. *Journal of Economic Literature* 20:529–63.

Smith, V. Kerry. 1983. The role of site and job characteristics in hedonic wage models. *Journal of Urban Economics* 13:296–321.

13 Interfamily Transfers and Income Redistribution

Donald Cox
Fredric Raines

13.1 Introduction

The issue of resource transfers among families and across generations has stimulated much concern among economists in recent years. Intergenerational and interfamily transfers have been investigated in a variety of contexts. One important line of research has been concerned with the connection between bequests and inequality in earnings or lifetime wealth. Menchik (1980) finds that bequests are equally shared among family members. In contrast, using a different data set, Tomes (1981) finds evidence that bequests perform a compensatory role; ceteris paribus, inheritances received tend to be inversely related to income. Though the bequest motive appears to be strong for those in upper-income strata (Menchik and David 1983), the scope for significant redistribution of economic welfare through bequests for the majority of individuals is limited, since the average inheritance received is small (Blinder 1973; Menchik 1980).

Another mechanism for income redistribution is inter vivos transfers. Because of data limitations, however, these transfers have received less attention in the literature compared to bequests. Parsons (1975) analyzes the connection between parental characteristics and schooling behavior but did not have access to direct measures of family support for students. Adams (1980) explores a similar problem and is forced to use educational attainment as a proxy for inter vivos transfers received. Lampman and Smeeding (1982), using fragmentary data culled from a variety of sources, investigate trends in interfamily transfers, finding evidence of a declining trend in such transfers relative to government transfers over the past thirty years.

Donald Cox is assistant professor of economics at Washington University, St. Louis. Fredric Raines is associate professor of economics at Washington University, St. Louis.

In this chapter we investigate a new data set that contains information for a variety of inter vivos transfers as well as bequests. We focus primarily on an analysis of inter vivos transfer behavior. The chapter is divided into three sections. In the first section, a descriptive overview of the interfamily transfer data is presented. In the second section, a life-cycle model of interfamily transfers is developed to analyze inter vivos transfer behavior among families. In the final section some implications of the model are tested using the interfamily transfer data.

13.1.1   Interfamily Transfers—A Descriptive Overview

Data for intergenerational transfers come from the President's Commission on Pension Policy (PCPP)—Household Survey. The main objective of the commission was to obtain information about retirement income and the effects of retirement income on saving. The data set contains information about the components of household balance sheets, income from various sources, pension information, and demographic data. In addition, survey respondents were asked to report on various types of interfamily transfers. (Kurz 1984 complements this study.)

The PCPP survey obtained data for 4,605 families. The sample was designed to be a representative cross-section of the U.S. population. (See the appendix for more information about respondent selection.) The survey information used in this paper was collected in August 1979, generally covering the first eight months of that year.

Information about interfamily transfers was gathered in the following way. Respondents were asked if they received any contributions toward their expenses from anyone outside of their immediate family. The immediate family is defined as parents and any children under the age of eighteen living at the same address. Survey respondents are the heads of each family unit, where the head of each family unit is defined as the individual most familiar with family finances. Respondents aged eighteen and over who are living at the same address were treated as separate family units. The respondents were first asked to report any payments received in the past month for mortgages, utility bills, property taxes or property insurance, or food. The families were then asked to report on an additional set of transfers received from January 1979 through August 1979. These transfers included: bill payments (such as medical or legal fees) not reported in the monthly categories above; contributions toward the purchase of durable goods; transfers for education; trust funds; stocks and bonds; gifts of durable goods or property; the value of use of goods or property; cash; inheritances; and miscellaneous transfers received. Then the respondents were asked to report any transfers given to individuals outside the immediate family unit from January 1979 through August 1979. The categories for transfers given match the categories for eight-month transfers received (except that no information was obtained for bequests given). For the "monthly" items, however (i.e., mortgages, utilities, taxes and insurance, and food), households were only asked to report receipts and not transfers given. (A facsimile of the type of question dealing with interfamily transfers is presented in the appendix.)

Further, survey respondents were asked to identify the source of transfers received and the recipient of transfers given according to generation. Transfers received were classified according to three different family generations: older, younger, and equal. Transfers received from friends were put into the "equal" category. Transfers given were classified in the same way as transfers received.

The interfamily transfer data offer a unique opportunity to examine many different types of private transfers between family units, but the data are limited in a variety of ways. First, about a quarter of all households surveyed contained more than one family unit, and there are many implicit transfers that could take place in shared living arrangements that would not be picked up in the interfamily transfer data. Members of two-family units living under the same roof could exchange a variety of services, such as home production activities (e.g., housework, baby-sitting, and running errands). Second, transfers to individuals under the age of eighteen are not recorded in the survey, because the survey only considers transfers among adults (those aged eighteen and over). Third, since only transfers between family units are counted, interspousal transfers are omitted from the analysis below.

The survey also contains a variety of information about assets, property income, income from government transfers, and earnings. Household balance sheet components are broken down according to a variety of types of assets (e.g., value of savings deposits, jewelry) and different types of liabilities (e.g., mortgage debt, debts owed to other families). The survey contains data for nonlabor income from many different sources (e.g., food stamps, private pensions, stock dividends). Families were asked to report earnings for the first eight months of 1979, weekly hours worked, and other work-related information such as years of employment. The PCPP survey contains a variety of demographic data including number of children, marital status, and education.

Of the 4,605 families surveyed, 727 (15.8 percent) reported that they gave one or more transfers to other family units during the first eight months of 1979 (see table 13.1).[1] The number of households receiving a transfer during that period was 840 (18.4 percent). There were 472 monthly transfers received (for food, mortgages, insurance, and utilities) and 610

---

1. The actual number of family units that reported giving transfers was 728. One of the givers reported giving an extremely large cash gift (over $200,000), and the value of this gift appeared inconsistent with the related earnings and asset information for this case. This outlier was removed from the sample.

Table 13.1   Families Giving and Receiving One or More Interfamily Transfers

	Number	Proportion of Sample (N = 4,605)
Families giving	727	15.8%
Families receiving	840	18.3
1. Monthly	472	10.2
2. Eight-month period	610	13.5
3. Both (1) and (2)	241	5.2
Families both giving and receiving	196	4.3

transfers received for bills, education, gifts, etc., during the first eight months of 1979.

The distribution of interfamily transfers is highly skewed (table 13.2). Among households giving transfers, those in the ninetieth percentile and above—in terms of the size of the transfer given—account for over half of all transfer dollars given. Among households receiving transfers, the size distribution of transfers is also highly unequal. The distribution pattern for transfers received is similar to that of transfers given.

The distribution of transfers given by type of transfer is presented in table 13.3.[2] The largest category in terms of total transfer dollars is transfers given for the payment of bills (25.4 percent). Bills could include payments for a variety of expenditures such as medical care or food, but a further breakdown of this category is not available in the data set. Expenditures for college education account for 16.8 percent of all transfer dollars, and the average transfer amount among givers (annualized) is $2,292. Note that the transfer categories in table 13.3 cover both investment-related expenditures (e.g., education, durables) and consumption goods (e.g., use of property).

The types of transfers received in the first eight months of 1979 are presented in table 13.4, and monthly transfers received are presented in table 13.5. The items in table 13.4 for transfers received match those in table 13.3 for transfers given, except that table 13.4 includes bequests and the types of bills reported in tables 13.3 and 13.4 do not match.[3] The largest component of total transfers received is bequests, but bequests in dollar terms account for only a quarter of all transfers received. The data in table 13.4 indicate that most of the interfamily income redistribution occurs through inter vivos transfers, rather than through bequests.

2. The transfer amounts reported in tables 13.3 and 13.4 are annualized figures. Because the eight-month survey period excludes the holiday season, however, the annualized figures may not reflect true annual figures for certain transfer categories, such as cash gifts.

3. In table 13.3 households were asked to report all transfers given for the payment of bills. In table 13.4 households were asked to report receipts of transfers for the payment of bills except for those covered under the monthly categories, which were reported separately.

Table 13.2   Size Distribution of Transfers

Percentile	Percentage of Total Transfer Dollars Given	Percentage of Total Transfer Dollars Received, Eight-Month Categories	Percentage of Total Transfer Dollars Received, Monthly Categories
95th and above	37.7	38.5	46.5
90th and above	54.4	52.7	56.5
Upper quartile	78.4	75.0	73.1
Second quartile	15.1	17.0	15.9
Third quartile	5.3	6.4	7.8
Lowest quartile	1.2	1.7	3.1
Sample size	727	610	472

Table 13.3   Distribution of Transfer Dollars, by Type of Transfer Given (annualized figures, 1979 dollars)

Transfer Category	Proportion Giving Transfers	Average Transfer Amount per Giver	Distribution of Transfer Dollars
1. Bill payments	6.2%	$1,344	25.4%
2. Durables	1.5	1,023	4.7
3. College education	2.4	2,292	16.8
4. Trust funds	0.2	2,067	1.2
5. Securities	0.1	5,717	2.3
6. Durables (in kind)	1.7	2,059	10.7
7. Use of property	4.4	1,284	17.2
8. Cash	3.3	1,211	12.2
9. Other	3.6	864	9.5
TOTAL	15.8	2,081	100.0

Table 13.4   Distribution of Transfer Dollars, by Type of Transfer Received (annualized figures, 1979 dollars)

Transfer Category	Proportion Receiving Transfer	Average Transfer Amount per Recipient	Distribution of Transfer Dollars
1. Bill payments	5.3%	$ 1,048	16.3%
2. Durables	1.1	1,296	4.3
3. College education	3.9	2,087	22.9
4. Trust funds	0.1	3,155	1.0
5. Securities	1.2	2,984	2.1
6. Durables (in kind)	1.1	1,010	3.2
7. Use of property	4.1	1,112	13.6
8. Cash	2.4	1,217	8.5
9. Inheritance	0.8	11,465	25.7
10. Other	0.4	1,395	2.5
TOTAL	12.3	2,753	100.0

Table 13.5   Distribution of Transfer Dollars, by Type of Monthly Transfer Received (monthly 1979 dollars)

Transfer	Proportion Receiving Transfer	Average Transfer Amount per Recipient	Distribution of Transfer Dollars
1. Mortgages	4.0%	$267	37.9%
2. Utilities	3.7	62	8.3
3. Insurance	0.6	420	8.8
4. Food	7.7	163	44.9
TOTAL	10.2	272	100.0

A comparison of similar categories in tables 13.3 and 13.4 is useful in order to assess the consistency of the transfer data reported in the survey. There is some evidence that transfers received might be underreported relative to transfers given. Aggregate transfer amounts from tables 13.3 and 13.4 from transfer categories that match (durables, college education, trust funds, securities, durables in kind, use of property, and cash) reveal that reported transfers given exceed transfers received by 11 percent. In addition, the average value for durables in kind among givers is twice as high as the value for durables received ($2,059 versus $1,010). Givers may place a greater value on those transfers compared to recipients.[4]

The distribution of monthly transfers by type is presented in table 13.5. The average transfer amount among recipients was $272, and most of the monthly transfers received were for food. It is not possible to determine whether or not the monthly transfers occurred on a regular basis during the first eight months of 1979.[5] The transfers reported in table 13.5 apply to August 1979.

An interesting comparison can be made between public and private transfers for food. Data for the value of food stamps received are available in the PCPP data. There were 412 family units who reported receiving food stamps, and the average value of food stamps received for this group was $581 over the first eight months of 1979. Dividing by 8 yields a monthly average food stamp figure of $73. This figure is less than half of the $163 private transfer average for food (table 13.5). It is difficult to compare these two figures because of differences in the time frame, however. The private food transfer amount applies to August 1979 only, and it

4. The reconciling of aggregate transfers received with transfers given may be affected by a sampling problem, however. We do not know whether or not students living in dormitories on college campuses were sampled in the household survey. An undersampling of this group would cause an underreporting of educational transfer receipts. This problem is mitigated by the fact that the survey took place during the month of August, when the number of students living in dormitories is expected to be low compared to the fall and spring months.

5. In table 13.2, six households (the ninty-ninth percentile and above) reported receiving monthly transfers of $3,000 and above, and one household reported receiving a monthly transfer for mortgage payments of $15,820. These large values are likely to be lump-sum payments such as transfers for a down payment on a house.

Table 13.6   **Transfers Received, by Student Status**

Recipients	Number	Average Transfer Received for Education	Average Transfer Received for Noneducational Items[a]	Average Transfer Received Monthly[b]
Students	179	$2,087	$1,174	$ 92
Nonstudents	661	0	1,503	169

Notes: Student status is defined in the following way: An individual is designated as a student if he or she receives interfamily transfers for education. Otherwise the recipient is designated a nonstudent. Those designated as nonstudents may still be students (e.g., enrolled in public universities or scholarship recipients). The word *student* is used here as convenient shorthand for "recipient of interfamily transfers for education." Educational transfers received are annualized, 1979 dollars.

[a]All items in table 13.4 except item number 3 (annualized, 1979 dollars).

[b]All items in table 13.5.

is impossible to measure private food transfers that took place in the earlier months of that year. Forty-two individuals in the sample received both food stamps and private transfers for food.

The values of average transfers received by student status is presented in table 13.6. An individual is defined as a student if he or she received interfamily transfers for education. Those receiving transfers for education also received an average of $1,174 for other items during the first eight months of 1979 and an average of $92 in monthly transfers. The average transfer received among nonstudents is lower. Nonstudents received an average of $1,503 in noneducational transfers and an average of $169 in monthly transfers.

13.1.2   Directions of Transfers

Transfer data are available according to generation. It is possible to distinguish among transfers given to younger, older, or same generations. Similarly, it is possible to distinguish among transfers received from different generations. The directions of transfers are presented in table 13.7. The distributions show that, while most of the flow of transfers is from older to younger generations, a substantial number of interfamily transfers take place among households of the same generation. Measured in dollars, transfers given to younger generations account for almost two-thirds of total transfer dollars, while transfers given to members of the same generation account for 27 percent of total transfer dollars given. The flow of transfers from younger to older households is small. Such transfers account for 9 percent of total transfer dollars given. The breakdown of transfers received according to direction reveals the same pattern. Almost 70 percent of all interfamily transfer income received originated with families from an older generation. In contrast, less than 3

Table 13.7   Directions of Transfers

A. Transfers Given (annualized, 1979 dollars)

Generation Given to	Number of Transfers Given	Percentage	Average Amount of Transfer	Percentage of Total Transfer Dollars
Older	161	18.9	841	8.9
Same	353	41.4	1,170	27.3
Younger	338	39.7	2,855	63.8
TOTAL	852	100.0	1,776	100.0

B. Transfers Received (annualized, 1979 dollars)

Generation Received from	Number of Transfers Received	Percentage	Average Amount of Transfer	Percentage of Total Transfer Dollars
Older	387	56.7	$2,791	69.1
Same	245	35.9	1,811	28.4
Younger	50	7.3	799	2.6
TOTAL	682	100.0	2,293	100.0

C. Transfers Received (monthly)

Generation Received from	Number of Transfers Received	Percentage	Average Amount of Transfer	Percentage
Older	275	55.4	$259	55.7
Same	157	31.7	264	32.4
Younger	64	12.9	237	11.9
TOTAL	496	100.0	259	100.00

Table 13.8   **Transfers by Age of Family Unit Head**

A. Transfers Given

Age	Proportion Giving Transfers	Average Transfer per Giver
18–21	10.7%	$ 383
22–40	16.7	920
41–61	19.6	1,950
62+	12.2	2,259

B. Transfers Received

Age	Proportion Receiving Transfers	Average Transfer Amount per Recipient
18–21	40.6%	$1,283
22–40	19.7	1,590
41–61	10.3	1,461
62+	9.0	624

percent of transfers received (measured in dollars) originated from younger households.[6]

Another way to examine the flow of transfers between generations is to look at the age profiles of transfers (table 13.8). The proportion giving transfers rises and falls with age. Among those giving transfers, the transfer-age profile rises over the life cycle. The proportion receiving transfers falls with age, but the average transfer per recipient first rises and then falls with age. The elderly (aged sixty-two and over) receive less transfer income than any other age bracket.

13.1.3 Characteristics of Families in the Sample

Selected characteristics of families in the sample are presented in table 13.9 according to transfer status. Transfer status is divided into givers, recipients, and those who neither give nor receive transfers. For convenience, let us denote the last group as "others." Because 196 families both gave and received a transfer, some recipients are included among the givers and some givers are included among the recipients.[7]

Earnings and asset levels among the transfer groups are ranked highest for givers and lowest for recipients. Average earnings among givers is

6. The amount of transfers received from members of a younger generation is less than half of the amount given to members of an older generation. This discrepancy may result from reporting bias. Older households may have been reluctant in some cases to report income received from younger families.

7. If families are divided according to net transfer status—that is, transfers given net of transfers received being positive, negative, or zero—the characteristics of the families in these groups are similar to the figures reported in table 13.9.

Table 13.9   Selected Characteristics of Families by Interfamily Transfer Status

	Givers	Recipients	Nongivers and Nonrecipients
Age	41.1	32.8	42.6
Percent married, spouse present	59.7	26.2	49.0
Percent with children aged 18 or under	40.9	27.0	35.9
Years of schooling	12.9	12.8	11.8
Years of schooling, spouse	12.5	12.7	11.7
Percent multiearner	38.2	15.0	24.5
Percent female headed	31.0	50.7	37.9
Earnings	32,067	16,816	19,976
Percent with earnings	89.8	84.5	70.0
Financial income	2,216	900	980
Percent with financial income	72.5	59.2	48.9
Retirement income	1,145	625	1,180
Percent with retirement income	17.2	16.2	23.4
Public transfer income[a]	434	697	561
Percent with public transfer income	19.0	30.7	21.6
Value of financial assets	28,417	11,372	14,654
Value of tangible assets	59,650	22,168	32,850
Value of expected inheritance	13,092	12,003	3,998
Mortgage debt, home	8,797	4,218	6,204
Mortgage debt, other properties	1,999	435	1,080
Debts owed to other families	517	225	136
N	727	840	3,249

[a]Includes income from private disability plans, alimony, and child support.

twice as high as average earnings among recipients. The average value of assets among givers (financial plus tangible wealth) is almost three times as high for givers compared to recipients, and the average value of assets for givers is almost double that of "others." Average income among "others" is higher than that of recipients, although a larger proportion of recipients have positive earnings (84 percent versus 70 percent). A greater proportion of "others" are retired compared to either of the other two groups. The proportion receiving public transfer income is highest among recipients and lowest among givers.

Recipients tend to be younger than other households, and relatively fewer of them are married. Average education levels for both recipients and givers, however, are higher compared to "others." In addition, the average value of expected inheritance reported among givers and recipients was three times higher compared to that reported among "others."

13.1.4   Transfers and Relative Income Inequality

Table 13.9 shows that average income is higher among households that give transfers compared to nongivers/nonrecipients, and that the average

Table 13.10   **Income Inequality before and after Transfers**

	Sample	1979 Income Inequality[a]		
		Labor Income	Total Income[b]	N
1. Givers	pretransfer	.55	.56	
	posttransfer	.52	.55	640
2. Recipients	pretransfer	.70	.60	
	posttransfer	.49	.47	700
3. (1) and (2)	pretransfer	.71	.69	
	posttransfer	.56	.56	1,169
4. All earners[c]	pretransfer	.58	.55	
	posttransfer	.52	.51	3,396

[a]Income inequality is measured by the variance of the natural logarithm of income.

[b]Total income is equal to labor income plus financial income, government transfer income, retirement income, plus the rental value of owner-occupied housing, minus federal, state, and local taxes.

[c]The sample is restricted to those families with $100 or more in labor earnings. If the sample is expanded to include those with less than $100 in labor earnings, the qualitative results reported in table 13.9 are still obtained but the absolute changes in variances are larger.

income of households that receive transfers is lower than either of these groups. The next issue to be explored is the effects of interfamily transfers on the distribution of income.

The measure of relative income inequality used here is the variance of the natural logarithm of income. Inequality measures for different subsamples are given in table 13.10. Two measures of income are used. The first is labor income. The second is total income, which includes financial income, income from government and other transfer programs, retirement income, and imputed rental income from owner-occupied housing,[8] and subtracts federal, state, and local taxes. Posttransfer income is defined as income minus transfers given plus transfers received. An income flow was imputed from bequests received.[9] The sample is restricted to those families having $100 or more in labor earnings.

Measured relative inequality declines when net interfamily transfers are added to income. For all households in the sample in table 13.10, the vari-

8. The income flow from owner-occupied housing is calculated by multiplying the value of housing in 1979 dollars by the ratio of aggregate rental income to the aggregate value of the U.S. housing stock (3.94 percent). Data are from the *Washington University Macroeconometric Model of the U.S. Economy* 1984.

9. The income from bequests was calculated by multiplying the bequest amount by the average nominal rate of return from financial assets in 1979 (7.54 percent). The average rate of return was calculated by dividing aggregate U.S. income flows from financial assets by the value of the aggregate U.S. stock of financial assets (*Washington University Macroeconometric Model of the U.S. Economy* 1984). No attempt was made to impute income flows from other transfers, although possibly some other transfers (such as gifts of durables) would be more appropriately treated as additions to the stock of wealth as opposed to income flows.

ance of the log of total income falls from .55 to .51 after interfamily transfers are taken into account. The decline in measured income inequality for the entire sample of earners is small, but for certain subgroups the narrowing of relative income inequality due to transfers is larger. For the group of recipients, for example, the variance of the log of labor income declines from 0.70 to 0.49 after net interfamily transfers are added. Among recipients the expanded measure of total income (which includes government transfer payments and subtracts taxes) is distributed more equally compared to labor income (with variances of 0.60 and 0.70 respectively). Once interfamily transfers are taken into account, measured income dispersion declines further to 0.47. These calculations suggest that both government tax and transfer programs and interfamily transfers play a role in narrowing relative income inequality.

13.2   A Life-Cycle Model of Intergenerational Transfers

The model to be presented is aimed at capturing the basic dynamics of life-cycle transfers across generations or across families within generations where altruism exists. The model assumes no uncertainty, and bequests are assumed to be zero (all transfers are inter vivos). The model also makes no distinction between transfers that subsidize consumption of the recipients and those that reflect human capital investments.

The model assumes a pattern of overlapping generations as follows. Each representative person in the model proceeds through two distinct life-cycle phases of length L—the "child" phase followed by the "parent" phase. The child phase ends when the parent dies and a new child is born; these two events occur simultaneously. Thus, a lifetime lasts for $2L$ years and successive generations overlap for L years. The key distinction between the child and the parent generations is that the child is assumed to be liquidity constrained whereas the parent is not. The child's current consumption in each time period is constrained to equal the sum of own earnings and transfers received from the parents. The parent, on the other hand, has access to capital markets. Altruism is introduced into the model by assuming that parent and child seek to maximize the time preference discounted value of joint utility over the L years in which the two generations overlap.

The basic model may be stated formally as follows: Indexing child variables by 1 and parent variables by 2, joint utility in year t, $U(t)$, is assumed to equal the weighted sum of the logs of consumption of the child and the parent, $C_1(t)$ and $C_2(t)$ respectively.

$$(1) \qquad U(t) = \beta \ln(C_1(t)) + \ln(C_2(t)),$$

where β is a nonnegative parameter reflecting the weight given to consumption of the child relative to that of the parent. The budget constraint facing the child is given by

(2) $$E_1(t) + T(t) = C_1(t),$$

while that confronting the parent is

(3) $$\dot{A} = rA(t) + E_2(t) - T(t) - C_2(t),$$

where E denotes earnings, T denotes net transfers received from the parent, $A(t)$ is the stock of the parent's earning assets (the dot over A denotes the time derivative of A), and r is the rate of interest. Maximizing the present value of utility over the L-year generational horizon, subject to the constraints posed by equations (2) and (3), then involves finding the optimal solution values for the following Hamiltonian function:

(4) $$\begin{aligned} H = &[\beta \ln C_1(t) + \ln C_2(t)]e^{-\rho t} \\ &+ \lambda_1(t)[E_1(t) + T(t) - C_1(t)] \\ &+ \lambda_2(t)[rA(t) + E_2(t) - T(t) - C_2(t)], \end{aligned}$$

where ρ denotes the subjective rate-of-time discount, and earnings of both child and parent are assumed exogenously determined.

The assumption that bequests from the parent to the child equal zero implies that the parent exhausts all assets accumulated over the L adult years in which the liquidity constraint is not binding. Alternatively, the asset exhaustion condition states that the discounted value of parent consumption plus the discounted value of net transfers equal the discounted value of adult earnings over the L-year horizon:

(5) $$\int_0^L C_2(t)e^{-rt}dt + \int_0^L T(t)e^{-rt}dt = \int_0^L E_2(t)e^{-rt}dt.$$

The assumption of exogenously determined earnings for both parent and child plus the asset exhaustion condition mean that the control problem posed by equation (4) reduces to solving for the optimal time path of two control variables: parent's consumption and net transfers. First-order conditions for the solution of the Hamiltonian reveal what is intuitively clear; net transfers are adjusted over time so as to maintain a proportional relationship between consumption by the child and consumption by the parent, as follows:

(6) $$C_1(t) = \beta C_2(t).$$

Equation (6) defines the essence of altruism in the present model. It does not depend on the particular time paths of (exogenous) parent and child earnings. It implies that intergenerational transfers will increase income and consumption equality across generations so long as β is closer to 1.0 than the ratio of E_1 to E_2. To solve for the precise time path of net transfers, it is necessary to specify the time paths of child and parent earnings. We assume that these grow at constant rates g_1 and g_2 respectively:

(7) $$E_1(t) = E_1(O)e^{g_1 t}.$$
(8) $$E_2(t) = E_2(O)e^{g_2(L + t)}.$$

Defining W_1 and W_2 as the present value of these earnings streams,

$$W_i = \int_0^L E_i(t)e^{-rt}dt_1, \qquad i = 1, 2.$$

The expression for net transfers can be written as follows:

(9) $$T(t) = \frac{\beta}{1 + \beta} \rho[W_1 + W_2] \frac{e^{(r-\rho)t}}{(1 - e^{-\rho L})} - E_1(0)e^{g_1 t}.$$

Equation (9) implies the following partial derivative effects on transfers:

(10) $$\begin{array}{ccccccc} T = T(W_1, & W_2, & E_1, & t, & r, & \rho, & \beta). \\ (+) & (+) & (-) & (?) & (+) & (?) & (+) \end{array}$$

The sign below each of the arguments in equation (10) represents the sign of the partial derivative of transfers with respect to that argument.

Some discussion of the above results is in order. First, note that equation (9) suggests that transfers from the older (parent) generation to the younger (child) generation will typically be positive; they can only become negative (i.e., transfers go on balance from the child to the parent) if child earnings are relatively large and joint utility favors parent consumption (a low value for β). This result can be seen from expression (10) in which the current level of child earnings, E_1, is inversely related to the level of current transfers while the weighting parameter, β, is positively related to the level of transfers. Also clear is the positive influence of parent's wealth, W_2, on transfers to the child. Less obvious is the result seen in expressions (9) and (10) that the present discounted value of child's wealth, W_1, also increases transfers. This result becomes plausible when it is recognized that child's earnings are held constant and that the child is liquidity constrained. In such a circumstance any factor that produces a higher level of child's wealth, other than a higher level of current income for the child, can only lead to greater consumption if transfers increase. What is interesting in the present model is the unambiguous nature of this prediction.

The influence of the passage of time on transfers (holding E_1 constant) depends upon the values of ρ and r. A rate-of-time preference greater than the interest rate leads to reduced transfers over time, while a relatively low discount rate produces the opposite result.

The influence of increases in earnings growth rates on wealth is positive, while a rise in the rate of interest causes a decline in wealth. Through wealth effects, then, a rise in the rate of interest is associated with a decline in transfers. Holding wealth levels constant, a rise in the rate of interest implies steeper consumption profiles and therefore higher transfers (equation 10). A rise in the subjective rate-of-time preference could either raise or lower the level of transfers. Ignoring the finite life correction ($L = + \infty$), from equation (9), the effect of a change in the rate-of-time preference on transfers is given by

(11) $$\frac{\partial T}{\partial \rho} = \frac{\beta}{1 + \beta}[W_1 + W_2]e^{(r - \rho)t}(1 - \rho t).$$

The effect of a rise in the subjective rate-of-time preference is positive if ρt < 1, and negative if ρt > 1. An increase in the subjective rate-of-time preference tilts the time profile of consumption (and therefore transfers) towards greater levels of consumption early in the life cycle and smaller levels of consumption later on in the life cycle.

Note that in this model the weighting parameter for child's consumption is assumed to be constant over time. If, instead, this parameter were to vary over time, the transfer profile would vary accordingly. A plausible generalization would be an increasing time profile as children become more efficient in consuming relative to parents over time. This modification would steepen the time profile of transfers.

Finally, while the above model poses the problem of transfers from older to younger generations, it can be applied to interfamily transfers among members of the same generation. The only behavioral assumptions that are necessary are (1) that altruism exists among families and (2) that one family is liquidity constrained and the other is not.

Although fairly simple in its structure, the model presented above provides a number of unambiguous predictions concerning the life-cycle determinants of interfamily transfers.

13.3   Empirical Implementation

13.3.1   Organization of the Data

The PCPP survey data will be used to test some implications of the interfamily transfer model. There are three types of observations in the data set. The first is the household, which is defined as a group of persons living at the same address. The 1979 survey covered 3,440 households. The households were then broken down into 4,605 family units. A family unit contains a head, his or her spouse, and children under the age of eighteen who live at home. All other individuals were considered as members of separate family units. Suppose, for example, a household is made up of a husband, wife, two children aged sixteen and twenty-one, and a grandparent. This household would be recorded as three separate family units: a primary family unit consisting of the husband, wife, and sixteen-year-old child, and two secondary units (the twenty-one-year-old and the grandparent). A household consisting of two unrelated individuals would be divided into two family units. The third unit of observation is the person. Demographic and work-related information was collected for each person age eighteen or over. In the above example, the primary family unit would consist of two persons, the husband and wife.

The structure of the data set is summarized below:

Households	3,440
Multifamily-unit households	846
Single-family-unit households	2,594
Family units	4,605
Primary family units	3,440
Secondary family units	1,165
Persons	6,578

The basic unit of observation used in the estimations below is the family unit. An interfamily transfer takes place if income or gifts in kind are transferred from one family unit to another. Thus, for example, a cash transfer from father to twenty-year-old son living at the same address, for example, would be recorded as an interfamily transfer. Transfers given by one family unit to an individual outside the sample or received from an individual outside the sample would also be recorded as an interfamily transfer.

For those family units that are sharing a residence with other family units, there may be many transfers in kind that will not be recorded as interfamily transfers. Respondents were asked to report the value of free usage of goods—property or services received from or given to other family units—but it is unclear whether the typical respondent would include the rental value of housing in a shared living arrangement as "use of property" because respondents were not explicitly asked about housing. Similarly, respondents were asked to report cash contributions toward food consumed, but not the value of meals given or received.

It is not possible, in general, to determine the exact source of a transfer received or the exact destination of transfers given. Individuals giving transfers were asked only to identify the generation of the recipient, and all recipients were asked only to identify the generation of the giver. Secondary family units can be matched to their primary counterparts to construct complete households, but a matching of sources and destinations of transfers is not possible.

Despite the lack of information about sources and destinations of interfamily transfers, some evidence shows that much of the *interfamily* transfers reported might also be *intrahousehold* transfers. Those households containing more than one-family units (multifamily-unit households) represent 25 percent of all households in the sample (846 of the 3,440 households). These multifamily-unit households account for 53 percent of the dollar amount of total transfer dollars reported given and 61 percent of total transfer dollars received.[10]

10. These percentages were calculated in the following way: Transfer dollars reported given, aggregated over all family units in the PCPP survey, amounted to $1,008,927 (not annualized). Transfer dollars given, aggregated over all family units that belong to multifamily-unit households equaled $532,196 (not annualized). The latter aggregate is 53 percent of the former. The aggregate for transfers received among all family units in the sample is $902,233 (not annualized, and monthly transfer amounts are added to eight-month items). The equiv-

13.3.2   Interfamily Transfers

First, the behavior of all givers and all recipients will be analyzed separately. Then, results from a matched subsample of secondary and primary family units will be presented. The matched subsample will be examined in order to determine whether characteristics of primary family units are associated with transfers received by secondary units. Definitions of variables that will be used in the estimations are given in table 13.11.

The theoretical section above relates transfers to the lifetime wealth of givers and recipients and the income of recipients. The empirical specification below suffers from two limitations, which preclude the estimation of a transfer function that is precisely analogous to that derived in the model. First, donors and recipients of transfers cannot be matched. Second, since cross-sectional data are used, the lifetime wealth of individuals in the file cannot be measured. Instead, components of a family unit's balance sheet are used as indicators of the wealth of the family unit. Education levels should also be correlated with lifetime wealth.

Both the giver and recipient equations are represented as Tobit models.[11] For givers the dependent variable is equal to gross transfers given (*TRAN*). In equation (12) the variable *TRAN* is equal to zero for all observations for which a transfer was not given. Among the 4,605 family units, 727 gave interfamily transfers. The Tobit equation for givers is specified as follows:

$$
\begin{aligned}
(12) \quad TRAN = {} & a_0 + a_1 \, HEDUC + a_2 \, SPEDUC + a_3 \, AGE \\
& + a_4 \, (AGE)^2 + a_5 \, FEMALE + a_6 \, KIDS \\
& + a_7 \, MARRIED + a_8 \, DUAL + a_9 \, INCOME \\
& + a_{10} \, FINC + a_{11} \, RETINC + a_{12} \, WELFINC \\
& + a_{13} \, FINASST + a_{14} \, TANASST \\
& + a_{15} \, INHEREXP + a_{16} \, MORTDEBT \\
& + a_{17} \, DEBTTO + a_{18} \, MORTOTHR - u_1 \\
& = \alpha X - u_1, \qquad \text{if } \alpha X - u_1 > 0, \\
TRAN = {} & 0, \qquad\qquad\quad\; \text{if } \alpha X - u_1 \le 0.
\end{aligned}
$$

---

alent figure for all family units that belong to multiunit households is $552,993. The latter figure is 62 percent of the former.

11. The Tobit model can be considered as a restricted version of a more general model in which the decision to give a transfer and the transfer amount are determined separately (see Heckman 1979). Suppose, for example, that the decision to give a transfer is determined by a positive value for the latent variable T_1, where $T_1 = \beta_1 X_1 - u_1$, and the transfer amount is determined by $T_2 = \beta_2 X_2 - u_2$. The Tobit specification amounts to the restriction that $u_1 = u_2$, $X_1 = X_2$, and $\beta_1 = \beta_2$. Alternatively, the process could be modeled as a two-stage procedure in which the decision to give is estimated by probit and the transfer amounts are estimated using Heckman's procedure for correcting censoring bias. This procedure was implemented using the same vector X in both the probit and the transfer equation. The instrument for the selection correction (inverse Mills ratio) was highly collinear with the other regressors in the transfer equations, resulting in unstable estimates. The two-equation model is tractable only if certain variables are excluded from the transfer amount equation. Rather than impose these restrictions, we instead impose the restriction that $\beta_1 = \beta_2$.

Table 13.11   Definitions of Variables

Mnemonic	Variable
HEDUC	Years of education, head.
SPEDUC	Years of education, spouse.
AGE, $(AGE)^2$	Age of head, age of head squared.
$(HEDUC) \times (AGE)$	Interaction between years of education of head and age of head.
$(SPEDUC) \times (AGE)$	Interaction between years of education of spouse and age of spouse.
FEMALE	Dummy variable = 1 if sex of head is female.
KIDS	Number of children under the age of eighteen in family unit.
MARRIED	Dummy variable = 1 if head is married.
DUAL	Dummy variable = 1 if dual-earner family unit (i.e., positive wage rates for both head and spouse).
INCOME	Total labor income of family unit, first eight months of 1979, measured in 1979 dollars.
HWAGE	Hourly wage rate, head of the family unit, 1979.
SWAGE	Hourly wage rate of spouse, 1979.
FINC	Income from financial assets of the family unit, first eight months of 1979, measured in 1979 dollars.
RETINC	Public and private retirement income of the family unit, first eight months of 1979, measured in 1979 dollars.
WELFINC	Income from government transfer payments plus private disability payments, alimony, and child support, first eight months of 1979, measured in 1979 dollars.
FINASST	Value of stock of financial assets of the family unit, measured in 1979 dollars.
TANASST	Value of stock of tangible assets of the family unit measured in 1979 dollars.
INHEREXP	Value of expected inheritance, undiscounted, 1979 dollars.
MORTDEBT	Stock of outstanding mortgage debt for home, 1979 dollars.
DEBTTO	Stock of outstanding debts owed to other family members, 1979 dollars.
MORTOTHR	Stock of outstanding mortgage debt for properties other than home, 1979 dollars.
TRAN	Interfamily transfers given, first eight months of 1979, measured in 1979 dollars.
TRANREC	Interfamily transfers received first eight months of 1979, including monthly items, measured in 1979 dollars. Inter vivos transfers only. Bequests are excluded.
TOTASST	Total assets; the sum of financial and tangible assets.

The Tobit estimates of equation (12) are presented in table 13.12. Transfers given are positively related to the family unit head's education, labor and retirement income, and assets. The income elasticity of transfers given, evaluated at mean argument values among givers, is 0.82. The elasticity of transfers given with respect to financial and tangible assets (evaluated at giver means) is .16 and .19 respectively. Note that the esti-

Table 13.12   **Tobit Estimates, Transfers Given (*TRAN*)**

Variable	Coefficient	t-statistic
INTERCEPT	− 8880.10	− 11.96
HEDUC	198.65	5.47
SPEDUC	− 18.88	− 0.36
AGE	69.46	2.20
(AGE)²	− 0.56	− 1.63
FEMALE	− 142.60	− 0.73
KIDS	− 163.78	− 1.85
MARRIED	− 104.56	− 0.16
DUAL	288.48	0.96
INCOME	0.053	7.51
FINC	− 0.028	− 1.45
RETINC	0.057	2.00
WELFINC	− 0.072	− 0.92
FINASST	0.0077	5.47
TANASST	0.0045	4.56
INHEREXP	0.0035	2.70
MORTDEBT	− 0.0139	− 2.13
DEBTTO	0.0515	2.01
MORTOTHR	− 0.0101	− 1.29
Limits		3878
Nonlimits		727
ln *L*		− 8029

mated coefficient for financial income is negative and significant at the margin of the .10 level. At reasonable values for the rate of return on financial assets the estimated net impact of an increase in financial wealth is positive, but a higher rate of return on financial assets is associated with a decrease in transfers given. The effect of an increase in expected inheritance (*INHEREXP*) on transfers given is positive, but the elasticity of transfers given with respect to *INHEREXP* evaluated among givers is small. A 10 percent increase in *INHEREXP* is associated with a 0.3 percent increase in transfers given. The two liability measures, *MORTDEBT* and *MORTOTHR,* enter the Tobit equation with negative signs, and the coefficient for *MORTDEBT* is significant at the .05 level. The positive coefficient for *DEBTTO*—the stock of outstanding debt owed to other family members—suggests that some of the transfers given might be repayments for past transfers received.

Gross transfers given increase at a decreasing rate over most of the life cycle. The difference, for example, between predicted transfers given at age fifty and transfers given at age forty is $191. The age profile of transfers given peaks at age sixty-two. Beyond age sixty-two the effect of age on transfers given is negative. The age variable captures the effects of some important omitted variables in the transfer equation. None of the characteristics of recipients or potential recipients are included in the equation for transfers given. The estimated age profile of transfers suggests that as households age, the scope for giving continually widens until the family unit head approaches retirement age.

The level of education of the head of the family unit is an important determinant of transfers. An additional year of education for the head adds an estimated $199 to gross transfers given. Since educational transfers are included among the various categories of transfers given, education in part may proxy the desire of more educated households to make transfers in the form of human capital investment. Higher levels of education should in addition be associated with increased lifetime wealth, however. If households making educational transfers are deleted from the sample, education is still positively related to transfers given (estimated equation not reported). An additional year of head's education raises noneducational transfers given by $170. The education level of the spouse enters the transfer equation (table 13.12) with a negative sign, but is statistically insignificant.

Finally, the dummy variables for marital status (*MARRIED*), sex of family unit head (*FEMALE*), and multiearner status (*DUAL*) are each statistically insignificant in the estimated equation for gross transfers given. An increase in the number of children under age eighteen in the family unit is associated with a decline in transfers given to other family units.

13.3.3 Transfers Received

The value of all inter vivos transfers received[12] is expressed as

$$
\begin{aligned}
(13) \quad TRANREC = {} & b_0 + b_1\,HEDUC + b_2\,SPEDUC \\
& + b_3\,((HEDUC){\times}(AGE) + b_4\,(SPEDUC) \times (AGE) \\
& + b_5\,AGE \\
& + b_6\,FEMALE + b_7\,KIDS + b_8\,MARRIED \\
& + b_9\,INCOME + b_{10}\,FINC + b_{11}\,RETINC \\
& + b_{12}\,WELFINC + b_{13}\,FINASST + b_{14}\,TANASST \\
& + b_{15}\,INHEREXP + b_{16}\,MORTDEBT + b_{17}\,DEBTTO \\
& + b_{18}\,MORTOTHR - u_2 \\
= {} & \beta Y - u_2, \qquad \text{if } \beta Y - u_2 > 0, \\
TRANREC = {} & 0, \qquad\qquad\ \text{if } \beta Y - u_2 \le 0.
\end{aligned}
$$

Estimates of equation (13) are presented in the first column of table 13.13. Of particular interest are the coefficients for the income variables—*INCOME, FINC, RETINC,* and *WELFINC.* The coefficient on labor income (*INCOME*) is negative and statistically significant at the .05 level. The elasticity of transfers received (evaluated at recipient argument

---

12. Bequests are excluded, and transfers from the monthly categories are included along with those of the eight-month categories. No attempt is made to put the monthly and eight-month transfers on an equivalent time scale.

Table 13.13   **Tobit Estimates, Transfers Received (TRANREC)**

Variable	Transfers Received		Noneducational Transfers Received	
	Coefficient (1)	t-stat (2)	Coefficient (3)	t-stat (4)
INTERCEPT	−6207.80	−8.94	−4200.62	−6.67
HEDUC	445.80	8.21	251.57	5.08
(HEDUC)×(AGE)	−7.43	−6.55	−4.42	−4.28
SPEDUC	119.08	2.59	109.30	2.59
(SPEDUC)×(AGE)	−0.25	−0.46	−0.44	−0.87
AGE	45.86	3.48	21.05	1.75
FEMALE	492.32	3.79	461.49	3.82
KIDS	−105.07	−1.58	−62.04	−1.04
MARRIED	−1943.09	−3.50	−1820.06	3.62
INCOME	−0.014	−2.17	—	—
HWAGE	—	—	−8.74	−0.59
SWAGE	—	—	2.51	0.13
FINC	0.035	2.10	0.036	2.38
RETINC	0.039	1.50	0.022	0.95
WELFINC	0.100	2.26	0.090	2.13
FINASST	−0.0004	−0.63	−0.0020	−1.22
TANASST	0.0005	0.51	0.0006	0.70
INHEREXP	0.0023	2.43	0.0021	2.47
MORTDEBT	−0.0075	−1.36	−0.0061	−1.22
DEBTTO	0.0067	0.30	0.0085	0.44
MORTOTHR	−0.0023	−1.96	−0.0196	−1.92
Limits		3785		3846
Nonlimits		840		759
ln L		−8668		−8002

means) is −.14. The estimate of the *INCOME* coefficient offers some support for the hypothesis that one of the functions of interfamily transfers is to redistribute resources towards family units with low-income levels. Taken at face value, the estimate appears to concur with the findings of Tomes (1981) for inheritance data.

The estimate for the coefficient on income should be regarded with some caution, however. First, the variable *TRANREC* contains transfers received for education, and these transfers are used to subsidize investment in human capital, rather than current consumption. Average earnings among those receiving transfers for education are lower than those of other recipients, so the negative income coefficient is in part picking up the relationship between proportions of time devoted to investment in human capital and transfers received for education. Second, if transfers received cause an increase in the demand for leisure, then the negative coefficient for income could in part reflect work disincentives associated with transfer receipts.[13] Each of these problems is addressed in an alternative specification of the equation for transfers received in which (1) educational transfers received are subtracted from *TRANREC,* and (2) wage rates for head and spouse (*HWAGE* and *SWAGE*) are substituted for family-unit income. The results are reported in the second column of table 13.13. The coefficient for *HWAGE* is of anticipated sign, but is not statistically significant.

A further finding associated with the connection between transfer receipts and income is the positive signs of estimated coefficients for other sources of income in the transfer equation. This finding is contrary to the theoretical prediction of the model. The other sources of income—financial income (*FINC*), retirement income (*RETINC*), and transfer income from public and private sources (*WELFINC*)[14]—are each positively associated with interfamily transfers received. One possible reason why financial income is positively related to transfers received is that some transfers (e.g., securities, cash) would be expected to produce financial income. The positive coefficient for *RETINC* suggests that retirement status is associated with increases in transfers received.

The coefficient of *WELFINC* is difficult to sign a priori in this single equation specification. Though *WELFINC* represents current income flows that the theoretical model predicts would "crowd out" interfamily transfers, the variable also acts as a surrogate for a host of other effects that are not measured in the data set. Eligibility for income from disability plans or food stamps implies that the family unit may be experiencing some financial distress that is not measured by other variables included in the equation.

The amount of transfers received rises with education. While education levels can be interpreted in part as indicators of lifetime earnings of individuals, the relationship between education levels and transfers received is more complex in the estimated equations. Most importantly, educational transfers are included among transfers received in the first column of table 13.13. To deal with the problem of spurious correlation between transfers received and education levels, years of education was interacted with age. Further, educational transfers were deleted from transfers received in the equation presented in the second column of table 13.13.

The estimates of the effects of education on noneducational transfers received indicate a $1,006 difference between predicted noneducational transfers for a family unit headed by a thirty-year-old college graduate as opposed to a thirty-year-old high school graduate. The same calculation

13. Tomes 1981 raises this issue, but finds no evidence of work disincentive effects due to inheritance.

14. The variable *WELFINC* includes AFDC and other public assistance income, food stamps, Supplementary Social Security Income, as well as income from private disability plans, alimony and child support, and other conditional transfer income.

using spouse's education indicates a predicted difference in noneducational transfers received of $437.

Estimated transfers decline with age. The age effect of noneducational transfers evaluated at twelve years of schooling is estimated at −$32.35 for each additional year.[15] The dummy for marital status indicates that estimated interfamily transfers received are much smaller for married individuals. Interfamily transfers are primarily targeted at family units in which the head is not married.

Estimated transfer receipts are higher for family units headed by females. Female status raises estimated transfers by almost $500 (table 13.13, cols. 1 and 2).

The influence of the asset variables (*FINASST, TANASST*) on transfers received is negligible; the coefficient for *FINASST* is of expected sign but not statistically significant. Family units that expect larger inheritances receive more inter vivos transfers. The causality may run the other way, however, if family units use current values of inter vivos transfers to gauge the expected value of their inheritance.

In sum, the estimates offer some support for the theoretical model above. Inter vivos transfers are targeted towards young, unmarried family units. Controlling for other factors that influence transfers, female-headed family units receive higher transfer amounts. The evidence is far from conclusive, however. Most importantly, the impacts of changes in wage rates on the level of noneducational transfers received are not statistically different from zero.

13.3.4   Primary and Secondary Family Units

A quarter of the 4,605 family units are secondary family units. Information for each secondary family unit can be matched with information from its primary counterpart. Aside from the matching aspects of the sample of secondary family units, these family units are different from the others because they are living in the same dwelling with a primary family unit. The purpose of this section is twofold. First, transfers received will be analyzed in the matched sample, where information is given both about primary and secondary units. Transfers received by secondary units will be expressed as a function of the characteristics of secondary units and the characteristics of the primary units with which they are matched. Second, an equation for transfers received will be estimated among the sample of all primary units, and this equation will be compared with the equation for the secondary units.

The Tobit equations for transfers received for each family-unit type are presented in table 13.14. Transfers received are limited to noneducational

---

15. A parabolic age profile was estimated, but the second-order term was not significantly different from zero.

Table 13.14   Tobit Estimates, Noneducational Transfers Received

Variable	Secondary Family Units				Primary Family Units	
	Coefficient (1)	t-stat (2)	Coefficient (3)	t-stat (4)	Coefficient (5)	t-stat (6)
INTERCEPT	-2584.40	-4.17	-1499.12	-3.13	-3302.44	-6.43
HEDUC	10.63	0.31	55.86	1.73	121.30	4.03
AGE	-31.52	-4.95	-30.50	-4.85	-27.01	-5.14
FEMALE	452.11	3.08	405.98	2.75	606.43	3.42
MARRIED	-451.69	-0.92	-477.08	-0.98	-582.98	-2.93
INCOME	0.026	2.11	0.021	1.71	-0.012	-1.72
FINC	0.140	3.33	0.126	3.16	0.011	0.30
RETINC	0.195	2.01	0.182	1.87	0.019	1.03
WELFINC	0.073	1.45	0.061	1.19	0.090	1.60
TOTASST	-0.0014	-0.51	-0.0004	-0.16	-0.0003	-0.33
HEDUCP	81.38	2.72				
AGEP	11.94	2.01				
INCOMEP	0.007	1.26				
FINCP	-0.029	-1.09				
RETINCP	-0.105	-2.10				
WELFINCP	-0.012	-0.19				
TOTASSTP	0.0008	1.04				
N	1165		1165		3440	
Limits	832		832		3014	
Nonlimits	333		333		426	
ln L	-3315		-3327		-4667	

transfers in order to avoid the possibility of a spurious relationship between educational transfers and recipients' income, as noted above. The equations that are estimated are simplified variants of equation (13). The equation for transfers received among secondary units, including characteristics of their primary-unit members, is presented in columns (1) and (2) of table 13.14. The variables for primary units are denoted by the suffix P. The variable $HEDUCP$, for example, denotes years of education for the head of the primary family unit for which there is also a secondary unit present.

When the sample is restricted to secondary family units, $INCOME$ is estimated to have a positive effect on transfers received. This finding is contrary to the predictions of the model. Actual transfers received by individuals in the same household may include services in kind that are not recorded in the transfer items measured in the PCPP data. If so, then there may be greater scope for mismeasurement of actual transfers received among secondary family units compared to primary family units.[16]

In columns (3) and (4) of table 13.14, transfers received by secondary units are estimated when characteristics of their associated primary units are permitted to vary. The reason for this experiment is that primary family units may be a source of many transfers received by their secondary counterparts. If this is true we can assess the possible "omitted variable bias" that may affect the recipient equations when characteristics of donors are not available. The estimated coefficients are similar, except that the coefficient for education for the secondary family unit is much larger when primary-unit variables are omitted from the equation. The estimated effects of own-education levels on transfers received in the previous section (table 13.13) may therefore in part be picking up the effects of donors' education on transfers.

The estimated equation for transfers received among primary households is presented in columns (5) and (6) of table 13.14. There are three major differences between the sample of primary family units and secondary family units with respect to transfers received. First, the proportion of recipients among secondary family units is much larger than among primary family units (29 percent versus 12 percent). Second, labor income among primary units is inversely related to transfers received. The elasticity of noneducational transfers received with respect to income (evaluated at recipient means) is equal to -0.2, and the estimated income coefficient is significant at the 0.1 level. Finally, the influence of education on transfers received is larger for primary units compared to secondary units.

The estimates of transfers received in the sample of primary family units tend to confirm the predictions of the theoretical model. If we inter-

---

16. In addition, a Tobit equation was estimated in which recipients were redefined as those receiving transfers in excess of transfers they gave. In this specification, the effect of income on these net transfers received is not significantly different from zero.

pret years of education as an indicator of lifetime wealth, the positive relationship between transfer receipts and education combined with the inverse relationship between income and transfer receipts indicate that, among primary family units, interfamily transfers serve a compensatory function that increases with lifetime wealth.

13.3.5 Conclusion

In this study we have attempted to gain understanding of the disposition of inter vivos transfers by means of data that measure a variety of such transfers. While the data set offers a unique opportunity to explore this aspect of economic behavior, the data have significant limitations that need to be emphasized. First, the data do not permit matching of transfer givers with transfer recipients. Second, while the theory is cast in terms of lifetime wealth, we are forced to use crude proxies for wealth in the empirical implementation.

Despite these limitations, the data provide qualified support for a model of interfamily transfers characterized by altruism in consumption. Inter vivos transfers tend to originate in older, high-income family units and are primarily targeted towards younger, single individuals. A positive female-male differential exists with respect to transfers. Interfamily transfers tend to narrow relative income inequality.

The data, however, do not provide the theoretical model with an entirely clean bill of health. Financial income is positively related to transfers received, and evidence for the relationship between earnings and transfers received is mixed. Indeed, the model predicts a dollar-for-dollar inverse relationship between income and transfers, and this hypothesis is clearly rejected by the data.

Despite some of the limitations of this study, we tentatively conclude that the direct examination of inter vivos transfers afforded by the PCPP data reinforces a solicitous view of the role of these transfers. This initial exploration generally supports the view that such interfamily transfers are substantial, altruistic, and egalitarian in direction.

Appendix
Interfamily Transfer Data

The PCPP survey respondents were asked questions about interfamily transfers in the following way. First, the respondents were reminded about the definition of the family unit. The person taking the survey began the section on interfamily transfers with the following statement: "Now I would like to talk about contributions toward your family expenses from someone other than a member of your family. Remember that your family only includes you [and if appropriate], your husband/ wife, and any children under eighteen-years-old who usually live at home."

Second, individuals were asked to report monthly transfers received (four categories), transfers received over the previous eight months (ten categories), and transfers given over the previous eight months (nine categories). An example of a question about monthly transfer receipts taken from the survey is the following: "Has anyone outside your family made contributions toward your mortgage payments or rent in the past month?" The respondent was then asked to report the number of people from whom he/she received such transfers, the relationship of the donors to him/her (e.g., father, sister), and the amounts contributed by each person. For recipients with multiple donors, the direction of the transfer is determined by the generation of the donor who gives the most.

An example of a question dealing with eight-month transfers received is the following: "Since January 1, 1979 has your family received any contributions toward college education expenses from anyone outside your family?" The survey was taken in August 1979, so this question covers an eight-month period. The respondent was then asked to report generations of donors and transfer amounts in the same way as was done with monthly categories.

Finally, the survey respondents were asked to report on transfers given. An example of a survey question for transfers given is the following: "Since January 1, 1979 has your family contributed to bill payments for such things as medical, dental and legal fees, vacations, clothes, and so on, to anyone outside your family?" Donors were asked to report the number of recipients, the relationship of each recipient to them, and the transfer amounts given.

Other data sets dealing with inter vivos interfamily transfers of income exist (see, for example, Lampman and Smeeding 1983). Differences in variable definitions and organization exist between the PCPP data set and others, however, so that ad hoc comparisons between the PCPP data set and others would not be very illuminating. The ultimate reliability of the interfamily transfers depends on the accuracy with which family units responded to the survey and their level of understanding of the survey questions. While this is a problem that affects most other data sets based on household surveys, the problem of survey response error is likely to be particularly acute for the PCPP survey. Survey respondents may be likely to overestimate their generosity and underestimate their dependence on other family units. The average value reported for durables given, for example, was much higher than the average value reported for durables received (tables 13.3 and 13.4). In addition, the PCPP survey was time consuming and complex. Respondents were asked a long list of questions dealing with their balance sheets, pension programs, earnings, other income, and demographic information. These observations suggest that the data for interfamily transfers in the PCPP survey must be interpreted with care.

Respondent Selection

Sampling and interviews were conducted by Market Facts, Incorporated. Stanford Research Institute (SRI) created the data tapes from the survey results. An original random sample of 6,384 dwelling units was selected, and this sample was designed to reflect a cross-section of the U.S. population. Of the 6.384 dwelling units, 829 (13 percent) were either vacant or not accessible. Of the remaining 5,555 dwelling units, 1,974 (35.5 percent) refused to participate in the survey. The remaining dwelling units contained data for 3,581 primary units and 1,172 secondary units. A portion of these units were judged by Market Facts to be unusable, leaving a final sample of 4,605 family units (3,440 primary family units and 1,165 secondary family units).

Imputations

Some of the values for interfamily transfers were imputed by SRI. Of the 728 family units reporting that they gave an interfamily transfer, 64 were unable to report the amount given for one or more transfer categories. Amounts given were imputed by SRI from a regression on income and demographic variables for those reporting amounts given (estimated equation not available in the documentation). Of the 840 family units reporting that they received an interfamily transfer, 141 were unable to report amounts received for one or more of the transfer categories. SRI imputed amounts received for these observations by using the same imputation method for amounts given.

In addition, a portion of the families indicating asset holdings in various categories did not report values for those assets. Of the 2,812 families reporting that they had balances in savings accounts, for example, 185 did not report the value of these assets. SRI imputed values for these variables using methods similar to those used for imputing interfamily transfers. However, SRI also included a wealth variable in the data set ($WEALTHQ$) which was constructed only from nonimputed values for assets.

To check whether or not the results reported above were sensitive to these imputations, equations (12) and (13) were reestimated with two modifications. First, those observations with imputed values for interfamily transfers were deleted from the sample. Second, $WEALTHQ$ was substituted for the asset and debt variables in the estimating equations. The results were similar to those reported in tables 13.12 and 13.13. In particular the elasticity of transfers given with respect to $WEALTHQ$ (evaluated among givers) in the reestimated equation is .17. In comparison, estimated transfer elasticities with respect to $FINASST$ and $TANASST$

from table 13.11 above are .16 and .19 respectively. In addition, income elasticities of transfers given and received in the reestimated equations were similar to those reported in tables 13.12 and 13.13, cols. (1) and (2). The estimated income elasticity of transfers given in the reestimated equation was 0.98 compared to 0.82 in the equation presented in table 13.12. The elasticity of transfers received with respect to income was -0.20 in the reestimated equation compared to -0.14 in the equation presented in table 13.13, cols. (1) and (2).

References

Adams, James D. 1980. Personal wealth transfers. *Quarterly Journal of Economics* 95:159–79.

Blinder, Alan S. 1973. A model of inherited wealth. *Quarterly Journal of Economics* 87:608–26.

Heckman, James J. 1979. Sample selection bias as a specification error. *Econometrica* 47:153–61.

Kurz, Mordecai. 1984. Capital accumulation and the characteristics of private inter-generational transfers. *Economica* 51:1–22.

Lampman, Robert J., and Timothy M. Smeeding. 1983. Interfamily transfers as alternatives to government transfers to persons. *Review of Income and Wealth* 29:45–66.

Menchik, Paul L. 1980 Primogeniture, equal sharing, and the U.S. distribution of wealth. *Quarterly Journal of Economics* 94:229–316.

Menchik, Paul, and Martin David. 1983. Income distribution, lifetime savings, and bequests. *American Economic Review* 83:672–90.

Parsons, Donald O. 1975. Intergenerational wealth transfers and educational decisions of male youth. *Quarterly Journal of Economics* 89:603–17.

Tomes, Nigel. 1981. The family, inheritance, and the intergenerational transmission of inequality. *Journal of Political Economy* 89:928–58.

Washington University macroeconometric model of the U.S. economy. 1984. Laurence H. Meyer and Associates, Ltd., St. Louis, Missouri.

Comment   Paul L. Menchik

In recent years a number of economists have tried to find the determinants and economic effects of private transfers. In the past the focus has been on charitable contributions of time and money, and on bequests. Very lit-

Paul L. Menchik is associate professor of economics at Michigan State University.

tle work has been done on inter vivos transfers—gifts between living people—presumably due to the lack of data. The chapter by Cox and Raines, which focuses on this issue, is an especially useful start at filling this gap in the literature.

The chapter employs a sample from the President's Commission on Pension Policy—Household Survey of 4,605 respondents. Although the survey was plagued by problems of nonresponse (in 13 percent of the dwelling units selected a respondent could not be located, and in 35 percent of the remaining dwelling units no respondent would participate in the survey), this survey represents one of the few available data sets containing figures on inter vivos transfers. The chapter first presents some descriptive statistics about those who give and those who receive, then provides an analytical model of the process of transfer from (largely) parent to child, and finally offers some econometric results in support of the model. I will discuss the chapter in the same order.

The PCPP survey obtained data from 4,605 families concerning sources of income, savings, and public and private transfers—gifts as well as inheritance received. The survey period is the first eight months of 1979. Respondents were asked if they made or received any contributions toward their expenses from outside their immediate family, which is defined as parents and any children under the age of eighteen living at the same address. Unfortunately the only identification of the recipient (source) of the transfer (except for a very nonrandom subsample) is the generation of the party, whether older, younger, or equal. Also transfers to those under eighteen and transfers to spouses were not counted.

Over the eight-month survey period 15.8 percent of the families report giving and 18.3 percent report receiving one or more transfers. Of these people about one-quarter report *both* giving and receiving a transfer.

The size distribution of transfers is rather concentrated over this short period, i.e., over half the transfers received (and given) were received (or given) by the highest 10 percent in the recipient (or giver) distribution.

There is some evidence that transfers received might be underreported relative to transfers given (it is better to report giving than receiving)—a result also found by James Morgan (1984). It appears that while most transfers flow to younger generations, 27 percent go to the same generation and only 9 percent are given to older generations.

If we compare those who make a transfer with those who receive one we see the givers are older, wealthier, less likely to be female heads, more likely to have labor earnings, and more likely to have higher earnings over the eight-month survey period. Also, the group labeled "others" (nongivers and nonrecipients) are older than the recipients. "Others" are more likely to be retired and to have earnings slightly higher than the recipients and lower than givers. What struck me was that although the recipients were younger and had lower current earnings than the givers, they were more like the givers than the "others" in several significant ways—years of schooling, expected inheritance, and percentage with financial income. Although the authors want to conclude that private transfers are egalitarian, the fact that the transfers go from the well schooled to the well schooled, from the wealthy to those expecting three times the inheritance of the "others" supports a different hypothesis. That is, transfers may go to those whose transitory income is low relative to life cycle and/or permanent income. That transfers are equalizing only in the narrow sense that they smooth instabilities out or allow consumption earlier in the life cycle than warranted by earnings alone (the way a well-functioning capital market would) is also an allowable inference from this evidence. Furthermore, that about one-fourth of those either giving or receiving did *both* supports the view of transfers as *instability* reducing as opposed to lifetime *inequality* reducing.

Using the variance of log income as a measure of inequality, the authors calculate the measure for those making a transfer, with the value of the transfer either added to or subtracted from income, then excluded. The measure is lower *post-* than it is *pre*transfer. Second, they compute the measure for recipients; once again the measure is lower (much lower) post- than pretransfer. Finally they compute the measure for all givers and recipients and for the entire sample including "others." As before, the measure *post* implies less inequality then the measure *pre*. Although the authors interpret this to mean that transfers reduce relative income inequality, some comments are in order.

First, the authors deduct or add the asset value of the transfer from the flow of labor earnings (or total income), not from the flow equivalent. If one transfers an asset to another, does it make sense to call earnings—plus or minus the asset—*net* labor earnings? (This problem is avoided by using the flow equivalent of the transfer as was done for inheritance received.) This makes sense if the flow is permanent, but with so many people both making *and* receiving transfers, can this assumption be expected to hold? Second, since the income measure is based on transitory income (eight months), the transfers may equalize only in the sense that bank loans equalize, e.g., reducing instability not permanent inequality of income. Finally, the transfers may not reduce *lifetime* inequality but (as the model in the next section reveals) allow consumption earlier in the life cycle than current earnings allow. Hence transfers to those early in their life cycle may *appear* to equalize income because recipients are in their relatively lower earning years, but may do the contrary.

The authors present an optimal control model of an overlapping generation world. Each person has a child phase and then a parent phase, with parents and children coexisting in time. A joint utility function is maximized with B—the weight put on log child relative to log parent consumption during the half-life when they both are alive. This specification of the utility function differs from the standard intergenerational model where the lifetime (not half-life) consumption or utility of parent and child is in the maximand.

The growth path of earnings is exogeneous, and, most critically, children can neither borrow nor lend. The behavior is referred to as "altruistic," but this means only that joint utility maximization is pursued; a B of zero (which is allowed by the model) implies that children will starve for the benefit of their parents. Their model predicts that the ratio of child-to-parent consumption, at any point of time, is B. The comparative static results—equation (10)—predicts transfers positively related to the wealths of parents and children and negatively related to the child's current earnings. However, wealth is defined as the discounted sum of earnings over the period. Hence for a given growth rate in earnings one cannot take the partial derivative of wealth, holding earnings constant; if one moves, the other must move as required by the identity defining wealth.

The point of the model, which is a valuable one, is that if children can neither borrow nor lend, i.e., are totally constrained by current earnings, their parents act as the bank allowing a child with growing earnings to consume more than current earnings warrant. Children are therefore able to get around this capital constraint by "banking" with their parents like a child actor might. Whether this severe constraint for children is of sufficient importance to explain all transfers is another matter. Note that the model differs from other "altruistic" models in the literature that base transfers on differences in lifetime (not half-life) resources or consumption between generations. Hence it is by no means clear that transfers equalize *lifetime* consumption, but rather half-life consumption. With secularly growing earnings this mechanism would likely dis-equalize lifetime income since parents would be transferring resources to a younger cohort that is poorer during the period of overlap, but richer than they over a lifetime accounting period.

The authors estimate Tobit models of transfers made and transfers received. They use the data set of 4,605 family units divided into primary and secondary, with (I think) the presence of the marital couple denoting primary and single individuals as secondary when all live at the same address. (It's not clear what is done when two married couples live together.) A Tobit regression of transfers made is presented in table 13.11 as a function of eighteen variables. Transfers received is positively related to transitory income with an elasticity of .82. Martin David and I (Menchik and David 1983) found that the earnings elasticity of bequests made could not be represented by a constant, with a markedly higher elasticity at higher rather than lower income. I would like to see if, for example, using a spline function, the same is true for gifts.

They also find that gifts made vary directly with assets but, interestingly, are negatively related to financial income. This finding is consistent with a strategy of giving away one's low yielding but greatly appreciated assets for tax purposes. Since the taxable basis is not stepped up for gifts, but is for bequests, it is certainly cheaper to give an appreciated asset rather than cash to someone in a lower tax bracket. Hence this behavior is consistent with tax avoidance. The results also show a positive and significant effect of education and age (up to age sixty-two) on transfers made.

Next they present, in table 13.12, regressions of both total transfers (excluding inheritance) received and noneducational transfers received. In the total equation, transitory income is used; in the second, wage rates are used as measures of the recipients' current position. First, years of education is a positive determinant of transfers received in both equations. Second, current income has a negative sign in the first equation which the authors claim supports an egalitarian view. (The authors note that since those currently attending school would have a low labor supply, this finding might be a spurious one.) In the second equation, noneducational transfers are regressed on wage rate not income. The sign is negative and insignificant for heads and positive and insignificant for spouses, which is counter to the model. It seems to me that the regressors were entered in a backwards fashion—that wage rate should be in the first and income in the second regression if the time cost of being a student is to be adjusted for. Transfers received rise with age and expected inheritance.

Finally, regressions for family units sharing living quarters are presented. The results are mixed on the sign of own income—positive for secondary units and negative for primary units.

The chapter is a start at filling an important gap in the literture. I would quibble with the authors' conclusion that the results supported an "altruistic, egalitarian" view of transfers. Transfers are made from and to well-educated people and (as in the model) can be used to get around an imperfect capital market, but may not be equalizing in a lifetime sense. Hence I would argue that the results more strongly support a "shock absorber" or "young Rockefeller" model rather than an equalizing or compensating one. Without data on lifetime earnings, their case cannot be made.

References

Morgan, James. 1984. The role of time in the measurement of transfers and well-being. In *Economic transfers in the United States,* ed. M. Moon. NBER Studies in Income and Wealth, No. 49. Chicago: University of Chicago Press.

Menchik, Paul L., and Martin David. 1983. Income distribution, lifetime savings, and bequests. *American Economic Review* 83:672–90.

14   Economic Consequences of Marital Instability

Greg J. Duncan
Saul D. Hoffman

14.1 Introduction

The precarious economic position of families headed by women and the explosive growth in the number of such families over the past two decades are well known. The women and children of these families constitute a disproportionate share of the poverty population and of welfare recipients; in the minds of some recent analysts, they also account for a large number of the members of America's "underclass." Although much has been discovered from cross-sectional surveys about the status of female- and male-headed families in the past few years, there is considerably less information about the dynamics of one of the most important events—divorce and separation—that produce families headed by women and about the nature of the adjustment process that takes place following a divorce or separation. Simple comparisons of families headed by married men with those headed by women ignore the selection process that leads some women to head their own families, and are apt to be a poor guide to the likely changes in the economic situation of a currently married woman if she were to divorce or of a currently unmarried woman if she were to marry.

More sophisticated attempts to gauge the economic consequences of divorce and remarriage have either estimated multiequation models with cross-sectional data (Danziger et al. 1982) or have used longitudinal data from the Panel Study of Income Dynamics (PSID) (Hoffman 1977; Banc and Weiss 1980; Weiss, forthcoming) and National Longitudinal Surveys

Greg J. Duncan is associate research scientist at the Institute for Social Research. Saul D. Hoffman is associate professor of economics at the University of Delaware.

The research reported in this paper was supported by a grant from the Ford Foundation. Helpful comments from Martin David, Martha S. Hill, Robert Hutchens, Tim Smeeding, Arland Thornton, and various conference participants are gratefully acknowledged.

(Nestel, Mercier, and Shaw 1982). Although based on smaller numbers of observations, longitudinal data make it possible to compare the economic status of the *same* individuals before and after such events as divorce and remarriage, thus providing the opportunity to look at the effects of persistent interpersonal differences, even if those crucial characteristics are not measured.

Longitudinal data solve some but by no means all of the modeling problems inherent in estimating the consequences of changes in marital status. The first attempts to use PSID data to assess the economic consequences of divorce (Hoffman 1977; and Holmes 1976) fixed the time period over which changes in economic status were measured and counted all divorces that occurred at any time in the interval. As a result, income changes were measured at varying lengths of time after the divorce or separation and thus were not easily interpreted.

In this chapter we extend the uses of the longitudinal data from the PSID to provide a more complete analysis of the income and labor supply changes that accompany divorce and remarriage. We use a method developed by Bane and Weiss in which divorces are observed over a period of several years; then data on income sources and labor supply are "lined up" around the divorce year. This procedure not only increases sample size compared to a single year—something that is crucial for a relatively rare event like divorce—but also provides a uniform time interval to assess the economic conditions and adjustments in the years just after a divorce.

Other important features of our descriptive analysis that distinguish it from past work are the following:

Previous studies have largely ignored the fact that many divorced people remarry, causing a vast improvement in their economic situation. More than 50 percent of divorced white women and considerably less than that fraction of black women remarry within five years following their divorce. The economic status of women who do not remarry is a potentially unreliable guide to the situation women are likely to encounter should they happen to divorce. Our approach integrates the probability of remarriage into an analysis of the economic consequences of divorce.

Unlike Weiss and Bane and Weiss, we have not limited our postdivorce samples to single-parent families. Instead, we use as separate analysis subgroups men, women, and children involved in divorce, as well as a comparison group of intact couples.

We adopt functional definitions of *marriage* and *divorce*, the former including instances where unmarried couples are living together and the latter covering cases where residential separation occurs without divorce, or where unmarried couples who had been living together have separated. Unlike Weiss (forthcoming), we were able to identify and include instances where both the divorce and remarriage occurred within the same year.

Like Weiss's study, our analysis focuses on the distributional consequences of marital dissolution by carrying out separate analyses of white women from the upper and lower halves of the family income distribution. Unlike Weiss, however, we choose a different year in which to define the high- and low-income segments than that used as a base year for measurement of predivorce economic status. There are truncation problems with Weiss's procedure which lead to an overstatement of the distributional consequences of divorce.

Since the economic situation of women and children involved in divorce depends crucially upon the event of remarriage, we focus a great deal of attention in this chapter on the process and consequences of remarriage. To address the policy questions of whether anything can be done to increase remarriage rates of women, especially black women, we must understand the process of remarriage and learn whether programs such as AFDC play a role in discouraging remarriage, why remarriage rates are lower for black than white women, and whether the experience of women who do remarry is a reliable guide to the likely economic benefits marriage would bring for women who are currently choosing not to remarry. Investigation of the latter point is fraught with potential problems of selection bias, and we develop and estimate a model of the likely improvement in status that adjusts for this consideration. Although sample-size limitations prevent us from estimating the selection effect with precision, we do find evidence that the likely favorable income consequences of remarriage are much smaller for women who had not remarried than for otherwise similar women who had remarried.

This introduction is the first of a total of six sections. Section 14.2 summarizes the general framework that guides our approach. In the third section the sample and data are described. The fourth section presents a descriptive analysis of the income and labor supply flows that surround divorce and separation for the men, women, and children concerned. The fifth section details our modeling and estimation of the likely gains associated with remarriage for women who have divorced. The results are summarized in the sixth section.

14.2   Framework

It is easy to understand why the economic consequences of divorce may be especially adverse for women and children. In most cases children remain with the mother, who has considerably less capacity for earning a generous income in the labor market than her former husband, partly because her responsibilities for the children may reduce her labor supply.

Alimony and child support are the principal mechanisms for transfers from the ex-husband to the ex-wife, but the frequency and amount of payments rarely make up for an appreciable amount of the labor income lost through the departure of the ex-husband (U.S. Bureau of the Census 1983). Human capital investments on the part of the mother are one way in which the economic situation of her family may be improved, but the main route to financial betterment for her has been remarriage.

As pointed out by Hutchens (1979), striking parallels exist between the process of divorce, remarriage, and "marital search" on the one hand, and job change and job search on the other. That comparison suggests one crucial but frequently overlooked idea. Although the short-run economic impact of unemployment and job search may be severe, unemployment is rarely permanent. Just as it would be inappropriate to assess the economic impact of job change by focusing exclusively on the period of unemployment between jobs or on a sample of permanently unemployed persons, it is equally inappropriate to ignore the possibility of remarriage in an analysis of the economic consequences of divorce. Many studies of the consequences of divorce do that, however, by focusing exclusively on a sample of still-divorced women. We do not mean to minimize the adverse economic situation of women and children involved in a divorce or separation. Indeed, as pointed out by Bane and Weiss (1980), a five-year spell of female headship may be a relatively short period in the life of the female head but it constitutes a major portion of the time that her children spend in their childhood. Adverse economic circumstances in childhood may leave lifetime scars. Nevertheless, an evenhanded assessment of the economic consequences of divorce should take account of the probability of remarriage and the economic gains associated with it.

These ideas are illustrated in figure 14.1 which shows hypothetical income flows surrounding a divorce or separation. Suppose that economic status is measured by family income, adjusted for family size and composition; call this measurement family income/needs.[1] If a couple remains married, some growth in economic status over time is likely, accompanying additional investments in human and financial capital. This growth is illustrated by the line labeled "continuously married" in figure 14.1. Some couples will choose to divorce or separate, however, and that event will likely entail a substantial decline in economic status for the ex-wife and children. But within any fixed period of time there is the possibility that the ex-wife will remarry and substantially improve her economic status. For a woman whose new spouse is more capable than the former one, the economic circumstances associated with remarriage may well be higher than the status that would have resulted from continuing the first marriage. If remarriage is a random event among divorced women, then the

1. Nonmoney income should be included in this analysis as well but it is ignored here and in the empirical sections of the paper.

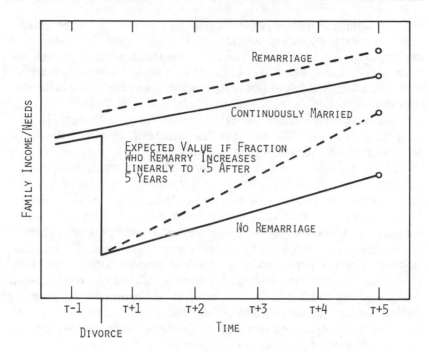

Fig. 14.1.   Hypothetical levels of family income/needs associated with divorce and remarriage.

expected economic situation following a divorce is the expected value of the income flows associated with the states of remarriage and no remarriage. Shown in figure 14.1 are expected values, associated with remarriage probabilities, that increase linearly with time from 0 to .5 over the first five years following divorce or separation.

Measuring status changes immediately after a divorce is likely to overstate considerably its longer-run effects because the measurement minimizes the chances of remarriage and thus its likely beneficial economic effects. It would be preferable to take an expected-value approach to economic status that weights the remarriage situation by the probability of occurrence. A crucial aspect of this procedure, however, is that remarriage may not be a random event across groups with different characteristics. Racial differences in remarriage rates are well known (Thornton and Rodgers 1983), and there may well be crucial but typically unmeasured characteristics of divorced spouses that affect remarriage chances. These issues are addressed in section 14.5 of the paper.

14.3   Data and Subsamples

The analysis presented in this paper was conducted on data from the Panel Study of Income Dynamics. The PSID provides a continuous representative sample of individuals in the population of the United States (except for recent immigrants), and thus also a representative subsample of adults and children undergoing a divorce or separation. All of the descriptive analyses reported here are estimated with sample weights that adjust both for differential initial sampling fractions and for differential nonresponse.

Samples were drawn from the fourteen-year family-individual file, covering the period from 1967 to 1981. The sample of women undergoing a divorce or separation was limited to sample women between the ages of twenty-five and fifty-four in the year prior to the divorce. A divorce or separation was defined as the transition from a state of living with a husband or long-term partner to a state of not living with that same person. Changes due to the death of a husband were excluded from the analysis. Remarriages are defined by the acquisition of a new husband or partner. The sample of men was drawn with analogous restrictions.[2] Corresponding criteria on their parents were used to determine the sample of children. The group of children was restricted to sample children who were between the ages of one and five in the year prior to the divorce.[3] The sample of children was further restricted to exclude those who were living with neither parent. In about one-tenth of the included cases, the children remained with the father rather than the mother after the divorce.

These samples were selected by scanning adjacent pairs of years from 1969–70 to 1975–76 for divorces or separations. Where there were multiple occurrences, the first such instance was taken. The first year of the adjacent pair in which a divorce or separation occurred was designated as year t. Income and employment information was then compiled from years $t - 2$ through year $t + 5$. References to these years in this paper concern statistics for the calendar year rather than for the interviewing year in which they were reported. Because the three subsamples of individuals involved in divorce are selected through a procedure that pools the data of various sets of years and because no marked differences in the incidence of divorces occurred over the business cycle, macroeconomic influences are averaged over all the relevant years.[4]

The sample of intact couples consists of all couples who were married continuously from 1971 to 1977, where the wife was between the ages of

2. Note that identical age restrictions on the sample of divorcing men and women will cause some ex-husbands to be included in the sample of men without their ex-wives being included in the sample of women, and vice versa.

3. Since the measurement of economic status extends for seven years, the age range for children was set narrowly to avoid situations in which the children would be old enough to set up independent households by the end of the measurement period.

4. The fraction of all divorces observed for the seven years between 1969 and 1975 were .168, .145, .120, .124, .094, .170, and .184, respectively. The largest fractions are indeed associated with the recession years of 1974 and 1975, but the third largest is associated with 1969, a period of exceptionally low unemployment and high growth.

twenty-five and fifty-four in 1971. For these couples, years $t - 1$ through $t + 5$ correspond to calendar years 1971 through 1977. Note that this span of years includes the severe recession of 1974 through 1976 (years $t + 2$ through $t + 4$, respectively) and thus provides some information about how income flows among intact couples are affected by macroeconomic fluctuations. All dollar figures have been inflated to 1981 prices using the Consumer Price Index. Contributions to the support of dependents outside the household have been subtracted from the family incomes of the subsample of men who have been divorced or separated.

As shown in the appendix in table 14.A.1, the resulting female subsample included 349 divorced or separated women, of whom 140 were black. Separate analyses are presented below by race and, for white women only, according to whether family income in year $t - 2$ was above or below the unweighted median.[5] Comparable distinctions are made for the subsamples of men, children, and intact couples. We also present separate calculations for women who remained divorced or separated in each year and for all of the initially divorced women, regardless of whether they had remarried. As table 14.A.2 shows, remarriage rates for all groups are substantial—for women they are about 20 percent after one year and over 50 percent after five years. Black remarriage rates are always lower than white rates.[6]

14.4 Descriptive Analysis

14.4.1 Changes in Total Family Income

The most dramatic economic effects of marital instability show up as changes in the total family income of the women and children involved. These changes are detailed in the appendix in tables 14.A.3 through 14.A.6 and are summarized in figure 14.2, which shows time profiles of income relative to year $t - 1$ for four groups—intact couples, divorced women who remained unmarried, and all divorced women and men re-

---

5. This division (at $23,000 in 1982 prices) is based on the year $t - 2$ because truncation on income in $t - 1$ would bias the analysis of income changes between year $t - 1$ and subsequent years.

6. The remarriage rates for whites are remarkably similar to those calculated from the June 1980 Current Population Survey's retrospective marital histories. Thornton and Rodgers 1983 calculated annual remarriage probabilities for white women, less than forty-five years of age, who separated between 1970 and 1974. Their figures, with comparable PSID figures in parentheses are: .22 (.21), .34 (.33), .43 (.46), .49 (.49), and .55 (.54). Comparable figures for blacks are not nearly as well matched: .05 (.18), .08 (.28), .12 (.31), .17 (.32), .20 (.42). A notable difference in the procedures used in computing these figures is that the CPS asks about official remarriages and the PSID does not distinguish between official remarriages and "living-together" situations. Thornton and Rodgers also note that there is substantial disagreement between the CPS figures and vital statistics calculated from official records.

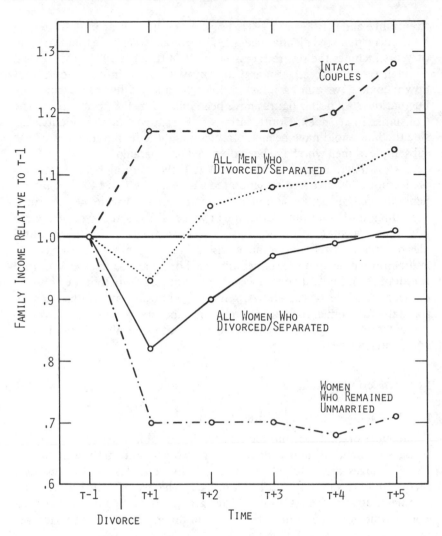

Fig. 14.2.   Family income of selected groups after a divorce or separation as a fraction of family income for the year prior to the divorce or separation.

gardless of their marital status in each subsequent year. Changes in a preferred measure of family economic status—total family income relative to needs—are described in the following section.

The average income level of women who divorce or separate falls from more than $26,000 in the year prior to divorce to less than $15,000 in the first full year after the divorce (table 14.A.3, row 4, cols. 1 and 2). Expressed as a fraction of family income in year $t - 1$ (table 14.A.4, row 4, col. 2 and figure 14.2), their income falls to 70 percent of its predivorce level in year $t + 1$ and, if they do not remarry, remains at about that level thereafter.[7] The 70 percent figure compares with 73 percent for children living with a parent who remained divorced in the first year following the divorce, 93 percent for men who divorced,[8] and 117 percent for intact couples. The relative drop for above-median white women and for black women is especially large.[9]

A closer look at the distribution of these ratios (tables 14.A.5 and 14.A.6) confirms the drastic drop in income for women (and their children) who remain divorced or separated after a year; over 40 percent of each group had family incomes cut by more than one-half (table 14.A.5, col. 1). Only about one-sixth of the divorced or separated men experienced so drastic a drop. Virtually none of the intact couples (2 percent) suffer such a fall, even during the recession years of $t + 2$ through $t + 4$.[10] While some of the women and children did actually experience an increase in real total family income between these two years (table 14.A.6, col. 1), the fractions who did so (11 and 15 percent, respectively) were smaller than comparable fractions for divorced or separated men (30 percent) and much smaller than for intact couples (65 percent). The relative decline in income was particularly severe for blacks and for women and children with family incomes above the median prior to the divorce.

The right-hand columns of the appendix tables show the income amounts and ratios for *all* individuals involved in divorce or separation, regardless of whether they had remarried. Including the possibility of remarriage dramatically improves the picture of the average postdivorce economic situation of women and children. More than one-fifth of the women and children involved in divorce remarried within one year, and their improved economic status raised the average ratio of post- to predivorce family income from .70 to .81 for women and from .73 to .85 for children.

7. The average of the individual ratios does not equal the ratio of the average income levels because the distribution of the individual ratios is skewed to the right. There is a natural truncation of these ratios from below at zero. Although a truncation from above was imposed at the value of 5.0, there is still enough skewness in this distribution to place the mean well above the median.

8. None of the calculations for the divorced or separated men distinguish between those who remarried and those who remained divorced or separated.

9. As large as the drop is for the above-median white women, it would be even larger if, as with Weiss (forthcoming), $t - 1$ had been the year used for stratification of the white women into the two income groups. Transitory increases in income in year $t - 1$ will push some of the women into the above-median group and lead to large decreases in income between $t - 1$ and $t + 1$. The ratio of $t + 1$ family income to $t - 2$ family income for the above-median white women was .51.

10. Recall that the divorced samples were drawn from a pooling procedure that roughly averages macroeconomic fluctuations across all years. Income information for the intact couples covers the years 1971–77, with years $t + 2$ through $t + 4$ corresponding to calendar years 1974 through 1976.

As shown in figure 14.2, family income of the women averages 97 percent of its predivorce level by the third year; after five years, when more than half had remarried, income rises above the predivorce level. Of course, these averages conceal great diversity in the experiences of subgroups. Few of the women and children who were *not* involved in a remarriage improved their status. And remarriage rates are substantially lower for black women and children, causing their average status to improve much more slowly than that of whites. The final columns of tables 14.A.3 through 14.A.6 show that the economic position of white women and children who were involved in a remarriage is often close to the $t + 5$ position of intact couples. The economic status of black women and children involved in a remarriage is considerably below that of intact black couples.

Taken together, the flat relative income profile of continuously unmarried women and the rising profile for all women clearly shows the relative unimportance of human capital adjustments relative to remarriage as a means to improved economic status. The important tasks of understanding why remarriage occurs in some cases but not in others and why the rates are lower for blacks is taken up in the fifth section of this paper.

14.4.2   Changes in Income/Needs and Poverty

Family income relative to needs is a preferred measure of family economic status because it adjusts for the number and composition of family members relying on family income. The need standard used here is the official government poverty standard, which takes into account family size and the ages and sex of family members. Income/needs is a simple ratio of total family cash income to this needs level.

It is expected that adjustments for family size will show a somewhat more optimistic picture of the economic status changes that accompany divorce for women and children, since the ex-husband's needs are no longer met. Figures 14.3 and 14.4 and tables 14.A.7 through 14.A.11 show that this is indeed the case. Family income/needs drops to 87 percent of its predivorce level for women who are still divorced in $t + 1$ and to 84 percent of its prior level for children in such situations (table 14.A.8, col. 2, rows 4 and 12). The comparable declines in family income from $t - 1$ to $t + 1$ for still-divorced women and children were to 70 percent and 73 percent, respectively, of their former average levels. The average adult man who became divorced or separated was actually better off one year later, although the improvements in his situation were less than that experienced by the average couple that remained intact.

As with family income, the relative drop in family income/needs is particularly severe for black women and children and for white women and children with predivorce income levels above the median. Also as with family income, including in the calculations women and children involved

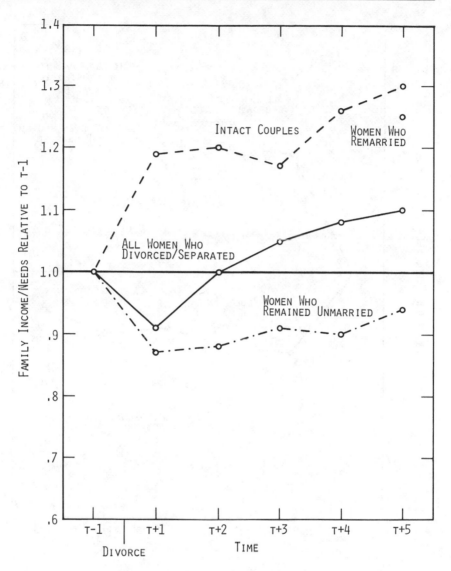

Fig. 14.3.   Family income/needs of women after divorce or separation as a fraction of family income/needs for the year prior to divorce or separation.

in a marriage improves their average position so much that virtually all of the groups are better off, on average, by the fifth year following the divorce or separation than they were before it. The average, of course, includes those who did remarry (the majority of whom are better off economically) and those who did not remarry (the majority of whom are worse off) (tables 14.A.9, 14.A.10).

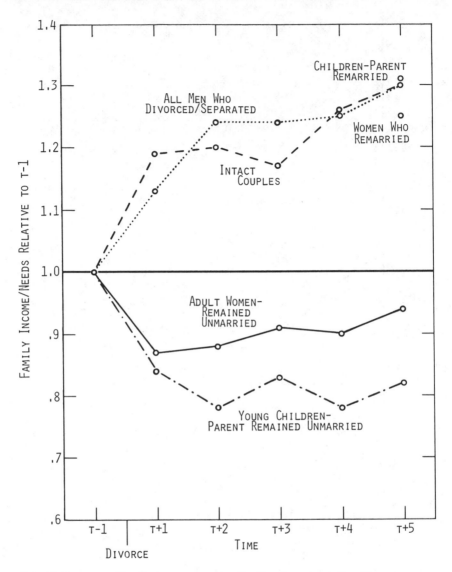

Fig. 14.4.   Family income/needs of selected groups after divorce or separation as a fraction of family income/needs for the year prior to divorce or separation.

Poverty rates rise dramatically for women and children involved in divorce or separation but actually fall slightly for men who divorce (figure 14.5 and table 14.A.11). A closer look at the distribution of the poverty figures shows that the higher incidence is limited almost exclusively to black women and children and to white women and children whose predivorce family income levels were below the median. The increases for

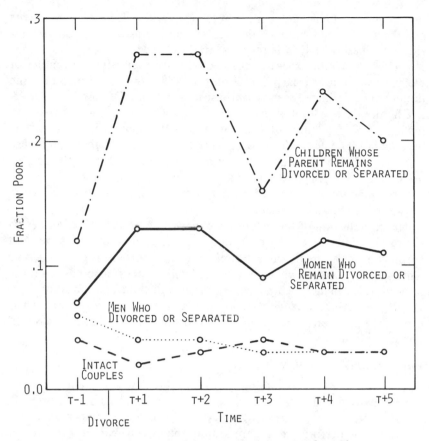

Fig. 14.5.   Incidence of poverty among intact couples and men, women, and children involved in divorce or separation.

these two groups are large indeed. Poverty rates for below-median white children jump from .14 in the year prior to the divorce to .41 in the year after (table 14.A.11, row 10, cols. 1 and 2). Comparable increases for black children are from .24 to .38. The situation of the white children improves substantially with time, even if no remarriage occurs, but poverty rates at the end of the period are still higher than they were before the divorce. Poverty rate changes are similar for women involved in divorce, although the absolute fractions for poor women are uniformly lower than the comparable fractions for children.

14.4.3   Changes in the Composition of Family Income: Earnings, Welfare, Alimony and Child Support

The composition of family income changes drastically for the women and children involved in divorce, as only part of the ex-husband's lost labor income is retained in the form of alimony and child support payments and the wife's own labor income, welfare, and transfers from others outside the household adjust in response to the change.

An examination of these various sources for the PSID subsamples of women and children clearly shows that the wife's own labor income is the dominant component for most of these new families. Of the $14,781 average family income level of divorced or separated women in the year following the divorce (table 14.A.2, row 4, col. 2), about three-fifths was the wife's labor income (table 14.A.12, row 12, col. 2), only about one-tenth consisted of alimony and child support (table 14.A.13, row 12, col. 2), about one-twentieth consisted of welfare income (table 14.A.14, row 12, col. 2), and only about 1 percent consisted of other private transfers from outside of the household (data not shown).[11]

The composition of the income packages is somewhat different across the racial and income subgroups and changes somewhat over time. Not surprisingly, welfare is considerably more important for low-income whites and for blacks, while alimony and child support is somewhat more important for higher-income white women and children. For all of these groups, however, the ex-wife's labor income constitutes more than 60 percent of the total, on average, and the importance of this income source increases with time.

Labor Supply and Labor Income

The labor force participation of women increases dramatically in response to divorce. The fractions of women working at least 1,000 hours in the year after a divorce is more than twenty percentage points higher than the fractions performing a comparable amount of market work in the year prior to the divorce. The size of this increase is almost identical for all three subgroups of women (figure 14.6 and table 14.A.12, rows 5 to 8). Virtually all of the divorced white women coming from above-median income families were working at least 250 hours in the year following the divorce and 85 percent worked at least 1,000 hours. The comparable fractions of black women and below-median white women working at least 250 hours are 65 and 72 percent, respectively. There is some tendency for the participation rates to increase with time for the women who remain divorced or separated. In contrast, women who remarry end up with participation rates that are not only lower than when they were divorced, but also lower than in the year prior to the divorce.[12] Labor income amounts associated with these work hours show a similar pattern (table 14.A.12, rows 9 to 12).

11. Private transfers from others outside the household never averaged more than $400 for any of the subgroups and do not appear in any of the appendix tables.

12. This latter fact raises the possibility that many women may increase their participation rates in anticipation of an upcoming divorce. Annual average work hours did increase between $t - 2$ and $t - 1$, but only by a modest amount—32 hours.

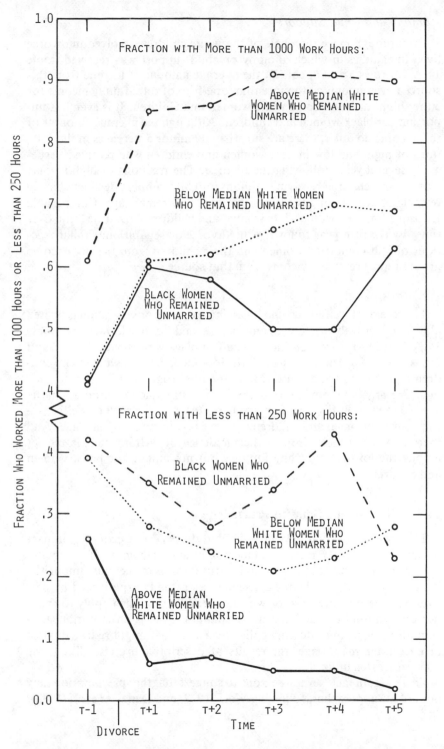

Fig. 14.6. Labor supply adjustments of women after a divorce or separation.

Alimony and Child Support

Even though more than half of the white children involved in divorce lived in families in which alimony or child support was received (table 14.A.13, rows 5 and 6, col. 2), the average amount of income from this source never amounted to more than one-fifth of total family income for either high- or low-income white women and children. It is even less important for black women and children. Although the average amounts of this income do differ, there are surprisingly minor differences in the fractions of high- and low-income women and children who receive it, especially several years following the divorce. The fractions of high-income women and children receiving alimony or child support declines sharply over time, even among those not involved in a remarriage. Comparable fractions for low-income white women and children show little trend over time; by the fifth year following the divorce or separation, similar fractions of still unmarried women and their children from the two income groups report receiving income from that source.

Welfare

The receipt of welfare income following a divorce or separation is limited almost exclusively to low-income white and to black families (table 14.A.14, rows 1–8, col. 2). Close to half of black women and children and between one-third and one-half of the low-income white women and children report receiving at least $250 in income from AFDC, general assistance, or any other noncontributory cash welfare income program in the year following the divorce. Remarriage often ends the spell of welfare receipt for the women and children who are involved in a remarriage. And there is a discernable drop in the incidence of welfare income receipt among the low-income white families but not among the black women and children.

14.5   Modeling the Gains to Remarriage

The previous sections have documented the pervasive economic impact of both divorce and remarriage. One potential shortcoming of this analysis, however, is that it treats marital status itself as exogenous. Implicitly, it suggests that the economic consequences actually experienced by persons who become divorced or who remarried would also apply to those persons who did not undergo those changes. That is an important presumption, since, in evaluating policy measures that might reduce divorce or encourage remarriage, the results of descriptive exercises like those above are often utilized.

There are, in fact, several reasons to suggest that that presumption may not hold. Suppose that, following Wolf (1977) and Danziger et al. (1982), we view choices about marital status as a function of the expected utility levels associated with being married or single. In neither case, of course, is utility solely a function of income, but ceteris paribus, it seems reasonable that a sample of divorced persons would consist largely of those who experienced relatively smaller income losses. Similarly, those who remarry may also be a nonrandom set of all divorced persons, in this case including those who had the most to gain economically from remarriage. In either case, inferences drawn from descriptions that treat the samples as if they were random would be in error. If the selection processes were as described above, the economic consequences of divorce would be understated and those of remarriage would be overstated—at least as far as drawing inferences to the rest of the population was concerned.

In this section we focus more carefully on issues of this kind. Specifically, we examine two related issues. First, we now treat the choice of marital status as endogenous. We restrict this analysis to the transition in marital status for women from divorced to married. Second, we reexamine the expected income consequences of remarriage, explicitly accounting for the potential nonrepresentativeness of that sample. To do that, we utilize the sample selection techniques developed by Heckman (1979).

4.5.1 A Simple Model of the Gains from Remarriage

Our basic ideas can be sketched as follows. Let Q stand for "husband quality," a concept analogous to Becker's child quality. We think of Q as having two components: potential labor market earnings (Y) and all else (A).[13] Q is an increasing function of both Y and A, but some components of A can be negative. We assume that a divorced woman seeks a new spouse of highest Q, but that this maximum Q value is conditional on her own personal characteristics. There may, for example, be certain personal characteristics of a divorced woman that enable her to acquire a spouse of higher quality. Letting Q_i^* be the maximum husband quality available to woman i and X_i be the set of her relevant personal characteristics, we can express this as:

(1) $$Q_i^* = f(Y_i^*, A_i^*) = g(X_i).$$

Presumably, remarriage occurs only if it is expected to increase utility. A minimum condition for this is $U(Q) > 0$; a stronger one, which accounts

---

13. In the model developed by Danziger et al. 1982, Y is one of the components of the expected earned income of the female household if the woman were to marry. The authors do not distinguish between her own labor income in the married state and the earned income of the husband, and they note, but do not incorporate, the possibility of selection bias in the estimation of this earned income component in their statistical analysis. Our analysis can be thought of as an elaboration upon one aspect of their model. The size of the future husband's labor income in the income package of married women is so large, however, that it is certainly the most important component and deserves a careful and separate analysis.

for the fact that some income sources (I_s) are withdrawn at remarriage, would be that:

$$(2) \qquad\qquad U(Q) > U(I_s).$$

AFDC and alimony payments would be examples of I_s. Since from equation (1), Q_i^* is a function of X_i, equations (1) and (2) together suggest that a woman's characteristics determine not only the maximum husband quality available to her, but also the probability of remarriage.

If all of the elements of X_i could be measured, equation (1) could be estimated by an OLS regression of Q^* on X_i for a sample of women who remarried. The results would be unbiased estimates of population parameters and would be appropriate for the sample of unmarried women as well. If, however, some relevant portions of X are not observable, estimation problems arise, since the unobserved components would affect not only the value of Q^* but also the probability that an individual would fall into the sample of remarried women. That is precisely the problem of selection bias; coefficient estimates derived from such a sample could no longer be meaningfully applied to the population as a whole or, more importantly, to the sample of unmarried women.

The well-known statistical solution to this problem, developed by Heckman (1979), involves estimating the sample selection process—in this case, remarriage—with a probit function.[14] Those results are then used to form the inverse Mill's ratio denoted as λ for each individual in the sample of unmarried women. Finally, the equation of interest—our equation (1)—can be estimated by OLS with $\hat{\lambda}$ included as an additional regressor. The sign of the coefficient on λ depends on the correlation of the error terms across equations. In this example, a positive (negative) coefficient would indicate that a woman who did not remarry would have a lower (higher) quality husband (if she were to remarry) than an otherwise identical woman (in terms of measured characteristics) who did remarry. A conventional t-test on the estimated coefficient on $\hat{\lambda}$ can be used to assess its statistical significance.

4.5.2 Model Specification

Although the model outlined above was cast in terms of husband quality, broadly defined, we focus in our empirical work only on the new husband's labor market earnings. There are two reasons for this. An obvious one is the lack of data on the components of A. While nonmonetary characteristics may well be important, we have no measures of them. The second justification is that the spouse's income is important as a means of escaping from poverty and increasing the family's standard of living.

---

14. A full treatment of these issues is in Heckman 1979.

Our full empirical model examines both the probability of remarriage and the labor income of the new spouse over a five-year period beginning with the onset of a divorce. The sample of women who divorce or separate is drawn from the PSID data and is identical to the one used in the descriptive analyses. The regression results we report are unweighted, although we use weighted means to make population projections.[15]

Remarriage Equation

The dependent variable in our remarriage equation is whether the initially divorced or separated woman remarried within five years after the divorce or separation.[16] The specification of the independent variables follows Hutchens (1979). All explanatory variables included in X apply to the woman: her educational attainment, health status (whether disabled), age, number of children, whether a child is less than age six, and dummy variables for whether she resided in large and small SMSAs. As measures of I_s, we use annual alimony income and monthly AFDC payments for a family of four in the state of residence.[17] We expect both of these to reduce the probability of remarriage. We also include a time trend to examine whether remarriage probability is different for more recent instances of divorce. Finally, we conclude after some preliminary experimentation that it is appropriate to pool black and white women using only an additive race variable (black = 1), but no interactions between race and any of the independent variables.

We think that our use of the data set is an improvement over previous work in several respects. First, the five-year time period for remarriage is more precise than the variable-length periods used in other studies. This time period is long enough for ample search to have occurred and thus allows us to assume that an equilibrium situation with respect to remarriage is being observed. Second, our analysis includes women in all fifty states; previous studies (Hutchens 1979) included only women in selected states or were unable to identify the exact state of residence (Danziger et al.

---

15. We used the method outlined in DuMouchel and Duncan 1983 to determine whether weighting was necessary. Sample weights, which are the inverse of the probability of sample selection, are always required for estimates of population means.

16. This specification of the dependent variable does lead to the loss of information concerning the time of remarriage within the five-year period. A potentially richer estimation technique that would require the imposition of assumptions about the distribution of completed spells longer than five years is event history analysis, developed by Tuma, Hannan, and Groeneveld 1979.

17. The data were taken from information published by the Department of Health, Education, and Welfare on the "largest amount paid for basic needs." Since women without children are ineligible for AFDC, we reassigned their potential AFDC payments to zero.

Region variables are excluded from the model because of the strong correlation with AFDC payment levels. Over half of the variation in AFDC levels was accounted for by three region dummy variables in an OLS regression. Although urban/rural measures may reflect remarriage opportunities, we see no similar argument for the inclusion of region variables.

1982). Finally, unlike all previous studies, all of the women in our sample are observed as of the beginning of a spell of divorce or separation. Previous studies have not been able to control for the length of a divorce spell and this may have affected their findings.

New Husband's Labor Income Equation

Ideally, the dependent measure of new husband's earnings capacity in our regression analysis should be his expected permanent labor market earnings. Lacking that, we use the natural logarithm of the new husband's labor income in the fifth year after her divorce or separation; for women who were married and divorced within the five-year period, we use the new husband's labor income in the last observed year of remarriage.[18] The independent variables include all of the variables from the remarriage equation except the time trend. A set of three dichotomous variables for region of residence is added, as is a measure of the labor income of each woman's previous husband. We interpret this variable as a proxy for her own unobservable characteristic that might affect the income of her new spouse. We continue to use only a dummy variable for race.

Table 14.1 presents the results of our analyses. Estimated coefficients from the probit model are in column (1), those from an OLS regression of husband's labor income are in column (2), and the adjusted OLS results, correcting for selection bias, are in column (3).

The remarriage equation is of interest both in its own right and as a prelude to the regression analysis. Considering the relatively small sample size and the inherent problems in modeling such a complex event, the equation performs well. Two sets of results are of special interest. First, the two financial variables—AFDC payments and alimony—reduce the probability of remarriage, although neither is significant at conventional levels. A more important finding is the very large, negative, and statistically significant effect of race. Substantial racial differences in remarriage persist even when the effects of a host of other factors that influence remarriage are taken into account. Evaluated at the means of the independent variables, the predicted five-year remarriage rates are 56 percent for whites and 25 percent for blacks.

Implicit in the labor income regression equation is both an assortative mating marriage process and a human capital earnings function. That is, we are attempting to predict the labor income of an unmarried woman's *prospective* spouse. We do so by using information on the women in our sample who did remarry and on their new husbands, adjusting the estimates with Heckman's technique for the possible nonrepresentativeness of that group. Thus, the independent variables in the earnings regression

18. To correct for extremely low income that may have been the result of an unusual circumstance (extended unemployment or illness, etc.), and thus not representative of long-run income, we imposed a minimum income level of $2,000.

Table 14.1 **Remarriage and the Gains from Remarriage (standard errors in parentheses)**

Independent Variable[a]	Whether Remarried	Ln (New Husband's Labor Income)	
	Probit	OLS	Adjusted OLS
Race	−.846[b]	−.302[c]	−.604
	(.162)	(.157)	(.488)
AFDC $(00s)	−.039	.026	.013
	(.037)	(.033)	(.039)
Alimony $(000s)	−.051	.006	−.008
	(.037)	(.030)	(.038)
Years of education	−.038	.092[b]	.081[b]
	(.034)	(.028)	(.033)
Disabled	−.272	−.288	−.359
	(.212)	(.209)	(.235)
Wife's age	−.032[b]	−.016[c]	−.026
	(.009)	(.009)	(.018)
No. of children	.015	−.064[b]	−.055[c]
	(.035)	(.030)	(.033)
Whether child younger than age 6	−.154	.036	−.005
	(.186)	(.156)	(.170)
Large SMSA	−.380[b]	−.093	−.213
	(.192)	(.153)	(.242)
Small SMSA	−.300	−.102	−.191
	(.190)	(.142)	(.201)
South	—	−.181	−.188
		(.173)	(.165)
West	—	−.117	−.126
		(.183)	(.175)
Northeast	—	−.270	−.279
		(.209)	(.198)
Ex-husband's income (000s)	—	.025[b]	.024[b]
		(.010)	(.005)
Time trend	−.054	—	—
	(.036)		
Constant	2.40[b]	8.79[b]	9.07[b]
	(.684)	(.98)	(.714)
λ	—	—	.507
			(.781)
Mean of dependent variable	.43	9.40	9.40
Sample size	345	150	150
$\bar{R}^2$		.386	
Log likelihood	−208.3		
Residual mean square error (adjusted)			.589

[a]Independent variables refer to the sample of divorced women.
[b]Significant at 5 percent confidence level.
[c]Significant at 10 percent confidence level.

are for the women who remarried, while the dependent variable is the labor income of their new husbands. It is important to note that this sample of men whose incomes are being predicted are not a random sample of all men because they are drawn from the pool of men who were eligible to marry these women.

The unadjusted OLS coefficients in table 14.1 reflect the labor income behavioral equation as it applies only to the sample of remarried women, while those coefficients in the final column, which have been adjusted for sample selection bias, can be interpreted as estimates of population parameters applicable to the entire set of divorced or separated women. In both equations it appears that the prospective husband's labor income is most strongly related to the wife's education and to the income of her ex-husband. The estimated coefficient on $\hat{\lambda}$ is positive, but it is less than its own standard error. The positive coefficient is, however, plausible; it indicates that those women who do remarry find higher-income spouses than would otherwise similar women who did not remarry. With the exception of the race and age variables, the other estimated coefficients in the two regressions are similar to each other. The race variable coefficient falls sharply from $-.302$ to $-.604$ when the selection bias adjustment is made. That change follows from the positive coefficient on λ and the very negative effect of race on remarriage. λ is itself inversely related to the probability of inclusion in the sample, so black women who remarried must have larger values for λ than otherwise identical white women in the sample. Since the unobservable traits measured by λ tend to increase the labor income of the spouse, failure to account explicitly for this selection effect mistakenly attributes that effect to the race variable. When the correction is made, the race coefficient becomes more negative, now reflecting the opportunities facing an average black woman in the population. This may reflect the characteristics of the group of unmarried black men who are potential remarriage partners. Similar reasoning explains the fall in the coefficient on age.

We can use the two sets of regression results as predictive equations to indicate the average husband's income that could be obtained by different groups of women.[19] These results are shown in table 14.2. The first column shows the actual new husband's income for women who remarried— $8,813 for black women and $15,125 for white. The next two columns give the predicted mean values for women who did not remarry, using both the unadjusted and adjusted coefficients. The difference between the figures in the second and third columns represents the effect of differences in measured characteristics, assuming that those characteristics would affect unmarried women exactly as they affected the sample of married women.

19. To obtain these values, we multiply each coefficient by the mean value of each variable for each group of interest.

Table 14.2   Actual and Predicted Mean of Husband's Income by Race

	New Husband's Income	Predicted Husband's Income	
		OLS[a]	Adjusted OLS[b]
Black women	$ 8,813	$ 8,292	$4,200
White women	15,125	13,494	8,408

[a]Based on OLS results from table 14.1.
[b]Based on OLS estimates, corrected for selectivity bias.

The numbers in the second column are lower, but the differential is not substantial. The predicted difference for blacks is only 6 percent, reflecting the fact that in terms of measured traits, remarried and still-divorced blacks are not very different. The much lower numbers in the third column include the additional effect of differences in the unmeasured traits summarized in the λ term, now valuing those traits using the parameters appropriate for a random person in the population. They also reflect the selection bias adjustments in some of the other coefficients, most notably race, age, and education. As shown, there is a sharp fall in the predicted mean value of husbands' earnings, especially for black women whose predicted value is only 48 percent of the figure for the remarried women. The implication is that the opportunities for a woman to increase her standard of living through marriage appear to be much worse for currently unmarried women than for similar women who did remarry.

A complete assessment of the impact of these low expected amounts of husbands' labor income on remarriage decisions would require building them into a model like that of Danziger et al. (1982). We hope to extend our work in that direction, but it appears likely that the low expected gains from remarriage will go a long way in explaining the low remarriage rates of black women.

14.5 Summary

A close look at the income and labor supply flows in the years following a divorce or separation reveals marked differences in the distribution of effects. Most men who divorce or separate are immediately better off because they retain most of their labor incomes, typically do not pay large amounts of alimony and child support to their ex-wives, and no longer have to provide for the level of needs associated with their former families. On the other hand, women and children involved in divorce are often much worse off. The fall is largest in relative terms for women and children whose predivorce incomes were above the median and for black women and children. In absolute terms, however, low-income whites and especially black children suffer the most.

Many of the women and children involved in divorce do improve their economic status with time. Half of the low-income whites and blacks rely on welfare to a certain extent after the divorce, and considerable numbers of whites from both income strata report receiving alimony and child support. The average size of these income sources is small, however, relative to the amount of labor income earned by the ex-wives. Labor force participation rates jump substantially for all groups of women. They approach unity for the high-income white women and are well above 50 percent for low-income white and black women. The importance of this earned income grows with time following divorce.

Much more important than growth in an ex-wife's income is the role of a new husband's labor income if she remarries. More than half of white women remarry within five years following a divorce or separation; the comparable fraction for black women is less than half. A crucial question is whether policies that might encourage the currently unmarried to marry would provide the same kind of economic benefits that are enjoyed by the women and children who were involved in a remarriage. Estimates from a model of the new husband's labor income, adjusted for selection bias inherent in the process of remarriage, indicate that there is not likely to be as much of a benefit for the currently unmarried if they were to remarry. The expected labor income of potential husbands of black women averages only about $5,000—a modest amount when compared to the alternatives that might be available to her.

Appendix Tables

(tables follow on pp. 451–466)

Table 14.A.1   Number of Observations

	Remained Unmarried						All (includes those who remarried)						Married in
	$t-1$	$t+1$	$t+2$	$t+3$	$t+4$	$t+5$	$t-1$	$t+1$	$t+2$	$t+3$	$t+4$	$t+5$	$t+5$
Women													
All white													
Above median	105	87	77	61	55	48	105	105	105	105	105	105	57
Below median	104	73	57	47	46	42	104	104	104	104	104	104	62
All black	140	122	115	112	108	103	140	140	140	140	140	140	37
All women	349	282	249	220	209	193	349	349	349	349	349	349	156
Men													
All white													
Above median							77	77	77	77	77	77	56
Below median							89	89	89	89	89	89	70
All black							84	84	84	84	84	84	36
All men							250	250	250	250	250	250	162
Children													
All white													
Above median	64	56	47	34	30	27	64	64	64	64	64	64	27
Below median	117	76	57	42	41	37	117	117	117	117	117	117	80
All black	182	161	158	155	146	141	182	182	182	182	182	182	41
All children	363	293	262	231	217	205	363	363	363	363	363	363	158
Intact couples													
All white													
Above median							668	668	668	668	668	668	668
Below median							460	460	460	460	460	460	460
All black							365	365	365	365	365	365	365
All intact couples							1,481	1,481	1,481	1,481	1,481	1,481	1,481

Table 14.A.2   **Weighted Fraction of Divorced or Separated Women, Men, and Children Who Were Involved in a Remarriage**

	Remarriage Occurred				
	1–2 Years	2–3 Years	3–4 Years	4–5 Years	5–6 Years
Women					
White	.213	.328	.460	.489	.544
Black	.182	.281	.309	.316	.416
All	.209	.322	.441	.468	.528
Men					
White	.394	.551	.641	.696	.761
Black	.350	.408	.565	.571	.572
All	.389	.536	.633	.682	.741
Children					
White	.242	.363	.542	.566	.607
Black	.117	.210	.307	.321	.441
All	.221	.337	.502	.524	.580

Note: Remarriage is defined as the acquisition of a permanent partner, regardless of official marital status.

Table 14.A.3 Family Income Level (in 1981 dollars)

	Remained Unmarried						All (includes those who remarried)						Married in
	$t-1$	$t+1$	$t+2$	$t+3$	$t+4$	$t+5$	$t-1$	$t+1$	$t+2$	$t+3$	$t+4$	$t+5$	$t+5$
Women													
All white													
Above median	34,756	17,719	17,975	18,762	18,411	17,934	34,576	20,369	22,856	27,457	26,584	28,579	37,994
Below median	18,282	12,501	12,723	12,807	13,311	13,094	18,282	15,280	15,912	16,376	18,576	18,235	22,264
All black	18,021	9,165	10,308	9,891	9,526	11,385	18,021	10,463	13,204	12,722	12,797	14,283	18,356
All women	26,168	14,781	15,229	15,417	15,240	15,178	26,168	17,168	18,958	21,317	21,765	22,781	29,566
Men													
All white													
Above median							33,508	26,533	28,431	30,728	30,661	31,937	33,762
Below median							18,539	16,843	19,270	19,947	19,925	21,546	22,883
All black							20,241	19,798	19,643	17,304	22,102	18,720	24,111
All men							25,403	21,488	23,398	24,470	24,952	25,874	27,728
Children													
All white													
Above median	33,960	19,025	17,786	18,929	18,366	18,466	33,960	21,663	23,671	26,187	26,581	29,337	37,566
Below median	16,837	10,376	12,703	13,348	13,507	12,302	16,837	13,370	13,956	15,441	18,402	18,850	22,600
All black	18,415	10,207	11,165	12,318	11,336	12,110	18,415	10,616	14,345	15,682	18,006	17,588	24,536
All children	23,213	13,822	14,436	15,243	14,761	14,511	23,213	15,866	17,488	19,317	21,254	22,380	28,096
Intact Couples													
All white													
Above median							38,828	41,265	41,451	39,293	41,710	41,735	
Below median							18,570	22,412	21,412	21,230	22,655	23,613	
All black							22,779	24,492	24,441	24,165	24,669	25,513	
All intact couples							30,604	33,483	33,237	31,903	33,838	34,248	

Note: Payments made to support outside dependents have been subtracted from income for men. For intact couples, $t-1$ is calender year 1969, t is 1970, etc.

Table 14.A.4   Family Income Relative to $t-1$

	Remained Unmarried						All (includes those who remarried)						Married in $t+5$
	$t-1$	$t+1$	$t+2$	$t+3$	$t+4$	$t+5$	$t-1$	$t+1$	$t+2$	$t+3$	$t+4$	$t+5$	
Women													
All white													
Above median	1.0	.61	.64	.69	.68	.69	1.0	.68	.78	.94	.89	.94	1.16
Below median	1.0	.88	.85	.76	.75	.74	1.0	1.03	1.08	1.06	1.15	1.13	1.44
All black	1.0	.54	.59	.59	.55	.74	1.0	.67	.83	.82	.82	.88	1.08
All women	1.0	.70	.70	.70	.68	.71	1.0	.81	.90	.97	.99	1.01	1.27
Men													
All white													
Above median							1.0	.82	.91	.95	.97	1.02	1.05
Below median							1.0	1.00	1.22	1.27	1.21	1.31	1.42
All black							1.0	1.02	.98	.87	1.09	.97	1.04
All men							1.0	.93	1.05	1.08	1.09	1.14	1.23
Children													
All white													
Above median	1.0	.62	.60	.67	.63	.68	1.0	.69	.76	.85	.85	.92	1.11
Below median	1.0	.87	.76	.74	.74	.67	1.0	1.01	1.06	1.17	1.30	1.29	1.65
All black	1.0	.65	.70	.78	.67	.90	1.0	.73	.89	.99	1.10	1.09	1.34
All children	1.0	.73	.68	.72	.68	.72	1.0	.85	.93	1.02	1.11	1.13	1.42
Intact couples													
All white													
Above median							1.0	1.11	1.11	1.04	1.14	1.12	
Below median							1.0	1.29	1.26	1.38	1.32	1.53	
All black							1.0	1.14	1.15	1.22	1.16	1.32	
All intact couples							1.0	1.17	1.17	1.17	1.20	1.28	

Table 14.A.5 Fraction with Family Income Less Than Half of $t - 1$ Level

	Remained Unmarried						All (includes those who remarried)						Married in
	$t-1$	$t+1$	$t+2$	$t+3$	$t+4$	$t+5$	$t-1$	$t+1$	$t+2$	$t+3$	$t+4$	$t+5$	$t+5$
Women													
All white													
Above median		.54	.55	.55	.49	.57		.42	.44	.36	.33	.34	.14
Below median		.40	.36	.23	.31	.18		.40	.22	.16	.21	.12	.06
All black		.41	.39	.48	.49	.33		.34	.28	.34	.34	.26	.15
All women		.47	.47	.43	.43	.39		.38	.33	.28	.28	.24	.11
Men													
All white													
Above median								.13	.10	.09	.11	.06	.08
Below median								.18	.10	.13	.10	.11	.10
All black								.17	.17	.28	.16	.18	.11
All men								.16	.11	.13	.11	.10	.09
Children													
All white													
Above median		.43	.50	.47	.48	.53		.38	.38	.34	.32	.35	.23
Below median		.43	.37	.08	.26	.21		.30	.25	.12	.20	.13	.08
All black		.43	.41	.33	.38	.22		.38	.33	.25	.28	.14	.05
All children		.43	.43	.29	.37	.33		.34	.31	.22	.26	.21	.13
Intact Couples													
All white													
Above median								.02	.02	.05	.05	.05	.05
Below median								.02	.04	.04	.05	.05	.05
All black								.01	.05	.04	.05	.06	.05
All intact couples								.02	.03	.05	.05	.05	.05

Table 14.A.6 Fraction with Family Income Higher Than $t - 1$ Level

	Remained Unmarried						All (includes those who remarried)						Married in
	$t-1$	$t+1$	$t+2$	$t+3$	$t+4$	$t+5$	$t-1$	$t+1$	$t+2$	$t+3$	$t+4$	$t+5$	$t+5$
Women													
All white													
Above median		.08	.12	.14	.13	.14		.12	.22	.35	.34	.34	.52
Below median		.16	.13	.14	.14	.17		.32	.36	.38	.43	.40	.61
All black		.04	.15	.12	.10	.16		.12	.34	.28	.30	.26	.39
All women		.11	.13	.14	.13	.14		.20	.29	.35	.37	.35	.55
Men													
All white													
Above median								.19	.29	.36	.39	.45	.48
Below median								.35	.43	.46	.50	.57	.63
All black								.52	.45	.37	.51	.47	.57
All men								.30	.37	.41	.45	.50	.56
Children													
All white													
Above median		.12	.10	.15	.16	.24		.15	.24	.32	.38	.37	.47
Below median		.17	.14	.09	.17	.03		.35	.35	.37	.49	.44	.67
All black		.14	.27	.22	.18	.27		.16	.39	.44	.41	.40	.56
All children		.15	.15	.14	.17	.16		.25	.32	.36	.44	.41	.58
Intact Couples													
All white													
Above median								.62	.57	.50	.56	.59	.59
Below median								.70	.64	.60	.67	.69	.69
All black								.69	.57	.56	.64	.62	.62
All intact couples								.65	.60	.54	.60	.63	.63

Table 14.A.7   Family Income/Needs Level

	Remained Unmarried						All (includes those who remarried)						Married in
	$t-1$	$t+1$	$t+2$	$t+3$	$t+4$	$t+5$	$t-1$	$t+1$	$t+2$	$t+3$	$t+4$	$t+5$	$t+5$
Women													
All white													
Above median	4.7	3.2	3.1	3.3	3.3	3.3	4.7	3.3	3.6	4.1	4.1	4.3	5.3
Below median	2.7	2.3	2.3	2.4	2.6	2.5	2.7	2.4	2.6	2.5	2.8	2.7	2.8
All black	2.3	1.5	1.6	1.5	1.5	1.8	2.3	1.6	1.9	1.9	1.9	2.0	2.3
All women	3.6	2.6	2.7	2.7	2.7	2.8	3.6	2.7	3.0	3.2	3.3	3.4	4.0
Men													
All white													
Above median							4.6	4.6	5.0	5.1	5.1	5.3	5.1
Below median							2.8	2.9	3.2	3.2	3.1	3.4	3.4
All black							2.9	3.5	3.3	2.6	3.4	2.9	3.5
All men							3.6	3.7	4.0	4.0	4.0	4.2	4.1
Children													
All white													
Above median	4.0	2.5	2.5	2.7	2.6	2.7	4.0	2.8	3.1	3.1	3.2	3.7	4.4
Below median	2.0	1.4	1.6	1.8	1.8	1.6	2.0	1.6	1.7	1.8	2.1	2.0	2.3
All black	1.9	1.3	1.3	1.3	1.2	1.3	1.9	1.3	1.5	1.6	1.8	1.8	2.3
All children	2.7	1.8	1.9	2.1	2.0	1.9	2.7	2.1	2.2	2.2	2.4	2.6	3.0
Intact Couples													
All white													
Above median							5.0	5.4	5.5	5.3	5.7	5.8	
Below median							2.5	3.0	2.9	2.8	3.0	3.1	
All black							2.7	2.9	3.0	3.0	3.1	3.1	
All intact couples							4.0	4.4	4.4	4.3	4.5	4.7	

Table 14.A.8 Family Income/Needs Relative to t − 1

	Remained Unmarried						All (includes those who remarried)						Married in
	$t-1$	$t+1$	$t+2$	$t+3$	$t+4$	$t+5$	$t-1$	$t+1$	$t+2$	$t+3$	$t+4$	$t+5$	$t+5$
Women													
All white													
Above median	1.0	.77	.81	.89	.88	.88	1.0	.80	.89	1.02	.98	1.04	1.17
Below median	1.0	1.07	1.04	1.00	.99	1.02	1.0	1.08	1.16	1.12	1.22	1.21	1.36
All black	1.0	.71	.77	.78	.74	.95	1.0	.80	.94	.97	1.00	1.03	1.13
All women	1.0	.87	.88	.91	.90	.94	1.0	.91	1.00	1.05	1.08	1.10	1.25
Men													
All white													
Above median							1.0	1.07	1.15	1.16	1.20	1.27	1.20
Below median							1.0	1.12	1.32	1.34	1.28	1.36	1.41
All black							1.0	1.40	1.30	1.08	1.36	1.19	1.08
All men							1.0	1.13	1.24	1.24	1.25	1.30	1.29
Children													
All white													
Above median	1.0	.73	.71	.78	.75	.81	1.0	.76	.84	.85	.87	.96	1.07
Below median	1.0	.99	.83	.86	.84	.76	1.0	1.02	1.06	1.12	1.22	1.23	1.50
All black	1.0	.75	.80	.86	.73	.94	1.0	.82	.94	.99	1.04	1.05	1.20
All children	1.0	.84	.78	.83	.78	.82	1.0	.89	.96	1.00	1.06	1.10	1.31
Intact couples													
All white													
Above median							1.0	1.14	1.16	1.13	1.23	1.27	
Below median							1.0	1.28	1.25	1.24	1.29	1.34	
All black							1.0	1.15	1.18	1.18	1.25	1.30	
All intact couples							1.0	1.19	1.20	1.17	1.26	1.30	

Table 14.A.9   Fraction with Family Income/Needs Less Than Half of $t-1$ Level

	Remained Unmarried						All (includes those who remarried)						Married in $t+5$
	$t-1$	$t+1$	$t+2$	$t+3$	$t+4$	$t+5$	$t-1$	$t+1$	$t+2$	$t+3$	$t+4$	$t+5$	
Women													
All white													
Above median		.31	.29	.22	.18	.26		.29	.25	.17	.16	.23	.20
Below median		.18	.14	.03	.14	.16		.13	.11	.10	.12	.15	.15
All black		.32	.31	.29	.44	.28		.27	.23	.20	.31	.27	.25
All women		.26	.24	.17	.21	.23		.23	.22	.15	.16	.20	.18
Men													
All white													
Above median								.06	.06	.02	.03	.04	.04
Below median								.13	.10	.11	.09	.08	.08
All black								.03	.08	.07	.08	.13	.11
All men								.09	.08	.07	.06	.07	.07
Children													
All white													
Above median		.26	.24	.21	.12	.34		.26	.18	.16	.10	.23	.15
Below median		.14	.19	.00	.20	.20		.11	.17	.14	.18	.19	.19
All black		.36	.35	.24	.34	.18		.33	.30	.18	.24	.17	.15
All children		.23	.24	.14	.21	.25		.20	.20	.16	.16	.20	.17
Intact couples													
All white													
Above median								.01	.02	.03	.03	.04	
Below median								.02	.04	.05	.07	.04	
All black								.01	.03	.05	.06	.05	
All intact couples								.02	.03	.04	.05	.04	

Table 14.A.10   Fraction with Family Income/Needs Higher Than $t-1$ Level

	Remained Unmarried						All (includes those who remarried)						Married in $t+5$
	$t-1$	$t+1$	$t+2$	$t+3$	$t+4$	$t+5$	$t-1$	$t+1$	$t+2$	$t+3$	$t+4$	$t+5$	$t+5$
Women													
All white													
Above median		.14	.17	.15	.24	.22		.19	.25	.32	.39	.35	.46
Below median		.34	.30	.32	.45	.44		.38	.41	.43	.54	.52	.58
All black		.20	.24	.21	.20	.26		.28	.36	.38	.36	.33	.53
All women		.22	.19	.22	.31	.30		.27	.33	.37	.45	.41	.51
Men													
All white													
Above median								.53	.55	.56	.57	.57	.50
Below median								.52	.60	.61	.55	.67	.64
All black								.65	.55	.47	.66	.54	.53
All men								.54	.57	.57	.57	.61	.57
Children													
All white													
Above median		.17	.10	.15	.19	.27		.19	.25	.22	.32	.34	.39
Below median		.26	.30	.36	.34	.19		.34	.37	.41	.49	.45	.61
All black		.24	.29	.28	.20	.29		.28	.40	.39	.43	.31	.35
All children		.22	.22	.26	.25	.24		.28	.33	.34	.42	.39	.50
Intact Couples													
All white													
Above median								.66	.63	.55	.62	.67	
Below median								.66	.61	.55	.63	.64	
All black								.58	.56	.61	.68	.67	
All intact couples								.66	.62	.56	.63	.66	

Table 14.A.11   Fraction Poor

	Remained Unmarried						All (includes those who remarried)						Married in
	$t-1$	$t+1$	$t+2$	$t+3$	$t+4$	$t+5$	$t-1$	$t+1$	$t+2$	$t+3$	$t+4$	$t+5$	$t+5$
Women													
All white													
Above median	.02	.04	.04	.02	.02	.07	.02	.04	.03	.01	.03	.06	.06
Below median	.10	.19	.21	.10	.10	.10	.10	.14	.16	.12	.10	.09	.09
All black	.13	.33	.32	.28	.47	.28	.13	.30	.30	.26	.33	.26	.22
All women	.07	.13	.13	.09	.12	.11	.07	.11	.11	.09	.09	.10	.09
Men													
All white													
Above median							.01	.01	.00	.00	.00	.01	.00
Below median							.08	.06	.05	.02	.04	.02	.03
All black							.18	.05	.15	.16	.17	.15	.06
All men							.06	.04	.04	.03	.03	.03	.02
Children													
All white													
Above median	.02	.07	.06	.03	.04	.10	.02	.06	.05	.03	.02	.08	.07
Below median	.14	.41	.36	.11	.19	.17	.14	.30	.29	.22	.23	.18	.19
All black	.24	.38	.50	.43	.63	.42	.24	.37	.42	.36	.45	.32	.19
All children	.12	.27	.27	.16	.24	.20	.12	.23	.22	.18	.19	.17	.15
Intact couples													
All white													
Above median							.00	.00	.00	.00	.01	.00	.00
Below median							.08	.04	.06	.07	.06	.05	.05
All black							.15	.12	.14	.13	.10	.11	.11
All intact couples							.04	.02	.03	.04	.03	.03	.03

Table 14.A.12 Labor Supply of Divorced or Separated Women

	Remained Unmarried						All (includes those who remarried)						Married in
	$t-1$	$t+1$	$t+2$	$t+3$	$t+4$	$t+5$	$t-1$	$t+1$	$t+2$	$t+3$	$t+4$	$t+5$	$t+5$
Fraction with Less Than 250 Work Hours													
All white													
Above median	.26	.06	.07	.05	.05	.02	.26	.07	.12	.15	.15	.19	.35
Below median	.39	.28	.24	.21	.23	.28	.39	.29	.29	.32	.32	.36	.43
All black	.42	.35	.28	.34	.43	.23	.42	.33	.27	.32	.34	.34	.50
All women	.33	.18	.15	.15	.17	.15	.33	.19	.21	.23	.24	.28	.39
Fraction with More Than 1,000 Work Hours													
All white													
Above median	.61	.85	.86	.91	.91	.90	.61	.83	.78	.79	.77	.71	.54
Below median	.42	.61	.62	.66	.70	.69	.42	.62	.59	.55	.53	.52	.38
All black	.41	.60	.58	.50	.50	.63	.41	.58	.57	.56	.56	.57	.48
All women	.51	.73	.74	.77	.77	.78	.51	.72	.68	.66	.65	.62	.47
Annual Labor Income (includes zeroes)													
All white													
Above median	7,562	11,327	11,880	12,693	13,422	12,957	7,562	10,709	11,180	11,258	11,019	10,236	7,830
Below median	4,444	6,639	7,671	8,454	9,174	8,668	4,444	6,353	6,680	6,471	6,814	6,342	4,520
All black	3,370	5,635	6,344	5,057	4,878	7,332	3,370	5,365	6,524	5,363	5,708	6,308	4,868
All women	5,829	8,937	9,757	10,113	10,603	10,541	5,829	8,350	8,848	8,663	8,723	8,230	6,169

Table 14.A.13   Alimony and Child Support Payments Received by Women and Children

	Remained Unmarried						All (includes those who remarried)						Married in t+5
	t−1	t+1	t+2	t+3	t+4	t+5	t−1	t+1	t+2	t+3	t+4	t+5	t+5
						Fraction Receiving More Than $250							
Women													
All white													
Above median	.01	.48	.46	.41	.36	.33	.01	.42	.39	.31	.26	.26	.20
Below median	.01	.36	.40	.36	.34	.35	.01	.30	.27	.22	.23	.23	.13
All black	.01	.17	.14	.14	.14	.20	.01	.14	.10	.12	.10	.14	.06
All women	.01	.39	.40	.36	.32	.32	.01	.34	.31	.25	.23	.23	.16
Children													
All white													
Above median	.02	.60	.69	.55	.52	.46	.02	.54	.61	.44	.39	.41	.37
Below median	.00	.54	.56	.57	.50	.56	.00	.38	.32	.29	.32	.35	.23
All black	.01	.15	.23	.26	.25	.31	.01	.13	.19	.23	.17	.31	.31
All children	.01	.49	.55	.49	.45	.47	.01	.39	.40	.34	.32	.37	.29

Table 14.A.13 (continued)

	Remained Unmarried						All (includes those who remarried)						Married in
	$t-1$	$t+1$	$t+2$	$t+3$	$t+4$	$t+5$	$t-1$	$t+1$	$t+2$	$t+3$	$t+4$	$t+5$	$t+5$
	Total Amount of Alimony and Child Support Received (includes zeroes)												
Women													
All white													
Above median	10	2,425	1,889	1,312	900	746	10	2,143	1,536	1,032	700	583	
Below median	19	940	1,119	1,090	888	764	19	770	762	700	565	509	
All black	9	449	276	486	589	232	9	367	199	375	403	177	
All women	13	1,646	1,423	1,113	847	675	13	1,388	1,070	821	611	505	
Children													
All white													
Above median	18	3,712	3,403	2,003	1,439	1,085	18	3,349	2,780	1,648	1,223	1,023	
Below median	0	1,685	2,238	2,352	1,487	1,632	0	1,159	1,232	1,233	967	939	
All black	16	389	463	957	1,090	381	116	300	366	737	740	481	
All children	26	2,243	2,361	1,891	1,374	1,152	26	1,796	1,639	1,298	1,020	892	

Table 14.A.14 Welfare Receipt

	Remained Unmarried						All (includes those who remarried)						Married in
	$t-1$	$t+1$	$t+2$	$t+3$	$t+4$	$t+5$	$t-1$	$t+1$	$t+2$	$t+3$	$t+4$	$t+5$	$t+5$
	Fraction Receiving at Least $250 in Welfare												
Women													
All white													
Above median	.00	.03	.04	.06	.04	.04	.00	.03	.03	.03	.02	.03	.02
Below median	.08	.35	.27	.31	.26	.23	.08	.29	.22	.24	.22	.17	.12
All black	.12	.53	.55	.61	.59	.53	.12	.50	.44	.48	.44	.39	.18
All women	.05	.21	.18	.22	.20	.18	.05	.19	.15	.17	.15	.13	.08
Children													
All white													
Above median	.03	.05	.04	.03	.04	.04	.03	.05	.03	.05	.05	.05	.05
Below median	.10	.50	.45	.33	.34	.34	.10	.41	.37	.31	.34	.25	.19
All black	.24	.48	.67	.63	.64	.64	.24	.50	.56	.48	.49	.38	.05
All children	.10	.32	.33	.29	.30	.30	.10	.29	.28	.25	.26	.13	.20

Table 14.A.14 (continued)

| | Remained Unmarried | | | | | | All (includes those who remarried) | | | | | | Married in |
	$t-1$	$t+1$	$t+2$	$t+3$	$t+4$	$t+5$	$t-1$	$t+1$	$t+2$	$t+3$	$t+4$	$t+5$	$t+5$
			Total Annual Amount Received (includes zeroes)										
Women													
All white													
Above median	0	73	81	136	108	64	0	61	61	80	60	35	9
Below median	350	1,586	1,413	1,245	1,169	1,194	350	1,402	1,115	991	875	818	523
All black	621	2,250	2,567	3,066	2,275	1,763	621	2,005	1,948	2,260	2,056	1,206	423
All women	213	887	847	951	896	733	213	824	704	702	623	484	262
Children													
All white													
Above median	244	306	280	120	85	94	244	269	214	236	211	270	403
Below median	524	2,368	2,291	1,735	1,713	2,046	524	2,103	1,794	1,434	1,267	1,193	705
All black	1,462	2,457	3,452	3,866	3,344	2,253	1,462	2,494	2,827	2,868	2,542	1,307	107
All children	582	1,556	1,696	1,617	1,509	1,379	582	1,514	1,404	1,248	1,105	823	523

References

Bane, M. J., and Robert S. Weiss. 1980. Alone together: The world of single-parent families. *American Demographics* 2:11–14, 48.

Danziger, Sheldon, George Jakubson, Saul Schwartz, and Eugene Smolensky. 1982. Work and welfare as determinants of female poverty and household headship. *Quarterly Journal of Economics* 98:519–34.

DuMouchel, William, and Greg J. Duncan. 1983. Using sample survey weights in multiple regression analyses of stratified samples. *Journal of the American Statistical Association* 78:535–43.

Heckman, James. 1979. Sample selection bias as a specification error. *Econometrica* 47:153–61.

Hoffman, Saul D. 1977. Marital instability and the economic status of women. *Demography* 14:67–76.

Hoffman, Saul D., and John W. Holmes. 1976. Husbands, wives, and divorce. In *Five thousand American families: Patterns of economic progress*, ed. Greg J. Duncan and James N. Morgan, vol. 4. Ann Arbor, Mich.: Institute for Social Research.

Hutchens, Robert. 1979. Welfare, remarriage, and marital search. *American Economic Review* 69:369–79.

Nestel, G., J. Mercier, and L. Shaw. 1982. Economic consequences of mid-life change in marital status. In *Unplanned careers: The working lives of middle-aged women*, ed. L. Shaw. Lexington, Mass.: Lexington Books.

Thornton, Arland, and Willard Rodgers. 1983. Changing patterns of marriage and divorce in the United States. Appendix 3. NICHD contract no. NO1-HD-02850.

Tuma, Nancy B., Michael T. Hannan, and Lyle P. Groeneveld. 1979. Dynamic analysis of event histories. *American Journal of Sociology* 84:820–54.

U.S. Bureau of the Census. 1983. *Child support and alimony, 1981.* Advance report. Special Studies series P-23, no. 124.

Weiss, Robert S. Forthcoming. The impact of marital dissolution on income and consumption of single-parent households. *Journal of Marriage and the Family*.

Wolf, D. A. 1977. Income maintenance, labor supply, and family stability. Ph.d. diss., University of Pennsylvania.

Comment   Isabel V. Sawhill

Due to the work of a number of analysts, it has now been established that changes in family composition are an important reason for flows into and

Isabel V. Sawhill is a senior fellow at the Urban Institute.

out of poverty and for changes in economic status more generally. Greg Duncan and Saul Hoffman have made significant contributions to this literature in the past, and their current chapter, "Economic Consequences of Marital Instability," is a useful addition to the evolving story.

The chapter contains a number of important findings. First, women and children involved in a divorce or separation experience a substantial drop in real economic welfare relative to their economic status before divorce—a drop that is particularly sharp for black women and women from higher-income families. This contrasts with men whose economic status improves after a divorce. Adjusted for family size, the gains experienced by divorced males are similar to those experienced by intact families. Second, after an initial drop in economic status, divorced women and their children gradually recoup some of the losses, so that at the end of five years they are actually better off than they were the year before divorce, although not as well off as women who remained in intact families throughout the period. Third, the major reason for these gains is remarriage. Although there is a sharp increase in labor force participation and earned income among women after they divorce, those who do not remarry experience little or no gain in income during the five-year period following divorce and thus end up considerably worse off than they were prior to divorce. Fourth, about half of all women and about three-quarters of all men remarry within five years. The probability of remarrying is much lower for blacks than for whites and for older than for younger women. Fifth, there is some evidence that women who remarry have more to gain from doing so than women who remain unmarried. Thus, one should be cautious about assuming that a higher remarriage rate would produce equivalent gains for currently unmarried women. In particular, black women's low remarriage rates appear to be related to the fact that the earnings of their prospective husbands are low relative to the alternative sources of income available to them.

These are the substantive findings in a nutshell. A wealth of more detailed information can be found in the tables. A number of methodological or conceptual wrinkles in the paper also distinguish it from previous work. These include the use of a Heckman technique to correct for selection bias in the sample of people who remarry, the pooling of observations according to their timing in relation to the event of divorce, and the adoption of a functional as opposed to a legal definition of marriage and divorce.

In my comments on the paper, I will focus on five issues: selection bias, child care expenses, investment in human capital, remarriage patterns, and policy implications.

With respect to selection bias, the authors give most of their attention to analyzing whether women who remarry are different (in ways that cannot be measured) from those who do. They found what appeared to me to be no evidence in favor of such selection bias. The estimated coefficient on the selection bias variable was positive but less than its own standard error. In spite of this they give a lot of attention to the results from the equation that includes this coefficient, attributing the shift in the race coefficient, for example, to a selection bias effect. I think they are misinterpreting what is probably just a case of unstable coefficients. In addition, if one is worried about selection bias, this may not be where one should look for it first. The counterfactual case for most of the analysis of changes in the economic well-being of men and women after divorce is, or should be, concurrent changes in the economic status of intact families. But suppose that people who divorce are different (either in measurable or nonmeasurable ways) from those who do not. Then all of the findings reported in the tables and summarized above would need to be modified to adjust for this fact.

Another kind of bias present in the authors' results stems from the failure to adjust gross income for child care expenses. If most divorced women with children have significant work-related expenses that their ex-husbands do not have, and we compare the relative economic status of the two groups after divorce without adjusting for this fact, we will underestimate the differences in net income. The authors are careful to adjust for differences in family size and in child support or alimony obligations. Although not a major omission, child care expenses should ideally be added to this list.

Turning to the human capital issue, as a member of the "second sex," I find it somewhat depressing that the only way to improve one's economic status after divorce is to find another man. But before I get too gloomy about this finding, I would want to see more analysis of how women who actually make investments in additional education or new careers after a divorce fare relative to those who do not, and what happens beyond the first five years. Earnings in the first few years after divorce might actually be depressed by a decision to go to school but be higher at a later point in time. I doubt that such an analysis would change the basic conclusions of this paper but it would be an interesting addition to someone's future research agenda.

Turning to the determinants of remarriage among women, we have not advanced far from where we were eight years ago when I first used the PSID to examine this question. Other than age and race, there are no robust predictors, and the reasons for the large race differential remain elusive. It might be instructive in this regard to analyze the remarriage rates of men to see if similar patterns hold and to develop better conceptual models for both sexes that involve examining transition probabilities between different marital states using a more creative set of independent variables. Although I doubt that we will ever be able to explain much of the observed variation among individuals, we should be able to do better than we have to date.

Finally, let me say something about the policy issue that appears to have motivated this research. Duncan and Hoffman note that "a crucial question is whether policies that might encourage the currently unmarried to marry would provide the same kind of economic benefits that are enjoyed by the women and children who were involved in a remarriage" (p. 450). I do not think this is the crucial question, or even the right question. It is only the Moral Majority, after all, that is advocating using government policies to encourage marriage. The right question is whether government policies are neutral or whether they are inadvertently destabilizing family life. And if the latter, is this a cost we are willing to pay to achieve some other benefit such as providing an income floor for dependent children? Duncan and Hoffman find weak evidence, at best, that the current AFDC program discourages remarriage. In my opinion, this is the issue to which more research should be devoted.

Let me conclude by saying that the authors have provided us with a lot of useful new information, most of it descriptive, about the economic consequences of divorce and separation. I hope they will continue to till this particular field because they do it quite well.

15 Variations in the Economic Well-Being of Divorced Women and Their Children: The Role of Child Support Income

Andrea H. Beller
John W. Graham

15.1 Introduction

Female-headed families are a large and growing proportion of all families. Special concern for this population stems from the limited amount of resources available to the family unit. Divorce almost always results in a decline in the level of living for all parties involved, but the decline is larger for women than for men (Hoffman 1977). Female-headed families make up a disproportionate share of the poverty population and many have little choice but to rely upon the welfare system (Bradbury et al. 1979).

Between 1970 and 1981 the number of married-couple families increased only 10.1 percent while the number of female-headed families increased 62.4 percent, so by 1981 over 15 percent of all families were headed by a woman only (U.S. Bureau of the Census 1982, table 60). This rising rate of female headship is of special concern in part because female-headed families have lower incomes and are more likely to be classified as poor than are married-couple families. In 1980 the median income of married-couple families was $23,180 compared to $10,830 for female-headed fam-

Andrea H. Beller is associate professor of family economics at the University of Illinois at Urbana-Champaign. John W. Graham is assistant professor of economics at the University of Illinois at Urbana-Champaign.

This research was supported by Hatch funds from the University of Illinois Agricultural Experiment Station and by funds from the University of Illinois at Urbana-Champaign Research Board. The authors gratefully acknowledge the excellent research assistance of Kee-ok Kim Han and Lorraine Maddox and the computer programming assistance of John Boyd. Thanks are also due to Elizabeth Peters for sharing her computer program with us for preparation of the data extract and to Morey MacDonald for some early discussions. This chapter has benefited from comments by Irwin Garfinkel and the editors of this book and from presentation at the Labor Workshop at the University of Illinois. The authors alone take responsibility for errors and omissions.

ilies (U.S. Bureau of the Census 1982, table 717). Of the 6.2 million families with incomes below the poverty level in that year, almost 3 million were female headed (U.S. Bureau of the Census 1982, table 735), a phenomenon recently dubbed the "feminization of poverty."[1] Female headship also may be of special concern because of the large number of children involved. Between 1970 and 1980 the number of children living with two parents (not necessarily their natural ones) declined 20.6 percent, while the number living with one parent (overwhelmingly their mother) increased 67.1 percent. By 1982, 15.3 percent of white and 47.2 percent of black children lived with only their mothers (U.S. Bureau of the Census 1983, p. 5). For most this is a temporary arrangement, since a large majority of divorced women remarry. However, it has been estimated that "children born in the mid-1970s have about 45 chances in 100 of living in a one-parent family for a period of at least several months before they reach the age of 18 years." (Glick and Norton 1977).

Most mothers with children from an absent father head their own families at least for a time. Figure 15.1 shows the distribution by household status in April 1979 of mothers aged eighteen and over with children (under twenty-one years of age) from an absent father.[2] Of these 6.4 million mothers, 5.5 million had previously been married to the child's father, while 0.9 million had not. Among the ever married, 3.5 million are divorced or separated: 3.2 million of these head their own families and 0.3 million live as subfamilies with parents or other relatives. Another 2.0 million are remarried and 54 thousand are widowed after remarriage. Among the never married, most head their own families. In this chapter, we focus on the two largest of these groups, divorced or separated mothers heading their own families and remarried mothers, excluding the widowed.[3]

We investigate variations in several key components of the economic well-being of ever-divorced or currently separated mothers with children from an absent father. In large measure, the economic well-being of a divorced mother depends upon the amount of family support (child support and alimony) she receives from her ex-husband, her labor force participation, and how quickly she remarries, if at all. Whether family support is received or not and how much is received is subject to considerable uncertainty, both in amount and regularity of payments. Because many divorced mothers are awarded child support while few are awarded ali-

1. National Organization of Women president, Judy Goldsmith, *New York Times*, 1 September 1983.
2. The idea for this figure comes from Bradbury et al. 1979.
3. Subfamilies pose special problems of income sharing that we cannot readily handle. Never-married mothers differ in significant ways from ever-married mothers and thus must be considered separately. Women who are widowed after remarriage form a small group whose economic position may depend more upon their current circumstances than upon having been divorced.

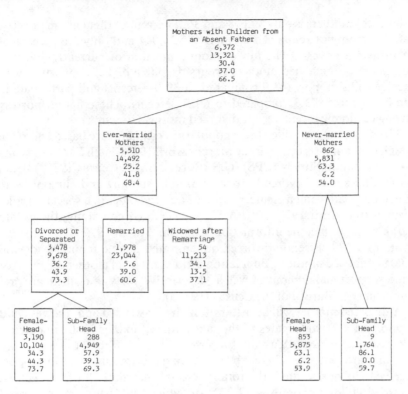

Fig. 15.1.   Mothers eighteen and over with children from an absent father
in 1979: number of women (in thousands); average total family
income; percentage in poverty; percentage receiving child
support; labor force participation rate. *Source:* Tabulations by
authors from the computer tapes of the March/April Match
File of the 1979 Current Population Survey.

mony, we shall devote much more attention to the former. A divorced
mother is more likely to participate in the labor force than a married
mother, since her earnings become crucial to the family's economic status.
She also can seek to improve the position of her family by searching for a
new mate to regain the economic well-being lost by divorce. One unique
aspect of our study is that we pay particular attention to the effects of
child support and alimony upon the probabilities of remarriage and labor
force participation.

Figure 15.1 presents four measures of well-being for each household
status group: average total family income; the percentage of families in
poverty; the percentage of families receiving child support; and the labor
force participation rate of mothers. In terms of economic status, ever-
married are better off than never-married mothers, and remarriage clearly
improves economic status. While the total family income of divorced (or

separated) mothers is only $9,678 and 36.2 percent of them live in poverty, family income of remarried mothers is $23,044 and only 5.6 percent of them live in poverty. The low economic position of currently divorced compared to remarried mothers occurs despite a higher proportion who receive child support (43.9 compared to 39.0 percent) and participate in the labor force (73.3 compared to 60.6 percent). These figures portray strong economic incentives for divorced mothers to remarry.

The data set upon which these population estimates are based and from which our sample is drawn is the March/April 1979 Match File of the Current Population Survey (CPS) (U.S. Bureau of the Census 1981b). Data on marital status, divorce history, and child support and alimony were collected on all women eighteen years of age and older in a special supplement to the April 1979 CPS. A file was created containing these data along with the income information from the March 1979 CPS. This file contains 1,579 currently divorced or separated female family heads and 1,005 remarried mothers. Population estimates for all mothers eligible for child support and alimony as well as descriptive analyses of them are presented in U.S. Bureau of the Census (1981a).[4]

A divorced mother will be better off if she is awarded and receives child support, if she participates in the labor force, and/or if she remarries. Women who are awarded child support are better off than those who are not, and their income is higher by more than the amount of child support received. In our sample, the total personal income in 1978 of women awarded child support was $7,970, of which child support comprised $1,115. For those not awarded child support, total personal income was $5,568. The difference is even greater between those who received child support and those who did not. Total personal income of those who received child support in 1978 was $9,425 while for those who did not it was $5,742. The average amount of child support received for those who received any was $1,901, much less than the difference in income. Women who participate in the labor market have higher personal income and receive more child support than those who do not. In 1978 the average personal income of currently divorced or separated mothers who worked outside the home was $9,632, while for those who did not it was $4,197; if they worked, they received $998 in child support, but if they did not, only $570. As shown in figure 15.1 above, although remarriage improves the economic well-being of divorced mothers the most, it appears to be associated with less child support received—$1,683 compared to $2,021 for currently divorced or separated mothers.

An important question raised by these figures is whether child support payments have a direct causal effect upon the decision to work and/or re-

---

4. The population estimates published in that report differ slightly from the ones we report in figure 15.1.

marry, or whether the observed association is simply simultaneously determined by other factors. To examine the interrelationships between child support and these other components of economic well-being, we postulate the theoretical model presented in section 15.2. Based upon that model, we examine in section 15.3 what factors influence the award and receipt of child support. Then in sections 15.4 and 15.5 we examine the impact of child support payments (holding constant other factors) upon remarriage and upon labor force participation, respectively.

15.2 Theoretical Framework

Before turning to our empirical work, we offer a short sketch of the theory upon which our analysis is based. We posit the following recursive system:

(1) $$CSDUE = f^1(H^1, W^1, L^1).$$

(2) $$CSREC = f^2(H^2, W^2, L^2, CSDUE).$$

(3) $$RM = g[Y_d(CSREC_d, \ldots), Y_r(CSREC_r, \ldots), C].$$

(4) $$LF_d = k[W_h(CSREC_d, \ldots), W_m, V_d(CSREC_d, \ldots)].$$

The first equation says that child support due ($CSDUE$) is a function of a vector of characteristics of the ex-husband's ability (and desire) to pay (H^1), the financial needs of the woman and children (W^1), and the legal environment at divorce (L^1).[5] The second equation says that support actually received ($CSREC$) depends upon the same three vectors of variables (H^2, W^2, and L^2) as well as upon the amount of support due. We label these vectors with different superscripts to suggest that they may contain somewhat different elements from those in the first equation. For example, W^1 may measure the judge's perception of the woman's needs, while W^2 measures the ex-husband's perception of her needs. A priori W^2 could depend in part upon the woman's current marital status (RM), but in our empirical work we offer evidence that this effect is limited. Past work (Gordon, Jones, and Sawhill 1978; Cassetty 1978) finds that the effect of H^2 upon $CSREC$ is particularly strong where H^2 refers to the absent father's current financial status, measured perhaps by his current income or current employment status. L^2 includes child support enforcement laws which vary from state to state.

---

5. Equation (1) might be viewed as a reduced form expression derived from equilibrating the mother's demand for with the absent father's supply of child support, where equilibrium is attained through either private negotiation or the court system. Viewed this way, one could investigate determinants of these demand and supply functions such as other anticipated sources of support (including alimony and property settlements) and the tax treatment of these alternative income sources. However, we choose not to pursue this line as our data are better suited to analyzing the reduced form than the structural equations.

Equation (3) states that the probability a divorced woman remarries (RM) depends negatively upon her real income (monetary plus nonmonetary) while divorced (Y_d), positively upon her expected real income if remarried (Y_r), and negatively upon the costs of marital search (C). Since child support payments are supposed to continue even after a woman remarries, $CSREC$ enters both Y_d and Y_r, although a priori we allow expected receipts to vary with marital status ($CSREC_d$ and $CSREC_r$). Ceteris paribus, an increase in child support payments will reduce the expected increase in income from remarriage (because, although portable, child support payments are a larger fraction of Y_d than of Y_r), but will raise the woman's attractiveness to potential marriage partners. Therefore, the net impact of child support on remarriage is ambiguous. It should be noted that public assistance benefits may be another important component of Y_d.

The final equation states that the probability a divorced woman is in the labor force (LF_d) depends negatively upon the value of her time at home (W_h), positively upon the value of her time in the market (W_m), and negatively upon nonlabor income (V_d), which itself depends upon child support payments ($CSREC_d$). If a woman uses child support payments to purchase for her children market goods that can be substituted for her home time, then W_h may depend negatively upon $CSREC_d$. In this case, the net effect of an increase in $CSREC_d$ on LF_d is ambiguous: it raises V_d which reduces LF_d, but it lowers W_h which raises LF_d.

To summarize, economic theory cannot determine the net impact of child support payments on either the probability of remarriage or the probability of labor force participation. Instead, this remains to be determined by empirical analysis.

15.3   Empirical Analysis of Child Support

Child support payments are in many cases an uncertain and inadequate source of income to divorced mothers. In this section we examine what factors determine whether a woman is awarded child support, and then, given its award, whether she actually receives it as well as how much she receives. Our study significantly improves upon previous studies of child support (Cassetty 1978; Gordon, Jones, and Sawhill 1978; and Sorensen and MacDonald 1981) by separating the question of award from receipt and by using a large national data set that samples the entire eligible population.

Excluding observations with missing values, our sample consists of up to 2,416 ever-divorced or currently separated women (eighteen years of age or over) with children (under twenty-one years of age) from an absent father. There are 389 black women and 2,027 nonblack, of which 7 percent are of Spanish origin. At divorce or separation, 72.6 percent of these women were awarded child support—77.5 percent of nonblacks and 47.6

percent of blacks.[6] For those who were due payment in 1978 the average annual amount due was $2,028.[7] Of these, 71.4 percent received partial or full payments averaging $1,899. While the large majority of those due support received at least partial payment, 45.4 percent reported receiving no payments or irregular payments. Means and standard deviations for various characteristics of this sample are summarized in the appendix, table 15.A.1.

In this section, we estimate determinants of the award and receipt of child support for currently divorced or separated and remarried women.[8] Because black women are much less likely than nonblack women to be awarded child support, we estimate the determinants of award probability separately by race. However, in analyzing the receipt of child support, we combine blacks and nonblacks because too few blacks are awarded child support to permit separate analysis.[9] The variables used in the regression equations are defined in the appendix, table 15.A.2.

15.3.1 Determinants of the Probability of Being Awarded Child Support

Child support awards may be either court ordered or informally agreed to, although even most voluntary agreements are formalized through legal contracts. Our theoretical analysis postulates that child support is more likely to be awarded the greater is the perceived need of the woman and children and the greater is the ability (or desire) of the absent father to pay. The probability of award also depends upon the legal environment at divorce which varies from state to state and over time, and may vary within a state across legal jurisdictions, as well as across individual judges. There is some evidence that in states with no-fault divorce, the amount of child support awarded is lower than in states without no-fault divorce (Peters 1982). For our sample we have only some of the desirable information on the needs of the mother and on the ability of the father to pay, and no information on the legal environment.[10]

6. Black mothers are significantly less likely to be awarded support even after controlling for other factors.

7. Around 17.2 percent of all mothers—16.8 percent of nonblacks and 21.6 percent of blacks—awarded child support were not due any in 1978 for a variety of reasons such as death of the previous spouse and children past the age of eligibility for support.

8. In separate regression equations we found no systematic differences between them in the estimated coefficients.

9. Equations estimated for the nonblack sample alone are nearly identical to those for all races combined, with the notable exception that the black intercept dummy is usually significant in the combined sample.

10. It would be especially desirable to have some direct information on the financial circumstances of the father at the time of divorce. For our sample, it is not possible to find a simple measure of the legal environment at divorce because the divorce year varies from 1945 to 1979. Ten percent of the sample were divorced in 1965 or earlier and 29 percent in 1970 or earlier. We could not in any case account for the individual variation from judge to judge in a study at the national level. For a study that takes account of such variation in a single state, see Chambers 1979.

Let P be the probability that child support is agreed to or awarded conditional upon a woman being ever divorced or currently separated. Then the logistic function

(5) $$P = 1/(1 + e^{-\beta X - u})$$

was estimated by maximum likelihood methods, where X is a vector of independent variables and β a vector of coefficients to be estimated. Table 15.1 presents the estimated partial derivatives of P with respect to each variable, found by multiplying the estimated βs by $\overline{P}(1 - \overline{P})$, where $\overline{P}$ is the mean of the dependent variable.

Variables that may reflect the new family's financial need include the mother's age at divorce (*AGEDIV*), education (*EDUC* and *COLLGRAD*), number of children by the absent father (*PATERNR*) and age of the children (*KID6TO17*). While no direct information is available on the father's financial status at the time of divorce, his ex-wife's age (at divorce) and education will be positively correlated with his own and, consequently, with his ability to pay. Another proxy for his ability to pay is the value of the property settlement reached in the divorce proceedings (*SETVAL*). Finally, geographic location variables (*NEAST, NCENTR, SOUTH, SMSA*, and *CC*) may control for some of the variation in the legal environment that we are unable to capture.

It is important to distinguish divorced from separated (*SEP*) women in our sample. Fourteen percent of the nonblacks are currently separated, while 48 percent of the blacks are separated. Separated women may but are less likely to be awarded child support. According to our estimates, ceteris paribus, separated nonblack (black) women are 21 (29) percent less likely than comparable divorced women to have been awarded child support.

For nonblacks, the probability of being awarded child support increases as the number of dependent children increases (*PATERNR*), by 4.1 to 4.7 percent per child, and as one or more of these children tends to be older (*KID6TO17*). For the black sample, however, neither variable is significant.

EDUC is positive for both groups but significant only for nonblacks. In addition, the dummy variable *COLLGRAD* is negative and significant for nonblacks, suggesting that college-educated women are between 2.5 and 5.0 percent less likely than otherwise similar high school graduates to be awarded child support. As noted above, *EDUC* may serve both as a proxy for ex-husband's lifetime earnings potential and as a measure of the new family's financial needs. Although more education may enable a woman to support the children herself, thereby reducing needs, it also raises the standard of living to which the family is accustomed, thereby increasing needs. The positive sign on *EDUC* may reflect both this second effect as well as her ex-husband's ability to pay, while the negative coeffi-

Table 15.1   **Child Support Award Probability**

Independent Variable	Nonblack		Black	
	(1)	(2)	(3)	(4)
EDUC	.025	.019	.020	.016
	(4.91)	(3.60)	(1.67)	(1.27)
COLLGRAD	−.125	−.126	.022	.027
	(2.79)	(2.60)	(0.14)	(0.17)
SPANISH[a]	−.088	−.089	—	—
	(2.46)	(2.44)		
NEAST	−.086	−.074	−.055	−.092
	(3.00)	(2.44)	(0.54)	(0.88)
NCENTR	.018	.004	−.040	−.063
	(0.64)	(0.10)	(0.41)	(0.63)
SOUTH	−.055	−.059	−.058	−.069
	(2.06)	(2.10)	(0.65)	(0.76)
SMSA	.014	.008	.160	.155
	(0.60)	(0.32)	(1.61)	(1.53)
CC	−.024	−.016	−.179	−.170
	(0.88)	(0.55)	(2.16)	(2.00)
PATERNR	.047	.041	.022	.019
	(4.01)	(3.38)	(1.02)	(0.84)
KID6TO17	.053	.042	.025	.017
	(2.28)	(1.69)	(0.30)	(0.20)
NUMMAR	−.033	−.024	.042	.053
	(1.38)	(0.96)	(0.50)	(0.64)
REMAR	−.040	−.023	−.073	−.094
	(1.69)	(0.91)	(0.86)	(1.06)
AGEDIV	.001	−.001	.008	.006
	(0.84)	(0.39)	(2.33)	(1.68)
SEP	−.207	−.129	−.291	−.207
	(7.50)	(4.39)	(4.62)	(3.13)
SETVAL	—	.094	—	.151
		(6.90)		(2.51)
Constant	−.097	−.051	−.439	−.389
	(1.13)	(0.57)	(1.70)	(1.49)
Likelihood ratio test				
(chi-square)	180.9	241.7	48.6	49.8
N	2,027	1,907	389	373
Mean of dependent				
variable	.775	.769	.476	.453

Notes: Table represents all ever-divorced or currently separated women, age eighteen and over, with children under twenty-one years of age from an absent father, as of spring 1979.

The logistic function $P = 1/(1 + e^{-\beta x - u})$ was estimated by maximum likelihood methods and the coefficients reported above are $\beta \overline{P}(1 - \overline{P})$ where $\overline{P}$ is the mean of the dependent variable reported in the last row of the table. Asymptotic t-values are shown in parentheses.

[a]*SPANISH* was omitted from the equation for blacks because less than 1 percent of the sample was Spanish.

cient on *COLLGRAD* may reflect the competing effect of less need for support.

The coefficient on the woman's age at divorce (*AGEDIV*) is positive for both races and significant for blacks. In part, her age is again a proxy for her ex-husband's ability to provide support. (It appears to be a better proxy for income of black ex-husbands than is her education.) But in addition, the variable is strongly positively correlated with the duration of the marriage.[11] Longer marriages may be more likely to result in child support awards for several reasons. Chief among them is that the father is likely to be more attached to his children and therefore more disposed toward providing them support. A longer duration of marriage might also suggest that the woman has invested more in this marriage, developing greater marriage-specific capital (Becker, Landes, and Michael 1977), and specialized more in home activities, developing less human capital valued in the market. Thus, she would be less able to support the children.

In neither racial sample of ever-divorced women is current marital status (*REMAR*) significant. This result is important in that it suggests that women who have remarried do not possess some unobserved traits that made them systematically more or less likely to be awarded child support at the time of their divorce.

For a slightly smaller sample of women, we were able to include an index of the value of property settlements (*SETVAL*) as a proxy variable for the financial well-being of the couple before divorce. Since property settlements and child support awards are determined together, the coefficient on *SETVAL* may be biased if any unobservable factors that affect the value of property settlements also affect the probability of being awarded child support. To the extent that *SETVAL* is a good proxy, its significant positive coefficient for both racial groups reinforces the hypothesis that father's ability to pay (and the original family's standard of living) is a strong determinant of child support awards. Note that the inclusion of *SETVAL* reduces the coefficients on *EDUC* and *AGEDIV*, other proxies for father's ability to pay.

For the sample of all women both awarded child support and expecting to receive it in 1978, we estimated equations on factors determining the amount due (results not shown). With a few notable exceptions, factors that determine whether or not child support is awarded also affect the amount due. Few child support awards are automatically indexed to the rising price level (Krause 1981, p. 24), and most are infrequently renegotiated; thus, we controlled for the number of years since the divorce (*YEARSDIV*) and found its coefficient to be negative and significant. We

---

11. We also estimated this equation for the sample of currently divorced (or separated) women only for which we know marriage duration (*DURMAR*). When we enter *DURMAR* as an independent variable in place of *AGEDIV*, its coefficient is positive and significant for nonblacks, but insignificant for blacks.

also introduced as an explanatory variable the woman's estimate of her ex-husband's current income (*HUSINC*); this considerably reduces the sample size because many women do not know *HUSINC*.[12] While the results from this smaller sample may be biased because of this self-selection, the means of the independent variables (reported in table 15.A.1) change very little from the full sample. We found the coefficient on *HUSINC* positive and significant, suggesting that each additional $5,000 in the absent father's 1978 income raises child support due by $219. The coefficient on *EDUC* declines in size, but remains significant, suggesting that *EDUC* stands for more than just his *current* ability to pay. We have argued that it serves as a proxy for his lifetime earnings potential upon which the support award is likely to be based. It may also indicate a higher standard of living to which the family is accustomed.

15.3.2   Determinants of the Probability of Receiving Child Support and of the Amount Received

Not all women due child support actually receive it. Of those expecting payment in 1978, only 71.4 percent received any. Moreover, those who receive it frequently receive less than what is due. Among women receiving some support, the mean receipt was $1,899 out of the $2,204 due them, around 86 percent. In this section we offer some evidence that the probability of actually receiving child support, unlike its award, depends less upon the needs of the woman and more upon the current financial status of her ex-husband.

This problem consists of two related issues: first, whether a divorced mother receives any child support and second, how much she receives. This second issue introduces the possibility of sample selection bias: estimates of the determinants of support received may be biased if some omitted factors that determine whether the woman gets into the sample (i.e., receives any child support) also determine how much she receives. To correct for this sample selection bias, we use a technique developed by Heckman (1979) that eliminates the bias by introducing a new independent variable λ (negatively related to the probability of receiving child support) into the regressions on amount of child support received. Using maximum likelihood probit, first we estimate determinants of the probability of receiving *any* child support in 1978, conditional upon some payment being due. Estimated partial derivatives of these factors are presented in columns (1) through (3) of table 15.2. Next we use the probit estimates to compute a

---

12. This variable is believed to be subject to considerable measurement error, which would increase its standard error. However, since the variable is measured in increments of $5,000, we believe that it provides a reasonably good indication of relative magnitudes of incomes among ex-husbands. If the woman knows what kind of job her ex-husband holds and whether or not he is employed, she should have a rough idea of what he earns, which is good enough for our purposes.

Table 15.2 Receipt and Amount of Child Support

	Probability of Receiving Child Support			Amount of Child Support Received for Those Who Received Any		
	(1)[a]	(2)[a]	(3)[a]	(4)[c]	(5)[c]	(6)[c]
BLACK	-.101	-.123	-.043	-299	-259	-56
	(2.69)	(3.03)	(0.73)	(2.49)	(1.70)	(0.38)
SPANISH	-.030	-.020	-.104	-346	-406	-926
	(0.61)	(0.38)	(1.39)	(2.83)	(3.02)	(3.60)
NEAST	.082	.081	.094	177	170	107
	(2.36)	(2.23)	(1.99)	(1.30)	(1.71)	(0.84)
NCENTR	.055	.065	.110	-50	-5	-139
	(1.85)	(2.12)	(2.83)	(0.67)	(0.05)	(1.08)
SOUTH	.042	.047	.060	-114	-71	-90
	(1.43)	(1.50)	(1.55)	(1.58)	(0.90)	(0.88)
SMSA	-.018	-.015	-.045	39	18	-67
	(0.70)	(0.54)	(1.35)	(0.66)	(0.29)	(0.77)
CC	.010	.012	.079	90	95	30
	(0.32)	(0.36)	(1.84)	(1.30)	(1.29)	(0.26)
EDUC	.015	.016	.013	0.2	6	-22
	(2.87)	(2.89)	(1.90)	(0.02)	(0.36)	(1.12)
AGE	.027	.022	.005	59	67	59
	(2.66)	(2.05)	(0.46)	(1.95)	(2.27)	(2.03)
AGESQ	-.0003	-.0002	-.0001	-0.6	-0.7	-0.6
	(2.12)	(1.52)	(0.45)	(1.64)	(1.90)	(1.61)
PATERNR	-.012	-.026	-.022	18	-13	83
	(1.05)	(2.13)	(1.54)	(0.63)	(0.38)	(2.03)
OTHERKID	-.079	-.069	-.087	89	49	140
	(2.78)	(2.35)	(2.35)	(1.01)	(0.51)	(1.06)
KID6TO17	.066	.087	.072	-64	-20	-253
	(2.02)	(2.55)	(1.76)	(0.74)	(0.19)	(2.18)
CSVOL	.222	.221	.155	173	271	-31
	(8.33)	(8.03)	(4.55)	(1.23)	(1.63)	(0.22)

NUMMAR	−.045	−.039	−.085	−198	−204	−180
	(1.59)	(1.40)	(2.73)	(2.69)	(2.74)	(1.47)
YEARSDIV	−.020	−.020	−.011	−7	−15	21
	(6.94)	(5.88)	(2.63)	(0.42)	(0.84)	(1.39)
REMAR	−.008	−.005	−.028	−159	−123	−53
	(0.30)	(0.17)	(0.80)	(2.63)	(1.92)	(0.62)
HUSCHD	—	−.012	—	—	−41	—
		(0.48)			(0.66)	
HUSINC	—	—	.027	—	—	−2.96
			(3.33)			(0.10)
CHSUPDUE	—	—	—	0.891	0.897	0.930
				(80.1)	(79.2)	(61.6)
λ(1)[b]	—	—	—	198	—	—
				(0.45)		
λ(2)[b]	—	—	—	—	433	—
					(0.82)	
λ(3)[b]	—	—	—	—	—	−1,000
						(1.70)
Constant	−.521	−.430	−.068	−1,199	−1,547	−574
	(2.89)	(2.30)	(0.32)	(1.51)	(1.88)	(0.86)
$\bar{R}^2$	—	—	—	.877	.886	.901
Likelihood ratio test	219.0	195.9	100.8	—	—	—
N	1,461	1,259	648	1,043	931	521
Mean of dependent variable	.714	.739	.804	$1,899	$1,918	$2,146

Note: Figures are for ever divorced or currently separated women due child support in 1978.

[a] The coefficients reported in these columns are the probit maximum likelihood estimates (β) multiplied by the sample mean of normal density functions evaluated at $X_i\beta$, where X_i is the vector of independent variables for the ith observation. These sample means are .297 for col. (1), .280 for col. (2), and .232 for col. (3).

[b] $\lambda = f(X_i\beta)/F(X_i\beta)$, where f and F are, respectively, the density and distribution function for a standard normal variable, and X_i and β are defined as in footnote a. See Heckman 1979, p. 156.

[c] Since we cannot reject the null hypothesis of no selection bias (i.e., that the coefficient on λ is zero), the usual OLS standard errors and t-statistics are appropriate. See Heckman 1979, p. 158.

λ-value for each mother who receives any child support and enter it in OLS regressions on amount of child support received, holding constant the amount due.[13] These results appear in columns (4) through (6) of table 15.2. Because previous researchers did not explicitly recognize the possibility of sample selection bias, their regression results on factors affecting child support received may be biased (see, for example, Cassetty 1978).

Ex post, we find only limited evidence of sample selection bias: the coefficient on λ is insignificantly different from zero in both columns (4) and (5) and only significant at a 10 percent level in column (6). The negative sign on λ in column (6) indicates that omitted factors that lower the probability of receiving child support (and therefore increase λ) also lower the amount received.

Black women are less likely to receive child support and, when they do, receive less than nonblack women, even after controlling for the lower amount they are due. However, these differences become insignificant for blacks who know their ex-husband's income. Although women of Spanish origin are equally likely to receive child support as non-Spanish women, they receive significantly less child support. The coefficient on SPANISH becomes even more negative for those few who know their ex-husband's income.

EDUC, AGE, and AGESQ may serve as proxies for the absent father's ability to pay. Education has a positive impact on the likelihood of payment but not on the amount. Advancing age increases both the probability of receiving payment and the amount paid at a decreasing rate (reminiscent of the manner in which earnings change with age). When HUSINC is included, these proxies for ability to pay become insignificant or less significant in the probability of receipt equation (col. 3), but age remains significant in the equation on the amount received (col. 6). Although HUSINC significantly increases the likelihood of payment, it has no significant effect upon the amount paid once we control for the amount due. Thus, we conclude that while the absent father's income is an important determinant of the amount of child support awarded (each $5,000 increment raises the amount by $219) and of whether or not he pays anything, it is not an important determinant of the portion of the award that he pays. This suggests that fathers with negative transitory income are likely to evade the support obligation altogether rather than pay a smaller portion of the amount due.[14]

13. The sample means (and standard deviations) for these λ variables are as follows:

λ(1)	.414(.246)
λ(2)	.378(.281)
λ(3)	.289(.212)

14. In a separate regression, we included child support due (CHSUPDUE) as an explanatory variable. Holding HUSINC constant, its coefficient is small but significantly positive: each additional $100 of support due increases the probability that some support will be received by .02 percent. If the absent father's permanent or lifetime income contributes posi-

Three measures of the impact of children are included. Holding constant the length of time since the divorce (*YEARSDIV*), having older children (*KID6TO17*) increases the probability of receiving support, consistent with the hypothesis that absent fathers are more likely to pay support for children whom they lived with longer. As the number of children due support increases (*PATERNR*), the probability that support will be paid appears to decline although this effect is significant only in the equation in column (2). This result is difficult to explain. If the woman has other children not fathered by her most recent ex-husband (*OTHERKID*), this significantly reduces by 7 to 9 percent the probability that he pays child support. This result is more understandable. Given the amount due, neither the number nor ages of the children affects the amount of support received, except in the sample that knows *HUSINC*. This group (col. 6) receives $83 more for each additional child but $253 less for older children, another result that is difficult to explain.

Women were asked whether their child support awards were court ordered or agreed to voluntarily. Those reporting voluntary agreements (*CSVOL*) are between 15 and 22 percent more likely to receive payments; however, given the amount agreed to, the effect of *CSVOL* on the amount received is positive but insignificant. Apparently voluntary initial agreement, which probably indicates something about the character of the father or of the relationship, has lasting effects.

If the marriage that ended in divorce was not the woman's first, her likelihood of receiving payment is reduced for each higher-order marriage (*NUMMAR*) by around 8.5 percent, at least when controlling for her ex-husband's income. Moreover, she receives up to $204 less support per higher-order marriage, controlling for the amount due. This is especially interesting in light of the finding that women in higher-order marriages seem to negotiate somewhat higher support awards (results not shown).

Absent fathers reported by their ex-wives to have other children to support (*HUSCHD*) are no less likely to pay child support. While new children may reduce his ability to support absent ones, the father's decision to remarry and have more children suggests he values family life and is apt to be more conscientious about providing support for his absent children.[15]

---

tively to the amount of child support awarded, then the significance of both *CHSUPDUE* and *HUSINC* in the same regression could indicate that his permanent income (*CHSUPDUE*) and current income (*HUSINC*) have separate effects upon his probability of paying support. Holding current income constant, absent fathers with higher permanent income are somewhat more likely to pay support. Holding permanent income constant, fathers with higher current income are much more likely to pay support. Again this is consistent with the hypothesis that current ability to pay has a strong impact upon child support payments.

15. Cassetty 1978 found that absent fathers who remarried were no more likely to pay child support, but paid significantly more. Since she does not control for amount due, her findings on amount received confound determinants of award amount with receipt amount, and thus are not directly comparable to ours.

Because of these competing effects, the insignificance of *HUSCHD* does not disturb our hypothesis that the probability of receiving child support is largely a function of the absent father's ability to pay.[16]

The variable *YEARSDIV* has a significant negative effect upon the probability of receiving child support, but not on the proportion received. Each additional year since the divorce reduces the probability of receiving support by approximately 2 percent. This relationship appears to be linear. The absent father may be less likely to pay support with each passing year if he loses physical or emotional contact with his children. (We have no information on whether he has visitation rights.) This explanation is reinforced by noting that the coefficient on *YEARSDIV* is much smaller in magnitude for the sample of women who know *HUSINC*, women who may be presumed not to have lost complete contact with their ex-husbands.

Whether the woman is remarried (*REMAR*) does not affect her likelihood of receiving any child support, but does appear to lower the amount she receives by up to $159, except for those (remarried) women who know *HUSINC*.[17] This suggests that when his ex-wife remarries, the absent father may reduce somewhat the amount of child support he pays, but not attempt to renegotiate the amount due (*REMAR* is insignificant in the equation on amount due—results not shown), nor stop paying altogether (*REMAR* is insignificant in cols. 1 through 3 of table 15.2). However, another possibility is that our regression suffers from reverse causality: women who receive less of the support they are due may be more likely to remarry. We examine this possibility in the next section.

15.4   Empirical Analysis of Remarriage

The majority of women in the United States who divorce eventually remarry. For example, in the 1979 CPS, 70 percent of divorced mothers remarried within fifteen years of their divorce. This identical remarriage rate for divorced women was found in the 1967 Survey of Economic Opportunity (SEO) data by Becker, Landes, and Michael (1977). In the CPS, one-half of all mothers remarried within five years of their divorce, and 29 percent within two years.[18]

16. Another reason why this coefficient is insignificant may be that this variable is measured with error.

17. Our results would appear to disagree with those of Cassetty 1978 which finds that remarried women are less likely to receive child support and also receive less child support. However, Cassetty's dependent variable combines child support and alimony income together. Since alimony stops with remarriage while child support is supposed to continue, her results would inevitably be negatively biased. We are fortunate to have data that enable us to separate child support from alimony income.

18. In the 1967 SEO, only 43 percent of women remarried within five years and 22 percent within two years. Either divorced mothers remarry more rapidly than divorced women in general or there has been a secular trend since 1967 toward shorter intervals between divorce and remarriage. We offer some evidence of the latter effect in our empirical estimates.

The modern theory of job search has recently been applied to marital search by, among others, Becker, Landes, and Michael (1977) and Hutchens (1979). Briefly, the probability of remarriage depends upon a woman's own search behavior and upon her attractiveness to potential marriage partners. A divorced woman can decide whether or not to engage in search, how intensively to search, and how long to search. These decisions depend upon her expected gain from remarriage, which is a function of her expected future flow of real income if single compared to her distribution of offers of real income if remarried, net of search costs. A divorced woman's distribution of offers will depend upon her attractiveness to potential mates, which will be a function of some characteristics we can observe such as age, some we cannot observe such as charm or beauty, and the amount of "marital-specific" capital (investments that are significantly less valuable when divorced, such as children) from her previous marriage. As Becker, Landes, and Michael (1977, p. 1155) point out, "positive" specific capital in one marriage may be "negative" specific capital in a subsequent marriage.

Some factors affect her search behavior and her attractiveness to others in opposite directions making it difficult to determine their net effect upon the probability of remarriage a priori. One example is a woman's portable (carries into marriage) nonwage income. A higher income if single would reduce the gain from remarriage, which might cause a woman to choose not to search or to search less intensely and longer. However, it also enhances her attractiveness to potential spouses, causing an increase in the mean of the offer distribution. This would tend to increase her probability of participation in search and have an indeterminant impact on intensity and duration of search (Hutchens 1979, p. 371). Hutchens cites Becker's theoretical analysis (1973, p. 891) as evidence that the latter effect tends to dominate the former. Thus, greater portable nonwage income is expected to increase both the probability of participation in and the duration of search.

The presence of children is another factor with competing effects. The greater the number of children, ceteris paribus, the greater the economic gain from remarriage; thus, the woman is likely to set lower standards for a new husband and to search more intensely. However, this greater specific capital from the previous marriage also reduces her attractiveness to potential marriage partners, which decreases the number and mean value of marriage offers.

We hypothesize that women will remarry quickly if they are either unusually attractive to potential mates or have established a low "reservation" set of characteristics for a new husband. Similarly, women will take longer to remarry (or never remarry) if they are either less attractive partners or have set a higher standard for a new husband.

We related the probability of remarriage by the nth year after termination of the previous marriage ($n = 2, 5, 10,$ and 15) to the expected gain from remarriage. We selected our sample so that all women were divorced (excludes separated) at least *n* years. (Thus, each successive sample is smaller than the previous one.)[19] We estimated a logistic function for each sample by maximum likelihood methods. Results for the *n* = 15 group are not shown because that sample contains less than 150 observations and because most of these women had remarried by *n* = 10. Partial derivatives of the logistic function with respect to each independent variable, evaluated at the sample mean, for divorce durations of two, five, and ten years are reported in table 15.3.

A higher age at divorce (*AGEDIV*) significantly reduces the probability of remarriage of divorced mothers at all three durations. The increase in the size of the coefficient with each successive duration suggests that age at divorce becomes an increasingly important determinant of remarriage probabilities at higher durations, possibly because it reduces a woman's attractiveness as a marriage partner. The greater her number of previous marriages (*NUMMAR*), the less likely a woman is to remarry, holding *AGEDIV* constant. Ceteris paribus, a greater number of previous marriages might reduce her attractiveness to potential marriage partners or her inclination to try again. This effect also becomes larger at higher durations.

We might expect to find a secular rise in the probability of remarriage because the divorce rate has been increasing, which makes available a greater pool of potential mates and reduces the stigma associated with being a divorced woman. Indeed, we find that for durations of five and ten years, given *AGEDIV*, the more recent the divorce (the lower *YEARSDIV*), the more likely is a woman to remarry. This effect is significant in the regressions in columns (3) and (5).

As discussed above, a greater number of children (*PATERNR*) will have the competing effects of raising search intensity but lowering potential marriage offers. (The former effect may be mitigated by the fact that a greater number of children probably increases her costs of search and reduces her need for additional companionship.) We find that the probability of remarriage within two years of divorce (col. 1) increases as the number of children increases to between two and three and decreases thereafter. The woman may have set her reservation standard low in order to remarry quickly for her children's sake, but too many children make it difficult to attract offers. At higher durations, the effect is linear: each additional

19. This structure is partly longitudinal in nature because we have marital histories for all divorced women, and partly cross-sectional because women who are recently divorced fall into the samples only for the shorter time intervals. Thus, this sequence of remarriage probabilities cannot be viewed precisely as the experience of a given cohort at two, five, or ten years after their divorce. Women divorced only two years today may behave differently by five years after divorce than women who today are already five years beyond their divorce. Within each equation, we control for differences in length of time since divorce, which should control for this cohort effect.

Table 15.3 Probability of Remarriage, by Duration of Time Since the End of Previous Marriage

| Independent Variables | Duration of Time Since End of Previous Marriage (in years) | | | | |
| | 2 | 5 | | 10 | |
	(1)	(2)	(3)	(4)	(5)
EDUC	−.010	−.014	−.011	−.010	−.008
	(1.78)	(1.89)	(1.47)	(0.97)	(0.73)
BLACK	−.215	−.312	−.320	−.178	−.149
	(4.20)	(5.21)	(5.46)	(2.25)	(1.93)
SPANISH	−.042	−.107	−.120	.097	.105
	(0.73)	(1.44)	(1.58)	(0.87)	(0.91)
NEAST	−.081	−.122	−.116	−.115	−.081
	(2.04)	(2.33)	(2.27)	(1.53)	(1.08)
NCENTR	.001	−.024	−.052	.043	.036
	(0.00)	(0.53)	(1.15)	(0.61)	(0.53)
SOUTH	.003	−.025	−.035	.089	.105
	(0.10)	(0.56)	(0.79)	(1.25)	(1.49)
SMSA	−.036	−.067	−.042	−.038	−.018
	(1.26)	(1.69)	(1.08)	(0.61)	(0.30)
CC	−.049	−.107	−.090	−.230	−.221
	(1.39)	(2.31)	(1.98)	(3.39)	(3.29)
PATERNR	.116	−.039	−.042	−.096	−.082
	(2.16)	(2.19)	(2.35)	(3.49)	(2.99)
PATSQ	−.024	—	—	—	—
	(2.16)				
AGEDIV	−.012	−.017	−.019	−.021	−.023
	(6.24)	(6.59)	(7.63)	(5.24)	(5.78)
YEARSDIV	−.0002	−.004	−.012	−.009	−.017
	(0.10)	(1.09)	(2.93)	(1.31)	(2.44)

Table 15.3 (continued)

Independent Variables	Duration of Time Since End of Previous Marriage (in years)				
	2		5		10
	(1)	(2)	(3)	(4)	(5)
NUMMAR	−.052	−.168	−.142	−.253	−.237
	(1.45)	(3.22)	(2.71)	(3.08)	(2.85)
AWARDAL	−.007	−.041	−.082	−.105	−.162
	(0.20)	(0.81)	(1.59)	(1.28)	(2.02)
SETVAL	−.007	.002	—	−.006	—
	(0.69)	(0.17)		(0.26)	
AWARDCS	−.053	−.042	.188	−.047	.180
	(1.72)	(1.00)	(3.42)	(0.80)	(2.39)
CHSUP78	—	—	−.227	—	−.291
			(3.81)		(3.40)
PCCSDUE	—	—	$-.834*10^{-4}$	—	$-.327*10^{-4}$
			(2.53)		(0.66)
Constant	.350	1.129	1.202	1.542	1.608
	(3.00)	(7.28)	(7.85)	(6.01)	(6.22)
Likelihood ratio test (chi-square)	123.2	170.0	237.1	112.2	132.0
N	1,570	1,069	1,150	474	500
Mean of dependent variable	.298	.512	.504	.658	.656

Note: See table 15.1, second paragraph of *Notes*.

Table 15.4   Likelihood of Labor Force Participation of Currently Divorced (or Separated) Women, March 1979

Independent Variables	(1)	(2)	(3)
BLACK	−.085	−.076	−.076
	(2.31)	(2.05)	(2.06)
SPANISH	−.101	−.103	−.105
	(1.99)	(2.02)	(2.06)
NEAST	−.130	−.127	−.126
	(3.36)	(3.28)	(3.25)
NCENTR	−.027	−.030	−.033
	(0.70)	(0.78)	(0.84)
SOUTH	.015	.028	.025
	(0.30)	(0.53)	(0.47)
SMSA	.021	.019	.019
	(0.60)	(0.54)	(0.55)
CC	−.062	−.057	−.059
	(1.73)	(1.58)	(1.62)
KIDLT3	−.127	−.128	−.128
	(3.21)	(3.22)	(3.23)
KIDLT6	−.063	−.062	−.062
	(2.19)	(2.13)	(2.16)
KIDLT18	−.026	−.025	−.025
	(1.81)	(1.75)	(1.72)
NUMMAR	−.037	−.033	−.040
	(1.27)	(1.17)	(1.38)
EDUC	.053	.053	.052
	(8.72)	(8.79)	(8.76)
NADULT	.044	.045	.044
	(1.75)	(1.76)	(1.73)
AGE	.023	.023	.024
	(2.33)	(2.25)	(2.35)
AGESQ	−.0003	−.0003	−.0003
	(2.57)	(2.43)	(2.52)

therefore reducing the probability of labor force participation. On the other hand, child support has a substitution effect of increasing the quantity of goods devoted to children, decreasing the amount of time spent on them, and therefore raising the likelihood of labor force participation.

Table 15.4 reports estimated partial derivatives from logistic models on factors affecting the likelihood of labor force participation in March 1979 for our sample of divorced mothers.[22] All three variations contain the same economic and demographic variables but different child support and alimony variables. The coefficients on the common set of independent variables change very little across functional forms.

22. We also estimated equations with labor force participation for any part of 1978 as the dependent variable. The results—particularly on the child support and alimony variables— were virtually identical.

child reduces the probability of remarriage within five years by 3.9 percent (col. 2) and within ten years by 9.6 percent (col. 4). When we control for child support due per child (PCCSDUE), the coefficient on PATERNR is still negative and significant at both durations. This suggests that what is unattractive about a greater number of children is more than just the cost of caring for them. The increase in the size of the coefficient on PATERNR with increasing divorce duration suggests that the woman's attractiveness as a marriage partner becomes an increasingly important determinant of remarriage the longer she has been divorced.

Alimony is nonportable income; that is, it stops with remarriage. As such, it should have a negative effect upon the probability of remarriage. AWARDAL is negative at all divorce durations, becomes larger at higher durations, but is significant only at ten years in the regression controlling for child support due (col. 5). Women awarded alimony are 8.2 percent less likely to have remarried five years after divorce and 16.2 percent less likely ten years after. This finding is consistent with findings by Hutchens (1979, p. 377) that nonportable transfers tend to reduce remarriage probabilities. Unfortunately, this is the only information about alimony we have that is relevant to the remarriage decision.

Child support income is legally portable between the single and married status. As such, it has the competing effects discussed above of decreasing the gain from remarriage but of increasing the woman's attractiveness to potential mates; therefore, theoretically its effect upon remarriage is indeterminate. Where Hutchens (1979, p. 377) was unable to draw any conclusions on the relationship between portable nonwage income and remarriage, we are able to do so. Two additional considerations make it likely that child support income will decrease the gain from remarriage more than other income. First, if a divorced mother spends child support income on the children, in part on goods and services substitutable for child care time, then it reduces the benefits to be derived from the sexual division of labor in the care of children. Second, although legally portable, in practice child support income may be only partly portable. We showed in table 15.2 that for otherwise identical women due the same amount of child support annually, remarried women receive up to $159 less than divorced women. If fully anticipated, this reduction in payments would serve to further reduce the expected gain from remarriage.

Women awarded child support (AWARDCS) are 5.3 percent less likely to remarry within the first two years after divorce, but this effect is significant only at the 10 percent level (col. 1). If not awarded child support, a woman stands to gain a great deal more from a quick remarriage than a woman awarded support. Consequently, she may search more intensely and set lower standards for a new husband.

In the equations of columns (3) and (5), we add measures of whether child support was due in 1978 (CHSUP78) and of the amount of child support due per child (*PCCSDUE*).[20] Women awarded child support *and* had it due to them in 1978 were 3.9 percent less likely to have remarried five years after the termination of their previous marriage and 11.1 percent less likely ten years after than women not awarded child support. For those awarded and due child support in 1978, each additional $500 due per child reduces the probability of remarriage within five years by 4.2 percent. Within ten years, the effect is smaller and statistically insignificant, but this may be due to the high correlation between *CHSUP78* and *PCCSDUE* in this sample. On net, child support income reduces the gain from remarriage more than it increases the woman's attractiveness to potential mates, probably because several factors work in this direction. Thus, we conclude from these findings on child support that this type of portable nonwage income reduces the probability of remarriage.

Holding constant whether and how much child support is due in 1978, *AWARDCS* becomes positive and significant. Women awarded child support but due none in 1978 (around 20 percent of the sample) are 18 to 19 percent more likely to remarry than women not awarded support, even though women both awarded and due support are less likely to remarry. If a woman is due child support or due more support, she searches longer before remarrying and may not remarry at all. But if her child support income stops, she is much more likely to remarry than if it were never awarded at all.

Two other variables that have the competing effects of reducing the woman's gain from remarriage but of increasing her attractiveness to others are her wealth at divorce (*SETVAL*) and her education (*EDUC*). *SETVAL* is insignificant in all regressions; *EDUC* is consistently negative, but significant only at the 10 percent level for durations of two and five years.

AFDC and other public assistance benefits available to single mothers are other important forms of nonportable income that would reduce the gain from remarriage and prolong the duration of divorce. Because remarriage occurs in many different years in our sample, we have no simple measure of the relevant public assistance benefits when each woman was deciding upon remarriage.[21] However, some of our variables may be interpreted as proxies for the likelihood a divorced woman received AFDC.

20. Theory would suggest that the relevant variable in the decision to remarry is dollars of child support (or alimony) received when divorced. But this variable is not available for women who have remarried. For remarried women, the best proxy for child support received when divorced is child support due now, since most child support awards are rarely renegotiated; for currently divorced women, child support due and child support received are correlated 0.88.

21. Had we restricted our sample to remarriages that took place within say the last two years instead of *n* years after divorce, we could have included measures of AFDC (as did Hutchens 1979). But for the problem we are interested in, our specification (similar to that of Becker, Landes, and Michael 1977) is more appropriate.

For example, by five years after termination of the marriage, black women (*BLACK*) are 32 percent less likely to have remarried than similar nonblack women. If black women, women in the northeast (*NEAST*) or in central cities (*CC*), and women with many children are somewhat more likely AFDC candidates than other women, then our results support previous findings (Hutchens 1979) that welfare reduces the probability of remarriage.

15.5 Empirical Analysis of Labor Force Participation

Although differences in female labor force participation rates have narrowed recently, unmarried women are still more likely to be in the labor force than married women. Among our sample of 1,503 currently divorced or separated mothers, 73.9 percent were either working or looking for work in March 1979, compared with 60.3 percent of our sample of 936 remarried mothers. The greater labor force attachment of divorced mothers is an obvious response to their loss of other family income. In this section we examine factors affecting the variation in labor force participation rates among divorced mothers, paying special attention to the influence of family support—child support and alimony.

The probability of labor force participation should depend negatively upon the value of a woman's time at home, positively upon the value of her time in the market, and negatively upon nonlabor income. The presence of younger children or more children raises her time value at home, while education and job experience raise her value more in the market than in the home. In addition, if market work imposes fixed entry costs, then a woman may elect not to participate unless her desired hours of employment exceed some critical minimum. And since hours of work depend negatively upon nonlabor income, a ceteris paribus increase in such income should reduce the likelihood a woman participates in the labor force. For divorced mothers, most nonlabor income consists of income from property, earnings of other family members, public welfare, and alimony and child support payments from her ex-husband.

In contrast to the other sources of nonlabor income, child support payments might exert an additional and opposite influence upon labor force participation. Since this income is awarded to support the children, a woman may feel explicitly or implicitly constrained to spend it entirely on goods and services for them. If these commodities (such as day care for small children) can substitute for her own home time, then she may be able to reduce her hours of work in the home and raise her desired hours of employment beyond the critical minimum required for labor force entry. If this occurs, then the net impact of child support payments on labor force participation is ambiguous. On the one hand, child support has an income effect of raising leisure, reducing desired hours of work, and

Table 15.4 (continued)

Independent Variables	(1)	(2)	(3)
YEARSDIV	−.006	−.006	−.007
	(2.07)	(2.08)	(2.19)
OTHFINC	−.115*10⁻⁴	−.117*10⁻⁴	−.120*10⁻⁴
	(2.98)	(2.98)	(3.04)
AFDCMAX	−5.35*10⁻⁴	−4.84*10⁻⁴	−4.87*10⁻⁴
	(2.77)	(2.51)	(2.52)
CHSUPDUE	.305*10⁻⁴	—	—
	(2.99)		
ALIMDUE	−.272*10⁻⁴	—	—
	(2.37)		
CHSUP78	—	.113	.144
		(3.70)	(4.12)
ALIM78	—	.006	−.040
		(0.10)	(0.88)
CHSUPREC	—	−.016*10⁻⁴	—
		(0.17)	
ALIMREC	—	−.254*10⁻⁴	—
		(1.75)	
CSREGULR	—	—	−.061
			(1.61)
Constant	−.448	−.506	−.508
	(2.22)	(2.49)	(2.51)
Likelihood ratio test (chi-square)	361.8	368.6	368.0
N	1,503	1,503	1,503
Mean of dependent variable	.739	.739	.739

Note: See table 15.1, second paragraph of *Notes.*

The pattern of coefficients on the number of children under eighteen years by age groups is consistent with findings from studies for married, spouse-present women (Smith 1980). Compared with having at home one child age eighteen to twenty, having one child age six to seventeen (*KIDLT18*) reduces the probability of participation by 3 percent; having one child age three to five (*KIDLT6*) reduces participation another 6 percent; and having one child under three (*KIDLT3*) reduces participation another 13 percent. Small children raise the value of the woman's home time and reduce her likelihood of labor force entry. Each additional adult in the household (*NADULT*) who might share in child care duties increases her labor force participation by up to 4.5 percent.

As the woman becomes more valuable in the market, her labor force participation increases. Each additional year of education (*EDUC*) raises her entry probability by over 5 percent. Advancing age (and presumably experience) raises entry at a declining rate (*AGE* is positive and *AGESQ* is negative). Finally, women who have been divorced a longer time

(*YEARSDIV*) are less likely to enter the job market. This result appears counterintuitive if labor market entry is viewed as one possible way to restore economic well-being lost at divorce (where remarriage is another possible way). One explanation consistent with this result is that mothers who are likely candidates for public assistance and therefore less likely to be working remain divorced (or separated) for a longer time than do other mothers to maintain their eligibility. Alternatively, this result may reflect the secular trend toward rising labor force participation among younger (more recently divorced) women.

Black women (*BLACK*) are around 8 percent and women of Spanish origin (*SPANISH*) around 10 percent less likely to participate in the labor force than other divorced mothers. This may reflect cultural differences and/or discrimination against minority women in the labor market. Women in the northeast (*NEAST*) are 12 to 13 percent less likely than other women to participate, while women in central cities (*CC*) are 6 percent less likely to participate. Since women with these characteristics make up a disproportionate share of the AFDC population, these results also suggest that an increased likelihood of being on public assistance reduces labor force participation, findings consistent with those of other studies such as Keeley et al. (1978).

AFDCMAX equals the maximum amount of monthly AFDC payments that a woman with a given number of children in a particular state could receive if she does not work (and has no other income) as of July 1978. (Data on *AFDCMAX* were obtained from U.S. Department of Health, Education, and Welfare 1979.) In other words, it represents potential, not actual, welfare benefits. Generous public assistance benefits, ceteris paribus, should be expected to reduce labor force participation. Our finding indicates that each additional $100 per month in benefits reduces the likelihood of labor force participation by around 5 percent. When these potential benefits are replaced by actual benefits received, the regression fits even better but it then suffers from an obvious simultaneity bias.[23]

As expected, the coefficient on other family income excluding child support, alimony, and public assistance (*OTHFINC*) is negative and significant; each additional $1,000 in annual income deters labor market entry by slightly more than 1 percent. The coefficient on amount of alimony due (*ALIMDUE*) is also negative and significant, but each additional $1,000 of alimony deters entry by 2.7 percent (col. 1). Controlling for whether or not alimony is due in 1978 (*ALIM78*), the coefficient on amount received (*ALIMREC*) is virtually identical to the one on *ALIMDUE* (col. 2). One reason that alimony appears to reduce participation more than other income is that its coefficient may be biased downward. Women

---

23. In addition, the size and significance of the coefficients on *BLACK*, *SPANISH*, *NEAST*, *CC*, *KIDLT3*, *KIDLT6*, *KIDLT18*, and *YEARSDIV* are reduced. This is consistent with our notion that each of these variables serves in part as a proxy for the probability of going on public assistance.

awarded alimony are probably less likely to have worked in the labor market during their marriage and thus, with less previous job experience, less likely to be working now. Therefore, the coefficient on alimony may reflect both an income effect and an "experience" effect.[24]

Unlike alimony, child support income appears to be positively associated with labor force participation. This is consistent with past work demonstrating a positive simple correlation between labor force participation and the receipt of child support (Grossman and Hayghe 1982), but extends it by showing that even when other characteristics (such as race, age, education, and family size) are held constant, the positive association persists. The coefficient of .0000305 on *CHSUPDUE* (col. 1) indicates that among women due child support in 1978, one who is due the average amount (slightly over $2,100) is 6.4 percent more likely to participate in the labor force than an otherwise identical woman due no child support. Furthermore, each additional $1,000 of support due raises participation by 3.0 percent. The positive sign is consistent with our hypothesis that child support payments are used to purchase goods and services that substitute for mother's home time and thus facilitate her labor force participation.

In columns (2) and (3) we enter alternative measures of child support due and/or received. Women due child support in 1978 (*CHSUP78*) are 11 to 14 percent more likely to participate in the labor force than women not due support. One reason why this effect appears so large is that the coefficient on *CHSUP78* may be biased upward. At divorce, women who anticipate future labor force participation may seek to obtain child support, which is nontaxable income, instead of alimony, which is taxable. Once we control for whether it is due, the amount of child support received (*CHSUPREC*) has no significant additional effect on participation (col. 2). However, for the 58 percent of divorced mothers due child support in 1978 who received it regularly (*CSREGULR*), the difference in labor force participation over women due no support is 6.1 percent less, but this effect is insignificant (col. 3). This suggests that the uncertainty created by receiving child support payments on an irregular basis may cause a greater increase in the labor force participation of divorced mothers than if payment were regular.

15.6   Summary and Conclusions

In this section we summarize our most important findings and discuss their implications for the formation of public policy. Also, we suggest promising directions for future research.

24. However, for a sample of recently divorced (or separated) mothers for whom we are able to control for whether or not they were in the labor force prior to the termination of their marriage (in March 1975), the coefficient on alimony due is virtually identical to the one reported here, suggesting that the "experience" bias may be negligible for this particular sample.

Like other forms of nonlabor income, child support payments were found to lower the probability of remarriage. But unlike other forms of nonlabor income, child support payments were found neither to raise nor to lower labor force participation. Each of these findings is consistent with our hypothesis that child support income serves as a substitute for the absent father. If a divorced mother receives child support, her economic incentive to remarry is reduced. This allows her to increase the duration of marital search which should improve the quality of the match and thus the likelihood that the new marriage will last. In addition to these long-run benefits, child support payments do not deter a divorced woman's labor force participation, which raises her family's income and well-being in the short run. Thus, child support payments are found to have both immediate and future benefits.

It is interesting to contrast the effects of child support, a private transfer, with AFDC payments, a public transfer. Previous work (Hutchens 1979) has found that AFDC reduces remarriage rates, just as we found that child support does. Other previous work (Keeley et al. 1978) has found that AFDC reduces labor force participation, unlike our finding that child support does not. While this may be evidence that child support income does not create the same work disincentive as AFDC, it is also possible that women not awarded child support, who are more likely candidates for AFDC, exhibit a fundamentally different response to nonwage income.

Within the limitations imposed by our data, we found that somewhat different factors affect the award of child support than its receipt. The likelihood of being awarded child support depends upon the needs of the mother and her children, and upon the absent father's long-term ability to pay. There appears also to be substantial racial differences: black women are less likely to be awarded support. In contrast, the likelihood of receiving child support due depends less upon the race or the circumstances of the woman and more upon the current financial well-being of the ex-husband. His income was found to affect whether or not any child support is actually paid, but not how much is paid. Apparently, absent fathers with low current incomes evade payment altogether, instead of partially cutting back on payments. This suggests that one effective strategy for child support enforcement may be to get nonpaying fathers to pay at least some portion of the child support they owe.

Given the beneficial effects of child support upon the well-being of female-headed families, it is unfortunate that such support is not awarded to or received by more divorced mothers and their children. Recent state and federal legislation has attempted to improve the enforcement of existing child support contracts. In future work we plan to study the effects of these new laws on child support receipts. However, no degree of enforcement can improve the well-being of a family never awarded child support in the first place. More effort needs to be placed on improving the system of awards. Initial work in this direction has been accomplished by Garfinkel (1982). Our analysis of determinants may help to provide a foundation for improving both the enforcement and award of child support.

Finally, let us conclude with an appeal for developing better data. The March/April 1979 CPS Match File (or the forthcoming 1982 version) represents the most comprehensive data base yet assembled for studying the determinants and consequences of child support payments, but it is far from ideal. We have argued that the award and receipt of child support depend upon both the needs of the mother-only family and the ability of the absent father to provide support. While data on the former are abundant, data on the latter are limited to a few responses provided by the woman. An ideal data set would match responses obtained directly from the woman on her family's well-being with responses obtained directly from her ex-husband on his financial condition. In assessing the impact of child support and alimony payments upon remarriage and labor supply, we were limited to data pertaining to the previous year only. An ideal data set would include a more complete history of family support awarded and received. It would include data on family support due and received in the year prior to remarriage for remarried women. It would also include the amount of family support awarded at the time of the divorce or separation, as well as whether the award was subsequently readjusted, and if so, why, and by how much. These data would permit us to investigate more fully the impact of past receipts (or nonreceipts) on current behavior of individuals in families headed by women.

References

Becker, Gary S. 1973. A theory of marriage: Part 1. *Journal of Political Economy* 81: 813–46.

Becker, Gary S., Elisabeth M. Landes, and Robert T. Michael. 1977. An economic analysis of marital instability. *Journal of Political Economy* 85: 1141–87.

Bradbury, Katherine, Sheldon Danziger, Eugene Smolensky, and Paul Smolensky. 1979. Public assistance, female headship, and economic well-being. *Journal of Marriage and the Family* 41: 519–35.

Cassetty, Judith. 1978. *Child support and public policy.* Lexington, Mass.: D. C. Heath.

Chambers, David L. 1979. *Making fathers pay.* Chicago: University of Chicago Press.

Garfinkel, Irwin. 1982. *Child support: Weaknesses of the old and features of a proposed new system.* Vol. 1. Institute for Research on Poverty.

Glick, Paul C., and Arthur J. Norton. 1977. Marrying, divorcing, and living together in the U.S. today. *Population Bulletin* 32: 3–39.

Gordon, Nancy M., Carol A. Jones, and Isabel V. Sawhill. 1978. The determinants of child support payments. Working paper no. 992-05. Washington D.C.: The Urban Institute.

Grossman, Allyson Sherman, and Howard Hayghe. 1982. Labor force activity of women receiving child support or alimony. *Monthly Labor Review* 105: 39–41.

Heckman, James J. 1979. Sample selection bias as a specification error. *Econometrica* 47: 153–61.

Hoffman, Saul. 1977. Marital instability and the economic status of women. *Demography* 14: 67–76.

Hutchens, Robert M. 1979. Welfare, remarriage, and marital search. *American Economic Review* 69: 369–79.

Keeley, Michael C., Philip K. Robins, Robert G. Spiegelman, and Richard W. West. 1978. The estimation of labor supply models using experimental data. *American Economic Review* 68: 873–87.

Krause, Harry D. 1981. *Child support in America: The legal perspective.* Charlottesville, Va.: Michie Co.

Peters, Elizabeth. 1982. The impact of regulation of marriage, divorce, and property settlements in a private contracting framework. Paper presented at the Workshop in Applications of Economics, University of Chicago.

Smith, James P., ed. 1980. *Female labor supply: Theory and estimation.* Princeton: Princeton University Press.

Sorensen, Annemette, and Maurice MacDonald. 1981. Child support: Who pays what to whom? In *Child support: Weaknesses of the old and features of a proposed new system*, vol. 3, appendixes. Institute for Research on Poverty.

U.S. Bureau of the Census. 1981a. *Child support and alimony, 1978.* Current Population Reports, series P-23, special studies no. 112. Washington, D.C.: GPO.

———. 1981b. Current Population Survey, March/April 1979 Match File [machine-readable data file]. Conducted by the Bureau of the Census for the Bureau of Labor Statistics. Washington, D.C.: Bureau of the Census [producer and distributor].

———. 1982. *Statistical abstract of the United States, 1982–83.* 103d edition. Washington, D.C.: GPO.

———. 1983. *Marital status and living arrangements, March 1982.* Current Population Reports, series P-20, no. 380. Washington, D.C.: GPO.

U.S. Department of Health, Education, and Welfare. 1979. *AFDC standards for basic needs, July 1978.* Social Security Administration, Office of Policy. ORS Report D-2. Washington, D.C.: GPO.

Appendix Tables

Table 15.A.1   Means and Standard Deviations for All Regression Samples

	All Ever-Divorced or Currently Separated Women		Women Supposed to Receive Child Support in 1978			Women Who Received Child Support in 1978			Women Who Have Been Divorced at Least N Years			Currently Divorced or Separated Women
	Nonblack	Black	All races			All races			$N=2$	$N=5$	$N=10$	All Races
Sample size	2,027	389	1,461	1,259	648	1,043	931	521	1,570	1,150	500	1,503
AWARDCS	.775 (.418)	.476 (.500)	1.0	1.0	1.0	1.0	1.0	1.0	.779 (.415)	.765 (.424)	.716 (.451)	—
RECCS	—	—	.714 (.452)	.740 (.439)	.804 (.397)	1.0	1.0	1.0	—	—	—	—
EDUC	11.920 (2.395)	11.026 (2.702)	12.069 (2.291)	12.087 (2.270)	12.389 (2.254)	12.270 (2.295)	12.286 (2.269)	12.582 (2.204)	11.957 (2.348)	11.902 (2.421)	11.546 (2.567)	11.685 (2.637)
COLLGRAD	.086 (.281)	.041 (.199)	—	—	—	—	—	—	—	—	—	—
SPANISH	.074 (.261)	.005 (.072)	.052 (.222)	.046 (.210)	.031 (.173)	.047 (.212)	.042 (.200)	.023 (.150)	.050 (.217)	.051 (.221)	.058 (.234)	.073 (.261)
NEAST	.188 (.391)	.180 (.385)	.171 (.377)	.168 (.374)	.159 (.366)	.183 (.387)	.177 (.382)	.165 (.372)	.159 (.365)	.169 (.375)	.172 (.378)	.226 (.418)
NCENTR	.259 (.438)	.237 (.426)	.273 (.446)	.280 (.449)	.292 (.455)	.272 (.445)	.280 (.449)	.301 (.459)	.257 (.437)	.272 (.445)	.288 (.453)	.248 (.432)
SOUTH	.256 (.436)	.460 (.499)	.262 (.440)	.260 (.439)	.270 (.444)	.260 (.439)	.259 (.438)	.271 (.445)	.283 (.451)	.279 (.449)	.280 (.449)	.279 (.449)
SMSA	.531 (.499)	.805 (.397)	.559 (.497)	.556 (.497)	.542 (.499)	.557 (.497)	.555 (.497)	.545 (.498)	.547 (.498)	.571 (.495)	.598 (.491)	.625 (.484)
CC	.207 (.405)	.663 (.473)	.235 (.424)	.228 (.420)	.207 (.405)	.228 (.420)	.221 (.415)	.213 (.410)	.248 (.432)	.254 (.435)	.278 (.449)	.341 (.474)
PATERNR	1.766 (.960)	2.229 (1.311)	1.878 (1.025)	1.851 (.993)	1.881 (1.031)	1.887 (1.013)	1.841 (.973)	1.871 (.997)	1.743 (.960)	1.741 (.989)	1.654 (.930)	—

Table 15.A.1 (continued)

	All Ever-Divorced or Currently Separated Women		Women Supposed to Receive Child Support in 1978			Women Who Received Child Support in 1978			Women Who Have Been Divorced at Least N Years			Currently Divorced or Separated Women
	Nonblack	Black	All races	All races	All races	All races	All races	All races	N = 2	N = 5	N = 10	All Races
KID6TO17	.787 (.410)	.828 (.378)	.821 (.383)	.817 (.387)	.804 (.397)	.831 (.375)	.830 (.376)	.814 (.390)	—	—	—	—
NUMMAR	1.155 (.412)	1.108 (.350)	1.146 (.399)	1.158 (.414)	1.164 (.428)	1.135 (.387)	1.147 (.403)	1.132 (.392)	1.129 (.373)	1.100 (.333)	1.088 (.311)	1.184 (.457)
REMAR	.426 (.495)	.144 (.352)	.371 (.483)	.369 (.483)	.355 (.479)	.345 (.476)	.347 (.476)	.336 (.473)	.298 (.458)	.504 (.500)	.656 (.476)	0
AGEDIV	29.246 (7.821)	30.319 (8.290)	29.758[d] (7.540)	30.024[e] (7.602)	30.714 (7.774)	—	—	—	28.645 (7.563)	27.946 (7.216)	26.922 (6.814)	—
DURMAR	10.285[a] (7.666)	9.915[a] (7.339)	—	—	—	—	—	—	—	—	—	—
SEP	.142 (.349)	.476 (.500)	—	—	—	—	—	—	0	0	0	—
SETVAL	.986[b] (1.544)	.257[c] (.867)	1.151[f] (1.600)	—	—	—	—	—	1.019 (1.504)	.854[g] (1.348)	.641[h] (1.081)	—
BLACK	0	1.0	.100 (.300)	.085 (.297)	.066 (.249)	.084 (.278)	.069 (.253)	.061 (.240)	.112 (.316)	.124 (.330)	.126 (.332)	.222 (.416)
YEARSDIV	—	—	5.518 (4.427)	5.289 (4.214)	4.556 (3.773)	4.949 (4.072)	4.811 (3.764)	4.280 (3.505)	7.638 (4.847)	9.731 (4.345)	13.568 (3.860)	4.970 (4.761)
NEWDIV	—	—	.173[d] (.378)	.188[e] (.391)	.223 (.416)	—	—	—	0	0	0	—
HUSCHD	—	—	—	—	.291 (.454)	—	—	.268 (.443)	—	—	—	—

	(1)	(2)	(3)	(4)	(5)	(6)	(7)	(8)	(9)	(10)
HUSINC	—	—	3.553 (1.877)	—	—	3.716 (1.923)	—	—	—	—
AGE	35.141 (7.928)	35.211 (8.023)	35.244 (8.198)	35.369 (7.776)	35.372 (7.888)	35.108 (7.961)	—	—	—	36.321 (9.245)
AGESQ	1,298 (604)	1,304 (612)	1,309 (636)	1,311 (596)	1,313 (606)	1,296 (617)	—	—	—	1,405 (730)
OTHERKID	.236 (.424)	.233 (.423)	.204 (.403)	.198 (.398)	.200 (.400)	.175 (.380)	—	—	—	—
CSVOL	.320 (.467)	.343 (.475)	.378 (.485)	.395 (.489)	.417 (.493)	.430 (.496)	—	—	—	—
CHSUPDUE	2,023 (2,080)	2,061 (2,184)	2,294 (2,243)	2,205 (2,344)	2,225 (2,434)	2,447 (2,398)	—	1,052 (1,360)	698 (1,040)	1,292 (1,883)
CHSUPREC	—	—	—	1,899 (2,263)	1,918 (2,345)	2,146 (2,399)	—	—	—	915 (1,755)
CSREGULR	—	—	—	.764 (.425)	.773 (.419)	.806 (.396)	—	—	—	.355 (.479)
AWARDAL	—	—	—	—	—	—	.129 (.335)	.130 (.337)	.108 (.311)	—
PATSQ	—	—	—	—	—	—	3.960 (4.773)	—	—	—
CHSUP78	1.0	1.0	1.0	1.0	1.0	1.0	—	.581 (.494)	.472 (.500)	.611 (.488)
PCCSDUE	—	—	—	—	—	—	—	654 (908)	442 (668)	—
ALIMDUE	—	—	—	—	—	—	—	—	—	247 (1,135)
ALIM78	—	—	—	—	—	—	—	—	—	.106 (.308)
ALIMREC	—	—	—	—	—	—	—	—	—	199 (1,041)
AFDCMAX	—	—	—	—	—	—	—	—	—	286 (113)

Table 15.A.1 (continued)

	All Ever-Divorced or Currently Separated Women		Women Supposed to Receive Child Support in 1978	Women Who Received Child Support in 1978	Women Who Have Been Divorced at Least N Years			Currently Divorced or Separated Women
	Nonblack	Black	All races	All races	N=2	N=5	N=10	All Races
INLF79	—	—	—	—	—	—	—	.739
								(.439)
KIDLT3	—	—	—	—	—	—	—	.153
								(.409)
KIDLT6	—	—	—	—	—	—	—	.410
								(.680)
KIDLT18	—	—	—	—	—	—	—	1.820
								(1.221)
NADULT	—	—	—	—	—	—	—	1.400
								(.716)
OTHFINC	—	—	—	—	—	—	—	2,222
								(4,253)

Note: Standard deviations appear in parentheses.

[a]For currently divorced women only.

[b]Sample size is 1,907.

[c]Sample size is 373.

[d]Sample size is 1,453.

[e]Sample size is 1,253.

[f]Sample size is 1,345.

[g]Sample size is 1,069.

[h]Sample size is 474.

Table 15.A.2 **Definition of Variables**

Variable	Definition
AWARDCS	= 1 if child support is awarded and 0 otherwise.
RECCS	= 1 if child support is received and 0 otherwise.
EDUC	= number of years of school completed by the woman.
COLLGRAD	= 1 if woman is a college graduate and 0 otherwise.
SPANISH	= 1 if woman is of Spanish origin and 0 otherwise.
NEAST	= 1 if woman lives in the Northeast and 0 otherwise.
NCENTR	= 1 if woman lives in North Central states and 0 otherwise.
SOUTH	= 1 if woman lives in the South and 0 otherwise.
SMSA	= 1 if woman lives within an SMSA and 0 otherwise.
CC	= 1 if woman lives within the central city of an SMSA and 0 otherwise.
PATERNR	= number of children under twenty-one, fathered or adopted by ex-husband, who are living with their mother.
PATSQ	= PATERNR squared.
KID6TO17	= 1 if there are one or more children age six to seventeen present and 0 otherwise.
NUMMAR	= number of the marriage that ended in divorce.
REMAR	= 1 for remarried women and 0 otherwise.
AGEDIV	= woman's age at divorce.
DURMAR	= duration of the marriage that ended in divorce.
SEP	= 1 for currently separated women and 0 otherwise.
SETVAL	= index of property settlement with 0 = none; 1 = less than $5,000; 2 = $5,000–9,999; 3 = $10,000–19,999; 4 = $20,000–29,999; 5 = $30,000–39,999; 6 = $40,000–49,999; 7 = $50,000–74,999; 8 = $75,000 plus.
BLACK	= 1 if woman is black and 0 otherwise.
YEARSDIV	= years since the divorce.
NEWDIV	= 1 if the divorce occurred since January 1978 and 0 otherwise.
HUSCHD	= 1 if ex-husband has other children to support and 0 otherwise.
HUSINC	= woman's estimate of her ex-husband's income in $5,000 increments, where 1 equals less than $5,000 and 6 equals $25,000 plus.
AGE	= woman's current age (April 1979).
AGESQ	= AGE squared.
OTHERKID	= 1 if woman has any children not fathered by her ex-husband and 0 otherwise.
CSVOL	= 1 if child support was agreed to voluntarily and 0 otherwise.
CHSUPDUE	= dollars of child support due in 1978.
CHSUPREC	= dollars of child support received in 1978.
CSREGULR	= 1 if child support received regularly and 0 otherwise.
AWARDAL	= 1 if alimony was awarded.
CHSUP78	= 1 if child support due in 1978 and 0 otherwise.
PCCSDUE	= CHSUPDUE/PATERNR.
ALIMDUE	= dollars of alimony due in 1978.
ALIM78	= 1 if alimony is due in 1978 and 0 otherwise.
ALIMREC	= dollars of alimony received in 1978.
AFDCMAX	= maximum monthly AFDC payments by state and number of children.

Table 15.A.2 (continued)

Variable	Definition
INLF79	= 1 if woman was working or looking for work in March 1979 and 0 otherwise.
KIDLT3	= number of children under three years old.
KIDLT6	= number of children under six years old.
KIDLT18	= number of children under eighteen years old.
NADULT	= number of adults in the household.
OTHFINC	= total family income excluding child support received, alimony received, and public assistance income.

Comment   Irwin Garfinkel

"Variations in the Economic Well-Being of Divorced Women and Their Children" by Andrea H. Beller and John W. Graham reports on a series of empirical investigations motivated by the observation that the economic well-being of divorced women is effected primarily by how much they work, how much child support and alimony they receive, and whether or not they remarry. Although the chapter examines the determinants of remarriage and labor force participation as well as the determinants of child support, the central focus is on child support. When child support is not the dependent variable, it is the key independent variable. This focus makes the chapter both original and interesting.

In view of the focus on child support, the data set used, the March/April 1979 Match File of the Current Population Survey (CPS), is appropriate. The April 1979 CPS contained a special supplement that gathered data from all women eighteen years of age or older on potential child support eligibility, child support and alimony awards and payments, property settlements, and the income of absent fathers as reported by custodial mothers. Data from the April supplement were matched with the March 1979 CPS.

Beller and Graham limit their sample to ever-divorced and separated women. They estimate: (1) the probability of receiving a child support award; (2) conditional upon having an award, the probability that child support is received; (3) conditional upon receiving some support, the amount of support received; (4) the probability of remarriage within two, five, and ten years of divorce; and (5) the probability of labor force participation. In all regressions, they use maximum likelihood to estimate logistic functions. Their independent variables include age, race, location,

Irwin Garfinkel is director of the School of Social Work and a research fellow at the Institute for Research on Poverty, University of Wisconsin, Madison.

number of children, several variables on marital history, a host of variables on child support, alimony and property settlements, and the custodial parents estimate of the absent father's income. The last is available for only one-third of the sample.

In summarizing their results, Beller and Graham stress three. First, a child support award is a function both of the absent father's ability to pay and the needs of the children and custodial mother, while child support payments depend primarily on the current financial status of the ex-husband. With respect to the second and third conclusion on remarriage and labor force participation, respectively, I quote from the conclusion "Like other forms of nonlabor income, child support payments were found to lower the probability of remarriage. But unlike other forms of nonlabor income, child support payments were found to raise labor force participation." I have trouble with all three major conclusions.

The most important piece of evidence in support of the contention that the needs of the children and custodial parent have no effect on child support payments is that remarriage of the custodial mother has no effect on the probability of receiving child support. Note, however, that they find that remarriage significantly decreases the amount of child support received for those who receive any at all. So at best the evidence they present is ambiguous. More important, by restricting the sample used to estimate the probability of receiving child support to those who were due support in 1978, the effects of remarriage on the probability of receiving child support are underestimated. Of all those who received child support awards at divorce about 20 percent responded that they were not due child support in 1978. The CPS did not ask respondents to explain the discrepancy. I have been puzzled about this off and on for quite some time. Two reasons are that the child was over age eighteen or twenty-one and therefore no longer eligible for support or that the ex-husband had subsequently died. After reading and puzzling over the Beller-Graham paper for the second or third time, I realized that a third and for this paper a critical reason was that the custodial parent had remarried. Child support awards may be adjusted any time there is a significant change in circumstances. In some cases, the new husband may formally adopt the children thereby legally releasing the absent father from any financial obligation. Even without formal adoption, the parties may agree to end the support obligation of the absent father. In any case, although remarried women make up just a bit over one-third of all those with support awards in the CPS, they account for one-half of all those with awards who are due no support in 1978.

One final comment on the conclusion that child support payments are unrelated to the needs of the custodial parent. Most absent parents, judges, researchers, and other people, would be reluctant to conclude that need has little effect on payments when the current income of the custodial parent is not included in the regression.

Although Beller and Graham assert that child support payments reduce remarriage and increase labor force participation, the results they report show significant effects on remarriage and labor force participation, not of child support payments but rather of child support awards at divorce or eligibility for support in 1978. Normally economists are concerned with the influence of income and prices on behavior. Child support payments are a form of income. Child support awards are obligations or promises. What the Beller-Graham analysis sheds light on, therefore, is not the effect of a particular kind of income on behavior but rather the effect on behavior of promises, promises, promises. No theoretical justification for their use of promises rather than payments is presented. Indeed, they treat the two as if they are interchangeable. As we shall see, however, they are not.

Beller and Graham find that having a child support award increases the probability of remarriage, while being due support in 1978 decreases the probability of remarriage by a larger amount than the award increases it. If as discussed above remarriage leads some with awards at the time of divorce to lose eligibility for child support, this is precisely what we would expect to find. Imagine that there is no relationship between child support awards and remarriage. By including dummy variables both for those with awards and for those due support in 1978, the awards variable picks up the positive correlation between remarrying and losing child support eligibility. The child-support-due variable picks up the corresponding negative relationship between not remarrying and retaining child support eligibility. I have no explanation for why the amount of the award per child is negatively related to remarriage within five years and unrelated to remarriage within ten years. And it may well be that child support payments decrease the probability of remarriage. Beller and Graham provide no evidence either way.

Finally, Beller and Graham recognize that in their labor force participation equation, the amount of child-support-due variable may be positively biased because women expecting to work would negotiate for child support rather than alimony. The former is not taxable while the latter is. For some reason they never consider that this same bias will lead the alimony-expected coefficient to be too negative. More important, given their countertheoretical finding that the child-support-due variable is positively correlated with labor force participation, why should we believe that there is anything more to this relationship than the bias? Indeed, when a dummy for child support due is entered along with a variable measuring child support received, the former is positive and significant while the latter is not significantly different from zero. A reasonable interpretation is that the former picks up most, but not all, of the positive bias. In any case, in this instance where Beller and Graham use child support received, they find no significant relationship between it and labor force participation. Perhaps if the child-support-due variable were not included in the regression, there would be a positive and significant relationship between payments received and labor force participation. Again Beller and Graham fail to present evidence on the most important relationship.

In short, although this chapter deals with an important and interesting topic, it suffers from a failure to define clearly the variable of central interest: child support.

Contributors

Andrea H. Beller
Department of Family and Consumer
  Economics
University of Illinois at Urbana-
  Champaign
274 Bevier Hall
905 South Goodwin Avenue
Urbana, IL 61801

Marcus C. Berliant
Economics Department
University of Rochester
Rochester, NY 14627

David Betson
Department of Economics
University of Notre Dame
Notre Dame, IN 46556

Richard V. Burkhauser
Department of Economics
Vanderbilt University
Box 1535 Station B
Nashville, TN 37235

J. S. Butler
Department of Economics
Vanderbilt University
Box 1535 Station B
Nashville, TN 37235

Donald Cox
Department of Economics
Washington University
Campus Box 1208
St. Louis, MO 63130

Sheldon Danziger
Institute for Research on Poverty
University of Wisconsin
1180 Observatory Drive
Madison, WI 53706

Martin David
Department of Economics
University of Wisconsin
1180 Observatory Drive
Madison, WI 53706

Greg J. Duncan
Institute for Social Research
University of Michigan
P.O. Box 1248
Ann Arbor, MI 48106

Pamela J. Farley
National Center for Health Services
  Research
Park Building, Stop 3-50
5600 Fishers Lane
Rockville, MD 20857

Gary S. Fields
New York State School of Industrial
    and Labor Relations
Ives Hall
Cornell University
Ithaca, NY 14853

Irwin Garfinkel
Institute for Research on Poverty
University of Wisconsin
1180 Observatory Drive
Madison, WI 53705

Carol C. S. Gilbert
Societal Analysis Department
General Motors Research Lab
Warren, MI 48090

John W. Graham
Department of Economics
University of Illinois at Urbana-
    Champaign
1206 S. 6th Street
Champaign, IL 61820

Edward M. Gramlich
Department of Economics
University of Michigan
Ann Arbor, MI 48109

Robert H. Haveman
Institute for Research on Poverty
University of Wisconsin
1180 Observatory Drive
Madison, WI 53706

Saul D. Hoffman
Economics Department
University of Delaware
Newark, DE 19711

Michael D. Hurd
Department of Economics
State University of New York at Stony
    Brook
Stony Brook, NY 11794

F. Thomas Juster
Institute for Social Research
University of Michigan
P.O. Box 1248
Ann Arbor, MI 48106

Arie Kapteyn
Department of Econometrics
Tilburg University
P.O. Box 90153
5000 LE Tilburg
The Netherlands

Frank Levy
School of Public Affairs
University of Maryland
College Park, MD 20742

Lee A. Lillard
Department of Economics
Rand Corporation
1700 Main Street
Santa Monica, CA 90406

Paul L. Menchik
Department of Economics
Michigan State University
East Lansing, MI 48824

Olivia S. Mitchell
New York State School of Industrial
    and Labor Relations
Ives Hall
Cornell University
Ithaca, NY 14853

Joseph P. Newhouse
Department of Economics
Rand Corporation
1700 Main Street
Santa Monica, CA 90406

Robert Plotnick
Graduate School of Public Affairs,
    DP-30
University of Washington
Seattle, WA 98195

Joseph F. Quinn
Department of Economics
Boston College
Chestnut Hill, MA 02167

Fredric Raines
Department of Economics
Washington University
Campus Box 1208
St. Louis, MO 63130

Lee Rainwater
Department of Sociology
William James Hall 530
Harvard University
Cambridge, MA 02138

Isabel V. Sawhill
Urban Institute
2100 M Street, NW
Washington, DC 20037

John B. Shoven
Department of Economics
Stanford University
Encina Hall, 4th Floor
Stanford, CA 94305

Timothy Smeeding
Department of Economics
University of Utah
BUO-314
Salt Lake City, UT 84112

James D. Smith
Institute for Social Research
University of Michigan
P.O. Box 1248
Ann Arbor, MI 48106

V. Kerry Smith
Department of Economics and
    Business Administration
Vanderbilt University
Box 52 Station B
Nashville, TN 37235

T. N. Srinivasan
Economic Growth Center
Yale University
P.O. Box 1987, Yale Station
New Haven, CT 06520

Eugene Steuerle
Treasury Department
15th and Pennsylvania Avenue, NW
Washington, DC 20220

Robert P. Strauss
School of Urban and Public Affairs
MMC 307
Carnegie-Mellon University
Pittsburgh, PA 15213

T. H. Tietenberg
Department of Economics
Colby College
Waterville, ME

Dan Usher
Department of Economics
Queen's University
Kingston, Ontario K7L 3N6
Canada

Sara van de Geer
Center for Mathematics and Computer
    Science
Amsterdam
The Netherlands

Huib van de Stadt
Central Bureau of Statistics
Amsterdam
The Netherlands

Jacques van der Gaag
Development Research Department
The World Bank
1818 H Street, NW
Washington, DC 20433

Harold W. Watts
Department of Economics
Columbia University
New York, NY 10027

Gail R. Wilensky
Domestic Division
Project Hope
Millwood, VA 22646

James T. Wilkinson
Department of Economics
University of Missouri
Columbia, MO 65211

Barbara L. Wolfe
Institute for Research on Poverty
University of Wisconsin
1180 Observatory Drive
Madison, WI 53706

Author Index

Allen, S., 135
Andrews, Frank M., 30
Antonides, G., 40
Arnett, Ross H., 333
Arriaga-Salinas, A. S., 371, 376
Arrow, Kenneth J., 326, 355
Asch, Peter, 389
Atkinson, A., 113, 181, 182, 239, 243, 245, 300

Bane, M. J., 427, 430
Becker, Gary S., 480, 486, 487
Berliant, M., 181, 184, 186, 193, 239, 241
Bishop, George F., 21
Blackorby, D., 181
Blinder, Alan S., 15, 342, 393
Bonham, Gordon Scott, 348
Boskin, M., 128
Bradbury, Katherine, 471
Brown, Charles, 371
Buyze, J., 39, 42

Campbell, Angus, 30
Cantril, Harley, 9
Carroll, Marjorie S., 333
Cassetty, Judith, 475
Chestnut, Lauraine G., 364, 369
Ciccheti, C. J., 221
Clark, R., 135
Cohen, Steven B., 348
Colasanto, D., 38, 41, 48
Converse, Phillip E., 16, 20, 22, 30
Cook, Phillip J., 367
Corder, Larry S., 348

Cowell, Frank, 239, 245
Cropper, Maureen L., 371, 376

Danziger, S., 38, 48, 427, 442
David, Martin, 96, 393
Davis, James A., 29, 30
Denison, Edward D., 15
Donaldson, D., 181
Dow, Greg, 237
Duncan, Greg J., 237
Duesenberry, James S., 9

Easterlin, Richard A., 9

Farley, Pamela J., 334
Fei, J. C. H., 181
Feldstein, M., 109, 182, 239, 337, 342
Fields, G. S., 181, 273
Fischoff, Bernard, 381
Franklin, Stephen D., 93
Freeman, A. Myrick, 221, 367, 367, 368, 377, 379

Galper, Harvey, 114
Garfinkel, Irwin, 499
Gerking, Shelby, 377
Glick, Paul C., 472
Goedhart, T., 36, 37, 41
Gordon, Nancy M., 475
Gordon, Roger Hall, 342
Gottschalk, Peter, 24
Graham, D. A., 221, 367
Greenwood, Daphne, 328, 350
Grossman, Allyson Sherman, 497

Hall, Robert, 276
Hammond, Peter J., 362
Harrison, A. J., 113
Hausman, J. A., 222
Hayghe, Howard, 497
Heckman, James, 443, 444
Henry, C., 222
Hershey, John C., 369
Hirschman, Albert, 11, 31
Hoch, Irving, 371, 376
Hoffman, Saul, 428, 471
Holmes, John W., 428
Holmlund, Bertil, 237
Holtmann, A. G., 372
Hurd, M., 125, 128
Hutchens, Robert, 430, 445, 491, 498

Ibbotson, Roger, 111

Jones, Carol A., 475
Jordan, Bruce C., 361
Juster, F. T., 237

Kalsbeek, William, 348
Kapteyn, A., 37, 38, 39, 40, 41, 42, 48
Keeley, Michael C., 498
Key, V. O., Jr., 10
Kilpatrick, R. W., 48
King, M., 181, 182, 183, 239, 241, 245
Kondor, Y., 181
Kotlikoff, Laurence J., 276, 342
Krause, Harry D., 480
Kunreuther, Howard C., 369

Lampman, Robert J., 93, 393
Landes, Elisabeth M., 480, 486, 487
Lazear, Edward P., 270, 276
Lebergott, Stanley, 331, 350
Leuchtenberg, William E., 18
Lichtenstein, Sarah, 381
Litai, Dan, 369
Lucas, Robert, 371

McClung, Nelson, 91, 113
McCurdy, Thomas, 361
Marquis, M. Susan, 357
Martin, David, 424
Mayers, David, 323
Menchik, Paul, 96, 393, 424
Mercier, J., 428
Michael, Robert T., 480, 486, 487
Mill, J. S., 182
Miller, Arthur H., 19

Miller, Warren E., 19
Mitchell, Olivia S., 273
Moon, Marilyn, 71
Morgan, James, 422
Moynihan, Daniel P., 10
Musgrave, P. B., 183
Musgrave, R., 94, 182, 183

Nestel, G., 428
Norton, Arthur J., 472
Nozick, Robert, 243

Okner, B. A., 184
Oldendick, Robert W., 21

Parsons, Donald O., 393
Pauly, Mark, 326
Pechman, J. A., 184
Pellechio, Anthony, 342
Phelps, Charles E., 357
Plotnick, R., 182, 239, 244, 245, 246
Portney, Paul R., 376
Projector, Dorothy S., 328

Rainwater, L., 10, 48
Richmond, Harvey M., 361
Rodgers, Willard, 30, 431
Rosen, H., 181, 239
Rosen, Sherwin, 365, 367, 371, 376
Ruckelshaus, William D., 359
Ruggles, Nancy D., 328, 352
Ruggles, Richard, 328, 352

Samuelson, Paul A., 182
Sawhill, Isabel V., 475
Schiltz, Michael, 20, 21, 22
Schmalensee, R., 222
Schneider, Edward J., 19
Schoemaker, Paul J. H., 369, 381, 387
Schulze, William D., 377
Schwartz, Marvin, 92
Sen, A., 181
Seneca, Joseph J., 389
Shaw, L., 428
Shephard, D. S., 364
Shoven, J., 125
Sinquefield, Rex, 111
Slovik, Paul, 381
Smeeding, Timothy, 91, 393
Smith, Clifford W., Jr., 323
Smith, Daniel, 276
Smith, James D., 93
Smith, James P., 495

Smith, Robert S., 365
Smith, Tom W., 14
Smith, V. K., 371, 372, 376
Starr, C., 369
Stein, Herbert, 21, 23
Steurle, Eugene, 91, 96, 113, 114
Stiglitz, Joseph, 243, 247
Strauss, R. P., 181, 184, 186, 193, 239, 241
Sumner, D., 135
Sundquist, James L., 10, 11

Thaler, Richard, 365, 367, 371
Thin, T., 182
Thornton, Arland, 431
Tomes, Nigel, 393, 413
Tuchfarber, Alfred J., 21

Ulph, Alistair, 362

van de Geer, S., 42
van der Gaag, J., 38, 41, 48

van de Stadt, H., 42
van Herwaarden, F. G., 39, 40
van Praag, B. M. S., 36, 37, 39, 41
Violette, Daniel M., 364, 369
Viscusi, W. Kip, 371, 377

Wansbeek, T. J., 40, 41
Weisbrod, B. A., 221
Weiss, Gertrude S., 328
Weiss, Robert S., 427, 430
Wertz, K. L., 179, 184, 186
Wilensky, Gail R., 334
Wise, Donald E., 342
Withy, Steven B., 30
Wolff, D. A., 442
Wolff, Edward N., 328, 350

Yancey, William L., 10

Zeckhauser, Richard, 364
Zellner, Arnold, 75

Subject Index

Accelerated Cost Recovery System, 95

Accidents, work related, 363–64

Age: and child support, 480; effect on interfamily transfers, 411, 415

Aged: concerns of, 69; federal aid to, 11; health insurance, 9; importance of intrafamily transfers, 70n; income realization of, 96; and inflation, 148–49; inflation vulnerability of, 150, 153, 155; and nominal interest rates, 149; real income of, 126; Social Security indexing as protection against inflation, 154; vulnerability of, 147–56

Aid to Families with Dependent Children, 24, 215, 429, 442, 446, 492, 496, 498

Air quality, 370; improvements in, 379; standards, 361; as variable in hedonic wage model, 371

Alimony, 430, 442, 446, 491; and labor force participation, 497

American Council on Education, 24

American Institute of Public Opinion, 8

Assets, preferred, 111

Atkinson Index, calculation of, 315

Bearer bonds, 121

Beneficiaries, 101

Benefit Amounts Survey, 273, 288

Benefit rules, 274

Bequests, and earnings inequality, 393

Blacks. See Minorities

Blind, federal aid to, 11

Capital, human, calculation of, 169–70

Capital income: relationship to inheritance, 101; and tax shelters, 109

Carbon monoxide, 362

Carcinogen exposure, as variable in hedonic wage model, 372

Carter, Jimmy, 11

Cash transfer system, horizontal inequity of, 247

Children: age of, and probability of receiving child support, 485; cost of, 48; financial effect of divorce on, 449

Child support, 430, 442, 474, 491; effect of race on, 477; empirical analysis of, 476–86; factors affecting amount of, 507; factors affecting payment of, 507; indexing of, 480; and labor force participation, 497; probability of being awarded, 477–81; probability of receiving, 481–86; and probability of remarriage, 498, 507; voluntary vs. court ordered, 485

Civil rights revolution, 23, 31

Clean Air Act, 360

College freshmen, attitudes towards life goals, 24–26

Consumer Price Index, 125, 135

Consumption power, 70

Consumption tax, 95, 114

Conventional pension plans, 280, 282, 289

Cost-of-living, 125; index, 342

Cost recovery, 95

Crime rate, as variable in hedonic wage model, 371
Current Population Survey, 304, 360, 474, 506

Deferred retirement, economic rewards of, 276–85. *See also* Retirement
Depreciation, 95; need for better measurement of, 114
Depression, 13
Disability Insurance, 316
Disabled: categories of, 305; differences in income between nondisabled, 295–304; and disability insurance, 316; earnings of, 293, 294; educational level of, and income, 296, 320; federal aid to, 11; and federal taxes, 298; income inequality of, 299–302, 309–11; income of white and nonwhite compared, 317–19; income status of, 297–99, 306–9; income uncertainty of, 302–4, 311–13; and railroad retirement, 316; relative economic status of, 314; and Social Security, 316; and Supplemental Security Income, 316
Divorce: financial effect on men, 449; income level of women following, 434–35, 436; and labor force participation rate for women, 440

Early retirement, 270. *See also* Retirement
Economic Report of the President, 170, 171
Economic status, perceptions of, 16–18
Educational level: of disabled, effect on income, 296, 320; effect on comprehensiveness of health insurance, 337; and interfamily transfers, 412, 414; and probability of receiving child support, 484; and remarriage, 448; and savings behavior, 342; as variable in hedonic wage model, 372
Eisenhower, Dwight, 12, 23
Elderly. *See* Aged
Environmental hazards, 4
Environmental policy, 370
Environmental Protection Agency (EPA), 361
Environmental risks, use of wage model in, 387
EPA, 361
Equilibrium wage rates, 380

Equity, horizontal: classification of, 186–88; concept of, 241–44; defined, 182; net, 328; vertical, 182, 186–88
Equity principle, 183
European Community, 35

Families, nonhuman wealth of, 145
Family income: changes in, with marital instability, 433–36; changes in composition with divorce, 439–40
Family size, and health insurance coverage, 334, 342
Family wealth. *See* Household wealth
Farms, percent of household wealth, 331
Financial status, perceptions of, 16–18
Flower children, 31
Food, price inflation of, 24
Food stamps, 11; and horizontal inequities, 255–56

Gallup poll, 8
Goals, attitudes of college freshmen towards, 24–26
Goldwater, Barry, 11
Government: distributive functions of, 183; public trust in, 19
Great Society, 9, 26, 31
Group health insurance, 333; effect of tax subsidy on, 337; and self-employed, 331

Happiness: assessments of, 8; evaluation in terms of social situation, 30
Health, effect on income, 85
Health insurance, 9, 69, 324, 333–42; and educational level, 337; effect of sex on premiums, 337; and family size, 334, 342; and geographic differences, 337; relationship to assets, 331–33; and tax subsidies, 347
Health Insurance/Employer Survey, 349
Hispanic women, 484, 496
Home ownership, 131
Hopkins, Harry, 18
Horizontal equity: classification of, 186–88; concept of, 241–44; defined, 182; and single taxpayers, 198, 199; theoretical considerations, 109–12
Horizontal inequity, measures of, 244–46
Household savings: empirical model of, 328–33; and insurance, 327; theoretical model of, 324–28

Household wealth, 342–46; definition of, 328, 349; effect of age on, 345; effect of family size on, 346; effect of marital status on, 345; farm percent of, 331; home equity, 350–51; income producing assets, 350; nonfarm percent of, 331; rental property percent of, 331; sociodemographic factors, 346
Household welfare, 212
Housing, owner occupied, as tax shelter, 109
Human capital: calculation of, 169–70; model, 77–81
Human life, value of, 359

Illness: last, cost of, 120; prolonged, 69
Income: growth of real, 18; of disabled, 293–304, 317–20; past, influence on present needs, 47; property, need for better measurement of, 114; realized, as basis for tax transfers, 123; relationship to amount of inheritance, 101; and tax shelters, 109; and unemployment, 236; welfare function of, 39; and welfare programs, 113; as well-being measure, 70, 92, 94–97, 123
Income inequality, 183; structure of, 192
Income levels, quantitative perceptions about, 65
Income maintenance program, 216–19; with unemployment uncertainty, 219–28
Income status, of disabled, 297–99, 306–9
Income tax: horizontal equity in, 114 horizontal inequity of, 195, 198; level of progressivity of, 180; measurement of progressivity, 182; progressivity of, 193, 195, 198, 202; replacement with consumption tax, 95
Indexing: of capital returns, 114; of child support payments, 480; of Social Security, 153, 154, 156
Individual behavior, under uncertainty, 381
Inflation, 15; effect on household wealth positions, 171; and the elderly, 148–49, 155; and interest rates, 111n; and Social Security indexing, 154; vulnerability: calculation of, 170–71
Inheritances, relationship to capital income, 101
Insurance, 323; demand for, 356–57; health, relationship to assets, 331–33; and savings, 327

Interest rates: effect of taxes on, 111n; and inflation, 111n; nominal, and the elderly, 149
Interfamily transfers, 394–99, 409–18; direction of, 399–401; and educational level, 412, 414; effect of age on, 411, 412, 415; and marital status, 412; and relative income inequality, 402–4. *See also* Intergenerational transfers; Intrafamily transfers
Intergenerational transfers, life cycle model of, 404–7
Intertemporal utility, 270–73
Intrafamily transfers, 70n. *See also* Interfamily transfers

Job hazards, as variable in hedonic wage model, 372. *See also* Risk valuation
Jobs, government provision of, 20
Job tenure, 276
Johnson, Lyndon, 10, 12, 14, 20, 23, 26

Kennedy, John, 12, 14, 23; assassination, 11
Korean War, 14, 18

Labor strikes, 14
Labor force participation: and alimony, 497; and child support, 497; empirical analysis of, 493–97; rates, 170; by women, following divorce, 440
Lead pollutants, 362
Leisure, 270, 272; in unemployment, 236; value of, 70n; and work, 237
Leyden Poverty Line, 39–41, 51–52
Life cycle, and family wealth, 331
Life-cycle concept, 71
Life-cycle consumption models, 71n
Life-cycle theory, 176, 342
Life expectancy, 148
Life goals, attitudes of freshman towards, 24–26
Life-style revolution, 31

Mandatory retirement, 291. *See also* Retirement
Marital instability, and changes in family income, 433–36
Marital status: and income, 128, 131; and income tax progressivity, 198; and interfamily transfers, 412; and nonhuman wealth, 145; and Social Security, 131; and wealth, 137
Market compensation effect, 110

Marriage. *See* Marital status; Remarriage
Medicaid, 24, 97, 137, 139, 175
Medical expenses. *See* Health insurance
Medical services, 120
Medicare, 24, 137, 139, 175
Men: financial effect of divorce on, 449
  health insurance premiums in families
  headed by, 337; income of compared to
  women, 128, 131; nonhuman wealth
  of, 145; and Social Security payments,
  131; wealth of, compared to women,
  137
Michigan Panel Study of Income
  Dynamics, 295
Minorities: and disability income, 317–19;
  and household wealth, 346; and labor
  force participation, 496; and
  probability of receiving child support,
  477, 484; and remarriage, 431, 446;
  and savings behavior, 342
Models: environmental risks, 387; hedonic
  wage, 365–76; of household savings,
  328–33; human capital, 77–81; of
  intergenerational transfers, 404–7; life-
  cycle consumption, 71n; occupational
  risks, 387
Mondale, Walter, 10n
Mortgage rates, 171

National Medical Care Expenditure Survey,
  348
National Opinion Research Center, 14
Needs, present, influence of past income
  on, 47
Net equity, 328
Nixon, Richard, 15, 17
Nonfarm business, percent of household
  wealth, 331
Nonwhites, and household wealth, 346

Occupational risks, use of wage model in,
  387
Occupational injury rate, as variable in
  hedonic wage model, 372
Oil, price inflation of, 24
Old Age, Survivors, and Disability Income.
  See Social Security
Option price, 221, 222
Organization of Petroleum Exporting
  Countries (OPEC), 7

Panel Study of Income Dynamics, 427, 431
Pattern pension plans, 280, 282, 289

Pension benefit rules, 274
Pension benefits, government mandated
  neutrality in, 285
Pension plans: conventional, 280, 282, 289;
  integration with Social Security, 290;
  pattern, 280, 282, 289
Pensions, private, 148, 278–82
Petroleum, price inflation of, 7, 24
Political activism, 31
Poor: and nontransfer wealth, 139; and
  welfare benefits, 139
Portfolio, vulnerability of, 150
Postwar period, 7; and private consumption
  hunger, 13
Poverty: feminization of, 472; relative
  nature of, 36, 48
Poverty line: definitions of, 37–41; Leyden,
  39–41, 51–52; political decision on,
  40–41; subjective, 37–39, 50–51
Poverty rates, and divorce, 438
President's Commission on Pension Policy,
  394, 422
Price controls, 14, 16
Property income: as measure of well-being,
  97; need for better measurement of, 114
Property ownership, as measure of ability
  to pay, 94
Property settlements, 480
Property tax, and horizontal inequities, 114
Public goods, 10; public opinion on, 18–26;
  taxation to provide, 183
Public sector, growth of, 9

Race. *See* Minorities
Railroad retirement, and the disabled, 316
Rank reversals, 264–68
Rationing, 13
Recessions, 14
Redistribution, process of, 243
Redistributive programs, 23
Relative income hypothesis, 9
Remarriage, 429; effect of alimony on, 491;
  effect of child support on, 491, 492,
  498; empirical analysis of, 486–93;
  gains from, 442–49; marital search
  behavior, 487–88; and probability of
  receiving child support, 507, 508; racial
  differences in, 431, 446; variables
  affecting, 476
Rental property, percent of household
  wealth, 331
Retirement: deferred, rewards of, 276–85;
  early, 270; income inequality of

Retirement (*continued*)
  disabled, 299–302; income uncertainty
  of disabled, 302–4; mandatory, 291
Retirement behavior, 270–73
Retirement History Survey, 72, 126, 161–66,
  167
Retirement leisure, 270, 272
Retirement wealth, 287
Riots, urban, 23
Risk, attitudes towards, 212
Risk management, 359; government
  involvement in, 385
Risk premium, 223
Risk reductions, estimated value of, 376–80
Risks, occupational, 387
Risk-taking behavior, policy analyses of,
  369
Risk-taking decisions, hedonic models for,
  365–70
Risk valuation: and hedonic wage model,
  370–76; policy demands for, 361–65;
  and socioeconomic groups, 391

Savings: and insurance, 327; precautionary,
  323, 324, 326–27, 333, 342, 345, 355,
  356
Savings behavior: educational differences
  in, 342; geographical differences in,
  342; racial differences in, 342
Savings bonds, 135
Self-employed, and group health insurance,
  331
Sex, and horizontal equity, 199–201
Singles: and horizontal equity, 199, 202;
  and income tax progressivity, 198, 199,
  202
Social Security, 31, 69, 72, 137, 271, 272,
  275, 291; changes in benefit levels, 81,
  83; and the disabled, 316; indexing of,
  153, 154, 156; and inflation
  vulnerability, 153; integration with
  pension plans, 290; as nonhuman
  wealth, 139; and the poor, 139; and
  taxation of benefits, 177
Social Security Primary Insurance Account,
  167
Social tension, sources of, 240
Social welfare: effect of horizontal inequity
  on, 242; effect of rank reversals on, 243
Statistics of Income—Estate Tax Returns,
  92, 118
*Statistics of Income—Individual Income
  Tax Returns,* 189

Strikes, 14
Sulfur dioxide, 362
Sunshine, as variable in hedonic wage
  model, 371
Supplemental Security Income, and the
  disabled, 316
Survey of Consumer Finances, 328
Survey of Economic Opportunity, 350, 486
Survivor's benefits, 168

Taxes: accelerated cost recovery system, 95;
  avoidance of, 212; on consumption,
  95, 114; cost recovery, 95;
  depreciation, 95; and disabled persons,
  298; evasion of, 212; and interest rates,
  111n; on Social Security benefits, 177
Taxpayers: itemization among, 181;
  married, and horizontal equity, 181;
  single, and horizontal equity, 181
Tax shelters, 109
Tax subsidies, and health insurance, 347
Tax system, 114; horizontal inequity in,
  112; voluntary nature of, 112. *See also*
  Income tax system; Property tax
Tax transfers, realized income as basis for,
  123
Tax transfer system, and disabled, 298,
  308–9, 311–14
Trust-in-Government Index, 19

Unemployment, 14, 15, 20; and income,
  236; and leisure time, 236; uncertainty,
  and income maintenance program,
  219–28. *See also* Income maintenance
Unemployment rate, as variable in hedonic
  wage model, 371
Union membership, as variable in hedonic
  wage model, 372
Unions, and strikes, 14
United States, postwar economic
  performance in, 7
University of Michigan Survey Research
  Center, 16

Vertical equity: classification of, 186–88;
  defined, 182
Veteran status, as variable in hedonic wage
  model, 372
Vietnam War, 15

Wage and price controls, 16
War on Poverty, 9, 31

Wealth: nonhuman, 137, 175; and well-being, 70

Welfare, 442; and property income as measure of well-being, 97; public opinion on, 22–23; relative nature of, 48

Welfare programs: evaluation of, 113; horizontal inequity in, 112

Welfare state, growth of, 18

Well-being: defined in terms of income, 70; future, influence of unexpected events on, 77–86; income as measure of, 94–97; individual, 2–3; measures of, 92, 97, 123, 246–49; social, 3–5

Widows, 131

Women: financial effect of divorce on, 433–39, 449; health insurance premiums in families headed by, 337; household wealth, 346; income of, compared to men, 128, 131; nonhuman wealth of, 145; and Social Security payments, 131; wealth of, compared to men, 137

Work: and leisure, 237; length of, and wealthy persons, 131

Workmen's Compensation, 388